KU-260-324

Elizabeth Grant (1797–1885) was born in Edinburgh's fashionable New Town. Most of her childhood was spent in London and on the family estate, Rothiemurchus, on Speyside. She was educated by governesses and in the social graces by various tutors, finally entering Edinburgh society at the end of the Napoleonic wars.

The trauma of a broken engagement was followed by the disastrous failure of her father's career. This involved a huge burden of debt which, in 1820, forced the Grants to retreat to their Highland home. As her contribution to improving the family fortunes, Elizabeth and both her sisters wrote articles for popular magazines of the day.

In 1827 the family left Scotland for India when her father was appointed to a Judgeship in Bombay. It was here that she met and married Colonel Henry Smith, seventeen years her senior. They left for Ireland the following year to live at Baltiboys, her husband's newly inherited estate situated near Dublin.

She devoted herself to raising a family and took the leading role in managing and improving their impoverished estate. For over half a century Baltiboys was to be her home, her life and her occupation, her resolve never failing even after the death of her husband and her only son. Between 1845 and 1854 she wrote her Memoirs for her family's pleasure; they were later edited by her niece Lady Strachey and published in 1898, thirteen years after her death. This Canongate Classic edition is the most complete ever to appear in print.

*Elizabeth Grant of Rothiemurchus*

# MEMOIRS OF A HIGHLAND LADY

*Edited with an introduction by*
*Andrew Tod*

10

**CANONGATE**
*Edinburgh · New York · Melbourne*

First published in 1898 by John Murray.
Revised edition first published in two volumes
in Canongate Classics in 1988. This edition
published in 2006 by Canongate Books,
14 High Street, Edinburgh, EH1 1TE

1

Introduction copyright © Andrew Tod 1988 and 2006
All rights reserved.

A catalogue record for this book is available
on request from the British Library.

ISBN 1 84195 757 7 (10 Digit ISBN)
ISBN 978 184195 757 9 (13 Digit ISBN)

CANONGATE CLASSICS
Series Editor: Roderick Watson
Editorial Board: Cairns Craig,
Dorothy McMillan, Kathleen Jamie

The publisher gratefully acknowledges
subsidy from the Scottish Arts Council towards
the publication of this volume.

 Scottish
**Arts** Council

Set in 10pt Plantin
by Hewer Text Composition Services,
Edinburgh.
Printed and bound in Denmark by
Nørhaven Paperback A/S

www.canongate.net

# Contents

# Introduction

*Memoirs of a Highland Lady* has long been recognised as a
classic of Scottish nineteenth-century literature. Elizabeth
Grant of Rothiemurchus wrote it between 1845 and 1854, in
the middle of a long life that began in 1797 and ended nearly
ninety years later. It was originally intended as a private
memoir for her family alone. The first public edition did not
appear until 1898, edited and abridged by her niece, Lady
Strachey, who explained in the introduction:

> These memoirs were written by Mrs Smith for her own
> children and the daughter of her sister, Mrs Gardiner,
> with no thought but to interest them in those scenes of
> her early life which she recalled so vividly, and has
> narrated with such lively simplicity.

The book's devoted readers would sing its praises rather
higher, for although it was, indeed, hastily written without
the use of journal or diary notes it is a masterpiece of
historical and personal recall, clearly organised, and so
vividly written that the attention of the reader is held to the
last page.

Lady Strachey's edition was so popular that it was
reprinted four times within the year, and a letter in the
archives of John Murray, the publisher, testifies to a demand
that was still unsatisfied:

> I should be greatly obliged if you could say if there is any
> likelihood of a new edition of the *Memoirs of a Highland
> Lady* being published in the near future. Second-hand
> copies of this book I am advised are now selling at high
> prices—a guinea to thirty shillings.

A second edition appeared in 1911, also edited by Lady

Strachey, who took the opportunity to reduce it still further—by almost a third, in fact—as she explained in a letter to John Murray . . . 'the whole of the journey to Holland is omitted and all of the Indian part, except what was necessary to finish up the fortunes of the family.' Reprinted in 1928, this was the text which Angus Davidson edited and prepared for the Albemarle Library in 1950.

The *Highland Lady* has remained in steady demand over the years, but in fact most of the copies of this acknowledged masterpiece contain no more than two thirds of the 1898 edition which was itself abridged from the original manuscript. The opportunity to publish the first complete and authentic edition of this perennial favourite has come about through the generosity of Mrs Ruth Forster, Elizabeth Grant's great-great-grand-daughter, to whom has descended the two vellum-bound, manuscript volumes that are undoubtedly the original. These were written in Elizabeth Grant's meticulous hand-writing, which seems effortlessly to flow over the sheets in her endearingly readable style. It is incredible that she managed to produce such consistency, as for the most part her *Memoirs* were produced, as she wrote herself, 'so much by snatches, never getting above a few done at a time since the idle days of Avranches.' Family tradition has it that they passed to the second daughter, Annie, because she was the favourite, but equally it might have been because she was the mother of most of the Highland Lady's grand-children. Alas, the first eight either died young or had no children, so it was, remarkably, through the ninth child, Lizzie, that the manuscript passed to Ruth Forster. Her magnanimous decision to donate them to the National Library of Scotland was the first step towards this new edition in the Canongate Classics series.

From the very first sentence of the original manuscript it was clear that there were many adjustments to be made. For example, Elizabeth Grant was born at 5 Charlotte Square, Edinburgh, and not at number 6, as all the earlier editions maintain. An accurate and complete edition involves a faithful return to the manuscript and therefore to the style and practices of an intelligent and hugely literate writer who had been born in the eighteenth century. Yet some changes, and some footnotes, do need to be introduced for the modern reader. One or two cases of repetition have been removed, abbreviations like *Edin.* for the city of her birth have been altered, and the manuscript use of & has been changed to *and* along with the conversion of *ʃs* to represent *ss*. The original chapters have been restored and where it seemed that her paragraphing was more effective, this too has been brought back. Elizabeth Grant's use of capitals is idiosyncratic. Another obvious change is her use of capitals for emphasis (so that a visit to a *Play* might appear in the same sentence as the adjective *french*), and her spelling has been returned to its period style. Sympathetick, puritanick and arithmetick; bachelour, mirrour and errour; cloke, dropt and skreen; cantilevres, burthens and accompt . . . these and many more give us the authentic voice of the Highland Lady. That voice has its own comment to make for example when she chooses in most cases to refer to her stern mother with a capital M.

Place names have been presented in their most immediately recognisable modern spelling. This was especially necessary for the many Gaelic place names around Rothiemurchus, for it is clear from these and other words that Elizabeth Grant's Gaelic was phonetic, suggesting that she had a reasonable comprehension of the language as it was spoken by most of Speyside at that time. The dance *Shean Trews* she writes as *Chantreuse* place names like *Drumochter*, the *Lairig Ghru* and *Carrour* she writes as *Dromouchta, Laigrew* and *Carower*. Her Father is recorded as *Ian Peck* rather than *Beag* (little), and *briach* (pretty) is written 'breach, breach (pronounced pree-ack)'. Slough Mouich, which she gives as 'the pass of the wild boars' is an accurate translation where Lady Strachey's Slochd More is obviously wrong.

Stylistic matters apart, there are a number of substantial benefits in a return to the full text. In the first place a much fuller, sharper and less ambiguous portrait is drawn of the Grant family. For the early reviewers in 1898, Elizabeth Grant's mother was 'unsympathetic, indolent and autocratic withall' (*The Times*) and *Blackwood's Magazine* concluded she was 'one of those unfortunate people in whom physical suffering has produced some curious twist of the moral nature.' The more complete portrait shows her mother to be even less likeable, and in some respects ill-tempered and cruel to her children. That this was an opinion she kept to the end of her mother's life is shown by the comment in her *Journal* for 26 September 1842:

> I had almost forgot there were evil passions in human nature, I have lived so long where none are either felt or met with and it jars against my temper to find suspicion, envy, spite, idle curiousity and unkind constructions all in full vigour, in an old woman, too, within a footstep of the tomb. Much, much mischief has she wrought during her life . . .

*Blackwood's Magazine* saw Sir John Peter Grant as 'one of those brilliant men who are not born to succeed.' *The Times* described him as 'sympathetic enough, but wayward, extravagant and, though not without shining parts, impracticable and unsuccessful in life.' His daughter adored him but she was not blind to his failings: her account of church collections, inter-family loans and legacies, not to mention the smuggling of china from Holland, show him to have been unreliable and evasive, with his financial affairs in such constant disrepair that he would resort to almost any means to improve them. Furthermore her younger brother, William, the future Laird, was clearly suspected of having mishandled some of the funds gathered for the family's flight to India, so that it comes as no surprise to learn that his future mother-in-law, the famous actress Mrs Siddons' daughter should have imposed such a heavy-handed wedding settlement.

With the restoration of such a family portrait, warts and all, there is a clear gain in historical value, and in readability, too. Elizabeth Grant's comments on society are shown to be equally trenchant, once the editorial discretion of the earlier versions is discarded. Her sympathetic comments on what she called the madness of George III, the full description of the deranged behaviour of the writer Basil Hall and Archdeacon Hawtayne, and the oddities of Lady Colville, the wife of the Governor of Mauritius, all help to produce a more interesting and complete picture. Not surprisingly, in the light of her time and station, Lady Strachey invariably pruned all references to sexual misdemeanours.

This removed the stories about Lord Archibald Hamilton; General Wynward's 'undisguised devotion' to General Anstruther's wife; Lady Wiseman, who sought 'safety in numbers' while her husband was at sea, and the Queen of Sweden's unseemly pursuit of her former lover, the Duc de Richelieu . . . 'we set the whole affair down to foreign manners.' All of these undoubtedly enliven the text. Perhaps the greatest loss was the full story of that engaging femme fatale 'Mrs X', now revealed as the wife of Colonel Henry Churchill, whose escapades so enlivened the voyage home from India.

Readers of previous editions will be able to discover further insights or points of detail to give new interest and impact to the familiar narrative. Thus the Highland Lady's scathing comments on Sir Walter Scott and his family (more than a matter of their different political and social backgrounds), adds an unexpected dimension to our understanding of Scott's contemporary reputation. Shelley's undergraduate shortcomings at her uncle's Oxford college; Sir Edward Barnes' misgovernment of Ceylon; and the unfailingly critical mentions of Eton, to which her brothers were sent, these and many other examples provide additional and welcome insights into a fascinating period.

*The Times*' first review saw Elizabeth Grant as 'simple, sincere, kindly and unaffected' and described her as an 'engaging chronicler of the ways, manners and experiences of her youth.' The unexpurgated edition demonstrates that there was a steelier and racier side to her reminiscences, less in tune with the moral complacencies and certainties at the end of the century. This is confirmed by the realistic and honestly matter-of-fact accounts, of servant immoralities at Rothiemurchus and the resulting regular pregnancies. The long saga of Peggy Davidson, and the apparent suicide of her former lover Simon Ross, is a good case in point. An otherwise puzzling mention of a pension awarded to a former servant, Mrs Sophy Williams is now revealed as reparation by her employer for the careless accident that left her with a

wooden leg. Elizabeth Grant never shirked her own responsibilities, not least to the truth.

The first volume of this edition tells of the Highland Lady's
childhood and adolescence in Rothiemurchus, Edinburgh
and London, set against the efforts of her father, Sir John
Peter Grant, to improve his family fortunes. He himself was
somewhat uneasily placed between the role of a traditional
highland chief and that of a substantial landowner with
ambitions to be an advocate in Edinburgh and an M.P. at
Westminster. As the original *Scotsman* review commented,
'The portraits of the numberless host of family connections
and retainers are drawn with spirit and humour,' and
Elizabeth Grant's reputation as a fascinating and reliable
chronicler of the first quarter of the century is enhanced by
this expanded account of her own family's trials and tribu-
lations. The volume ends as the decision is taken to move to
Edinburgh, a city then in the last glow of the Scottish
Enlightenment. There she met and came to know many of
the movement's leading figures, especially those whose Whig
political sympathies were shared by her father. It was hoped
that the change to Edinburgh would bring prosperity to the
father and enhance the marriage prospects of the daughter.

The second volume begins in 1814, when the author was
seventeen, and it shows that these new hopes did not last.
Elizabeth suffered a broken engagement and her own
unhappiness only echoed the difficulty encountered by her
father as he pursued his legal and political ambitions. The
summer of 1819 was spent in a family tour of Holland, after
which the decision was taken to return to Rothiemurchus as
Sir John Grant retreated from political aspiration in the face
of his financial problems and a life increasingly dominated
by pressing creditors. The Grant sisters played their part by
writing articles and stories for the popular magazines of the
day. Elizabeth was proud to record what the owner and
publisher of *Fraser's Magazine* said about her first attempts:
'the very best things of the kind I ever read . . . if these are
the first productions of a Writer, what must her future efforts
produce?' Rescue for the Grants was to come in the
somewhat unexpected form of a Bombay judgeship, which

Elizabeth believed to be a reward for certain favours her father managed for George IV on the occasion of his celebrated visit to Scotland in 1822. The *Memoirs* end with an Indian section during which the thirty-three years old Elizabeth Grant finds the chance of future happiness in marriage to an Irish landowner, Colonel Henry Smith, then in the East Indian Company Cavalry. After all the problems of youth and maidenhood, it looked at last as if the Highland Lady's future was secure, 'an end indeed to Eliza Grant.'

These recollections have had a devoted following amongst all sections of the reading public for nearly ninety years. Their publication now, in a form faithful to the original intentions of the writer, means that a full text is available for the first time outside the immediate family. Elizabeth Grant's witty eye never fails to animate the manners, fashions and events of her day; more than that, her manuscript is an inexhaustible document of social and historical value. *Memoirs of a Highland Lady* has confirmed its reputation as a masterpiece of nineteenth-century Scottish writing.

Andrew Tod

Another reprint, with a new cover, belatedly gives me the opportunity to thank my Perthshire friends Nick Du Boulay, Richard Fitzsimmons, Robert Proctor, Alastair Thomson, Emily Roy and Nicola Turnbull for their unstinting encouragement and infectious enthusiasm over the years. It should be noted that all *Dictionary of National Biography* (thereafter D.N.B.) references are to the original, not the new Oxford D.N.B. There is one addition Elizabeth Grant made to her original text. This takes the form of a somewhat rambling, occasionally repetitive post script of some six hundred words, which nevertheless contains interesting ideas and comments and it has therefore been added to the text.

A.M.T., October 2005

# *Preface*

After breakfast and my little walk I write the recollections of my life, which I began to do on my birthday to please the girls, who eagerly listen to the story of their mother's youth, now as a pleasing tale, by and bye it will be out of a wish to feel acquainted with people and places I shall not be at hand to introduce them to. This effort of memory amuses me extremely. I live again my early years, among those who made the first impressions on my mind, many of them gone where I am perhaps slowly but very surely following, and I recall places very dear to my imagination, which were I now to see I should probably, from the changes made in them, know no more. I am glad I thought of this way of occupying my quiet day, a part of it at least, the hour or two thus employed steals easily away. The pleasure of talking over these bygone times with my children attaches us the more to one another. As we become more confidential in our intercourse, we make the tale profitable too by the comments we engraft upon it, and best of all it encreases my content with the present, the contrast between my maiden days and married life being to all rational feelings so much in favour of the latter.

from the *Irish Journals of the Highland Lady*
8 June 1845

VOLUME I


MEMOIRS OF MY LIFE
BEGUN TO PLEASE MY CHILDREN
AND MY NIECE
AVRANCHES
MAY 1845[1]


1. The families of Elizabeth and Mary Grant
   spent 1843–1845 in Pau and Avranches.

# CHAPTER ONE

# 1797-1803

I WAS born on the 7th of May 1797 of a Sunday evening at No. 5 N. side of Charlotte Square, Edinburgh, in my father's own lately built house and I am the eldest of the 5 children he and my Mother reared to maturity.

My parents had married young. My father wanted a few weeks of 22 and my Mother a very few of 21 when they went together for better for worse, my poor Mother! They were married on the 2nd of August 1796 in the church of the little village of Houghton le Spring in the County of Durham. I have no genealogical tree of either family at hand, so not liking to trust to memory in particulars of this nature, I must be content with stating that my father was descended not very remotely from the Chief of the Clan Grant and that these cadets of that great House having been provided for handsomely in the way of property and having also been generally men of abilities in their rude times, had connected themselves well in marriage, and held rather a high position among the lesser Barons of their wild country.

My mother was also of ancient birth, the Ironsides having held their small estate near Houghton certainly from the times of our early Norman kings, the cross they wear for arms having been won in the holy wars; the tradition in the family indeed carried back their origin to the Saxon era to which their name belongs, and it may be so, for Saxon remains abound in that part of England.

My parents met in Glasgow in their dancing days and there formed an attachment which endured to the very close of their long lives through many troubles, many checks, and many changes. But they did not marry immediately, my father at the period of their first acquaintance not being exactly his own master. His childhood had been passed strangely without any

3

fixed plan and in various homes under widely differing systems, but with the certain future of wealth and station if he lived. The beautiful plain of Rothiemurchus, with its lakes and rivers and forest and mountain glens, offered in those old days but a few cleared sunny patches fit for tillage. Black cattle was its staple produce – its real wealth, its timber, was unthought of, so that as its sons multiplied the Laird of the period felt some difficulty in maintaining them. The result in the generation to which my Grandfather, Dr William Grant, belonged, was that he with another brother [Dr George], and a set of half Uncles much about their own age, were all shoved off about the world to scramble through it as they best could with little but their good blood to help them. The fortunes of this set of adventurers were various; some fared well, others worse, but all who survived returned to end their days where they began them, for no change of circumstances can change the heart of a highlander. Faithful to the impressions of his youth wherever he may have wandered, whatever may have befallen him, to his own hills he must return in his old age, if only to lay his bones beneath the heather. At least it was so in my Grandfather's day, for he died at the Doune,[1] still but the Laird's brother, surrounded by his relations. He had prospered in his struggle for independence, beginning his medical studies at Aberdeen and pursuing them thro' several of the continental hospitals, remaining some time at Leyden and then fixing in London, where he got into good practice; turned authour so successfully that one of his works, a treatise on fever,[2] was translated into both French and German; and then married an heiress of the name of Raper of a very respectable and highly talented family.

1. The name of the principal house on the Rothiemurchus estate.
2. *Observations on the late Influenza, the Febris Catarrhalis Epidemica of Hippocrates as it appeared in London in 1775 and 1782*, by William Grant m.d. (printed for the author and published London 1782, price one shilling). An earlier work on fever had been translated into French in 1773 and an essay of 1775 on 'Jail Fever' into German in 1778 (Dictionary of National Biography).

They were for some years childless, 12 I think. Then came my father and 4 years afterwards his only sister, my Aunt Mrs Frere, at whose birth her mother died. Good Mrs Sophy Williams, my father's attendant, Bonne or nursery Governess, soon removed with both her charges to their Grandfather Raper's country house at Twyford, near Bishop's Stortford, where they remained till his death. My Aunt was then adopted by other Raper relations and my father went back to his father, who just at that time was retiring from his profession. In due course he accompanied the Doctor to Rothiemurchus on his father's death, which happened very suddenly and very shortly; his Uncle Rothy took entire charge of his heir. The summers were passed at Inverdruie,1 the winters at Elgin and a succession of Tutors – queer men enough, by their pupils' account of them – were engaged to superintend the studies of this wilful boy and a whole host of cousins, who helped to spoil them. This plan not exactly answering, one country school after another was tried, and at last the High School of Edinburgh, where his time wore away till the period of College arrived. He was sent to Glasgow with the intention of being prepared for the Bar; there he met my Mother. She was on a visit to her elder sister, Mrs Leitch, a very beautiful woman, the wife of one of the principal merchants of that eminently mercantile city.

My Mother's education had been a very simple matter. She had grown up healthy and happy in her own village among a crowd of brothers and sisters and cousins amounting to a multitude, learning the mere rudiments of knowledge from the village schoolmistress, catching up stray bits of better things from the lessons of her brothers, and enjoying any chance gaiety that now and then wakened up the quiet but very sociable neighbourhood. My Grandfather Ironside was a clergyman, rector of an adjoining parish, curate of his own, and with his little private income might have done more for his children had he not had so many of them, and been besides a man of rather expensively hospitable habits. My Aunt Leitch's marriage opened the world to the family and my Mother's engagement to my father was the first result.

1. A small house on the property.

As I have mentioned, the marriage was deferred awhile, and before it took place both the Bride's father and the bridegroom's Uncle died. My Grandfather Ironside had been so long helplessly paralytick, that his death was really a release from a very pitiable existence. My Uncle Rothy died suddenly in the full vigour of a green old age. He was found in his study, leaning back in his chair, a corpse, with his large Bible open before him. This event much altered my father's position, it enabled him to marry when he liked, and it would have released him from his legal studies had he been inclined to give them up; but besides that he thought a knowledge of law necessary to the usefulness of a country gentleman, he really liked the profession; and the French revolution, in the startling shake it had given to the aristocracy of all Europe while it was annihilating its own, had made it a fashion for all men to provide themselves with some means of earning a future livelihood, should the torrent of democracy reach to other lands. He therefore, during the year of mourning requisite on both sides, took a lodging in Edinburgh, where he gave a succession of bachelour entertainments, got through his Law trials, and then, to make sure of the fidelity of his attachment, went over to Ireland with an Irish College friend, and made a gay tour thro' Cork, Limerick, Wicklow etc. before appearing at Houghton. My Mother expected him, but she had not thought herself justified in formally announcing this; she had therefore to meet some frowns for having rejected noble and wealthy suitors, for the sake of him who was considered to have been trifling with her, and whom she must have loved for himself alone—for mind and manner only—as neither he nor she had any idea of the extent of his inheritance, and in person he was not handsome.

On their marriage my parents settled in Edinburgh, which was to be their home and where my father had purchased one of the only three houses then finished in Charlotte Square. Here he was to pursue his profession, spending the summer vacations either on the beautiful highland property, or in travels which were sometimes to extend to the south of England, a pretty estate in Hertfordshire having fallen to him just at this time by the death of an Uncle Raper.

The house at Thorley Hall was so small as to be inconvenient, but its furniture was valuable. A fine library, some good pictures, portfolios of prints, and all sorts of philosophical instruments formed part of it, all of which were removed to the Doune. The land was worth about £1200 a year. The rents of Rothiemurchus were small, not more than £800, but the timber was beginning to be marketable; 3, or 4,000 a year could easily have been cut out of that extensive forest for ever and hardly have been missed the while.[1] My Grandfather Grant had left his son £10,000 in ready money and my Aunt Frere inherited her mother's fortune, so that life began with these happy young people well. To assist in the spending of what was then a fine income, there were numberless relations on both sides to bring gay spirits, a good deal of talent, a good deal of beauty, with healthy appetites to the hospitable board where they were so welcome. Bachelour friends, too, were not wanting and as at that time gentlemen seldom re-appeared in the drawing-room after dinner, they made, as the wine merchant thought, excellent use of their freedom from ladies' society.

My memory, however, does not go back to these scenes, it is very indistinct as to all that happened before I was four years old. I remember nothing of Edinburgh but a certain waggon full of black sacks which represented coals, and which I vainly attempted to pull or push up some steps in the garden, and which I think was taken from me for crying, so that its possession must have been very near my baby heart when the impression was so vivid on it. I have a dreamy recollection of at about this time beating a boy in a red jacket who was playing with me and of shutting up another in some cupboard, while I went about with his drum which he had refused me. My victims were my regular companions, the children of the houses on each side of us. The red jacket was the present Sir George Sinclair, agricultural Sir John's eldest

1. The Hon. Mrs Murray Aust of Kensington visited Rothiemurchus during the tour that led to her *Companion and Useful Guide to the Beauties of Scotland* (1803); in it she described how 'Mr Grant annually cut down perhaps £1500 of timber; and yet when riding through his woods, not a tree to the eye is missing.'

son,[1] and the drum boy was poor little Johnny Redfearn, who died at five years of age, to the abiding grief of his parents. He was the last survivor of their once well-filled nursery. But beyond this, I have no remembrance of Charlotte Square, which, considering that I was but three years and a half old when we left it for ever, is not surprising.

Of the highlands, that dear home of all our young hearts, I have more perfect glimmerings. My father and mother had spent there the summer following my birth, and I fancy the winter also, and the next summer, at the end of which in September my brother William was born. I had been named Elizabeth after my two Grandmothers and two Aunts, one of each side, Mrs Leitch and Mrs Frere. William Patrick was called after both Grandfathers and my great Uncle Rothy whom my father had immediately succeeded. He was christened by the presbyterian parson and nursed by my mother, so that perhaps that nursing winter was the one they all spent at the Doune, with my two Aunts, Mrs Frere and Mrs Bourne, then Lissy Grant and Mary Ironside, for company.

It was when I was weaned there had come a tall randy kind of woman from Forres, a Meg Merrilies,[2] to take care of me; our much-loved Betty *Glass* in those days, Betty Campbell afterwards when she married the grieve. She had William from his birth and to test the strength of the young heir, she gave him, before she washed him, a spoonful of gin in highland fashion, which medicine he survived to my great sorrow; for spoiled as I had been, the darling of so many, I so much disliked the arrival of this brother near the throne, that I very early tried to make away with him. One day that I had been left alone in his room before his dressing time I seized his clothes, which had been all stitched together and laid upon the bed ready to put on him and carrying the bundle to the fire tried to throw it on the flaming peats, saying with all the spite of a baby not a year and a half old could give way to,

1. Sir John Sinclair (1754–1835), was the celebrated agricultural improver, first President of the Board of Agriculture and organiser of the Statistical Account.
2. From Sir Walter Scott's *Guy Mannering*. Six feet tall, she is 'a kind o' queen among the gipsies' . . . Beelzebub's post-mistress . . . a harlot, thief and witch.

'Dere! Burn! nassy sing!' which exclamation brought in an Aunt, horrourstruck. But all this is hearsay. Of my own impressions I have a clear recollection of some West Indian seeds, pretty, red, shiny and with black spots on them, sweet-smelling beans and a variety of small shells, all of which were kept in a lower drawer of a japanned dressing table in my Mother's room, for the purpose, it appeared to me, of my playing with them.

I recollect also the bookcases in my father's study, a set of steps by which he used to reach the upper shelves and up which I used to climb in terrour not of a fall, but of being set in the corner as a punishment—a fox-tail for dusting dirty volumes and a dark place in the wall where the peats were kept, so that I think while my Mother was taken up with her baby boy I must have been the companion of my father. I also remember building materials lying about, an old woman with a wooden leg warning me from some mischief, and a lady in a blue gown assisting me to play at see saw, she and I sitting on the ends of a plank laid across a trestle, and a clapping of hands around answering my laughter. I have also a painful remembrance of a very tearful parting from our dear Betty, who declined accompanying us when we left the Doune.

All these clearer visions of the past must relate to a summer spent in the highlands after the birth of my sister Jane, which event took place in Edinburgh in the month of June of the year 1800. I don't imagine we ever returned to Charlotte Square afterwards.

My Mother nursed Jane herself, and Betty, unassisted, took charge of us all three. Our nursery at the Doune was the room at the head of the backstairs my Mother afterwards took for her own. It had two windows looking towards Inverdruie, a fire on the hearth, two wooden cribs made by Donald Maclean, a cot cradle, a press bed for Betty into which we all of us scrambled every morning, a creepie apiece for William and I, and a low table of suitable height on which our porridge was set in the mornings. I hated mine and Betty used to strew brown sugar over it to make it more palatable. She washed us well, dressed us after a fashion, set us to look at pictures while she tidied the room and then set off out of doors, where she kept us all day. We were a great deal in the fields with John Campbell the grieve and we talked to every body we met, and Betty sang to us and told us fairy tales, and made rush crowns for us, and kept us as happy as I wish all children were. I don't feel that I remember all these details accurately, there is just an idea of some of them fixed by after allusions.

In the winter of 1802, after a season of all blank, I wake up in a gloomy house in London in Bury Place. There were no Aunts, no Betty, a cross nurse, Mrs Day, who took us to walk somewhere where there was gravel, and nothing and nobody to play with; the few objects round us new and disagreeable. William and Jane were kept in great order by Mrs Day. William she bullied. Jane she was fond of; every body was fond of Jane, she was always so good. Me she did not like, I was so selfwilled. I therefore gave her very little of my society, but spent most of my time with Mrs Lynch, my Mother's maid, an Englishwoman who had been with us some time, engaged in London soon after my Mother's marriage when they first visited Thorley Hall. Mrs Lynch taught me to sew, for I was always very fond of my needle and my scissors too. I shaped and cut out and stitched up my doll's clothes from very early days. I used to read to her too, she was so good natured! I fancy my Aunts had taught me to read, though I do not remember this or them up to this date.

My books had very gaudy paper backs, red and green and all manner of colours, with dashes of gold dabbed on, in size vigesimo quartos,[1] paper coarse, printing thick, and the contents enchanting! Puss in boots, Riquet with the tuft, Blue Beard, Cinderella, the geni and the fisherman; and in a plain marble cover on finer paper, full of prints, a small history of Rome, where one print so shocked me—Tullia in her car riding over the body of her father—that I never would open that classic page again.

It is here in Bury Place that the first distinct notion of the appearance of my parents presents itself. I see my father in his study at a table writing; a little sallow brisk man without any remarkable feature, his hair all drawn back over his head,

1. The size of a book in which each sheet is folded into 24 leaves.

powdered and tyed in a queue with a great bow of black ribbon. He has on drab coloured stocking pantaloons and little boots up to the knee, from the two pointed front of which dangles a tassel. The last Duke of Gloucester wore the very dittos, stocking pantaloons and all, when we saw him in the year '32 at Cheltenham. Strange, as this figure now rises before my mental eye, it is one which always produces recollections of happiness, for my father's voice was the herald of joy to us children. He was the King of all our romping plays, had always something agreeable to say, and even when too much occupied to attend to us, would refuse our petitioning faces with a kindness and an air of truthful regret so sympathetick that he gave us nearly as much pleasure as if he could have assented. There was a charm in his manner I have never known any one of any age or station capable of resisting under any circumstances, and which my dear sister Mary inherited. My Mother, though accounted such a handsome person, impresses my memory much less agreeably. A very small mouth, dark hair curling all over her head in a bush down close to her eyes, white shapeless gowns, apparently bundled up near the chin without any waist visible, her form extended on the sofa, a book in her hands, and a resident nervous headache which precluded her from enduring noise, is the early recollection that remains with me concerning her. She had probably been ill in Bury Place, which had contributed to make our residence there so melancholy.

The reason of our removal from Edinburgh to London was my father's having determined on giving up the Scotch for the English bar. Why, with his large fortune, and plenty to do both on his Highland and his Hertfordshire properties, he should have followed any profession but that of managing them, nobody could very well tell. But as his wish was to be a great lawyer, some of his dear friends, in whose way he stood in Edinburgh, easily persuaded him that his abilities were too superiour to be frittered away in a mere provincial town, and that Westminster Hall was the only sphere for such talents—the road to St. Stephen's! the fit arena for display! No thought of their country's good in those days, the general interest was of little account compared with the individual's fame for speaking!—very little being *done* in Pitt and Fox days. I have often thought my poor Mother's headaches had something to do with all these mistakes of her young, much loved husband. She had certainly, as far as I remember, very little of his company, only just during dinner, and for the little while he sat to drink his wine afterwards. William and I always came to them at that time, and when my Mother went up to the Drawing room to make the tea we two went on further to bed. Though so young, we were always sent upstairs by ourselves to our nursery at the top of the house in the dark; that is, we had no candle, but a glimmering light fell in rays on the windings of the crooked stairs from a lamp on some landing above. On the small gallery on the second floor, which we had to pass on our ascent to our atticks, there stood a big hair trunk into which I had often seen Mrs Lynch dive for various necessaries required in her needle works. Poor William, who was kept in the nursery by Mrs Day, and who during his periodical descents and ascents seldom looked beyond his own two little feet, which he had some difficulty in placing and pulling up and down after him while she was tugging him along by whichever unfortunate arm she had hold of, had never noticed in the sunlight this object, which appearing large and dark in the gloomy evenings, and feeling rough to the touch, he took for a wild beast, the wolf, in fact, which had eaten up Red Riding Hood. He began at first to shrink and then to shudder and then to stop, till soon I could not get him past the trunk at all. Our delay being noticed by Mrs Day, that enlightened person, on being informed of the cause, took upon herself to put an end to all such nonsense in a very summary manner. She shook me out of the way, and well thumped poor William. The next night the terrours of the journey and his probable warm reception at the end of it so worked upon the poor child's mind that he became quite nervous long before bedtime, and this sort of agony encreased so much in the course of a day or two that my father noticed it. My Mother noticed nothing but as we kept our disgraceful secret faithfully our misery continued a little longer, till my father, certain there was something wrong, followed us as hand in hand we very slowly withdrew. He found William stifling his sobs and trembling in every limb some steps below the fatal landing, and I, with my arm round him, kissing him and trying to encourage him to proceed. My father called for lights and without a word of anger or mockery shewed his boy the true nature of this object of dread. He was led gently to it, to look at it, feel it, sit on it, see it opened, not only then, but in the morning; and though we had still to go to bed by ourselves, the drawing room door was henceforward left open till our little steps were heard no more.

About this time, that is during the course of the two years which followed our arrival in London, various perceptions dawned on my young mind to which in recollection I can prefix no date, neither can I remember the order in which I learned them. My Aunt Lissy became known to me. She had lived generally with my father since his marriage; it was her home; but though she was the lady in the blue gown, I have no distinct idea of her before this, when she returned from some visit she had been paying and brought to Jane and me a pretty basket apiece. Mine went to bed with me, was settled at my feet that I might see it the first thing in the morning. I see it now, as plainly as then, an oval open basket of fine straw, not by any means small and with a handle apparently tied on by two knots of blue ribbon.

In the summer of this year we must have gone to Tunbridge Wells, for I remember perfectly a house near the Common there upon which we were allowed to run about all day, and where to our delight we found some heather which we greeted as an old friend. I recollect too a green paper on the walls of the room in which I slept covered all over with sprigs in a regular pattern, that it amused me extremely to wake up in the morning and fall a-counting. In the autumn we must have gone to Eastbourne, for I well remember the seashore, splashing my feet into the cool green water in the little pools between the rocks, picking up seaweed, star fish and jelly blobs, and filling my dear basket with quantities of shells. At some inn on our way either to or from one of these places, while we little people were at our bread and milk supper at one table, and the elders at their dinner at another, we were all startled by the sounds of a beautiful voice outside, clear and sweet and very tuneful, singing 'Over the mountains

and over the moors, Hungry and barefoot I wander forlorn.'
It was one of the fashionable ballads of the day out of a
favourite farce—'No song no supper,'[1] I think, and not
inappropriate to the condition of the poor creature who was
wandering about singing it. My father opened the window
and threw out 'some charity,' when the 'kind gentlefolks'
were rewarded by another verse which enabled me to pick
up the air, and it became my favourite for many a month to
come, 'piped in a childish treble'[2] very unlike the silvery
tones I had learned it from.

William and I were taken to see a ruin near Eastbourne,
and what was called the field of Batile [Battle] Abbey, and my
Mother, in that sack of a white gown with a little hat stuck
round with bows of ribbon on one side of her head, showed us
the spot where brave King Harold fell, for she was a Saxon in
name and feeling, and in her historical lessons she never
omitted the scanty praise she could now and then truthfully
bestow on the race she gloried in descending from. It is
curious that I have no recollection of learning anything from
any body except thus by chance as it were, though I have
understood I was a little wonder, my Aunts having amused
themselves in making a sort of show of me. I read well at 3
years old, had long ballads off by heart, counted miraculously,
danced heel and toe, the highland fling, and highland shuffle,
and sang, perched upon the table, ever so many Scotch
songs, 'Tommin soo ze eye' and such like, to the amusement
of the partial assembly. I fancy I was indebted to Aunt Mary
for these higher accomplishments; counting I know my Aunt
Lissy taught me, with a general notion of the four first rules
of arithmetick by the help of little bags of beans, which were
kept in one of the compartments of an immense box full of all
sorts of *tangible* helps to knowledge. My further progress in
the art might have been checked had my father and mother
been so unwise as to carry out an intention they frequently
reverted to: that of going over from Eastbourne to France.
The short peace with France had been signed early in the
year. I can perfectly remember the illuminations in London

1. Dialogue Opera (1790) by Stephen Storace (1762–96).
2. *As You Like It*, II, v. 162.

on account of it. On a clear day the French coast was distinctly visible through a telescope from Eastbourne and so many fishing-boats came off from thence with cheap poultry, eggs, and other market wares that people were quite bit with a wish to make so short a voyage. Some that did never returned, war having been again declared, and Buonaparte retaining all travellers unlucky enough to have trusted themselves to his ill temper.

Before Christmas we were established in the tall house in Lincoln's Inn Fields, which continued for 10 years to be the principal home of the family. 1803 therefore saw us settled in this new abode, where our fine, airy nurseries, though reached at the expense of a weary climb, were a delightful change from the gloom of Bury Place. We had the Square to play in, were allowed to run about there without a maid, and soon made acquaintance with plenty of children as well pleased with new companions as ourselves. From this time our town life was never an unhappy one. In the winter my Aunt Mary, who had been away, returned with Aunt Fanny, my Mother's only other unmarried sister. They remained some months, which we children liked. Aunt Mary was dearly loved by us all. She knew how to manage us, could amuse without letting us plague her—an art poor Aunt Fanny did not understand so well. My Mother's youngest brother, my Uncle Edward, who was pursuing his studies at Woolwich with the intention of proceeding to India, spent his vacations frequently with us. Besides these there were highland cousins innumerable, who, on their periodical flights from the wild hills where they could find nothing, to the broad world where they never failed to gather plenty if they lived, were sure of a resting-place on their passage with my father. It was a strange household for London, this hotel for all relations. We were play things for every one, and perhaps a little more made of than was good for some of us.

Amongst other indulgences this spring I was taken twice to the play and once to Sadler's Wells with William. The first play was 'The Caravan.' John Kemble[1] acted in it—the

1. John Kemble was ⅙ proprietor and actor-manager of
   Covent Garden in 1803; John Bannister was acting
   manager of Drury Lane.

lover, and a very lugubrious one he seemed to be. The actor that delighted me was a dog, a real Newfoundland trained to leap into a cataract and bring dripping out of the water, real water, a doll representing a child which had spoken in the scene a few minutes before, and had then appeared to be dropt by a lady in distress while flying across a plank up at the top of the stage, the only bridge across the torrent. They could not persuade me the doll was not the real child; I thought it dead, drowned, and cried and sobbed so violently I was hardly to be pacified—not till all the audience had been attracted by the noise. The other play was 'The busy body.' Bannister in all sorts of scrapes, doing mischief continually from over officiousness, hid in a chimney, discovered when least welcome, etc., a collection of *contretemps* that fidgetted and annoyed much more than they amused me. The horsemanship with the tumblers, ropedancers, etc., I did not like, they frightened me. William, little as he was, was in extasies.

In the month of May of this year, 1803, on the 21st, in the evening, my sister Mary was born. From this I date all my perfect recollections. All that happened stands clearly before me now at the end of so long a life as if that one event had suddenly wakened up a sleeping intellect. It was indeed a matter of some moment to me, for in some way the new baby and I were thrown upon each other from her birth. Jane was so engrossingly the pet of my mother and the companion of my brother, that she was less my associate than the mere difference in our ages warranted. My father was always busy, my mother generally ill, William, the heir, was the child of consequence to all the family connexions of course more noticed by them than either of us his sisters were. I was not romp enough for him so that he did not seek me unless Jane was out of the way; therefore when my Aunts were away I was often lonely. The baby just suited me for a playmate— to watch her, amuse her, help to attend upon her, and by and bye to work for her and teach her, was my delight, and as I was six years old when she was born, I was quite a little mother to her, preferring her infinitely to the dolls which had hitherto chiefly occupied me. I was never weary of watching her. Cross Mrs Day had been replaced by a very good natured

Mrs Herbert, a Widow, who had seen better days, and whose son, her only child, was in the blue coat school [Christ's Hospital]. He was now and then allowed to come and see his mother in his curious dress—the queer petticoat, coat, yellow stockings and little wee cap. Mrs Lynch was still with us. We spent most of our time in the Square with plenty of companions, so that altogether this spring in London has left a sweet memory behind it.

My mother had been alarmingly ill after the birth of this her finest child. She had lost the use of her limbs, and was carried up and downstairs, and to and from the carriage, when she took her airings on a sort of King's cushion. As my father found it necessary to proceed to the highlands in the summer and had to attend Circuit somewhere in the north of England, it was resolved that she and we should have a few weeks of sea bathing at Scarborough on our way. A sort of couch was contrived for her, on which she lay comfortably in the large *berline*[1] we had hitherto used, and which the four horses must have found heavy enough when weighted with all its imperials, hat boxes, and the great hair trunk that had been poor William's terrour in Bury Place. Mrs Lynch and McKenzie, who had been my father's valet before he married, were on the outside; my father, Jane, and I within with my mother, and we travelled with our own horses driven by two postillions in green jackets and jockey caps, leaving London, I think, in July. In the heavy post chariot behind were the two nurses, the baby in a swinging cot, William, who was too riotous to be near my mother, and a footman in charge of them. What it must have cost to have carried such a party in such a style from London to the Highlands and how often we travelled that north road! Every good inn became a sort of home, every obliging Landlord and Landlady an old friend. We had cakes here, a garden with a summer-house there, a parrot further on, all to look forward to on every migration, along with the pleasant flatteries of surprise at our growth and our looks of health, as if such a train would not have been greeted joyously by every publican. We travelled slowly, 30 miles a day on an average, starting late and

1. A four-wheeled covered carriage, with a hooded seat
   behind.

stopping early, with a bait soon after noon when we children dined. I forget when we reached Scarborough, neither can I recollect any particular impression made by the town itself or the country around, but I do remember feeling astonishment at the sight of the sea, and also surprise and *annoyance*—who would have believed this in such a child—at our not having a whole house to ourselves, but lodging in the lower and very upper part of a house, the rest of which was occupied by the family of Sir Thomas Liddell. Another merry set of children to play with might have reconciled me to the humiliation of sharing our temporary abode with 'our neighbour,' had we then been able to secure such companions as the first few days promised. Overtures on both parts were answered on both parts, and Lady Williamson, Lady Normanby,[1] Lady Barrington and two little white faced brothers had arrived at blowing soap bubbles most merrily with William, Jane and me, when laughing too loud one unfortunate morning, our respective attendants were attracted by the uproar and flew to separate our happy group. They shook us well, shook Grants and Liddells, and scolded us well, and soon divided us, wondering what our Mammas would say at our offering to make strange acquaintance, when we knew we were forbid to speak to any one they did not know. So we Grants used to listen to the Liddells, who monopolised the garden, and to their mother who played delightfully upon the Harp, and amuse ourselves as we best could, alone.

We were a great deal out upon the beach, sometimes wandering about the sands with the nurses, and always taking one drive along that beautiful shore close to the sea with my mother. The sands are very extensive at Scarborough, very firm and very even, and there are caves and curiously shaped rocks, and an old Castle on a height, if I recollect rightly.

My father returned to us some time before we left, for I remember his explaining all about the Life Boat, taking us to see it, and telling us tales of wrecks and storms in which it had

1. One of these children, Lady Normanby's son (who was
   to be Lord Lieutenant of Ireland 1835–39 when
   Elizabeth Grant and her husband resided on their
   estate in Co. Wicklow) married Maria, daughter of Sir
   Thomas Liddell.

been useful, reading to us about the sea, and about ships and sailors and commerce, using the occasion to impress upon our minds all sorts of information on these subjects, which was indeed the way he generally taught us. There was a violent storm of thunder and lightning about this time, which introduced *us* to electricity and Dr Franklin,[1] and did an immensity of damage in and around Scarborough, killing cattle and people and destroying a great deal of property. It was quite unusually terrific, so as often to have been alluded to in after years as the frightful thunderstorm of 1803, a point of comparison with others.

A company of strolling players happening to arrive in the town, William and I were taken to see them. The state of their play house not a little astonished us. The small dirty house, though wretchedly lighted, brought the audience and the stage so close together that the streaks of paint on the actors' faces were plainly visible, also the gauze coverings on the necks and arms of the actresses. Then the bungling machinery, the prompter's voice, the few scenes and the shabby scene shifters, all so revealed the business that illusion there was none, and we who at Drury Lane and Astley's and Covent Garden had felt ourselves transported to Fairy Land, were quite pained by the preparations for deception which the poor Strollers so clumsily betrayed to us. The Play was Rosina, an opera,[2] and the *prima donna* so old, so wrinkled, so rouged, that had she warbled like my own Janey she would have been ill selected as the heroine; but she sang vilely, screamed and I must have thought so, for I learned none of her songs, and I generally picked up every air I heard. Soon after the Play I was laid up with scarlet fever, which I notice as I had it twice afterwards and have had returns of the scarlatina throat all my life.

Upon leaving Scarborough we proceeded to Houghton, where I must have been before, as many changes in the place struck me. I have no recollection, however, of a former visit.

1. Benjamin Franklin (1706–90), the American statesman and scientist, was the author of *Experiments and
   Observations on Electricity* (1751).
2. Ballad opera by William Shield, first produced at
   Covent Garden in 1782.

As I remember it from this one, the village consisted of one long, wide, straggling, winding street, containing every variety of house, from the Hall standing far back beyond the large Court yard, and the low, square, substantial mansion even with the road, to the cottage of every size. A few shops here and there offered a meagre display of indifferent wares. About the middle of the village was the church half concealed by a grove of fine old trees, the Rectory, and the then celebrated boys' school near it. The finest looking of the Court dignified Halls belonged to the Nesham family, from amongst whom my Grandfather Ironside had chosen his wife. She had had but to move across the little street to the most ancient looking of the low substantial houses which offered a long double row of windows and a wide doorway to the dusty path, only protected by posts and chains from the close approach of passengers. A kitchen wing had been added on one side; behind this were piled the roofs of the offices. A clump of old trees sheltered the east end. A large well filled garden at the back stretched down a long slope to a small brook that drained the neighbouring banks, and all around lay the fields which had descended from *father to son*, they said, *at least* for 700 years. In this quiet abode my Grandmother Ironside had passed her life of trials. Her Nesham home had not been happy. A violent, positive, money making father, no mother, one sister who never married, and two brothers, one at sea, the other as busy in the coal mines as her father, these composed the interior of the second house in size in the village, Houghton Hall, belonging to the Huttons, being the first. My Grandfather's ranked third. My Grandmother's love was another Romeo and Juliet story. The rich coal owner despised the Curate suitor, while the pride of seven centuries, collected in the bosoms of all having the remotest affinity to that much prized holy cross, revolted at so inferiour a connection for an Ironside as the gentle, graceful daughter of an upstart who had built his own house himself. Temper was very uncontrouled in those days. People, moving little, got into a set of prejudices they had no means of shaking by intercourse either with men or books, the reading of the period being of the most limited kind. And after habit had a little softened bitter feelings, children came fast and quick and noisy, funds were small, and my Grandfather, an hospitable careless man, leaving his farm to his man Jacky Bee, and his tithes to his clerk, Cuddy Kitson, his children to the pure air of his fields, and his wife to herself—her cares as soon as he found it pleasanter to be elsewhere was rather an encrease than a help to her difficulties. And for ten years the poor man was bed rid, paying assistants to do his duty, and thus still further diminishing the little my Grandmother could reckon on for the support of their numerous offspring. Only nine of her fifteen children grew up to be provided for. My Mother and three sisters, the eldest of whom was married when very young to Mr Leitch. The eldest son, my Uncle William, went early into the army; Uncle Ralph was in the Law. My Uncles John and Edmund were taken into Mr Leitch's Counting house; Uncle Edward was a boy at school when my Grandfather died. His wife did not long survive him, she lived but to bless me; and in the old family house at Houghton she had been succeeded by a pretty young woman of most engaging manners but small fortune, who had persuaded my Uncle William to give up his profession for her sake, and in the full vigour of his manhood to settle down for life on the few acres he had not the skill to make productive, and which in a less luxurious age had been found insufficient for the decent wants of a family.

My Mother always went to Houghton well provided with trifling presents for her numerous connexions there. There had never been any lack of daughters in the household of the reigning Ironside, and they formed quite a Saxon Colony by their marriages. We had a Great Aunt Blackburn, Horseman, Potter, Goodchild, with cousins to match, all the degradations in name possible bestowed on the Serf Saxon by his conquering Norman lord—with one redeeming Great Aunt Griffith who, however, had never recovered caste among her relations for her misalliance with, I believe, a schoolmaster, though had they followed my clever Welsh Great Uncle to his mountains his maligners might have heard of a princely ancestry.

Two Maiden sisters of this generation, my Great Aunts Peggy and Elsy, lived in the village in a square low house very near to and very like my Uncle's, but it stood back from the road, and was kept delightfully dark by some large elm trees which grew in front in a court yard. This retreat was apparently sacred to the ancient virgins of the family, for *their* Aunts Patience and Prudence had been established there before them. I hardly remember these old ladies, Aunt Elsy not at all, though it was in their house that Jane and I were domiciled. Aunt Peggy made more impression. She was fat, rosy, merry, idle, told funny stories, made faces, and winked her eyes at good jokes when sometimes her laughing listeners rather blushed for her. My mother was much more attached to her Aunt Jane Nesham, the only and the maiden sister of her mother; her house was just opposite to my Uncle's and it was the home of my two unmarried Ironside Aunts, my Mother's sisters, Mary and Fanny. Aunt Mary was not often there, she went on long visits to Mrs Leitch and to my Mother, and to an Indian Colonel and Mrs Ironside, distant relations who lived in London in Brook Street. Aunt Jane Nesham was a charming little old lady with powdered hair turned over a cushion and a little white muslin turban stuck up on the top of it. She wore tight fitting cross folded gowns with full skirts, much as we wear them now, the whitest and the clearest muslin handkerchiefs puffed over her neck, a row of pearls round her throat, and high heeled shoes. Her house was order itself, her voice gentle and her smile the kindest. She had been in the highlands with my father and mother before my recollection. The cousins Nesham lived in the village, at least the then head of the family with one or two of his unmarried sisters and his young wife. Mrs Griffith and a disagreeable daughter had a small house there, and the clergyman, the schoolmaster, the Doctor and Squire Hutton, and there was a very populous neighbourhood. Such was Houghton as I first remember it. How different from what it is now. There are no gentry, the few neat rows of Pitmen's houses of that time have grown into streets belonging to a town. It is all dirt and bustle and huge machinery and tramways, one of which cuts through the fields of the Ironside inheritance. These frightful tramways were our childish delight; such a string of waggons running along without horses reminded us of our fairy tales, and the splendid fires blazing on all sides enchanted us, after the economical management of scanty fuel we had been accustomed to in

London. We liked our young cousins too, three or four of whom were old enough to play with us.

The next stoppage on our northern journey was at Edinburgh, where we remained long enough for an abiding impression of that beautiful city to be made on a young mind. The width of the streets, the size of the houses, the brightness and the cleanliness, with the quantity of gooseberries to be bought for a penny, impressed me before I was capable of appreciating the grandeur of its position. It was then very far from being what it became a few years later, how very very far from what we see it now! The new town was but in progress, the untidy appendages of building encumbered the half finished streets, and where afterwards the innumerable gardens spread in every quarter to embellish the city of palaces, there were then only unsightly *greens* abandoned to the washerwomen. My father had always business to detain him here. We put up at Blackwood's hotel, at the corner of the north bridge in Princes Street, where my Mother received a quantity of visitors of all degrees, amongst whom was my nurse, an ill conducted woman, never a favourite, yet who managed to keep up a claim to assistance by dint of persevering pretence of tenderness for her nursling. The same scene was rehearsed regularly—she had always a long string of misfortunes to bewail, disappointments and losses and cares of one sort or another, the death of five children amongst the rest. But somehow my foster sister 'bore a charmed life,' for not only did she exist and flourish, but she actually got younger occasionally, even to my father's short seeing eyes—my Mother was always clearer sighted—a miracle that at length put an end to our forbearance.

The Queen's ferry was the next landmark!, to speak in Irish fashion. No steamer in those days, no frame to run the carriage on from quay to deck. Ugly, dirty, miserable sailing vessels, an hour at the quickest crossing, often two or three, it was the great drawback to the journey. The landing at Inverkeithing was as disagreeable as the embarking, as tedious too. We seldom got on beyond Kinross that night, where Queen Mary, the Castle, the lake, red trout, and a splendid parrot all combined to make it one of our favourite resting places. At Perth we were always met by my father's only surviving Uncle, Sandy, the parson, his mother the Lady Jean's favourite son, and her youngest. He was of the episcopalian church, and had at this time the care of a chapel at Dundee. He was a popular preacher, had published very fair sermons,[1] was an accomplished person for his times, gentlemanly in manner, taller than the 'little Grants,' more of a Gordon, in fact, in his appearance. He had had a good deal to do with my father's education, and his own five ill brought up sons had been my father's principal companions towards his College days. My mother never thought kindly of this uncle, to whom my father was much attached. She judged him perhaps harshly, an easiness of temper may have been fully as much the cause of the loose discipline he maintained as want of principle, which she ascribed his errours to, errours they were and errours of evil consequence proving him to have been unfitted for the charge of youth. He probably had been deficient in the capacity to avoid them.

It took us three days to reach home from Perth, Blackbird, Smiler, and their *pairs* who met us there, and whose names I have not remembered not being in as great a hurry to return to the Doune as we were. There was no good ford near the house in those days, the shifting river not having revealed the rather deep one near the offices we used so constantly afterwards; besides, there was then no road from the bridge of Alvie down the heathery bank to the bogach and so round its shallow waters to the riverside. We had to drive on, after a good peep of our dear home, two or three miles past the burn at Lynwilg, towards Aviemore, and then turn off down a seldom travelled road through the birch woods—I smell them now—to the ford at Inverdruie, where there was a carriage boat at the ferry a little higher up the stream, so that travellers could cross in all states of the river.

Once 'over the water' we were at home in Rothiemurchus, our beloved Duchus,[2] which, through all the changes of our

---

1. *Sermons on Various Subjects and Occasions*, by Alexander Grant D.D., Minister of the English Episcopal Chapel at Dundee; two volumes, published in 1800 at Dundee.
2. A Gaelic word having much the same signification as *domain*. The crest of the family is an armed hand holding a broadsword, with the motto 'For my Duchus.'

lives, has remained the spot on earth dearest to the heart of every one of us. We have been scattered far and wide, separated, never now *all* to meet again. We children have grown up and married and have had new interests engrafted on our old feelings, and have changed our homes and changed all our surroundings, and most of us have lived long, busy years far away from the Highlands, yet have we never any one of us ceased to feel that there was the magnet to which all our purest, warmest, earliest, and latest affections were steadily drawn. No other place ever replaced it, no other scenery ever surpassed it, no other young happiness ever seemed to approach within a comprehensible distance of our childhood in Rothiemurchus.

# CHAPTER TWO

# 1803–1804

It was in July or August 1803 when we crossed the Spey in
the big boat at Inverdruie in a perfect fever of happiness.
Every mountain, every hill, every bank, fence, path, tree,
cottage was known to us, every face we met revealed a
friend's, and our acquaintance was by no means limited, for
the 'wide plain of the fir trees,'[1] which lies in the bosom of the
Grampians, cut off by the rapid Spey from every neighbour,
has its beautiful variety of mountain scenery, its heights, and
dells, and glens, its lakes and plains and haughs, and it had
then its miles and miles of dark pine forest through which
were little clearings by the side of rapid burnies, and here and
there a sawmill. We were expected, so from the boathouse to
the Doune it was one long gathering, all our people flocking
to meet us and to shout the 'welcome home!'—the only time
that I remember so great an assemblage on our arrival, the
custom becoming obsolete, warm and hearty as it was.
William and I knew every one, remembered every thing. Our
dear Betty waited for us at the house anxiously. She had
married the grieve, John Campbell, and was now a great lady
in her high cap and shawl, and she had a baby to shew us, a
little daughter, the only child she ever had, called after me, to
whom I was bringing a real silver coral with more than the
usual complement of bells. She had been left in charge of the
house and beautifully clean she delivered it. We thought the
floors so white, the polish so bright, the beds so snowy, all so
light, so airy, our nursery so enchanting with its row of little
plain deal stools, creepies, and our own dear low table, round
which we could ourselves place them. We were certainly

1. James B. Johnston, *Placenames of Scotland* (1892),
   suggests 'Fort of the big firs'—rath mhòir ghuithais.

26

easily pleased with any thing Highland, for a less luxurious abode than the charmingly situated Doune at that date could hardly have been the residence of a lady and gentleman.

It took its name from a long low hill in the form of a boat with its keel upwards, at the end of which it had been rather ill advisedly built, and which had been fortified in the ruder ages when the dwelling of our ancestors had been upon the top of it. I never saw the vestige of a ruin there, but the moat is perfect and two or three steep terraces along the side. When improving times permitted our ancestors to descend from their 'Doune,' a formal Scotch house was built at the foot of it, with a wide door in the centre, over which were emblazoned the arms in a shield, and as many narrow windows were stuck in rows over the wall as were required to light the rooms within. A kitchen built of black turf was patched on to one end which had an open chimney and bare rafters overhead. A green duck pond and such offices as were at the period necessary were popped down any where in front and all round, wherever and whenever they were wanted. There were a barn and a smithy, and a carpenter's shop and poultry houses, all in full view from the principal rooms, as was the duck pond. A perfect network of sluggish streams, back water from the Spey, crept round a little knot of wooded islands close at hand, and a garden lay at the foot of the hill. My Uncle Rothy had not latterly lived here; he had married a very delicate woman, a daughter of Mr Grant of Elchies, commonly known as a Lord of Session by his legal title of Lord Elchies. She had persuaded him that the situation of this old family mansion was unhealthy, which, considering all the wood and water on this side of the Spey, and the swamp of the bogach on the other, was probably a correct opinion. He had therefore built at Inverdruie, to please her, a modern mansion very like a crab with four extended claws, for there was a dumpy centre to live in, with four low wings, one at each corner, for offices; and this was set down on a bare heath, with a small walled garden behind and a pump standing all alone some little way off in front. Here with them my father had spent his boyhood, always, however, preferring the Doune, which had been, when deserted, let to various half Uncles and second cousins, retired half pay

Captains and Lieutenants, who all, after their wandering youth, returned to farm out their old age in the highlands. A few years before his death my grandfather, the Doctor, had taken possession of it and anticipating a much longer tenure, undertook many improvements. To the end of the old house opposite the black kitchen he stuck an outrigger of an overwhelming size, containing a cellar to which the descent was by stone steps outside, a large dining room on the ground floor and a couple of good bedrooms above reached by a turning stair. As an additional object from the windows he erected a high stable, where as long as it stood my brother William spent his leisure, and he encreased the old garden, laid it out anew, and stocked it from Hertfordshire. The entrance to this paradise of our childhood was by a white gate between two cherry trees, such cherry trees, large white heart, still standing there to prove my taste, and by no means dwarfish looking even beside the fine row of lime trees that extended on either side. The old house had a few low rooms on the ground floor with many dark closets; the principal apartment was on the first floor, and reached by a wide and easy stair; the family bedroom was on the one hand, a large hall on the other for the reception of guests, and the state bedroom through it. Up in the atticks, beneath the steep grey roof, were little rooms again. This was the highland home to which my mother had been brought a Bride.

I imagine that the furniture had been very much suited to the style of the house; there was some plate, some fine old china and glass and a few valuables of little use but as curiosities. The state bed and bedroom were curtained with rich green silk damask heavily fringed, and the japanned toilette table in which was my drawer of shells with a mirrour to match, and numberless boxes, trays, and baskets of japanned ware belonged to this chamber; the other rooms were, I fancy, rather bare. There was, however, never any lack of living furniture. My Mother found established there my great Uncle Sandy the Parson with his English wife, her sister and all their carpet work, two of the five sons, an old Donald, a faithful servant of my grandfather's, who had been pensioned for his merits, an old Christy who had gone from Strathspey to wait on my father and my Aunt Lissy, and their

*Bonne* good Mrs Sophy Williams. She had had her leg shot off in the garden at Twyford by some unlucky Raper cousin, while she was wandering about there in her double employment of frightening the birds with a rattle from the cherry trees, while watching Master Jack's operations in the strawberry beds. She had her pension and her attick and so had Mr Dallas, one of the line of tutors, when he chose to come to it. Then there were College friends, bachelour cousins, and it was the fashion of the country for any of the nearer neighbours, when they came in their full dress to pay their occasional morning visits, to expect to be pressed to remain the day, often the night, as the distances are considerable in that thinly peopled district. My father and mother never wanted for company, and the house was as full of servants as an Indian or an Irish one, strange, ignorant creatures, running about in each other's way, wondering at the fine English Maids who could make so little of them. Amongst the rest was a piper, who, for fear of spoiling the delicacy of the touch of his fingers, declined any work unconnected with whisky, which with plenty of oatbread and cheese was given to all comers all day long.

Most of the farms in Rothiemurchus were occupied by relations. Colonel William Grant was at the Croft, Captain Lewis Grant at Inverdruie. These were my father's great Uncles. Lieutenant Cameron, a cousin, came to Kainapool from Kinrara as soon as a former tenant left it. Up in Badenoch and down in Strathspey there were endless humble connexions most attentive in observing the visiting customs of the country. Relations at a greater distance were not wanting,—Cummings in Morayshire, McKenzies in Ross-shire, Grants in Urquhart, etc. Of great neighbours there were few. Highland properties are so extensive that there can neither be walks nor rides in general to the homes of equals. Each proprietor holds, or *held* perhaps I should say, his own little court in his own domains and when he paid a brother Laird a visit it was in a stately manner befitting the rareness of the event, and the number of miles he had to travel. Our great house then was Castle Grant, the residence of our Chief. It was about twenty miles off down Speyside. My father and mother were much there when they first married, my Aunts

Mary and Lissy delighting in the gaiety of so new a scene to them. Generally about fifty people sat down to dinner there in the great hall in the shooting season, of all ranks. There was not exactly a 'below the salt' division so marked at the table, but the company at the lower end was of a very different description from those at the top, and treated accordingly with whisky punch instead of wine. Neither was there a distinct 'yellow drawing room' party, though a large portion of the guests seldom obtruded themselves on the more refined section of the company unless on a dancing evening, when all again united in the cleared hall. Sir James Grant was hospitable in the feudal style; his house was open to all; to all and each he bade a hearty welcome; and he was glad to see his table filled and scrupulous to pay fit attention to every individual present. But in spite of much cordiality of manner it was all somewhat in the king style, the Chief condescending to the Clan, above the very best of whom he extremely considered himself. It was a rough royalty too, plenty, but rude plenty, a footman in the gorgeous green and scarlet livery behind every chair, but they were mere gillies, lads quite untutored, small tenants' sons brought in for the occasion, the autumn gathering, and fitted into the suit that they best filled. Lady Grant was quiet and ladylike, Miss Grant a favourite, the rest of the family of less account. This was my Mother's description to me years afterwards, when all connexion between us and the head of our house had unhappily ceased.[1]

A permanent member of our family at this time I must not forget, for I bore her great affection. She was indeed very kind to us, and very careful of us the few years she remained in the household. She was a natural daughter of my Grandfather's, born long after his Wife's death and had been brought up by his sister the Lady Logie. When this great Aunt of mine died, 'Miss Jenny' removed as matter of course to the family asylum, as I may call my father's house. She was entrusted with the storeroom keys, and was employed as a

1. Sir James Grant was born in 1738 and died in 1811 'at Castle Grant where the greater part of his useful life had been spent' (D.N.B.); see I, pp. 71–2 for an explanation of this dispute.

general superintendent of the family business till she married, which event, luckily for her, poor thing, was not very long delayed. A red haired Forres beau, a Mr Arthur Cooper, learned in the law, thought the connexion would make his fortune and her little money set him up, which they did and so relieved my Mother of one of her burthens. It was indeed a strange mixture of ranks and positions and interests that she was the Head of and I don't imagine that all was always harmony among them. My parents were both too young, too inexperienced, to be very patient with such an heterogeneous assemblage. It might do very well in the bright summer weather when an outdoor life in the pure air occupied all the day and produced a glow of spirits for all the night, but there were wintry weeks in this gay sphere of theirs, clouds and storms and chills, when annoyances gloomed into grievances, and worry brought on ill humour. I have the recollection of many a tart word that had better have been left unsaid, of eyes red and swollen with weeping, of gaiety repressed and happiness checked and constraint engendered—temper—temper—take every gift we covet most, take health and wealth and skill and talent, take all that all most long for, leave me but temper—temper to bear and temper to *forbear* and where that Christian temper is even in one member only of a household, there will be comfort, comfort attainable by each of us, requiring less of energy than we expend on things that by comparison with it are valueless. A little self controul for one week and we ensure the happiness of ourselves and all depending on us. In those days, unluckily, education had not extended to the temper. My Mother's family cares were principally confined to such as she could reach with her needle, in the use of which she was very dexterous. As for the rest, after the dinner was ordered and the windows opened, matters were very much left to the direction of the chances.

My father was a much more active person, very despotick when called on to decide, yet much beloved. An eye every where, nursery, kitchen, farm, stable, garden, tenantry, but not a steady eye, no prevention in it, fitful glances seeing sometimes too much, and very summary in the punishment of detected offences. He was principally occupied at this time with his mason and carpenter, as he was making great changes in and about the Doune. These changes, indeed, employed him all his life, for he so frequently altered in the present year what had been executed the year before, that neither he nor his allies, Donald McLean and the Collys, were ever out of work.

The changes effected up to this period, the autumn of 1803, when we all reached our beloved highland home from Scarborough and Houghton, were of some importance. My Grandfather's outrigger had been heightened and lengthened, and carried back beyond the old house, the windows in it had all been changed and enlarged, and ornamented with cut granite; in fact, a very handsome modern wing appeared in place of an ill contrived ugly appendage. It was intended at no very distant time to have matched it with another, and to have connected the two by a handsome portico, all in front of the old house, which would have been entirely concealed, and being single, was to have had all its windows turned to the back, looking on a neat square of offices, some of which were now in progress. My Grandfather's new dining room was thus made into a pleasant drawing room, his turning stair was replaced by an easier one in a hall which divided the drawing room from a new dining room, and in which was the door of entrance to this modern part of the house. Above were the spare bedrooms and dressing rooms, and over them two large atticks, barrack rooms, one for the maids, the other for visiting maidens, young ladies who in this primitive age were quite in the habit of being thus huddled up in company. In the old part of the house my father's study, the ancient reception hall, had been cut short by a window to give him a dressing room and the black kitchen outside had vanished, much to the satisfaction of my Mother and Mrs Lynch, who declared no decent dinner could by possibility be dressed in it. It was indeed a rude apology for a set of kitchen offices. A mouse one day fell into the soup from the open rafters, a sample merely of an hundred such accidents.

To make room for the new range of servants' rooms, part of the end of the hill had to be cut away, spoiling entirely the boat shape of our Doune. The soil thus removed was thrown into the nearest channel of the backwater, it being my father's intention to fill these up by degrees; an improvement to which William and I were decidedly opposed, for on the broom island, the largest of the group amidst this maze of waters, our very merriest hours were spent. A couple of wide, well worn planks formed the bridge by which we crossed to our elysian field; two large alder trees grew close to the opposite end of this charming bridge, making the shallow water underneath look as dark and dangerous as 'Annan Water' did to Annie's lover; an additional delight to us. Between the two large alders hung in gipsy fashion the large caldron used for the washing; a rude open shed, just sufficient to protect the officiating damsels from the weather; tubs, cogues,[1] lippys, a watering pot and a beetle, a piece of wood, bottle shaped, with which the clothes were thumped, Indian and French fashion, lay all about among the yellow broom under the alders and hazels on this happy island, the scene of as much mirth and as much fun as ever lightened heavy labour, for be it remembered the high stable was in very close neighbourhood. William and I were never failing parts of the merry group, for our time was pretty much at our own disposal, Jane only joining us occasionally. We two elder ones were of an age to say our lessons every day to my Mother, and we always faithfully learned our twelve words, that is, I did, out of a red marble covered book filled with columns of words in large, black print. But my Mother was not often able to hear us—sometimes she was ill, and sometimes she was busy, and sometimes she was from home, and sometimes she had company at home, and sometimes she was not up, so our lessons had often time to be got pretty perfect before we were called upon to say them. But we had plenty of story books to read on rainy days, and we had pleasure in reading to ourselves, for even Jane at three years old could read her 'Cobwebs to catch flies' and she or I read to William. I was fond, too, of dressing my doll by the side of Mrs Lynch, and of learning to write of McKenzie. On fine days we were always out, either by ourselves or with a son of the old gardener's, George Ross, to attend us. There was also

1. A wooden vessel for carrying water.

a highland nursery maid and Mrs Acres, the baby's nurse, superintending. Amongst them they did not take very good care of us, for William was found one sunny morning very near the Spey, sailing away in a washing tub, paddling along the backwater with a crooked stick in his hand for an oar, and his pocket handkerchief knotted on to another he had stuck up between his knees for a flag. A summerset into the rapid river stream, had he reached it, would have made an end of him, but for my voice of rapturous delight on the bank where I stood clapping my hands at his progress, which directed some one to our doings, and thus saved the young Laird from his perilous situation.

So passed our summer days. We grew strong and healthy, and we were very happy, revelling among the blackberries on the Doune till we were *tattooed*, frocks and all, like the American Indians; in the garden, stung into objects by the mosquitoes in the fruit bushes; in our dear broom island, or farther off sometimes in the forest, gathering cranberries and lying half asleep upon the fragrant heather, listening to tales of the fairy guardians of all the beautiful scenery around us. I was a tall, pale, slight, fair child to look at, but I seldom ailed anything. William, fat and rosy and sturdy, was the picture of a robust boy. Jane was the beauty, small and well formed; with a healthy colour and her Ironside eyes, she was the flower of the little flock, for Mary was a mere large, white baby, very inanimate, nor anyway engaging to any one but my Mother, who always made the youngest her favourite.

In winter we returned to Lincoln's Inn Fields and then began our sorrows. Two short walks per day in the Square, sauntering behind a new nurse, Mrs Millar, who had come to wean the baby; an illness of my Mother's, whose room being just beneath our nursery, prevented all the noisy plays we loved; and next, a governess, a young pretty timid girl, a Miss Gardiner, quite new to her business, who was always in a fright lest neither we nor herself were doing right, and whom we soon tyrannised over properly; for my father and my Mother and my Aunts went to Bath to meet Mr and Mrs Leitch; and we were left with this poor Miss Gardiner, who from the beginning had always lived up in the schoolroom with us, and never entered the drawing room unless invited.

How well I remember the morning after her arrival. She had charge of William, Jane, and me. We were all brought in by Mrs Millar and seated together upon a low sofa without a back which had been made for us. Our schoolroom was the large front nursery, curtained anew and carpeted. There were besides the sofa, four chairs, two tables, one in the middle of the room, one against the wall; a high fender, of course, two hanging bookcases, six framed maps, one on Mercator's projection, which we never could understand; a crib in which William slept—I slept in my mother's dressing room, Jane in the nursery—and between the two windows a large office desk, opening on each side, with two high stools belonging to it. To encrease the enjoyment of this prospect, into my hands was put the large edition of Lindley Murray's grammar,[1] William was presented with 'Geography by a Lady for the use of her own Children,' not one word of which he was capable of reading, and Jane, who had fine easy times of it in our eyes, though I question whether at three years of age she thought so, had a spelling book given to her. Such was the commencement to us of the year 1804. We were soon as thoroughly miserable as our anxious parents from this method of instruction could expect. The lessons were hard enough and numerous enough, considering the mere infants who had to learn them, but for my part, though I would rather not have had them, they were very little in my way, although the notes of the *whole* musick gamut were included, with the names of all the keys and the various times, etc., all at a blow, as it were. It was never any trouble to me to have to get whole pages off by rote; I was not asked to take the further trouble of thinking about them. No explanations were either asked or given, so that the brain was by no means overexcited, and the writing and cyphering and piano forte lesson which followed the drier studies of the morning pleased me extremely. Hook's easy lessons[2] were soon heard in great style, played by ear after the first painful reading,

1. *English grammar adapted to the different classes of learners. With an appendix, containing rules and observations for assisting the more advanced students to write with perspicuity and accuracy* (5th edition, York, 1799).
2. *Guida di Musica* (c.1785) by James Hook.

without any one but the performer being the wiser. But what we wanted was our fun, flying from crib to crib on awaking in the morning, dancing in our night clothes all about the room, making horses of the overturned chairs, and acting plays dressed up in old trumpery. We had only sedate amusements now. How delighted I was to escape sometimes to my Aunts, from one of whom, my Aunt Mary, I heard stories, sometimes real, now fabulous, always containing some moral, however, which I had wit enough to apply silently, as occasion offered. By my Aunt Lissy I was diverted and instructed through the contents of the big box full of every sort of object likely to interest a child.

Poor Miss Gardiner! She was neither reasoning nor reasonable, too young for her situation, without sufficient mind, or heart, or experience for it, a mere school girl, which at that time of the day meant a zero. Her system of restraint therefore became intolerable, when from the absence of the heads of the family we had no relief from it—for about this time my father and Mother had gone to meet Mr and Mrs Leitch at Bath. Still a certain awe of a person placed in authority over us had prevented our annoying her otherwise than by our petulance, till one day that she desired us to remain very quiet while she wrote a letter, rather a serious business with her. It was to my mother to give an account of our health and behaviour. She took a small packet of very small pens from a box near her, and a sheet of very shiny paper, and after some moments of reflexion she began. I observed her accurately. 'What do you call those pretty little pens?' said I. 'Crow quills, my dear,' said she, for she was in manner very kind to us. 'William,' said I in a low aside, 'I don't think we need mind her any more, nor learn any more lessons, for she can't really teach us. She is a fool, I shan't mind her any more.' 'Very well,' said William, 'nor I, nor I shan't learn my lessons— he never yet had learned one, for a more thorough dunce than this very clever brother of mine in his childish days never performed the part of booby in a village school, but it was very disagreeable to him to have to try to sit quiet behind a book for half an hour together two or three times a day, poor child! He was but five years old and he was of course satisfied with any suggestion that would release him.

Some weeks before, my mother had received a note in my father's absence, which appeared greatly to irritate her. The contents were never made known to me, but on my father's return home she imparted them to him with some lively comments to the disparagement of the writer. 'I always knew she was a fool,' cried she, for she spoke strongly enough when excited; 'but I did not expect such an extreme proof of her folly.' 'My dear,' replied my father, in his quietest and calmest voice, 'what *did* you expect from a woman who writes on satin paper with a crow quill!' In my corner with my doll and pictures I saw and heard a great deal that passed beyond it. Miss Gardiner fell her proud height on the day she wrote her letter, and she never regained a shadow of authority over us, for I led all, even 'the good little Jane.' Like Sir Robert Peel, Louis quatorze and other dictators, *'je fus l'état, moi!'*[1] and respect for our poor governess had vanished. The next time the crow quills and satin paper occupied her, William and I provided with the necessary strings got ready beforehand, tied her by her dress and her feet and the hair of her head to the legs of the chair and the table, so that as she rose from her engrossing composition the crash that ensued was astounding, the fright and even pain not small. She was exceedingly agitated, almost angry, but so gentle in her expostulations that, like Irish servants, we were encouraged to continue a system of annoyance that must have made her very uncomfortable. We behaved very ill, there was no doubt of it, and she had not the way of putting a stop to our impertinence. When Mrs Millar found out these proceedings and remonstrated, I told her it was of little consequence how we acted, as I knew my Papa would send her away when he came home; which he did. She was not supposed to be equal to the situation and her father came to take her home. The state of anarchy the schoolroom exhibited was perhaps as much against her remaining as the finely penned account of it, but I have since thought that her extreme beauty and my Uncle Edward's very undisguised admiration of it had as

1. Her severe judgement on Peel is explained by his 'betrayal' of party principles with the repeal of the Corn Laws in 1846, the time she began her *Memoirs*.

much to do with her departure as the crow quills. We heard a few years afterwards that she had married very happily and had a fine set of children of her own who would be all the better managed for the apprenticeship she had served with us.

Uncle Edward was now studying at Woolwich, expecting to proceed to India as a Cadet. Fortunately old Charles Grant was able to change his appointment and give him a writer-ship,[1] so he came to us to prepare his equipment. Being quite a boy, full of spirits and not the least studious, he romped with his little nephew and nieces to our hearts' content, particularly after the departure of the governess, when William and I resumed our spellings with my Mother, and Jane roamed 'fancy free.' Lindley Murray and Geography by a Lady retired from our world, but a Mr Thompson who was teaching Uncle Edward mathematicks was engaged to con-tinue our lessons in writing and cyphering. A young Mr Jones took charge of my musick, in which I really progres-sed, though I never practised. I rattled away so mercilessly, wrong notes or right ones, as it happened that I was considered to have great execution, and brilliant fingers and I was actually not ashamed to receive this most undeserved praise when in point of fact I deserved censure for extreme incorrectness—the fingers rattled away at a great rate but the listeners had to be indebted to the ear belonging to them for the few wrong notes they touched; as to the number missed out, no one took any account of them. I had a turn for drawing, too, as was discovered by the alterations I made one rainy day in my young Uncle's designs. He had been studying fortifications; his plans were said to be very neatly executed, but they were not sufficiently finished to please me. I therefore extended the patches of colour laid on here and there, round the whole works, filled up vacant spaces, etc., and I wonder now when I know all the mischief I did how my good natured Uncle could ever have forgiven me, for he had been much flattered on his skill as a draughtsman. He blamed himself for having left his plans within my reach and for having given me leave to amuse myself with his paint box.

1. One of the most influential East India Company
   directors; see A. T. Embree, *Charles Grant and the
   British Rule in India* (London, 1962).

He got into a great scrape himself during this spring. He slept in my Mother's dressing room, I being removed to Miss Gardiner's room. The shower bath stood there, altho' my Mother had given up the use of it, and it was of course supposed to be empty. We were all in this room at play with our Uncle, of whom we were very fond, and I suppose teasing him, for he suddenly caught up Jane, the most riotous of the set, and popt her into the shower bath, threatening a ducking, and touching, to prove his sincerity, the string. Down came the whole bucket full of water on the poor child's head. Both the man and the baby were frightened near to death. He actually waited till the deluge was over before his presence of mind returned, and then the piteous object he rescued, stunned almost and dripping wet, at last she spoke. 'Oh my red soos, my red soos!' it was a new pair she had had put on that morning. I suppose no words ever gave more relief to an anxious listener. The hubbub brought my Mother, who, in the impartial manner customary in nursery dealings at that time, scolded us all round, and very heartily. We three departed in tears to have 'that naughty little girl' dried, leaving Uncle Edward at the shower bath looking very sheepish.

My three maiden Aunts were with us at this time, and Uncle Ralph came for a short visit, then Mr and Mrs Leitch, all to take leave of poor Uncle Edward, whom we observed begin to look very grave. He went often out in the carriage with my father, sometimes they remained away a long time, once, all the day; and trunks came, and parcels to fill them, and Mrs Lynch was marking stockings, changing buttons, and sewing on strings for ever. She made also a long, large chintz housewife full of pockets, with an attached thread case, and a curiously nicked leaf of scarlet cloth filled with needles; it was her modest offering to Mr Edward, who truly promised to keep it for her sake, for he shewed it to me more than twenty years afterwards at his house at Cambala in Bombay.

At length came a quite sad day; all the eyes in the house were red. On meeting, every one talked with assumed cheerfulness on indifferent subjects, to which no one seemed really to attend. A sort of nervousness spread from old to young; we children felt afraid of what was coming and as the hours wore away the gloom spread. We were all in the dining room when McKenzie opened the door; Uncle Edward rose and kissed each child; Mary was his darling, he doted on her with a love that never left him. 'When shall I see you again, little woman?' said he as he set her down out of his arms;— little any one of us there thought then where the next meeting would be, or when—his heart was too full for another word; he folded my Mother silently to his breast, I remember no one else present, and followed my father out, while she fell back in a passion of tears very rare in a woman of her calm, reserved nature. I watched through the blind and saw them turn the corner of Sir Giffin Wilson's garden wall next door to us, my father leaning on my Uncle's arm, and my Uncle with his hat slouched over his brows and his head held down. It was my first idea of grief; I had never lost any body I had loved before, and it was long ere even *my* gay spirits recovered from the first scene of distress I had noticed.

One of my employments at this time was to hold the skeins of cotton thread which my mother wound off very neatly on two square pieces of card placed one over the other, so as to form eight corners between which the thread was secured. This cotton sewing thread was a great invention, a wonderful improvement on the flax thread in previous use, which it was difficult to get of sufficient fineness for some works, and hardly possible to find evenly spun. When one thinks of the machinery spinning of these days, the cotton and flax threads like the fibres of spiders' webs which we produce in ton weights now, we may indeed wonder at the difficulties in needle works overcome by our mothers.

'Evenings at Home,'[1] 'Sandford and Merton,'[2] and a short Roman history in which very little mention was made of Tullia, were added to our Library. In imitation of my Aunt Mary I began to take upon myself to tell fairy tales to 'the little ones,' sometimes relating, sometimes embellishing, sometimes inventing, choosing historical heroes to place in situations of my own imagining, turning all occurrences into romance. We acted too occasionally, dramatised striking

1. *Evenings at Home or The Juvenile Budget Opened*, by Dr Aikin and Mrs Barbauld.
2. *The History of Sandford and Merton for the Use of Juvenile Britons*, by Thomas Day.

incidents, or only played at ladies and gentlemen, copying the style of my Mother's various visitors, supporting these characters for days together at our playhours. We began to feel great interest in Shakespeare's plays, several of which we were taken to see, my father talking them over with us afterwards. I remember believing they were all extemporised by the players as they proceeded in their parts, like as we did ourselves in our own improvised dramas, and wondering whether we should ever, any of us, attain to the dignified declamation of John Kemble.

This spring of 1804 Aunt Mary had a long, serious illness. She was so weakened by it that country air was immediately recommended, so she and Aunt Fanny took lodgings at Richmond and I was sent with them. We lived in the house of a widow who had a parrot which talked to me just as much as ever I wished, and a maid who was quite pleased to have my company on all her errands. I recollect perfectly, delighting in the view of the river with so many pretty boats on it and gardens down to its edge. I liked to hear the sound of my jumping steps on the hard pathway, and I was charmed with what I called Rosamond's labyrinth—two high walls turning off at angular corners for ever, between which a narrow road led, I think, to Kew, and where the view was limited the whole way to a few yards before us. Then I only wondered when we should escape out to the open country again, now a feeling of suffocation would come over me in such a place.

Mrs Bonner, our landlady, also allowed me to help her to make my Aunt's puddings, the family preserves, pickles, etc., an honour I was extremely proud of and turned to good account in after days when recollection served me in the stead of experience. She also lent me an old tea caddy to put my work in; the sugar bowl and cannister had been broken, so the empty compartments exactly suited the patches I was engaged on, and made me as perfectly happy as if it had been the handsomest in the land. I was so improved by this visit to Richmond, that as my Aunts determined on remaining there during the summer, my father resolved to leave his two youngest children near them under the care of Nurse Millar, in whom they had full confidence. Lodgings were taken for them not far from Mrs Bonner, where they were to sleep and be sent whenever my Aunts were tired of them in the day, and William and I were to accompany our restless parents to the Doune.

I can't remember where Aunt Lissy was all this time. I often recollect her with us, and then I miss her for long whiles. Though my father's house was nominally her home she was perfectly independant, being now of age, and inheriting all that would have been her mother's property by the Will of her Grandfather Raper. She had Twyford House, near Thorley Hall, in Hertfordshire, and a considerable sum of money from the savings during her minority. I have always heard her income called about £800 a year. She was not a beauty, short, thick made, plain features, with an agreeable expression, a clear but not a fair skin, and quiet manners. She was not a genius though possessed of a good understanding—her intellect had been undeveloped, afterwards it was cramped; her temper was charming, yet she and my Mother never got on well together. She had odd, quaint old maidish ways adopted from old Raper relations, with whom she very much lived. She had also continued an acquaintance with School friends, the results of which appeared again. She certainly did not go with us this year to the highlands.

# CHAPTER THREE

# 1804–1806

WE set off then some time in July, my father and mother, William and I, Mrs Lynch and McKenzie, in a new carriage, a sociable with a cane body, a roof on four supporters hung round with leather curtains, which we were constantly letting down and tying up according to the weather, and which we never managed to arrange in time either for wet or dry, and which, in spite of hooks and buttons, let in the rain whenever the showers were heavy. A very superiour description of horses replaced the Smiler and Blackbird of earlier years, and the four bloods which formed the present team—two bays and two grays, cross cornered—were driven by the smart coachman, William Millar, from the box. These horses for beauty were each a picture; they had cost proportionate sums, and they did their work, as the Coachman said, like jewels, never giving in nor shirking when once a start—but to make the start was the difficulty. Mr Coxe, named after his last master, and the most sedate of the set, merely indulged in a few plunges; but Highflyer, the other bay, regularly lay down, and it took all the hostlers and half the postboys at every inn, with plentiful applications of William Millar's long whip, to bring him to his feet again. He was cured of this trick afterwards, I remember, by having lighted straw placed under him. The two grays were merely awkward, setting out different ways, the one to the right, the other to the left, instead of going straight forward. Such a crowd as used to gather round us. To add to the tumult, my mother, the most nervous woman that ever lived, kept screaming at the top of her voice all the time, standing up in the sociable and throwing herself half out at either side, entreating all the collected mob to have pity on her and open the door. This scene continued during the whole journey till we got quite accustomed to what at first had frightened William and me. We were pleased with our new queer carriage, glad to see our Landlady acquaintance, the boats at Boroughbridge, and other recollected objects, but we were not happy. We missed our little sisters, we talked over and over again when we were put to bed at night of all the tears shed on both sides at parting, particularly by poor Jane, who was always a most affectionate little creature. William was long before he became reconciled to the want of his favourite companion, and I regretted equally dear Mary, my live doll. It was not till we reached the Doune that we at all got over this painful separation. We were a less time than usual upon the road, luckily for our spirits, as we did not go to Houghton at all and were but a short time in Edinburgh.

On this journey I first remember old Neil Gow[1] being sent for to play to us at the inn at Inver—not Dunkeld: that little village we passed through and went on to the ferry at Inver, which we crossed the following morning in a large boat. It was a beautiful ferry, the stream full and deep and dark, the banks overhung by fine timber trees, a glimpse of a newly planted conical hill up the stream, only thick wooding the other way. I don't know whether this did not make more impression on me than Neil Gow's delightful violin, though it had so over excited me the evening before that my father had had to take me a little walk by the river side in the moonlight before I was rational enough to be left to sleep. We were odd children, full of nonsense my mother said. Left to her, a good scold and a slap would have apparently quieted her little frantick daughter, though a sobbing sleepless night would have left but a poor object for the morrow. My father understood my temperament better. As for William, he took all in an easy Ironside way, remarking nothing but the peat reek, which neither he nor I had noticed before.

We passed a very happy season at the Doune. We did no lessons; we had a Jock McKenzie to play with us in the stead of George Ross, who had been made a groom of. We rode on the old gray pony; we paid quantities of visits to our friends

1. The age of Neil Gow (1727–1807) has been called 'the golden age of Scottish fiddling'.

all through Rothiemurchus, and we often had a brace of muirfowl for our dinner, each carving our bird. A dancing master taught us every variety of wonderful highland step—that is taught me, for William never could learn anything, but he liked hopping about to the fiddle—and we did 'Merrily danced the quaker's wife' together, quite to the satisfaction of the servants, who all took lessons too, in common with the rest of the population, the highlanders considering this art an essential in the education of all classes, and never losing an opportunity of acquiring a few more flings and shuffles. The dancing master had, however, other most distinguished pupils, the present Duke of Manchester and his elder sister, Lady Jane Montague, who were then living in our close neighbourhood with their grandmother, the Duchess of Gordon.

This beautiful and very celebrated woman[1] had never, I fancy, lived very happily with her Duke. His habits and her temper not suiting, they had found it a wise plan to separate, and she had for the last few years spent her summers at a little farm on the Badenoch property, a couple of miles higher up the Spey than our Doune, and on the opposite side of the water. She inhabited the real old farmhouse of Kinrara, the same our good cousin Cameron had lived in, and where I have heard my mother say that the Duchess was happier and more agreeable, and the society she gathered round her far pleasanter, than it ever was afterwards in the new cottage villa she built about a mile nearer to us. It was a sort of backwoods life, charming to young people amid such scenery, a dramatick emancipation from the forms of society that for a little while every season was delightful, particularly as there was no real roughing in it. In the but and the ben, constituting the small farm *cabin* it was she and her daughter Lady Georgina dwelt in, by the help of white calico, a little white wash, a little paint, and plenty of flowers they made their apartment quite pretty. What had been kitchen at one

1. Jane, daughter of Sir William Maxwell of Monreith, Bart., (1749–1812) married the fourth Duke of Gordon; for *The Scots Peerage* she was 'the beautiful, witty, eccentric and daring Duchess of Gordon, the heroine of innumerable anecdotes'.

end of the 'house' was elevated by various contrivances into a sitting room; a barn was fitted up as a barrack for ladies, a stable for gentlemen; a kitchen was easily formed out of some of the out offices, and in it, without his battery, without his stove, without his thousand and one assistants and resources, her French cook sent up dinners still talked of by the few remaining partakers. The *entrées* were all prepared in one black pot—a large potato *chaudron*, which he had ingeniously divided within into four compartments by means of two pieces of tin sheet crossed, the only inconvenience of this clever plan being that the company had to put up with all white sauces one day and all brown the next. Her favourite footman, Lang James, a very handsome, impudent person, but an excellent servant for that sort of wild life, able to put his hand to any work, played the violin remarkably well, and as every tenth highlander at least plays on the same instrument tolerably, there was no difficulty in getting up a highly satisfactory band on any evening that the guests were disposed for dancing. Half the London world of fashion, all the clever people that could be hunted out from all parts, all the north country, all the neighbourhood from far and near without regard to wealth and station, and all the kith and kin both of Gordons and Maxwells, flocked to this encampment in the wilderness during the fine autumns to enjoy the free life, the pure air, and the wit and fun the Duchess brought with her to the mountains.

Lady Georgina Gordon, the youngest of the fair sisters of that, the last generation of that noble name, and the only one unmarried, was much liked; kind hearted she has all through her life shown herself to be; then, in her early youth, she was quiet and pleasing, as well as lively. Unchangeable in amiability of manner, she was very variable in her looks; one day almost beautiful, the next day, almost plain; so my mother described her when she described those merry doings in the old cottage at Kinrara in days quite beyond my memory. Lady Georgina had been some years married to the Duke of Bedford, and the Duchess of Gordon was living in her new house in this summer of 1804 when I first recollect them as neighbours. Our two dwellings were little more than a mile apart, but as I have said, the river was between us, a river not always in the mood for assisting intercourse. There were fords which allowed of carriage and pony communication at several points, but only when the water was low. At flood times passengers had to go down the stream to Inverdruie, or up the stream to near Loch Inch to the big boats, when they carried their equipages with them; those who walked could always find a little boat near every residence, and our ferries were in constant requisition, for no day passed without a meeting between the Doune and Kinrara. When the Duchess had miscalculated her supplies, or more guests arrived than she could possibly accommodate, the overplus as a matter of course came over to us. All our spare rooms were often filled even to the many beds in the barrack, and at Kinrara shakedowns in the dining room and the sofas in the drawing room were constantly resorted to for gentlemen who were too late for a corner in the 'wooden room,' a building erected a short way from the house in the midst of the birch thicket upon the banks.

Many changes had happened in our family since my baby recollections of the members of it. Old Donald was dead, old Christy was pensioned and settled with some relations in Duthil; Miss Jenny was married, my Uncle Sandy's five sons were all sent abroad about the world, and my father's first cousins, Glenmoriston and Logie, who used to be a good deal with us while bachelours, were both of them married and fixed in their beautiful homes and so the style of our house was a good deal altered, improved. There were still the Captain and Mrs Grant at Inverdruie, and the Colonel at the Croft, and Mr Cameron at Kainapool, and there were at a little distance, up in Badenoch, old Invereschie and his niece, and young Belleville and his bride. Cluny beyond in Laggan; down the Spey, Castle Grant, Ballindalloch, Arndilly and Altyre; Moy, Burgie, etc., in Morayshire; parties from which houses were frequently with us—all except our Chief. I don't remember my father and mother going much from home this season, or indeed at all, except to Kinrara; they had not time, for so many English travellers were in the habit of making hotels of the houses of the highland proprietors, there was a sort of running stream of them during the latter part of summer. Mrs Thrale and her daughters,[1] and Mr and Mrs Murray Aust,[2] my mother afterwards continued an acquaintance with. In general, these chance guests were hardly agreeable enough to be remembered.

William and I joined in all the fun of this gay summer. We were often over at Kinrara, the Duchess having perpetual dances, either in the drawing room or the servants' hall, and my father returning these entertainments in the same style. A few candles lighted up bare walls at short warning, fiddles and whisky punch were always at hand, and then gentles and simples reeled away in company till the ladies thought the scene becoming more boisterous than they liked remaining in; nothing more, however, a highlander never forgets his place, never loses his native inborn politeness, never presumes upon favour. We children sometimes displayed our accomplishments on these occasions in a very prominent manner, to the delight, at any rate, of our dancing master. Lady Jane was really clever in the Killie callum and the 'chantreuse', I little behind her in the single and double fling, the shuffle and the heel and toe step.[3] The boys were more blundering, and had to bear the good natured laugh of many a hard working lass and lad who, after the toil of the day, footed it neatly and lightly in the Ballroom till near midnight. Lord Huntly was the life of all these meetings; he was young, gay, handsome, fond of his mother, and often with her, and

1. Mrs Thrale (1741–1821), later Hester Lynch Piozzi, was celebrated for her literary friendship with Dr Samuel Johnson (the D.N.B. comments 'she cast off her daughters as decidedly as she did Dr Johnson'.)

2. In her *Companion* (1803, p. 7), 'sketching in some detail the social condition of the northern peasantry', she wrote: 'I had the pleasure of spending a fortnight at that most enchanting place in 1801 . . . the proprietor and his lady have great taste!'

3. Killie callum: the *Gille Caluim* (two pence) is a traditional sword dance. Chantreuse: the *Seann Triubhas* (old trews) 'according to a popular tradition was the only dance that the Gaels would condescend to perform in the dress imposed by the Disclothing Act' after the '45. See John MacInnes, *Companion to Gaelic Scotland*, edited by Derick S. Thomson (Oxford, 1983).

so general a favourite, that all people seemed to wake up as it were when he came amongst them. Kinrara had to us come in lieu of Castle Grant. There had been some coolness between my father and Castle Grant about Election matters; the Chief and the Chieftain differed in politicks, and had in some way been opposed to each other, a difference that very foolishly had been allowed to influence their social relations. Many and many a family jar was caused in those times by the absurd violence of party feeling.

We were now to travel back to London in the sociable, rather cold work in cold autumn weather. We had to drive unicorn, for one of the gray horses was gone; the other therefore had the honour of leading the equipage, a triangular style not then common and which ensured us an abundant amount of staring during our journey, a long one, for we made a round by 'the west countrie' in order to pay two visits. My Uncle Leitch had bought a pretty place near Glasgow, and made a very handsome house out of the shabby one he found there by adding to the front a great building in very good taste. We two were quite astonished with the first aspect of Kilmerdinny. Large, wide steps up to a portico, a good hall, and then a circular saloon the height of the house, out of which all the rooms opened, those on the upper floor being reached by a gallery which ran round the saloon. Fine gardens, greenhouse, hothouses, hot walls, plenty of fruit, a lake with two swans upon it—and *butter* at our breakfast!—made us believe ourselves in paradise! There was a beautiful drawing room and a sunny little parlour, and a window somewhere above at which more than once our handsome aunt appeared and threw out pears to us. We were sorry to go away, although there were no children to play with. The house was full of company, but they did not interfere with us, and when we did see any of these strangers they were very kind. But the day of departure came, the sociable was packed, and we set off for Tennochside in Lanarkshire, near the Clyde, and near to Hamilton, about eight miles from Glasgow.

Uncle Ralph, my Mother's second brother, had been bred to the Law; he had entered the office of a friend, Mr Kinderley, an Attorney of repute in London, but he never liked the business, and on one of his visits to Aunt Leitch, an acquaintance of old standing with the heiress of Tennochside suddenly blazed up into a lovefit on her part, which he, vain and idle, could not resist, and they were married. My poor Aunt Judy, a good excellent woman, not the very least suited to him, plain in person, poor in intellect, without imagination or deep feeling or accomplishment, she had not money enough to make up for the life of privation such a man has had to lead with such as her. He was certainly punished for his mercenary marriage. Still, in an odd way of their own they got on, each valuing the other, though not exactly agreeing, save in two essential points—love for Tennochside and their two children. Eliza, the elder, was at this time nearly five years old, Edmund, still in arms, a mere baby. Here we had no fine house, but a very comfortable one, no finery, but every luxury, and the run through the woods or by the river side was something like our own dear home to us. We did not like our cousin Eliza, though she was a pretty child, and seemingly fond of us; she was so petted, and so spoiled and so fretful, that she teased us extremely. The night that I danced my chantreuse—in a new pair of yellow slippers bought at Perth on our way for the purpose—she cried so much because she could not do the same, that she had to be sent to bed. Next day therefore I was called to help my Aunt Judy in the storeroom, where she made all the sweet things for the second course at dinner, and she had a great cry again; a lesson that did neither of us any good, for I was conceited enough without any additional flatteries, and she only ran away to the low parlour where her great Aunt old Miss Jopplin always sat, and who petted her up into a sort of sulky good humour again. We did not leave Tennochside with as much regret as we had quitted Kilmerdinny.

Aunt Mary and our two little sisters were in Lincoln's Inn Fields to receive us. How we flew to them, Jane and William were in extasies—they had always been inseparable playfellows and were overjoyed to be together again. Mary did not know us, at which I cried. She was amazingly grown, quite a large child, as tall almost as Jane and stouter, quiet, silent, heavy yet loved by all of us. Jane and William had a deal to say. She really was a boy in all her tastes. She played top, bat, leapfrog, fought, boxed, climbed trees, rode on the sofa and the rocking horse astride, and always put on her spencers and pinafores the wrong way to make believe that they were jackets. I was forced to turn to Mary, who became very dear to me and who in her quiet way understood my quiet plays with my doll, her dress, and meals, and visitors. I daresay we were as happy as were our more boisterous companions, who, indeed, sometimes tamed down to associate with us, for we all in the main agreed very well together. We were loving and happy children.

For the next three years we lived entirely in England. My father went north during this time once, if not twice, to look after the various matters; none of us went with him. Our winters were all passed in Lincoln's Inn Fields, our summers at Twyford in Hertfordshire, which place my father rented of my Aunt Lissy, having let his own, Thorley. We were also one spring again at Tunbridge Wells, the bracing air and the steel waters being necessary for my Mother, whom I never remember well for long together. I don't see how she could be, she sat up very late, she laid in bed a great part of the morning, she took no exercise but in her carriage and that not regularly. She had no occupation of any particular interest. She visited very little and she saw very little of my father. She ordered dinners, paid the weekly bills, read the newspapers or a novel. She did a great deal of plain work, but when in London she very seldom got up off the sofa in the back drawing room, a dark dull place looking on the back windows of a low commercial hotel in Serle Street, the near neighbourhood of which obliged her always to keep the blinds down. The front drawing room was cheerful, large, airy, light, looking to the Square, one of the largest open spaces in London, with the gardens belonging to the Inns of Court on one side instead of a row of houses. It was prettily furnished in the untasteful style of the day, and kept for company, never entered except upon occasion of the three or four solemn dinner parties, which repaid the eating debts of the winter; dismal days for us, McKenzie and Mrs Lynch both too busy to be plagued with us, my Mother less disposed for noise than ever; and on the melancholy day itself we were dressed so early to be ready that we had to stay still in all our finery a full hour, till the formal circle invited had been seated long enough to be glad of such a break in the stately proceedings as the introduction of four timid children, who, after a bow and three curtseys at the door, had then to make the round of the awful circle.

In the cold, empty looking best drawing room there were chairs, tables, sofas, lights, looking glasses, and the company. How the evening was passed I know not. When they went down to dinner, we went up to supper, a miserable meal, for we were tyed up to our chins for fear of spilling the milk on our dresses. We appeared again at dessert, to give annoyance by having room made for us, and to be hurt ourselves by flattery and sweetmeats. When the ladies left the gentlemen, we accompanied them to the drawing room door, when we bade good night, and after some kissing were let away to bed, a little sick and very tired. These formal inflictions apart, my Mother had little society, the large family connexion to whom ours was certainly a home house, not affording many brilliant companions. It must have been often dull for her. When she was well enough she diversified her sober life by taking us to the Play, and me to the Hanover Square and other Concerts. She very rarely went out to private parties. Once I remember sitting up to help her toilette on a grand occasion—a rout at the Duchess of Gordon's; the hours were then more rational than they now are, she was dressed and off by nine o'clock, very little later than my bed time. Her appearance has often recurred to me, for she was very lovely; her gown was white satin trimmed with white velvet, cut in a formal pattern, then quite the rage, a copy from some of the Grecian borders in Mr Hope's book,[1] she had feathers in her hair and a row of pearls on her neck, from which depended a large diamond locket. The gown was short waisted and narrow skirted, but we thought it beautiful. A touch of rouge finished matters and then Mrs Lynch taking up a candle, preceded her lady downstairs. My Mother stooped to kiss me as she passed, and to thank me for holding the pins so nicely, an unusual attention it must have been, it so delighted me.

1. Thomas Hope: *Costume of the Ancients.*

One candle carried away, there remained another lighted, which had been moved from the toilette to a small table close to the wardrobe where Mrs Lynch had been searching for some piece of finery wanted. A book lay near it, I took it up. It was the first volume of the Letters of Lady Hertford and Lady Pomfret,[1] the old edition, good sized print and not over many lines in the octavo page. I read a line, some more lines, went on, sat down; and there, heaven knows how long afterwards, I was found tucked up in the arm chair absorbed in my occupation, well scolded of course—that followed as a matter of necessity for wasting the candle when every one supposed me to be in bed. Why my nurse did not see that I was safe there she did not explain. I was half afraid to allude to my book in the morning, but finding no complaints had been made, took courage and asked permission to read it, which being readily granted, many a happy hour was spent over those delightful volumes. They were read and read again, and my father, finding I understood them, and could give a good reason for preferring Lady Hertford's charming way of telling her home news to the more exciting letters of her travelling correspondent, gave me Lady Mary Wortley Montagu.[2] We were also introduced this spring of 1805 or 6, I am not sure which, to Miss Edgeworth's Parent's Assistant,[3] and the Arabian Tales. I somehow mix up the transactions of these three years, recollecting only the general progress we made and confusing the details. The three winters in London are all jumbled together somehow, the summers stand out more prominently.

My Mother's large family circle was now reduced to three brothers and three sisters, my Uncles John and Edmund

1. *Correspondence between Frances, Countess of Hertford and Henrietta Louisa, Countess of Pomfret, between 1738 and 1741* (London, 1805).
2. (1689–1762): Adversary of Pope and Walpole, and an indefatigable writer ('Letters from the East') whose collected works were published in five volumes in 1803.
3. Published in 1796, this was an early work on education by Maria Edgeworth (1768–1849), the well-known Irish writer E.G. much admired.

having both died in the West Indies, and my Uncle Gilbert while at College. My father had one only sister, but the cousinhood on both sides was extensive, and we saw so much of so many of these near relations, that on looking back to our London life, I do not think my Mother could have found it as dull as she fancied afterwards when talking of it; gay, it was not, but she was far from being lonely. In the spring of 1805 four highland cousins, the orphan children of Glenmoriston, came to London to my father's care. He was their joint guardian, with their Uncle James Grant, a Writer to the Signet in Edinburgh, and as he wished to educate them in the best manner, he determined to put them to school in the south. Patrick and James, who were the youngest, were placed with a Dr Somebody at Kensington, Harriet and Anne at a school of reputation in the same neighbourhood; their holidays they sometimes spent with us. There was also a pretty Annie Grant, whose parentage I shall allude to again.[1] She had been apprenticed to the Miss Steuarts, the great dressmakers in Albemarle Street; generally passed her Sundays with us. Sometimes, when work was slack, she got leave to come on a week day, and her short summer holiday was always spent with us while we remained in England. She was a nice dear creature, very popular with every one, she played highland reels delightfully, we liked no music so well to dance to. Miss Bessy Maling, a first cousin of my Mother's, was another of the home circle. Her father was a man of fortune in the Houghton neighbourhood; his first wife, my Mother's Aunt, died in giving birth to this, their only child—he had married again and come to live in London with his second wife, a clever woman and a fine musician. She brought him two or three sons and many handsome daughters—Mrs Welch, Mrs Ward (Tremaine), Mrs Hunter, Lady Warre, Lady Jackson, Lady Mulgrave—who had all so well connected themselves that they would have been great additions to my Mother's society, had not adverse politicks prevented intimacy. Politicks were 'war to the knife' in those bickering times. Bessy Maling, however, kept clear of them. We had Cousin James Griffith too, a clergyman, son of the

1. See I, pp. 175–6.

Welsh schoolmaster, who drew in every sort of style beautifully. He had a small Living which he held along with a Fellowship at Oxford, yet often contrived to spend a good deal of time with us, both in town and country, particularly if Aunt Mary was to be met with. There was also a clever and very queer clergyman, cousin Horseman, and an old sailor cousin Nesham, whom we did not like, he found so much fault with us. Another sailor cousin Raper was a favourite, with his merry Irish wife and two sons who were great allies of ours; a spoiled daughter we did not approve of. Young Harry Raper, who was determined on a sea life, brought us Robinson Crusoe, the charm of many an after hour. He thought it would determine William to fix his affections on the Navy, but no such thing. William was not adventurous— Jane was much more impressed by Harry's book and Harry's enthusiasm, and had she been a boy, might have been tempted even to a desert island in such company.

Besides these occasional companions, we children had a large acquaintance in the Square. We played at every game that ever children tried, in large merry bands, seldom watched by our attendants; indeed we were so safe when locked within those creaking iron gates, there was no need for other care, all sides being upon honour to keep faith. Our nurse Mrs Millar used to signal for us when we were wanted. She was a very respectable woman for her class, though I did not like her. She could see that we learned our lessons, she taught my sisters and me to sew; and she sang, with a voice that Mrs Billington[1] could have equalled, so clear, and so full and sweet it was though quite untaught, all the old English ballads about Robin Hood, all the favourite English opera songs of the day—'Bonny tawny Moor,' 'When the hollow drum,' 'Betsy Blowsy,' etc. Above all, Dibdin's sea songs,[2] 'All in the downs,' 'A sweet little Cherub sits up aloft,' 'By the deep nine,' and a hundred others—with the inspiration of a sailor's wife—widow, poor thing! for her young husband, whose long black curls and merry eye and love for her we almost daily heard of, had been drowned at sea many

1. See p. 141.
2. Charles Dibdin (1745–1814): 'English composer, dramatist, novelist, actor, singer and entertainer' (*Groves*).

years before, soon after their early marriage. I could not like Millar, for she was not just to me. She thought my father and my Aunts spoiled me. I had been six months in Scotland almost my own mistress, away from her, and did not bear quietly returning under controul. I was too quick too, and too pert, for a servant to manage. She took very good care of us, better than any one we had had about us before, although her temper was imperfect. Mr Thompson came as before. In addition to writing and cyphering, we now learned geography, astronomy, and History with him; to my mother we read and *spelt*—a part of education unwisely given up now—those arranged columns of words alike in sound, *black, hack, track*, etc., were great helps to memory. Mr Jones taught me musick. Mr Foothead began William with Latin. Good old Mr Beekvelt was our French master. One way or another we picked up a good deal. As my Mother's health improved we were more with her, and tho' she took little trouble with us herself, she was never alone, and as our eyes and ears were always open, we made the most of our advantages in this respect.

Our principal London pleasure was the play, to which we went frequently, generally at Covent Garden, which we soon learned to consider as more decidedly our House. We had the Duke of Bedford's private Box, sometimes meeting the Duchess of Gordon there,[1] which we liked above all things, for then we had ices, fruits, and cakes in the little ante room adjoining—in spite of all these amusements, the first note of preparation for the country caused a sort of delirium in our nursery; it was as if we had been prisoners expecting freedom, so much more natural to the young are green fields and shady lanes than the confinement of a city.

In the spring of 1805 we went for a few weeks to Tunbridge Wells, while some of the servants were getting Twyford ready. We lodged in a gloomy house near the pantiles, with no garden, merely a court yard before it, which got very slippery in showery weather. But Mr Beekvelt was with us and took us long wandering walks over the heath, and to the rocks, and up to Sion Hill, and as happy as we were

1. Bedford was her youngest son-in-law.

ourselves, as much a child too. He laughed and chattered French, and ran and climbed and gathered flowers as we did, always in the tight nankins,[1] with the snuff box and the powdered hair. I know not what he had been before the revolution in his own country—only a *bourgeois* he told us—but he was a dear, kind old man, like the good fathers or tutors we read about in *L'ami des enfants*. He brought some *Contes de fées* down with him to Tunbridge, with which we got on very quickly; we made, however, greater progress in *Le boulanger*, which we danced on the heath like witches, screaming out the chorus like possessed things; the people must have thought us crazy when any passed our magick circle. I think the Phipps's were here at this time with Lady Mulgrave. I recollect meeting and speaking, and nothing more, so I fancy the two families had not commingled. They were very plain, all but Henry, the present Lord Normanby.

The Wells were very pretty, two bubbling springs rising uncovered from small round marble basins; rows of little glasses stood on tables near, and were dipt into the fountains by neat old women, who presented them with a spring of sage to the drinkers; the sage was for rubbing the teeth, as the steel water discoloured them. I do not recollect much more of Tunbridge this visit—a toy shop I remember and the musick and the long covered walks on one side called the pantiles—all else is confused with later memories of this most enjoyable place. We soon left it this year and went to Twyford.

The remainder of this summer of 1805 and the two following summers of 1806 and 1807, we spent entirely at Twyford, the winters in Lincoln's Inn Fields, as I said before, never all this time going near the highlands. My father took a run to the north when he thought it necessary, but my Mother was glad to remain quiet with her children in the south, which part of the world, I think, she had begun to prefer to her more romantick home, now that the novelty of her Highland life had worn off a little. In London she had frequent opportunities of seeing many of her own relations, most of whom, at one time or another, had to pass the capital on their journeys. At Twyford she had a good house, and

1. Yellow cotton trousers.

quiet, both of which luxuries she valued, for though there were neighbours, she saw little of them. I never remember her dining out there, and as there was plenty of accommodation, she had always some of her own friends with her.

Twyford was about the most comfortable, modernised old residence that ever any one need wish to live in. It was ugly enough on the outside, a heavy, square, red brick building with little windows and dumpy chimneys; a small, squat dome upon the top, within which was a great church clock, and an observatory stuck up at one end like an ear, or a tall factory chimney, ending in a glass lantern. In front was a small bit of shrubbery hardly hiding the road, and beyond a short double avenue of lime trees stretching across a green field. Behind was a more extensive shrubbery and flower garden, divided by a light railing from pretty meadows dotted over with fruit trees. On one side was a walled garden and the farm offices, on the other the kitchen court, stables and stableyard, and an immense flour mill, all upon the river Stort, a very sluggish stream moving along, canal fashion, close to the premises. Barges heavily laden plied all day long backwards and forwards on this dingy water, and as there was a lock just underneath the laundry windows, scenes as merry as any that ever were known in the broom island took place on ᵗhe flat banks of the lazy Stort among the bargemen, the du ᵗɣ millers, and the men and maids of the kitchen court. To the elder part of the family all this commotion must have been a nuisance, to us children such noisy doings were a great delight. We had a post of observation contrived by ourselves in the middle of the wide yew hedge which bounded the back shrubbery on the riverside, and there, from what we called our summer parlour, we made many more observations than were always agreeable to the observed. There was a large establishment of servants, and no very steady head over them, for Lynch had married McKenzie, and they had gone to keep the inn at Aviemore, a melancholy change for we little people; but we had to bear a worse.

In the summer of 1806 Aunt Lissy married. Her particular friend was a Miss Susan Frere, who had been her favourite companion at the celebrated school in Queen's Square where she had been educated. Miss Frere's father, a gentleman of consideration in the County of Norfolk, had seven sons, and it was his fourth son, George, who was lucky enough to gain the heart of one of the best of women. The courtship had been begun by means of letters through the sister; it had been carried on at the Hanover Square Concert rooms at rare intervals, for no one was aware of the progress of this seldom noticed lover till the engagement was announced. My Mother thought the pair had met in Wimpole Street, and Mrs Raper was sure he visited in Lincoln's Inn Fields, and both houses felt amazed at such an affair having been managed unknown to either. The first time that I became aware of what was going on was one day in the spring shortly before our removal to Twyford in 1806. I was sitting near an open window in the front drawing room beside my Aunt Lissy, who had been ill, and was only sufficiently recovered to be nursed up carefully. Some humble friend had called to see her, and while they were conversing on their charity affairs, I was amusing myself watching the progress down along the dead wall which supported the terrace walk of the Lincoln's Inn gardens, of the tall Mr Frere who had lately begun to appear among us, and whose nankins always attracted me. As I expected, he was lost to sight for a moment only to emerge the brighter, for he soon appeared round the corner of the Giffin Wilsons' garden, and across our court yard up to the door. His knock brought the colour into my aunt's pale face; she also dismissed the humble friend, telling her she was too tired for further conversation, and then, forgetting me, for I could be very quiet, she rose up briskly to receive Mr Frere, and told him laughing how she had sent away an inconvenient third. Of course my turn soon came too, but I was so busy arranging all my conjectures that they had twice to bid me run away and play before I recollected to obey. When I gained the nursery I announced without more ado the impending marriage, which soon after was officially proclaimed when both bride and bridegroom set about the preparations for their change of condition in a quiet, straight forward, business like manner that much amused my Mother and my Aunt Mary. Mr Frere took a house in Brunswick Square, which Aunt Lissy went with him to see. After due consideration they decided on buying all the furniture left in it by the late proprietor, to which my Aunt added a great deal belonging to herself from the stores at Twyford of beautiful Indian wares, and all that she had gathered together for her own Comfort while her home was with us. Her bedroom looked very bare when all in it belonging to her had left it; and the back drawing room we usually lived in, deprived of pictures, flower stands, bookcases, china and other pretty things, with really a pretty collection of books, was nearly empty, and it never quite recovered the loss, for my Mother had no turn for adornments. She kept a clean house, a good table, a tidy room, always putting in the stitch in time, but she did not care for knick knacks, at least she did not care to buy them; parting with them was a different affair; she was angry enough at the loss of what she had been used to see around her, and while my imperturbable Aunt Lissy day by day continued her dismantlings and her careful packings, my Mother's surprise grew to indignation, as Jane and I were quick enough to find out by means of certain never ending mysterious conversations between her and our Aunt Mary. They fancied that the low tone of voice in which they spoke and the curious language they employed effectually veiled the meaning of their gossip. Instead, therefore, of sending us away when they had private communications to make to one another, they merely bid us go to some other part of the room, while they tried to conceal the subject of their whisperings by the ingenious addition of '*vus*' to every word they spoke, as 'Did*vus* you*vus* ever*vus* hear*vus* of*vus* any*vus* thing*vus* so*vus* queer*vus* as*vus*,' etc. etc. At first we supposed this was another Continental language different from French, which we were ourselves learning, but the proper names sometimes unwisely employed instead of '*he*vus* she*vus*' they generally used gave us a clue to the cypher, which soon enabled us to translate all the oddities attributed to the Aunt we loved so dearly.

The marriage took place at Twyford in the month, I think, of August, and my father was not present at it, for I remember that some of the wedding cake was kept for him; he was in the North canvassing busily for the representation of Morayshire, a dissolution of parliament being expected.

Who gave his only sister away I don't recollect, I suppose it must have been Mr Matthew Raper, the then Head of the family. An old Mr Pickering performed the ceremony in Thorley Church; he had christened both my Aunt and my father, and his sisters had had the charge of my Aunt for some years before she went to Queen's Square. It was a very private wedding, Aunt Mary and Harriet Grant Glenmoriston the bridesmaids, and one or two of the brother Freres to attend them. The bride and bridegroom drove off in a carriage and four to make a lazy journey of it to Roydon, the father's place in Norfolk, and we were all left in spirits the very reverse of gay to think over their departure.

Our first summer at Twyford had been very happy. Both our aunts, Mary and Lissy, were with us, and cousin James Griffith, who was a great favourite. The queer old house particularly pleased us. There was the long garret under the roof, a capital place for romping, and such hiding-places!— The great clock chamber, turrets and turret stairs and back stairs and the observatory and crooked corners, and odd closets, it was all charming. Then such a yew hedge, a famous gravel Walk beside it, a garden so well stocked, such an orchard, fruits hardly known by more than sight showering down their treasures when we shook the trees. Another good amusement of that first year was the bat hunts; the house had been so long shut up, so little looked after, that the cellars and even the kitchen offices were actually swarming with bats; they hung down from the rafters in hundreds, and were infinitely more difficult to dislodge than the mice in the highlands. We were so used to them flapping about our ears within and without after dark, that even the servants gave up complaining of them, and only that they were unpleasant to the sense of smell, vigorous war would hardly have been waged against them, disgusting as they were. We had merry walks, too, through the fields, a firm pathway, and stile after stile all the way to Bishop's Stortford; and in the autumn such nutting parties, the hedges full of blackberries, sloes, nuts, bullaces,[1] and then the walnuts we were stained to the colour of gipsies merely picking off the husks. The second

1. Wild plum, larger than the sloe.

summer was even happier, for good Mr Beekvelt came for a
month or more. He took us long walks all over the country, to
Thorley Wood and Thorley Hurst, and among the pretty
shady lanes abounding in every direction. We greatly
preferred him to the nursery maids, for he really had no
pleasure but ours.

The peasantry were uninteresting, so after a few Cottage
visits we gave up any attempt at acquaintance in that sphere,
but the fields were charming. We went to church at Thorley
always, sitting in the old Raper pew, and so pretty was that
old church, so very pretty the old Raper Hall in which my
father's tenant Mr Voules lived, that we used to wonder we
did not live there ourselves. Mr Frere came frequently to see
us, and sometimes a tall brother with him. These were our
gala days, for they played bat and ball, battledore and
shuttlecock, cricket, hunt the slipper, puss in the corner, and
a hundred other games, which they had the knack of making
every one, young and old, join in out on the lawn in the back
shrubbery, under the shade of a fine chestnut tree. They
seldom came either without a little cargo of presents for the
children; the Clan Frere therefore was so much in favour
that we hardly felt the parting from our kind Aunt, little
understanding then how much our childish happiness had
depended on the little quiet woman who seemed to be of no
account with any one.

Our dear Aunt Lissy had never interfered with the baby,
little Mary. She was now at three years of age Mrs Millar's
principal charge and my Mother's pet. We three elder ones
had been her care, and how she had managed us we only
found out by comparing it with the mismanagement that
followed. Having few lessons and no employment but such as
we contrived for ourselves, our play hours were so many as to
tire us, our tempers suffered, and Mrs Millar, not possessing
the best herself, sadly annoyed ours. I was active, pert,
violent, Jane indolent and sulky, William impracticable,
never out of humour, but quietly and thoroughly self willed.
One mode was applied to all; perpetual fault finding,
screams, tears, sobs, thumps, formed the staple of the
nursery history from this time forward. We were as little
upstairs as we could help, though we were not always much

better off below, for if my Mother or our Aunt Mary were not in the vein for hearing our lessons, they had very little patience either with our mistakes or our enquiries; my Mother would box our ears well with her pretty white hand that sometimes had the book in it and Aunt Mary had a spiteful fillup with the thimble finger which gave a very painful sting to the tender skin of a child. Bursts of crying, of course, followed, when the delinquents were despatched to dark closets, where they were sometimes forgotten for hours. There was no kind Mrs Lynch to watch us, steal to our prison door and carry us off to her room to be employed and so amused and kept from mischief. She was as great a loss to us as our Aunt Lissy, in one particular,—a very serious matter to me, my breakfast—she was a greater. Our nursery breakfast was ordered, without reference to any but Houghton customs, to be dry bread and cold milk the year round, with the exception of three of the winter months, when in honour of our Scotch blood we were favoured with porridge. The meal came up from the highlands with the kegs of butter and barrels of eggs and bags of cheese, etc., but it was boiled by the English maids in anything but our north country fashion. Had we been strong children this style of food might probably have suited us, many large healthy families have thriven on the like; but though seldom ailing much, we inherited from my father a delicacy of constitution demanding the most fostering care during our infancy. In those days it was the fashion to take none. All children were alike plunged into the coldest water, sent abroad in the worst weather, fed on the same food, clothed in the same light manner. From the wintry icy bath Aunt Lissy had saved us; our good nurse Herbert first, and then Mrs Lynch, had always made us independant of the hated milk breakfast; but when they were gone and the conscientious Mrs Millar, my Mother's 'treasure,' reigned alone, our life was one long misery, at least to William and me who were not favourites. In town, there was a large, long tub stood in the kitchen court, the ice on the top of which had often been broken before our horrid plunge into it. We were brought down from the very top of the house, four pair of stairs, with only a cotton cloak over our night gowns, just to chill us completely before the dreadful shock. How I have screamed, how I have begged, prayed, entreated to be saved from such horrour, half the tender hearted maids in tears beside me; all no use, Millar had her orders—so had our dear Betty, but did she ever mind them when they revolted her! Nearly senseless I have been taken to be dried in the housekeeper's room at hand, which was always warm; there we dressed, without any flannel, and in cotton frocks with short sleeves and low necks. Revived by the good fire, we were enabled to endure the next bit of martyrdom, an hour upon the low sofa without a back, so many yards from the nursery hearth, our books in our hands, while our cold breakfast was preparing. My stomach utterly rejecting milk, bread and tears generally did for me, a diet the consequences of which soon manifested themselves. From being a plump, bright, merry, though slight, child, I became thin, pale and peaky, and wofully changed in disposition, slyness being added to my natural violence, as I can recollect now with shame on many occasions. William told fibs by the dozen, because he used to be asked whether he had done, or not done, so and so, and did not dare answer truthfully on account of the extreme severity of the punishments to which we were subjected. We began our ill behaviour soon after our Aunt Lissy's marriage. On my father's return from his canvas in Morayshire he received bad accounts of our misconduct.

The recapitulation of all our offences to my father drove us to despair, for we loved him with an intensity of affection that made his good opinion essential to our happiness. We also dreaded his sternness, all his judgments being *à la* Brutus, nor did he ever remit a sentence once pronounced. The milk rebellion was immediately crushed. In his dressing gown, with his whip in his hand, he attended our breakfast—the tub at this season we liked, so he had no occasion to superintend the bathing—but that disgusting milk! He began with me. My beseeching look was answered by a sharp cut, followed by as many more as were necessary to empty the basin. Jane obeyed at once and William after one good hint. They suffered less than I did. William cared less, he did not enjoy this breakfast with the whip accompaniment, but he could take it. Jane always got rid of it, she had therefore only hunger to endure. I, whose stomach was either stronger or weaker, it little mattered to me which, had to bear an aching head, a heavy, sick often painful feeling which spoilt my whole morning, and prevented any appetite for dinner, where again we constantly met with sorrow. Whatever was on the table we were each to eat, no choice was allowed us. The dinners were very good, one dish of meat with vegetables, one tart or pudding. On broth or fish days no pudding, these days were therefore not in favour; but our two *maigre* days in the week during summer, we delighted in, fruit and eggs being our favourite dishes. How happy our dinner hour was while Aunt Lissy presided. A scene of distress often afterwards. My Mother never had had such an idea as that of entering her nursery, I never remember her shadow in it. When she wanted either her children or her maids she rang for them; Aunt Mary, of course, had no business there. The cook was pretty sure of this, the broth got very greasy, the vegetables were heavy with water, the puddings were seldom brown. Mrs Millar allowed no oughts, our shoulders of mutton—we ate up all the shoulders—were to be cut fair, fat and lean, and to be eaten fair, a hard task for either Jane or me. The stomachs which rejected milk could not easily manage fat except when like the West Indian Negroes we were under the lash, then indeed the fat and the tears were swallowed together; but as my father could not always be found to act overseer, we had sometimes a good fight for it with our upright nurse, a fight ending in victory as regarded the fat, which we would not touch, though we suffered in another way the pains of defeat, as on these occasions we were always deprived of our pudding; and then when I was saucy and Jane in a sulky fit, the scene often ended in the dark closet where we cried for an hour or more, while William and little Mary finished the pudding. This barbarity only lasted a short time, owing to my ingenious manufacture of small paper bags which we concealed in our laps under the table, and took opportunities of filling with our bits of fat; these we afterwards warily disposed of, at Twyford through the yew hedge into the river, in town elsewhere.

Another serious grief we had connected with our food. We

could refuse nothing that was prepared for us; if we did we not only got nothing else, but the dish declined was put by to appear again at the next meal, and be disposed of in the first instance before we were permitted to help ourselves to what else there was. Jane greatly disliked green vegetables, spinach or cabbage in particular. It was nature speaking, poor nature! so unheeded in those times, for these indigestible plants really disagreed with her, yet she must eat them. I have known a plate of spinach kept for her from dinner one day to supper the next, offered at each meal and refused, and not even a bit of bread substituted all those long hours, till sheer hunger got the better of her dislike and her obstinacy, and she gave herself a night of sickness by swallowing this acid mess. Fancy a young child kept 30 hours without food and then having poison given her. The dungeons of feudal days were in their degree not more iniquitous than these proceedings.

Of course under this *régime* the rhubarb bottle became a necessary appendage in the nursery. I had my French beans antipathy, nobody that had seen the half boiled pods swimming in salt and water would have wondered at it, and it was to be overcome in the same way, and followed by the same cure for its effects. In addition to the dose of rhubarb, nauseous enough by itself, our breakfast on medicine mornings was water gruel—I can see it now, unstrained, thick, black, seasoned with salt and made with water only—how unlike the delicious mess prepared by Margaret Fyfe[1] on which I have half lived for so long. This frightful bowl gave me an obstinate fit in Jane's style, from which I suffered in the same manner; breakfast, dinner, and supper passed, and the cold gruel remained untouched for the very look sickened me. Faint from hunger I lay down in the evening upon the floor of the closet where I had passed the summer's day, and I sobbed out that I wished to die, I was so miserable. One of the housemaids on her tour of window shutting, a Hertfordshire girl named Sally Witham, whom I remember

1. She was the Scots servant who had accompanied the
   Smith family to France, and was to follow them to
   Ireland as housekeeper at Baltiboys.

with gratitude to this hour, unturned the key which kept me prisoner, and threw beside me some red streaked apples. I have liked apples ever since. Good humoured, light hearted, rosy cheeked Sally Witham! She told me all the servants were scandalised at the 'barbariousness of master' and that if she could find that nasty gruel, it should not plague her sweet young lady no more, she'd answer for it. I was not slow to give the hint, and certainly on being called to bed, whither I went without a kiss or a goodnight or even appearing downstairs, fresh gruel, better made it seemed to me, warm at any rate, and a slice of bread, were thankfully received after the miserable day of dark closet fasting. Dotheboys hall is not so unnatural.

Even poor little Mary did not escape the Spartan rules of my father's discipline; for her little baby errours she had to bear her punishment. She used to be set upon the bottom step of the stair at 'naughty times,' and not be allowed to move from thence till permission was given her. One night my father forgot her, so, I suppose, had every one else, for on ringing for wine and water at mid night, the footman who brought it up found the poor little thing lying there asleep. She had sat there since dinner. We used to comfort one another in our troubles when we could manage it, for interference with punishment was not allowed, and many a goody the good children stole and carried to be given with kisses and hugs to the poor desolate culprit, who all the time honestly believed him or herself to be disgracefully guilty.

This is the dark side of the picture. We had very happy hours as well. Despotically as we were ruled in some respects, we were left much to our own devices in other ways. We disposed of our own time very much according to our own fancies, subject to certain rules. We were always to appear at the breakfast table of our father and mother some time between ten and twelve o'clock; the last of the three regular ringings of my father's dressing room bell was our signal for leaving our plays. We ran off to brush our hair, wash our hands, and seize our books, with which provided we repaired to the breakfast room, where our duties were to go on messages, in winter to make the toast, in summer to amuse ourselves quietly till called upon to stir. Breakfast over, we said our few lessons and read in turns to my Mother, who had certainly very little patience with dunce, poor William. I was supposed to have practised the pianoforte early. If we were wanted again during the day we were sent for, though very frequently we passed the whole morning in the drawing room, where we employed ourselves as we liked, provided we made no noise. The prettily wound cotton balls had already superceded the skeins, so that we were saved that piece of business. In the hot summer days Aunt Mary sometimes read to us fairy tales, or bits from the Elegant extracts,[1] latterly Pope's Homer, which with her explanations we enjoyed extremely, all but the shield of Achilles, the long description of which I feared was never to end. When my father was away my Mother dined with us early, and in the evenings we took long drives in the open landau and four. When he was at home, and the late dinner proceeded in full form, and what a tedious ceremony it was, we all appeared at the dessert in full dress like the footmen, or rather at the second course for it was part of our education to be disciplined spartan fashion. We sat in a row—we four, little Mary and all, on four chairs placed against the wall—trained to perfect quiet. We were to see and to smell, and to taste nothing. We were to hear and not to speak, but on the dessert appearing we were released, called forward to receive a little wine, a little fruit, and a biscuit, and then to have our game at romps. The riot generally forced our nervous Mother to retire, and then quite at ease, in right good earnest began the fun.

Sometimes my father was an ogre groping about for little children, whom he caught and *tickled* nearly into fits. Sometimes he was a sleeping giant whom we besieged in his Castle of chairs, could hardly waken, and yet dreaded to hear snore. Whatever the play was it was always charming, redeemed all troubles. We looked forward to this happy hour as to a glimpse of heaven. Milk, spinach, cabbage, fat, rhubarb, and gruel were all forgotten, and the whippings too; he was no longer the severe master, he was the best of play fellows. We dreaded hearing of his absence, as all our joy

1. Improving literature written by Vicesimus Knox
   (1752–1821).

went with him. We hailed his return as our chief blessing. He soon found out that no punishment had such effect upon any of us as exclusion from the romping hour. Once or twice it was my fate to remain upon my chair in that row against the wall, while the romp went on around me, to be told to remain there as unworthy of my share in the fun. I don't think I ever needed a third lesson, although the faults had not been very heinous; the most flagrant was my having provided myself with a private store of apples, gathered only from underneath the trees, but it had been done slily, it was said, that is without assistance, and the hoard had been consigned to, they said again concealed in, one of the queer little triangular corner cupboards scattered up and down the turret stairs. I had never meant to regale in secret, the store was for all, it was to furnish out our play banquets up in the haunted attick, but publick opinion was against me and I was misjudged. It was probably as well to make a clearance of such unwholesome fruit—Aunt Lissy would have said so at once without attributing any improper motives to a thoughtless act, but Aunt Lissy was gone and nobody else thought it worth while to study character, to educate on a plan, to make a proper business of their proper duty. She was a greater loss to us than we were at all aware of.

# CHAPTER FOUR

1806–1807

THE summer of 1807 was the last we spent at Twyford. Annie Grant was a few weeks with us, and Bessy Maling and James Griffith and Aunt Mary—not all at the same time, there would not have been room for them. Harriet Grant, too, came for a long visit. She was grown up and had left school. The one she and her sister had first gone to at Kensington did not turn out good, so Harriet had been placed with a very ladylike Mrs Pope in Bloomsbury Square, who took only a certain number of pupils; and Anne, who was very delicate, had been sent to the sea under the care of Mrs Peter Grant, a Cousin, the Widow of one of the five ne'er do weel sons of my great Uncle Sandy. By the bye we wore mourning for the first time this very summer for Uncle Leitch, such mourning as suited my mother's economy. Our coloured frocks were put away and in the afternoons our white frocks were decorated with black crape sashes, the long tails of which did charmingly for playing at horses. There were black ribbons on our bonnets too, and round William's straw hat.

Just before leaving town we had seen our dear Aunt Lissy's little boy, poor John Frere, a fine plain, healthy baby, when as a secret I was told to expect a little brother or sister shortly at home, for whose arrival many preparations were making. Jane hemmed some new soft towels for it—very badly—and I made all the little cambrick shirts so neatly, that I was allowed to begin a sampler as a reward, and to go to Bishop's Stortford to buy the canvas and the coloured worsteds necessary.

There was less disturbance in the nursery this summer. Whether we were better children, or Millar more occupied working for the expected baby, or that private instructions had been given her to forbear such very strict inforcement of her rules, I know not, but we were all in better humour certainly. For one thing, we had more to do. Harriet Grant undertook the lessons, and under her they were not quite child's play; besides this, a Mr Morris came over from Epping, I think, where he was organist, to give me a musick lesson twice a week. My Mother gave him a good luncheon always, and he in return let William have a scamper on his poor little tired pony, for he was goodnatured to every body but me.

On our first introduction I seated myself in full confidence before Pleyel's Concertante,[1] and rattled it off in my own peculiar style, looking for the usual amount of praise as a matter of course. Old Mr Morris gravely put on his spectacles, and after surveying the musick, the instrument, and me, he soberly asked me who had been my teacher. He said no more, but the tone was quite enough. I knew as well as if I had been his pupil for a twelvemonth that no sleight of finger practices would pass under his severe eye. We turned back to Clementi's first book of instructions, and beginning with the scales again I may say I then began to learn the pianoforte, with more trouble to both of us than if I had never touched its keys before. I felt thoroughly ashamed of myself, I don't know why, except that old Mr Morris had laid peculiar stress on what he called *honest* playing, so true it is that *truth* should be carried out in all things. 'Play by yourself,' he said, 'as if I were beside you, leave no difficulty behind, get every passage smooth.' As I distrusted myself and my old bad habits, I got Harriet to watch the practisings, and for the single hour a day allowed for this purpose really made good progress, delighting my father on his return with many neatly given passages from his favourite Corelli.[2]

He had been in the north, of course: Parliament had been dissolved, and he had set up for Morayshire. His opponent was Colonel Francis Grant, the second son of his Chief, who had all the Tory interest and a deal of clannish help besides;

1. Ignaz Joseph Pleyel (1757–1831); his 'Celebrated Concertante' was a demanding test piece.
2. He shared this love for Corelli with Neil Gow, who played the Italian's sonatas at home.

feudal feeling being still strong in the highlands, although personally there was no doubt as to the popularity of the two Candidates. My father ran up to within two votes of his Cousin; all the consolation he had for setting the country in a flame, losing his time, and wasting his money, and dividing irremediably the House of Grant against itself. Years before, he had canvassed Inverness,[1] Sir James giving all his interest to the East India Director, Charles Grant, who to secure his seat promised my father unlimited Indian appointments if he would give in. This was the secret of my father's Indian patronage, through which he provided ultimately for so many poor Cadets. How much each of such appointments cost him unluckily he never calculated. He was very little cast down by his ill success, having probably arranged the road to ruin and knew where next to fling his gold.

My father turned the remainder of his time in the highlands to farming account, for he was exceedingly interested in agricultural improvements, particularly anxious to open the eyes of the Hertfordshire people, who at that time pursued the most miserable of the old fashioned English systems. The first year we went to Twyford he had established a Scotch grieve there; he built a proper set of offices, introduced rotation crops, deep ploughing, weeding, hay made in three days, corn cut with a scythe, and housed as cut, cattle stall fed; and I remember above all such a field of turnips as all, far and near, came to look and wonder at—turnips in drills, and two feet apart in the rows, each turnip the size of a man's head. It was the first such field ever seen in those parts, and so much admired by two footed animals that very little of it was left for the four footed. All the lanes in the neighbourhood were strewed with the green tops cut off by the fortunate depredators. The Scotch farming made the Hertfordshire bumpkins stare, but it produced no imitators during the short period it was tried by us. The speculation did not enrich the speculator. We ate our own mutton, poultry, and vegetables in town, as well as in the country, the market cart coming to Lincoln's Inn Fields

1. This was in 1802; in the close defeat in Morayshire in 1807 only 11 constituents voted.

weekly with all supplies. We had a cow, too in the London stables, changed as required. But Mr Reid got to drink too much gin, Mrs Reid lay in bed in the mornings and saw company in the evenings. The laundry maids also entertained a large acquaintance with the dairy produce in our absence for they united the two conditions; so that though we lived in luxury we paid well for it, made no friends, and were cheated by our servants, for besides the liberal way in which they helped themselves they neglected their master's business.

My father had gone to the Trysts after losing Moray, and bought a large drove of fine young black cattle, for no small penny. These were sent South under the care of two highland drovers. The fine field of turnips during the winter and the rich grass of the Hertfordshire meadows being expected to feed such beef for the London market as, to say the truth, the English people of that day had very little notion of. There was above an hundred head. They were put to rest in the small paddock between the orchard and the river bordered on the shrubbery side by the *yew* hedge. Poor beasts! I forget how many survived; it was heart breaking to see them all next day dropping one after the other, lying about the field dying from the effects of the poison. Reid might not have known the ill qualities of a shrub very little seen in Scotland but my father or my Mother could hardly have been so ignorant—it was just the usual want of thought that characterised all our proceedings.

This unfortunate business disgusted my father with his English improvements; at least after this summer we never saw Twyford again. He sold Thorley Hall to Lord Ellenborough for £30,000, I have heard, £10,000 of which bought Kinloss near Forres, the remainder helping off the accounts of the Morayshire canvass.

Had we known when we left for Lincoln's Inn Fields in November that we were never to run wild in those happy gardens again, we should have grieved bitterly, for life was very bright to us in the summers there. Green and flowery, and sweet scented, sunny, dry and comfortable; all home pleasures were perfect. It was easy to run in and out, it was warm and cheerful everywhere, and the farm labours, the fruit harvest, the nutting, all close round us, coming in a rotation of enjoyment, with sunshine pervading the atmosphere, left a glow over the remembrance of our childhood there that lives still through every recollection of Twyford. To our parents it could not have been so rose coloured. The few neighbours of their own degree within visiting distance were extremely uninteresting, primitive families, rich, self important, ignorant of the world, which indeed they despised, for they were illiberally limited in all the few ideas they had. We kept up no after acquaintance with any but one house, the Archer Houblons, originally Dutch, who had come over as Merchants in the reign of the third William, and had been some way connected with the Rapers, and were not considered altogether on an equality with the older and stupider County families.

The clergyman of our parish, a tall thin Mr Pennington, was clever in an odd way, and agreeable, but he had so very queer a wife, and such an ill brought up daughter, that his visits when accompanied by them as was mostly the case for he was intensely fond of them, were any thing but agreeable. He lives chiefly in my recollection as the donor of the first quarto volume I had ever held in my hands, and to actually read a book of this size, know it was my own, and lay it myself upon its side on the shelf in the nursery bookcase appropriated to my literary property, was a proud pleasure only equalled by another afforded me at the same time, which I will mention presently. The book was the letters of that prodigy Mrs Elizabeth Carter, with some notice of her studious life, not very interesting to me, for my turn did not lie in the scientifick line; but the lady being a relation of Mr Pennington's, good breeding kept me silent as to my opinion of his gift.[1] They lived, this thin dreamy old clergyman, his managing wife, and spoilt child, in a baby house of a parsonage standing actually *in* one of the shady lanes leading to Thorley, for the line of the front wall of the house was the line of the hedge that stretched along on either hand. The

1. *A Series of Letters between Mrs Elizabeth Carter and Miss Catherine Talbot for the years 1741–1770* (London, 1808).

entrance was into the parlour without any passage or hall, and a staircase in the parlour led up to a play room over it, where we could have passed many happy hours, it was so filled with children's treasures, had not the wayward humours of its young mistress turned it generally into a scene of strife. As we had no other acquaintance of our own age, we deplored this the more, for the walk to the parsonage, first through fields and along the shady lane, was delightful, and there were a thousand objects in that little curiosity shop which interested us. Above all, a microscope, and good Mr Pennington ever ready to let us peep into it.

I do not remember any other neighbours of whom we saw anything. And of a low degree I recollect none, they were all stupid, cloddish drones, the peasantry thereabouts, speaking a language we could not understand, and getting vacantly through their labouring lives as if existence had no pleasures. There were no old family retainers save one ancient pair, farmer Dugard and his neat old wife, and their pretty tidy niece Nancy Raymus, who lived in a picture of a cottage close to our offices, with only the road between their little flower garden and the Grieve's. I forget now whether their cottage was thatched or tiled, but I remember it had several gable ends with latticed windows, and high peaked roofs; and that the entrance was into a kitchen kept for shew, with sanded floor, and bright barred grate, and shelves loaded with glittering brass and pewter. Other rooms used by the family opened out of this, the glory of Nancy's busy hands, where too she had her bird in its cage, her geraniums in the window, shaded from the summer's sun by the white muslin curtain so daintily trimmed with a plaited frill.

We sometimes drank tea here, a real fête, for we had syllabub made with currant wine spiced, and we helped to hold the real china bowl under the cow, whose name was Cherry. On Sundays we used to see these good friends proceed to church in real English county fashion; old Dugard always first, in his brown bob wig, large coat, and gold headed cane, with gloves on. Next came the wife in a black mode cloke and sharp pointed shoes, carrying her prayer book in a handkerchief; and last came Nancy, of whom I recollect only her rosy cheeks and bright kind eyes, and that she held both her own prayer book and her uncle's and an umbrella. They used to whisper that one of the Miller's men used to like attending Thorley church, and so would meet the little party at the first stile. Whether more came of this I cannot tell.

Dear sunny Twyford! it was not always what I remember it. My father altered both house and grounds to suit the times, improved them probably, though as we have lived to see taste return in some degree towards the measured formality of our Ancestors, we might perhaps in so old and quaint a place have retained a little more of the broad yew hedge than he did.

The Rapers are an old Buckinghamshire family of Norman descent, as their name anciently spelt Rapier attests. Where they came from, or when they came, or what they were, I really do not know, but so strange a leaven of puritanism pervaded the Christian names of the family, that I cannot but think they were known in the days of the Commonwealth for more stirring deeds than suited them in after times. They descended to us as scientifick men, calm, quiet, and retired, accomplished oddities. How any of them came to settle in Hertfordshire was never explained, but it so happened that two brothers established themselves in that County within a mile of one another; Matthew at Thorley Hall, John at Twyford, Moses the elder remaining on the family inheritance. Matthew never married, John took to wife Elizabeth Beaumont, the sister if I mistake not of the wife of Chief Justice Hailes, descended in the direct line from Sir John Beaumont, the authour of Bosworth Field and the elder brother of the dramatist.[1] I remember mentioning this with no little pride to Lord Jeffrey[2] when he answered quietly he would rather himself be able to claim kindred with Fletcher; and soon after he announced in one of his Reviews that

1. Sir John Beaumont (1583–1627): his collected works,
   *Bosworth Field, with a Taste of the Variety of Other
   Poems*, were published by his son in 1629.
2. Lord Francis Jeffrey: the *Edinburgh Review* 'under his
   rule became indisputably the leading organ of public
   opinion and the most dreaded of critical censors'
   (D.N.B.). He was a close friend of the family.

Beaumont was but the French polish upon the fine sound
material of Fletcher—or something to that effect; which may
be, though at this distance of time, I don't see how such
accurate division of labour could be tested; and what would
the rough material have been unpolished. I myself believe
that Beaumont was more than the varnish, he was the edge
tool too and I request of you children to feel like me, proud of
such parentage, and to value the red bound copy of Bosworth
Field with my great great grandmother's name in it, and the
little silver sugar basket with the Lion of England in the
centre of it, which she brought with herself into the Raper
family.

She must have been a person of rare acquirements too, for
her death so affected her husband that he was never seen out
of his own home afterwards. I do not know how he managed
the education of his only child, his daughter, my grandmother; for she was well educated in a higher style than was
common then, and yet he lived on at Twyford alone almost,
except for visits from a few relations. His horses died in their
stables, his carriages decayed in their coach house, his
servants continued with him till their death or marriage,
when the supernumeraries were not replaced, and he lived on
year after year in one uniform round of dulness till roused by
the arrival of his Grandchildren.

Aunt Lissy did not remain long with him, but my father
was his charge till his death. He did not appear to have
devoted himself to his charge, and yet the boy was very
constantly his companion within doors, for all the old man's
queer methodical ways had impressed themselves vividly on
the boy's mind. When altering the house my father would
permit no change to be made in the small room on the ground
floor of the hall, which had been his grandfather's dressing
room, and which was now his own.

We generally attended on my father towards the end of his
toilette, on the third ringing of that startling bell—a sound
that acted through our house like the 'Sharp' in the Royal
palaces, sending every one to their duty in all haste—and
there we found the same oddly contrived wardrobe which
had been made so many years ago. Two or three broad
shelves were below, and underneath the bottom one a row

of small pegs for hanging boots and shoes on; at top were innumerable pigeon holes, employed by my father for holding papers, but which in Raper days had held each the proper supply of linen for one day—shirt, stock, stockings, handkerchief, all along in a row, tier above tier. My Great Grandfather began always at No. 1 and went on regularly through the pigeon holes, the washerwoman refilling in proper time those he had emptied. This methodical habit pervaded all his actions; he walked by rule at stated times, and only in his garden, and for a definite period; so many times round the formal *parterre*, bounded by the yew tree hedge. He did not, however, interrupt his thoughts to count his paces, he filled a pocket of his flapped waistcoat with so many beans, and each time that he passed the door he dropped a bean into a box placed upon the sill of the window for the purpose of receiving them. When the beans had all been dropt the walk was done.

He was a calm and placid man, and acted like oil on waves to the impatient spirit he had to deal with. Some baby fury had excited my father once to that degree, he took a fine new handkerchief that had been given to him and threw it angrily upon the fire, then seeing the flames rise over it, he started forward as suddenly to rescue what he had valued. 'No, Jack,' said his Grandfather, 'let it burn, the loss of a handkerchief is little, the loss of temper is much; watch it burning and try to remember what irremediable mischief an uncontrolled temper works.' My father said this scene constantly recurred to him and checked many a fit of passion, fortunately, as his highland maid Christy and others did their best to spoil him.

The Thorley brother, Matthew, was equally as eccentrick as my Great Grandfather. They were much together, and he it was who built the observatory at Twyford, that when he dined there and took a fancy to consult the stars, he need not have to return home to spend an hour with them, for he was a true lover of learning. He had built a large room to hold his books at Thorley. The best of those we loved so much at the Doune came from thence, and the maps and prints and volumes of rare engravings, mathematical and other instruments, coins and curiosities.

He played both on the violin and violincello. Our poor cousin George Grant took possession of the violincello, on which I have heard he was a proficient. The violin was lent to Duncan McIntosh, who enlarged the sound holes, as he thought the tone of this true Cremona too low for the proper expression of Highland musick!

There was an observatory at Thorley too, from whence my great Uncle surveyed the earth as well as the heavens—a favourite occupation of his being the care of some grass walks he was very particular in defending from the feet of passengers. He had planted a wood at a short distance from his house, laid out a kind of problem in action; an oval pond full of fish for centre, and gravel walks diverging from it at regular intervals towards an exteriour square; the walks were bordered by very broad turf edging, and thick plantations of young trees were made between. It was a short cut through this mathematical plantation from one farm house to another, and in rainy weather the women in their pattens destroyed the grass borderings when they disobeyed the order to keep to the gravel path. From his tower of observation Matthew Raper detected every delinquent, and being provided with a speaking trumpet, no sooner did a black gypsey bonnet and red cloke beneath it appear on the forbidden edge, than 'Off with your pattens' echoed in rough seaman's voice to the terrour of the sinners, who hearing such a voice as they never heard before, and seeing no one, thought the devil lay hid among the bushes.

These two old brothers, the one a bachelour, the other a widower, had their hearts set upon the same earthly object, my Great Grandfather's only child, my grandmother. To judge of her from the fragments of her journals, her scraps of poetry, some copied, some original, her pocket books full of witty memoranda, her receipt books, songs and the small library, in each volume of which her name was beautifully written, she must have been an accomplished woman and passing clever, with rather more than a touch of the coarseness of her times.[1]

1. See *The Receipt Book of Elizabeth Raper and Portion of her Cypher Journal* edited by Bartle Grant (1924), and illustrated by Bloomsbury luminary Duncan Grant.

She had a temper! for dear, good Mrs Sophy used to tell us, as a warning to me, how every one in her household used to fly from her presence when it was up, hiding in any corner till the brief storm was finished. She was not handsome, short in figure, with the Raper face, and undecided complexion; yet she had lovers. In early youth a cousin Harry figured in her private MS., he must have been the Admiral's father,[1] and after came a more serious business, an engagement to Bishop Horsley,[2] an illness delayed the ceremony, and when the heiress recovered she married her Doctor!—my grandfather[3]—whether with or without the consent of her family I do not know; it certainly was not with their approbation, for they looked on my grandfather as a mere Scotch adventurer, and never thoroughly forgave my grandmother for years; not till my great Uncle Rothy, with his graceful wife, came to London to visit their brother the Doctor, when the Raper connexion was relieved to see that the honour of the alliance was at least mutual.

Although my grandfather lived to get into great practice as a physician, his income at the time of his marriage was not considerable; the Raper addition to it was extremely welcome. Her father allowed Mrs Grant a guinea a day, paid punctually to herself in advance on the first of the month in a little rouleau containing thirty gold pieces, or thirty one, or

1. He was (as Lady Strachey pointed out) the Admiral himself, Lord Howe (1726–99). When informed of the then Captain Richard Howe's marriage, the Journal's entry for 15.2.1758 reads: 'Heard ... Dick was married ... thought I should have died. Cried heartily, damned him as heartily and walked about loose with neither life nor soul.'

2. Samuel Horsley (1733–1806), an eccentric polemical career clergyman later to become Bishop of St. Asaph, seemed to find Elizabeth Raper's father's offer of only £200 a year the main stumbling block to marriage; she condemns him as acting 'villainously, mercenarily and so very prudently'.

3. Her first impressions: 'He had the appearance of a clergyman about 50, was a Scotchman by his tongue, seemed to have seen a great deal of the world and by his behaviour to have been used to the best of company.'

twenty eight or nine as the case might be. As I understood, this was never promised, but never failed. The Uncle at Thorley, too, kindly assisted the housekeeping. On new year's day he regularly gave or sent his niece a piece of plate and a hundred pounds, so regularly that she quite reckoned on it, unwisely; for one day the Uncle, being with her talking confidentially upon the Doctor's improved ways and means, trusting matters were really comfortable; 'Oh dear, yes,' replied his niece; 'fees are becoming plenty, and the Lectures bring so much, and my father gives so much, and then, uncle, there's your hundred pounds.' 'True, niece,' answered the odd Uncle, and to the hour of his death he never gave her again a guinea. He saved the more for my father, little thinking all his hoards were destined for that odious Sandy Grant and the electors of Great Grimsby.

My Grandfather and grandmother were married twelve years before they had a child, then came my father, and four years after, my aunt Lissy; in giving birth to her, her mother died. The highlanders saw the hand of a rewarding providence in the arrival of these children to a lonely home, my grandmother having signally approved herself in their eyes by her behaviour on a memorable occasion; I don't know how they accounted for the poor woman's early death, in the midst of these blessings, on the same principles.

The visit that the Laird and the Lady of Rothiemurchus had paid to Doctor and Mrs Grant at their large house in Lime Street in the City of London was to be returned, but, after repeated delays, his professional business quite preventing the Doctor from taking such a holiday. His Wife was to go north alone, that is without him, but with his younger brother, Alexander the clergyman, who was then Curate at Henley, where he had been for some time with his Wife and her sister Miss Neale. Besides his clerical duties, my great Uncle Sandy at this time took pupils, who must have been at home for their midsummer holidays, when he could propose to escort his wife and his sister in law to the highlands. My great Uncle Rothy was unluckily living at Elgin, his delicate wife having fancied the mountain air too keen for her, but the object of the journey being principally to see Rothiemurchus, the English party proceeded there under the charge of their cousin, Mr James Cameron, of Kinrara, Kainapool, and latterly, in my remembrance, of the Croft.

My grandmother rode up from Elgin on a pillion behind Mr Cameron. She wore high heeled, pointed toed shoes, with large rosettes, a yellow silk quilted petticoat, a chintz sack or fardingale bundled up behind, and a little black hat and feather stuck on one side of her powdered head. She sang the Beggar's Opera through during the journey with a voice of such power that Mr Cameron never lost the recollection of it. I fancy the sound was rather close for pleasant effect for he was a highlander and musical. One of the scenes they went to view was that from the churchyard. The old church is beautifully situated on a rising ground in a field not far from the house of the Doune, well backed by a bank of birch wooding, and commanding a fine prospect both up and down the valley of the Spey. My grandmother looked round in admiration, and then, turning to Mr Cameron, she lamented in simple good faith that the Laird had no son to inherit such a property. 'Both a loss and a gain,' said Mrs Alexander in a blithe voice, 'the parson and I have five fine sons to heir it for him.' Where are they now? she might have added not many years after, for she outlived them all, poor woman! and my Grandmother the following year produced the delicate boy, whose birth ended all their expectations.

The Doctor and his rather eccentrick, true Raper Wife lived happily together, barring a slight occasional coolness on his part, and a little extra warmth now and then on hers. From the time of her death, Mrs Sophy told us, he never entered her drawing room, where all remained precisely as she had left it; her harpsichord on one side of the fireplace, and her japan cabinet on the other, both remained locked: her bookcases were undisturbed; a small round table that held a set of real egg shell china out of which her favoured guests had received their tea, had been covered with a cambrick handkerchief by his own hand, and no one ever ventured to displace the veil. All her wardrobe, which was very rich, and her trinkets which were very handsome, were left as she had left them, never touched till they were packed in chests when he left London, which chests were never opened till Aunt Lissy came of age, and then the contents were fairly divided between her and my handsome father.

More than all, he laid aside his violin. They had been many years married before she knew he played. She had seen the violin hanging up in its case, and often wondered what it did there. At last she asked, and was surprised and pleased to find him no mean performer. How very odd, how individualised were those odd people of those old days. On the death of her whom he had never seemed to care to please, he laid aside the instrument he was really fond of, nor ever resumed it till he retired to the Doune, when my father remembered his often bringing sweet musick from it in an evening. I can't tell why, but I was always much interested in those old world days—my father never liked speaking of his childhood, it had probably not been happy. He was ever exceedingly reserved, too, on all matters of personal feeling. Not till I had nearly grown up did I ever hear much from him of his boy hood, and even then it was drawn from him by my evident pleasure in the answers this cross questioning elicited. He had one only recollection of his mother, seeing her dressed in long diamond earrings on some company occasion, and sleeping with her by an accident when, tired out with his chattering, my silent father!, she invented a new play—a trial of who should go to sleep first. Her voice, he said, was like Aunt Lissy's, low and sweet. Aunt Lissy was quite a Raper, and she loved Twyford, and after her marriage tried to live there, but before the railway crossed the orchard, the distance was great from chambers for so complete a man of business as uncle Frere, and after that thundering iron way cut the farm yard in two, it became quite disagreeable as a residence so it is let to some one belonging to the Line.

That last summer at Twyford, how fresh it comes back to me! My father was of course away. We lived entirely with my Mother, Harriet [of Glenmoriston], Bessy Maling, Aunt Mary, Cousin James, and Annie Grant. Harriet was not a demonstrative person, but she had a warm Scotch heart beneath her cool manner. She was very kind to us, and amused us often when we should otherwise have been in the way. She made us half a dozen ladies and gentlemen of pasteboard, whose arms and legs were all made in separate joints, just held together by a stitch of silk—through the bodies was passed a stronger thread, one end of which was pinned to the carpet, the other was held in the hand and jerked up and down in time to musick, when the loose limbed figure capered like the wildest opera dancer. They were refined Souple Tams.[1] Harriet painted their faces, we helping to mix the colours, my first lesson in tinting, compounding etc. Annie dressed them in bits of finery brought from Albemarle Street, and what shouts of merry laughter accompanied the pianoforte which set our *corps de ballet* dancing!

We were sometimes troublesome, however, in spite of all the pains taken to amuse us. I remember Jane and Mary persisting in standing by the table where Cousin James was drawing, and Aunt Mary patching—two arts we never tired of watching; no delicate hints sufficing to remove them, when my Mother at last bid them go off and gather their Aunt Mary some green frogs. Aunt Mary was always a nervous person so much so as to be constantly called both affected and fine, and above every other antipathy of the many she indulged in, was her utter horrour of frogs. She never strolled out on moonlight evenings for fear of seeing these harmless creatures nor set her foot upon the soft grass of a meadow for fear of them jumping over it. Pleasant was the laugh, therefore, with which the unconscious children were dismissed, none of the party being more amused than Aunt Mary. She very soon, however, changed to a scream, gave an appalling shriek, for back came Jane and Mary, their little pinafores held well up in hand and Mary, advancing first, opened her burden upon Aunt Mary's knee—a dozen of little green frogs! 'Dere Aunt Mamy, plenty flogs!' It banished her from the drawing room for the evening—the Aunt, not the child; no one could persuade her those odious animals had not hidden under all the chairs—poor little Mary, next came a sobbing scene.

We dined with my Mother, early for her, but late enough for us, and following up the wise discipline to which we had been accustomed, whatever dainties might adorn the table,

1.  Jointed wooden toy figure, which is manipulated by pushing a string so that it seems to dance (S.N.D.).

our plain dishes were always there. One day at the bottom was placed boiled mutton, to which William, Jane, and I were helped. At the top was a roast goose, extremely savoury with its stuffing and rich gravy and apple sauce. It was a favourite dish with the whole Houghton connexion, and as tastes descend by inheritance, little Mary quite naturally affected the goose. She declined the offered mutton. 'What's the matter, little Mary? not hungry, my dear? she looks very red!' etc. No answer. There she sat, flushed certainly, but not otherwise remarkable, except for her empty plate. At last the truth dawned upon my Mother, who rose from her seat and, seizing the poor child, she began to box the tiny ears, first the one and then the other, calling names between the slaps 'till her own face became scarlet and her eyes flashed. These scenes always made me shiver whether I were victim or spectator; they deranged me for the day, yet it was the ordinary routine of education in all nurseries then, and still retains its place in our schools. Mary cried, but never spoke. She went without her dinner, and she passed an hour or two in our usual place of punishment, our condemned cell—the large dutch tiled fire place in the entrance hall—but she never gave up her secret, except to Annie Grant, who after a little tender coaxing, learned that 'I wanted *duck*.' Annie could make any of us do or not do anything—she never tried any other form but that of gentleness.

The entrance hall was a large, low, square dark room panelled in dark oak; floor the same, in a diced pattern bright rubbed, with an old fashioned fire place that my father had left untouched. It had a hanging chimney, a small settle within on each side of the hearth; two dogs with Antelopes heads on the ends of them—the Raper crest—the whole lined with clean blue dutch tiles representing Bible history, especially the Apocrypha for there was Tobit and his dog and the whole story of his blindness and its cure, and a great deal more that much amused the culprits placed on the settle of repentance. My Mother sometimes dined in this hall when the dinner was early in the very height of summer, for the eating room looked to the south, and in spite of closed venetians was often very oppressively over heated. The grape parlour was cool too, but the narrow windows very high on the wall made it dreary, so we used to bear the sun in the dining room and the drawing room which was over it, rather than the gloom of the north aspect. The prettiest room in the house was my mother's bedroom looking on the orchard. It had three windows in a bow, and on one side at either hand of the fire place were the two light closets in two turrets, one she used as her washing closet, the other was neatly fitted up for reading in. No wonder she ever after regretted the comforts of Twyford.

# CHAPTER FIVE

## 1807–1809

EARLY in November 1807 we removed to town and before the end of the month my brother John was born, the youngest, and most talented of us all.[1] He was a small, thin, ugly baby, and he remained a plain child, little of his age for many years, no way remarkable nor ever much noticed except by my Mother. In the spring of 1808 William was sent to Eton, not ten, poor child, very unfit for the buffetings of that large publick school, where the little boys were utterly neglected by the Masters, and made mere slaves and drudges by the elder boys, many of whom used their fags unmercifully. William was fortunate in this respect, his first master was the present Duke of Leinster, a very good natured lad; his dame, too, Mrs Denton, was kind to all her boys in a sort of way; but poor William was far from happy, he told us in confidence at mid summer, though it would have been incorrect to allow this publickly. We were proud of having a brother at Eton then. Now I look back with horrour on that school of corruption, which the strongest minded could not enter without being polluted and where weaker characters made shipwreck of all worth.

We passed a very happy winter. My Mother was more out in society than usual, having Harriet to introduce into it. We had hardly any lessons except such as we chose to do for our masters, Mr Beekvelt, Mr Thompson, and Mr Jones, which very often was little enough. We were a great deal in Brunswick Square with Uncle and Aunt Frere, we had the two babies to play with, John Frere and our own Johnny, and we had now a large acquaintance in the Square. We had great

1. He was to become Lieutenant Governor of Bengal and Governor of Jamaica.

games of 'Tommy Tickler,' 'Thread the needle,' 'Follow the Leader,' 'Hen and Chickens,' and many more, our merry laughter ringing round the gardens, where we were so safe, so uncontrouled, and so happy, though we were not among the *élite* of our little world. An elder set kept itself quite distinct from the younger ones, and a grander set walked in stately pride apart from either. Sir John Nicholls' daughters and Mr Spencer Percival's[1] never turned their exclusive looks upon meaner neighbours, while Justice Park's, with Daniels, Scarletts, Bennets, and others growing up, would only smile upon the children they passed occasionally. We, all unknowing and equally uncaring, romped merrily on in our gleesome play hours, Tyndales, Hultons, Grants, Williams, Vivians. Besides, we had a grade or two below ourselves with which on no account were we to commingle; some coarse shoed, cotton gloved children, and a set who entered with borrowed keys, and certainly appeared out of their proper place. Home was quite as pleasant as the Square, the baby made us so merry. I worked for him too; this employment was quite a passion with me; from very early days down to this very hour generations of little people might have thanked my busy needle for their outfit. My box of baby clothing has never been empty to my knowledge since I first began to dress my doll. Many a weary hour has been beguiled by this useful plain work, for there are times when reading, writing, or more active employments only irritate, and when needlework is really soothing, particularly when there is an object in the labour. It used as a child to give me a glow of delight to see the work of my fingers on my sisters and brothers, and on the Rothiemurchus babies; for it was only for our own poor that I busied myself, every body giving me scraps for this purpose, and sometimes help and patterns, my sisters requiring none as they never worked from choice; they much preferred to the quiet occupations, the famous romps in Brunswick Square, where, Aunt Lissy having no nerves, her tall brothers in law, who were all uncle

1. He was to have six sons and six daughters; for her reac-
tion to his assassination when Prime Minister in 1812 see
1, p. 199.

Freres to us, made perfect bedlam in her drawing room, and after dinner made for us rabbits of the doileys, cut apples into swans and wells, their pips into mice and oranges into no matter what.

Uncle John, the ambassador,[1] was rather stately; but Uncle Bartle, his Secretary, was our grand ally; William, the serjeant, came next in our esteem; Edward was quieter; the two younger, Hatley and Temple, were all we could wish. The two sisters we hardly knew, Lady Ord was in the country, and Miss Frere, my Aunt's friend Susan, was generally ill. There was a friend, however, Sir Robert Ainslie, whom we thought charming, and a Lady Laurie and her brother, Captain Hatley, who were very likeable. We were pretty well off for friends at home; Captain Stephenson and his brother Colonel Barnes were famous playfellows, and our cousin Harry Raper, and the old set besides. Also we helped to dress my Mother and Harriet for their parties, and had once great fun preparing them for a masquerade, when, with the assistance of some friends, they all went as the country party in the Journey to London, my Mother being such a pretty Miss Jenny.[2] Another time Harriet went as a highland girl, in some fantastick guise of Miss Steuart's invention, and meeting with a kilted, belted, well plumed Highlander, had fun enough to address him in gaelick, and he, not understanding one word of what should have been his native tongue, retreated confounded, she following, till he turned and fled!, to the delight of the lookers on who somehow always seem to enjoy the discomfiture of a fellow creature. It was Harriet's last exploit in London. She went north to some of her highland aunts, in company with her brother Patrick the Laird this spring; her sister Anne

1. John Hookham Frere (1769–1846): Fellow of Caius
   College Cambridge, M.P. for Westloo, Under Secretary of
   State for Foreign Affairs 1799, Envoy to Lisbon 1800 and
   Madrid 1802 and 1808. As a minor poet (*Whistlecraft*), his
   use of *ottava rima* influenced Byron. Bartle Frere, the
   statesman and colonial administrator, (1815–1884), was
   his nephew.
2. *The Provok'd Husband or A Journey to London*, by Sir John
   Vanbrugh.

remaining with her far away cousin, Mrs Peter Grant, at Ramsgate. Anne was a stiff, formal, reserved girl, good-natured enough, yet not a favourite with any of us. I remember admiring the beauty of her needlework. She generally brought little presents of embroidery for my Mother, dolls' clothes for us, and a pincushion or penwiper for the study table when she came to visit us but she gave them all so coldly we hardly cared for them. Mrs Peter Grant was a great amusement to us, a very pretty, obliging little woman, dissolved in excess of feeling. The Malings were soft and gentle and sighing and sentimental, but she was sentiment run mad. Her widowed griefs were perpetually paraded, she nursed her sorrows and got fat on them, for she was quite a comfortable round about body, and both astonished and diverted us by this habit she had got into,—it did not seem much more. And we, who were brought up to annoy no one, to put self out of the way, to keep our own feelings to our own selves, to sacrifice them if necessary, could not understand this perpetual whining over the memory of a scape grace of a cousin whom we had never known. She was a good creature after all, worth a thousand of her impossible pupil.

Early in the summer of 1808, we all started together for the highlands. The greater part of the furniture had been sent from Twyford to the Doune, where, truth to say, it was very much wanted. The servants all went north with it by sea, excepting those in immediate attendance on ourselves. A new barouche landau was started this season, which served us for many a year, and was a great improvement upon either the old heavy close coach or the leather curtained sociable. Four bays in hand conducted us to Houghton, where after a visit of a few days my father proceeded on his Circuit, and my Mother removed with the children to Seaham, a little bathing hamlet on the Coast of Durham, hardly six miles from Houghton. She had often passed an autumn there when a child, with some of her numerous brothers and sisters, and she said it made her feel young again to find herself there once more, wandering over all the ground she knew so well. She was indeed in charming spirits during the whole of our sojourn at this pretty place. We lived entirely with her, she bathed with us, walked with us, we gladly drove in turn with her. We took our meals with her, and she taught us how to make necklaces of the sea weed and the small shells we found, and how to clean and polish the large shells for fancy works she had done in her own childhood, when she, our grave, distant mother, had run about and laughed like us. How very happy parents have it in their power to make their children. We grew fat and rosy, required no punishments, hardly even needed a reprimand; but then Mrs Millar had left us, she had gone on a visit to her friends at Stockton, taking the baby with her, for as far as care of him was concerned she was quite to be trusted.

We lived in a little publick house, the only inn in the place. We entered at once into the kitchen, bright and clean, and full of cottage valuables; a bright 'sea-coal' fire burned always cheerily in the grate, and on the settle at one side generally sat the old grandfather of the family, with his pipe, or an old well worn newspaper, or a friend. The daughter, who was mistress of the house, kept bustling about in the back kitchen where all the business went on, which was quite as clean, though not so handsomely furnished, as the one where the old man sat. There was a scullery besides for dirty work, such as baking, brewing, washing, and preparing the cookery. A yard behind held a large water butt and several outhouses; a neatly kept flower garden, a mere strip, lay beneath the windows in the front, opening into a large kitchen garden on one side. The sea, though not distant, could only be seen from the upper windows; for this and other reasons we generally sat upstairs. Roses and woodbine clustered round the lattices, the sun shone in, the scent of the flowers, and the hum of the bees and the chirp of the birds, all entered the open casements freely; and the polished floors and furniture, and the clean white dimity hangings, added to the cheerfulness of our suite of small atticks. The parlour below was dull by comparison. It could only be reached through the front kitchen; tall shrubs overshadowed the window, it had green walls, hair bottomed chairs set all round by them. One round table in the middle of the room oiled till it was nearly black, and rubbed till it shone like a mirrour; a patch of carpet was spread beneath this table, and a paper net for catching flies hung from the ceiling over it. A corner cupboard full of tall glasses and real old china teacups, and a large china punch bowl on the top, and a cornerset arm chair with a patch work cover on the cushion, are all the extras I remember. We were very little in this 'guest-chamber,' only at our meals or on the rainy days. We were for ever on the beach, strolling along the sands, which were beautiful; sitting on the rocks or in the caves, penetrating as far into them as we dared. When we bathed we undressed in a cave and then walked into the sea, generally hand in hand, my mother heading us. How we used to laugh and dance, and splash, and push, anything but *dip*, we avoided that as much as possible; then in consideration of our cold bath we had a warm tea breakfast and felt so light. It was a very happy time at Seaham. Some of the Houghton cousins were often with us, Kate and Eliza constantly. We had all straw bonnets alike, coarse dunstables lined and trimmed with green, with deep curtains on the neck, pink gingham frocks and holland pinafores, baskets in our hands, and gloves in our pockets. We did enjoy the seashore scrambles. On Sundays we were what we thought very fine, white frocks all of us; the cousins had white cambrick bonnets and tippets, and long kid gloves to meet the short sleeves. We had fine straw bonnets trimmed with white, and lilack silk spencers. My Mother wore gypsey hats, in which she looked beautiful; they were tied on with half handkerchiefs of various colours, and had a single sprig of artificial flowers inside over one eye. We went to church either at Seaham or Houghton, the four bays carrying us quickly to my Uncle Ironside's, when we spent the remainder of the day there always, our own feet bearing us to the little church on the cliff when it suited my mother to stay at home.

The name of the old Rector of Seaham I cannot recollect; he was a nice kind old man, who most goodnaturedly, when we drank tea at the parsonage, played chess with me, and once or twice let me beat him. He had a kind homely wife too, our great ally. She had many housekeeping ways of pleasing children. The family, a son and two or three daughters, were more aspiring; they had annual opportunities of seeing the ways of more fashionable people, and so tried a little finery at home, in particular drilling an awkward lout of a servant boy into a caricature of a lady's page. One evening, in the drawing room, the old quiet Mama observing that she had left her knitting in the parlour, the sprucest of the daughters immediately rose and rang the bell and desired this attendant to fetch it, which he did upon a silver salver; the thick gray woollen stocking for the parson's winter wear! presented with a bow—such a bow! to his mistress. No comments that ever I heard were ever made upon this scene, but it haunted me as in some way incongruous. Next day, when we were at our work in the parlour, I came out with, 'Mamma, wouldn't you rather have run down yourself and brought up that knitting?' '*You* would, I hope, my dear,' answered she with her smile—she had such a sweet smile when she was pleased—'you would any of you.' How merrily we worked on, though our work was most particularly disagreeable, an economical invention of our Aunt Mary's. She had counselled my Mother to cut up some fine old cambrick petticoats into pocket handkerchiefs for us, thus giving us four hems to each, so that they were very long in hand. Jane never got through one during the whole time we were at Seaham; it was so dragged, and so wetted with tears, and so dirtied from being often begun and ripped and begun again, I believe at last it went into the rag bag, while I, in time, finished the set for both, not, however, without a little private grudge against the excellent management of Aunt Mary. Aunt Mary was then living at Houghton with her maiden Aunt, Miss Jane Nesham. She and Aunt Fanny had been there for some months, but Aunt Mary was to go on to the highlands with us whenever my father returned from Circuit, and in the meanwhile she often came over for a day or two to Seaham.

Except the clergyman's family there was none of gentle degree in the village, it was the most primitive hamlet ever met with, a dozen or so of cottages, no trade, no manufacture, no business doing that we could see: the owners were mostly servants of Sir Ralph Milbanke's. He had a pretty villa on the cliff surrounded by well kept grounds, where Lady Milbanke liked very much to retire to in the autumn with her little daughter, the unfortunate child granted to her after eighteen years of childless married life.[1] She generally lived quite privately here, seeing only the Rector's family, when his daughters took their lessons in high breeding; and for a companion for the future Lady Byron at these times she selected the daughter of our landlady, a pretty and quite elegant looking girl, who bore very ill with the publick house ways after living for weeks in Miss Milbanke's apartments. I have often wondered since what became of little Bessy. She liked very much being with us. She was in her element only when with refined people, and unless Lady Milbanke took her entirely and provided for her, she had done her irremediable injury by raising her ideas beyond her home. Her mother seemed to feel this, but they were dependants, and did not like to refuse my Lady. Surely it could not have been that modest graceful girl, who was 'Born in a garret, in a kitchen bred.'[2] I remember her mother and herself washing their hands in a tub in the back yard after some work they had been engaged in, and noticing sadly, I know not why, the bustling hurry with which the one pair of red, rough hands was yellow soaped, well plunged, and then dried off hard on a dish cloth; and the other pale, thin delicate pair was gently soaped and slowly rinsed, and softly wiped on a towel brought down for the purpose. What strangely curious incidents make impression upon some minds. Bessy could make seaweed necklaces and shell bags and work very neatly. She could understand our books too, and was very grateful for having them lent to her. My Mother never objected to her being with us, but our Houghton cousins did not like playing with her, their father and mother, they thought, would not approve of it. So when they were with us our more humble companion retired out of sight, giving us a melancholy smile if we chanced to meet with her. My Mother had no finery.

1. Annabella Milbanke married Lord Byron on 1.1.1815; a tempestuous year of marriage ended with the birth of their daughter, Augustus Ada, on 10.12.1815; they separated a month later and never met again.
2. The opening lines of Byron's *A Sketch for Private Life* (written on 30 March, 1816):
   Born in the garret, in the kitchen bred,
   Promoted thence to deck her mistress' head.

She often let us, when at Houghton, drink tea with an old Nanny Appleby, who had been their nursery maid. She lived in a very clean house with a niece, an eight day clock, a chest of drawers, a cornerset chair, and a quantity of bright pewter. The niece had twelve caps, all beautifully done up, though of various degrees of rank. One was on her head, the other eleven in one of the drawers of this chest, as we counted, for we were purposefully taken to inspect them. The Aunt gave us girdle cakes, some plain, some spiced, that is with currants in them, and plenty of tea, Jane getting hers in a real china cup, which was afterwards given to her on account of her possessing the virtue of being named after my Mother.

There were grander parties, too, in Houghton, among the Aunts and the Uncles and the cousins. At these gayer meetings my great Aunts Peggy and Elsy appeared in the very handsome head gear my Mother had brought them from London, and which particularly impressed me as I watched the old ladies bowing and jingling at the tea table night after night. They were called dress turbans, and were made alike of rolls of muslin folded round a catgut headpiece and festooned with large loops of large beads ending in bead tassels, after the most approved prints of Tippoo Sahib.[1] They were considered extremely beautiful as well as fashionable, and were much admired. We also drove in the mornings to visit different connexions, on one occasion going as far as Sunderland, where the iron bridges so delighted Jane and me, and the shipping and the busy quays, that we were reproved afterwards for a state of over excitement that prevented our responding properly to the attentions of our great Aunt Blackburn, a very remarkably handsome woman, although then upwards of eighty.

It was almost with sorrow that we heard Circuit was over; whether sufficient business had been done on it to pay the travelling expenses, no one ever heard, or I believe enquired, for my father was not communicative upon his business matters; he returned in his usual good spirits. Mrs Millar and

1. 'The Tiger of Mysore' (1749–99), who opposed British expansion in Central India.

Johnny also reappeared; Aunt Mary packed up; we took rather a doleful leave of all and started. There had been a great many mysterious conversations of late between my Mother and Aunt Mary, and as they had begun to suspect the old *how-vus do-vus* language was become in some degree comprehensible to us, they now substituted a more difficult style of disguised English. This took us a much longer time to translate into common sense. 'Here*thegee* is*thegee* a*thegee* let*thegee* ter*thegee* come*thegee* from*thegee*,' etc. I often wondered how with words of many syllables they managed to make out such a puzzle, or even to speak it, themselves. It baffled us for several days; at last we discovered the key, or the clew, and then we found a marriage was preparing—whose, never struck us—it was merely a marriage in which my Mother and my Aunts were interested, the arrangements of which were nearly completed, so that the event itself was certain to take place in the course of the summer. We were very indifferent about it, almost grudging the pains we had taken to master the gibberish that concealed the parties from us, no fragment of a name having ever been uttered in our hearing.

At Edinburgh, of course, my father's affairs detained him as usual. This time my Mother had something to do there. Aunt Mary had been so long rusticating at Houghton—four months, I think—that her wardrobe had become very old fashioned, and as there was always a great deal of company in the highlands during the shooting season, it was necessary for her to add considerably to it. Dress makers consequently came to fit on dresses, and we went to silk mercers, linen drapers, haberdashers, etc. Very amusing indeed, and no way extraordinary; and so we proceeded to Perth, where, for the last time, we met our great Uncle Sandy. This meeting made the more impression on me, not because of his death soon after, for we did not much care for him, but for his openly expressed disappointment in my changed looks. I had given promise of resembling his handsome mother, the Lady Jean Gordon, with her fair oval face, her golden hair, and brilliant skin; I had grown into a Raper, to his dismay, and he was so ungallant as to enter into particulars—yellow, peaky, skinny, drawn up, lengthened out, every thing disparaging; true enough, I believe, for I was

neither strong in health nor exactly happy, except during the
Seaham interlude, and many a long year had to pass before
a gleam of the Gordon beauty settled on me again. It passed
whole and entire to Mary, who grew up an embodyment of
all the perfection of the old family portraits. Jane was a true
Ironside then and ever, William ditto, John like me, a cross
between Grant and Raper.

They did not understand me, and they did not use me
well. The physical constitution of children nobody thought
it necessary to attend to then, the disposition was equally
neglected. No peculiarities were ever studied; how many
early graves were the consequence. I know now that my
constitution was eminently nervous. This extreme suscepti-
bility went by many names in my childhood, and all were
linked with evil. I was affected, sly, sullen, insolent, every
thing but what I really was, nervously shy when noticed.
Jealous too, they called me, jealous of dear good Jane,
because her fearless nature, fine healthy temperament, as
shown in her general activity, her bright eyes and rosy cheeks,
made her a much more satisfactory plaything than her timid
sister. Her mind, too, was precocious; she loved poetry,
understood it, learned it by heart, and expressed it with the
feeling of a much older mind, acting bits from her favourite
Shakespeare like another Roscius.[1] These exhibitions and her
dancing made her quite a little show, while I, called up on
second thoughts to avoid distinctions, cut but a sorry figure
beside her; this inferiority I felt, and felt it still further
paralyse me. Then came the unkind, cutting rebuke, which
my loving heart could ill bear with. I have been taunted with
affectation when my fault was ignorance, called sulky when
I was spirit crushed. I have been sent supperless to bed for
not, as Cassius, giving the cue to Brutus, flogged by my father
at my Mother's representations of the insolence of my
silence, or the impudence of the pert reply I was goaded on
to make; jeered at as the would be modest, flouted as envious.
How little they knew the heart thus outraged or guessed
the depth of that affection they tortured. They did it

1. First century B.C. Roman actor and friend of Cicero. See
    I, p. 192 and *Hamlet*, II, 11, 419.

ignorantly, but how much after grief this want of wisdom caused. A very unfavourable effect on my temper was the immediate result, and health and temper go together. Well, will our children profit by their better training.

On reaching the Doune a great many changes at first perplexed us. The stables in front of the house were gone, also the old barn, the poultry house, the duck pond; every appurtenance of the old farm yard was removed to the new offices at the back of the hill; a pretty lawn extended round two sides of the house, and the backwater was gone, the broom island existed no longer, no thickets of birch and alder intercepted the view of the Spey. A green field dotted over with trees stretched from the broad terrace on which the house now stood to the river, and the washing shed was gone. All that scene of fun was over, pots, tubs, baskets and kettles were removed with the maids and their attendants to a new building, always at the back of the hill, better adapted, I daresay, for the purposes of a regular Laundry, but not near so picturesque, altho' quite as merry, as our beloved broom island. I am sure I have backwoods tastes, like my Aunt Frere, whom I never could, by letter or in conversation, interest in the Rothiemurchus improvements. She said the whole romance of the place was gone. She prophesied, and truly, that with the progress of knowledge all the old feudal affections would be overwhelmed, individuality of character would cease, manners would change, the highlands would become like the rest of the world, all that made life most charming there would fade away, little would be left of the olden time, and life there would become as uninteresting as in other little remarkable places. The change had not begun yet, however. There was plenty of all in the rough as yet in and about the Doune, where we passed a very happy summer, for tho' just round the house were alterations, all else was the same. The old servants were there, and the old relations were there, and the lakes and the burnies, and the paths through the forest, and we enjoyed our out of door life more this season than usual, for Cousin James Griffith arrived shortly after ourselves with his sketch books and paint boxes, and he passed the greater part of the day wandering through all that beautiful scenery, Jane and I his constant companions. Mary was a fat, heavy, lumpy child unable to move very far from the side of the nurse. She was a mere baby too, but William, Jane, and I, who rode in turns on the gray pony, thought ourselves very big little people, and expected quite as matter of right to belong to all the excursion trains, were they large or small. Cousin James was fond of the Lochans with their pretty fringe of birch wood, and the peeps through it of the Croft, Tullochgrue, and the mountains. A sheep path running along by the side of the burn which fed these picturesque and small lakes was a favourite walk of Aunt Mary's, and my father had christened it by her name. It started from the Polchar, and followed the water to the entrance of the forest, where, above all, we loved to lose ourselves, wandering on amongst the immense roots of the fir trees, and then scattering to gather cranberries, while our artist companion made his sketches. He liked best to draw the scenery round Loch an Eilein; he always talked to us if we were near him, explaining the perspective and the colouring and the lights and shadows, in a way we never forgot, and which made those same scenes very dear to us afterwards. It was, indeed, hardly possible to choose amiss; at every step there lay a picture. All through the forest, which then measured in extent nearly twenty square miles, small rivers ran with sometimes narrow strips of meadow land beside them; many lakes of various sizes spread their tranquil waters here and there in lonely beauty. In one of them, as its name implied, was a small island quite covered by the ruins of a stronghold, a memento of the days of the Bruce, for it was built by the Red Comyns, who then owned all Strathspey and Badenoch. A low square tower at the end of the ruin supported an eagle's nest. Often the birds rose majestically as we were watching their eyrie, and wheeled skimming over the lake in search of the food required by the young eaglets, who could be seen peeping over the pile of sticks that formed their home. Up towards the mountains the mass of fir broke into straggling groups of trees at the entrance of the Glens which ran far up among the bare rocky crags of the Grampians. Here and there upon the forest streams rude sawmills were constructed, where one or at most two trees were cut up into planks at one time. The sawmiller's hut close beside, a cleared field at hand with a slender crop of oats growing in it, the peatstack near the door, the cow, and of course a pony, grazing at will among the wooding. Nearer to the Spey the fir wood yielded to banks of lovely birch, the one small field expanded into a farm; yet over all hung the wild charm of nature, mountain scenery in mountain solitude beautiful under every aspect of the sky.

Our summer was less crowded with company than usual, very few except connexions or a passing stranger coming to mar the sociability of the family party. Some of the Cumming Gordons were with us, the Lady Logie, and Mrs Cooper, with whom my Mother held several mysterious conferences. There were Kinrara gaieties too, but we did not so frequently share in them, some very coarse speeches of the Duchess of Manchester having too much disgusted Cousin James to make him care for such company too often repeated. He had a very short time before been elected Head of his College at Oxford. As Master of University with a certain position, a good income, a fine house, and still better expectations through his particular friends Lord Eldon the Chancellor, and his brother Sir William Scott, he was now able to realise a long cherished hope of securing his Cousin Mary to share his prosperous fortunes. This was the expected marriage that the *hethegee-shethegee* language had attempted to conceal from us, and did, in fact, till very near the time of its completion, when we found it out more by the pains my Mother took to leave the lovers alone together than by any alteration in their own imperturbably calm deportment. They were going together in middle age, very sensibly on both parts, first loves on either side, fervent as they were, having been long forgotten, and they were to be married and be at home in Oxford by the Gaudy day in October. The marriage was to take place in the episcopal chapel at Inverness, and the whisperings with Mrs Cooper had reference to the necessary arrangements.

It was on the 19th of September, my brother William's birthday, that the bridal party set out; a bleak day it was for encountering Slough Mouich; that wild, lonely road could have hardly looked more dreary. I accompanied the Aunt I was so very much attached to, in low enough spirits, hating the thought of losing her for ever, dreading many a trial she had saved me from, and Mrs Millar, who feared her searching eye. My prospects individually were not brightened by the happy event every one congratulated the family on. Cousin James was to take his wife by the coast road to Edinburgh, and then to Tennochside. Some other visits were to be paid by the way, so my Aunt had packed the newest portion of her wardrobe, much that she had been busied on herself with her own neat fingers all those summer days, and all her trinkets, in a small trunk to take with her on the road; while her heavy boxes had preceded us by Thomas Mathieson, the Carrier, to Inverness, and were to be sent on from thence by sea to London. We arrived at Grant's Hotel, the carriage was unpacked, and no little trunk was forthcoming. It had been very unwisely tied on behind, and had been cut off from under the rumble by some exemplary highlander in the dreary waste named from the wild boars.[1] My *poor* aunt's little treasures! for she was far from rich, and had strained her scanty purse for her outfit. Time was short, too, but my Mother prevailed on a dressmaker—a Grant—to work. She contributed of her own stores. The heavy trunks had luckily not sailed; they were ransacked for linen, and on the 20th of September good Bishop McFarlane united as rationally happy a pair as ever undertook the chances of matrimony together.

We all loved Aunt Mary, not as we had loved Aunt Lissy—she did not merit the same unreserved affection and children know just as well as older people how to appreciate character. Aunt Lissy was thoroughly truthful, uncompromisingly truthful, she had no idea of deception of any kind. Aunt Mary was not so honestly simple. She had company manners and company temper and company conversation like my Mother, all put on with their company dress. We were never certain that either of them meant what they said on these state occasions, even though a smile of softness preceding sweet gentle words were part of the pantomime.

1. *Slough Mouich* (on the previous page) is Gaelic for 'pass of the wild boars'.

To *appear* this that or the other, to *acquit* oneself well, was the Ironside endeavour, so different from the straightforward Grant way of just being what one seemed. Aunt Mary, too, kind and good and amusing as we generally found her, was not strictly just. We were punished sometimes for being in the way more than for having done wrong, her punishments were not always well advised. Amongst several similar transactions the affair of the Workbox, as Jane and I always called it, when sitting in judgement on this circumstance of my life, made a great impression to her disadvantage. Children can define the limits between right and wrong very correctly. My Uncle Frere in his courting days at Twyford had given me a workbox with a lock and key, the first key I had ever possessed—of course to the quick feelings of a sensitive child this was a treasure invaluable. The box had a sliding lid on the outside of which was painted a very full rigged ship sailing over very mountainous waves. It was divided within into many small compartments, certainly particularly suited to Aunt Mary's favourite patch work—all those little nests she said would so exactly hold the different cuttings of her chintzes and papers. Had she asked me to lend the box, although my dolls' rags were already in it and the lid locked safely down and the key on a ribbon round my neck, I should have been pleased to have been useful to her, proud to oblige her, but she set to work otherwise. She waited for my first fault, not long in coming I daresay, and decreed as a punishment the loss of my workbox for so many weeks—an unlimited number it proved, for it never was returned to me from the moment when in an agony of tears and sobs and stifled passion I had to deliver up my key. The patches were immediately installed in all the neat divisions and there they may have remained for years for all that I knew or cared, for my corruption rose and pride or anger prevented my ever alluding to this 'unprincipled affair' again. Still we loved our Aunt and soon had reason to regret her. Mrs Millar, with no eye over her, ruled again, and as winter approached and we were more in the house, nursery troubles were renewed. My father had to be frequently appealed to, severities were resumed. One day William was locked up in a small room used for this pleasant purpose, the next day it was I, bread and water the fare of both. A review of the Volunteers seldom saw us all collected on the ground, there was sure to be one naughty child in prison at home. We were flogged too for every errour, girls and boys alike, but my father permitted no one to strike us but himself. My Mother's occasional slaps and boxes were mere interjections taken no notice of. It was upon this broken rule that I prepared a scene to rid us of the horrid termagant, whom my Mother with a gentle, self satisfied sigh announced to all her friends as such a treasure. William was my accomplice, and this was our plan.

My father's dressing closet was next to our sitting nursery, and he, with Raper regularity, made use of it most methodically, dressing at certain stated hours, continuing a certain almost fixed time at his toilette, very seldom indeed deviating from this routine, which all in the house were as well aware of as we were, Mrs Millar among the rest. The nursery was very quiet while he was our neighbour. It did sometimes happen, however, that he ran up from his study to the dressing room at unwonted hours, and upon this chance our scheme was founded. William was to watch for this opportunity; as soon as it occurred he secretly warned me, and I immediately became naughty, did something that I knew would be particularly disagreeable to Mrs Millar. She found fault pretty sharply, I replied very pertly, in fact as saucily as I could, and no one could do it better. This was followed as I expected by two or three hard slaps on the back of my neck, upon which I set up a scream worthy of the rest of the scene, so loud, so piercing, that in came my father to find me crouching beneath the claws of a fury. 'I have long suspected this, Millar,' said he, in the cold voice that sunk the heart of every culprit, for the first tone uttered told them that their doom was sealed. 'Six weeks ago I warned you of what would be the consequences; you can retire and pack up your clothes without delay, in an hour you leave this for Aviemore,'—and she did. No entreaties from my Mother, no tears from the three petted younger children, no excuses of any sort availed. In an hour this odious woman had left us for ever. I can't remember her wicked temper now without shuddering at all I went through under her care. In her character, though my father insisted on mentioning the cause for which she was dismissed, my Mother had gifted her with such a catalogue of excellences, that the next time we heard of her she was nurse to the young Duke of Roxburghe—that wonder! long looked for, come at last—[1]and nearly murdered him one day, keeping him under water for some childish fault till he was nearly drowned, quite insensible when taken out by the footman who attended him. After this she was sent to a lunatick asylum, where the poor creature ended her stormy days; her mind had probably always been too unsettled to bear opposition, and we were too old as well as too spirited to have been left so long at the mercy of an ignorant woman, who was really a tender nurse to an infant then. In some respects we were hardly as comfortable without her as with her, the good natured highland girl who replaced her not understanding the neatnesses we had been accustomed to. And then I, like other patriots, had to bear the blame of all these inconveniences; I, who for all our sakes had borne these sharp slaps in order to secure our freedom, was now complained of as the cause of very minor evils. My little brothers and sisters, even William my associate, agreeing that my passionate temper aggravated 'poor Millar,' who had always been 'very kind' to them. Such ingratitude—'Kill the next tiger yourselves,' said I, and withdrew from their questionable society for half a day, by which time Jane having referred to the story of the soldier and the brahmin in our *Evenings at home*, and thought the matter over, made an oration which restored outward harmony; inwardly, I remained a little longer angry—another half day—a long period in our estimate of time. My Mother, however, discovered that the gardener's young daughter would not do for us undirected, so the Coachman's wife, an English Anne, a very nice person who had been nurse before her marriage, was raised from the housemaid's place to be in Millar's, and it being determined we were all to stay over the winter in the highlands, a very good plan was suggested for our profitable

1. The first marriage of the fifth Duke was childless and eight days after his wife died he married again; nine years later, when he was eighty, his only child, the sixth Duke (1816–1879) was born (*The Scots Peerage*, Volume VII).

management. We were certainly running not a little wild as it was.

The minister of the united parishes of Duthil and Rothiemurchus was a curious, tall, thin, shy, worthy, and rather clever man, commonly known among us as Mr Peter of Duthil. His surname was Grant of course, his duties far from light, his cure extending for about twenty miles down along Spey side, with all the plains and Glens on either hand of the river. The births and marriages alone of all this district were work enough for one man, considering the distances he had to travel to these ceremonies. Funerals he had little to do with unless he chose to attend them out of any particular respect, the Presbyterians not requiring of necessity any form of prayer at the grave, nor in humble cases the blessings of the clergy at the preceding feast. Private exhortations were never thought of, all who could read preferring the Bible itself to man's exposition of it; and for preaching, the Service was long enough certainly, two psalms, two prayers, and a sermon first in gaelick, then in English; but it was only once in the day, and when he officiated in the one kirk, the other kirk was closed. We were entitled to Mr Peter only once in three weeks, being given over to the heathen the other two Sundays, unless the Laird exerted himself to provide spiritual comfort for his people otherwise. There were what were called Queen Anne's bounty clergy, a class of men ordained but not beneficed, educated in the usual Divinity classes at Aberdeen, picking up the crumbs of such learning as was taught there, and generally of inferiour birth even to the humble class from which the Scotch clergy were then taken. One of these, good old Mr Stalker, with his poor, very poor Government allowance, and some assistance from my father, and the further help of a mob of scholars, for he kept the parish school, was then settled in a cabin not a bit better than his neighbours, and gave us Sermons on the two blank Sundays—on all, I believe, when 'the family' was absent, Mr Peter, honest man, indulging himself with home during the winter snows and frosts at any rate. Such a home! We used to hear him sometimes talk of it, not in complaint—he never dreamed of complaining; it used to come out that he was neglected and lonely there, and very happy at the Doune.

Mrs Peter, or rather Mrs Grant of Duthil, for she was dignified and literary, in fact a blue stocking, had but one aim in life—to rival the fame of Mrs Grant of Laggan.[1] She began by two volumes of letters, full of heather and sunsets, gray clouds and mists, and kindred feelings with the half pay officers around her and their managing wives; which volumes not succeeding, though the Clan 'stood to her' and bought half of the edition, she determined to try a school on the wild moor among the mountains, a school of pretention, not a sensible, practical place of improving education for the children of those of her own degree, the owners of the little farms around her. She imagined the fame of her talents would procure her distinguished pupils from a distance, whose tastes she, tasteless, was to cultivate; and she had in-veigled a poor English girl, a Miss Ramsay, from Newcastle to come to act the part of principal teacher in her rather singularly conducted establishment. There was no account made of poor Mr Peter, no pleasant breakfast, nor cozy parlour, nor tidy dinner, nor well swept hearth with its good fire, nor cheerful companion for the Minister—his little closet of a study was his world, where he reigned in solitude, content with such scanty attendance as two barefooted, overworked lasses could find a moment to give him. Every body pitied poor Mr Peter, and he in his turn pitied the poor disappointed English girl, who had found, instead of a well ordered place of instruction, a most distracted sort of Bedlam; wild, rebellious, mindless girls, an ignorant fantas-tick Head, and not a comfort on earth. Between him and my Mother it was arranged, therefore, that when the year of her engagement at Duthil was up, Miss Ramsay should remove to the Doune, a happy change for her and a very fortunate hit for us. She was a kind, cheerful creature, not capable of giving us much accomplishment, but she gave us what we wanted more, habits of order. She employed our day busily and rationally, not interfering with our play hours or our

1. 1755 to 1838: left a Minister's widow with eight
    children to support, she turned to writing and her
    *Letters from the Mountains* (1806) is a celebrated
    forerunner to the *Memoirs of a Highland Lady*.

active out of doors pursuits, on the contrary joining in them when business was over, reading to us while we worked or drew on rainy days, thus entirely banishing fretfulness from our Schoolroom. Drawing was a new pleasure, and one we took to heartily, every one of us, little Jane and all. She and I were Miss Ramsay's pupils, waited on by Grace Grant the souter's daughter. Mary and the baby Johnnie remained under the care of Mrs Bird.

The autumn and winter passed very happily away, under these improved arrangements. The following summer of 1809 was quite a gay one, a great deal of company flocking both to the Doune and Kinrara, and at midsummer arrived William whom we had not seen since that time twelve-month—the little fellow, only ten, eleven nearly, years old *then* had travelled all the way south after the summer holidays from Rothiemurchus to Eton, by himself, paying his way like a man; but they did not put his courage to such proof during the winter. He spent both his Xmas and his Easter with the Freres, and so was doubly welcome to us in July. He took care of himself as before on this long journey, starting with many companions in a postchaise, dropping his friends here and there as they travelled, till it became more economical to coach it. At Perth all coaching ended, and I don't remember how he could have got on from thence to Dalwhinnie, where a carriage from the Doune was sent to meet him.

During the winter my father had been very much occupied with what we considered mere toys, a little box full of soldiers, painted wooden figures, and tin flags belonging to them, all which he twisted about over the table to certain words of command, which he took the same opportunity of practising. These represented our Volunteers, about which, ever since I could remember, my father, had whilst in the highlands, been extremely occupied. There was a Rothiemurchus company, his hobby, and an Invereschie company, and I think a Strathspey company, but really I don't know enough of warlike matters—though a Colonel's *leddy*—to say whether there could be as many as three. There were officers from all districts certainly. My father was the Lieutenant-Colonel; Ballindalloch, the major; the captains, lieutenants, and ensigns were all Grants and Macphersons, with the exception of our Cousin Captain Cameron. Most of the elders had served in the regular Army, and had retired in middle life upon their half pay to little highland farms in Strathspey and Badenoch, by the names of which they were familiarly known as Sluggan, Tullochgorum, Ballintomb, Kinchurdy, Bhealiott. Very soldierly they looked in the drawing room in their uniforms, and very well the regiment looked on the ground, the little active highlander taking naturally to the profession. There were fuglemen[1] in those days, and I remember hearing the Inspecting General say that tall Murdoch Cameron the miller was the most superb model of a fugleman. I can see him now in his picturesque dress, standing out in front of the lines, a head above the tallest, directing the movements so accurately followed. My father on Field days rode a beautiful bay charger named Favourite, covered with goatskins and other finery, and seemingly quite proud of his housings. It was a kilted regiment, and a fine set of smart well set up men they were, with their plumed bonnets, dirks, and purses, and their lowheeled buckled shoes. My father became his trappings well, and when, in early times, my Mother rode to the ground beside him, dressed in a tartan petticoat, red jacket gaudily laced, and just such a bonnet and feathers as he wore himself, with the addition of a huge Cairngorm on the side of it, the old gray pony might have been proud in turn. These displays had, however, long been given up. I recollect her always quietly in the carriage with us bowing right royally on all sides.

To prepare himself for command, my father, as I have said, spent many a long evening manoeuvring all his little figures; to some purpose, for his Rothiemurchus men beat both Strathspey and Badenoch. I have heard my Uncle Lewis and Mr Cameron say there was little trouble in drilling the men, they had their hearts in the work; and I have heard my father say that the habits of cleanliness, and habits of order, and the sort of waking up that accompanied it, had done more real good to the people than could have been achieved

---

1. An expert soldier placed in front of the regiment as an example to the others in their exercises.

by many years of less exciting progress. So we owe Napoleon thanks. It was the terrour of his expected invasion that roused this patriotick fever amongst our mountains, where, in spite of their distance from the coast, inaccessibility, and all other advantages of a hilly position, the alarm was so great that every preparation was in train for repelling the enemy. The men were to face the foe, the women to fly for refuge to Castle Grant. My Mother was all ready to remove there, when the danger passed; but it was thought better to keep up the volunteers. Accordingly they were periodically drilled, exercised, and inspected till the year '13, if I remember rightly. It was a very pretty sight, either on the moor of Tullochgorum or the beautiful meadows of Dalnavert, to come suddenly on this fine body of men and the gay crowd collected to look at them. Then their well executed manoeuvres with such exquisite scenery around them, and the hearty spirit of their cheer whenever the *Leddy* appeared upon the ground; the bright sun seldom shone upon a more exhilarating spectacle. The Laird, their Colonel, reigning in all hearts. After the 'Dismiss,' bread and cheese and whisky, sent forward in a cart for the purpose, were profusely administered to the men, all of whom from Rothiemurchus formed a running escort round our carriage, keeping up perfectly with the four horses in hand, which were necessary to draw the heavy landau up and down the many steeps of our hilly roads. The officers rode in a group round my father to the Doune to dinner, and I recollect that it was in this year 1809 that my Mother remarked she saw some of them for the first time in the drawing room to tea—and sober.

Miss Ramsay occupied us so completely during this summer, we were much less with the autumn influx of company than had been usual with us. Happy in the schoolroom, still happier out in the forest, with a pony among us to ride and tie, and our luncheon in a basket, we were indifferent to the more dignified parties whom we sometimes crossed in our wanderings. To say truth, my father and mother did not understand the backwoods, they liked a very well cooked dinner, with all suitable appurtenances in their own comfortable house. Neither of them

could walk, she could not ride, there were no roads for
carriages, a cart was out of the question, such a vehicle as
would have answered the sort of expeditions they thus
seldom went on was never thought of, so with them it was
a very melancholy attempt at the elephant's dancing. Very
different from the ways of Kinrara. There was a boat on Loch
an Eilein, which was regularly rowed over to the old ruined
Castle, then to the pike bay to take up the floats that had
fish to them, and then back to the echo and into the carriage
again; but there was no basket with luncheon, no ponies to
ride and tie, no dreaming upon the heather in pinafores all
stained with blaeberries. The little people were a great deal
merrier than their elders, and so some of these elders
thought, for we were often joined by the 'lags of the drove,'
who perhaps purposely avoided the grander procession.
Kinrara was full as usual. The Duke of Manchester was there
with some of his children, the most beautiful statue like
person that ever was seen in flesh and blood.[1] Poor Colonel
Cadogan, afterwards killed in Spain,[2] who taught us to *play
the devil*, which I wonder did not kill us; certainly throwing
that heavily leaded bit of wood from one string to the opposite, it might have fallen upon a head by the way, but it never
did.[3] The Cummings of Altyre were always up in our
country, some of them in one house or the other, and a Mr
Henville, an Oxford clergyman, Sir William's Tutor, in love
with the beautiful Emilia, as was young Charles Grant, now
first seen among us, shy and plain and yet preferred; and an
Irish Mr Macklin, a clever little, flighty, ugly man, who
played the flute divinely, and wore out the patience of the
Laundry-maids by the number of shirts he put on per day;
for we washed for all our guests, there was no one in all
Rothiemurchus competent to earn a penny in this way. He

1. When young William, Duke of Manchester, had been
   painted as Cupid by Reynolds; he married Susan,
   daughter of the Duchess of Gordon; Governor-General of
   Jamaica, 1808–1827.
2. Colonel Henry Cadogan died at the battle of Vittoria in
   1813.
3. *Diabolo*: a wooden double cone worked on a string
   between two sticks.

was a 'very clean gentleman,' and took a bath twice a day, not in the river, but in a tub—a tub brought up from the washhouse, for in those days the chamber apparatus for ablutions was quite on the modern French scale. Grace Baillie was with us with all her pelisses, dressing in all the finery she could muster, and in every style; sometimes like a flower girl, sometimes like Juno; then she was queen like, then Arcadian, then *corps de ballet*, the most amusing and extraordinary figure stuck over with coloured glass ornaments, and by way of being outrageously refined; the most complete contrast to her sister the Lady Logie. Well, Miss Baillie coming upstairs to dress for dinner, opened the door to the left instead of the door to the right, and came full upon short, fat, black Mr Macklin in his tub! Such a commotion! we heard it in our Schoolroom. Miss Baillie would not appear at dinner. Mr Macklin, who was full of fun, would stay upstairs if she did; she insisted on his immediate departure, he insisted on their swearing eternal friendship. Such a hubbub was never in a house before. 'If she'd been a young girl, one would a'most forgive her nonsense,' said Mrs Bird, the nurse. 'If she had had common sense,' said Miss Ramsay, 'she would have held her tongue; shut the door and held her tongue, then no one would then have been the wiser.' We did not forget this lesson in presence of mind, but no one having ventured on giving even an idea of it to Miss Baillie, her adventure much annoyed the ladies, while it furnished the gentlemen with an excuse for such roars of laughter as might have almost brought down the ceiling of the dining room.

Our particular friend, Sir Robert Ainslie, was another friend who made a long stay with us. He brought to my mother the first of those little red morocco cases full of needles she had seen, where the papers were all arranged in sizes, on a slope, which made it easy to select from them. He had with him his Swiss servant, the best valet, the best cook, the best aid to the housekeeper, the kindest companion to children that ever entered a house. William was his especial favourite, and in after years owed much at his Xmas holidays to the unfailing attentions of this excellent friend, when he spent those holidays in London which were too short to warrant the long journey to his Scotch home. It is odd I should forget the name of this favourite of ours, for he was quite our especial attendant during his stay at the Doune, up in the guigne[1] trees showering down that most delicious of fruits to the expecting flock below, and excelling on the water either in rowing or fishing. How well I remember the day that we all came exulting home from a very successful expedition to the pike bay, William with an immense fish on a stick laid over his shoulder, the tail of it touching the ground! It was measured and then weighed, and turned out quite a wonder, stuffed and baked and eaten, and most surprising of all, was really good. The pike in Loch an Eilein were very uncommonly large, living there so little disturbed; but I never remember our catching another to equal to this.

This was the first season I can recollect seeing a family we all much liked, ever after, Colonel Gordon and his tribe of fine sons. He brought them up to Glentromie in a boat set on wheels, which after performing coach on the roads was used for Loch fishing in the hills. He was a most agreeable and thoroughly gentlemanly man, full of amusing conversation, always welcome to every house on the way. He was said to be a careless father, and not a kind husband to his very pretty wife, who certainly never accompanied him up to the Glen. He was a natural son of the Duke of Gordon's, a great favourite with the Duchess! much beloved by Lord Huntly whom he exceedingly resembled, and so might have done better for himself and all belonging to him, had not the Gordon brains been of the lightest with him. He was not so flighty, however, as another visitor we always received for a few days, Lovat, the Chief of the Clan Fraser, who was indeed a connexion. The peerage had been forfeited by the wicked lord[2] in the last rebellion, the lands and the Chieftainship had been left with a cousin, the rightful heir, who had sprung from the common stock before the attainder. He was an old man, and his quiet, comfortable looking wife

1. *Scots* gean, the wild cherry.
2. This was Simon, the eleventh Lord Lovat, whose colourful career ended in his eightieth year on the execution block after the '45.

was an old woman. They had been at Cluny, the Lady of the Macpherson Chieftain being their niece, or the laird their nephew, I don't exactly know which; and their servants told ours they had had a hard matter to get their master away, for he was subject to strange whims, and he had taken it into his head when he was there that he was a Turkey hen, and so he had made a nest of straw in his carriage and filled it with eggs and a large stone, and there he sat hatching, never leaving his station save twice a day like other fowl, and having his supplies of food brought to him. They had at last to get the Lady Cluny's henwife to watch a proper moment to throw out all these eggs and to put some young chickens in their place, when Lovat, satisfied he had accomplished his task, went about clucking and strutting with wonderful pride in the midst of them, running about to collect his flock, flapping the tails of his coat as the hens do their wings in like circumstances. He was quite sane in conversation generally, rather an agreeable man I heard them say, and would be as steady as other people for a certain length of time; but every now and then he took these strange fancies, when his wife had much ado to bring him out of them. The fit was quite over when he came to us. It was the year of the Jubilee when George the 3rd had reigned his 50 years. There had been great doings at Inverness, which the old man described to us with considerable humour. His lady had brought away with her some little ornaments prepared for the occasion, and kindly distributed some of them among us. I long kept a silver buckle with his Majesty's crowned head somewhere upon it, and an inscription in pretty raised letters com-memorating the event surrounding the medallion. By the bye it was on the entrance of the old king upon his 50th year of reign that the jubilee was kept, in October I fancy 1809, for his state of health was such he was hardly expected to live to complete it; that is, the world at large supposed him to be declining. Those near his person must have known that it was the mind that was diseased, and not the strong body, which lasted many a long year after this, though every now and then his death was expected, probably desired, for he had long ceased to be a popular sovereign. John Bull respected the decorum of his domestick life, and the ministerial Tory party of course made the best of him. All we of this day can say of him is, that he was a better man than his son, though, at the period I am writing of, the Whigs, among whom I was reared, were very far indeed from believing in this truism.

# CHAPTER SIX

# 1809

I CAN'T recollect whether it was in this year of the jubilee, 1809, or the year before, that of Aunt Mary's marriage, that the whole world blazed up, like a tap o' tow,[1] on account of the doings of Mrs Mary Anne Clarke and Colonel Wardle. She was a worthless woman, who in the course of her professional life became for a while the mistress of the Duke of York, and during her reign of power made use of his name to realise large sums of money by the sale of Army patronage.[2] Colonel Wardle, disappointed like many others, for she did not always manage to get the commissions she had been paid for promising, was yet the only one bold enough to shew her and himself up, by bringing the matter before the publick. The pleasure of finding royalty in half a dozen scrapes, made this said world wonderfully patriotick, and of course virtuous. Colonel Wardle's own delinquencies were quite overlooked, the sin of having tried his own luck by these very dirty back stairs was shrouded by the glory of coming forward to throw such a set of bones upon the publick arena. He was made a hero of, addresses voted to him from every where. Meetings to praise him held all over the country—even at Inverness—it was quite a rage. My father and a stout band of Whigs attended our highland demonstration, and superlatived the Duke's infamy in great style, his folly would have been the juster term, for of actual criminality nobody accused him as far as his honour as Commander in

1. 'Flaxen hair, hence fiery-tempered, irritable person'
   (S.N.D.).
2. As M.P. for Oakhampton (1807–12) he brought eight
   charges against Frederick, Duke of York, for corrupt
   use of his military patronage.

Chief was concerned. As a christian man and a husband there was no justifying his immoral life, though from what clean hands the stones so heartily thrown at him could come, we might leave to the rigid to discover. The outcry was so violent the ministry was obliged to deprive the Duke of his office, although it was not very long before there was as great an outcry to have him back again, everything having gone wrong at the Horse guards without him. Colonel Wardle was discovered and dethroned, Mrs Clarke and her influence forgotten, and after judgments pronounced that throughout the whole transaction only one person had behaved well, and that was the little quiet, trifling, generally insignificant Duchess of York, who for the most part living separate from her husband in the retirement of Oatlands, with her rouge, her flowers and her poodles, upon this occasion came to his house in London, drove out daily with him, and gave him her countenance in every way possible. There was a deal of low party spirit at the bottom of the hubbub; party governed all actions. The exposure, however, did some good, it put an end to the system of jobbing which had been the scandal of the profession hitherto. And the Duke, wise enough to profit by the lesson, so effectually reformed the service when he returned to power, that he is always considered the best Chief ever placed in authourity.[1] The wants of the common soldiers he more particularly attended to; they got to speak of him as their best friend, and justly. But during the Wardle epidemick his character in all respects was sadly maligned. Every now and then people hunt up a scapegoat, and load him well before they are done with it.

It was this autumn that a very great pleasure was given to me. I was taken on a tour of visits with my father and mother. We went first to Inverness, where my father had business with his Agent, Mr Cooper. None of the Lairds in our north countrie managed their own affairs, all were in the hands of some little writer body,[2] who to judge by consequences ruined

1. He was C. in C. from 1798 to 1827 (apart from these years 1809–11) and, in the opinion of the D.N.B., he had 'the greatest influence on the history of the British Army'.
2. Many lawyers in Scotland are *Writers to the Signet*.

most of their clients. One of these leeches generally sufficed for ordinary Victims. My dear father was preyed on by two or three, of which honourable fraternity Mr Arthur Cooper was the most distinguished for iniquity. He had married Miss Jenny and made her a very indulgent husband; there was nothing to say of him on that score; her few hundreds and the connexion might have been her principal attractions, but once attracted, she retained her power over him to the end. She was plain but ladylike, she had very pretty, gentle manners, a pleasing figure, beautiful hand, dressed neatly, kept a very comfortable house, and possessed a clear judgment, with high principles and a few follies; a little absurd pride, given her perhaps by my great Aunt, the Lady Logie, who had brought her up and was very fond of her. Who he was, nobody rightly knew. Betty Campbell always declared his father was a shoemaker 'in a good way of business, who had given a fine education' to his only son, and set him up first in Forres, his native place, whence he afterwards removed to Inverness. He was a most vulgar body, short and fat and red haired, and a great beau, clever enough, I believe, very plausible and so full of a quaint kind of really amusing gossip, that he made his way even with my Mother. We were all very fond of Mrs Cooper, and so was my father and she adored him. While we were at Inverness we paid some morning visits too characteristick of the highlands to be omitted in this true chronicle of the times; they were all in the Clan. One was to the Miss Grants of Kinchurdy, who were much patronised by all of their name, although they had rather scandalised some of their near relations by setting up as Dressmakers in the County town. Their taste was not perfect, and their skill was not great, yet they prospered. Many a comfort earned by their busy needles found its way to the fireside of the retired Officer their father, and their helping pounds bought the active Officer, their brother, his Majority. We next called on Mrs Grant, late of Aviemore, and her daughters, who had set up a school, no disparagement to the family of an innkeeper although the blood they owned was gentle, and last we took luncheon with my great Aunt, the Lady Glenmoriston, a handsome old lady with great remains of shrewdness in her countenance. I thought her cakes and custards excellent; my mother, who had seen them all come out of a cupboard in the bedroom, found her appetite fail her that morning. Not long before we had heard of her grandson our cousin Patrick's death, the eldest of my father's wards, the Laird. She did not appear to feel the loss, yet she did not long survive him. A 'clever wife,' as they say in the highlands, she was in her worldly way. I did not take a fancy to her.

We left Inverness nothing loth, Mrs Cooper's small house in the narrow, dull street of that little town not suiting my ideas of liberty; and we proceeded in the open barouche and four to call at Nairn upon our way to Forres. At Nairn, comfortless dreary Nairn, where no tree ever grew, we went to see a sister of Logie's, a cousin, a Mrs Baillie, some of whose sons had found 31 Lincoln's Inn Fields a pleasant resting place on the road to India. Her stepson—for she was a second wife—the great Colonel Baillie of Bundelcund![1] and of Leys, often in his pomposity, when I knew him afterwards, recalled to my mind the very bare plenishing of this really nice old lady. The small, cold house chilled our first feelings. The empty room, uncurtained, half carpeted, with a few heavy chairs stuck formally against the walls, and one dark coloured, well polished table set before the fireplace, repressed all my gay spirits. It took a great deal of bread and marmalade, and scones and currant wine, and all the kind welcome of the little, tidy, brisk old lady to restore them; not till she brought out her knitting did I feel at all at home—a hint remembered with profit. Leaving this odious fisher place very near as quick as King James did, we travelled on to dine at five o'clock at Burgie, a small, shapeless square of a house, about two miles beyond Forres, one of the prettiest of village towns, taking situation into the account. There is a low hill with a ruin on it, round which the few streets have clustered; trees and fields are near, wooded knolls not far distant, gentlemen's dwellings peep up here and there; the Moray firth, the town and Souters of

---

1. John Baillie (1772–1833), an exotic character:
    'Colonel, orientalist, political agent and director of the
    East India Company' (D.N.B.).

Cromartie,[1] and the Ross-shire hills in the distance; and between the village and the sea extends a rich flat of meadow land, through which the Findhorn flows, and where stand the ruins of the ancient Abbey of Kinloss, my father's late purchase. I don't know why all this scene impressed me more than did the beautiful situation of Inverness. In after years I did not fail in admiration of our northern Capital, but at this period I can't remember any feeling about Inverness except the pleasure of getting out of it, while at Forres all the impressions were vivid because agreeable; that is I, the perceiver, was in a fitter fame of mind for perceiving. How many travellers, ay, thinkers, judges, should we sift in this way, to get at the truth of their relations. On a bilious day Authours *must* write *very* tragically.

The old family of Dunbar of Burgie, said to be descended from Randolph, Earl of Moray—though all the links of the chain of connexion were far from being forthcoming—had dwindled down rather before our day to somebody nearly as small as a bonnet Laird; his faraway collateral heir, who must have been a most ungainly lad, judging from his extraordinary appearance in middle age, had gone out to the West Indies to better his fortunes, returning to take possession of his inheritance just a little before my father's marriage. In figure something the shape of one of his own sugar hogsheads, with two short thick feet standing out below, and a round head settled on the top like a picture in the penny magazine of one of the old English punishments, and a countenance utterly indescribable—all cheek and chin and mouth, without half the proper quantity of teeth; dressed too like a mountebank in a light blue silk embroidered waistcoat and buff satin breeches, and this in Pitt and Fox days, when the dark blue coat, and the red or the buff waistcoat, according to the wearer's party, were indispensable. Mr Dunbar presented himself to my father, to be introduced by him to an Edinburgh Assembly. My father, always fine, then a Beau, and to the last very nervous under ridicule. But

1. 'The two hills enclosing the entrance to the Cromarty
   Firth on the north and the south, and resembling
   cobblers bent over their work' (s.n.d.).

Burgie was a worthy man, honest and upright and kind hearted, modest as well, for he never fancied his own merits had won him his wealthy bride; their estates joined, and 'that,' as he said himself, 'was the happy coincidence.' The Lady Burgie and her elder sister, Miss Brodie of Lethan, were co-heiresses. Coolmenie, a very picturesque little property on the Dulnan, was the principal possession of the younger when she gave her hand to her neighbour, but as Miss Brodie never married, all their wide lands were united for many a year to the names and titles of the three contracting parties, and held by Mr and Mrs Dunbar Brodie of Burgie, Lethan and Coolmenie during their long reign of dulness; precedence being given to the gentleman after some consideration. They lived neither at very pretty Coolmenie, nor at very comfortable Lethan, nor even in the remains of the fine old Castle of Burgie, one tall tower of which rose from among the trees that sheltered its surrounding garden, and served only as storehouse and tool house for that department; they built for themselves the tea cannister like lodge we found them in, and placed it far from tree or shrub, or view of any object but the bare moor of Macbeth's witches. My spare time at this romantick residence was spent mostly in the tower, there being up at the top of it an apple room, where some little maiden belonging to the household was employed in wiping the apples and laying them on the floor in a bed of sand. In this room was a large chest, made of oak with massive hasps, several padlocks, and a chain; very heavy, very grand looking, indeed awful, from its being so alone, so secured, and so mysteriously hidden as it were. It played its part in after years, when all that it did and all that was done to it shall take the proper place in these my memoirs, if I live to get so far on in my chroniclings. At this time I was even afraid to allude to it, there appeared to be something so supernatural about the look of it.

Of course we had several visits to pay from Burgie. In the town of Forres we had to see old Mrs Provost Grant and her daughters, Miss Jean and Miss—I forget what name—but she, the nameless one, died. Miss Jean, always called in those parts for distinction Miss Jean Pro, because her mother was the widow of the late Provost, was the living frontispiece

to the 'world of fashion.' A plain, ungainly, middle aged
woman, with good Scotch sense when it was wanted,
occupied every waking hour in copying the new modes in
dress. No change was too absurd for Miss Jean's imitation,
and her task was not a light one, her poor purse being scanty,
and the Forres shops, besides being dear, were ill supplied.
My mother, very unwisely, had told me her appearance
would surprise me, and that I must be upon my guard and
shew my good breeding by looking as little at this figure of
fun as if she were quite like other people. And my father
repeated the story of the Duchess of Gordon, who receiving
at dinner at Kinrara some poor Dominie, never before in
such a presence; he answered all her civil inquiries thus,
''Deed no, my Lady Duchess; my Lady Duchess, 'deed yes,'
she looking all the while just exactly as if she had never been
otherwise addressed—not even a side smile to the amused
circle around her, lest she might have wounded the good
man's feelings. I always liked that story, and thought of it
often before and since, and had it well on my mind on this
occasion; but it did not prevent my long gaze of surprise at
Miss Pro. In fact, no one could have avoided opening wide
eyes at the caricature of the modes she exhibited. She was
fine, too, very fine, mincing her words to make them English,
and too good to be laughed at, which somehow made it the
more difficult not to laugh at her. In the early days, when her
father, besides his little shop, only kept the post-office in
Forres, she, the eldest of a whole troop of bairns, did her part
well in the humble household, helping her mother in her
many cares. And to good purpose, for of the five clever sons
who grew up out of this rude culture to honour in every
profession they made choice of, three returned 'belted
knights' to lay their laurels at the feet of their old mother. Not
in the same poor but and ben in which she reared them—they
took care to shelter her age in a comfortable house, with a
drawing room upstairs!, where we found the family party
assembled, a rather ladylike widow of the eldest son, a Bengal
Civilian, forming one of it. Mrs Pro was well born of the
Arndilly Grants, and very proud she was of her lineage,
though she had made none the worse wife to the honest man
she married for his failure in this particular. In manners she

could not have been his superiour, the story going that in her working days she called out loud, about the first thing in the morning, to the servant lass to 'put on the parritch for the pigs and the bairns,' the pigs as most useful coming first.

We went next to a very old Widow Macpherson, belonging to the Invereschie family, who had likewise two unmarried daughters living with her, Miss Maddie and Miss Bell, the greatest gossips in Forres. A third daughter, Mrs Clark, was married at Milltown in Badenoch of whom we shall hear much more ere long. Next we drove out to Kincorth, a new bare place, where dwelt another Widow Grant, with her four children, wards of my father's, Robina and Davina, girls of my own age, and twin sons much younger, whom we often saw in after days, and to one of whom, excellent Lewis Grant, we owe a debt of gratitude it will be a pleasure to me to the end of my life to remember. He it was who saw us safe from London to Portsmouth, and on board our Indiaman, in 1827, on our melancholy way to Bombay. The little red headed Kincorth laddie was then a confidential clerk in Sir Charles Forbes' house, and well deserving of his good fortune.

From Burgie we went back a few miles to Moy, an old fashioned house, very warm and very comfortable, and very plentiful, quite a contrast! where lived a distant connexion, an old Colonel Grant, a cousin of Glenmoriston's, with a very queer wife, whom he had brought home from the Cape of Good Hope. This old man, unfortunately for me, always breakfasted upon porridge. My Mother, who had particular reasons for wishing to make herself agreeable to him, informed him I always did the same, so during the three days of this otherwise pleasant visit a little plate of porridge for me was placed next to the big plate of porridge for him, and I had to help myself to it in silent sadness, for I much disliked this kind of food as it never agreed with me, and though at Moy they gave me cream with it, I found it made me just as sick and heavy afterwards as when I had the skimmed milk at home. They were kind old people these in their homely way. In the drawing room stood a curiously shaped box, through a sort of telescope end belonging to which we looked at various scenes, thus magnified to the size of nature—a very amusing pastime to me. One of these scenes depicted St Helena so accurately that, forty years after, the reality came upon me as an old friend—the town, the ravine, the shingly shore, and the steep sides of the rock as they rise inaccessible from the sea. I wonder why this particular view made so vivid an impression.

From Moy we went straight to Elgin, where I only remember the immense library belonging to the shop of Mr Grant the Bookseller, and the ruins of the fine old Cathedral. On our way, by the bye, we rested a few minutes at Kinloss, the farm there being tenanted by the husband of Mr Cooper's sister. The ruins of the old Abbey were still of some size, the remains of the monks' garden rich in fruit trees, all planted upon a pavement, as is our modern fashion, with a sufficiency of soil above the stones for the side roots to find nourishment in. We got to Duffus to dinner, and remained there a few days with Sir Archibald and Lady Dunbar and their tribe of children. Lady Dunbar was one of the Cummings of Altyre—one of a dozen—and she had about a dozen herself, all the girls handsome. The house was very full. We went upon expeditions every morning, danced all the evenings, the children forming quite a part of the general company, and as some of the Altyre sisters were there, I felt perfectly at home. Ellen and Margaret Dunbar wore sashes with their white frocks, and had each a pair of silk stockings which they drew on for full dress, a style that much surprised me, as I, at home or abroad, had only my pink gingham frocks for the morning, white calico for the afternoon, cotton stockings at all times, and not a ribbon, a curl, or an ornament about me.

One day we drove to Gordonstone, an extraordinary palace of a house lately descended to Sir William, along with a large property, when he had to add the Southron Gordon to the Wolf of Badenoch's lone famed name,[1] not that it is quite clear that the failing clan owes allegiance to this branch particularly, but there being no other claimant Altyre passes for the Comyn Chief. His name is on the roll of the victors at Bannockburn as a chieftain of his race indubitably. I

1. Alexander Stewart, Earl of Buchan (d. 1405), whose
   reputation came from his ruthless extension to his
   power during the reign of his brother, Robert III.

wonder what can have been done with Gordonstone. It was like the side of a Square in a town for extent of façade, and had remains of rich furnishings in it, piled up in the large deserted rooms, a delightful bit of romance to the young Dunbars and me. Another day we went greyhound coursing along the fine bold cliffs near Peterhead, and in a house on some bleak point or other we called on a gentleman and his sister, who shewed us coins, vases, and spearheads found on excavating for some purpose in their close neighbourhood at Burghead, all Roman. On going lower the workmen came upon a bath, a spring enclosed by cut stone walls, a mosaick pavement surrounding the bath, steps descending to it, and paintings on the walls. The place was known to have been a Roman Station with many others along the South shore of the Moray firth. We had all of us therefore great pleasure in going to see these curious remains of past ages thus suddenly brought to light. I remember it all perfectly as if I had visited it quite lately, and I recollect regretting that the walls were in many parts defaced.[1]

On leaving Duffus we drove on to Garmouth to see Mr Steenson, my father's wood Agent there; he had charge of all the timber floated down the Spey from the forest of Rothiemurchus where it had grown for ages, to the shore near Fochabers where it was sorted and stacked for sale. There was a good natured wife who did me a present of a milk jug in the form of a cow, which did duty at our nursery feasts for a wonderful while, considering it was made of crockery ware; and rather a pretty daughter, just come from the finishing school at Elgin, and stiff and shy of course. These ladies interested me much less than did the timber yard, where all my old friends the logs, the spars, the deals and my Mother's oars were piled in such quantities as appeared to me endless. The great width of the Spey, the bridge at Fochabers, and the peep of the towers of Gordon Castle from

1. The promontory-fort of Burghead is, in fact, between Forres and Lossiemouth. O. G. S. Crawford, *Topography of Roman Scotland*, writes sternly (p. 125) of the 'very thorough ransacking of 1809', and doubts its Roman origin.

amongst the cluster of trees that concealed the rest of the building, all return to me now as a picture of beauty. The Duke lived very disreputably in this solitude, for he was very little noticed, and, I believe, preferred seclusion.[1]

It was late when we reached Leitchison, a large wandering house in a flat bare part of the country, which the Duke had given, with a good farm attached, to his natural son Colonel Gordon, our Glentromie friend. Bright fires were blazing in all the large rooms, to which long passages led, and all the merry children were jumping about the hall anxiously watching for us. There were five or six fine boys, and one daughter, Jane, named after the Duchess. Mrs Gordon and her two sisters, the dark beautiful Agnes, and fat, red haired Charlotte, were respectably connected in Elgin, had money, were well educated and so popular women. Mrs Gordon was pretty and pleasing, and the Colonel in company delightful; but somehow they did not get on harmoniously together; he was eccentrick and extravagant, she peevish, and so they lived very much asunder. I did not at all approve of the ways of the house after Duffus, where big and little people all associated in the family arrangements. Here at Leitchison the children were quite by themselves, with porridge breakfasts and broth dinners, and very cross Charlotte Ross to keep us in order. If she tried her authourity on the Colonel as well, it was no wonder if he preferred the highlands without her to the lowlands with her, for I know I was not sorry when the four bays turned their heads westward, and, after a pleasant day's drive, on our return through Fochabers, Elgin, and Forres, again stopt at the door at Logie.

Beautiful Logie! a few miles up the Findhorn, on the wooded banks of that dashing river, wooded with beech and elm and oak centuries old; a grassy holm on which the hideous house stood, sloping hills behind, the water beneath, the Darnaway woods beyond, and such a garden! such an orchard! well did we know the Logie pears, large hampers of them had often found their way to the Doune; but the Logie

1. The fourth Duke, after his estrangement from the Duchess, the Grants' great friend, lived here with Mrs Jane Christie, 'by whom he had a large family' before marrying her in 1820 (D.N.B.).

guignes could only be tasted at the foot of the trees, and did not my young cousins and I help ourselves. Logie himself, my father's first cousin, was a tall, fine looking man, with a very ugly Scotch face, sandy hair and huge mouth, ungainly in manner yet kindly, very simple in character, in fact a sort of goose; much liked from his hospitable ways, respected for his old Cumming blood (he was closely related to Altyre), and admired for one accomplishment, his playing on the violin. He had married rather late in life one of the cleverest women of the age, an Ayrshire Miss Baillie, a beauty in her youth, for she was Burns' 'Bonnie Leslie,'[1] and a bit of a fortune, and she gave herself to the Militia Captain before she had ever seen the Findhorn! And they were very happy—he looked up to her without being afraid of her, for she gave herself no superiour wisdom airs, indeed she set out so resolutely on St Paul's advice to be subject to her husband, that she actually got into a habit of thinking he had judgment; and my Mother remembered a whole roomfull of people hardly able to keep their countenances, when she, giving her opinion on some disputed matter, clinched the argument as she supposed, by adding, 'It's not my own conviction only, but Mr Cumming says so.' She was too southron to call the Laird 'Logie.' Logie banks and Logie braes—how very very lovely ye were on those bright autumn days, when wandering through the beech woods upon the rocky banks of the Findhorn, we passed hours, my young cousins and I, out in the pure air, unchecked of any one. Five sons and one fair daughter the Lady Logie bore her Laird; they were not all born then at the time I write of. Poor Alexander and Robert, the two eldest, fine handsome boys, were my companions in these happy days; long since mourned for in their early graves. There was a strange mixture of the father's simplicity and the mother's shrewdness in all the children, and the same in their looks; only two were regularly handsome, May Anne and Alexander, who was his mother's darling. Clever as she was she made far too much distinction between him and the rest; he was better

1. 'O saw ye bonie Lesley' (tune, The Collier's Bony Dochter).

dressed, better fed, more considered in every way than the younger ones, and yet not spoiled. He never assumed and they never envied, it was natural that the young Laird should be most considered. A Tutor, very little older than themselves, and hardly as well dressed, tho' plaiding was the wear of all, taught the boys their humanities—he ate his porridge at the side table with them, declining the after cup of tea, which Alexander alone went to the state table to receive. At dinner it was the same system still, broth and boiled mutton, or the kain fowl[1] at the poor Tutor's side-table. And yet he revered the Lady; everybody did; every one obeyed her without a word, or even, I believe, a thought, that it was possible her orders could be incorrect. Her manner was very kind, very simple, though she had an affected way of speaking; but it was her strong sense, her truthful honesty, her courage—moral courage, for the body's was weak enough—her wit, her fire, her readiness that made her the queen of the intellect of the north countrie. Every one referred to her in their difficulties; it was well that no winds wandered over the reeds that grew by the side of the Lady Logie. Yet she was worldly in a degree, no one ever more truly counselled for the times, or lived more truly up to the times, but so as it was no reproach to her. She was with us often at the Doune with or without the Laird, Alexander sometimes her companion, and he would be left with us while she was over at Kinrara, where she was a great favourite. I believe it was intended by the families to marry him, Alexander, to Mary, they were very like and of suitable ages, and he was next heir of entail, presumptive, to Rothiemurchus after my brothers. It had also been settled by the seniors to marry first Sir William Cumming and afterwards Charles, to me. Jane oddly enough was let alone, though we always understood her to be the favourite with every body.

My father had a story of Mrs Cumming that often has come into my head since. He put her in mind of it now, when she declined going on in the carriage with him and my mother to dine at Relugas, where we were to remain for a few days. She had no great faith in four in hands on highland roads, at our

1. A payment in kind (s.n.d.).

English Coachman's rate of driving. She determined on walking by the riverside, that lovely mile with Alexander and the girlie, me, as her escort. Her dress during the whole of our visit, morning, noon, and night, was a scarlet cloth gown made in habit fashion, only without a train, braided in black upon the breast and cuffs, and on her head a black velvet cap, smartly set on one side, bound with scarlet cord, and having a long scarlet tassel, dangling merrily enough, as my father reminded her of what he called the passage of the Spey. It seemed that upon one occasion when she was on a visit to us, they were all going together to dine at Kinrara, and as was usual with them then, before the ford at our offices was settled enough to use when the water was high, or the road made passable for a heavy carriage up the bank of the Bogach, they were to cross the Spey at the ford below Kainapool close to Kinrara. The river had risen very much after heavy rain in the hills, and the ford, never shallow, was now so deep that the water was up above the small front wheels and in under the doors, flooding the footboard. My Mother sat still and screamed. Mrs Cumming doubled herself up orientally upon the seat, and in a commanding voice, though pale with terrour, desired the Coachman, who could not hear her, to turn. On plunged the horses, in rushed more water, both ladies shrieked. My father attempted the masculine Consolation of appealing to their sense of eyesight, which would shew them 'returning were as tedious as going o'er,'[1] that the next step must be into the shallows. The Lady Logie turned her head indignantly, her body she could not move, and from her divan like seat she thus in tragick tone replied—'A reasonable man like you, Rothiemurchus! to attempt to appeal to the judgment of a woman while under the dominion of the passion of fear!'

At Relugas lived an old Mrs Cuming, with *one* m, the Widow of I don't know who, her only child her heiress daughter, and the daughter's husband, Tom Lauder. He had some income from his father, was to have more when the father died, and a large inheritance with a Baronetcy at an uncle's death, Lord Fountainhall. It had been a common

1. Macbeth, III, iv, 138.

small Scotch house, but an Italian front had been thrown before the old building, an Italian tower had been raised above the offices, and with neatly kept grounds it was about the prettiest place that ever was lived in. The situation was beautiful, on a high tongue of land between the Divie and the Findhorn—the wild, leaping, rocky bedded Divie and the broader and rapid Findhorn. All along the banks of both were well directed paths among the wooding, a group of children flitting about the heathery braes, and the heartiest, merriest welcome within. Mr and Mrs Lauder were little more than children themselves, in manner at least; really young in years and gifted with almost bewildering animal spirits, they did keep up a racket at Relugas. It was one eternal carnival. Up late, a plentiful Scotch breakfast, out all day, a dinner of many courses, mumming all the evening, and a supper at the end to please the old lady. A Colonel Somebody had a story—ages after this, however—that having received an appointment to India, he went to take leave of his kind friends at Relugas. It was in the evening, and instead of finding a quiet party at tea, he got into a crowd of Popes, Cardinals, jugglers, gypsies, minstrels, flowergirls, etc., the usual amusements of the family. He spent half a lifetime in the east, and returning to his native place thought he would not pass that same hospitable door. He felt as in a dream, or as if his years of military service had been a dream—there was all the crowd of mountebanks again. The only difference was in the actors; children had grown up to take the places of their elders, some children, for all the elders were not gone. Sir Thomas Dick Lauder! wore as full a turban, made as much noise, and was just as thin as the Tom Lauder of twenty years before, and his good lady, equally travestied and a little stouter, did not look a day older with her grown up daughters round her, than she did in her own girlish times. It was certainly a pleasant house for young people. Sir Thomas, with all his frivolity, was a very accomplished man. His taste was excellent, as all his improvements shewed—no walks could have been better conducted, no trees better placed, no views better chosen, and this refinement was carried all through, to the colours of the furniture and the arrangement of it. He drew well, sketched very accurately from nature, was clever at puzzles, *bout rimés,*[1] etc.—the very man for a country neighbourhood. Her merit was in implicitly following his lead—she thought, felt, saw, heard as he did, and if his perceptions altered or varied, so did hers. There never was such a patient Grizzle; and the curious part of their history was that being early destined to go together by their parents, they detested one another, as children did nothing but quarrel, agreed no better as they grew, being at one on one only point, that they never would marry. How to avoid such a catastrophe was the single subject they discussed amicably. They grew confidential upon it quite, and it ended in their settlement at Relugas.

This merry visit ended our tour. We drove home in a few hours over the long, dreary moor between the Spey and the Findhorn, passing one of the old strongholds of the Grants, the remains of a square tower beside a lonely lake—a very lonely lake, for not a tree nor a shrub was near it; and resting the horses at the Bridge of Carr, a single arch over the Dulnan, near which had clustered a few cottages, a little inn amongst them sheltered by trees; altogether a bit of beauty in the desert. I had been so extremely good all this tour, well amused, made of, and not worried! that Miss Ramsay was extremely complimented on the improvement she had effected in my naturally bad disposition. As if there were any naturally bad dispositions. Don't we crook them, and stunt them, and force them, and break them, and varnish them, and do every thing in the world except let them alone to expand in pure air to the sun, and nourish them healthfully.

We were now to prepare for a 'journey to London.'[2] I recollect rather a tearful parting with a companion to whom we had become much attached, Mr Peter of Duthil's youngest son—or only son, for all I know, as I never saw any other. Willie Grant was a fine handsome boy, a favourite with every body and the darling of his poor father, who had but

1. 'A List of Words that rhyme to one another, drawn up by another Hand, and given to a Poet, who was to make a poem to the rhymes in the same order that they were placed upon the List' (Addison's definition in the O.E.D.). See I 159.
2. See footnote 2, 1, p. 89.

this bright spot to cheer his dull home horizon. All this summer Willie had come to the Doune with the parson every third Sunday; that is, they came on the Saturday, and generally remained over Monday. He was older than any of us, but not too old to share all our out of doors fun, and he was full of all good, really and truly sterling. We were to love one another for ever, yet we never met again. When we returned to the highlands he was in the East India Military College, and then he sailed, and though he lived to come home, marry, and to settle in the highlands, neither Jane nor I ever saw him more. How many of these fine lads did my father and Charles Grant send out to India? Some that throve, some that only passed, some that made a name we were all proud of, and not one that ever I heard of that disgraced the homely rearing of their humbly positioned but *gentle* born parents. The moral training of those simple times bore its fair fruits: the history of half the great men in the last age began in a cabin.

Sir Charles Forbes was the son of a small farmer in Aberdeenshire. Sir William Grant, the Master of the Rolls,[1] was a mere peasant—his Uncles floated my father's timber down the Spey as long as they had strength to follow the calling. General William Grant was a footboy in my Uncle Rothy's family. Sir Colquhoun Grant,[2] though a woodsetter's child, was but poorly reared, in the same fashion as Mrs Pro's fortunate boys. Sir William Macgregor, whose history should we tell it was most romantick of all, was such another. The list could be easily lengthened did my memory serve, but these were among the most striking examples of what the good plain schooling of the dominie, the principles and the pride of the parents, produced in young ardent spirits; forming characters which, however they were acted on by the world, never forgot home feelings, although they proved this differently. The Master of the Rolls, for instance, left all his

1. Sir William Grant (1752–1832), Attorney General for Canada, M.P. for Banffshire and Master of the Rolls 1801 to 1817 (D.N.B.).
2. Sir Colquhoun Grant (1764–1835): 'One of the most dashing hussars in the service', he had 'several horses killed under him at Waterloo' (D.N.B.).

relations in obscurity. A small annuity rendered his parents merely independant of hard labour; very moderate portions just secured for his sisters decent matches in their own degree; an occasional remittance in a bad season helped an Uncle or a brother out of difficulty. I never heard of his going to see them, or bringing any of them out of their own sphere to visit him. While the General shoved on his brothers, educated his nephews and nieces, pushed the boys up, married the girls well—such of them at least as had a wish to raise themselves—and almost resented the folly of Peter the Pensioner,[1] who would not part with one of his flock from the very humble home he chose to keep them in. Which plan was wisest, or was either quite right? Which relations were happiest—those whose feelings were sometimes hurt, or those whose frames were sometimes over wearied and but scantily refreshed? I often pondered in my own young enquiring mind over these and similar questions; but just at the time of our last journey from the Doune to London less puzzling matters principally occupied my sister Jane and me.

We were not sure whether or no Miss Ramsay were to remain with us; neither were we sure whether or no we wished it. We should have more of our own way without her, that was certain; but whether that would be so good for us, whether we should get on as well in all points by ourselves, we were beginning to be suspicious of. She had taught us the value of constant employment, regular habits, obliging manners, and we knew, though we did not allow it, that there would be less peace as well as less industry should we be again left to govern ourselves. However, so it was settled. Miss Ramsay was dropt at Newcastle amongst her own friends, and for the time the relief from restraint seemed most agreeable. She was not capable of teaching us much, neither was she an intelligent person, so that probably she was no loss had her place been better supplied; but from my recollections of nursery gossip, nursery misrule, wasted time, neglected studies, ill used masters, I should say that as far as our progress was concerned the sums my father paid to our several teachers might as well have remained in his pocket. It

1. See I, p. 326.

was an idea of my father's that we were better unguided; characters self formed were to his mind more brave, more natural, than could ever be the result of over tutoring. We were therefore very little directed in our early days. We were always informed of our wrong doings, sometimes punished for them, but we were very much left to find out the right for ourselves; and so once more unshackled we proceeded on our way to town.

# CHAPTER SEVEN

## 1809–1810

Baltiboys, November 1845[1]

HAVING got so far in these memorials of past life, the pleasure of the many half forgotten incidents now revived induces me to proceed in stringing together such recollections of our generation as can hardly fail, dear children, to be interesting to you. The feebleness of my health at present confines me so much to my room that I am neglecting nothing else while thus employing myself, so, though I have lost one listener to the chapters as they are concluded, dear Janie Gardiner being no longer among us, on I go as at Avranches, feeling that if any of you are like me, this history of one of yourselves of the past age will be a curious family legend to refer to.

We left the highlands, then, late in the autumn of 1809, and leaving our good natured Governess with her friends at Newcastle, reached London in about three weeks from the time we set out. During the winter, and the spring of 1810, we were occupied as usual with our several masters, under whom we could not fail to make a certain degree of progress, because we were quick children and they were clever instructors, but we by no means duly improved our time, or conscientiously worked out the value of my father's money and kindness. For want of a steady Director we got into habits of dawdling, idling, omitting, and so on, and we were very irregular in our hours, setting the authourity of our maid, Margaret Davidson, at defiance. She waited on my Mother as well as on us, and might have made a good deal of

1. The Smith family returned to Ireland in the summer of 1845 ; Baltiboys was her husband's estate ; Janie Gardiner was her niece.

mischief had she been given to tale bearing. My musick fell *really* back, though not apparently. Miss Horn was not Mr Morris. I recollect too that I took no trouble—nobody was there to make me. That is, in musick a difficult passage was slurred, in singing an uneasy note omitted, in drawing chance directed the pencil, in writing translations I never looked out in the dictionary for the meaning of such words as I did not know, I just popt in any word that struck me as suitable, and it was quite a bright idea given me by one of our companions in the Square, to read the rule before making the exercise; this had never struck me as necessary, so poor Mr Beekvelt must have taught us oddly; he was extremely pleased with the marked improvement caused by this study of the grammar, and I daresay gave himself all the credit of it. Mr Thompson, from whom we learned the most, did not take matters so easily. The dining room was given up to us, and there we lived by ourselves, as it was never wanted by any one else till about an hour before my father and mother's dinner. We got up late, studied as little and amused ourselves as much as we could manage. My Mother was often ailing, she also hated the worry of children, and she did not herself understand the various accomplishments we were trying to learn. She therefore occupied the back drawing room; where, however, I made her breakfast, she being seldom down in time for my father, who required his early. Either Jane or I took it down to him in his study, and when my Mother had hers up in her room, we helped ourselves with great delight to the remains, our detestable porridge having been barely tasted. After this we always walked our two hours in the Square, then we returned to our studies, we dined, studied again by way of, and when the Butler entered with his plate trays we bundled up all our books, and departed to change our dress. In the evenings, when we were at home, we occupied ourselves pretty much as we liked, being reproved when we did foolishly.

This kind of half haphazard education may preserve originality of character, or indeed produce some good effects in some cases, but I do not think it improved any of us, either physically or mentally. I am sure we should all have been stronger women had there been a better system pursued with our diet and general training; most certainly we should have been happier then and afterwards had we been more looked after, and so better understood; and it is likely that we should have been more skilled in all we were taught, our minds and memories much better stored, had there been some eye over us. I know for myself that I, all quickness and eagerness and volatility, required a steady hand to keep me back, to make me finish as I went on, complete what I had begun, *think* of what there was to do, how to do it, and why it was done. Naturally active, lively, negligent, capricious, vain, all good qualities verged too nearly upon bad for me to be safely left to my own impulses; for I never reflected. Jane, slow, cautious, conscientious, very sensitive and rather awkward, required encouragement and direction, and occasional shaking up. We had both to educate ourselves long years after, when taught by sufferings how much discipline we wanted. Dear Mary was petted one minute, repulsed the next, called idle when she was ill, stupid and obstinate for want of help in her childish difficulties, the seeds of evil were fostered till they grew to bear their bitter fruit—melancholy reflections! Common to many of us of the last age when the duties of our several stations were neither taught nor known. Mothers were ignorant of their responsibilities, assistants were incapable of supplying their place, the world in general as far behind in economick morals as in less momentous things. Our children have numberless advantages over us, their parents, they are benefitting by our sad experience, passing happy youths, learning without effort what we bought by tears. I cannot reflect on the mistakes of our day and their consequences without a feeling that is very painful. I really think I must have turned out badly but for two people, Mr Thompson and Annie Grant. Mr Thompson did not suit Jane. She was plodding herself and wanted enlivening. Mary pretended utter dulness and would never attend to him. He vexed me with his chronological order, and his pricknickity neatness and his rigid arithmetick, but these methodical proceedings were just exactly what my volatile nature required. The man had not an idea, but he somehow caught and made me look after mine. How hard he worked for the wife and half dozen children. Up every morning summer and winter at four, to get his breakfast and walk to Kensington by six, and then teach on till nine at night.

We had an excellent dancing Master, an Irish Mr Blake, of whom we learned the good old minuet style of moving, which I wish from my heart were the fashion again, for I neither think the manner of the present day so graceful, nor the carriage by any means so good, nor the gestures so easy as in the days of the stately sinkings and risings and balancings of the body required in the minuet. We formed a small dancing class, which met once a week at alternate houses. We were three—four at William's holidays; there were five Hultons, Mary, Sophy, Emily, Edward, and Henry, and a Miss and two Master Williams; all inhabitants of the Square, as we called Lincoln's Inn Fields, the children of brother barristers! We had encreased our acquaintance in our playground. We had little Diana Wilson and her cousins Hotham next door to add to our list of friends; the younger Vivians, a set of Wyndhams—very nice children; three Tyndales, not so well born as some of the others, but clever girls—their father was an Attorney, vulgar enough, their mother a daughter of Mrs Rundell (Cookery book),[1] an extremely accomplished woman, without an approach to refinement. My favourite companion was Julia Hankey, now the Widow of my brother William's Schoolfellow, Seymour Bathurst. Her mother was an Alexander of Ballochmyle, and she lived with her two maiden sisters, honest Scotch gentlewomen, and their Uncle the Chief Baron, in one of the best houses in our then fashionable law situation. She was the Widow of the Alderman Hankey who died from putting brandy in his shoes when his feet were sore and hot with walking through the City, canvassing to be Lord Mayor: the chill of the evaporation produced apoplexy. They were all immensely rich on all sides, and Julia and her three brothers and one Cousin, Frederick, the only heirs of all. We also saw sometimes the Welshs and the Wards at the Admiralty, Fanny Hunter, and our cousin Raper. My father did not encourage young society for us.

1. *A New System of Domestic Cookery* (1807) by Maria Eliza Rundell.

We were extremely fond of a visit to Brunswick Square; the baby cousins there, of whom there were now three, John, Lizzy, and George, were charming playthings, and all our aunt's tall brothers in law were so very kind to us. Another particular friend was Mrs Sophy Williams, my father's old Governess, who very often came to see us and never empty handed, and we used to go to visit her where she then lived at Kensington as companion to old Mrs Anguish, the mother or the Aunt of the Duchess of Leeds, and a relation of Mrs Raper's. It was one of those old fashioned households now hardly remembered, where the fires were all put out, the carpets all taken up, and curtains down upon the first of May, not to be replaced in those shivery rooms until the 1st of October; where the hard highbacked chairs were ranged against the wall, and a round, club legged, darkly polished table stood quite bare in the middle of the room. In one window was a parrot on a perch, screaming 'How d'ye do' for ever. In the other the two old ladies with their worsted work, their large baskets, and their fat spaniel. Mrs Anguish talked a great deal of scandal to my mother about the Court of the good Queen Charlotte, the Prince and the Duchess of Devonshire, the Duke of ditto and Lady Elizabeth Forster, sundry irregularities amongst the nobles of past and present days; while dear Mrs Sophy described Twyford and Thorley, told of my Grandmother's warm heart and warmer temper, of my father's quaint sayings, aunt Lissy's goodness. We used also to visit Mrs Thrale (Dr Johnson's), who was then Mrs Piozzi—her house a sort of Museum—and Lady Keith, her daughter, and Mrs Murray Aust in a beautiful villa looking on Rotten Row, whose tour in the highlands had made her rather celebrated; and dear old Mrs Raper in her melancholy back drawing room in Wimpole Street, where I never yet found her doing anything whatever, though her mind must have been well filled at some former time, for she drew upon its stores in conversation most agreeably; and Mrs Charles Ironside, and old Mrs Maling I remember. What other acquaintances my Mother called on I do not know, for we were always left in the carriage except at the foregoing houses. She generally drove out every day, and some of us were always with her. On the week days she made her visits and went shopping—to Green the glover's in Little Newport Street, next door to such beautiful dolls, a whole shop of no other toy, some of the size of life, opening and shutting their eyes, as was then a rare virtue; to Roberts and Plowman; to Gray the jeweller; to Rundall and Bridge, so dirty and shabby without, such a fairy palace within, where on asking a man who was filling a scoop with small brown looking stones what he was doing, he told me he was shovelling in rubies; to Miss Steuart's, our delight, cakes and flattery and bundles of finery awaiting us there; and then the three or four rooms full of *hoops* before the Court days, machines of Whalebone, very large, covered with silk, and then with lace or net, and hung about with festoons of lace and beads, garlands of flowers, puffings of ribbon, furbelows of all sorts. As the waists were short, how the imprisoned victims managed their arms we of this age can hardly imagine. The heads for these bodies were used as supports for whole faggots of feathers, as many as twelve sometimes standing bolt upright forming really a forest of plumage; the long train stretched out behind very narrow, more like a prolonged sashend than a garment. Yet there were beauties who wore this dress, and looked in it beautiful. We went to Churton's for our Stockings, to Ross for my mother's wigs—that was another queer fashion—every woman, not alone the gray and the bald, wore an expensive wig instead of her own hair; to Lowe for shoes, to St Paul's church corner for books. I can't remember half the places.

On Sundays we went to Lincoln's Inn Chapel in the morning, Sir William Grant looking kindly down upon us from his window. We dined, said our Catechism, and then all set out for Rotten Row, where the amusement consisted in one long file of carriages at a foot's pace going one way, passing another long file of carriages at a foot's pace going the other, bows gravely exchanged between the occupants, when any of the busy starers were acquainted. All London was engaged in this serious business. We sometimes prevailed on my Mother to make a diversion round the ring, that we might see the swans on the water, but she only now and then obliged us, much preferring that long procession up and down a mile of dusty road—the greater the crowd, the slower the move, the greater the pleasure. 'Delightful drive in the park to-day' meant that there was hardly a possibility of cutting into the line, or moving much above a yard in a minute. 'Most dreadfully stupid in the park to-day' meant that there was plenty of room for driving there comfortably.

On Sunday evenings my father took his tea upstairs. Other evenings we carried him down a large breakfast cup full of very strong tea to his study, where he was always seated immersed in papers with his Secretary, little horrid Sandy Grant, whose strange voice sounded as if he spoke through a paper covered comb. It was not Law business that occupied them; the poor clerk in the outer office had but an idle time. Lawsuits of his own, dreams of political influence,[1] money loans, and all the perplexities and future miseries consequent on these busy evenings were being prepared in that study where we carried the cup of tea. How kindly my poor father smiled on his young messengers, how bright his room looked, how warm his fire. We liked to go there, and we loved to linger there. Even Sandy Grant was a favourite.

We were very seldom allowed to go to children's parties, nor did my Mother ever give any for us at home. One ball only I remember at the Walsh's in Harley Street, where I danced all night with two partners, Henry Ward and Abercrombie Dick, the first rather a great man now among a secondary set,[2] the last a Lieutenant Colonel at twenty seven; and another at Mr Blake's, our dancing Master, where I so far forgot the orthodox English style of regular four in a bar style of evenly goosestepping the scotch reel, as in our happy excitement to revert to good Mr Grant's Strathspey fashion, of springing through in time to the musick, at which, as both my sister Jane and myself were exceedingly admired by the elders of the company, no remark was made either by Mr

1. Sandy Grant was her father's Agent in the successfully fought election for Great Grimsby in 1812.
2. It is likely that this was the Sir Henry Ward (1797–1860) who was Governor of the Ionian Islands and later Ceylon.

Blake or his assistant; but we received a sufficient lecture during our next lesson at home for so disgracing his teaching. We went very often to the Play, we three elder ones, and to Sadler's Wells and Astley's, and to some of the Concerts. Also this spring for the first time in my life I went to the Opera. At the Hanover Square Concerts Saloman was the Leader,[1] the singers were Bartleman, Braham, Kelly, the Knyvetts, Mr and Mrs Vaughan, Mrs Bianchi—afterwards my teacher—and Mrs Billington. Mrs Mountain I heard, but not there. The first song I ever heard Mrs Billington sing was Handel's 'Sweet Bird that shunn'st the noise of folly,'[2] accompanied on the violin by Saloman. I was sitting next to my father, behind whom I slunk, holding down my head to conceal the soft tears whose shedding relieved my heart. We were always taught to restrain all such exhibitions of feeling, which indeed my Mother would have characterised as mere affectation, and therefore I was ashamed of the overpowering sensations which made me so utterly full of delight; something exquisite in the feeling there was which I have not yet forgotten. How I practised my own shakes and runs and holding notes, for the two following days only, giving up from despair of ever pleasing myself. She was the enchantress of my first Opera too. We were all in the Square one afternoon, at a grand game of Tom Tickler's ground, when one of my playmates told us that the white flag, our homeward signal, was flying from our high windows. We ran off at once and were met at the gate by the footman, who said that I only was wanted. I was to dress as quick as possible in my best white frock to go to the Opera. How old was I that happy night?— thirteen within a week or two. My dress was a plain white frock with plenty of tucks at the bottom, a little embroidery

1. John Peter Saloman (1745–1815) was the brilliant
   violinist and impresario whose concerts in Hanover
   Square Rooms, for example, had premiered Haydn's
   London symphonies. The most interesting of his
   talented singers were Mrs Billington (see over) and
   Michael Kelly, the famous Irish tenor who worked
   with Mozart.
2. Aria from *L'Allegro il Penserosa ed il Moderato* (1740),
   Handel's setting of Milton's poems.

on the waist, white calico long gloves, and a cropt head, the hair brushed bright with rose oil, which to me made the toilette complete. The Opera was 'Il fanatico.' Naldi the father, with his full low notes, Mrs Billington his pupil daughter.[1] She sang her solfeggi, all the exercises, and 'Uno trillo sopra là'— nothing ever was so beautiful, even the memory of those sounds, so clear, so sweet, so harmonious, that voice that ran about like silver water over pearls. There is no enjoyment equal to good musick, simple or complicated, so as it be truthfully, earnestly given; it has ever afforded to me the most intense pleasure I am capable of receiving, and how little I have heard, and how very vilely I made it.

We had had a great fright this year by the very severe series of illnesses that attacked poor William. He brought the whooping cough with him from Eton at Xmas, which we all caught from him, and a pleasant time we had, condemned to one side walk in the Square, from any approach to which all other children were strictly forbidden. It was not very bad with us, and towards the end we became rather attached to our visitor, for we had no lessons, no milk, delicious tea breakfasts, and dinners of puddings and such good things, with long daily drives far out into the country. William had not been long returned to school when he took the measles; this turned to scarlet fever, and my Mother went down to nurse him, with very faint hopes at one time of bringing him through. When he could be moved he was taken to Kensington to be under the care of Mrs Mary Williams, the elder sister of Sophy, who, with a blind sister, Anne, lived in a very neat house not far from the gardens. My Mother went every day to see him, taking care to take off the dress she wore before allowing any of the rest of us to come near her, while any risk of infection was thought to remain; and yet both Jane and I got, not the measles, but the scarlet fever and severely too; the younger ones escaped.

1. Simon Mayr's 'Il fanatico per la musica' (1798); Guiseppe Naldi was a fine bass but Mrs Elizabeth Billington (1768-1818) has been described as 'the greatest singer England has ever produced' whilst for Haydn she was 'ein grosses Genie' (*Groves*).

It was about this time that I began to take more notice of any remarkable persons occasionally dining at my father's. The three eccentrick brothers, Lord Buchan, Lord Erskine, and Harry Erskine, by far the most brilliant of the three, stand out foremost.[1] It was a real treat to the whole family when this last with his agreeable wife came for a few weeks from Scotland, as we always saw a good deal of them. The Duchess of Gordon I remember with her loud voice, and Lady Madelina Sinclair, talking of Rothiemurchus and Kinrara. Lord Gillies and Mrs Gillies, in his Advocate days, when Appeal cases brought him to London. The Redfearns, whom I never saw, the sight of me recalling her lost boy (with the drum) so vividly that she could not bear the shock: so no children appeared when she did—no great disappointment to us. There were the Master of the Rolls and some few English Lawyers, Mr Ward (Tremaine), Sir Giffin Wilson, and William Frere; and upon one occasion his intended, Miss Gurdon, who sang with a voice and in a style only equalled by Catalani (see II 181).

This year, after all the sickness, we went early to Tunbridge, my Mother having suffered herself severely in consequence of her fatigue and anxiety. A large dull house, but a very comfortable one, was taken for us at the top of Sion Hill. It belonged to Mr Canning's mother,[2] and had a really good garden, with a fine clump of shady trees in it, under which we children used to pass our day. My Mother had some dislike to this place which suited all the rest of us so admirably, so, in the fiery month of June, we removed from

1. These three sons of the tenth Earl of Buchan were all well-known public figures at this time. The eleventh Earl (1742–1829) was much involved in the history and antiquities of Scotland; the Hon. Henry Erskine (1746–1817) was Lord Advocate for Scotland at the same time his brother Thomas (1750–1823) was Lord Chancellor during the 'Ministry of All the Talents' of 1806–07.
2. She had been a moderately successful actress, who was able to leave the stage when her son arranged for his pension (he had been Under Secretary of State for the previous five years) to be paid direct to her.

this quiet, roomy, old fashioned house to a smartened up Grosvenor Lodge, a new bow windowed villa on the London road, a full mile from the Wells, where the sun shone on us unmolested till we in the atticks were nearly grilled; but we were in the world as well as in the sunshine, and the dust besides. Every evening we went out in the open carriage and four, driving in every direction all round that beautiful country, where well wooded hills and dales, with fields, lanes, villages, peeping spires, and country seats, combined to present a succession of views of surpassing richness, wanting only water to make the style of scenery perfect. We made parties to the Rocks, to the Repository on the heath, to Frant, and many other places, and we often walked up and down the pantiles listening to a very respectable Band. There was something so very pretty about those simple Wells; they struck me again, as they struck me before, as so much more to be admired—the pure water just bubbling up fresh as it sprung, merely caught in small marble basins into which the clear glasses were dipt, and then offered to the drinkers by a few tidily dressed old women—than the pump room style of Cheltenham and other places, where from a row of brass cocks flows no one knows what sort of mixture, served by flaunty girls from behind a long counter. Then the water was so pleasant, clear and sparkling and very cold, the taste of iron far from disagreeable, and I at least, like my Mother, so strengthened by it, that I love the very name of the Wells to this day. It was a *dry* bracing climate that suited me; I felt as if I could have jumped over the moon there.

Aunt Leitch spent a short time with us at Grosvenor Lodge, and Annie Grant and Miss Maling. Mrs Giffin Wilson, our neighbour, was in the next house to us for a while, attending the death bed of her sister Lady Edward O'Brien. A pleasant cousin James Blackburn, rather sweet we thought upon Aunt Leitch, was also of our party. Aunt Leitch had been for some time a Widow. She had given up Kilmerdinney to her husband's heir for a consideration, and had joined in housekeeping with Uncle Ralph, who had determined on letting Tennochside and coming South for a few years, in order better to educate his two children. We had our highland neighbours, Belleville and Mrs Macpherson, also here; of them we saw a great deal, having from first to last been always on the most friendly terms with them. My brother John, then Johnny, a little creature in a nankin frock, and Belleville were so inseparable, that people soon began to look for them as one of the Shows of the place, for they walked together the greater part of the day in rather a singular manner. Belleville went first with his hands crossed behind his back, holding out his long stick, the end of which was taken by the child, who trotted on thus for hours, few words passing between the pair. Mrs Macpherson, who preferred the carriage, generally went an airing with us, my Mother calling for her at her lodgings near the pantiles. We were really very happy this season at Tunbridge Wells, and so set up by the fine air that we could not have looked more healthy had we been in our own Duchus.

Upon looking over the doings of this year so far, I find I have forgotten to mention quite a remarkable circumstance. Some time before we left town Mrs Charles Grant, the old Director's wife, invited we three little girls to accompany my father and mother to a great party she was giving in Russell Square—a rout—and we went. It was to meet the Persian Ambassador, the same who was Mr Morier's friend, and who got on in every way so well in this country that many years afterwards he was sent here again. I can't at this moment recollect his name—he was a tall handsome man, not very dark, he spoke English quite well enough to be understood, and turned all the women's heads with his beautiful eastern dress and flatteries. He was remarkably fond of children, always liked to have some in the room with him, which was the reason we had been distinguished by this invitation. There was wonderful commotion in the green room which Jane and I shared in common, little Mary venturing to shew herself there, as she had been included among the company. Our dancing shoes, drab jean, were to do quite well, and cotton stockings, but we got new frocks of soft clear muslin, very full, with several deep tucks and open behind. All the three heads were fresh cropt and oiled, and as our toilettes were completing my Mother entered, so beautifully dressed in white spotted muslin over strawcoloured silk, holding in her hands three pairs of white kid gloves, and three cairn gorm crosses dangling to gold chains. Duncan McIntosh[1] had given us the stones which had been found on our own hills and she had had them set for us purposely to wear this evening. The Persian Ambassador took a great deal of notice of us and of our sparkling crosses. Jane, of course, he most distinguished, her bright eyes and her rosy cheeks, and her lively natural manner equally free from forwardness or shyness, always ensured her the attention of strangers. Both she and I behaved extremely well, we were told next day, Papa and Mama quite satisfied with us, and with our propriety in the cake line, just helping ourselves once, as we had been told, and no more. Mary was suspected of more frequent helpings, also she tired and fell asleep on Belleville's knee, for he and Mrs Macpherson were there. Mrs Macpherson said laughing to my Mother when the great *Mirza* (I am sure now one of his names was)[2] was occupied so much with Jane, not very far from where sat an elderly Miss Perry, another Director's daughter, with an enormous turban on her head, and a fine cachemire on her shoulders: 'What would *she* give to be the object of such attention?' the shawl and turban having been adopted, it was said, to attract the stranger, who had a wife and one little girl at home.

Aunt Mary had invited me to be present at a great solemnity at Oxford, the Installation of Lord Grenville as Chancellor of the University, which ceremony was to take place in the month of July of this summer, 1810.[3] It was quite an era in my life, the first indeed of any moment, and it filled my young heart with a tumultuous pleasure I was for some days unable to controul. It was lucky for me that my father was from home, as he would have been very likely to have kept me there for shewing myself so utterly unfit to be trusted with my own conduct. We were never to annoy others with any excess of emotion, probably a good rule for such very excitable children, and yet it might have made us artificial, and it did afterwards make me appear affected, the struggle

1. The Rothiemurchus forester.
2. In fact this was a common title of honour in Persia.
3. Former Prime Minister ('Ministry of All the Talents' 1806–07), he was installed on 14 December, 1809.

between feeling and fearing. I certainly did run a little wild on receiving Aunt *Griffith's* letter—she liked us to call her by her husband's name. To visit alone! To go to the *Theatre*! Concerts, Inaugurations! See degrees conferred! Among such a crowd of great and noble, in classick Oxford, where stood Great Tom! It really half turned a head not then very steady. We had been reading Miss Porter's Scottish Chiefs,[1] to initiate us into the realities of life and the truth of history; and such visions of display had been brought before us, of plumed helmets, coats of gilded mail, kings, queens, trains, escorts, etc., that, my Aunt indulging a little in poetical anticipations of the splendid scenes she was asking me to witness, I took my seat beside my father in his post chariot, with some idea that I had grown suddenly six feet high, twenty years older, and was the envy of every one. My father had come to us for a week's holiday after my first transport had cooled a little. The parting with them all made me grave enough, and it was soon quite unnecessary to caution me about repressing any exuberance of spirits.

The first disappointment in this dream of pleasure was the conveyance we travelled in. Accustomed to the Barouche and four, the liveried servants, and all the stir of such an equipage, my father's plain post chaise, a pair of horses, and one only man outside, made no sensation along the road, neither at the inns nor in the villages. No one stared at so plain a carriage, nor was there any bustle in the inn yards on our changing horses. The landladies were all very kind to the dear young lady but no one seemed to be surprised that she was journeying. Arrived in London, the large empty house in Lincoln's Inn Fields was intolerable, not a creature there but the housemaid in charge of all the displaced furniture, so that I wandered from one bare melancholy room to another in very tearful mood. In the Square it was no better, few of our young companions having remained in town—none that I at all cared for. Aunt Lissy was in Norfolk, my father occupied the whole day, so that except at meals I never saw him. There

1. Jane Porter: *The Scottish Chiefs—A Romance* (five
volumes, the first of many editions published in
London 1810).

were plenty of books, however, and the pianoforte, and I had always work with me, but it was very lonely. One new delight reconciled me in some measure to this dull week of nearly solitude. My Mother had trusted me to buy myself shoes, gloves, ribbons, etc., required as additions to my moderate equipment, and I had the satisfaction of purchasing these supplies myself, entering the shops in Fleet Street, in great state, in front of my attendant the housemaid, asking for what I wanted, choosing and *paying* like a grown up young lady. I was thirteen, Annie's present age,[1] but how far behind what she is, so ignorant of all useful things, so childish, so affected in many ways, so bewildered at having to act for myself; all our wants having been hitherto supplied without any trouble to us. Aunt Leitch had made me a present of a pound note to spend as I liked without question. I parted with it for a *parasol* with a plated stick and a carved ivory handle and a pagoda summit, of a pea green silk with a dazzling fringe, all together big enough to have acted as an umbrella, and under this canopy I strutted away with the dignity of a peacock, to the amusement, I should suppose, of every one that passed me.

I and my Chinese parasol were one morning in the Square, figuring before the nursery maids, when an unusual sound yelled up from a corner of the gardens,—the Searle Street corner,—and a mob of dirty looking men tumbled in over one another to the amount of hundreds, nay I believe thousands. They had hardly rushed on as far as Lord Kenyon's high house, when from the Long acre corner a troop of dragoons rattled in, all haste, advancing towards the surgeons' hall, with gleaming sabres. The mob retreated, steadily enough and slowly and unwillingly, but the horses moving on in their peculiar way, turning their hind legs to the multitude occasionally, made good their determined press-ure on the crowd, amid yells and shouts and many hisses. But the dragoons prevailed as the imposing cavalry advanced so did the great unwashed[2] retire, and soon the whole pageant

1. E.G.'s eldest child, born 1832.
2. Attributed to her father's Scottish legal contemporary Lord Brougham.

vanished, the noise even, gradually dying away in the distance. As quickly as we could recover our composure, all who had been sauntering in the Square regained their houses. At the corner gate I flew to, I and my precious parasol, I found my father's man, Mr Sims, waiting to escort me home. All the windows of the two lower storeys of all the houses in the Square were immediately closed, and the housemaid and I had to mount up to the very top of ours, to the barred windows of the nursery, to study the horsetailed helmets of our patrol. Early next morning I was taken to Sandy Grant's chambers in Sergeant's Inn, the iron gates of which retirement were kept fast closed till Sir Francis Burdett had left the Tower, for he had been the cause of all this commotion.[1] He was then the perfect idol of the people, their ideal of an English country gentleman. He supported this character in breeches and topboots, and having a fair handsome person and goodhumoured manners, he remained for many a year the King of the fiddlers. What his crime had been on this occasion, I forget, some disrespect to the House of Commons, I think, for they ordered him into custody, and sent him to the Tower, by water, to avoid ill consequences, his friends being above all things excitable. On the day of his release they had him to themselves, and had all their own way, filling the streets from end to end.[2] Never was there such a *pack* of heads wedged close together, like Sir Walter Scott's description of the Porteous mob.[3] Every window of the long, tall row of houses on either side was filled with women waving handkerchiefs and dark blue flags, the Burdett colour. The roar of voices and the tread of so many feet sounded awful even in the enclosed Court; it penetrated to the back room where Mrs Sandy Grant and I were sitting.

1. A prominent M.P. advocate of reform. He seconded
   Colonel Wardle's motion censuring the Duke of York
   and at this point of his career had been sent to the
   Tower for breach of privilege.
2. In fact he chose to leave the Tower by water thus
   leaving the mob of his supporters without their idol;
   this helps to explain the riot.
3. *Heart of Midlothian*, ch. VII.

She was a good natured woman, lame from a short leg with a club foot, which prevented her moving much. Though she had a very handsome face, it was supposed her husband had married her for her money, as she had not been well educated, and so not suited for the companion of a clever man. He was hardly kind to her, though he did not positively ill use her. She was very good natured to me, doing her best to amuse me while I remained her guest. She had a friend on a visit with her, a young lady deficient in the number of her fingers; on neither hand had she more than the thumb and the index, concealing this difformity by always wearing gloves, the empty fingers of which were well stuffed. Thus defective, and thus shackled, she wrote, drew well, embroidered beautifully, and cut paper with minikin scissors, as if determined to show what could be done under difficulties; I often thought of her dexterity and perhaps all unconsciously laid the lesson to heart.

I was to travel to Oxford with two friends of my Uncle Griffith, Dr and Miss Williams. They accordingly called for me in a hack post chaise, the first I had ever entered, and when I found myself seated within it, bodkin, my feet on straw, my little trunk corded on outside, the lining dirty, the windows rattling, the whole machine so rickety, and began to jolt along the paved streets with these very uninviting strangers, I could not help having rather melancholy regrets for Grosvenor Lodge, sunny as it was, my brothers and sisters and their merry spirits, the open landau and four skimming over the roads, my Mother's silk dresses, the well bred servants, the polished luxury of home. I was indeed subdued, I sat quietly and silent, looking vacantly out at all the ugliness we travelled through. Dr Williams was reading a pamphlet, I am sure I wondered how he could keep his eyes steady on the lines; he made notes from time to time with a pencil on the pages of a pocket book he kept open on his knee, then he would lay back as if in deep thought, and begin to read and write again. That was my left hand. Miss Williams had a squeaky voice, quite an irritant to a sensitive ear. She did not speak much, which was well, but what she did say was very kindly meant; I daresay I was a great bore to her and all her bags and parcels; that was my right. Straight before was an Humphrey Clinker[1] whipping on two much abused horses, very very unlike the four bays. At last we stopt at a pretty country inn near a wood, where we had luncheon, and then we all went out to gather wild flowers, for Dr Williams was a Botanist and had gone this, not the usual, road for the purpose of collecting 'specimens.' We grew much more companionable; when he took my nosegay from me he seemed much pleased, he told me a great deal that I never forgot, shewing me the form and the beauty of the simple flower and telling me what valuable qualities it sometimes lost when cultivation rendered it more lovely to the eye. He pressed among the leaves of a thick packet of blotting paper such flowers as he had selected from our gatherings, and then we resumed our journey in, I thought, a very much more comfortable chaise; the Doctor read less, the sister, though she still squeaked, talked more, and I chattered away very merrily. The latter part of the journey therefore passed pleasantly to me, while both answering and asking questions. A little packet of change with a memorandum of my share of the expenses was put into my hands as we were about entering Oxford, and in a few minutes, late in the evening, we stopt at my Uncle's door.

Not the grand door opening on one of the quadrangles, approached by broad steps up to great gates kept by a porter in his lodge, all grand as a College should be. But a back door in a narrow lane, letting me in to the kitchen passage, up a stair to the hall, and so to the kindest welcome from both Aunt and Uncle who were standing there to receive me. I was just in time, they said, the house was to be full of company in a day or two, when the little housekeeper would find herself extremely useful. In the mean while I was introduced to all the apartments, made acquaintance with the different closets and their various keys, and was established myself in my Aunt's dressingroom with a sofa bed to sleep on, and two drawers in her chest and my own trunk for my clothes, she taking charge of my balance of cash, remarking that it was very shabby of Dr Williams to have charged me with any

1. The eponymous hero of Smollet's novel (1771) was a coach boy.

expenses, as he must have had the chaise for himself and his sister at any rate, and he might have treated me to my luncheon, just eighteen pence, without any violent liberality. My highland pride preferred having paid my share, but I said nothing. I was silent about the balance too, which I knew my father had intended I should have kept in my own pocket; not that I wanted money, we had never been used to have any.

The Master's Lodgings at University College formed two sides of a quadrangle—no, not quite, one side and the half of another. The other half of the second side and the third were occupied as Students' rooms; the fourth was the high wall of my Uncle's garden. It was a large house containing a great many rooms of a good size, but inconveniently planned, several of them opening one out of another with no separate entrances and not proportioned properly, the whole of the one long side being wedge shaped, the space twenty feet wide at the street end, and only ten at the garden end, the outer wall humouring the lane, instead of the lane having been made to follow the wall. The private apartments were on this side and very comfortable, though oddly shaped. There were on the other side two spare bedrooms with dressing rooms for company, and at the head of the front staircase a nice cheerful room which was afterwards mine, but wanted at this time for Sir William Scott. Besides this great man a cousin Horseman arrived, and Aunt Leitch and Uncle Ralph and Aunt Judy. Both ladies had been dressed by Miss Steuart for the occasion. Aunt Leitch always wore black, a Scotch fashion when a widow is no longer young; besides, it suited her figure, which had got large, and her rather high colour. She had good taste so looked extremely well, never wearing what did not become her, choosing always what was plain and rich and fresh and well fitting. A white chip bonnet and feathers made a great impression on me just now, so did a straw coloured silk of my aunt Judy's, as she altered it to please herself. It was to be worn with handsomely embroidered white muslin gowns and a small cloke of like material trimmed with lace, and all the broad hem round, lined with straw coloured satin ribbon; the shape of the bonnet was such as was worn at the time, rather a close cottage, if I remember, with a long feather laid across it very prettily. My Uncle had chosen the whole dress and spared no expense to have his oddity of a little wife made to look somewhat like other people. The first day it was all very well, but the second no one would have known her; both cloke and bonnet were so disfigured by the changes she had made in them, that their singularity and her high heeled shoes—for she had never yet been persuaded to lay her stilts aside—really made us all feel for my Uncle, who was certainly very angry, though he was prepared for the exhibition, she never having then nor since received any article of any description from any person, however cele-brated, without altering it, if it could be done; her own taste being, according to her, unimpeachable, and all these lower natures requiring the finishing touch of her refinement to make her the most perfect object that ever vexed a sensitive husband.

I have a much more distinct recollection of this affair, of nipping the sugar, setting out the desserts, giving out the linen, running all the messages, than I have of all the Classick gaieties of the week, though I was kindly taken to all of them. In fact I fancy they had disappointed me, read me another lesson, for, as far as I remember, hope never intoxicated me again; I never felt again as I had felt at Grosvenor Lodge, on the day of receiving my Aunt's invitation. The Theatre, for one thing, had been a shock, where I had expected to be charmed with a play, instead of being nearly set to sleep by discourses in Latin from a pulpit. There was some purple and some gold, some robes and some wigs, a great crowd and some stir at times, when a deal of hum drum speaking and dumbshow was followed by the very noisy demonstrations of the students as they applauded or condemned the honours bestowed; but in the main I tired of the heat and the mob, and the worry of these mornings, and so, depend upon it, did poor Lord Grenville, who sat up in his chair of State among the dignitaries, like the Grand Lama in his temple guarded by his priests. The Concerts, though, were delightful. There, for the first and only time in my life, I heard Catalani. I don't think her singing, her 'Rule Britannia,' above all her 'Got safe the King,' will ever go out of my head. She was the first Italian woman I had noticed, and much her large, peculiarly set eyes, her open forehead, pale dark complexion and vivacity of countenance struck me. She was very handsome. We had Braham, too, with his unequalled voice and fine bravura style, and my old acquaintance from the Hanover Square Rooms; Mrs Bianchi indeed always went about with Catalani to teach her her songs, the great singer not knowing a note of musick; indeed her ear was defective, it was a chance her gaining the pitch of the accompaniment; if she did, all was right, for she kept on as she set out, so it was generally sounded for her by her friend, and then off she went like nobody else that ever succeeded her.[1]

Well, all this over, the Company gone, the actors and the spectators departed, the term over, Oxford deserted, my regular life there began. In the morning I read both in French and in English to my Aunt, took one walk a day with old Anne, who dressed herself in a black mode cloke that had arm holes to let the arms through, and a small black bonnet, to attend upon me. I gave out the good things from the store room, sometimes naughtily helping myself, played in the garden at walking like a lady with a phantom companion, to whom I addressed some very brilliant observations, went visiting sometimes with my Aunt, and helped her to patch, for that favourite work still continued although the whole house was decorated with her labours. Borders of patchwork went round all the sofa and chair covers, and my room went by the name of the patchwork room because the bed and the window curtains were all trimmed with this bordering. My Aunt kept her house very neat and very clean, as it deserved to be kept, for my Uncle and the College together had fitted it up handsomely. The woodwork was all dark oak highly polished and carved. The chimney pieces were of stone, of antique form, suited to a College of *Alfred's*? days, and then with his ingenious turn for nicknacketies of his own production it was filled with ornamental trifles, all in keeping with

1. John Braham ('a beast of an actor but an angel of a singer' according to Sir Walter Scott) was well-known but Angelica Catalani (1780–1849), despite 'very little formal musical instruction', was a huge London success 1806–14.

the grave air of his College residence. The walls of some rooms were hung with his 'poker paintings,' pictures burned on wood by hot irons; others had his drawings framed; the plants were in pots painted Etruscan; some windows screened by transparencies. He was never idle, sketching or finishing his sketches filling up any unoccupied time. They had three old servants, a man and two maids, who did all the work of that large house. William and old Anne had lived with my uncle at his Living at Whitchurch in his bachelour days. Nanny was added on his marriage, and the three remained with him till his death, when William was made Porter of the College, and Anne and Nanny accompanied my Aunt to her small house in Holywell.

I was beginning to tire of being 'burd alane,' kind and indulgent as my Uncle and Aunt were to me, when a letter arrived from my Mother that caused a number of mysterious consultations. Though I was never admitted to the secret tribunal in the Study, I heard afterwards up in my Aunt's boudoir most of all that had been there discussed. The question at this moment was concerning a proposition made by my Mother to this effect, that instead of reclaiming me, my sister Jane should be sent to bear me company. My father found it necessary to proceed immediately to the highlands, and not intending to remain there long, it being now late in the season, he did not wish to encumber his party with all his children and a governess, for we elder ones could not well be let to run wild any longer; and if our Uncle Griffith would let us stay with him and my Aunt would take the trouble to look a little after us, and choose us good masters, we were anxious enough to learn to ensure our making good profit of such instruction. A delay of two or three days resulted in an answer such as was expected. I had a peep of father, Mother, brothers, and little sister, for William's holidays enabled him to travel with them, and then Jane and I were left by ourselves to make the best of it.

# CHAPTER EIGHT

# 1810-1811

IT was a very great trial, this arrangement, to have to give up the highlands, to be still separated, we who were all so happy together, and whose hearts were in Rothiemurchus. Many a passion of tears our little patchwork room witnessed for the first week. Afterwards our young spirits revived and we set ourselves to work in earnest to be busy and happy under our new circumstances.

University College is said to be the most ancient of all the Colleges in Oxford, as may be supposed from King Alfred getting the credit of being its founder. The two quadrangles which form the principal part of the Edifice occupy a considerable space in the High Street. Each quadrangle is entered through large arched gateways approached by flights of broad steps.[1] The line of building separating the two quadrangles extends sufficiently behind to separate the Master's gardens from the Fellows'. It is appropriated to the kitchen offices principally. My Uncle's Lodgings forming a larger house than he required, he let some of the upper rooms of the side looking to the Street, retaining on the ground floor a dining room, drawing room and pantry, two bedrooms, with two dressing closets above. The upper storey he let. The other side, the *wedge*, contained on the ground floor the hall and staircase, back passage and back staircase, the study, and through the study the Library, a very long room filled with old dusty books in cases all round, reaching from the ceiling to the floor; most of these books were unreadable, being a collection of divinity from very ancient times, belonging to

---

1. The gothic centrepiece in the Front Quad was designed by E.G.'s uncle when Master; for Pevsner it is 'somewhat barbaric in detail'.

the College, and not of late much added to. In this room there was no furniture, neither curtains, nor carpet, nor fireplace; but three chairs, one table, and a pianoforte were put into it for us, and this was our Schoolroom. Through this Library was a small room with a fireplace, used by my Uncle to heat his irons for his poker pictures. This little room opened into a very pretty garden, where our happiest hours were spent. Over this suite were the private apartments of my Uncle and Aunt, and our patchwork room over the study. Above again were the servants' rooms, storerooms and lumber rooms. The kitchens were all underground. It was all very nice, except that long melancholy Library, which was always like a prison to us; there was no view from the windows, no sun till quite late in the day, not an object to distract our attention from our business. A judicious arrangement perhaps; we lost no time there certainly.

Mr Vickery, the Organist of Magdalen, taught us Musick, he was clever, but perfectly mad; half his lesson he spent in chattering, the other half in dancing. So except my Aunt came in, or he thought she was coming, we got very little instruction from him. Jane made no progress at all, I not much, but I don't think I lost what I had formerly learned, because I was so fond of playing that I kept myself up for my own pleasure, spending at least two hours a day at the pianoforte. Our writing master was an elderly man of the name of Vincent, much in the same style as our old friend Mr Thompson; he, however, taught nothing beyond writing and arithmetick and the mending of pens, which last accomplishment we found about as useful an art as any of the many we learned. A young Mr Neale taught us drawing remarkably well; he drew before us during the lesson, and left us to copy what we had seen him do, an excellent plan. Our Aunt was so kind as to keep us up in History, Geography, French, etc., and our Uncle, with his refined tastes, his many accomplishments, was of the utmost use to us in fixing our attention on wiser things than had hitherto chiefly employed us. For one thing, he opened to us what had been till then a sealed book—the new testament. He taught us to make its precepts our rule of life, shewed us that part of our Saviour's mission here on earth was to be to us an example, and he explained the catechism so clearly that we, who had always just learned it by rote every Sunday most grudgingly, now took pleasure in repeating what we comprehended and found was to be of use. My little artifices and equivocations were never passed by him, but they were so kindly checked, so reproved as a duty, that I soon disliked to pain him by employing them. Neither did I find such subterfuges necessary. No one punished me for accidental faults, nor was a harsh word ever addressed to me, I therefore insensibly lost the bad habits given by our nursery miseries. Truly this visit to Oxford was one of the fortunate chances of my life.

My uncle was invariably good to me, but Jane was his favourite, honest, natural, truthful Jane. Her love of reading, drawing, gardening and poetry, kept them constantly together, whilst I was more my Aunt's companion. Still, we were often dull, for they were a good deal out at dinner with the other Heads of Houses, and we had then long evenings alone in the Study, Anne popping up every now and then to look after us. We were allowed to make ourselves tea, however, and we had tea to breakfast, and butter upon our bread, and a small glass of good ale—College home brewed ale—at dinner. How fat we got. Our regular walk was our only grievance. Neither my Aunt nor Anne would let us run, it was not considered correct to run in Oxford, not even in the parks or the Christ Church meadows; we were to move sedately on, arm in arm, for our arms were not allowed to fall naturally. They were placed by my Aunt in what she called a graceful position, and so they were to remain, and when we remonstrated and said Mama had never stiffened us up so, we were told that our Mother was by no means a model of elegance, a sort of heresy in our ears, we being persuaded she was as near perfection as mortal woman could be as far at least as appearance went. We were quite shocked to find her not appreciated. How we skipt upstairs for our bonnets when my Uncle proposed to walk out with us. No graceful arm in arm for him. The moment we were out of the town, away we raced just as we liked, off to Joe Pullen's tree, or along the London road, nay round the Christ Church meadows. If old Anne could but have seen us. We told her of our doings though, which was some satisfaction. Sometimes our walks with him were quieter. He took us into the different Colleges, to shew us the hall of one, the stained glass windows of another, the Chapel of a third. He told us the histories of the founders, with the dates of their times, and he gave us short sketches of the manners of those days, adverting to the events then passing, the advance of some arts since, the point at which a certain style of architecture, for instance, had stopt. We went over the Bodleian and the Radcliffe Libraries, and to the Museum and the Theatre! and the Schools, and very often we returned to the chapel window at New College, and the picture over the Communion table at Magdalen—Christ bearing the Cross—supposed to be Spanish, and perhaps by Velasquez; it had been taken in a ship that had sailed from a port in Spain.[1] Sometimes he made us write little essays on different subjects in prose, and even try to rhyme, beginning with *bouts-rimés*, at which my Aunt beat us all. I cannot say that my versifying ever did him or me much credit, I never could confine either ideas or expressions in metrical bondage, but I poetised capitally in prose, while Jane strung off couplets by the hundred with very little trouble beyond writing them down.

My Uncle could versify by the hour. There was an horrifying fragment in our 'Elegant Extracts' which we used to read over for ever with great delight—the ride of a certain Sir Bertram, his arrival at an enchanted Castle, with the beginning of fearful adventures there, cut short just at the exciting moment. This in the course of a forenoon he made an ancient Ballad of, in order to amuse us, in this style:—

> Sir Bertram did his steed bestride
> And turned towards the Wold
> In hopes o'er those wild moors to ride
> Before the curfew tolled.

He had an immensity of fun in him besides this readiness, and was the authour of many satirical pleasantries and political squibs called forth by the events of the day, some of which found their way into the newspapers, as—

1. Pevsner attributes it to the seventeenth-century
   Spanish artist Valdés Leal.

> Sir Arthur, Sir Arthur, Sir Hew and Sir Harry
>> Sailed boldly from England to Spain,
> But not liking there long to tarry,
>> They wisely sailed all back again.

Sir Arthur was the Duke of Wellington! His second sailing did better. Then there was—

> The City of Lisbon.
> The gold that lay in the City of Lisbon.

which in our home had little coloured vignettes all down the page, representing the subject of each new announcement. 'The Court of Enquiry,' with little officers in regimentals seated all round a table; the 'fraternal hug' of the french ally to the poor overwhelmed Portuguese, etc. Never a letter almost went to the Doune without containing either in pen or pencil some clever allusion to the times. His caricatures were admirable, particularly of living characters, the likenesses were so perfect. Some of these he composed *on* the common playing cards, the hearts and diamonds being most humorously turned into faces, hands, furniture, etc. He began a series from Shakespeare, which are really fine as compositions. His graver style, whether in water colour, chalks, reeds, pencil or burned in, are considered to have shewn great genius, his many sketches from nature being particularly valuable, from their spirit and truthfulness. There were portfolios full of these in their ruder states, hundreds finished, framed, and dispersed among his friends. We had a great many at the Doune taken in Rothiemurchus, Dunkeld and the West Highlands. My Aunt's little boudoir was hung with others. In his dining room were more; there were some at the Bodleian, and the altarpiece in his own College chapel—Christ blessing the bread—was of his own poker painting. In the Museum was a head, I think of Leicester; and while we were with him he was busy with a tiger the size of life, the colouring of the old oak panel and the various tints burned on it so perfectly suiting the tiger's skin. Jane was his great assistant in this work, heating the irons for him in the little end room, and often burning portions of the picture herself. A print was taken from his water colour drawing of part of the High Street, in which his own College figures conspicuously. They are rare now, as he sold none. One was afterwards given to me, which we have framed and hung in our entrance hall.

Two facts struck me, young as I was, during our residence at Oxford; the ultra Tory politicks and the stupidity and frivolity of the society. The various *Heads*, with their respective wives, were extremely inferiour to my Uncle and Aunt. More than half of the Doctors of Divinity were of humble origin, the sons of small gentry or country clergy, or even of a lower grade; many of these, constant to the loves of their youth, brought ladies of inferiour manners to grace what appeared to them to be so dignified a station. It was not a good style. There was little talent and less polish and no sort of knowledge of the world, and yet the ignorance of this class was less offensive than the assumption of another, where a lady of high degree had fallen in love with her brother's tutor and got him handsomely provided for in the church that she might excuse herself for marrying him. Of the lesser clergy there were young witty ones, odious—and young learned ones, bores—and elderly ones, pompous. All, of all grades, kind and hospitable. But the Christian pastor, humble and gentle, and considerate and self sacrificing, occupied with his duties, and filled with the 'charity' of his Master, had no representative, as far as I could see, among these dealers in old wines, rich dinners, fine china, and massive plate. The religion of Oxford appeared in those days to consist in honouring the King and his *ministers*, and in perpetually popping in and out of chapel. All the Saints' days and all the eves of Saints' days were kept holy. Every morning and every evening there were prayers in every College chapel, lengthened on Wednesdays and Fridays by the addition of the Litany. My Uncle attended the morning prayers regularly, Jane and I with him, all being roused by the strokes of a big hammer, beat on every staircase half an hour before by a scout. In the afternoons he frequently omitted this duty, as the hour, six o'clock, interfered with the dinner parties, the company at that time assembling about five.

The education was suited to the divinity. A sort of supervision was said to be kept over the young riotous community, and to a certain extent the Proctors of the University and the Deans of the different Colleges did see that no very open scandals were committed. There were rules that had in a general way to be obeyed, and there were Lectures which must be attended, but as for care to give high aims, provide refining amusements, give a worthy tone to the character of responsible beings, there was none ever even thought of. The very meaning of the word education did not appear to be in the very least understood. The College was a fit sequel to the School. The young men herded together, they lived in their rooms, or they lived out of them in the neighbouring villages, where many had comfortable establishments. Some liked study, attended the Lectures, and read up with their tutors, laughed at by others who preferred hunting, gaming, supper parties, etc. The Chapel going was felt to be an 'uncommon bore,' and was shirked as much as possible, little matter, as no good could possibly follow so vain a ceremony. All sorts of contrivances were resorted to, to enable the dissipated to remain out at night, to shield a culprit, deceive the dignitaries. It was a drive at random of a low and most thoughtless kind; the extravagance consequent on which often ruined parents who had sacrificed much to give a son the much prized University education. The only care the Heads appeared to take with regard to the young minds they were supposed to be placed where they were and paid well to help to form, was to keep the persons of the students at the greatest possible distance. They conversed with them never, invited them to their homes never, spoke or thought about them never. A perpetual bowing was their only intercourse; a bow of humble respect acknowledged by one of stiff condescension limited the intercourse of the old Heads and the young, generally speaking. Of course there were exceptional cases, and the Deans and the Tutors were on more familiar terms with the students, but quite in the Teacher and pupil style, very little of the anxious improver on the one side, and the eager for knowledge on the other. I do not know what encouragement was given to the Excelsior few, but I well remember the kind of punishment inflicted on the erring many, sufficient perhaps for the faults noticed. Too late out, not at Chapel, noise at Lecture—these delinquencies doomed the perpetrators to an 'imposition.' A certain number of pages from a classick authour *transcribed*, that was all, in a legible hand. A task that really was of some use, though no one would think it, for several decent young men belonging to the town made a livelihood by writing them, at so much a page. There was a settled price, and when the clean looking leaves had been turned over by my Uncle, for it was into the study of the Head that these mockeries had to be delivered, my Aunt claimed them, as she found them invaluable for patch papers. Mr Rowley, the Dean, had drawn for her, with a great array of compasses, a small hexameter, which she had had executed in tin, and after this pattern she cut up all these papers, sitting between dinner and tea, while my Uncle finished his port wine.

Our breakfast hour was at nine o'clock; dinner was at four, except on company days, when it was half an hour later, and such dinners! The College cook dressed them. The markets were ransacked for luxuries, the rich contents of the cellar brought out. Port, sherry, and Madeira of vintages most prized some twenty years before. Beautiful plate, the best glass and china and table linen. Desserts of equal costliness. It was a great affair a dinner, sixteen the table held: big men in wide silk cassocks that would have stood alone, scarves besides, and bands; and one or two of the older ones in powdered wigs. The ladies were very fine, quite as particular about their fashions, and as expensive too, as the husbands were about the wines, very condescending in manner to one another as if each were a princess holding her court. Mr Moises used to say that the two little girls in white frocks were the only live creatures that looked *real* amongst them all. It was certainly an unnaturally constrained life that these people passed at Oxford. To us the dulness was intolerable; we were often oppressed by it even to tears, as our pillows and a large red mulberry tree in the garden could have testified, for to the garden we generally repaired to recover from these occasional fits of melancholy and to read over and over again our mother's letters from the Doune. She had found a boat load of Altyre Cummings by the side of the river the day she reached home. The Lady Logie and Alexander had been up on a visit. All the old servants had asked so much after Jane and me. All the old people so regretted our absence. Never was such a season for fruit, the guignes superb, and William and little Mary on the ponies riding all over the country. What a contrast to our company dinners, our walks with Anne, the bare, dull Library, and our masters, and the little bit of garden where we tried to play.

We were one sunny afternoon sitting under the mulberry tree, tired with searching on the grass round its trunk for the fine ripe fruit which had fallen thickly there, and which, after all, we thought, came next to guignes, when a window at the end of that side of the quadrangle to which the College kitchens were attached opened, and a curly head was thrust out, to which belonged very bright eyes and very blooming cheeks, and a mouth wide opened by laughter. It was an upper window belonging to a suite of rooms let to the students. 'Little girls,' said the head, 'how do you sell your mulberries?' 'They are not ours, Sir,' said Jane—she was always the spokeswoman—'we cannot sell them.' 'You can only eat them? eh?' said the head again, and many voices from behind joined now in the laughter. 'Jane,' said I, in a low voice, 'don't go on talking to that young man, you know my Aunt would not like it.' 'What nonsense!' said Jane, 'where's the harm of answering a question.' 'Well! little girls! won't you sell me some mulberries? I'll give you a tune on the french horn for them.' And thereupon our new acquaintance began to play, we thought beautifully, upon an instrument that we thought charming. 'A basket full of mulberries for a tune? eh? My aunt won't be angry.' A basket with a string to it dangled quite coquettishly from the window. But we were firm! we refused to fill it. And because we were such very good, honest little girls, we had a great many tunes on the french horn played to us for nothing, till I, who was always a coward, coaxed Jane away. It was getting near the dinner hour. My uncle's man William, regularly as old Anne began to dish, crossed the garden to the private door of the buttery, where he went daily for Ale. We thought it best, therefore, to retire from this first interview with our musical acquaintance, although we were not sufficiently modest to avoid the chance of succeeding ones. Indeed that corner of the garden was so shady, so out of the way of my Aunt's windows and so near the mulberry tree, that we naturally preferred to amuse ourselves there; the head and the horn as naturally continued to appear to us, till at length we grew so friendly as to take their acquaintances into the alliance, and we found ourselves chatting and laughing merrily with about a dozen 'Commoners.'

'Pray, Mr Rowley,' said my Uncle the Master one day to the Dean, 'who plays the french horn here in College? No very studious young gentleman, I should think.' 'Mr So-and-So,' said Mr Rowley—Is it not strange that I should have completely forgotten our friend's name—'He is no bad performer, I believe, and a very quiet young man,' etc. etc. We were crimson, we bent over our work in very shame, certain that our highly improper flirtation had been discovered, and that this conversation was meant as a hint for us to behave ourselves. I daresay however neither my Uncle nor Mr Rowley had the least notion of our musical propensities, and were only mentioning a simple fact, but conscience terrified us too much to allow of our ever haunting the buttery steps again.

This recreation being at an end, we began another. My Aunt obliged us to darn our stockings every week when they came from the washing, up in our own room. That is, obliged me to darn them, for Jane couldn't work and wouldn't work,—the only specimen of her abilities in this feminine accomplishment during our Oxford visit being the rather singular piece of patchwork which always stays on the chimney piece in my room, and which I use as a kettle holder, but she read to me while I worked, and this made the time pass more pleasantly. My Uncle's lodgings, as I have mentioned, occupied two sides of the Square of buildings forming the inner quadrangle. Our room was close to the corner, at right angles with the spare apartments he had let for College rooms. The nearest set to us was occupied by a Mr Coxe, a very tall young man from Yorkshire, with a remarkably loud voice, as we knew by the tone in which it was his habit to read aloud, for the weather being warm and the windows open, we could distinctly hear him spouting either from book or from memory as he paced up and down his study. We could see him too, for we were very close neighbours, when either he or we looked out of our casements, and as he acted the parts he was speaking with such emphasis, I found it much more amusing to watch Mr Coxe's anticks than to fill up the great holes Jane thumped out in the heels of her stockings. Down therefore went my hands, and forward stretched my long neck, intent as I was on the scene enacting, when Mr Coxe, finding himself noticed, so encreased the force with which he ranted, that I could not contain my laughter. At this he humbly bowed, his hand upon his heart. I laughed the more. He shook his head; he clasped his hands; he threw his arms here and there, starting, stamping, and always roaring. In short, the panto-mime proceeded with vigour to a most amusing height before Jane, who was sitting below me faithfully reading through the pages of the Spectator, perceived what was going on. Some one else must have perceived it too, probably Mr Rowley, for he was always prowling about, for though neither he, nor my Uncle, nor my Aunt ever mentioned the subject to us, muslin blinds were fastened to our windows next day, which we were on no account to displace, and we were ordered in future to take all our mendings down to that horrid and most melancholy library, where she said, my Aunt I mean said, that we were more within her reach should she want us. Mr Coxe was really very diverting, I regretted losing his theatricals extremely.

The young men had a hundred ways of amusing them-selves, quite independent of the Master's childish nieces. Mr Rowley having made himself disagreeable to some of his pupils who found it suit their health to take long rides in the country, they all turned out one night to hunt the Fox under his window. A Mr Fox, in a red waistcoat and some kind of a skin for a cap, was let loose on the grass in the middle of the quadrangle, with the whole pack of his fellow students barking around him. There were cracking whips, shrill whistles, loud halloos, and louder harkaways, quite enough to frighten even the dignitaries. When those great persons assembled to encounter this confusion, all concerned skipped off up the different staircases, like so many rats to their holes, and I don't believe any of them were ever regularly discovered, though suspected individuals were warned as to the future. Mr Fox, I remember, was found quietly reading in his room, undisturbed by all the tumult, although a little flurried by the very authoritative knocks which forced him, at that hour of the night, to unlock his door. My Uncle was very mild in his rule or very indolent, yet there were circumstances which roused the indignation of the quietest Colleges.

The ringleader in every species of mischief within our grave walls was Mr Shelley, afterwards so celebrated for better things, though I should think to the end half crazy. He began his career by every kind of wild prank at Eton, and when kindly remonstrated with by his Tutor, repaid the well meant private admonition by spilling an acid over the carpet of that gentleman's study, a new purchase, which he thus completely destroyed. He did no deed so malicious at University, but he was very insubordinate, always infringing some rules, the breaking of which he knew could not be overlooked. He was slovenly in his dress, neither wearing garters nor suspenders, nor indeed taking any pains to fasten any of his garments with a proper regard to decency, and when spoken to about these irregularities, he was in the habit of making such extraordinary gestures, expressive of his humility under reproof, as to overset first the gravity, and then the temper, of the lecturing tutor. Of course these scenes reached unpleasant lengths, and when he proceeded so far in his improprieties as to paste up atheistical squibs on the Chapel door,[1] it was considered necessary to expel him, privately, out of regard for Sir Timothy Shelley, the father, who, being written to concerning his wayward son, arrived in much anxiety, had a long conference with my Uncle in the Study, to which presently both the young man and Mr Rowley were admitted, and then Sir Timothy and his son left Oxford together. Quiet was restored to our sober walls after this disturber of its peace had been got rid of, although some suspicious circumstances connected with the welfare of a

1. Percy Bysshe Shelley spent the two winter terms of 1810–11 at University College ; the D.N.B. believed he arrived with 'the passion for research into whatever the university did not desire him to learn'—his 'spirit of aggressive propaganda' was best shown by this pamphlet entitled *The Necessity of Atheism*.

principal favourite of my Aunt's still required to be eluci-
dated, as Mr Rowley said, and at once checked.

Our inner quadrangle had buildings on only three of its
sides, the fourth side was a wall, a high wall, the wall of the
Master's garden. The centre part of this wall was raised a few
feet higher than the lengths on either hand, carved in a sort of
scroll. Against this more elevated portion on the garden side
was trained a fruit tree, a baking pear, very old and very
sturdy, with great branching arms spread regularly at equal
distances from bottom to top, a perfect step ladder! The
defences of the garden on the Stable side next the lane were of
no moment, very easily surmounted, and the vigilant eyes of
Mr Rowley had discovered, on the College side of the high
pear tree wall, certain indications of the pear tree's use to
those tenants, steady or unsteady, who returned from their
rambles later than suited the books of the porter's lodge. The
pear tree must come down, beautifully as it was trained,
splendid as the fruit was—large brown half pound weight
pears on which my Aunt reckoned for her second course
dishes. The wall, too, looked so bare without it. My Aunt
never thoroughly forgave Mr Rowley for this extreme of
discipline, and, like Mrs Balquhidder's cow, the pears grew
so in size and flavour, and the tree became so wonderfully
fruitful after its decease, that my Uncle, after enduring a fair
allowance of lamentations for it, had to forbid the subject. I
have often thought since when on my hobby—as my brother
John calls my educating mania—that if we were to make wise
matters more lovable, young ardent spirits would not waste
the activity natural to their age on follies. Too much work we
hardly any of us have, but work too dry, work too absorbing,
work unsuitable, is the work cut out for and screwed on to
every young mind of every nature that falls under the iron
rule of School or College. *Learning* is such a delight, there
must be errour in the teaching when the scholars shirk it and
debase themselves to merely sensual pleasures, of a low order
too. Drinking, gambling, and the like were the pursuits
which caused the destruction of the pear tree.

I am setting down all my Oxford experiences together,
without regard to vacation or term time, an unclassical
proceeding, which, if I had thought about, I would not have

done. The long vacation began soon after the Commemoration was over in July, and lasted till October, and though some reading men remained to study, and some of the Fellows came and went, Oxford was empty for the time of all the hubbub I had gone to form a part of till close upon Gaudy day. My Uncle and Aunt remained there however till the month of September, when they went to Cheltenham for a few weeks on account of my Uncle's health, and took us with them. William, the man servant, attended us, but neither of the maids; we were to wait on our Aunt and on each other. Our lodgings were small but very neat, as every lodging was, and is, at Cheltenham. We had a good drawing room and small dining room over a Cabinet maker's shop, and bedrooms above. We were just opposite to a chemist's, beside whose house was the paved alley which led past the old church to the walk up to the old wells at the end of the Avenue. We all drank the waters and we all ate famous breakfasts afterwards, and Jane and I, out most of the day with my Uncle, were so happy wandering about the outskirts of what was then only a pretty village, that we very much regretted remaining here so short a time. My Aunt, who walked less, and who could patch away any where, of course, preferred her comfortable home, for she had found no acquaintances almost in Cheltenham; only old Mrs Colonel Ironside, the Widow of the Indian Cousin in whose gay London house she had spent such happy times in her young days, and Admiral Ricketts, Mrs Ironside's nephew, with his very kind Irish wife. We saw very little of any of them; I fancy morning calls had been the extent of the civilities. What I recollect of Cheltenham is the beautiful scenery. The long turning High Street, the rich well wooded plain the little town was settled in, the boundary of low hills, Malvern in the distance, and that charming well walk, always shady, where we were told the King and Queen had appeared by seven o'clock in the morning, when His Majesty King George the third had been ordered by his physicians to try the waters. Half a lifetime afterwards, when I returned married from India and revisited this pretty place, I remembered it all as it had been, even found my way about it, though so altered, and I must say I regretted that the lovely rural village had grown into a large town, beautiful still with its hundreds of handsome villa residences and long streets of excellent houses, but not half so pleasing to me as it was in the 'olden time.' I hear now that they have cut down the fine avenue that shaded the old well walk, built rows of shops from the Crescent up to the old pump room, and that the town extends through the fields beyond. The children then of these times will be tired before getting to their country walks. Jane and I had green fields to run in.

On returning to Oxford we all resumed our graver habits. Jane and I had that odious Library and our Masters. My Uncle and Aunt the duties of society. All the great people having reassembled, they had all to interchange their calls and then to invite one another to dinner. In the evenings sometimes there were routs – thirty or forty people to tea and cards, refreshments handed round before separating. Jane and I were spared appearing at the desserts; we were found in the drawing room by the ladies, dressed in the fine muslin frocks bought for the Persian ambassador, with the gold chains and the cairngorm crosses, of course. We also sat up as late as the company staid, and were much noticed; luckily the home parties were not many. The ladies were really all so common place, they made very little impression. There was a handsome, very vulgar and very good natured Mrs Lee, from Ipswich; an extremely pretty Mrs Hodson from Lancaster; a fat Mrs Landon, whose husband was uncle to L. E. L.; a tall Mrs Marlow and the Misses Williams, all three with squeaky voices, and all elderly. No young women seemed to live in Oxford. A single Miss Eveleigh, by no means good looking, but rich, soon married. The Principal of Jesus College, Dr Hughes, a most huge mishapen mountain of a Welshman, was our particular favourite among the gentlemen, I believe because he let each of us sit in the large silver punch bowl belonging to his headship. It held Jane easily. Dr Williams never got into my good graces, nor Mr Rowley, he was such a little ugly and very pompous man. Mr Moises we were very fond of.[1] A particular

1. Hugh Moises (1722–1806) was Headmaster of the grammar school at Newcastle for 38 years; his son Hugh (1763–1822) was the College Don.

friend of my Uncle's, the son of that Newcastle Schoolmaster who educated Lord Eldon and Lord Stowell, Mr Collins, then rather a Beau, was another great ally of ours. They were all clergymen, as were most of the travellers who paid passing visits, such as our two cousins Horseman, whom we distinguished as the 'clean and the dirty' one, both odd, but John, the elder and the dirty one, much the queerer. James was just going to be married, for which John called him a great fool. Mr Surtees came several times, once with his wife, such a pretty little woman, very small, one of those half dozen Miss Allans, who were all rich. Three of them married three Wedgwoods, and one of them married Sir James MacKintosh. Miss Allan, the nicest of them, remained single. Mr Surtees was brother to Lady Eldon,—of course got well up in the Church. In early life he had been in love with Aunt Leitch, though she had never smiled on him. Lord Eldon never happened to come to my Uncle's while I was there, though they were so intimate as to correspond. Lord Chancellors have not much time for travelling; besides, the King was in very uncertain health just then, giving everybody about him a good deal of uneasiness. Lord Stowell, then Sir William Scott, was often with us, and a very agreeable old man he was.

What very strange women those two clever brothers married. Lady Eldon's was a runaway affair and she had not a penny, but she was very beautiful, and to the last hour of her life retained her husband's affections, in spite of her eccentricities. Latterly she was never seen but by him. She lived up in her own rooms dressed in a hat and habit, and was called too much of an invalid to see visitors. But she got up to make his breakfast every morning, however early he required it, as she had done from the day of their marriage; nothing ever prevented this but her two or three confinements, her layings in; on other occasions, when indisposed with colds or headaches, she still waited on him, and returned to bed when he went off to Court or Chambers. She never learned that they were rich.[1] When he was making thousands at the Bar,

1. D.N.B. quotes Eldon's maxim that a lawyer should live like a hermit and work like a horse. He eloped with the heiress Elizabeth Surtees in 1772; they got married at Blackshiels near Edinburgh.

and later when his official salary was so large, she continued the careful management of their early struggling days, locking up stores and looking after remains, and herself counting the coalsacks, making the carters hold up the bags and shake them as they were emptied into the cellars, she standing at the window of her Lord's handsome house in her hat and habit, giving a little nod as each empty sack was laid upon the pavement.

Lady Scott was still more thrifty, at least we heard a great many more stories concerning her oddities. She had money and no beauty; and if there ever had been any love it did not last long, for they were little together. He was said to be miserly too, but he was not miserable. She grudged him his clean shirt daily, and used to take a day's wear out of the cast one herself, putting it on instead of a bedgown, thereby saving that article in her own wardrobe. Then she allowed him but one towel a week, and Mr Collins had a story of her, that on closing a visit to a friend of his, she entered her hostess's presence before taking leave, laden with a great pile of towels, which she thought it her duty to bring into view, in order to expose the extravagance of the servants who had supplied them with linen so profusely, priding herself on having used but two, one for herself and one for Sir William. There were tales of her serving up chickens reheated continually and having wings and legs of some fictitious kind skewered on in the places of the real ones which had been eaten; of a leg of mutton doing duty all the week, roast, cold hashed, minced, made into broth at the end and I rather think boiled at the beginning; of her cutting a turkey in two when she found her son dined out, and on his unexpectedly returning, sewing the turkey up again. Mr Collins and Mr Moises, both north country men, used to keep us laughing by the hour at all the oddities they told of her. She died at last, but long after this, and he made a second unlucky venture. Old Lady Sligo, the dowager of her day, was a worse wife than this first one. What they married for at their advanced age no one could fancy. She was near seventy, and he was past it. He had both a son and a daughter, the daughter very agreeable. She was often at Oxford as Mrs Townsend, and occasionally after becoming Lady Sidmouth; and as she had been at school with aunt Lissy, we imputed this also as a merit to her.

We remained at Oxford until the spring of 1811. My father and mother had left the highlands before Christmas, intending to proceed to London, whither they had sent on most of the servants, with the heavy luggage, by sea. They were delayed, however, in Edinburgh by either business or pleasure, perhaps a mixture of both, so it was in the month of March they called for us. A young friend, Mary Balfour, was with them; a nice, kind, very accomplished, though exceedingly plain girl. She was going on a visit to some friends in London, and took advantage of a spare seat in their carriage. There was no one in it but my father, my mother, the two children Mary and Johnny, and Miss Balfour. Mary Creake, the maid, and the footman were outside. Whether my father travelled with his own horses this time I forget. I daresay he did, and had kept them all four and the Coachman all this time at the hotel in Edinburgh. He did not hurry away as was his usual habit every where, he stayed a few days in order to shew the beauties of Oxford to Miss Balfour. Amongst other sights they went to see Great Tom, which I had no mind to do; hearing him every night booming so grandly over the quiet around quite satisfied me, for the sound was very fine, coming in too just after the little 'merry, merry Christ Church bells.' Jane, who was of a very inquisitive turn, decided upon mounting up all those long stairs in order to understand the real size of this wonder. Once up, she would go in and under it, and remain within it just to hear one toll. Poor child! she dropt as if shot, was carried out into the air, brought home, laid in bed still senseless, Dr Williams sent for, the whole house in despair. She lay as one dead, only she breathed very lightly. Dr Williams recommended her being left to nature, he apprehended no danger; the nerves had received a shock and they must be left to recover, and they did recover. She wakened up next morning as if she had merely had a good night's sleep, recollecting nothing, however, beyond her last expressed wish to see the great tongue moved by the men who pulled it with a rope, so very differently from the way of ringing other bells. This little agitating scene so well over, we fell to our packings, assisted by Mary Creake, who had a way of getting very quickly through this and every other kind of work.

We were sorry to leave our kind Aunt and Uncle, but we were not sorry to resume the freedom of our home life, after the restraints in fashion at University. We found the house in Lincoln's Inn Fields in great order, which was strange, considering that the servants had had nothing to do but to clean it for months back. We liked all our London masters and were glad to meet our young acquaintance, and then we had our happy days in Brunswick Square, and were to see our brother William at the Easter holidays. Besides, a great pleasure was preparing for us. Annie Grant came to live with us, and as the changes consequent upon this agreeable addition to our home party had much influence over the well being of we the younger members of the family, I will make a pause here in this particular era of my career—draw one of the long strokes between this and more trifling days, and begin again after this resting point.

# CHAPTER NINE

# 1811–1812

ANNIE GRANT was the 'accidental' daughter—to use a very delicate expression a very refined lady once used to me, when compelled to employ some term of this sort—the 'accidental daughter' of old Colonel William Grant with the long queue, my father's half great Uncle, my great grand Uncle, who had long lived at the Croft. The first time my Mother ever saw her she was herding some cows in the Lochan Mor, a boggy swamp, afterwards drained by Mr Cameron, standing beneath the shelter of a high bank of hanging birch, no shoes upon her feet nor hat upon her head, her knitting in her hands, her short dark petticoat, white jacket, and braided snooded[1] hair combining to present a perfect model of highland beauty. I wonder if Mrs General Need when the great lady at Cawnpore, the most favoured guest at Newstead Abbey, the honoured of Kensington Palace, where more than once she dined with the Duke of Sussex—did she ever wander back in thought to the days of her simple youth. In those early days she was not taught to expect much notice, neither did she receive much; her mother was her father's housekeeper, and she brought her children, Annie and brother Peter, up in her own station, sending them to the parish School, and never obtruding them or herself on any of the 'family.' After the old Colonel's death she, still a very beautiful woman, married his Grieve, and went to settle in another part of the country. The Colonel had been married in middle life to an Irishwoman, a Mrs Dashwood; they had never had any children, so he left his savings, these highlanders have always savings, to Annie and her brother,

1. A ribbon on the forehead binding the hair, the snood was a symbol of maidenhood.

175

some £2000 or better. My father as head of the house was their guardian. Peter was sent off to a better school. Annie was taken by Captain Lewis Grant and his odd wife to keep the keys of their small establishment, an office regularly filled in every household then by such stray maidens of the race as were in want of a home. When Mrs Grant died the Lady Logie took charge of Annie, who seemed never to be lost sight of among her kith and kin, however irregularly she arrived among them. The Lady Logie 'had her to school' at Forres, where she received a good plain education, and as much instruction in musick as, assisted by the ear of her race, enabled her to play the airs of her own country, grave or lively, with an expression very delightful. Lady Logie, my father's aunt, dying, it was determined the poor girl should earn a home for herself. She was accordingly brought to London to our house, and after being a few weeks with us she was bound apprentice to the Miss Steuarts, the celebrated dressmakers. May be, in their work room, she well remembered her free hours in the Lochan Mor. For her own happiness, herself and her little fortune would probably have been better bestowed on some young farmer in her native north, but this was an age of unnatural notions; accomplished girls, portionless and homeless, were made into governesses, and for the less instructed there was nothing dreamed of but the dress making, a trade never overstocked, its victims dying off quite as quickly as the vacant places were demanded. For some years all went smoothly. Annie was a favourite, and never overworked except at extra busy times. Every Sunday while we were in town she spent with us, often coming to us on a Saturday. Every summer she had her holiday, which all of us enjoyed as much as she did, for not only we, but every one who came to our house, were fond of her. At length came the time when the two old Miss Steuarts were to resign the business, as had been agreed on, to Annie Grant and Jessie Steuart, on terms which had been previously agreed on. A word of dissatisfaction had never been uttered on their part, till out came the astounding fact that they had sold their house and business more advantageously. Jessie Steuart had no refuge but the arms of a lover, to whom through many years of poverty she made the most exemplary wife, bearing severe trials with patience and afterwards an exalted position meekly. Her husband has long been a leading man, living in the best society. Annie Grant was received by my father and Mother, I may say, gladly, for they had begun to grudge her to the needle and thread. Very early for her one morning my Mother drove to Albemarle Street, and brought a great blessing to our home back.

Without, as far as we knew, any regular arrangement, Annie Grant slid somehow into the charge of us. She took lessons with us from all our masters, was so attentive while with them, so diligent in working for them, so anxious to improve, that we caught her spirit. There was no more idling in our dining room; when the prescribed lessons were over other occupations started up; she and I read history together daily, Goldsmith, Robertson, Rollin.[1] We also had Shakespeare given to us, and some good novels, all Miss Edgeworth's fashionable tales,[2] and we walked a great deal, sometimes taking the carriage to the Green park or Kensington gardens, and taking a turn there. We were really busy, and so happy, for Annie's gentle, steady rule was just what we all wanted; she soothed me, encouraged Jane, coaxed Mary. Her great art was removing from us all that was irritating; we had no occasion to set up our backs. We actually forgot to feel angry. Upon the phrenological system of influences, could we have been under better—had she been carefully trained in physiological principles she could not have acted more wisely than her mere kindly nature prompted. In the matter of our breakfast she gained for us quite a victory, persuading my Mother that, now she had no cow in the stable, weak tea was cheaper than milk, a small bit of butter good for the chest, so that we began our day so pleasantly all went smoothly on. In the evenings we reeled away for an hour to her spirited Strathspeys, the big people often joining the little, and turning with us to magick musick and other games we had before confined to our own more peculiar sphere. Every

1. Oliver Goldsmith's and William Robertson's reputations have survived; Charles Rollin was the French author of a well-known *History of Rome*.
2. Six volumes of her *Tales of Fashionable Life* were in the Grant library.

body seemed happier since Annie lived with us. She made extraordinary progress with the masters, particularly with Mr Nattes, who taught us drawing. He said she would be an artist if she chose. She more than overtook us in a very few weeks, a fact that first set me thinking about the folly of making children study while very young, that is, of giving them expensive masters for pursuits beyond their ability in general. Plenty of occupation better suited to their ordinary capabilities can be found which would give present employment, and prepare the way for future success in higher things at a more profitable age.

Mr Nattes had another pupil in whom he was much interested. He said she would never draw much nor be first rate in any art, but she was so excellent a person that he had recommended her as Governess to a family in which he taught. This was our old friend Miss Ramsay, who had come up to London to improve herself. She often came to see us both before and after she went to live with a rich Mrs Smith, sister to the Marchioness of Northampton, with whom and her very nice daughters she lived for many years, in fact till she died, tended by them in all her failing health with all the affectionate care her good conduct merited. Mr Nattes was a handsome Italian, elderly, most agreeable, who had been a Jesuit, it was said, and did give the idea of not being just what he seemed. He was married, and in some repute as an artist, though never high up among his brethren; he had been sketching in the highlands when my father fell in with him and brought him to Doune, where he filled a portfolio with beautifully executed sketches most accurately drawn. Some of these he reproduced in water colour, and we framed them and hung them up, and they were pretty enough, but no more like the scenes they were meant to represent than if they had been taken from any other place on the artist's tour; they were, indeed, mere fancy pieces with names below them fully as much travestied as the scenery.[1] He taught well so far,

1. John Nattes (1765-1822) produced his *Scotia Depicta* in 1804 but his reputation fell after his expulsion from the Old Society of Painters in Watercolours (which he had helped to found) for exhibiting work shown not to be his own.

made us handle our pencils neatly, and gave us a most thorough knowledge of perspective. We drew according to rule from models, attending accurately to position and to light and shade, and soon sketched quickly and truthfully from Nature. It was a great pity I had so little application, wearied so soon of any work I set about, idled my time away laughing and chattering. Easy come, easy go is a very wise proverb, and then I was in character fully half a dozen years younger than my age, and nobody considered this. People did not consider much in those days. Jane, on the contrary, had the sense of a much older girl. She was so conscientious, too, that she would not have neglected her duty for any consideration. She was naturally very slow in acquiring, and most particularly awkward in executing any one thing in the world to be done by the fingers; her sketches were all crooked, her shading was all blurred, her needle work was abominable, her playing dreadful, her writing was wretched, her figures could not be read; and yet in time she overcame most of these difficulties, for her industry was unfailing. It was almost a pity so much time passed so painfully with her, yet she was a happy child, and she was none the worse in after life for this discipline. They could not discipline me; binding the wind would have been about as easy. My spirits were at times quite flighty, nothing ever sobered them down to usefulness except the kind reproving look of dear Annie Grant. She, however, failed with Mary; the indomitable stupidity of that strange heavy child had hitherto rendered every attempt to rouse her vain. She was eight years old, and she could not read, hardly even knew her letters, count she never would try, writing she did on a slate her own way, but not the least in Mr Thompson's. She even romped listlessly, would not dance at all, liked sitting quiet with her doll cutting up cakes and apples into dinners for it. When she washed the old block of wood without arms or legs which she preferred to any wax baby, she seldom dried and never dressed it, but called to me to render her these services; and if I were out of the way would roll a pinafore round the beauty and be content. She was tall and large, and fair, as big nearly as Jane, and looked as old. I was excessively fond of her; so was my Mother. I believe every one else thought the poor child deficient.

My Mother was very ill again this spring, confined for many weeks to her room, and then ordered off to the seaside as soon as she had recovered strength enough for the long journey to the Coast. Those were not railroad days. To prepare her for her travels she took constant evening drives with us, getting out beyond Southwark, beyond the parks, towards Epping, etc., occasionally making a day of it to Kew, Richmond, and even Windsor. I had been once at Windsor before to see William, as I have, I think, mentioned, when we went to Eton Chapel, and afterwards met the King and Queen and the Band of the Blues upon the Terrace. We did some of this again, and went to the King's private Chapel and saw him say his prayers in his little bobwig, his short wife in a black silk cloke and plain straw bonnet beside him. We also this time saw the Castle thoroughly, private apartments and all, for the Queen and the Princesses had gone for the day to Frogmore. My father's tenant at Thorley Hall was a Mr John Vowles, who had a brother William a corn factor at Windsor; they were of German extraction, in some way connected with some of the personal attendants of the Queen. Mrs William Vowles, indeed, was a German born, and had been brought up by her parents in the palace; she had been educated and portioned by her Majesty, and not thrown off upon her marriage. She it was who took us up the back stairs and shewed us through most of the rooms in common use by the family, when for the first time my mind wakened up to the knowledge that real Kings and Queens were not like the royalties of fairy tales, always seated upon thrones receiving homage and dispensing life and death, but quiet, simple, actively industrious human beings. I could have made myself very comfortable in Queen Charlotte's bedroom, and should have felt entirely at home in the business like morning room occupied by herself and her daughters. Books, musick, painting, works plain and fine, each with a small table beside it; these were for Mr and Mrs Guelph, as they called themselves in the happy privacy of their family.

Another time that we were at Windsor we dined early with Mr and Mrs Vowles, and went over to Frogmore in the evening—the Queen's hobby, her garden house. It was a pretty villa in pretty grounds, too low for health, I should say, were people to have lived there, at least till the mere or pond was drained, but it did perfectly for the royal amusement by day. The walls of one room were painted by one Princess; all the tables and cabinets of another were japanned by a second; carpets, stools, and rugs were the work of a third; while the knitting, and knotting, and netting and patching of the old Queen, if she did it all herself, must have ensured her a busy lifetime. And it was well that she had these domestick habits, for long years of anxiety were before her. The king had been taken seriously ill shortly before this second visit of ours to Windsor, or rather his madness had become too confirmed, too violent in its outbreaks to be any longer concealed.[1] There was no old man to be seen now at Chapel in the mornings with a rolled curl above each ear, the ornaments of his bob wig, or on the terrace with his gold headed cane in the evenings, his odd little Queen by his side and the long train of their handsome children with quantities of attendants behind. His wing of the Castle was shut up, his windows barred and darkened, no one suffered to walk on the terrace, a gloom pervaded even the town—never was a place more changed, yet we were merry enough at the Star Inn where William met us with one or two of his particular friends. Much as the vice now known to reign there makes me at this present time abhor the name of Eton, it brought then most pleasant memories—the grounds belonging to the School were so spacious and so pretty, the old College, its chapel, the quadrangle, the noble river and that grand Windsor Castle behind all together formed a beautiful scene to find a dear brother in.

By the middle of July my Mother was able to be removed to Ramsgate, where she very soon recovered her looks and strength; she was always fond of the sea, and throve near it. Mrs Peter Grant had taken a house for us on the East Cliff, a very fine situation with a splendid seaview. We were at some

1. George III, approaching his 75th year, had been blind for eight years, suffered probably from porphyria and had a severe relapse in July 1811. John Brooke's *George III* describes him as becoming senile and living in a world of his own.

distance from the town, a sort of Common all round us, and one house only near; it was indeed attached to ours, the two stood together alone, out of the way of all the rest of Ramsgate. Our neighbour was Lady Augusta Murray, called by her friends the Duchess of Sussex,¹ although her marriage to the Duke, which really did take place abroad, was null in this country. She had been created Baroness D'Ameland, and had a pension settled on her of £3000 a year, on which to bring up her two children, a boy and girl, fine, large, handsome young people, *un*duly imbued with the grandeur of their birth. She never committed herself by calling herself or them by any title: 'My boy, my girl,' she always said in speaking of or to them. The Servants, however, mentioned them as the Prince and Princess, as did all the acquaintances who visited at the house. Prince Augustus was about 17, extremely good looking, though rather inclined to be stout; very good natured he was too, amiable and devoted to his mother. He was going into the army under the name of D'Este, a bitter pill to the Duchess, although it was one of the royal surnames, and had been chosen for his son by the Duke himself. Princess Augusta was some years younger than her brother though she looked nearly as old. She was but 12, and particularly handsome on a large scale, a fine figure, and fine features, with a charming expression of countenance. The Duchess's house was small, though larger than ours, for she had turned the whole ground floor into one room, a library, and built a large dining room out behind. The drawing room floor was her own apartment, containing bedroom, sitting room, and her maid's room; the floor above was equally divided between her son and daughter. She kept no horses, for she never drove out. She passed most of her time in a very large garden, well walled in, which covered a couple of acres or more, and extended all down the slope of the cliff to the town. Our two families soon became intimate, the younger ones especially passing the greater part of the day together,

1. The Duke of Sussex, sixth son of George III, married
   Lady Augusta Murray in Rome, contravening the
   Royal Marriage Act of 1772; he was aged 20, on his first
   Grand Tour, and she was ten years older.

a friendship beginning then which never entirely ceased while opportunity served to bring any of us together. The advances, however, were amusing. The Duchess, as a royal personage, must be waited on. My Mother, who was very retiring, would not take such a step forward as the leaving her name at the great lady's door. My father, who had bowed, and been spoken to when gallantly opening gates, could do no more without his wife; so all came to a full stop. Meanwhile, Jane and I, who had made acquaintance out on the free Common of the downs with the little Princess, untroubled by any notions of etiquette, enjoyed our intercourse with our new acquaintance amazingly; Jane and she soon becoming fast friends. One evening she approached the paling which separated our two small gardens just as my Mother was stepping over the gravel towards the carriage to take her airing. I shall never forget the picture; she leaned on the top rail, her large leaved Tuscan hat thrown back off her dark close cropped hair, and her fine countenance brightened by the blush of girlish modesty, while she held up a small basket full of fine peaches, an offering from her mother. A visit of thanks was of course necessary, and found agreeable. A few days after the Duchess bade Jane tell her Mama that she had returned her call when her Mama was unluckily out, and that she hoped they would be good neighbours. On this hint we all acted. We never expected H.R.H. to call nor even believed in the reported first call. My Mother occasionally went in there with some of us. My father constantly, indeed he soon became her confidential adviser in many of her difficulties, trying to get her through some of the troubles which harrassed her existence. We were all made very happy by this addition to our Ramsgate pleasures; we liked the place itself and our life there, and above all we liked our neighbours.

Early in the morning we all went down to the sands to bathe, not in Seaham fashion, but in a respectable business like manner, suited to a crowded watering place. A little table on which lay a great book stood within a railing enclosing all the bathing machines. Each party, on entering the gate of this enclosure, set their names down in the book, and in their turn were conducted to a bathing machine, roomy boxes upon wheels, at one end shaded by a large canvas hood that reached the water when the horse at the other had proceeded with it to a sufficient depth; the driver then turned his carriage round with the hood to the sea, and unhinging his traces went in search of another fare, leaving the bathers to the care of a middle aged woman in a blue flannel jacket and petticoat and a straw bonnet, who soon waded into view from a neighbouring machine, and lifting up the balance of the canvas shade stood ready to assist the fearful plunge. The shock of the dip was always an agony both to Mary and me; that over, we would have ducked about much longer than the woman let us. Jane delighted in the whole, and Annie Grant bore it; Johnny always bathed in the machine with my Mother. It was rather frightful bathing when the waves were high, at least to the timid ones. Some people really went into the sea when they might have been carried away by it, when they and the women had to keep hold of ropes while the waves went over them. We never emulated these heroines; but certainly Jane sometimes urged us all on with her when the rest would rather have turned back. Either in going or returning we encountered our friend the little Princess walking right royally before her very strange looking elderly maid, Mrs Deadman. Annie used to be amused at the dignity with which she used to approach the little table and dash down a very flourishing 'P,' the single letter that served to mark her name; then she would smile most courteously upon us, but never came near or spoke on these publick occasions.

We all breakfasted together, then studied for three hours, dined early with my father and mother, and drank tea with them late. In the intervals we were either next door, or on the downs, or on the sands. The sands were very firm, and of considerable extent when the tide was out; there was a charming subterranean passage by which we reached them without going round by the steep hill near Albion Place; it had been excavated by a strange sort of man who had built a Castle on the Cliff—a castle with battlements and towers, and a curtain flanked by turrets, and a moat, and what not. A prose Walter Scott who could not see the absurdity of defences when there were no longer any assailants, he thought the style suited to the scenery. This passage he made for the purpose of bringing up manure to his fields; it was quite dark about the middle of the descent, a particular merit to us. Annie and I used to take books down to the sands and sit on the rocks with them in our hands, but we never read; watching the waves, listening to them, looking at the crab hunters and the shrimpers, and far out at sea straining our eyes after the shipping, little boats, larger craft, huge merchantmen, all moving over the face of the waters, and the Downs in the distance—all this was book enough, at least for a dreamy nature. Mary and Johnny were often with us, and sometimes my mother, who, however, rather objected to such idling; and as Jane was almost always with the Princess, quite as great a favourite with the Duchess as with her daughter, a plan was struck out for the better employment of my time, that was acted on immediately.

Mrs Peter Grant, the widow of one of my great Uncle Sandy's sons, who had had charge of Anne Grant of Glenmoriston, and lived in a small house at Ramsgate, had been found so competent to the task of superintending the education of young ladies, that she had been prevailed on by first one friend and then another to receive their delicate children. At last her house became too small for her family. She took a larger one in Albion Place, engaged a clever governess, to whom she was shortly obliged to give an assistant, and soon had quite a flourishing school. She limited the number of pupils to eighteen, and generally had applications waiting for a vacancy. She was an honest hearted kind person, a little given to 'sentiment,' well read for her day and accomplished, having been originally intended for a governess by her parents, in whose house her husband had lodged while walking the hospitals in London; her beauty, much of which still remained, had changed her destiny—whether for better or worse, who can say. She fondly cherished the memory of her young husband, lost soon after her marriage by some accident at the Cape; he was Surgeon in a man of war. To Mrs Peter Grant's school I was to be sent every day for so many hours, ostensibly to learn flower painting, and be kept up in french and singing; but in reality to take down a deal of conceit which unavoidably sprung up in the mind of a quick girl without the means of fairly testing her abilities by an equal standard. Jane was so much younger, and naturally so slow, her attempts in all our occupations were of course very inferiour to mine, and as we had no companions except at play hours, I could not find out that, clever as I thought myself, there were girls of my own age very much more advanced. This I learned very quickly at Albion Place, where three or four of my new friends were very far beyond me. We were taught flower painting by a very pretty Mrs Abrams, a celebrated artist, the daughter of a Landscape painter and the wife of an architect, who had come to Broadstairs to give sea bathing to her pictures of children, and thought she might as well try to earn what would pay the expenses of the trip. She had taught at Mrs Pope's School in Bloomsbury Square, where Harriet Grant had gone when Anne went to Ramsgate; she afterwards gave Harriet lessons at our house in Lincoln's Inn Fields, so that I knew her quite well, and was delighted to see her again and be taught her pretty art, which, however, I never afterwards pursued. Yet it was of great use to me. Brought my drawing into order, accuracy of outline, minuteness of detail, delicacy in shading, and close observation of nature both as to form and colouring were all essential in this minute style of painting—the mixing of the colours and the undertinting for the several shades opened a new range of ideas that in after times was the source of unfailing pleasure. We mostly prepared our own colours, that is from the few primitive ones we mixed the rest according to the hues of the flowers we were representing, attending to blue as yellow greens, blue as pink lilack etc. till these *slight apparently* differences became quite interesting, enhancing to us the beauty of the commonest flowers.

Mrs Grant herself taught us singing, in a class. We stood behind her, all intoning the scales at once, and then executing the turns, runs, shakes, etc., in succession. A little ugly Miss Hodges had the finest voice, and so we let her do most of the work, Mrs Grant, busy with her accompaniment, not always detecting the tricks we played her. Miss Wishart the governess was not so easily deceived. Her Schoolroom lessons were difficult to evade; so when I tired of her grammar, and history, and french dictations, I used to get up a little fun to break the dulness of the morning. Poor Miss Wishart! She bore a good deal from me; many half hours of funny songs, droll stories, laughing, dancing, acting, mimicking, her own anger and Mrs Grant's melancholy remonstrances being done to the life before them. She often banished me to a certain back parlour where distressed members of the establishment were wont to expiate their offences in solitude, declaring it was impossible either to learn or teach while that flighty little creature was in the study; and then she would recall me herself, and say she had punished me only for my good, in a voice and manner she was sure to hear and see next day, the first offence that was committed amongst us so that I am not quite sure that I derived much benefit from my schooling after all. Sarah Backhouse, one of the elder pupils, whose roses and crocuses far surpassed mine, did her utmost to tranquillise my volatile nature. I liked her extremely, as I did a Miss Wintle; we kept sight of one another for several years, though we were far parted.

Lord Cochrane was at Deal this summer;[1] he came to see our friend the Duchess, and prevailed on her to go to sea with him for a day; he brought the barge, very nicely fitted up for her and her party, which, as a matter of course, included Jane. He had a Collation on board his ship for her and presented every lady with french gloves; a pair or two fell to me, as compensation, I suppose, for being left behind. But my turn came. Admiral Raper,[2] then a captain commanding the Bellerophon, arrived in the Downs; it was just before the old ship was broken up. My father, my mother, and William who was with us for the holidays, and I, all went to Deal to see him. Harry was there too, on a visit to his father for a day or two. How much I was struck with the parlour we were shewn

1. Thomas Cochrane, tenth Earl of Dundonald (1775–1860); this was shortly after the quarrel with his Commander-in-Chief Lord Gambier as a result of which he campaigned for three years (1809–12) against abuses in the Navy; he is credited later with helping to found the navies of Chile, Brazil and Greece; see Ian Grimble, *The Sea Wolf*, 1978.
2. Admiral Henry Raper (1767–1845); the 'old' Bellerophon was the predecessor of the ship that took Napoleon to St Helena.

into at the Inn. It was called the Dolphin, and it had a bow window actually built out into the sea; it had all the effect of looking out from the stern cabin, of course much admired by 'all in the Downs.' From this bow window we had perfect command of the beach, and were able to observe with admiration the wonderful dexterity of the Deal men in landing passengers from their clumsy shaped boats. The beach is so steep that it is deep water immediately, and whether coming in or going out, the boats always appeared to stand almost up on end just as they neared or left the shore. None of them ever upset, however difficult as it would seem to be to prevent it. I think it was in one of these that we made our start, and yet I have a perfect recollection of the Captain's gig and the smart boatscrew which manned it. We dined on board, and then proceeded to inspect the ship, one of the most interesting sights in the world. The ingenious comforts of the Cabins, the light, airy, cheerful aspect of the Captain's in particular, the excessive cleanliness, every board so white, every bit of a metal so brightly polished, the order, the quiet, the neatness, the most made of each small space, the real elegance of some of the arrangements,—all altogether produced an effect on persons unaccustomed to the interiour of a man of war, that every one of us were loud in expressing our surprise at. All I demurred at was the lamps in the cockpit, no daylight penetrating to the abode of the middies down below on the third deck; and yet Harry persisted in going to sea, because, as he said, he should rise in time to where his father stood; which he did not, for taking some disgust at the usual ill usage of the Admiralty he retired from the service a lieutenant.[1] He was, by the bye, on board the ship that carried Lord Amherst to China for the purpose of declining to make all the bows to the Emperour customary by the étiquette of that queer country,[2] and he was wrecked near Loo Choo! lost

1. He retired from the Navy in 1825 aged 26; his scientific interests led to the standard navigational text book of its day – *Practice of Navigational Nautical Astronomy.*
2. William Pitt Amherst was the British envoy sent to the Emperor Ken K'ing in 1815; he was ready to bow the statutory nine times but not to prostrate himself, or 'Kotow'.

all his beautiful drawings, scientifick Memoranda, etc.; for he was a true Raper, even to their eccentricities: but at this time a fine merry boy, full of spirits and hope.

We remained all night at Deal, and next day drove to a pretty parsonage in the close neighbourhood, where lived the father of my new friend, Miss Backhouse. He was in some way connected with the House of 'Forster, Cooke, and Frere,' had a son in it I think, and so made acquaintance with us. He was an agreeable man with a large family of well brought up children and a kind wife, and he lived in a picture of a country clergyman's house, all overgrown with honeysuckles, jasmines, roses, and vines, large clusters of grapes hanging down round the dining room windows, out of which we leaned to gather them. This part of Kent is very rich, a good soil and mild climate combining to make the vegetation very luxuriant. Beyond this sort of beauty and the sea there is however no fine feature in the scenery; of its sort it is however perfect, with its neat hamlets, church spires, old wooding, and such hedges! very high, twelve or even fifteen feet in some places, trimmed like green walls, not a break in them; little narrow cross roads running between two of these shady boundaries in all directions. Along such we drove to Walmer Castle and home by Sandgate; a sunny excursion that was cherished for many a day in a bright corner of my memory.

The next incident that rests there is the very exquisite singing of a Miss Walker, a young person not otherwise prepossessing, nor much known in Ramsgate, where they had come for the health of Mrs Walker, a fantastick woman, rather superiour in manner to her underbred husband; his forwardness was against the progress of the family rather. They were introduced to us by Mrs Peter Grant, and most certainly the eldest daughter's very remarkable talent made many of our summer evenings pass delightfully. Her voice was both sweet and powerful, of great extent, and I heard my father say wanted only practice to make it flexible and that she only wanted to *hear* better musick than had yet fallen in her way to be a really fine singer. She had hitherto been taught by one of the Choir of a Cathedral town in which they lived, her style was therefore the Sacred, and very beautiful. Quite extraordinary for so young a girl. I never heard what became of her—it was a voice with which much might have been done. Another fresh acquaintance was an old dashing Mrs Buckley, who made up to my Mother, I hardly know how; she had the remains of a great beauty, but was bold and noisy. She had two handsome daughters, and a fine looking son, a Lieutenant Colonel of a regiment of Cavalry, quartered at Canterbury. One of the daughters was dark, the other fair, to suit either taste in the market they were diligently prepared for; they were models of the class shabby genteel. Their aim was to appear what they were not, rich and fashionable, and to achieve this make believe reputation every energy of their clever heads was employed, and every moment of their busy day. They darned net to look like lace, they dyed, and turned, and revived, and remade; bought cotton satin and cotton velvet, made one dress do duty for three by varying the slip, the trimming, or the body, wore calico gloves, painted pasteboard for fans; every sort of expedient inexhaustible ingenuity could devise was resorted to, in order to make £10 effect an appearance which would have required £100 to have been expended on realities. The result of which hard labour was to give them the look of ladies any thing but respectable. The mother was seldom seen in the morning. She was generally occupied darning, clear starching, and cooking, for they gave evening parties at an expense they could not have afforded had a confectioner been employed to furnish the refreshments. It was for the benefit of the world at large that all this toil was gone through, or rather for two, any two, members of the world at large who were men, and bachelours. Whether two such ever rewarded the indefatigable endeavours of this Mother and daughters we, at least, never knew. A very different specimen of the military was introduced to us by the Malings; Colonel and Mrs Gossipp also from Canterbury. He was a fine soldierly looking man, she a plain woman, but so nice, kind, gentle, merry, clever, quite a soldier's wife. She had four healthy, happy boys, and three gowns, a 'heightem, a tightem, and a scrub,' with which she perambulated the world, none of the wardrobe department likely to be hurt by her travels if we were to judge of the inferiour degrees by a comparison with the 'heightem,' the one always exhibited at Ramsgate. But no matter what Mrs Gossipp wore she always looked like a lady, and she was so lively and agreeable it was always a white day when the Colonel's dog cart, his wife by his side and a boy or two parked up behind, drove up to the door of our small house on Albion Cliff.

Mrs Gossipp was full of fun, and to please her a party was made, including the handsome Miss Buckleys to attend a ball at Margate, at that time the summer retreat of the City of London, and held more wealth than any place out of it. Miss Louisa Buckley was quite wrong in carrying her pink cotton satin, tho' covered by muslin of her own embroidering, to such an assemblage as she found there. Lace dresses and lace flounces of fabulous value fluttered all round the room. Velvets and satins, feathers and jewels! such jewels as would have shamed the Queen's Drawing room were in profusion there. Large, fat, Dowager *Aldermanesses*, with a fortune in Mechlin[1] and diamonds on them, sat playing cards with tumblers of brandy and water beside them; the language used possessed a grammar of its own; the dancing was equally original, a Miss St George, the Belle of the ball and six feet high, cutting capers up to the moon. The extravagances of this 'fashionable' resort formed one of the sights to be seen from aristocratick Ramsgate. How different now. That race of civick dignitaries sleeps with their fathers. It would be hard to know the Tradesman from the noble now, at a glance at any rate. My father said the finery of the Margate ladies had excited my Mother's envy, for she set about smuggling vigorously at this time, very much to his annoyance; bargain making and smuggling were his aversion.[2] He always said, 'What is wanted, get, of the best quality, at the best place, and take care of it. What is not wanted, don't get, however cheap; it is wasting money, in fact real extravagance; and have nothing to do with rogues, eh.' Wise preaching—'tis so easy for the man who lavishes thousands on *his* whistle, to lift

1. Black funereal lace, produced at Mechelin, or Malines, near Brussels.
2. His principles were more elastic than this suggests; at the end of the family tour to Holland, he successfully smuggled china back to Scotland; see II, pp. 145–6.

his eyebrows at the cost of his Wife's. My dear mother found it hard to resist those melodramatick sailors with their straw hats smartly bound with a ribbon, the long curled love lock then generally worn by the more dashing among the seamen, the rough, ready, obligingly awkward manner, and all their silks, laces, gloves and other beautiful French goods so immeasurably superiour to any in those days fabricated at home. She was not to be deterred by the seizures now and then made of all these treasures, miles and miles away; carriages stopt and emptied, ladies insulted, fined, and so on, as really frequently happened when their transactions had been too daring. She could not resist a few purchases, though half believing my father's assertion that the smugglers were all in league with the Custom House, themselves giving information of any considerable purchaser. However, her doings were never thus brought to light.

Meanwhile, we had our occupations, we young people. The Duchess of Sussex, to amuse herself, got up the Tragedy of Macbeth. She was a Scotchwoman, one of the Dunmore Murrays, and very national; she was, besides, intellectual and intelligent, as all her pursuits evidenced, and she was very proud of the beauty of her daughter. It was all to be amongst ourselves, we four, the little Princess, and two quiet little girls sometimes our companions, whose father lived in Ramsgate and was the Duchess's man of business. We all therefore 'played many parts,' which necessity we considered a pleasure, as it kept us in one character or another constantly upon the Stage. During the preparations we were incessantly rehearsing either at one house or the other, each, for the benefit of the rest, learning the whole play; thus impressing on our young memories, never to be effaced, some of the finest poetry in the language; the sentiments actually became endeared to us, wise trains of reflection following the pains of learning those favourite passages by heart. Jane was Macbeth and a second Roscius, my father, who had a good idea of acting, having been taught to read by Stephen Kemble,[1] taking great pains with her. Lady Macbeth was ranted a little

---

1. Brother of John Kemble and Mrs Siddons, whose grand-daughter married E.G.'s brother William.

by the Princess, yet she looked the part well; I was a shocking stick in Banquo, but a first rate witch, a capital Hecate. The Duchess painted one Scene for us, which did for all—a bit of an old tower and some trees—and Deddy, as we called Mrs Deadman, superintended the dresses. My father was the prompter, the Library was the theatre, and a very respectable audience of dowager peeresses and other visitors and residents applauded every speech we made. The musick master played martial airs on an old wretched pianoforte between the acts, and there was a grand supper, followed by a good merry dance at the end, all having gone off well. Yet that crowning night was nothing near as pleasant as all the busy hours we had preparing for it. 'Dreamer, dream not that fruition,' etc., as the wise of all ages have repeated, none of them in prettier lines than these, written by my father to 'Rousseau's dream,' composed as he was walking round the Ord Bàn many a day after this.[1]

This was the year of the great Comet;[2] night after night we watched it rising over the town of Ramsgate, spreading its glorious train as it rose, and thus passing slowly on, the wonder of all, and terrour of some, a grand sight only equalled by the northern lights as we used to see them in the highland winters. And this was the season of the return of the China fleet, single merchantmen not daring in those war times to venture out to sea as in these happier, peaceful times. The east India shipping therefore made sail together under the convoy of a couple of frigates, an imposing evidence of the strength and wealth of the country, which had the most beautiful effect on the wide sea view they entirely filled that ever could have been gazed at from any shore. The Downs, always beautiful because never deserted, and often very crowded, were on this occasion close packed with huge Indiamen, their tall masts seeming to rake the skies; and when the anchors were weighed, and the dark mass moved

1. A dance from *Le Devin du Village* by Jean Jacques
   Rousseau in 1752.
2. According to authorities like *Flammarion*, the 1811
   comet was one of the most famous of modern times; it
   was used as a propitious omen by Napoleon before his
   invasion of Russia.

out to sea, each vessel carrying all her canvas to meet the breeze, all distinctly seen from the balcony of our house, I don't think a grander sight ever met wondering eyes. The frigates, much smarter looking ships, kept outside as Convoy, and on they moved like some fine pageant in a scene, till, hours after we had seen them leave the roads at Deal, the last of the long line was lost to us behind the North Foreland, or the *South* I fancy it must have been as nearer to us, although it was the lesser projection of the two.

Soon after the passing of the China fleet we left our pretty lodgings on the Cliff and moved into an excellent house on a less exposed situation, one of a row on the other, the town side of our friend the Duchess's garden. Our only acquaintance in it was Mr Vince the Astronomer, a kind old man, who often let us look through his large telescope by day, and watch the moon through a smaller by night.[1]

About the middle of November we returned to Lincoln's Inn Fields, and then Annie Grant and Jane and I set to work in earnest with all our old masters, and this winter really made good progress. As for Mary, there seemed to be no use in trying to teach her any thing, for she would not learn, not even to read; she was therefore, by the advice of old Dr Saunders, a friend of my grandfather Grant's, left to amuse herself as she liked with our baby brother Johnny, and they were generally kept out in the Square all the fine hours of the day. Our cousins Eliza and Edmund were a good deal with us. The winter before, when Aunt Leitch was with him, Uncle Ralph had a very good house in Somerset Street, Portman Square. This year, Aunt Leitch having left him, he took a very pretty house, an old fashioned half cottage, half villa, with a charming garden, out at Turnham Green, where we spent many a happy day. Edmund was at school in the neighbourhood; Eliza had a governess sometimes, and sometimes masters, and once she also went to school, but that whim did not last long. She was very quick, and learned what she had a fancy to without trouble, excelling in musick, that

1. Samuel Vince (1744–1821), son of a bricklayer, was Professor of Astronomy and Experimental Philosophy at Cambridge (1796–1821).

is playing, from infancy. She had no head to understand thoroughly any thing. We were very often in Brunswick Square, oftener than formerly, because Annie could go with us there through the quiet of those lawyer streets, crossing Holborn being our only difficulty. Mrs Charles Ironside's handsome sister, a widow, Mrs Lernault, married this year Mr Robert Calvert, the very rich Brewer; and our very handsome Cousin, Ursula Launder, married William Norton, the natural son of Lord Grantley, a mere boy to her, for he was not more than two and twenty and she was *at least* twice his age. Her large fortune was her charm, but her young husband treated her with marked attention during her whole life, long after every vestige of her remarkable beauty had left her. Aunt Mary was one of the Bridesmaids, Lord Dursley the Bridegroomsman, and soon came on the great Berkeley case, which was decided by stripping him of name and fame and giving that old title to a third brother.[1] Uncle Frere was the Solicitor employed to get up the case for the Defendant, and so over worked was he by it, between fatigue and anxiety, that he took a fever before it was over, and frightened us all seriously. It was a brain fever, and in his delerium he kept calling for little Eli to sing him Crochallan, so I was sent to him, to sit by his bedside and 'gently breathe' all the plaintive Scotch and gaelick airs I could remember, no small stock into his 'vexed' ear, thus soothing him when most excited. He would insist on sending messengers here, and there, on writing letters, and consulting on law points with me and the bed clothes, and I was never to thwart him, but to pretend to second all his whims and then to sing in a low murmuring tone the airs I found he liked best. At last he fell asleep one day to Crochallan, the oft repeated 'Hanour ma vourgne' having quite composed him.[2] My Aunt, who was always watching us, sat down and wept. 'Even little children can be of use,' said she as she kissed me, though I was no

1. The Committee of Privileges of the House of Lords decided in 1811 (after ten years' deliberation) that the fifth Earl of Berkeley's marriage was not proved; the title therefore went to his brother, Colonel William Berkeley, and not to his son 'Lord Dursley'.
2. Crochallan: gaelic Crodh Chailean (Colin's Cattle).

child, but very near fifteen. Too old, my Mother thought, to
be again exhibited in Macbeth, which, having succeeded so
well at Ramsgate, the Duchess was determined to get up
again in Arklow Place.

Jane and I were very much with our young friend the
Princess. Her mother's very handsome house looking into
the Park near Cumberland gate was a very agreeable change
to us, and we were so at home there we were quite at ease
among all the family circle. Jane was still the favourite, the
one most paraded, most spoke of, but I was the one applied
to when help was wanted, in fact, the real A. No. 1 whatever
they pretended and feeling my growing importance, a very
comfortable position, visiting there was much pleasanter to
me than formerly. Prince Augustus was with his regiment
in Jersey, from whence he had sent a box of little French
curiosities to his mother, two of the toys marked for Jane and
me, so goodnaturedly. Jane's was an ivory knife grinder,
mine a frenchwoman in a high cap, spinning—it is at the
Doune yet and instead of him we had our friend Lord
Archibald Hamilton, who spent most of his time with his
cousin 'Augusta,' and *his* son Henry Hamilton, a fine boy
then, tho' 'accidental.' There was scandal going about the
extreme attachment of the Duchess to this handsome lad and
I remember my father, long after this, telling my Mother
what that old gossip Lord Lauderdale[1] had told him. Lord
Archibald, one day talking of this dearly loved son of his,
consulting Lord Lauderdale about his destination and
thinking himself but coldly listened to, said rather testily as
an addition to whatever argument he was using 'I can assure
you he has in his veins by both sides some of the best blood in
Europe.' 'I never heard it doubted,' replied Lord Lauderdale
gravely and with a low voice. The blood of 'Princely
Hamilton' we all know sufficiently to value. The Murray
blood of that one family is purer still, more ancient and more
of royalty in it. Henry was very like the race. 'Deddy' was
particularly fond of him, [young Henry], he could do any

1. James, eighth Earl of Lauderdale: known as 'Citizen
   Maitland' on account of his sympathies with the
   French Revolution.

thing with her, when any of us offended her, we always deputed him to make the peace and never unsuccessfully. She was certainly a curious kind of old nurse body for a fine lady to keep as her only personal attendant and her influence was great even to our young apprehensions. Lord Lauderdale might have liked cross questioning some of us on these subjects. I must in fairness add that the pair whose intimacy was so commented on were first cousins and had been very much brought up together and that very little sets people atalking sometimes.

Well, the Play went on without me. I was only dresser and prompter. Lucy Drew replaced me as Banquo, and Georgie Drew as Hecate; the other characters remained the same. Our scenery was borrowed from the theatre, our dresses were very superiour, as was our Orchestra, and our audience was half the peerage! Jane outdid herself, but William's Macduff outdid her Macbeth, it was really fine acting. We waited for the Easter holidays in order to secure him. I remember that old Lady Dunmore, who had, like a frenchwoman, taken to religion in her old age by way of expiating the sins of her youth, would not attend our play in publick—her principles condemned the theatre—but she saw it in private nevertheless. We all went to her small house in Baker Street dressed, and acted before her, and a capital good dinner she gave us afterwards, all her plate out, and lots of fruit. She must have been very beautiful in her day; quite a picture she was now, in a high cap like that in the prints of the Duchess of Argyle, the Irish beauty. Lucy and Georgina Drew were the grand daughters of Lady Dunmore, and lived with her, brought up by Lady Virginia their Aunt, their Mother Lady Susan having on her third marriage made them over to this maiden sister. Lady Susan's first husband was a very rich West Indian, Mr Thorpe, by whom she had one son, an idiot. Who Mr Drew was I really do not know. The third husband was Mr Douglas, the Revd. Archibald Douglas, brother to Lord Miltown's mother, Lady Cloncurry. We often saw him in Connaught Place. He was much taken with Jane, as every one else was; but in after days, when we met here in Ireland, he insisted it was *me* that had so attracted him 'as a lovely intelligent girl'—I, at that time extremely plain, and so shy I never spoke to strangers. He was a remarkably handsome man then as now, and quite a crack preacher, all London flocking round any pulpit he consented to mount. Lady Virginia Murray had the ugliest face I ever looked on, seamed, scarred with the small pox, her figure perfect, and her general kindness unfailing. Lady Susan was scorbutick, but might have been handsome once. Lord Dunmore was very nice, and his wife too—a Hamilton, a cousin; Fincastle and Charley Murray charming boys. Many others there were whom I forget. I just remember Lady Georgina Montague being there one day—a handsome, very dark, and very thin girl in a black frock, put on for the first time for her Grandmother the Duchess of Gordon, whose funeral procession had that morning left London for the highlands. My Mother would hardly believe that the child could have been allowed to go out to spend a merry day with young companions at such a time, and attributed it to the ignorance of the governess who had charge of this poor deserted family. The Duke of Manchester was repairing his fortunes as Governor of Jamaica; the Duchess had left home years before with one of her footmen. Both my father and Mother grieved sincerely for the death of their old friend and neighbour with whom they had spent so many happy hours. Indeed, the whole of the highlands mourned for her, as with all her oddities she was the soul of our northern society.

The remaining events of this, our last season in London, come but hazily back to me. We acted our Macbeth in Brunswick Square, I taking Lady Macbeth's part badly enough, I should think, on this mere family occasion. And Duncan McIntosh, the Rothiemurchus forester, came to town on some of my father's lawsuits, and was a perfect delight to every body, with his shrewdness, his simplicity, his real astonishment, and the highland idea of good breeding which precluded the expression of wonder at any novelty. Aunt Leitch, who was on a visit with us, seized on him as her beau, and treated him and herself to the play two or three times a week, for it was the last appearance of Mrs Siddons; she went through all her great parts, and took her leave of the Stage as Lady Macbeth. Uncle Ralph ventured to Covent Garden that night; he did get in, but soon came out, returning to us nearly exhausted, his hat crushed, his coat and shirt torn, his face so pale that he quite frightened us. Never had there been such a crush at the doors of the pit; it had so overcome even his strength, that he was unable to endure the heat of the closely packed house. We heard next day that the Audience would listen to no other performer. When she was on the stage a pin could have been heard to fall; when she was off, all was uproar, Kemble even himself unattended to, and when she walked away at the last from her Doctor and the waiting gentlewoman, they would bear no more; all rose, waving hats and handkerchieves, shouting, applauding, making such a din as might have brought the house down, never was there such a scene before.[1] All passionless as was that great actress's private nature, she was overcome. Uncle Ralph ever regretted being unable to remain to see the last of fine acting. She has had no successor. I am quite sure that *we*, we young people I mean, owed more to Covent Garden than to any other of our teachers. We not only learned Shakespeare by heart, thus filling our heads with wisdom, our fancy with the most lovely imagery, and warming our hearts from out that rich store of good, but we fixed, as it were, all these impressions; John Kemble and Mrs Siddons embodying all great qualities, becoming to us the images of the qualities we admired. An excuse this for the statues and pictures in the churches of *infant* times.

In May or June poor Mr Perceval was shot, our neighbour in the Square, whose three daughters, disdaining other associates, only walked with the three Miss Nicholls, Sir John Nicholls' equally exclusive ladies.[2] Lady Wilson ran in to tell my Mother, she having just had an express from Sir Giffin, who was in Westminster Hall. It was a great shock to every one, though he had been an unpopular man; the suddenness of the blow and the insufficiency of the cause making the deed the more afflicting. It set all the politicians to work

1. This was her last performance (29 June, 1812); the play ended when she left the stage at the end of Act v scene i.
2. The Prime Minister was shot in the lobby of the House of Commons on 11 May, 1812 by the deranged bankrupt, John Bellingham.

again, but nothing came of all the commotion. The Prince Regent went on with the same Tory party amongst whom he had thrown himself as soon as he had became head of the government. One place was easily supplied; his former friends were just as far from power as before. They might and did abuse him, and the *man* deserved abuse, whatever the regent did. Moore enchanted the town with his witty newspaper squibs, looked for as regularly every morning as the breakfast was.[1] Whigs blamed and Torys could not praise, but they all ate their leek thankfully, and on went the world with its generalities and individualities, its Buonaparte and its Wellington, 'the most profligate Ministry that ever existed,' holding the whiphand over at least, an equally profligate Opposition. Whatever sins were going, we three little girls had worn mourning for all. While we were at Ramsgate the old king's delirium had become so alarmingly violent it was supposed his bodily strength must give way under the continual paroxisms; his death was therefore daily expected. So my 'careful' Mother, fearing black would rise, bought up at a sale there a quantity of bombazeen.[2] The King calmed, recovered his strength, but his mind was hopelessly gone, in which state properly attended to he might live for years. What was to be done with all the bombazeen? We just had to wear it, and trimmed plentifully with crimson it really looked very well.

But now a great change was to come over the family. The English Bar had never answered, and was now to be given up. It remained to be seen how parliamentary business would answer, for my father was elected member for the thoroughly rotten borough of Great Grimsby,[3] at an expense he and the electors, and his Agent little Sandy Grant, were

1. It was over a month before the Prince Regent and the customary political processes produced Lord Liverpool's government, ample time for the Irish poet and satirist Tom Moore to comment.
2. Twilled or corded dress funeral cloth made of silk or worsted.
3. 'Few boroughs in England were more corrupt than Great Grimsby' (J. Holladay Philbin, *Parliamentary Representation, 1832, England and Wales*).

not one of them fully able to acknowledge. To meet some of
the difficulties thus produced, economical measures were to
be resorted to, which in a couple of years would set every
thing to rights. Thorley Hall had been sold some time before
to Lord Ellenborough, and Kinloss bought with part of the
purchase money. The house in Lincoln's Inn Fields was to
go now and all the furniture not wanted to make the Doune
more comfortable, for, to our delight, it was there we were
to spend these two years of retirement. My father was to run
up to town for the session at a very trifling expense. We were
a little disturbed by the news that Annie was not to go north
with us. My mother hoped that before the winter she would
settle herself in some house of business, but in the meanwhile she was to pay a visit to a Mrs Drury, a rich widow,
the sister of Mr William Hunter, who had been married to
one of the Malings, and who had taken a very great fancy
to our dear Annie. Next came worse tidings. We were to have
a Governess. And very great pains our poor Mother took to
choose one. I could not count the numbers she saw, the
notes she wrote, the references she visited. At last she fixed
upon a little bundle of a woman recommended by Lady
Glenbervie. The father had been sub-ranger of Bushy Park
[to the Duke of Clarence]; the daughter, said to have been
well educated and left unprovided for at his death, had been
all winter in London taking lessons from various masters
with a view to teaching in private families. It all seemed satisfactory; a high salary bribed Miss Elphick to engage for one
year to go to so remote a country, and she came every other
day to sit with us from the time she gave her consent to the
bargain, that she might learn our ways and we get accustomed to her. My father also engaged a little french girl, a
protégée of Mr Beekvelt, and about Jane's age, to go north
as our Schoolroom companion. She went by sea with most
of the servants and the luggage, and had a very tearful
parting from good M. Beekvelt, whom we also were very
sorry to leave. He was up a bit in the world since we had
first known him. The dingy house in Rathbone Place was
exchanged for a pretty sunny house and garden at
Paddington; two of his daughters were well married, the
other two in good situations as governesses; he, just the same

as in less prosperous days. We were also in great grief when we said farewell in Brunswick Square. All the pretty presents waiting for us there could not pacify either Jane or me. To me my aunt Lissy was inexpressibly dear, and the little cousins, of whom there were then four, John, Lissy, George and Anne, were great pets with us. It required to have Rothiemurchus in prospect.

# CHAPTER TEN

# 1812

EARLY in July of the year 1812 my Mother set out with her children for the Doune, bidding a final adieu, though she knew it not, to England. I cannot quite remember whether my father travelled with us or not. Yes, he must—for he read Childe Harold to us; it had just come out, and made its way by its own intrinsick merit, for popular prejudice set strong against its authour. 'To sit on rocks,' etc.,[1] arrested the attention even of me, for I was not given to poetry generally; then, as now, it required 'thoughts that rouse, and words that burn' to affect me with aught but weariness; but when, after a second reading of this passage, my father closed the pamphlet for a moment, saying 'This is poetry!' I felt he was quite right, and resolved to 'look the whole poem over' some day more at leisure. We had also with us Walter Scott's three first poems, great favourites with us, The Seven Champions of Christendom, Goldsmith's History of England, and his Animated Nature, and in French, Adèle et Théodore.[2] This was our travelling library, all tumbled into a brown holland bag kept under the front seat of the barouche. At the inns where we had long rests, our own horses doing but few stages in the day, we amused ourselves in spouting from these

1. To sit on rocks—to muse o'er flood and fell
   To slowly trace the forest's shady scene . . .
   This is not solitude—'tis but to hold
   Converse with Nature's charms and view
      her stores unrolled.
         Canto II, stanza xxv
2. *The Famous History of the Seven Champions of Christendom*
   (c. 1597) by Richard Johnson; Goldsmith's *An History of
   the Earth and Animated Nature* (1774); *Adèle et Théodore*
   (1782) by Madame de Genlis.

volumes, Jane and I, acting Macbeth, singing Operas of our own invention, and playing backgammon when we met with tables, a style of thing so repugnant to the School ideas of propriety befitting the reign of the new governess, that she got wonderfully grave with her unfortunate pupils. We had picked her up as we left town, and thinking more of ourselves than of her felt quite disposed to quarrel with any one who wept so bitterly at leaving London and her own friends, when she was going to the highlands amongst ours. She was a little fat dumpling of a woman, with fine eyes, and a sweet toned voice in speaking, strangely dressed in a fashion peculiar to the middle classes in England in that day, when the modes were not studied all through society as they are now, nor indeed attainable by moderate persons, as the expense of a careful toilette was quite beyond the means of poorer people. Her provision for the long journey was a paper of cakes, and a large thick pocket handkerchief, which was very soon wetted through; not an auspicious beginning where two such monkeys as Jane and I were concerned. Mary and Johnny ate the cakes and were satisfied.

The play thus opened seldom flagged nor did it want for shifting scenes enough. Poor Miss Elphick, she had troubled times. Her first grand stand was against the backgammon— shaking dice boxes in a publick inn! We were very polite but we would not give in, assuring her we always were accustomed to shake dice boxes where we liked out of lesson hours. Next she entreated to be spared Macbeth's dagger! Hamlet's soliloquys! Hecate's fury! So masculine to be strutting about in those attitudes and ranting in such loud tones, etc. etc. We were really amazed. Our occupation gone! the labour of months to be despised after all the applause we had been earning by it! What were we to do? Sit silent with our hands before us? not we indeed! We stood amazed! We pitied her! and left her! thinking that my Mother had made a most unfortunate choice of a governess, and perhaps we were not wrong.

We entered Scotland by the Kelso road. We passed the field of Flodden; neither of us remembered why it should be celebrated. 'Miss Elphick will tell us, I am sure,' said I, pert unfeeling child that I was. I had taken her measure, and knew full well she knew less of Flodden field than I did. 'Decidedly not,' said my father, 'take the trouble to hunt out all the necessary information yourself, you will be less likely again to forget it; I shall expect the whole history a week after we reach home.' Whether suspecting the truth, he had come to the rescue of the governess, or that he was merely carrying out his general plan of making us do all our own work ourselves, I did not stay to think. My head had begun to arrange its ideas. The flowers o' the forest and Marmion[1] were running through it. 'Ah, Papa,' said I, 'I needn't hunt, it's all here now, the phantom, the English lady, the spiked girdle and all; I'm right, ain't I?' and I looked archly over at our governess, who, poor woman, seemed in the moon altogether. The family conversation was an unknown language to her. 'What could have made Mama choose her?' said Jane to me.

We went to see Melrose, dined at Jedburgh, passed Cowdenknows, Tweedside, Ettrick schawes, Gala Water, starting up and down in the carriage in extasies, flinging ourselves half out at the sides each time these familiar names excited us. In vain Miss Elphick pulled our frocks. I am sure she feared she had undertaken the charge of lunaticks, particularly when I burst forth in song at either Tweedside or Yarrow braes. It was not the scenery, there is much finer, it was the 'classick ground' of all the border country.

A number of french prisoners, officers, were on their parole at Jedburgh. Lord Buchan, whom we met there, took us to see a painting in progress by one of them; some battle field, all the principal figures, portraits, from memory, minutely executed and well grouped and pencilled I believe, but so vivid in colouring that the glare offended my eye, all unpractised as it was. The picture was already sold, and part paid for, and another ordered, which we were all so glad of, the handsome young painter having interested us. The ingenuity of these french prisoners of all ranks was amazing,

1.  The famous song about Flodden by Jean Elliot (1727–1805). Scott's *Marmion* (1808) is sub-titled 'A Tale of Flodden Field' and, with *The Lay of the Last Minstrel* and *The Lady of the Lake*, was part of the Grants' 'travelling library'.

really only to be equalled by their industry. Those of them unskilled in higher arts earned for themselves most comfortable additions to their allowance by turning bits of wood, and bones, straw, almost any thing in fact, into neat toys of many sorts, eagerly bought up by all who met with them. At Ramsgate we had provided ourselves with work boxes, work baskets and various other nicknacks, all made at the prisoners' dépots in the neighbourhood. We felt quite friendly therefore to all of the same sort we found at Jedburgh.

We rested a few days in Edinburgh and then journeyed leisurely by the highland road home, still crossing the Queensferry in a miserable sailing boat, and the Tay at Inver for the last time in the large flat boat. When next we passed our boundary river the handsome bridge was built over it at Dunkeld, the little inn at Inver was done up, a fine hotel where the civilest of Landlords reigned, close to the bridge, received all travellers; and Neil Gow was dead, the last of our bards—no one again will ever play Scotch musick as he did. His sons in the quick measures were perhaps his equals, they gave force and spirit and fine expression to Strathspeys and reels, but they never gave the slow, the tender airs with the real feeling of their beauty that their father had.[1] Nor can any one hope to revive a style passing away. A few true fingers linger amongst us, but this generation will see the last of them. Our children will not be as national as their parents—reflections made like some puns, *à loisir*, for at the time we last ferried over the Tay I was only on the look out for all the well remembered features of the scenery. We baited the horses at Moulinearn, not the pretty country inn of the rural village which peeps out on the Tummel from its skreen of fine wooding now, but a dreary, desolate, solitary stone house, dirt without and smoke within, and little to be had in it but whiskey. The road to Blair then passed over the summit of the hills, overlooking the river, the valley in which nestled Fascally, and allowing of a peep at Loch Rannoch in

1. All his five sons were accomplished players; Nathaniel came closest to his father's achievement, according to *Groves*.

the far distance; then on through Killiecrankie, beautiful then as now, more beautiful! for no Perth traders had built villas on its sheltered banks, nor Glasgow merchant perched a Castle on the rock. Hardly a cabin broke the solitude in those days, to interrupt the awe we always felt on passing the stone set up where Dundee fell, 'Bonny Dundee,' whom we Highlanders love still in spite of Walter Scott.[1] Miss Elphick, poor soul, was undoubtedly as innocent of any acquaintance with him as she had been with James the 4th, but there had been something in my father's manner on the Flodden field day which prevented any future display of my ill breeding. I therefore contented myself with a verse of the song, and a little conversation with my mother, who was a perfect chronological table of every event in modern history.

The old inn at Blair was high up on the hill, overlooking the park, the wall of which was just opposite the windows. We used to watch through the trunks of the trees for the antlered heads of the herds of deer, and walk to a point from whence we could see the Castle far down below, beside the river, a large, plain, very ugly building now, that very likely looked grander before its battlements were levelled by order of the government after the rebellion.[2] Here we were accustomed to a particularly good pudding, a regular soufflé that would have been no discredit to a first rate French cook, only that he would have been amazed at the quantity of whiskey poured over it. The German brandy puddings must be of the same genus, improved, perhaps, by the burning, except to the taste of the highlander. The 'Athole lad' who waited on us was very awkward, red haired, freckled, in a faded, nearly thread bare tartan jacket. My father and mother had a bedroom, Johnny and the maid a closet, but we had three and our governess slept in the parlour, two in a bed,

1. Major-General John Graham of Claverhouse, Viscount Dundee, led the first Jacobite rising in 1689; Scott's poem was 'Bonnie Dundee'.
2. *The Ordnance Gazeteer of Scotland* (1894), explains that after the '45 the castle was 'docked of two upper stories, and white-washed' so that for Queen Victoria, one hundred years later, it was merely 'a large, plain, white building.'

and the beds were in the wall shut in by panels, and very musty was the smell of them. So poor Miss Elphick cried, which we extremely resented as a reflexion upon the habits of our country. Next day was worse, a few miles of beauty, and then the dreary moor to Dalnacardoch, another lone house with very miserable steading about it, and a stone walled sheep fold near the road; and then the high hill pass to Dalwhinnie very nearly as desolate. Nothing can exceed the dreariness of Drumochter—all heather, bog, granite, and the stony beds of winter torrents, unrelieved by one single beauty of scenery, if we except a treeless lake with a shooting box beside it, and three or four fields near the little burn close to which stands the good inn of Dalwhinnie. We felt so near home there that we liked the lonely place, and were almost sorry we were to push on to sleep at Pitmain, the last stage on our long journey. We never see such inns now; no carpets on the floors, no cushions on the chairs, no curtains to the windows. Of course polished tables, or even clean ones, were unknown. All the accessories of the dinner were wretched, but the dinner itself, I remember, was excellent; hotch potch salmon, fine mutton, grouse, scanty vegetables, bad bread, but good wine. A mile on from Pitmain were the indications of a village—the present town of Kingussie, then a few very untidy looking slated stonehouses each side of a road, the bare heather on each side of the Spey, the bare mountains on each side of the heather, a few white walled houses here and there, a good many black turf huts, frightful without, though warm and comfortable within. A little farther on rose Belleville, a great hospital looking place protruding from young plantations, and staring down on the rugged meadow land now so fine a farm. The birch woods began to show a little after this, but deserted the banks about that frightful Kincraig where began the long moor over which we were glad to look across the Spey to Invereschie, from whence all that, the Rothiemurchus side of the river was a succession of lovely scenery. On we went over the weary moor of Alvie to the Loch of the same name with its kirk and manse, so singularly built on a long promontory, running far out into the water; Tor Alvie on the right, Craigellachie before us, and our own most beautiful 'plain of the fir trees' opening out as we

advanced, the house of the Doune appearing for a moment as
we passed on by Lynwilg. We had as usual to go on to the big
boat at Inverdruie, feasting our eyes all the way on the fine
range of the Cairngorm, the pass of the Lairig Ghru between
Cairngorm and Braeriach, the hill of Kincairn standing
forward to the north to enclose the forest which spread all
along by the banks of the Spey, the foreground relieved by
hillocks clothed with birch, fields, streams, and the smoke
from the numerous cottages. Our beloved Ord Ban rose right
in front with its bald head and birch covered sides, and we
could point out our favourite spots to one another as we
passed along, some coming into sight as others receded, till
the clamour of our young voices, at first amusing, had to be
hushed. We were so happy. We were at last come home;
London was given up, and in our dearly loved Rothiemurchus we now fully believed we were to live and die.

We found the Doune all changed again, more of the
backwater, more of the hill, and all the garden, gone. This
last had been removed to its present situation in the series of
pretty hollows in the birch wood between the Drum and the
Miltown moor; a fashion of the day, to remove the fruit and
vegetables to an inconvenient distance from the Cook, the
kitchen department of the garden being considered the
reverse of ornamental. The new situation of ours, and the
way it was laid out, was the admiration of every body, and
there could not well have been any thing of the sort more
striking to the eye, with the nicely managed entrance among
the trees, and the gardener's cottage so picturesquely placed;
but I always regretted the removal. I like to be able to lounge
in among the cabbages, to say little of the gooseberries; and a
walk of above a quarter of a mile on a hot summer's day
before reaching the refreshment of fruit is almost as torment-
ing to the drawing room division of the family as is the
sudden want of a bit of thyme, or sage or parsley to those in
authority in the offices, and no one beyond the swing door
idle enough to have an hour to spare for fetching some. A
very enjoyable shrubbery replaced the dear old formal
kitchen garden, with belts of flowering trees, and gay beds of
flowers, grass plots, dry walks, and the Doune hill in the
midst of it, all neatly fenced from the lawn; and so agreeable a

retirement was this piece of ornamental ground, that I can't but think it very bad taste in my brother John and the Duchess of Bedford to take away the light green paling and half the dressed ground, and throw so large an open space about that very ugly half finished house : for I am writing now after having been with my husband and my children and three of my nephews in the highlands, a few really happy weeks at Inverdruie ; finding changes enough in our Duchus, as was to be expected after an absence of twenty years ; much to regret, some things to praise, and many more to wish for. In my older age it was the condition of the people that particularly engaged me ; in 1812 it was the scenery, or the locality, for I had not arrived at distinguishing the landscape artificially.

It has always seemed to me that this removal to Rothiemurchus was the first great era in my life. All our habits changed—all connexions, all surroundings. We had been so long in England, we elder children, that we had to learn our highland life again. The language, the ways, the style of the house, the visitors, the interests, all were so entirely different from what had been latterly affecting us, we seemed to be starting as it were afresh. I look back on it now even as a point to date up to and a point to date on from ; the beginning of a second stage in the journey. Our family then consisted of my father and mother, we three girls and our governess, and our young French companion Caroline Favrin, William during the summer holidays, Johnny, and a maid between him and my Mother, poor Peggy Davidson. Besides her there were the following servants : Mrs Bird the Coachman's wife, an Englishwoman, as upper housemaid and plain needle woman ; under her Betty Ross, the gardener's youngest daughter ; Grace Grant, the beauty of the country, only daughter of Sandy Grant the *Greusaich* or shoemaker, who waited on the school room ; old Belle Macpherson, a soldier's widow who had followed the 92nd all over the world, and had learned to make up the Marquis of Huntly's shirts remarkably well at Gibraltar, box plaiting all the frills—he never wore them small plaited, though my father did for many a long day after this ! She was the Laundry maid. The Cook and housekeeper was an English Mrs Carr from Cumberland, an excellent manager; a plain cook under her from Inverness; and old Christie as kitchen maid. The men were Simon Ross, the gardener's eldest son, as Butler, and an impudent English footman, Richard, with a flat bottle nose, who yet turned all the women's heads; William Bird the Coachman, and George Ross, another son of the gardener's, as groom; and old John Mackintosh who brought in all the peats and wood for the fires, pumped the water, turned the mangle, lighted the oven, brewed the beer, bottled the whiskey, kept the yard tidy, and stood enraptured listening to us playing on the harp 'like David'! There was also a clerk of Mr Cooper's generally, my father requiring assistance in his study, where he spent the greater part of his time managing all his perplexed affairs himself.

At the Farm were the steward, called there Grieve, and as many 'lads' as he required for the work of the farm under him, who all slept in a loft over the stables, and ate in the farm kitchen. Old George Ross No. 1, not the gardener, had a house and shop in the offices; he was turner, joiner, butcher, weaver, lint dresser, wool comber, dyer, and what not; his old wife was the henwife, and had her task of so many hanks of yarn to spin in the winter. Old Jenny Cameron, who had never been young, and was known as Jenny Dairy always, was supreme in the farm kitchen. She managed cows, calves, milk, stores, and the spinning, assisted by an active girl whom I never recollect seeing do any thing but bake the oaten bread, and scour the wooden vessels used for every purpose, except on the washing and *rinsing* days called by the maids *ranging*, when Jenny gave help in the Laundry, in which abode of mirth and fun the under housemaid spent her afternoons. Besides this regular staff, John Fyffe, the handsome smith, came twice a week to the forge with his apprentices, when all the maids were sure to require repairs in the ironworks; and the *greusaich* came once a week for the cheque he carried in his bosom to the Bank at Inverness, walking the 36 miles as another man, not a highlander, would go three, and 36 back again, with the money in the same safe hiding place, my father at this time paying most of the wages in cash. And there was the Bowman, who had charge of the cattle, surnamed, I suppose, from the necessity of arming him in the olden time with the weapon most used, when he had to guard his herd from marauders. John Macgregor was our bowman's name, though he was never spoken of but as John Bhain or John the fair, on account of his complexion. He was married to George Ross the orraman's daughter, orraman means the jobber or Jack of all trades, and, like almost all the rest of them, lived with us till he died. The Gardener, with those of his family who were not married or in our service, lived in the pretty cottage at one entrance to the new garden, which also served as lodge to the white gate. The game keeper had an ugly little hut at the Polchar, a tall, handsome John Macpherson I think he was. The Foxhunter, little, active Lewie Gordon, had part of the Kainapool house. The principal shepherd, John MacGregor, known as the Muckle shepherd from his great stature, had the remainder; the under shepherd, also a MacGregor, lived nearer the mountains. The Carpenter, Donald Maclean, who had married my Mother's first cook Nelly Grant, she who could make so many puddings, 99 if I remember right, had another part of Kainapool. The Colleys, the Masons, were at Riannachan; far enough apart all of them, miles between any two, but it little mattered; we were slow coaches in our highlands. Time was of little value, space of no account, an errand was a day's work, whether it took the day or only an hour or two of it. Three or four extra *aids*, Tam Mathieson the Carrier, Tam McTavish the smuggler, and Mary Leosach and the Nairn fisher wives, with their creels on their backs, made up the complement of our highland servitors.

Poor Miss Elphick. All this assemblage could not reconcile her at first to the wild country she had got into. Between the inns, the bleak moors and the gaelick she had been overpowered, and had hardly indeed articulated since we had traversed Drumochter. Her eye had yet to be taught to comprehend the grand features of mountain landscapes. She had yet to awake to the interest of her situation, to accommodate herself besides to manners so entirely different from any she had been accustomed to. How my Mother could have taken a fancy to this strange little woman was ever an enigma to Jane and me; she was very uneducated, had lived amongst a totally low set of people, and had not any notion of the grave business she had under taken. Her temper was passionate and irritable. We had to humour, to manage her, instead of learning from her to discipline ourselves. Yet she was clever, very warm hearted, and she improved herself wonderfully after being with us a little time. Her father, of German extraction, had been bailiff to the Duke of Clarence at Bushy Park. He lived jollily with a set of persons of his own station, spending freely what was earned easily, and so leaving nothing behind him. His son succeeded him in his place; his elder daughters were married poorly; this youngest had nothing for it but the usual resource of her class, go out as Governess, for which responsible situation she had never been in the least prepared. Her childhood had been mostly passed under Mrs Jordan's eye, among all her FitzClarences;[1] she then went to a third rate school, and at eighteen she went to keep her rather dissipated brother's house during the interval between his first and second marriage. Lady Glenbervie, who was in some way interested about the family, recommended her to my Mother. She had found her in old Mrs Wynch's apartments in Hampton Court Palace, recommended her removing to London for a few months for masters, and promised to do all she could for her. We got on better with her after a while, but at first her constant companionship made us very miserable. Oh, how we regretted Annie Grant.

It was the intention of my father and mother to remain quietly at the Doune for the next two years, that is, my father intended the Doune to be the home of his wife and children. He could only himself be with us occasionally, as he had to carry his Election, and then in the proper season to take his place in Parliament. I can't bring to mind whether he wrote M.P. after his name this year or the next, but in either the one or the other Great Grimsby was gained—at what cost the ruin of a family could certify. Whether he were with us or no, visitors poured in as usual; no one then ever passed a friend's

1. The Duke of Clarence (1765–1837), later William IV,
   lived here with the famous actress Dorothea Jordan
   between 1790 and 1810; she had ten FitzClarence
   children, whilst continuing her career on stage.

house in the highlands, nor was it ever thought necessary to send invitations on the one part, or to give information on the other; the doors were open literally, for ours had neither lock nor bolt, and people came in sure of a hearty welcome and good cheer. The Lady Logie I remember well; I was always fond of her, she was so fond of me; and her old father, and her sister Grace Baillie, whom I overheard one morning excusing my plain appearance to my mother—pale and thin certainly, but very ladylike! 'which is always sufficient.' No Mr Macklin and his flute, how beautifully he played it!—he was in India recommended to the good graces of Uncle Edward! for he had gone as a Barrister to Bombay. And Burgie and Mrs Dunbar Brodie paid their regular visit. She measured all the rooms, and he played the flageolet in the boat upon the lake, not badly, though we young people preferred hearing Mrs Bird, the Coachman's wife, sing the 'Battle of the Nile' in that situation; her voice really rang round the hill in such a style that the echo must have been very dull indeed not to have repeated the strain. Then we had poor Sir Alexander Boswell,[1] not a Baronet then, 'Bozzy's' son, his wife, wife's sister and quiet husband, Mr Conynghame—new acquaintances made through the Dick Lauders, who lived near them; they were also with us, and all the old set. Amongst others, Sir William Gordon Cumming, newly come to his title and just of age; some of his sisters with him. He was the queerest creature. Ugly, yet one liked his looks, tall and well made, and awkward more from oddity it seemed than ungracefulness; strange, extraordinary in his conversation between cleverness and a kind of want of it. Every body liked Sir Willie, and many years afterwards he told me that he at this time very much liked me, and wanted my father to promise me to him in a year or two; but my father would make no promises, 'sawtie,[2] ye see', only just a warm welcome on the old footing when this oddity should return from his Continental travels. He was just setting out on them, and I never heard of this early conquest of mine, for

1. Well known as an antiquary and poet, he died in a famous duel in 1822. See Cockburn's *Memorials*.
2. Sarcastic (S.N.D.).

he fell in with Elizabeth Campbell at Florence; 'And ye see, Lizzy, my dear,' said he to me, as he was driving me in his buggy round the beautiful grounds at Altyre, 'Eliza Campbell put Eliza Grant quite out of my head, the more's the pity perhaps!' We had no Kinrara; that little paradise had been shut up ever since the death of the Duchess of Gordon, except just during a month in the shooting season, when the Marquis of Huntly came there with a bachelour party.

We girls saw little of all this company, old friends as some of them were, as, except at breakfast where Miss Elphick and I always appeared, we never now left our own premises. We found this schoolroom life at first very irksome; it was so very different from what we had been accustomed to in some respects it never became agreeable but we bore it better after a while. Governess and pupils slept in one large room up at the top of the new part of the house, the barrack room where I so well remembered Edwina Cumming combing her long yellow hair. We had each of us a little white curtained bed, made to fit into the slope of the roof in its own corner, leaving space enough between the bedstead and the end wall for the washing table. The middle of the room with its window, fireplace, toilettes, and book table, made our common dressing room—there were chests of drawers each side of the fireplace, and a large closet in the passage, so that we were very comfortably lodged. Miss Elphick began her course of instruction by jumping out of bed at six o'clock in the morning, and throwing on her clothes with the haste of one escaping from a house on fire. She then wiped her face and hands, and smoothed her cropped hair, and her toilette was over. Some woman, I forget who she was, telling Sir William Cumming, who was seated next her at breakfast, that she never took more than ten minutes to dress in the morning, he instantly got up, plate and cup in hand, and moved off to the other side of the table. He would not then have sat near me, for Miss Elphick considered ten minutes quite sufficient for any young lady to give to her dressing upon week days. We could 'clean ourselves' properly, as she did, upon Sundays. She could not allow us time for such unnecessary dawdling. We must get an hour of the harp or the pianoforte before breakfast, and our Papa chose that we should be out another;

therefore, we must give ourselves a 'good wash' upon Sundays, and make that do for the week, as she did and as she made her shift do, for that only went on clean after the thorough scouring and then served by night and by day till cleaning day came again. Her stock of linen indeed would not have permitted a more profuse use of it. We were thoroughly disgusted. In after days I am sure she herself would have had difficulty in believing she had ever had habits so unseemly.

Her acquirements were on a par with this style of breeding. She and I had a furious battle the first week we commenced business, because during a history lesson she informed dear Mary that Scotland had been conquered by Queen Elizabeth, and left by her with her other possessions to her nephew, King James. I was pert enough, I daresay, for the sort of education we had received had given us an extreme contempt for such ignorance, but what girl of fifteen, brought up as I had been, could be expected to shew respect for an illiterate woman of very ungovernable temper, whose ideas had been gathered from a Class lower than we could possibly have been acquainted with, and whose habits were those of the servant. She insisted too that there never had been a Caliph Haroun al Raschid—our most particular friend—that he was only a fictitious character in those eastern fairy tales; and when, to prove his existence, we brought forward the list of his presents to Charlemagne, we found she did not believe in him either.[1] And she could run off a string of dates 'could that ar, ooman' like Isabella in The Good French Governess. I thought of her historical recollections a good many years afterwards, when visiting General Need's nephew, Tom Walker, at Aston Hall, in Derbyshire, whom we had known very well in Edinburgh when he was in the Scots Greys. He was publick school and College bred, had been a dozen years in the army, was married to a marquis's granddaughter, and had a fortune of £3000 a year, not bribe enough for Jane by the way. He was shewing his collection of coins, some of them very valuable, he had several very perfect of the reign of

1. Caliph of Baghdad, through whom Charlemagne was trying to protect the Eastern Christians; the exchange of ambassadors and presents took place in 801.

Elizabeth, and after calling attention to them, he produced some base money which she had coined on some emergency—to cheat the publick in plain terms. 'And here, you see,' added he, picking up other equally base pieces, 'Philip and Mary, *following her example!* cheated the publick too!' What a queer look that odd Count Lapâture gave across the open drawer of the cabinet.

It was not to be supposed that we could get on very comfortably with poor Miss Elphick. We were ungovernable, I believe, but she was totally unfit to try to direct us; and then, when we saw from the windows of our Schoolroom, a perfect prison to us, the fine summer pass away, sun shining, birds singing, river flowing, all in vain for us; when we heard the drawing room party setting out for all our favourite haunts, and felt ourselves denied our ancient privilege of accompanying it, we, who had hitherto roamed really fancy free! no wonder we rebelled against being thus cooped up, and detested the unfortunate governess who thus deprived us of liberty. It was heart breaking, spirit breaking, or spirit *stirring* at any rate for we did stand up for our ancient rights, insisted on more out of doors exercise and refused to stay so much within, let come what might.

Miss Elphick determined to leave. She felt herself quite unequal to the highlands and the highland children together so she went to make her complaint to my Mother. She returned after a long conference, seemingly little improved in temper by the interview. However she had fared, we fared worse; she was, to all appearance, civilly treated, which we were not. I was first sent for, and well reproved, but not allowed to speak one word to excuse myself; called impudent, ignorant, indolent, impertinent, deprived of all indulgences, threatened with still heavier displeasure, and sent back to my duties in such a state of wrath that I was more decided than ever on resisting the governess, and only regretted my powers of annoyance could not also be brought to bear on my Mother. Jane then had her maternal lecture, which gave her a fit of tears, so bitter that she had to be sent to bed to recover from them; she was silent as to what had passed, but she was more grieved perhaps than I was. My father had been from home during this commotion, but I

suppose he was informed of what had taken place on his
return, for an entire reform in every way was the result of
this 'agitation.' Till he came back we were very miserable.
Miss Elphick never spoke to Jane or me but with mock
respect. She doubled our lessons, shortened our walks,
threw our books at us, pens, and pencils in our faces, contradicted our every wish, to make us know, she said, that she
was over us; her excessive vulgarity made us shudder. My
Mother soon forgave Jane; I, who was never a favourite, was
rather unreasonably continued out of favour—not a style of
management this that much improved a naturally passionate
temper.

My father met us with his usual affection. Next day his
manner was so stiffly dignified we were quite prepared for a
summons to attend him in the study. He had changed his
sitting room for our accommodation, and given up to us the
part of the old hall he had fitted up for himself and which
was now our Schoolroom; the room within, once the state
bedroom and then my Mother's room, was now the nursery
where Johnny, the French girl, and Peggy Davidson slept,
and my Mother had taken our old nursery at the head of the
stairs looking over the shrubbery to Inverdruie, while the
room exactly underneath was newly done up for my father.
Into this lower chamber I was first ordered to appear. I had
determined with Jane to tell my father boldly all our grievances, to expose to him the unsuitability of our governess,
and to represent to him that it could not be expected we
would learn from a person whom we felt ourselves fitted to
teach. Alas, for my high resolves! There was something about
my father so imposing when he sat in judgment that awe
generally overcame all who were presented to him.
Remonstrances would besides have been useless, as he
addressed me very differently from what I had expected as I
stood before him, all my courage gone, just waiting my doom
in silence. I forget the exact words of his long harangue; he
was never very brief in his speeches, but the purport is in my
head now as clear as the day he spoke to me, for he told me
what I felt was the truth. He said Miss Elphick was not
exactly the sort of governess he could have wished for us, but
that she was in many respects the best out of many my

Mother had taken the trouble to inquire about. She had great natural talents, habits of neatness, habits of order, and habits of industry, in all of which we were deficient; all these she could teach us, with many other equally useful things. We must also by this time be aware that we had considerably improved in our various studies under her steady superintendance, more particularly Mary who could hardly read before, was thought a dunce and was actually turning out clever. That this sort of methodical occupation was of immense importance in forming the character of young people he thought we must be aware of—it was what he and my mother had more especially taken pains to secure in a governess. A more correct knowledge of history, a more cultivated mind, would have been a great advantage certainly, but we could not expect every thing, particularly from school educated young women. What he did expect, however, was that his children should act as became the children of a gentleman, the descendants of a long line of gentlemen, and not by rude unfeeling remarks, impertinence and insubordination prove themselves to be more ill bred than those much their inferiours. A gentleman and a gentlewoman he told us were studious of the feelings of all around them; they were characterised by that perfect good breeding which would avoid inflicting the slightest annoyance on any human being. How could we expect if we forgot the dignity of our own character so far as to upbraid the lady placed over us with the deficiencies she herself must begin to be sensible of, that her temper would be proof against such extreme indelicacy— more to the same purpose in the same style, in which indeed one element of good, the highest of all was wanting, but so far as the teaching went, it could not have been better.

This lecture had considerable effect on me. I dreaded compromising my gentle blood by indecorums of any nature; I also fully believed in the difficulty of procuring a suitable governess. My conduct therefore improved in politeness, but I can't say that I ever learned to esteem poor Miss Elphick or to consider that she was wisely selected for her situation.

Jane's private interview with my father did not last so long as mine and it had proportionably less effect. She had never been so pert as I had been, nor so intractable, she had therefore less to reform. She said my father had quite failed to convince her that they had got a proper governess for us, she was therefore sure he had some doubts on the point himself; but as there seemed to be a determination not to part with her we could only try to bear with her, make the best of it; she and Jane got on from this time very well together; I think, at last, Jane really liked her. She improved wonderfully. Her conversation in the study lasted an hour or more, and she left it much more humble than she had entered it, this was the first step—she was beginning to 'know herself.' What passed never transpired, but her manner became less imperious, her assertions less dogmatick. Dictionaries, Biographies, Gazetteers, Chronologies were added to our bookcase, and these were always referred to afterwards in any uncertainty, though it was done by way of giving us the trouble of searching in order that we might remember better—for sincerity was not the fashion in those times. It would have been simpler for her to say 'I don't know so and so, *let us* look for it.' We should have respected her the more, but this kind of candour towards children at least, was never then practised. People in general knew so little they were ashamed of their ignorance and so affected wisdom beyond their reach, tried to impose in fact and sometimes succeeded.

Schoolroom affairs went on much more smoothly after this settlement of knotty questions. We were certainly kept very regularly at work, and our work was sufficiently varied, the heads were properly rested for the most part, and we had battled out a fair amount of exercise. We rose at six, in the summer, practised an hour, walked an hour, and then the younger ones had breakfast, a plan Dr Combe[1] would have changed with advantage. Miss Elphick and I had often to wait two hours longer before our morning's meal was tasted, for we joined the party in the Eating room, and my father and mother were very late in appearing. We took a bit of bread always before the early walk, all of us, a walk that tired me. Study went on till twelve, when we went out again. At two we

1. Dr Andrew Combe (1797–1847), physician and phrenologist, author of *The Physiological and Moral Management of Infancy* (1840).

dined, and had half an hour to ourselves afterwards. We studied till five again, and spent the rest of the evening as we liked, out of doors till dark in summer, or in the drawing room afterwards for we had 'agitated' to get rid of learning any lessons overnight and had succeeded. In winter we rose half an hour later, without candle, or fire, or warm water. Our clothes were all laid on a chair overnight in readiness for being taken up in proper order. My Mother would not give us candles, and Miss Elphick insisted we should get up. We were not allowed hot water, and really in the highland winters, when the breath froze on the sheets, and the water in the jugs became cakes of ice, washing was a cruel necessity, the fingers were pinched enough. As we could play our scales well in the dark, the two pianofortes and the harp began the day's work. How very near crying was the one whose turn set her at the harp I will not speak of; the strings cut the poor cold fingers so that the blisters often bled. Martyr the first decidedly sat in the dining room at the harp. Martyr the second put her poor blue hands on the keys of the grand-pianoforte in the drawing room, for in these two rooms the fires were never lighted till near nine o'clock—the grates were of bright steel, the household was not early and so we had to bear our hard fate. Mary was better off. She always, being quite a beginner practised under Miss Elphick's own superintendance in the schoolroom, where, if Grace Grant had not a good fire brightly burning by seven o'clock, she was likely to hear of it. Our *al fresco* playing below was not of much use to us; we had better have been warm in our beds for all the good it did.

As we had no early walk in winter, we went out at half after eleven, and at five we had a good romp all over the old part of the house, playing at hide and seek in the long garret and its many dependencies, till it was time for Miss Elphick, who dined in the parlour, to dress. We had a charming hour to ourselves then by the good fire in the schoolroom, no candle allowed, till we had to dress ourselves and take our work down to the drawing room, where I had tea; the rest had supped upstairs on bread, Johnny and Caroline Favrin alone being able to take the milk. Poor, dear Jane, how I longed to give her one of the cups of tea I was allowed myself; she was too honest to go in with Mary to the nursery and take one from Peggy Davidson.

We learned the harp, the pianoforte, and singing after a fashion, drawing in several styles, geography, with map-making well taught, and arithmetick very well, more knowledge of the heavens than I cared for; lists of stars, and maps of the sky, and peerings of a frosty night out of the barrack room window after Orion's belt, his sword, and neighbours, were not in my line at all. We had chronological tables to make which delighted me, pieces of poetry to learn by heart, and French translations and exercises. And every Saturday after dinner we mended our clothes. We really soon got to like the regularity of our life. Once accustomed to its discipline we hardly felt it as such, and we got very much interested in most of our employments, quite anxious to shew our father that we were making good use of our time. We generally played to him every evening whether there were guests or no, and once a week we had each to give him something new, on the execution of which he passed his judgment, not unsparingly, for he was particular to a fault in finding fault. Once a week we had a French evening when there was no company, and we read aloud occasionally after tea, in turns, such bits as he had himself selected for us out of good authours, the same passage over and over till we had acquired the proper expression. He often read aloud himself any passage that struck him, either from books, reviews, or newspapers. We had a good command of books, a fair Library of our own, and really a good one collected by my father. It was from these silent teachers that we very much received an education. The sentiments of those excellent writings laid in our way became ours from the habit of imbibing them without our being aware that we were learning. My father always commented on the passages selected, ever in a spirit of liberality and kindness; I never heard an illnatured remark from his lips, on either dead or living, nor noticed the very slightest interest in gossip of any sort; he meddled in no man's business, was charitable, in St Paul's sense, in all his judgments. It was no common privilege to grow up under such a mind.

My Mother, when in health, was an example of industry.

She kept a clean and tidy house, and an excellent table, not doing much herself, but taking care to see all well done. She was very kind to the poor, and encouraged us to visit them and work with them, and attend to them when sick. She was a very beautiful needlewoman, and she taught us to sew and cut out, and repair all our own, our father's, brothers', and family linen. She had become highland wife enough to have her spinnings and dyings, and weavings of wool and yarn, and flax and hanks, and she busied herself at this time in all the stirring economy of a household 'remote from cities,' and consequently forced to provide for its own necessities. Her evening readings were her relaxation; she was very well read, thoroughly read in English Classicks, and she possessed a memory from which neither fact nor date once entered ever escaped. We used to apply to her, when idle, and never found her wrong. She used to employ us to go her errands among the people, and we soon got Miss Elphick broken in to like the long wanderings through the fir wood. We had two ponies, which we rode in turns; a tent in the shrubbery in the summer, the garden in the autumn, the poultry yard in the spring, the farm yard at all times, with innumerable visits to pay to friends of all degrees. Such was our highland home; objects of interest all round us, ourselves objects of attention all round, little princes and princesses in our Duchus, where the old feudal feelings get paraded all in their deep intensity. And the face of nature so beautiful—rivers, lakes, burnies, fields, banks, braes, moors, woods, mountains, heather, the dark forest, wild animals, wild flowers, wild fruits; the picturesque inhabitants, the legends of our race, fairy tales, the raids of the Clans, haunted spots, the cairns of the murdered—all and every thing that could touch the imagination, there abounded and acted as a charm on the children of the Chieftain who was so adored; for my father was the father of his people, loved for himself as well as for his name.

# CHAPTER ELEVEN

# 1570–1813

ROTHIEMURCHUS at this period contained four large farms only, the Doune, where we lived ourselves, to which my father was constantly adding such adjoining scraps as circumstances enabled him now and then to get possession of; Inverdruie, where lived his great Uncle Captain Lewis Grant, the last survivor of the old race; The Croft, where now was settled his cousin James Cameron; and The Dell, occupied by Duncan McIntosh, the forester, who had permission to take in as many acres of the adjacent moors as suited his husbandry. Quantities of smaller farms, from a mere patch to a decent steading, were scattered here and there among the beautiful birch woods, near swiftly running streams, or farther away among the gloom of the fir forest, wherever an opening afforded light enough for a strip of verdure to brighten the general carpet of cranberries and heather. The Carpenter, the Smith, the Foxhunter, the Sawmillers, the Wheelwright, the few Chelsea pensioners, each had his little field, while comparatively larger holdings belonged to a sort of yeomanry coeval with our own possession, or even some of them found there by our Ancestor the Laird of Muckrach, the second son of our Chief, who displaced the Shawes, for my father was but the seventh Laird of Rothiemurchus. The Shawes reigned over this beautiful property before the Grants seized it, and *they* had succeeded the Comyns, lords not only of Badenoch but of half our part of the north besides.

The forest was at this time so extensive there was little room for tillage through the wide plain it covered. It was very pretty here and there to come upon a little cultivated spot, a tiny field by the burnside with a horse or a cow upon it, a cottage often built of the black peat mould, its chimney, however, smoking comfortably, a churn at the door, a girl bleaching linen, or a guid wife in her high white cap waiting to welcome us, miles away from any other spot equally tenanted. Here and there upon some stream a picturesque saw mill was situated, gathering its little hamlet round; for one or two held double saws, necessitating two millers, two assistants, two homes with all their adjuncts, and a larger wood yard to hold, first the logs, and then all they were cut up into. The Wood manufacture was our staple, on it depended our prosperity. It was at its height during the war, when there was a high duty on foreign timber; while it flourished so did we, and all the many depending on us; when it fell, the Laird had only to go back to black cattle again 'like those that were before him.' It was a false stimulus, said the political economists. If so, we paid for it.

Before introducing you, dear children, to our Rothiemurchus Society, we must get up a bit of genealogy, or you would never understand our relationships or our manners or our connections in the north countrie.[1] In the reign of the English popish Mary and of the Scotch Regencies, I fancy during the nonage[2] of our beautiful and unfortunate queen, in the year 1556, I think, but am not sure, the Chief of the Clan Grant presented his second son Patrick with the moor of Muckrach in Strathspey, on which he built a tower. The mother of Patrick was a Lady Steuart, daughter to the Earl of Athole, and cousin to the Queen. Whom he married I forget, but I rather believe his wife was a daughter of Fraser of Lovat. He had been a clever enterprising man, for the Shawes having displeased the Government by repeated acts of insubordination, a common offence in those times, their lands were confiscated, and the Rothiemurchus portion presented to the Laird of Muckrach—'gin he could win it'— which without more ado he did, and built himself a house at the Dell, the door stone of which he brought from his tower on the moor, and to this day there it is, with the date cut deep into it. The Shawes, though subdued, remaining troublesome, he repaired the ruins of an old Castle of the

1. The standard clan history is *Chiefs of Grant* (three
   volumes privately published in 1883) by William Fraser.
2. Minority.

Comyns on an Island in Loch an Eilein in case of any extraordinary mishap, and he pulled down and quite destroyed an old fort of the Shawes on the Doune hill, leaving his malediction to any of his successors who should rebuild it. He must have had stirring times of it, yet he died peaceably in his bed, and was succeeded by sons, for some generations of no great note, a Duncan, a James, a Patrick, etc., none of them remarkable except Duncan, who was surnamed of the Silver Cups from possessing two valuable drinking vessels, probably a rare piece of splendour in a highland household. A second James, the fifth Laird, inherited more of the qualities of the first Laird; his father, whose name I am not sure of, was but a poor body; he let the Shawes get rather ahead again, married badly, and was altogether so unfit to rule that his rather early death was not regretted. He either fell over a rock or was drowned in a hunting party—nobody ever inquired into particulars.

The reign of his son opened unpleasantly. The Shawes were very troublesome, and the Laird's mother, the Widow of the drowned or 'foolish Laird' for that was what they called him in gaelick, behaved herself scandalously. She married her son's tutor, a young man of the name of Dallas, very unsuitable in age or estate to the Lady Rothiemurchus. As she would not give him up, there was nothing left for it but to take him from her, which her sons accordingly did. I tell it as "twas told to me, they waylaid the poor Tutor and murdered him in the Little Dell, where the pump is in the new garden and where the smell of the blood rises every August in memory of the deed—committed in that month. Laird James had next to fight the Shawes, who of course, got the worst of it, though they lived through many a fight to fight again. At last their Chief was killed, which sobered this remnant of a Clan, but they had to bury him, and no grave would suit them but one in the kirk yard of Rothiemurchus beside his fathers'. With such array as their fallen fortunes admitted of, they brought their dead and laid him unmolested in that dust to which we must all return. But oh, what horrid times. His widow next morning on opening the door of her house at Dalnavert caught the corpse in her arms, which had been raised in the night and carried back to her. It was buried again, and again it was raised, more times than I care to mention, till Laird James announced he was tired of the play. The corpse was raised again, but carried home no more. It was buried deep down within the kirk, beneath the Laird's own seat, and every Sunday when he went to pray he stamped his feet upon the heavy stone he had laid over the remains of his enemy.

The last battle of the Clans was in this wild Laird's days. It took place on the Cambus More between the Grants and the remnant of the Comyns. The graves may yet be seen in the hollow just beyond the hill of the Callert. One larger than the rest is said to be the Leader's of the hostile band. Spearheads and other warlike weapons have been found there but not in our day. Laird James took to wife a very clever woman, the daughter of McIntosh of Killachy, nearly related to the McIntosh Chief (Sir James McIntosh [*sic*], the famed of our day, is that Killachy's). Her name was Grace, but on account of her height, and perhaps of her abilities, she was always called in the family Grizel Mhór. I don't know what fortune she brought beyond herself and the contents of a great green chest, very heavy, with two deep drawers at the bottom of it, which stood in the long garret as far back as my recollection reaches, and held the spare blankets well *peppered*, and with bits of tallow candles amongst them. She was the mother of McAlpine—Patrick Grant, surnamed McAlpine, I don't well know why, the great man of our line, who would have been great in any line. He removed from the Dell to the Doune, built what was then a fine house there, and had the family arms sculptured and *coloured* set over the door. I remember regretting the shutting up of that old door, and the dashing over of that coat of arms with stones and yellow mortar. [His brothers were Colonel William Grant, who married in 1711 Anne, a daughter of Ludovic Grant of Grant, and was the founder of the Ballindallochs,[1] and Mr John Grant, who died unmarried.] Whether he had any brothers and sisters I am not clear about but he had plenty of sons and daughters and his Wife was the daughter of the Laird of

---

1. He raised one of the original companies of the Black Watch.

Grant, his Chief, one of whose sisters was married to Lovat. McAlpine ruled not only his own small patrimony, but mostly all the country round. His wisdom was great, his energy of mind and body untiring. He must have acted as a sort of despotick sovereign, for he went about with a body of four and twenty men, picked men, gaily dressed, of whom the principal and the favourite was his foster brother, Ian Bàn or John the fair, also a Grant of the family of Achnahatnich. Any offences committed any where this band took cognisance of. McAlpine himself was judge and jury, and the sentence quickly pronounced was as quickly executed, even when the verdict doomed to death. A corpse with a dagger in it was not infrequently met with among the heather, and sometimes a stout fir branch bore the remains of a meaner victim. I never heard the justice of a sentence questioned.

He was a great man in every sense of the word, this stout Baron of old, tall and strong made, and very handsome, and a Beau; his trews, he never wore the kilt, were laced down the sides with gold, the brogues on his beautifully formed feet were lined and trimmed with feathers, his hands, as soft and white as a lady's and models as to shape, could draw blood from the finger ends of any other hand they grasped, and they were so flexible they could be bent back to form a cup which would hold without spilling a large table spoonfull of water. And he was an epicure, as indeed are all highlanders in their own way. They are contented with simple fare, and they ask no great variety, but what they have must be of its kind the best, and cooked precisely to their fancy. The well of which McAlpine invariably drank was the Lady's Well at Tullochgrue, the water of which was certainly delicious. It was brought to him twice a day in a covered wooden vessel, a cogue or lippie. There is no end to the stories of McAlpine's days—*was* none rather, for old world tales are wearing out in the highlands as every where else, and since we, the old race, have had to desert 'the spot where our forefathers dwelt,' the literal translation of our motto, Mo Duchus, there is less going to keep alive those feudal feelings which were so exclusively concentrated on the Laird's family.

McAlpine had by his first wife, the Lady Grace or Marjorie, several sons—James who succeeded him, Patrick who went into the army, married some one whose name I forget, and retired after some years of service to Tullochgrue, and John, surnamed Corrour, from having been born at the foot of the rock of that name up in the hill at Glen Einich. The young cattle were always sent up in the summer to eat the fine grass in the glens, and the lady having gone up at this time to the Sheiling (a mere but and ben which the herds inhabited), either to bleach her linens, the water there having priceless qualities, or for mere change of air, was suddenly taken ill in that wilderness. Without nurse or doctor she got as suddenly well, and brought her fine young son back with her to the Doune. The army was Corrour's destination of course; he saw a good deal of Service, and I believe died somewhere abroad, a distinguished officer, though he began life by fighting a running duel, that is, challenging two or three in succession, rather than acknowledge his highland ignorance. He had brought with him to the south, where he joined his regiment, a horse accoutred; the horse died, and John Corrour went about looking about for another to fit the saddle, which he insisted was the correct method of proceeding, and any one who questioned this had to measure swords with him. He had never seen asparagus; some being offered him he began to eat it at the *white* end, which provoking a laugh at the mess table, he laid his hand on the hilt of that terrible sword, and declared his undoubted right to eat what best pleased him. It is said that to his dying day he put aside on every occasion all the tender green points of asparagus. What marriages all the daughters of McAlpine made I never heard; one I know married Cameron of Glenevis.

A few years after the death of Lady Marjorie, when her family had long been grown up and settled, McAlpine, then in his 78th year, made what was considered to be a very low connection, although this second Bride of his was a handsome woman, the daughter of Grant of Tullochgorum, a respectable Tacksman. She bore him four sons, who were younger than some of his grandsons, Colonel William Grant, Captain Lewis Grant, George who was a sailor, a very uncommon profession for a highlander, and who died at sea, and Alexander who died young. Colonel William had been a good deal abroad, he had been in the West Indies, Canada, etc. He married in Ireland a Widow of the name of Dashwood, who died childless, and the Colonel soon after retired to the Croft, where he lived happily, but not altogether respectably, to a good old age, for his very handsome housekeeper, Jenny Gordon, bore him two children, our dearly loved Annie Grant and her brother Peter McAlpine Grant, whom my father sent out as a Cadet to India. Being the eldest living member of the family, Colonel William was tacitly elected to conduct my Mother to the kirk on her arrival as a Bride in Rothiemurchus. On this occasion he dressed himself in full regimentals, sash, belt, sword and all, etc., and wore a queue tyed with very broad black ribbon and which nearly reached down to his chair when he was seated. With cocked hat beneath his arm, he led her by the point of a finger, and walking backwards on tiptoe up the aisle in the face of the congregation, relinquishing her with a bow so low as made her feel much smaller than the little man who thus honoured her. He was the man of fashion of the circle, excelling in those graces of manner which belonged to the Beau of his day. He piqued himself on the amount of noise he made when rinsing out his mouth after dinner, when he squirted the water back into his finger glass in a way that alarmed all his neighbours. I have no recollection of the Colonel, he must have died when I was very young, but Captain Lewis I remember perfectly.

He had fought at the siege of Gibraltar, and was I daresay an excellent Officer, a little, handsome, dapper man, very gentlemanly, gay in manner, neat in habits, and with all the pride and spirit of his race. He had been given Inverdruie by my father when he resolved to make the Doune his own residence, and there I remember him from our earliest days till the autumn of 1814, when we lost him. His first wife, a Duff from Aberdeenshire, a pretty little old lady, had lived very unhappily with him, particularly since the death of their only child, a son, who had also gone into the army. They lived together for many years without speaking, though occupying the same rooms and playing backgammon together every night; when either made a disputed move the adversary's finger was silently pointed to the mistake, no word was ever spoken. My Mother and my Aunts rather liked the Captain's lady. She was a picture of a little old gentlewoman, riding every Sunday to church in a green joseph[1] and black bonnet, her pony led by a little maiden in a jacket and petticoat, plaid and snood. She also wore the hat perpetually, in the house and out of it. The joseph was her habit of ceremony, put on when she made her calls or dined with the Laird. She wore a sort of shirt beneath the joseph with neatly plaited frills and ruffles. The Captain made a much happier second choice, the wife I remember, Miss Grace Grant, Burnside, an elderly and a plain woman who had for some years kept house for her uncle, McPherson of Invereschie, and whom the Captain had always liked and had *toasted*, as was the fashion of his day, whenever after dinner he had proceeded beyond his second tumbler. She was installed at Inverdruie when we came back in 1812 to make our real home of Rothiemurchus; and at the Croft, instead of the Colonel was the cousin James Cameron, the grandson of McAlpine, his mother having been the Lady Glenevis; and he had married his cousin, the grand daughter of McAlpine, her father being Peter or Patrick Grant of Tullochgrue, a brother of Laird James.

But we must return to McAlpine himself, who died at 92, of some sore in his toe which the Doctors wished to amputate; but the Laird resolved to go out of the world as he had come into it, perfect, so the foot mortified. His eldest son James succeeded him; he was called the Spreckled Laird on account of being marked with the small pox which prevented his having turned out what nature intended, a very handsome man. He had some of the sternness of his grandfather James, the cruel Laird, and some of the talent of McAlpine, for in very troubled times he managed to steer clear of danger and to transmit his property unimpaired. He had married highly, a Gordon, a niece of the Duke's, who brought him a little money, and a deal of good sense, besides beauty. She was of course a Jacobite, sent help to Prince Charlie, secreted her cousin Lord Lewis, the Lewie Gordon of the ballad[2] in the woods, and fed him and his followers secretly, setting out

1. An eighteenth-century lady's riding coat.
2. Ballad by Alexander Geddes (1737–1802).

with her maids in the night to carry provisions up to the forest, which, while she was preparing them, she persuaded the Laird were for other purposes. Mr Cameron showed us the very spot near Tullochgrue where the rebels were resting when an alarm was given that the soldiers were in pursuit; they had just time to go through the house at Tullochgrue, in at one door and out at the other, and so got off to a different part of the forest, before the little pursuing detachment came up to the fire they had been seated round, the embers of which were still burning.

The Lady Jean, though so fast a friend, could be, highland like, a bitter enemy. She was systematically unkind to the widowed Lady Rachel, whose marriage indeed had been particularly disagreeable, not only to the family but to the people; and she upon every occasion slighted the four young sons of McAlpine's old age, who were some of them younger by a year or two than the Lady Jean's own boys, their nephews. Poor Lady Rachel, not the meekest woman in the world, bore this usage of her children with little placidity. Once after the service in the Church was over she stept up with her fan in her hand to the corner of the kirk yard where all our graves are made, and taking off her high heeled slipper she tapt with it on the stone laid over her husband's remains crying out through her tears, 'Oh McAlpine McAlpine! rise up for ae half hour and see me richted!' She had indeed, poor body, need of some one to act as her protector if all tales be true that were told of the usage she met with. Her sons, however, were honourably assisted by their half nephews, and helped by them all, well on in the world. The Spreckled Laird keeping clear of family disputes, as of public disagreements.

Three sons and two daughters were born to the Spreckled Laird and the Lady Jean; Patrick, called the White Laird from his complexion, always known to us as our uncle Rothy; he married a daughter of Grant of Elchies, a good woman and a pretty one, though nicknamed by the people the yellow *yawling*, their name for the little bird the yellow hammer, because her very pale skin became sallow as her health gave way; they had no children. The second son, William, the Doctor, was my Grandfather. Alexander, the third, and quite his Mother's favourite, with his Gordon name, was a clergyman, married as I think I mentioned to an English Miss Neale. She bore him five sons, who all died before their parents. Grace, the eldest daughter, married Cumming of Logie, Henrietta, the younger, and a great beauty, married Grant of Glenmoriston; both had large families, so that we had highland cousins enough; but of the elder set, all that remained when we were growing up were Mr Cameron, his Wife, and her sister Mary, and our great grand Uncle Captain Lewis.

Mr Cameron, though only a lieutenant, had seen some service; he had been at the battle of Minden,[1] and had very often visited my grandfather in London, who seemed to have been strongly attached to this cousin. I have several of my grandfather's letters to Mr Cameron, charming in themselves from the spirit of benevolence which shines through them, and proving a perfect affection, founded on similarity of disposition, to have existed between them. They were considered to have strongly resembled each other in countenance, person, and manner. If so, my grandfather, with his superadded undoubted abilities, must have been a very irresistible person. Poor Mrs Cameron was nearly blind, worn down too by the afflicting loss of all her children save one, a merchant in Glasgow. Miss Mary, therefore, managed the establishment, a very primitive one, and kept the household from stagnating, as very likely would have been the case had the easy master and mistress been left to conduct the affairs of the Croft.

The Dell was after a very different style, the largest farm of any, but only tenanted by the forester, a handsome, clever, active little man of low degree. He had gained the heart of one much above him, the very pretty daughter of Steuart of Pityoulish, a tacksman on the Gordon property, of some account in the country, who made many a wry face before he could gulp down as a son in law the thriving Duncan McIntosh. The marriage turned out very happy; she was another Mrs Balquhidder for management—such spinnings,

1. 1759, one of the turning points of the
Seven Years' War.

and weavings, and washings, and dyings, and churnings, and yearnings[1] and knittings, and bleachings, and candle makings, and soap boilings, and brewings, and feather cleanings, never were seen or written of even in these days, as went on in those without intermission at the Dell. And this busy guidwife was so quietly gentle, so almost sleepy in manner, one could hardly suppose her capable of thinking of work, much less of doing an amount of actual labour that would have amazed any but a Scotchwoman.

I have written these memoirs so much by snatches, never getting above a few pages done at a time since the idle days of Avranches, that I can't but fear I often repeat myself, so many old recollections keep running through my head when I set about making notes of them, and not always in the order of their occurrence either. The two years and a half we spent in Rothiemurchus after giving up England don't always keep quite clear of the summer visits to the dear old place afterwards, and about dates I am sure I am sometimes incorrect, for there are no memoranda of any sort to guide me, and such a long life to look back through now, the later years passed in such different scenes, I can only hope to give you a general impression of my youth in the highlands. It was well we were so very happy within ourselves, had so large an acquaintance of all ranks of our own people, for except during the autumn months, when we were certainly in a bustle of gaiety, we had very little intercourse with any world beyond our own, having at this time hardly a neighbour even at the great distances we were accustomed to go to them. Up the river there was Kinrara deserted; Mr McPherson Grant, afterwards Sir George, who had succeeded his uncle at Invereschie, never lived there; Kincraig, where dwelt Mr and Mrs McIntosh of Balnespick, we had little intercourse with. They were not rich, had a large family, he was a zealous farmer, and she a very stiff reserved woman. Belleville and Mrs Macpherson were in England, Miss Macpherson in Edinburgh, Clunie and his wife nobody knew. Down the river Castle Grant was shut up, the old General at Ballindalloch dead, and his heir, also the heir of Invereschie, we were never very cordial with, although

1. Old Scots word for rennet, used for cheese-making.

he was married to the sister of Mrs Gillies. Having none, therefore, of our own degree almost to associate with, we were quite thrown upon the *little bodies*, of whom there was no lack both up and down the Spey. They used to come from all parts ostensibly to pay a morning visit, yet always expecting to be pressed to stay to dinner, and even all night. The 'Little Laird,' for so my father was called—in the gaelick Ian Beag[1]—and his 'foreign lady' were great favourites. My Mother, indeed, excelled in her entertainment of this degree of company, acted the highland hostess to perfection, excelled in the conversation suited to her guests, leading it to such topicks as they were most familiar with, as if she had primed herself for the occasion. If they merely paid a visit, she reconducted them on their homeward way, quite like the French of these times, to the door, or the outer door, or the gate according as was necessary. If they staid to dinner, she heaped up their plates with delicacies long after their solemn assurances of being already satisfied and her table was so well provided, her self so handsome at the head of it, they certainly would have been ill to please had they been fault finders.

Betty Campbell used to tell us that at first the people did not like their 'Little Laird' bringing home an English wife. But when they saw her so pretty, so tall! they softened to her; and then when came the chubby boy (for I was not accounted of, my uncle Rothy's deed of Entail cutting me and my sex off from any but a very distant chance of the inheritance), a fine healthy child, born at the Doune, baptized into their own faith, she soon grew into great favour; and when, in addition to all this, she set up wheels in her kitchen, learned to count her hanks, and dye her wool, and bleach her web, 'young creature as she was,' she perfectly delighted them. At this time in the highlands we were so remote from markets we had to depend very much on our own produce for most of the necessaries of life. Our flocks and herds supplied us not only with the chief part of our food, but with fleeces to be wove into clothing, blanketing, and carpets, horn for spoons, leather to be dressed at home for various purposes, hair for

1. E.G. wrote 'beag' as she heard it, 'peck'.

the masons. Lint seed was sown to grow into sheeting, shirting, sacking, etc. My Mother even succeeded in common table linen; there was the 'dambrod' pattern, supposed to be the highland translation of *Dame board* or backgammon,[1] the 'bird's eye,' 'Snowdrop,' 'chain,' and 'single spot,' beyond which neither the skill of old George Ross nor the weaver in Grantown could go. We brewed our own beer, made our own bread, made our own candles; nothing was brought from afar but wine, groceries, and *flour*, wheat not ripening well so high above the sea. And yet we lived in luxury, game was so plentiful, red deer, roe, hares, grouse, ptarmigan, and partridge; the river provided trout and salmon, the different lakes pike and char; the garden quite abounded in common fruits and common vegetables; cranberries and raspberries overran the country, and the poultry yard was ever well furnished. The regular routine of business, where so much was done at home, was really a perpetual amusement. I used to wonder when travellers asked my mother if she did not find her life somewhat dull.

You will now be able to follow us in our daily rambles, to understand the places and the people whom in our walks we went to see. On rainy days we paced about the shrubbery, up the river to the green or west gate, over the Drum, back again to the white gate and so home or out at the white gate and along Tomnahurich to turn at the burn of Aldracardoch. But in fine weather we wandered much further afield, first coaxing Miss Elphick a little further than she liked, and then as her walking powers improved getting her onto great distances, particularly when cooler weather made exercise pleasanter. She soon became interested in our visits to all around, and felt pleasure in yielding to our wishes to have some point as the aim of every journey. Indeed, people high and low were so civil to the odd little woman, she would have been inexcusable had she not met their advances civilly. When we went to Inverdruie we passed the burn at Aldracardoch, over which a picturesque wooden bridge for footpassengers was thrown. The saw mill and the miller's house were close to the road, too close, for the mill when

1. Dambrod is Scots for a draughts board.

going had often frightened horses fording the stream. The miller's name was again McGregor, that dispersed Clan venturing now to resume the name they had been constrained to drop. They had, as was usual on all such occasions, assumed the patronymick of whatever Clan adopted them, remembering always that loved one which was their own. James McGregor's father had been known as Gregor Grant, so the son slid the easier back into that of right belonging to him. The road held on under high banks of fine fir trees, then came the lighter birch, and then a turn brought us to the Lios Mór, a swampy field of some size backed by the forest—the view of which, as he drained it year by year, was so pleasant to the Captain that he had built himself a covered seat among the birch in front of it, which used to be the extent of his walk on a summer's evening. Ten minutes more brought us up a rugged brae and past the offices upon the moor at Inverdruie, in the midst of which bare expanse stood the very ugly house my uncle Rothy had placed there. It was very comfortable within, and the kind welcome, and the pleasant words, and the good cheer we found there, made it always a delight to us to be sent there.

The Captain and Mrs Grant lived in the low parlour to the left of the entrance, within which was a light closet where they slept; the hall was flagged, but a strip of home made carpet covered the centre, of the same pattern as that in the parlour, a check of black and green. The parlour curtain was home made too of linsey woolsey,[1] red and yellow. A good peat fire burned on the hearth; a rug knit by Mrs Grant kept the fireplace tidy. A round mahogany table stood in the middle of the room; a long mahogany table was placed against the wall, with a large japanned tray standing up on end on it; several hair bottomed chairs were ranged all round. A japanned corner cupboard fixed on a bracket at some height from the floor very much ornamented the room, as it was filled with the best tall glasses on their spiral stalks, and some tea china too fine for use. A number of silver edged punch ladles, and two silver edged and silver lined drinking horns were presented to full view on the bottom shelf, and outside

1. Coarse linen fabric.

upon the very top was a large China punch bowl. But the cupboard we preferred was in the wall next the fire. It was quite a pantry; oat cakes, barley scons, flour scons, butter, honey, sweetmeats, cheese, and wine, and spiced whiskey, all came out of the deep shelves of this agreeable recess, as did the great key of the dairy. This was often given to one of us to carry to old Mary the Cook, with leave to see her skim and whip the fine rich cream, which Mrs Grant would afterwards pour on a whole pot of jam and give to us for luncheon. This dish, under the name of 'bainne briste,' or broken milk,[1] is a great favourite wherever it has been introduced, though it somehow eats better in the highlands than in any other part of the world.

In the centre of the ceiling hung a glass globe to attract the flies. Over the chimney piece was the Captain's Armoury, two or three pairs of pistols, safely encased in red flannel bags very dusty from the peats they burned, several swords of different sorts in their scabbards crossed in different patterns, and a dirk or two. On the chimney slab was a most curious collection of snuff boxes of all sorts of shapes and sizes intermixed with a few large foreign shells. The Captain, in a wig, generally sat in a cornered chair with arms to it, never doing any thing that ever I saw. He was old and getting frail, 85 or 86, I believe. Sometimes when he was not well he wore a plaid cloak, and a night cap, red or white, made by his industrious wife in a stitch she called Shepherd's knitting. It was done with a little hook which she manufactured for herself out of the tooth of an old tortoiseshell comb, and she used to go on looping her homespun wool as quick as fingers could move, making not only caps, but drawers and waistcoats for winter wear for the old husband she took such care of. She was always busy when in the house, and out of doors she managed the farm, and drove the Captain out in a little low phaeton I remember my father buying for them in London. Occasionally this first summer they dined with us, and then the old great grand Uncle looked very nice in his best suit. Mrs Grant was really charming, full of highland lore, kind and clever and good, without being either refined

---

1. Following her ear, E.G. wrote 'pagne a priesht'.

or brilliant, and certainly plain in person. She had a fine voice, and sang gaelick airs remarkably well and any Scotch airs indeed but the wild gaelick ballads were her forte. My Mother was extremely attached to this excellent woman, and spent many a morning with her; we used to watch them convoying each other home after their visits, turning and returning upon the Tomnahurich road ever so many times as each lady neared her own premises, wondering which would be first to give in and take final leave of the other. It was my Mother's only walk for she was indolent about exercise and therefore these gossips with her Aunt were of use to her.

It was a good mile beyond Inverdruie to the Dell, and we had to cross five streams of rapid running water to reach it, for into so many channels did the river Druie divide about a couple of miles below the bridge of Coylum. The intervening strips of land were all thickets of birch, alder, hazel, and raspberries, through which the well trodden paths wound leading to the simple bridges of logs without a rail that crossed the water, a single log in all cases but one, where the span being very wide two were laid side by side. We skipped over them better a great deal then than I at least could do it now, but poor Miss Elphick, to get her over the best of them, the one with the two logs, was no easy matter, the others she did not attempt for many a day unless assisted by some of the saw miller's lads who abounded in this neighbourhood and obligingly waded the water by her side. One day we had a charming adventure on Druie side; just as we were preparing to cross one of the single logs an old woman in a high crowned cap, a blanket plaid, and a bundle on her back, stept on it on the opposite side. We were generally accompanied in our walks by an immense Newfoundland dog called Neptune, an especial favourite whose particular business it was to guard the garden where he lived in a very pretty wooden house in the midst of flowers. Neptune happened to be marching in front and knowing his way as well as we did, proceeded to cross the log. On he stept, so did the old woman, gravely moved the dog, and quietly came on the old woman, till they met in the middle where both stood still. To pass was impossible, to turn back on that narrow footway equally difficult; there they stood, the old woman in considerable uncertainty. The dog made up his mind more quickly, he very quietly pushed the old woman out of his way. Down she fell into the river, and on he passed as if nothing extraordinary had happened. She was a good old creature, just as much amused as we were, and laughed as heartily, and she spread the fame of Neptune far and near, for every body had the story before the day was over. Miss Elphick and her sawmiller got over in safety that morning, but on another occasion, the first time she tried to cross alone, both she and Mary, who was leading her, lost their balance and got well ducked. The leading was a foolish plan, the free use of the arm being necessary to the balance.

The Dell was an ugly place, a small low house, only two or three stunted trees in the garden behind it, and a wide, sandy, stony plain all round, never a bit the more fertile for the regular inundation at the Lammas tide when the Druie always overflowed its banks. A narrow passage ran through the house from which on the one side opened the kitchen and the spare bedroom; on the other the family room and the parlour into which most melancholy state apartment we were always ushered. Over head were two garrets, one for children the other for servants, lighted by small windows in the gables. Here the first lairds of Rothiemurchus had lived after a fashion that must have been of the simplest. It then became the jointure house, and in it the Lady Jean passed her widowhood with a few fields and a hundred pounds a year. Mrs McIntosh was a tidy guidwife, cleaner than the generality of her country women, but she was nothing beyond the thriving farmer's helpmeet. She had no curtains in her best parlour, nor any furniture except a large dining table and some chairs, and a square of carpet in the middle of the room. She and her husband lived either in the kitchen or in their bedroom, and each in their own department quite did the work of a head servant. The cheer she offered us was never more than bread and cheese and whiskey, but the oaten bread was so fresh and crisp, the butter so delicious, and the cheese—not the ordinary skimmed milk curd, the leavings of the dairy, but the Saturday's kebbock[1] made of the overnight

1. Home-made cheese, sometimes made from a mixture of ewe and cow milk.

and the morning's milk, poured cream and all into the yearning tub. The whiskey was a bad habit, there was certainly too much of it going. At every house it was offered, at every house it must be tasted or offence would have been given, so we were all taught to believe. I am sure now that had we steadily refused compliance with so incorrect a custom on the real proper ground of its unsuitableness, it would have been far better for ourselves, and might all the sooner have put an end to so pernicious a habit among the people.

Whiskey drinking was and is the bane of that country; from early morning till late at night an eternal dram drinking was for ever going. Decent gentlewomen, Mrs Cameron of the Croft, for instance, always began the day with a dram. Whiskey was presented to every visitor of every degree. In our house the bottle of whiskey, with its accompaniment of a silver salver full of small glasses, was placed on the side table with cold meat every morning. In the pantry a bottle of whiskey was the allowance per day, with bread and cheese in any required quantity, for such messengers or visitors whose errands sent them in to that direction. The very poorest cottages could offer whiskey. The floaters, indeed, all the men engaged in the wood manufacture, drank it in goblets three times a day, yet except at a merry making we never saw any one tipsy. We children were extremely fond of the tastes we got every where, particularly when the dram was well spiced and sweetened, but most assuredly it was not good for us though the quantity we took at a time was but small.

We sometimes spent an evening at the Dell. Duncan McIntosh played admirably on the violin, he was a second Neil Gow for all lively musick, it was quite delightful to dance to it. Many a happy hour we have reeled away both at the Doune and at the Dell, servants and all included in the company, with that one untiring violin for our orchestra.

A walk to the Croft led us quite in another direction. We generally went to the white gate, and through the new garden on to the Milltown muir past Peter the Pensioner's wooden house, and then climbing over the railing wandered on among the birch woods till we reached the gate at the Lochan Mór; that passed, we got into the fir wood, refreshed ourselves in the proper season with blaeberries and cranberries, then climbing another fence re-entered the birch wood in the midst of which nestled the two cottages called the Croft. A few very small fields surrounded the houses separated by innumerable wooded knolls breaking the ground into beautiful bits of wild scenery and a little burn leaped down from a rocky height to wander away along a green holm where there was generally to be seen a bleaching. The cottages were not adjoining; the upper one connected with the farm offices was the dwelling of the family, the lower and newer one at a little distance was for strangers. Old Mrs Cameron, who was by this time nearly blind, sat beside the fire in a bonnet and shawl as if ready for walking, never occupied, talking little, but sighing a great deal. Miss Mary bustled about in her way of managing, kind as her nature would let her be, for hospitable or generous she was not; there was little fear of our getting a Saturday's kebbock at the Croft or a bowl of cream for our cranberry jam, a little honey with a barley scon was the extent of Miss Mary's liberality. Curtains or carpet or a cushioned chair none of them would have valued. They had always a good fire and a kind welcome for the Laird's children and that satisfied us for we liked going to see them, and when Mr Cameron was not too busy with his farm and could stay within and play on the Jew's harp to us, we were quite happy. He played more readily and better at the Doune, the tender airs which suited the instrument affecting his poor melancholy wife, of whom he was passionately fond. He was a constant guest at the Doune, dining with us at the least three times a week, but no weather ever prevented his returning to the old wife at night; well wrapped in his plaid he braved wind, rain, hail or snow, walking his two or three miles in the dark winter evening as if he had been six and thirty instead of seventy six. He was thoroughly a gentleman; no better specimen of a highlander and a soldier ever adorned our mountains. Old and young, gentle and simple, all loved Mr Cameron—how he had seen so much of the bitter of life could hardly be explained, perhaps he had suffered from an over softness of disposition. His pretty cousin fell in love with him and he married her. She disliked his profession and he gave it up. Their numerous children were spoiled as infants and died young, all but one who failed in every undertaking.

Poor my father took care he should not be, for he made him his Factor. In addition to the salary of this office, he had a lieutenant's halfpay and his farm at a very reasonable rate. He and Mrs Grant, Inverdruie, were two flowers in the wilderness; other society could well be dispensed with when theirs was attainable. There was a charm in their very simplicity, in their ignorance of what we call the world. A strength in their natural acuteness, in the use they made of their good common sense which must have been more satisfactory to those capable of appreciating them than any amount of more brilliant yet more everyday characteristics.

Almost all my Stories of the olden time were learned either at Inverdruie or the Croft. They never wearied of telling what I never wearied of listening to. John Grant of Achnahatnich was also one of the chroniclers of the past, but he never interested me so much in his more fanciful stories as did my old Aunt and my old Cousin in their more apparently accurate relations. They may have insinuated a little more pride of race than was exactly suited to the 'opening day,' yet it did no harm so far as I was concerned, and the younger ones had no turn for these antiquities  There was never one highland feeling either in John or Mary. Jane in childhood was more taken up with the scenery than the people. William solely occupied with the idea of future power. All was to be some day his and that was sufficient to him. Little as they suspected it, I was the dreamer, could have been the Bard to the family as far as love for the race and a knowledge of their deeds could have qualified a candidate.

# CHAPTER TWELVE

# 1812–1813

THE small farms in Rothiemurchus lay all about in various directions, most of them beautifully situated; the extent of the old forest was always said to be 16 square miles, and it was reckoned that near ten more was growing up, either of natural fir, or my father's planted larch. The whole lay in the bosom of the Grampians in a bend of a bow, as it were, formed by the mountains, the river Spey being the string and our boundary. The mountains are bare, not very picturesquely shaped, yet imposing from their size. Many Glens run up through them all richly carpeted with sweet grass peculiarly suited to the fattening of cattle, one or two of these ending in a lake dropt at the bottom of a skreen of precipices. One pass, that of Lairig Ghru, leads to Braemar, Lord Fife's country, with whose lands and the Duke of Gordon's, ours march in that direction. Several rapid streams run through the forest, the smaller burnies rattling along their rocky course to join the larger, which in their turn flow on to be lost in the Spey. The Luineag and the Beanaidh are quite rivers, the one rises north from Loch Morlich in Glenmore, the other south from Loch Einich in Glen Einich; they join just above the bridge of Coylum and form the Druie, an unmanageable run of water that divides, subdivides, sometimes changes its principal channel and keeps a fine plain of many acres in a state of stony wilderness. The vagaries of the Druie were not alone watched with anxiety by the Crofters on its bank. There was a tradition that it had broken from its old precincts on the transference of the property to the Grants from the Shawes, that the Grants would thrive while the Druie was tranquil, but when it wearied of its new channel and returned to its former course, the fortunes of the new family would fail. The change happened in the year 1829, at the time of the great

Lammas floods so well described, not by our pleasant friend Tom Lauder, but by a much greater man, Sir Thomas Dick Lauder of Fountainhall, the Grange, and Relugas, author of Lochandhu and the Wolf of Badenoch! We used to laugh at the prediction in our unthinking days.[1]

Besides the streams, innumerable lakes lay hid among the pine trees of that endless forest. On one of these was the small island completely occupied by the ruins of the Comyn fortress, a low building with one square tower, a flank wall with a door in it and one or two small windows high up, and a sort of house with a gable end, attached, part of which stood on piles. The people said there was a zigzag causeway beneath the water, from the door of the old castle to the shore, the secret of which was always known to three persons only. We often tried to hit upon this causeway, but we never succeeded. A great number of paths crossed the forest, and one or two cart roads; the robbers' road at the back of Loch an Eilein, 'the lake of the island,' was made by Rob Roy for his own convenience when out upon his cattle raids, and a decayed fir tree was often pointed out to us as the spot where Laird James, the Spreckled Laird, occasionally tied a bullock or two when he heard of such visitors in the country; they were of course driven away and never seen again, but the Laird's own herds were never touched. It has been the fashion of late to father all moss trooping throughout the highlands on Rob Roy, but there was a Macpherson nearer to us, and a Mackintosh equally clever at the gathering of gear—Mackintosh of Borlam, of whom I shall have a tale to tell anon.

In a country of such remarkable beauty, and with so many objects of interest and legends of interest to add to the mere pleasure of exercise, our long walks became delightful even to such a Cockney as Miss Elphick. She was a clever woman, she soon came to appreciate all the worth of her new

---

1. Sir Thomas Dick Lauder (1784–1848) was a close friend whose literary reputation has not survived. The description tion she refers to is *An Account of the Great Floods of August 1829 in the Province of Moray and Adjoining Districts*. It does not mention Rothiemurchus.

situation. She actually studied up to it, and though an innate vulgarity never left her, the improvement in her ideas was very perceptible. She corresponded occasionally with her only surviving sister, a poor little woman who kept a day school at Teddington and regularly with a Mr Somebody, a Builder. When she became more sociable with her pupils she used to read to us her letters descriptive of the savage land she had got into, and what was worse for us, she recounted this and every other adventure of the like kind she had ever had, love adventures of course. What English girl of her age and class was ever without a whole string of them, told to every acquaintance I believe as the fittest subject of conversation. No beauty, no heiress, ever had been the heroine of more romances than had fallen to the share of this little bundle of a body, by her own account. It never entered our young heads to doubt the catalogue. Mr Thomas Herbert's replies did not come very frequently from the beginning, neither were they very long, nor were such parts as we were favoured with very loving, and by degrees they ceased. She did most of the writing and really I remember now her description of our first *kirk* Sunday was both cleverly and truthfully and very amusingly told; it must certainly have astonished a Londoner.

The unadorned but neat small kirk is very different now, when hardly any one sits in it, from what it was then, when filled to overflowing.[1] It was very much out of repair; neither doors nor windows fitted, the plaister fallen from the roof lay in heaps about the seats, the walls were rough, the graveyard overgrown with nettles, even the path from the gate was choked with weeds in many places and in others was worn, over the sods that were laid upon the dead. Far from there being any ceremony about this highland style of worship, there was hardly even decency, so rude were all the adjuncts of our Sermon Sunday. Mr Stalker was dead—the good man who drank so many cups of tea, whom my wicked Aunt Mary

1. This difference between the later Free Church and
   E.G.'s Church of Scotland was celebrated in the rhyme:
   The wee Kirk, the Free Kirk/The Kirk wi'out the
   steeple/The auld Kirk, the cauld Kirk/The Kirk
   wi'out the people.

used to go on helping to more, cup after cup, till one evening they counted nine, always pressing another on him by repeating that his regular number was three! It was a luxury that probably in those dear times the poor Dominie seldom could afford to give himself at home, for there was a wife and children, and his income must have been economically managed to bring them all through the year. He had £5 from Queen Anne's bounty, a house and garden and a field and £10 from my father, and he taught the school. My Mother got the wife £4 additional for teaching sewing, which they hailed as a perfect godsend. I suppose the people were all kind to them, made them little presents. He was gone, and he had not been replaced, so we had sermon only every third Sunday in our own Kirk. The devout attended the neighbouring parishes on the blank days, some of the kirks being at no great distance, speaking highlandly, two to five or six miles and indeed for all they heard in our own, it was hardly worth coming so far as some did to listen in it.

Good Mr Peter of Duthil was gone, he had died in the winter. His Widow and her school removed to Inverness, and another Grant had succeeded him, for of course the patronage was very faithfully kept in the Clan. The new minister was a perfect contrast to his predecessor; he was fat, thickset, florid, with a large cauliflower wig on his large head. Within the head was more learning than may be half a dozen professors could boast of among them, but it was not in the divinity line. His turn was acutely satirical; he had been both a poet and an essayist, what he was now it would be hard to say; he seemed to have no particular employment; his wife managed the Glebe, the parishes managed themselves, and he certainly gave himself little trouble about his sermons. What he did in gaelick I cannot say; in English he had but two, although he altered the texts to give them an air of variety. The text did not always suit the discourse, but that was no matter. The sermons were by no means bad, though from constant repetition they grew tiresome; it was lucky we had six weeks to forget each of them in. One was against an undue regard for the vanities of life, and always contained this sentence: 'Behold the lilies of the valley they toil not neither do they spin yet Solomon in all his glory was not arrayed like one of those.' The other was on Charity and the 13th Chapter of the 1st Epistle to the Corinthians was all of it dextrously interwoven with the various divisions of the subject. A violent Tory, detesting the House of Hanover, yet compelled to pray for the reigning family, he cut the business as short as possible—'God bless the King, and all the Royal Family; as thou hast made them great make them GOOD,' with great emphasis, and then he hurried on to more agreeable petitions, all, sermon and prayer and psalm appearing to be a task to him that he was just getting through. Yet he was liked. On the day he was expected, the people began gathering early, forming little knots moving slowly on, visiting sometimes by the way, always stopping to have a talk with passing friends. The Kirk was very near our house, on a height in the field below the Drum, prettily sheltered by planting, and commanding from the gate a fine view of the valley of the Spey. The Bell tolled from time to time, and as the hour for the service approached the crowd began to pour in from either side, the white caps and the red plaids gleaming through the birch woods on the bank between the kirk field and the Drum, through which the path lay. Our farm people moved up from the low grounds to join them, and such of the house servants as understood the gaelick. The rest followed us an hour or more afterwards to the English portion of the Ceremony.

I think the gaelick service began with a psalm, then a long prayer, then a sermon, then a prayer again and then another psalm, during the singing of which, accompanied by the toll of the bell, the Laird's family entered the Kirk. We generally walked from the house along the flowdyke by the only piece of the backwater left, under the shade of natural alder to the right and a thriving plantation of larch to the left; a small gate painted green opened on the road to the west lodge; we had to cross it into the field and then step up the long slope to the kirk yard. My father opened the gate to let my mother pass; Miss Elphick next, we three according to our ages followed. Then he went in himself. We sat in a long pew facing the pulpit, with two seats, one in front for the Laird, and one behind for his servants. There was a wooden canopy over it with a carved frieze all round and supporting pillars flat but fluted, and with Ionick capitals like moderate ram's horns. McAlpine's seat was at the end, nothing to mark it but his scutcheon on a shield; the Captain, his surviving son, sat there. My father would not have moved him from it for the world. There were 160 years between the birth of that father and the death of that son, more than five generations. It is near 200 years now since Annie Need's grandfather was born. The Captain did not set his feet upon the Shawe—the Spreckled Laird had taken advantage of some repairs proceeding to move that ill used carse once more. He did not dare to lay it by the dust of his Ancestors, he buried it close to the kirk, very slightly raised above the mould and with a plain flat stone upon it. How they came there who could say but as by magick—four chiselled stones rose at each corner of the grave, in shape, be it said reverently, not unlike Stilton cheeses and about that size and the sough[1] ran that while they there kept watch, no evil would happen to Rothiemurchus. If they disappeared woe was approaching: not a soul in the country but firmly believed in the fulfilment of this prophesy, not one but turned to the Shawe's grave every Sunday when they passed it. I looked on it regularly, old and time worn it was, no inscription on it, no workmanship, nothing but the four guardian stones to mark the resting place of the last of an old brave race, numerous still as a name, but without a Chief.

The stir consequent on our entrance was soon hushed, and the minister gave out the psalm; he put a very small dirty volume up to one eye, for he was near sighted and feeble sighted and read as many lines of the old version of the rhythmical paraphrase (we may call it) of the Psalms of David as he thought fit, drawling them out in a sort of sing song that was very strange. He stooped over the pulpit to hand his little book to the precentor, who then rose and calling out aloud the tune—'the St. George's tune,' 'Auld Aberdeen,' 'hondred an' fifteen,' etc.—began himself a recitative of the first line on the key note, then taken up and repeated by the congregation; line by line he continued in the same fashion, thus doubling the length of the *exercise*, for really to some it was no play—serious severe screaming quite

1. Sound of the wind, hence rumour or gossip.

beyond the natural pitch of the voice, a wandering search after the air by many who never caught it, a flourish really, of difficult execution and plenty of the *tremolo* lately come into fashion with the tenor singers in particular. The dogs seized this occasion to bark, for they always came to the kirk with the rest of the family, and the babies to cry. When the minister could bear the din no longer he popt up again, again leaned over, touched the precentor's head, and instantly all sound ceased. The long prayer began. Every body stood up while the minister asked for us such blessings as he thought best: with closed eyes it should have been, that being a part of the 'rubrick'; our oddity of a parson closed but one, the one with which he had squinted at the Psalm book, some affection of the other eyelid rendering it unmanageable. The prayer over, the sermon began; that was my time for making my observations, 'Charity' and 'Solomon's Lilies' soon requiring no further attention.

Few save our own people sat around; old gray haired rough visaged men that had known my grandfather and great grandfather, black, red, and fairer hair, belonging to such as were in the prime of life, younger men, lads, boys—all in the tartan. The plaid as a wrap, the plaid as a drapery, with kilt to match on some, blue trews on others, blue jackets on all, that was the style of the male part of the assemblage. The women were plaided too, an outside shawl was seen on none, though the wives wore a large handkerchief underneath the plaid, and looked picturesquely matronly in their very high white caps. A bonnet was not to be seen among them, no young highland girl ever covered her head; the girls wore their own hair neatly braided in the front, plaited up in Grecian fashion behind, and bound by the snood, a bit of velvet or ribbon placed rather low on the forehead and tied beneath the plait at the back. The wives were all in homespun, homedyed linsey woolsey gowns, covered to the chin by the modest kerchief worn outside the gown. The girls who could afford it had a sabbath day's gown of like manufacture and very bright colours, but the throat was more exposed, and generally ornamented by a string of beads, often amber or a bit of black ribbon. Some had to be content with the best blue flannel petticoat and a clean white jacket, their ordinary and most becoming dress, and few of these had either shoes or stockings; but all had the plaid, and they folded it round them very gracefully. They had a custom in the spring of washing their beautiful hair with a decoction of the young buds of the birch trees, a cleanly habit at any rate. Whether it improved or hurt the hair I really do not know, but it most agreeably scented the kirk, which at other times was wont to be overpowered by the combined odours of snuff and peatreak, for the men snuffed up an immensity during the delivery of the English sermon; they fed their noses with quills fastened by strings to the lids of their mulls, spooning up the snuff in quantities and without waste, none ever dropping by the way. The old women snuffed too, and groaned a great deal, expressive this of their mental sufferings, their grief for all the backslidings supposed to be thundered at from the pulpit; lapses from faith was their grand self accusation, lapses from virtue were, alas, little commented on, perhaps because they were too common among them; temperance in man, and in woman chastity are not in the Highland code of morality.

The sermon over, the concluding prayer, a thanksgiving, brought us all to our feet again. Another psalm, then the blessing and a general bow to the pulpit ended the whole. After a pause we all dispersed—but I am forgetting the Collection. This was made just after the second psalm when every one, excepting such as were to receive an alms, put in an alms however small the amount—halfpence was the coin most frequently dropt into the oblong box with half a lid and a long handle carried round to every individual. The Captain and Mrs Grant put in pennies, so did Mr Cameron and our upper servants, so did the minister. We were always each given a sixpence for this purpose, my Mother gave a shilling and my father some unknown sum written on a bit of paper, in value I suppose equal to all the rest that was there. Who ever had the keeping of this fund, and it is strange that I should forget who this was, carefully preserved these bits of paper—my father redeemed them at the proper time, the beginning of winter when the gatherings of the year were divided in just proportions among all who wanted help. This was the way we provided for our poor before we were provided with poor laws. The dispersion of the crowd was a pretty sight, taking into account the landscapes, such picturesque groups filled with life—you must remember our own Sundays there and the scattering of the small flock the free kirk had left. The year I write of dreamed of no free kirk doings,[1] the full kirk near filled the field, so many groups, filing off north, south, east and west, up the steep narrow road to the Drum, by the path through the bank of birchwood to the garden gate, along the green meadow beneath the guigne trees to the Doune farm offices—the servants by the green gate under the crooked beech tree to the house; the family, after shaking hands and speaking and bowing and smiling all round, returning by the flowdyke and the alders as they went. The minister dined with us, and thus ended our Sunday, but not our acquaintance with him. We got very much to like this strangely eccentrick man. His head was so well filled, and his heart, in spite of the snarl, so kindly, that old and young we took a fancy to him, and often prevailed on him to spend a few days with us. He was a disappointed man, equal to a much, or rather I should say to a very different, position, and he was lost in the manse of Duthil, far from any mind capable of understanding his, and not fitted by inclination or principles to go actively through the duties of his calling.

Far different, yet no truer or better divine, in one sense of the word, was his neighbour, our prime favourite, the Minister of Abernethy, known through all the country as Parson John. He was a little merry man, fond of good eating, very fond of good drinking, no great hand at a sermon, but a capital hand at either the filling or the emptying of a bowl of punch. He was no scholar; his brother of Duthil used to wonder how ever he got through the University, he had so little skill in the humanities—of learning. For good practical sense, honesty of purpose, kindness of heart, tender feeling combined with energetick action, Parson John could hardly have been surpassed. He found his parish a nest of smugglers,

1. It was with the Disruption of 1843, when 470 of the
   1,200 ministers of the Church of Scotland seceded, that
   the Free Church of Scotland was founded.

cattle stealers, idlers, every species of immorality rife in it. He left it filled by the best conducted set of people in the country. He was all the more respected for the strictness of his discipline, yet a sly joke against the minister was much relished by his flock. There was no very deep religious feeling in the highlands up to this time. The clergy were properly reverenced in their capacity of pastors without this respect extending to their persons unless fully merited by propriety of conduct. The established form of faith was determinately adhered to, but the *kittle questions*,[1] which had so vexed the puritanick south, had never yet troubled the minds of their northern neighbours. Our mountains were full of fairy legends, old Clan tales, forebodings, prophecies, and other superstitions, quite as much believed in as the Bible. The shorter catechism and the fairy stories were mixed up somehow together to form the innermost faith of the highlander, a much gayer and less metaphysical character than his Saxon tainted countryman. Parson John therefore suited his parishioners, none the worse for his occasional lapses from the dignity befitting his station.

The other clergyman of our acquaintance was Mr McDonald of Alvie, our nearest neighbour of the three. He was a clever worldly man, strictly decorous, not unfriendly, although most careful in his management, particular in ascertaining the highest price of meal, his stipend depending on the fluctuation of the market, the ministers being paid in kind, so many 'bolls of victual'—meaning corn.[2] He preached well, rather at length perhaps, and made very fervent tiresome prayers and immensely long graces, and of all people in the world he was detested most heartily by our friend the minister of Duthil; his very name was an abomination, why we could never make out. He had been married twice, in neither case happily, both wives having become invalids. It never struck any one that the situation of his manse, nearly surrounded by water, could have affected the health of women not naturally strong. The second Mrs McDonald was

1. Intractable.
2. Approximately six imperial bushels amounted to one
   boll of corn, 48 gallons overall.

dying at this time. We often sent her delicacies, but never saw her; indeed, we never saw any of the parsons' wives, they seemed to keep quietly at home, like Mrs Balquhidder, 'making the honey.' We heard, however, plenty of the wife of Parson John, an excellent, managing woman, who kept her husband in great order. They had a large family of children, the bolls of victual were not many, and the glebe lands were small. She had to keep her eyes open, and water the ash tree betimes in the morning. One of her most prolifick sources of income was her dairy. She piqued herself on what she made of it, and was accused by the minister of a very economical use of its produce in the house, in order to send the more to market. Now, of all simple refreshments Parson John loved best a drink of fine milk, well coated with cream; this luxury his wife denied him, the cream must go into the churn, the skimmed milk was the fittest for the thirsty. In spite of her oft repeated refusals and her well hidden key she suspected that the minister privately contrived to visit the dairy, sundry cogues of set milk at sundry times having the appearance of being broken into. She determined to watch; and she had not long to wait before she detected the culprit in the act, met him face to face in the passage as he closed the door. She stoutly charged him with his crime, he as stoutly denied his guilt, hard words passed; but the poor minister! he had on his hat, he had forgotten to take it off, he had put his mouth to the cogue, the brim of the hat had touched the cream—there it was fringed with her treasure! Before her eyes, an evidence of his crime, and he denying it! What Highland wife could bear such atrocity. 'Man,' said the daughter of Dalachapple, ten acres of moor without a house on it, 'how daur ye! before the Lord! and you his graceless minister! see there!' He told the story himself, with remarkable humour, over the punchbowl, when Mrs Grant was not by.

The Captain had another story of him which used to be told to us by his Mrs Grant. His sermons were mostly practical, he was unskilled in scholastick learning. Sometimes when he had gone his round of moral duties he would, for 'lack of matter,' treat his congregation to a screed from the papers. They were very stirring times, revolutions and battle by sea and land. The minister was a keen politician, his people by no means unwilling to hear the news, although they very earnestly shook their heads after listening to it. False intelligence was as largely circulated then as now, it came and it spread, and it was then to be contradicted. The parson gave it as he got it, and one Sunday delivered a marvellous narrative of passing events. Finding out his errour during the week, he hastened honestly to correct it. So, on the following Sunday, after the psalm and the prayer and the solemn giving out of the text, he raised his hands and thus addressed his flock, 'My brethren, it was a' lies I told you last Sabbath day.' How the Minister of Duthil enjoyed this story! It was nuts and walnuts to him!

I will now go back to our every day and introduce the rest of our acquaintance as we meet with them. The first incident that comes back on memory is the death of old George Ross, not the gardener, the henwife's husband. He was not so very old a man but he had never been a strong one and, catching cold, inflammation came on; a bottle of whiskey, or may be more, failed to cure him, so he died, and was waked, after the old fashion shaved and partly dressed and set up in his bed, all the country side collecting round him. After an abundance of refreshments the company set to dancing, when, from the jolting of the floor, I suppose, out tumbled the corpse into the midst of the reel, and away scampered the guests screaming and running about the farm yard declaring the old man had come to life again. As the bereaved wife had not been the gentlest of helpmates, this was generally supposed to be a warning—of what however was not declared; all that was plain was that the spirit of the deceased was dissatisfied. Some of the spectators had seen his eyes roll, his hand raised, his head shake. Many extraordinary signs were spoken of, Caroline the French girl told us, for she heard a great deal more than we did from being so much with my Mother's maid.

Before winter we heard of the death of our cousin Patrick Grant of Glenmoriston, while walking on the banks of his own beautiful river, of disease of the heart, which complaint is an heirloom in our family. I learned a great lesson from this event. Some one told it to me, and I, all unthinking, and very sorry, for Patrick had been very kind to us, went straight to the drawing room with my sad news. My Mother immediately went off into hystericks, was carried to bed, and lost her baby; all which was represented to me by my father as a consequence of my extreme want of consideration. I was to remember never in future to tell any ill tidings to any one suddenly, but in particular not to married ladies who were frequently in a condition to be seriously injured by having their nerves startled. I had no nerves then (like the famous Duchess of Marlborough),[1] and could not myself comprehend the misery caused by their derangement. I wish I could say the same now. I was very much grieved at my thoughtlessness, however, and with many tears promised to be for ever more cautious in all cases. We had none of us had an idea that another baby was expected and the affliction in the Schoolroom was quite distressing at the disappointment—for a day.

The next death was the Shawe. He was not the lineal heir of the old race, he was descended collaterally from a former Chief of the ruined Clan, of whose once large possessions nothing now remained but the little farm of Dalnavert on Speyside. It was on the long meadow there that the Volunteers were so frequently exercised, Mr Shawe having a commission in the Regiment. He was the Major, and, for so old a man, a good officer. He had served in the line in his youth. When we went to the Reviews we always called at the house of Dalnavert, a mere black peat bothy, no better outside than the common huts of the same material, already falling into disuse about the country. It was larger, for it contained three rooms, each of which had a window of four panes, not made to open, however; and it had two chimneys, or rather only one chimney and two chimney tops, open wooden ones, for the kitchen fire place was as usual, a stone on the floor and a hole in the roof. Between the parlour and the bedroom a chimney stalk was built. Both these rooms too were wainscotted, so that they looked neat within and were

1. A reference to her astonishing ability to survive in the complicated political conditions ten years either side of 1700.

extremely warm. It was the old house that had come down with the few fields around it to this only survivor of his Line, and he would not change it. He had one child, a daughter married away from him to a half pay Captain of marines, the son of a Schoolmaster up in Badenoch, and one sister near his own age who lived with him. She it was that presented my mother with the sugared whiskey, giving her the same spoon she herself had more than tasted with, and which dose my Mother escaped by preferring her whiskey plain. Well, Major Shawe died, and was buried with military honours, in the kirk yard of Rothiemurchus, by the side of 'them that went before him,' up close to the graves of the Grants, just outside the wall enclosing our ancestors. The Invereschie and Rothiemurchus Companies formed a very imposing part of the funeral procession, the body being borne in the midst of the soldiers, and a volley fired over the grave. My father had a neat stone slab on four short pillars placed over it afterwards with a short inscription, and so ended this ancient feud—a lesson and a sad one. I never could see any of the Shawe's descendants, in the lowly state to which they were then reduced without an uneasy feeling, although when the male heirs were gone, the highlanders consider all gone, females being of no account with them, Chieftainships not being transmissible through daughters.

Miss Jean Shawe did not long survive her brother; when she died the niece and her husband, Captain and Mrs Clarke, left the farm they had rented at Invernahavon and came with their large and wonderfully handsome family to Dalnavert, where they built a small stone and lime house, and from their connexion with Belleville! the old Shawe blood raised its head a bit. A change indeed was coming over the old feudal feelings. Belleville was the son of Ossian, of the Mr Macpherson who pretended to translate Ossian, and made a fine fortune out of the Nabob of Arcot's debts. Who this Macpherson was I do not rightly know. A lad of parts, however, though of very lowly birth, not even a little farmer's son.[1] His sister was married to the Schoolmaster Clarke,

1. James Macpherson (1736–96) began the controversy with his publication in 1760 of his *Fragments of*

whose son, the marine, married the Shawe's daughter. Ossian Macpherson, highland to the very heart, helped his sister, educated her son, bought land around his birth place, and built the fine house on the heights near Kingussie, which for many a year looked so bleak, and so bare, and so staring, while the planting on the hill sides was young and is now really improving, rising from the shelter of skreens of hard wood overlooking the plain and backed by mountains. He never married. But he had four acknowledged children brought up most carefully. To his eldest son, James, our friend, he left his large estates in land. The second, Charles, he sent to the Civil Service in India, where he died. His two daughters he portioned handsomely. Our Belleville, who had also been in India, returned to take possession of his highland property about the year 1800. He married the summer my sister Mary was born, and brought a young Edinburgh wife home to the two London sisters, none of the three very particularly easy to live with. Juliet Macpherson, the youngest sister, very pretty and very clever, soon provided another home for herself, she married Dr, afterwards Sir David Brewster.[1] The more intractable Anne continued to battle on through many a long year of struggle against the somewhat despotick authority of her sister in law, till not very lately her brother died, and she herself became the Lady Belleville, when she certainly repaid with usury the slights of former days.

Ossian had left his affairs in some confusion. He had got entangled in several lawsuits and there was some claim made against him by the Directors. Our Belleville inherited many vexations, knowing little of business he left it too much to his

---

*Ancient Poetry Collected in the Highlands*. Although doubts were expressed about their authenticity, thanks to the patronage of the Prime Minister Lord North, he continued in public life and in 1781 was appointed Agent for Mohammed Ali, Nabob of Arcot; this post was both the source of his fortune and the explanation of the East India Company Directors' legal actions against him.

1. Sir David Brewster (1781-1868) was knighted for his services to science in 1831.

different Law Agents. Believing his resources inexhaustible he lived ostentatiously—open house—a crowd of servants—handsome equipages—and tours of pleasure. A thunderclap at his elbow would have startled him less than the announcement received by post the morning that his accompt at his banker's had been overdrawn. Often in our confidential conversations of after times, Mrs Macpherson described the effect of this shock on her husband—his amazement, his horrour, his despair, the difficulty of rousing him to meet his position. But it was done—and both putting their shoulders at once to the wheel they were set agoing again after some years of comparative poverty. They gave up Belleville, let the farm, shut up the house, sold the stock, and thus furnished with small funds, removed to a lodging in the neighbourhood of London, where in two or three rooms with one highland maid they watched the unravelling of their tangled skeins. Almost all their law difficulties were over in this year I am writing of. They had returned to Belleville before the winter to practise the most severe economy, he to farm, she to save, and thus to try again to get their heads above water. From this time they were our kindest neighbours, living like ourselves, winter and summer, in our highland homes. We became mutually dependant on the resources of each other; never a shadow of disagreement came between us. Upon us young people, the intimacy had a most favourable effect. Belleville, though a weak man, was thoroughly a gentleman, his tastes were refined, his desultary reading extensive, his kindness unfailing. There was a harshness in the character of Mrs Macpherson that we could have wished to soften; her uncompromising integrity was applied to weaker vessels sternly. Her activity, and her energy, and her industry, all admirably exerted in her own sphere of duties, rose up against any tolerance of the shortcomings in these respects of less vigorous temperaments. She measured all by her own rigid rules, her religious feelings partaking of this asperity. She was her own sister to old Mause in the strength and the acrimony of her puritanism.[1] I used so to wish

1. An old lady of severe principle in Allan Ramsay's *The Gentle Shepherd* (1725).

her to say to herself, 'God be merciful to me, a sinner.' But she had no idea then that there was a doubt of her being justified. She was right in principle, though ungentle, and so unchristian, in practice. She had learned no better in the house of her odious Mother. And this fault apart, a better woman never existed, anxious to help all around her of all degrees. She had a clear understanding, good quick abilities, and a warm heart. We owed much in many ways to Mrs Macpherson, and we ended the year with her, my father and Mother, and Jane and I, spending the Christmas new style with these good neighbours. We ourselves, who did every thing highland fashion, always kept the old style at home.

We had three harvest homes to keep in Rothiemurchus: a very small affair indeed at the Croft; a luncheon in the parlour for us children only, and a view of the barn prepared for the dinner and dance to the servants. It was a much merrier meeting at the Dell; my father and mother and all of us, stuffed into the carriage, or on it, drove there to dinner, which was served in the best parlour, my father at the head of the table, Duncan McIntosh at the foot, and those for whom there was not room at the principal board went with at least equal glee to a side table. There was always broth, mutton boiled and roasted, fowls, muirfowl—three or four pair in a dish—apple pie and rice pudding, such jugs upon jugs of cream. Cheese, oatcakes and butter; thick bannocks of flour instead of wheaten bread, a bottle of port, a bottle of sherry, and after dinner no end to the whiskey punch. In the kitchen was all the remains of the sheep, more broth, more mutton, haggis, head and feet singed, puddings black and white, a pile of oaten cakes, a kit of butter, two whole cheeses, one tub of sowans,[1] another of curd, whey and whiskey in plenty. The kitchen party, including any servants from house or farm that could be spared so early from the Croft, the Doune, or Inverdruie, dined when we had done, and we ladies, leaving the gentlemen to more punch, took a view of the

1. Oats and meal steeped in water for a week until sour, when they are strained; the jelly-like liquor is left to ferment and separate; the solid matter is sowans.

kitchen festivities before retiring to the bed chamber of Mrs McIntosh to make the tea. When the gentlemen joined us the parlour was prepared for dancing. With what extasies we heard the first sweep of that masterly bow across the strings of my father's Cremona. It had been my grandfather's. A small very sweetly toned instrument lent to Mr McIntosh to be kept in order. He thought it wanting in power, his reels could not be given with spirit from it, so he enlarged the S holes. What became of this valuable instrument I know not. It had been spoiled. The first Strathspey was danced by my father and Mrs McIntosh; as the principal personages. The other pair to form the foursome was of less consequence. If my mother danced at all, it was later in the evening. My father's dancing was peculiar; a very quiet body and very busy feet, they shuffled away in double quick time steps of his own composition, boasting of little variety, sometimes ending in a turn about which he imagined was the fling; as English it was altogether as if he had never left Hertfordshire. My Mother did better, she moved quietly in highland matron fashion, 'high and disposedly' like Queen Elizabeth and Mrs McIntosh, for however lightly the lasses footed it, étiquette forbade the wives to do more than 'tread the measure.' William and Mary moved in the grave style of my Mother; Johnny without instructions danced beautifully; Jane was perfection, so light, so active, and so graceful; but of all the dancers there, none were equal to little Sandy, the present Factor, the son of Duncan McIntosh, though no son of his wife.

Some years before his marriage the forester had been brought into our country by what was called the Glenmore Company, a set of wood merchants from Hull, who had bought the forest of Glenmore from the Duke of Gordon for, I think, £30,000. They made at the very least double off it, and it had been offered to my uncle Rothy, wood and mountain, glen and lake, for £10,000, and declined as a dear bargain. Mr Osborne, the gentleman superintending the felling of all this timber, brought Duncan McIntosh from Strathspey as head of the working gangs, and left him in that wild isolated place with no companion for the whole winter but a Mary, of a certain age, and never well favoured. The result was the birth of Sandy, a curious compound of his young handsome father and plain elderly mother. It was this Mary who was the cook at Inverdruie, and a very good one she was, and a decent body into the bargain, much considered by Mrs McIntosh. There was no attempt to excuse, much less to conceal her history; in fact, such occurrences were too common to be commented on. She always came to the Dell harvest homes, and after the more stately reels of the opening of the dance were over, when the servants and labourers and neighbours of that degree came in turns into the parlour, Mary came among the others, and I have seen her often, figuring away in the very same set with Mr McIntosh, his guidwife looking on with a very peculiar smile: too pretty and too good she was to fear such rivalry. She had brought little Sandy home at her marriage and as much as lay in her power acted a mother's part by him; her children even accused her of undue partiality for the poor boy who was no favourite with his father. If so, the seed was sown in good ground, for Sandy was the best son she had. It was a very curious state of manners, this. I have often thought since of it.

We were accustomed to dance with all the company, just as if they had been our equals; it was always done and without injury to either party. There was no fear of undue assumption on the one side, or low familiarity on the other; a vein of thorough good breeding ran through all ranks, of course influencing the manners and rendering the intercourse of all most particularly agreeable. About midnight the carriage would be ordered to bring our happy party home. It was late enough before the remainder separated.

The Doune harvest home was very nearly like that at the Dell, only that the dinner was in the farm kitchen and the ball in the barn, and two fiddlers stuck up on tubs formed the orchestra. A whole sheep was killed, and near a boll of meal baked, and a larger company was invited, for our servants were more numerous and they had leave to bring a few relations. We always went down to the farm in the carriage drawn by some of the men, who got glasses of whiskey apiece for the labour, and we all joined in all the

reels the hour or two we staid, and drank punch to every
body's health made with brown sugar, and enjoyed the fun,
and felt as little annoyed by all the odours of the atmosphere
as any of the humbler guests to whom the Entertainment was
given.

We had no other ploy till Xmas eve, when we started for
Belleville. Even now, after all the years of a pretty long life, I
can bring to mind no house pleasanter to visit at. They were
without servants, so to speak at this time, having now but a
couple of maids of Kingussie breeding and the upstairs
Drawing room floor had not been refurnished; they lived in
their handsome dining room and the small library through it.
The company, besides ourselves, was only one or two of the
young Clarkes and a 'Badenoch body.' But we had so very
kind a welcome. Belleville was a host in a hundred, Mrs
Macpherson shone far more in her own house than she did in
any other. For, being stiff in manner and shy in disposition,
she had to be drawn out of her shell when from home. At
home, her wish to put every one at ease produced ease in
herself and then her lively conversation, and her good musick
and her desire to promote amusement made her altogether a
very agreeable hostess. We young people walked about all the
mornings, danced and laughed all the evenings till the whist
for the elders began, Belleville liking his rubber; and what
particularly delighted Jane and me, we sat up to supper,
surely a very sociable meal, one we never saw at our own
house where the dinner was late. At Belleville they still dined
early—five o'clock, and as the card playing was seldom over
before midnight, the appearance of a well filled tray was not
mistimed. Roasted potatoes only, fell to our share, and a bit
of butter with them. We were quite satisfied, so much indeed
did we relish them that we privately determined, when
talking over our happy evenings up at the top of that large
house in one of the attick rooms no amount of peats could
warm, that when we had houses of our own we would
introduce the supper tray, and roasted potatoes should, as at
Belleville, be piled in the centre dish.

Miss Macpherson, who liked all of us and particularly
liked their Badenoch acquaintance, was in extreme good
humour during our whole visit. We remained till after the

new year, and then returned home to make grand preparations for the passing of our Christmas time, Old style, the
season of greatest gaiety in the highlands. It is kept by
rejoicings and merry makings amongst friends, no religious
services being performed on any day but Sunday.

# CHAPTER THIRTEEN

# 1813

CHRISTMAS, Old style, 1813 Belleville and Mrs Macpherson
spent with us. They were company easily entertained. She
worked and gossiped with my mother all the mornings, till
the regular hour for her duty walk, a task she performed
conscientiously as soon as it was too dark to thread her
needle. He had one or two little strolls during the day, and
plenty of old plays and newspapers to read. In the evenings
they enjoyed our merry games and a little musick, before we
young ones were sent to bed, almost as much as they did
the rubber of whist afterwards. Miss Macpherson, also of
the party, was quite our companion, being little accounted
of by the rest. We had two dinner parties for our guests for
it was an open Xmas, as indeed it mostly is in the highlands,
the cold seldom setting in till the 10th or so of January.
Balnespick and Mrs Mackintosh were with us one day,
people who should have taken a higher place in the country
than they actually occupied. He was highly born, his father
very near a kin to the Chief of this old Clan, his mother sister
to him, and Mrs Mackintosh was no very distant relation of
the Chisholm. She was really a beautiful woman—fair, tall,
slight and graceful, but oh so still—a word she never spoke,
a look she never gave, a statue could not have been more
impassive. When criticising her immobility and the excessive ugliness of her husband, a great big ungainly man with
the head and face and *teeth* of the 'Wolf of Badenoch,'[1] how
little did we dream that one of the sons of this slightly

1. In 1827 Sir Thomas Dick Lauder wrote a prose romance
   on this notorious Earl of Buchan who burned Elgin
   Cathedral in 1390; much is made of the uncommon size
   and unsullied lustre of his hero's teeth.

regarded couple would be married to a granddaughter of
my father—married dear Janie M. to you, who first set me
upon writing fair out of these memories of our race.[1]
Balnespick was a clever man, very useful in the neighbourhood, respected by all ranks, though hardly popular; he was
a good father, a kind husband, an active farmer, he had
married the beauty of Inverness, and was very proud of her.
She had made a good marriage and turned out an excellent
wife, all sides approving of the connexion. Her sister, of
keener feelings, ran off from a northern Meeting, which my
father and my Aunt Mary attended, with a young Subaltern
of the regiment in garrison at Fort George, a crime quite
inexcusable in her, such extreme of love being very rare in
the calm characters we deal with, but perfectly excusable in
him, for she was just as handsome a brunette as her sister
was a lovely blonde; and the stolen wedding turned out,
romance fashion, quite a hit—the poor Lieutenant was the
heir of Rokeby.[2] I have heard my Aunt say that the young
runaways were kindly received and forgiven by the affluent
friends in Yorkshire. Sir Thomas Lauder confessed to Jane
and me that he had drawn the features of his Comyn hero[3]
from Balnespick's countenance. The tusks were there,
immense ones, and really gave the look of a wild boar or a
wolf to the whole head. The peculiarity ran in the family, his
only sister shewed these tusks very remarkably. She and her
husband dined with us the same day and Mrs Macpherson
declared that when she looked from the one mouth to the
other, she felt as if she were sitting at table with wild beasts.

Balnespick's sister was married to William Cameron, the
only remaining child of our dear old Cousins at the croft.
He had been unfortunate in business, his mercantile career
in Glasgow had proved full of troubles although his father,
my father and his wife had at different times stept in to save

1. Her niece, Jane Mackintosh, her sister Mary's daughter.
2. J.B.S. Morritt: he succeeded his uncle of the same name,
   for whom Scott had written his poem *Rokeby* in the
   previous year, 1812.
3. It is surprising that E.G. does not comment on this confusion between the Stewart Lord of Badenoch and a
   Comyn.

him. The bankruptcy came at last and there was no resource left but a return to the home his ill success had impoverished. He was really a good man William Cameron with a warm highland heart that beat true to the last of his kith and kin—it was the head that failed him. The wife, on the contrary, the niece of 'my uncle Sir Eneas,' had head enough. She failed in the heart line, keeping the poor one she owned rigidly within the limits of a small maternal horizen. She bore very ill the change from the flat in the city of Glasgow to the most modern of the two pretty cottages at the Croft, ever complaining of the loneliness of the country, though she had half a dozen children to look after, and of the uncomfortable ways of the old parents who had given her a home when upon the face of the earth she had no other. She amused Mrs Macpherson with her town airs, Glasgow airs, and not a little worried her brother.

The other dinner was to guests of less degree, Duncan McIntosh, his Wife, and one or two of the half pay Strathspey gentlemen. Mrs McIntosh never dined with us but once a year; it was quite enough for both parties, the poor good woman being quite astray playing company in a drawing room, away from her wheels, reels, kirns, and other housewifery. She could not read, she brought no work, had no conversation, so that the time must have hung very heavy after a sort of catechism between her and my mother was over—a whole string of questions concerning the webs[1] and the diary, duly answered in very simplicity.

The great event of the Christmas time was the floaters' ball. As the harvest home was given to the farm, this entertainment belonged to the forest—all engaged in the wood manufacture, their wives and families, being invited. The amusements began pretty early in the day with a game at Ba', the hockey[2] of the Low country, our Scotch substitute for cricket. It is played on a field by two parties, which toss a small hard ball between them by means of crooked sticks called clubs. The object of the one party is to send this ball to

1. Woven cloth.
2. Hockey is Lady Strachey's suggestion; E.G. actually wrote 'Gough', but she is describing an early form of shinty.

a certain place, a home, generally marked by a pile of plaids. The object of the other party is to prevent its getting there—a matter of difficulty on either side when the opponents are equally matched. The highlanders are extremely fond of this exciting sport, and continue it for hours on a holiday, exhibiting during the progress of it many feats of agility. There are always spectators in crowds applauding the fine strokes, many of the women taking a pride in the success of their particular friends at the Ba' playing. Our people kept up the game till dark, when all the men, above a hundred, went to dinner in the barn, a beef and several sheep having been killed for them. The kitchens both of house and farm had been busy for a couple of days cooking this entertainment. The women, as they arrived, were carried into the Grieve's house to tea, a delicate attention, fully appreciated. We delighted in the floater's ball, so very large a party, such a crowd of strangers. Some splendid dancers from Strathspey, the hay loft and the straw loft, and the upper floor of the threshing mill all thrown open *en suite*. Two sets of fiddlers playing different tunes, punch made in the washing tubs, a perfect illumination of tallow dips. It is very surprising that the boards stood the pounding they got; the thumping noise of the many energetick feet could have been heard half a mile off.

When a lad took a lass out to dance, he led her to her place in the reel and 'pried her mou' before beginning, kissed her, she holding up her face quite frankly though with modesty to receive the customary salute, and he giving a good sounding smack when the girl was bonnie that could be heard generally above the warning scrape of the fiddler's bow. At the conclusion of the set the same ceremony was repeated; seats being scarce, the ladies mostly reclined on their partners' knees while resting—as the evening advanced the pairs were wont to cuddle up comfortably together in the plaidie, warm work I should suppose considering the temperature of the ball room. There was certainly some reform required in the very primitive manners of our society. Many happy hearts came to these merry makings that most surely ached before the year came to an end.

The number of people employed in the wood manufacture

was very great. At this winter season little could be done in the forest beyond felling the tree, lopping the branches, barking the log, while the weather remained open, before the frost set in. Most of this work indeed was done in the autumn, and was continued while practicable. This was not a severe winter, but it set in early. We had a deep fall of snow, and then a degree of frost only felt among the mountains, putting a stop while it lasted to all labour. It was not unpleasant, for it was dry, and the sun shone brightly for the few hours of daylight, and after the first slap of the face on going out, sharp exercise made our walks very enjoyable. We bounded on over the hard ground for miles, indeed the distances people were able to overtake in weather of this sort would not be believed by those who had not tried it. Five weeks of frost and snow brought us over the worst of the winter, and then came a foretaste of spring which set us all at work again. The spade and the plough were both busy, and in the wood the great bustle of the year began.

The logs prepared by the loppers had to be drawn by horses to the nearest running water, and there left in large quantities till the proper time for sending them down the streams. It was a busy scene all through the forest, so many rough little horses moving about in every direction, each dragging its tree, attended by an active boy as guide and remover of obstructions. The smack of the whip used to sound quite cheerful in those otherwise solitary spots, and when we met, the few gaelick words we interchanged seemed to enliven us all. This driving, as it was called, lasted till sufficient timber was collected to render the opening of the sluices profitable. Formerly small saw mills had been erected wherever there was sufficient water power, near the part of the forest where the felling was going forward, and the deals when cut were carted down to the Spey. It was very picturesque to come suddenly out of the gloom of the pine trees, onto a little patch of cultivation near a stream with a cottage or two and its appendages and a saw mill at work, itself an object of singular interest in a rude landscape. A fuller concentration of labour was, however, found to be more advantageous to the wood merchant; they were finding out that it answered better to send the logs down nearer to the

Spey by floating them, than the deals by carting them. The prettily situated single saw mills were therefore gradually abandoned, and new ones to hold double saws built as wanted, within a more convenient distance from the banks of the river where the rafts were made.

In order to have a run of water at command, the sources of the little rivers were artificially managed to suit floating purposes. Embankments were raised at the ends of the lakes in the far away Glens, at the point where the different burnies issued from them. Strong sluice gates, always kept closed, prevented the escape of any beyond a small rill of water, so that when a rush was wanted the supply was sure. The night before a run, the man in charge of that particular sluice set off up to the hill, a walk of miles partly over an untracked moor, and reaching the spot long before daylight opened the heavy gates; out rushed the torrent, travelling so quickly as to reach the deposit of timber in time for the meeting of the woodmen, a perfect crowd, amongst whom it was one of our enjoyments to find ourselves early in the day. The duty of some was to roll the logs into the water; this was effected by the help of levers—like Harry Sandford's snow ball, Johnny screamed out the first time we took him with us. The next party shoved them off with longer poles into the current, dashing about often up to the middle in water when any cases of obstruction occurred. They were then taken in charge by the most picturesque group of all, the younger, more active of the set, each supplied with a clip, a very long pole extremely thin and flexible at one end, generally a young tall tree; a sharp hook was fixed to the bending point, and with this, skipping from rock to stump, over brooks and through briers, this agile band followed the log laden current, ready to pounce on any stray lumbering victim that was in any manner checked in its progress. There was something peculiarly graceful in the action of throwing forth the stout yet yielding clip, an exciting satisfaction as the sharp hook fixed the obstreperous log. The many light forms springing about among the trees, along banks that were some times high, and always rocky, the shouts, the laughter, the gaelick exclamations, and above all, the roar of the water, made the whole scene one of the most inspiriting that either Spectators or Actors could be engaged in.

One or two of these streams carried the wood straight to the Spey or to some saw mill near it. Others were checked in their progress by a lake. When this was the case, light rafts had to be constructed, so many logs bound loosely together, and then paddled or speared over by a man holding a 'sting' in his hand standing on nothing more than a couple of small logs laid across the float of larger ones. The lake crossed, the raft was taken to pieces, some of the logs left at a saw mill, the rest sent down the recovered stream to the Spey. There the Spey floaters took charge of them. Our people's task was done.

The Spey floaters lived mostly down near Ballindalloch, a certain number of families by whom the calling had been followed for ages, to whom the wild river, all its holes and shoals and rocks and shiftings, were as well known as had its bed been dry. They came up in the season, at the first hint of a speat, as a rise in the water was called. A large bothie was built for them at the mouth of the Druie in a fashion that suited themselves; a fire on a stone hearth in the middle of the floor, a hole in the very centre of the roof just over it where some of the smoke got out, heather spread on the ground, no window, and there, after their hard day's work, they lay down for the night, in their wet clothes—for they had been perhaps hours in the river—each man's feet to the fire, each man's plaid round his chest, a circle of wearied bodies half stupefied by whiskey, enveloped in a cloud of steam and smoke, yet sleeping soundly till the morning. They were a healthy race, suffering little but in their old age from rheumatism. They made their own large rafts themselves, seldom taking help from any of our woodmen, yet often giving it if there were an over quantity of timber in the runs.

My Mother and my Aunt when we were in arms had often enlivened the different scenes of the floating. We were now quite as much interested in all the exciting variety of the different stages in the wood manufacture. Mr McIntosh, who dined very frequently at the Doune, usually contrived to come the day before a log run, our particular delight, so we were sure of appearing in the very height of the business just before the noontide rest. When the men met in the morning they were supposed to have all breakfasted at home, and perhaps had had their private dram, it being cold work in a dark wintry dawn, to start over the moor for a walk of some miles to end in standing up to the knees in water; yet on collecting, whiskey was always handed round; a lad with a small cask, a quarter anker[1] on his back, and a horn cup in his hand that held a gill, good measure, appeared three times a day among them. They all took their 'morning' raw, undiluted and without accompaniment, so they did with the gill at parting when the work was done; but the noontide dram was part of a meal. There was a twenty minutes' rest from labour, and a bannock and a bit of cheese taken out of every pocket to be leisurely eaten after the whiskey. When we were there the horn cup was first offered to us, and every one of us took a sip to the health of our friends around, who all stood up on the cup being returned to Duncan McIntosh, and gave the Laird and all belonging to him a round of cheers right heartily. Sometimes a floater's wife or bairn would come with a message to him at this time; such messenger was always offered whiskey. Aunt Mary had a story that she one day being of the Doune party to some of the forest business, a woman with a child in her arms, and another bit thing at her knee, came up among them; the horn cup was in due course handed to her, she took a 'gey guid drap' herself, and then gave a little to each of the babies. 'My goodness, child,' said my Mother to the wee thing that was trotting by its mother's side, 'doesn't it *bite* you?' 'Ay, but I like the bite,' replied the creature that could hardly speak. A young English girl like my Aunt could hardly fail to be astonished at the whole proceeding.

There were many laughable accidents happened during the merry hours of the floating; the clips would sometimes fail to hit the mark, when the overbalanced clipper would fall headlong into the water. A slippery log escaping from cold hands would cause as cold a sommerset, shouts of laughter always greeting the dripping victims, who goodhumouredly joined in the mirth, raised by their awkwardness. As for the wetting, it seemed no way to incommode them; they were really like a set of water rats. Sometimes the accident was

1.  This would contain 2 gallons or 64 gills.

beyond a joke. I know we were all sobered enough by one that befell us one day. Just below the bridge on the Loch an Eilein road, over the burn that flows out of the lake, a small basin of water had been allowed to form during a run, for the purpose of holding together a large quantity of logs to prevent them from going down farther too quickly, as from this point the stream was conveyed by a narrow conduit formed of wood, across the Milltown moor and on down a steep bank into the first of a pretty set of miniature lakes, concealed by the birch wood on the one side and the fir trees on the other, known as the Lochans. This conduit, called the Spout, was in particular favour with us, as along its course the fun was always at its highest, it was so difficult in that rush of water to keep the great hulking logs in order, send them singly on in regular succession. One would rise up here over a lazy leader, another there; above, two or three mounting up on end and choking the passage, stopping all progress and wasting the water. The clips were very busy here, the men jumping about with them hooking this log and sending it forward, hooking that log and keeping it back, screaming to one another as they skipped over the Spout. All of a sudden, Mary, the least active child I have ever seen, in fact heavy limbed and heavy headed, who never on any occasion exerted any one faculty of mind or body, made a spring and cleared the conduit. The shouts of applause this daring action was greeted with inspired her afresh, and actually laughing herself she prepared to spring back. This time she miscalculated the distance and fell plump into the stream, along which she was carried more rapidly than we could follow her, without a hope of rescue. Did she even escape being crushed by a following log she must have been drowned in that rushing torrent before being tossed down the steep bank into the lake. The presence of mind of one person often saves a life; hers required the presence of mind of two. The accident happened very near the little basin where the logs were collected previous to being sent off down the spout, by a narrow outlet in charge of a tall Murdoch Murray who stood there directing them with his clip. He had the wisdom to draw one log quite across the mouth of the conduit so that none could move, and thus all danger of her being followed by one and so stunned or crushed was at an end. A lad, whose name I have forgot but he died, poor fellow, of consumption, carefully tended by us all while he lived, leaped from his place, waited for her a little lower, seized her clothes, and dragged her out. She was insensible. Mr McIntosh then came up, carried her in his arms into a saw miller's house close by, Sandy Colley's it was, had her undressed, rubbed, laid on the bed wrapped in warm blankets, and then when she opened her eyes he gave her a glass of whiskey. Jane, as the sensible one of the party, was sent home to order up dry clothes, which she was to do privately, without going near my mother. Johnny and I sat by Mary, doing whatever Duncan McIntosh bid us, and Miss Elphick cried.

As soon as it was ascertained that 'the *bonny burd*' was living, grand cheering rent the air, and a dram all round, an extra, was given in honour of her rescuers. That dram was the highland prayer, it began, accompanied, and ended all things. The men wanted to make a king's cushion and carry her home, but Mr McIntosh thought it better for her to walk. We were abundantly cheered on setting forth, and well scolded on getting home, though none of us but Mary herself had had any hand in the accident.

A more tragical event than most happily this 'vaulting ambition'[1] of poor Mary's had turned out, occurred a year or two before at this same season. The only child of a poor Widow, a Christian Grant, a fine young man named Allan, had charge of the Loch Ennich sluice gates. A quantity of timber being wanted at Druie mouth for the Spey floaters who had come up to make their rafts, a run was determined on, and this lad was sent up to the Glen to open the sluice. It was a wild night, wind and hail changing to snow, and he had eleven or twelve miles to go through the forest, full of paths, and across the heath that was trackless. Poor old Christy. She gave him a hot supper, put up a bannock and a little whiskey for him, and wrapped his plaid well round him. She looked after him in the driving sleet as he left the warm house. Such risks were common, no one thought about them. Early in the morning down came the water, the weather had

1. *Macbeth*, I, vii, 27.

taken up, and the floating went merrily on, but Allan did not return. He had reached the Loch, that was plain; where then had he wandered? Not far. When evening came on and no word of him, a party set out in search, and they found him at his post, asleep seemingly, a bit of bannock and the empty flask beside him. He had done his duty, opened the water gate, and then sat down to rest. The whiskey and the storm told the remainder. He was quite dead. The mother never recovered her reason. The shock brought on brain fever, and that left her strangely excited for a while. After that she calmed, was always harmless, sometimes a little restless, but never either wiser or sillier than the half simple state in which she existed to extreme old age. She had always been a tidy body, and had been called in often by Betty Campbell to help at the farm whenever there was a press of business. Once or twice at Company times she had assisted in the scullery at the House. The first sensible action she did after her long months of darkness was to arrive at the Doune one morning and set herself to pluck the fowl. Every one was of course kind to her, so she came next day, and from that time never failed to arrive regularly when the family was at home, about the breakfast hour, and remain till after dinner when the kitchen was put in order. She never would remain all night, preferring her little cabin on Druie side, to which she returned cheerfully except on stormy nights, when the maids said she would shake her head very sadly, and sometimes let fall tears. She never mentioned her son. My Mother never let her want for any thing; clothes, tea, snuff, all she wished for was supplied whether we were at home or absent, till the really good hearted Duchess of Bedford succeeded us at the Doune,[1] when she took charge of Christy, gave her just what she had always got, and reinstated her as head of scullery. I can see her now, with her pale anxious face, her linsey gown, check apron, and very white cap always bound by a black ribbon, seated beside the old japanned clock in our cheerful

1. The youngest daughter of the Grants' great friend and neighbour, the Duchess of Gordon; she married the sixth Duke in 1803, and was therefore step-mother to Lord John Russell the statesman.

kitchen, at some of her easy labours. She had very little
English, just enough to say 'my dear' or 'my jewel' when any
of us children passed. She always rose when my mother
entered and kissed her hand, sometimes saying 'bonnie'
when she saw how white it was. Poor old Christy, we used to
work for her, help the maids to make her caps and aprons and
handkerchiefs. It was Johnny's privilege to carry to her the
week's supply of snuff. After her misfortune the men were
always sent up the hill in pairs, for it had not come alone. The
shepherds had their mournful tales to tell as well as the
floaters, and here is one of them.[1]

They were not Rothiemurchus people, the young people of
whom I am to speak. They lived up in Glen Feshie, a great
way from our March, and they had not long been married.
He was either a small farmer, or the son of one, or merely a
shepherd to a wealthier man, I am not sure which, but his
business was to mind a large flock that pastured on the
mountains. During the summer when their charge strayed
up towards the very summit of the high range of the
Grampians, the shepherds lived in bothies in the hill, miles
from any other habitation, often quite alone, their Colly dog
their only companion, and with no provisions beyond a bag
of meal. This they generally ate uncooked, mixed either with
milk or with water as happened to suit the establishment, the
milk or the water being mostly cold, few of these hardy
mountaineers troubling themselves to keep a fire lighted in
fine weather. This simple food, called brose, is rather
relished by the highlanders; made with hot water or with
good milk they think it excellent fare; made with beef *broo'*,
the fat skimmings of the broth pot, they consider it quite a
treat. Beef brose is entertainment for any one. The water
brose must be wholesome; no men looked better in health
than the masons, who eat it regularly, and the shepherds.
These last come down from their high ground to attend the
kirk sometimes, in such looks as put to shame the luxurious
dwellers in the smoky huts with their hot porridge and other
delicacies. They learn to love the free life of the wilderness,

1. Such stories were collected by Sir Thomas Dick
Lauder in his *Legendary Tales of the Highlands*.

although there are many rainy days. Somehow rain don't much interfere with the comfort of the highlander.

In the winter the flocks feed lower down, and the shepherd leaves his bothie to live at home, but not at ease. A deep snow calls him forth to wander over miles of dreary waste, in case of drifts that overwhelm, or cold that paralyses, or landmarks mistaken. In spring there come the early lambs, on whose safety depends the profit of the Sheepowner, and our highland springs retain so much of winter in them that the care of a flock at this harsh season entails about the hardest of all labouring lives on man. It was at this critical time, at the beginning of a heavy snow storm, that our young husband departed on his round of duty.

The wife was preparing for her first baby. She was also busy with her wheel, the first work of a newly married notable highland girl being the spinning and the dying of a plaid for the husband. She baked her bread, she trimmed her fire, she busked[1] her house, then took her wheel, and by the light of a splinter of quick fir laid on a small projecting slab within the chimney, she wore away the long dark hours of that dreary winter's night. Ever as the storm lulled for a while, she bent to listen for the voice she expected at the door, and which, poor young thing, she was never to hear again, for he never returned from those wild mountains. They sought him for days; no trace of him could be discovered. When the snow melted away, and the summer flowers burst into bloom, party after party set out in quest of his remains, all unsuccessfully. It was not till late autumn, when our gamekeeper was on the Braeriach shooting grouse, that he saw seated on a shelf of rock midway down a precipice a plaided figure. It was all that was left of the missing shepherd, little more than a skeleton, and his Colly dead beside him. He had wandered miles away from his own ground, deceived by the snow and must have died from exhaustion after a fall on to this sheltered spot. His Widow was past all knowledge of his fate ; her anxiety had brought on premature child birth, fever ensued, and though she recovered her strength in a degree, her mind was quite gone. She

1. Scots: to prepare or make ready.

lived in the belief of the speedy return of her husband, went cheerfully about her usual work, preparing all things for him, going through the same round as on the day she lost him; baking, sweeping, putting on fresh peats, and ending with her wheel by the side of the clean hearth in the evening. She would shew her balls of yarn with pride to the kind neighbours who looked in upon her, and the little caps she was trimming for the baby that was lying alongside the bones of its father in the kirk yard. Sometimes towards the evening, they said, she would look wearily round and sigh heavily, and wander a little in her talk, but in the morning she was early up and busy as ever. She was never in want, for every one helped her; but though she was so much pitied, she was in their sober way much blamed. The highlanders are fatalists; what is to be, will to be—philosophers—what happens must be borne and patiently. We must 'dree our weird,'[1] all of us, and 'tis a 'flying in the face of providence' to break the heart for God's inflictions. They feel keenly too; all their affections are very warm and deep; still, they are not to be paraded. A tranquil manner is a part of their good breeding, composure under all circumstances essential to the dignity of character common to all of the race. How would a matron from Speyside be astonished, scandalised, at the impulsive nature and consequent exhibitions of her reputed kindred in dear Ireland.

I have wandered very far away from the floating—and the forest work did not end with the arrival of the logs at their different destinations. Those of them that went straight to Spey were seized on by the Ballindalloch men, bored at each end by an auger, two deep holes made into which iron plugs were hammered, the plugs having eyes through which well twisted wattles were passed, thus binding any given number firmly together. When a raft of proper size was thus formed it lay by the bank of the river awaiting its covering. This was produced from the logs left at the saw mills, generally in the water in a pool formed to hold them. As they were required by the workmen, they were brought close by means of the clip, and then by the help of levers rolled over up an inclined

[1]. To endure one's fate, to submit to one's destiny.

plane and on to the platform under the saw; two hooks attached to cables kept the log in its place, the hooks being hammered into the end of the log, and the other end of the cable being fixed to the frame of the saw. The sluice was then opened, down poured the water, the great wheel turned, the platform moved slowly on with the log, the saw frame worked up and down, every cut slicing the log deeper till the whole length fell off. The four outsides were first cut off; they were called backs, and very few of them went down to Garmouth; they were mostly used at home for country purposes, such as fencing, out offices, even houses were made of them, roofing, or firing. The squared logs were then cut up regularly into deals and carted off to the rafts, where they were laid as a sort of flooring. Two rude gears for the oars to move in, and rude oars they were, completed the appointments of a Spey float. The men had a wet berth of it, the water shipping in, or more, properly, over, with every lurch; yet they liked the life, and it paid them well, and then they had idle times great part of the year, could live at home and till their little crofts their own old lazy way, the rent being always made up by the floating.

Near Arndilly there was a sunken rock sometimes difficult to pass; this furnished a means of livelihood to several families living on the spot. It was their privilege to provide ropes, and arms to pull the ropes!, and so to help the floats through a rapid current running at high floods between this sunken rock and the shore. The dole they got was small, yet there was hardly more outcry in Sutherland when the Duke wanted his starving cottars to leave their turf huts on the moors to live in comfortable stone and lime houses by the sea,[1] than my father met when some years after this he got leave to remove this obstacle by blasting.

The oars were to my Mother and us, Jane and me, the most important items of the whole manufacture. She had discovered that in the late Laird's time, when the sales of timber were very small, a dozen rafts in each season, worth a few hundreds annually, the oars had been the perquisite of the

1. Perhaps the most notorious of all the incidents of the
'Highland Clearances.'

Lady. A little out of fun, partly perhaps because she had begun to find money sometimes wanting, she informed good Mr Steenson that she meant to claim her dues. He used to listen quietly, answer with a smile blandly that next time he came up her claims should be remembered, but never a penny she got. Mr Steenson fell sick and died. A new wood agent had to be appointed, and he being an old friend, my Mother applied with more confidence to him. The new Agent was Dalachapple, Mr Alexander Grant of Dalachapple, nephew to the thrifty wife of Parson John—their son in law as well, but thereby hangs a tale. He had been connected in business with William Cameron in Glasgow, and failing like him had been living like him, with wife and bairns, plenty of bairns, at Abernethy waiting to see what would turn up for him. I declare these unfortunates all getting round my father and helping to manage his affairs when they had so signally failed in managing their own, always seemed to me like the lame leading the blind,—all in the end must fall into the ditch, for William Cameron had taken charge of the books as Factor to relieve his father of that part of the business and gradually he proceeded to relieve him of all the rest, salary included. He kept the books beautifully, in true mercantile order, and I never heard him complained of in his active duties on the property. Moreover, poor man, when money fell to his wife by the death of 'my Uncle Sir Eneas,' he lent it all to my father in the sure belief that whatever little difficulties might beset him at the moment, the forest would redeem all. Dalachapple, in like manner, invested the few thousands he inherited afterwards from good Parson John in the same bottomless pit, equally satisfied with the security and sure like his friend of a good rate of interest in the meanwhile, a matter of much consequence to them under present circumstances.

Dalachapple not only listened to my mother about the oar money, but he acted in accordance with the old established usage, and with a degree of delicacy quite amusing. In the most mysterious manner, and only when she was quite alone, did he approach her with her perquisite in the form of a Bank note folded into the smallest possible size. The oars were sold for half a crown apiece, a pair only to each float, and one season he gave her upwards of forty pounds and this was long before the great felling. She opened her eyes a little wider, and certainly felt the money a great comfort. She seldom had any in purse or pocket book, indeed 'twas of no use in the highlands. All we did not produce ourselves was ordered in large quantities on credit and paid by drafts on a Banker. We had no shops near us but one at Inverdruie, kept by a Jenny Grant, who made us pay very dear for thread and sugarplums and our charities were given in the form of meal or clothing; fuel every one had plenty of for the mere gatherings, the loppings all through the forest were never turned to any other account. They made a brilliant fire when well dried, owing to the quantity of turpentine in the fir timber. Still, those who could afford it laid in a stock of peats for the dead of the winter as the wood burned quickly out and so failed to give as much heat as turf.[1] My father had an objection to turf, and would not burn it up at the house even in the kitchen. Coals we never thought of; they could be had no nearer than Inverness, were dear enough there, and the carriage from thence, thirty six miles, would have made them very expensive; yet the wood fires were very costly; the wood itself was of no value, but it had to be carted home, cross cut by two men, split up by two more, and then packed in the wood sheds. It was never ending work, and at the rate of wages given, including the horse and cart, could never have come to less, when we lived the year round at the Doune, than £100.

In the huge kitchen grate, in the long grates with dogs in them made expressly for the purpose of supporting the billets, the cheerful wood fires were delightful. But in our part of the house, where my Mother in her English tidiness had done away with the open hearth and condemned us to small Bathgrates, we were really perishing with cold; three or four sticks stuck up on end, all that the small space would hold, either smouldering slowly at the bottom if wet or blazing up to the danger of the chimney if dry, gave out no heat equal to warm the frozen fingers and toes during a highland winter. We held a Council upon the subject in the

1. The word used throughout Ireland for peat.

Schoolroom and decided upon taking steps ourselves to render ourselves more comfortable. Whenever we went out to walk, before returning home we visited the farm offices, and there from the famous peat-stacks provided for the farm servants we helped ourselves, each carrying off as much as we could carry. We got old John McIntosh to chop our long billets in two, and thus we contrived a much better fire; the grate was quite unsuited to the sort of fuel, but we made the best of it. When we told our dear old great grand Uncle of our bright thought, he started up, a little angry, not with us though and forthwith sent down for especial Schoolroom use two carts of the fine hard peats from the far off famous Rhinruy moss; they burned almost like coal, having but one fault, very light red ashes. We made some dusters, enjoyed our fire, and had to keep good watch over our store of fuel to prevent any being stolen by the kitchen, never failing every day to take an accurate measurement of our own peat stack, neatly built in one of the wood houses by the Captain's men.

And so our winter glided away.

# CHAPTER FOURTEEN

## 1813

IN the spring, as soon as the hill was open, my father went to London to attend his duties in parliament. My Mother then changed our arrangements a little. We did not get up till seven, dark of course at first, but a whole hour gained on a cold morning was something. Miss Elphick, Jane and I breakfasted with her at half after nine. We used to hear her go downstairs punctually ten minutes sooner, opening her bedroom door at the end of the passage with a deal of noise, and then making a most resounding use of her pocket handkerchief—our signal call, we said. We all dined with her at four. After that there were no more lessons; we passed the evening beside her reading and working. The work was the usual shirting, sheeting, shifting, towelling, etc., required in the family, the stock of linen of all kinds, being kept up to the statutory number by a regular yearly addition. The whole was then looked over, some mended to serve a time, some made up for the poor, the rest sorted into rag bundles constantly wanted where accidents among the different labourers were so frequent. We read through all Miss Edgeworth's works, Goldsmith's histories, most of the Spectator, and a few good Standard novels from the dusty shelves in the Study. On Saturday nights we were allowed a fire in the barrack room, after which indulgence my hair was admitted to shine much more brightly. After dinner, in an hour we had to ourselves, Jane and I generally read to the 'little ones.' Mary was hammering through 'Parent's Assistant' herself, two pages a day for her lesson, enough as she slowly spelt her way along the lines, but not enough to interest her in the stories, so she seemed pleased to hear them to an end with Johnny. We often had to repeat a favourite tale, so much approved were Lazy Lawrence, The Little

Merchants, The basket woman, and some others. And then when we demurred to going over them again we were so assailed by our listeners that we began Evenings at Home, leaving out the Tutor, George, and Harry. What excellent books these are for children—ay and for those beyond childhood, how they form the mind, enlarge it and the heart as well, make virtue so lovely, teaching to shun the vile, excuse the sinner, filling the head so with good that there is no room left for evil. There are no orphans where such teaching surrounds the nursery. Yet it was not while I was young that I was fully aware of the value of the library chosen for us. It was when I was again reading these old favourites to childish listeners, to you, my own dear children, that the full extent of their influence struck me so forcibly. They have not been surpassed by any of our numerous Authours for the young since. This was a very happy time with us, even though poor William was away. We only saw him at midsummer, the journey being too long for the Christmas holidays to be spent with us; he passed them always with the Freres.

One April morning Grace Grant, the Greusaich's daughter, the pretty girl who waited on us, drew aside the white curtains of my little bed and announced that 'Mr Cameron's two houses were in ashes.' A fire had broken out in the night at the Croft in the new house occupied by Mr and Mrs William Cameron; it had spread to the stack yard and the offices, and even to the upper cottage in which the old people lived, and when my mother reached the scene, for she had been roused by the news, had got up, and dressed, gone off walking those two or three miles, she who seldom went farther than her poultry yard in the day time, she found the homeless family on the green watching the destruction of their property.

About half of this news was true. The fire had broken out and the lower house was burnt to the ground. Some of the corn stacks were destroyed, and one young horse was injured, but the rest of the stock and the better part of the crop and the old cottage were safe. My Mother had gone up, but before her bed time, the tidings having been brought to her while she was reading as usual after we had left her, and she brought back with her the two eldest of William Cameron's boys, who lived with us for the next eighteen months, there being no room for them at home. The loss to their parents was great. All the handsome Glasgow furniture was gone, as well as sundry little stores of valuables saved by poor Mrs William from the wreck of her City splendour. It was quite melancholy to see the blackened ruins of that little lovely spot; much of the offices had fallen, and though at this season they were less necessary than they would have been at any other time, the heaps of scorched timber and broken walls we had to pick our way through on our first visit made us feel very sad. The old people received us as if nothing had happened. Miss Mary was neither more nor less fussy, more nor less cross than usual. Mrs Cameron sat in her chair by the fire in her bonnet and shawl, and her green shade over her eyes just as she had ever done; a monument of patience in idleness, sighing in her accustomed manner, no change whatever in her. I am certain she had been equally immovable on the night of the fire. Mr Cameron talked to us cheerfully as usual of all matters going, the fire amongst the rest, as if he and his had no concern in it, except when he raised his fine head towards the sky in humble gratitude that there had been no lives lost; he even played on the Jew's harp to us, Lochaber, which we called his own tune, for he came from that part of the country, and Crochallan, beautiful Crochallan, which we considered more peculiarly our own, for we had all been sung to sleep by it in our infancy. I learned to sing it from his playing and he taught me to pronounce the gaelick words with the pretty, soft Lochaber accent, so very different from the harsh, guttural of Strathspey. Years after at Hampstead, my Uncle Frere, who remembered my childish 'crooning' of it when he had his fever, made me sing it again not only once, but for ever; and one day that Francis Cramer[1] was there he made me sing it to him; never was there a musician more delighted; over and over and over again was repeated this lovely gaelick air till he thought he had quite

1. Second generation (1772–1848) of a distinguished German musical family settling in England; he was appointed Master of the King's Music in 1837.

caught it, and when he went away he bade me farewell as Crochallan mavourgne!, little suspecting he was addressing a young lady as the favourite *cow* of one Allan!

I never myself admired the Croft so much in its improved state as I did in the days of the two small detached thatched cottages, the stack yard here, the stables there, the peat stack near the burn, and the garden paled with backs, wherein grew the sweetest, small, black-red hairy gooseberries that were ever gathered. My father, on his return from London, immediately began to plan the present very pretty two storeyed Cottage, as I may well remember, for I had to make all the drawings for it architecturally from his given dimensions; inside and outside working plans, and then a sketch of its future appearance in the landscape, and I was so awkward, so unskilful, and he was so very particular, required all to be so neatly done, so perfectly accurate, without blemish of any sort, that I'm sure I could not tell how many sheets of paper, how many hours of time, how many trials of a then easily chafed temper were gone through before the finished specimens were left to be tyed up with other equally valuable designs, in a roll kept in the lower closed book shelves to the left of the Library fireplace, docketted by his saucy daughter 'Nonsense of Papa's.' The new house was placed a little in advance of the óld in a situation very well chosen. It looks most particularly well from Aunt Mary's favourite walk round the Lochans. My father cut down some trees at one point to give a full view of it, and we made a rough seat there, as we did in many a pretty spot besides, where a summer hour could be dreamed away by lake, or stream, or bank, or brae, and mountain boundary, the birch leaves and the heather scenting the air.

They were very stupid boys those sons of William Cameron. James the elder, was a real lout, there was no making any thing of him, though Caroline the french girl, true to the coquettish instincts of her nation, tried all her fascinations on him, really toiled to elicit a single spark of feeling of some sort from this perfect log. In vain. Jane was more successful with the second boy, Lachlan. Both brothers went daily to the School at the bridge of Coylam, the common parish School, and a very good one, where all the boys in the place were taught, and could learn Latin if they liked it. The present master piqued himself on his English. He came from Aberdeen, and was great in the English Classicks; whole pages from our best poets, first read out in the proper style by him and then learnt by heart by the pupils, formed part of the daily lessons of the more advanced Classes. Lachlan Cameron, taught privately by Jane, quite electrified the Master by his fine delivery of the 'Deserted Village' at the rehearsal previous to the Examination.[1]

My father examined the School. I don't know what there was that my father did not do; so busy a man could hardly have been met with. He did his work well while the whim for that particular employment lasted; the misfortune of it all was that there were too many irons in the fire; fewer of them he would have managed perfectly. Poor Sir Alexander Boswell, Bozzy's very clever son, wrote a brilliant Tory squib once ridiculing the Edinburgh Whigs, and my father's share of it ended thus—'Laird, lawyer, Statesman, J. P. Grant in *short*.'[2] This superactive tendency was very strong in me. Without being a meddler, for that I never was, I was naturally inclined to attempt too much. In my youth I was versatile, seized on some new occupation, pursued it to weariness, gave it up unfinished, and took with equal zeal to something else. My father was quite aware of this defect *in me*. He first insisted on every work begun being finished, however distasteful it might have become; next he exacted a promise from me to this effect as soon as the habit was a little formed. And to this promise I have faithfully adhered, sometimes at no small cost of patience, the love of being up and doing, making me even in more advanced age, undertake many labours, the completion of which was far from agreeable. Jane had none of this volatility; fond of employment, never indeed idle, she was endowed from the beginning with a perseverance that has carried her bravely through difficulties that would have then disheartened me. I was educated into equal diligence, but it was a work of time, and

1. Oliver Goldsmith was a favourite author of the family.
2. They knew each other well; his *Edinburgh Squibs* was to be published in 1823.

shews what can be done by judicious supervision. We always
went with my father and mother to the examination of the
School—no short business; my father was very methodical,
no flash pupil could have imposed on him. Backwards and
forwards he cross examined, requiring the reasons for all
things, much as in the national systems[1] now, as was never
practised then. I have heard him say the boys were fair
Scholars, but beat by the girls. The Latin class was very
respectable, the arithmetick very creditable of course, the
recitations had to be applauded, and Lachlan Cameron was
rewarded for action as well as emphasis—Jane having John
Kembled him to the utmost of her ability—by receiving a
handsome Copy of Goldsmith's works. The prizes were
wisely chosen, indeed almost any standard work would have
been appreciated. Mrs Gillies, during a visit to us at the
Circuit time, taking a walk with my Mother one morning,
went to rest a bit in a saw mill; the saw was at work grinding
slowly up and down, while the log it was slitting moved lazily
on, the man and boy reading till they were wanted. The Boy's
book was Cornelius Nepos[2] in the original, the man's
Turner's Geography. I question whether that dear good
Lady Rachel [Russell]'s little mannie at Druie Side, trained
though he be by six months of the normal school in
Edinburgh, will send forth such an order of minds. When I
saw him he could hardly explain his ideas out of the gaelick,
and the staff was small.

The Schoolmaster's wife taught sewing, very badly my
mother said. She objected extremely to the fineness of the
thread used for stitching, and she would take hold of a knot
at the end of a hem and draw the whole up as if ready for
gathering, as a proof of the incorrect manner in which the
girls had been allowed to ravel over this most essential
element of the science of needlework. Peggy Green was
certainly better fitted to trim up a cap, dance at a harvest
home, or preside at a tea drinking, then to teach white seam,
or guide a poor man's house. She had been Mrs Gordon's

1. This refers to the system of primary education set up in
   Ireland in the 1830s; E.G. organised two such schools on
   her husband's estate.
2. Roman historian, author of *De excellentus ducibus*.

maid, used to go up to Glentromie in the boat with the
Colonel and the children, and at some of the merry makings
fell in love with the handsome Schoolmaster, the very best
dancer in Badenoch—for he was at Glen Feschie then. I
cannot recollect his name. He got 'wonderful grand presents' at his marriage, a hurried one—but he and the fine wife
did not suit, they were not happy, tittle tattle having
contributed to make them unhappy.

These forensick displays of poor Lachlan had turned our
thoughts back to our nearly forgotten theatricals. We
amused ourselves in the shrubbery re-acting several of our
favourite scenes in Macbeth. My father coming upon us
one day proposed that, as we were so well acquainted with
Shakespeare in tragedy, we should try our hands on his
Comedy, and if we liked he would prepare his own
favourite for us 'As you like it.' We were delighted. He set
to work, and leaving out objectionable passages and
unnecessary scenes, made the prettiest three act drama of
this pretty play. We learned our parts out among the birch
wooding on the Ord Ban, selecting for our stage, when we
had made progress enough to arrive at rehearsals, a beautiful spot upon a shoulder of the hill not so far from
Kainapool, about a couple of miles from the Doune, so
that we had a good walk to it all along the river side,
through the planting. Still, though charmed with Rosalind
and Celia, we could not bear giving up our older friends;
we therefore persuaded my father to curtail Macbeth, and
allow us to act both, before him and a select audience, as
soon as ever William should come home for the holidays.
We could not have got on without him, he and Jane being
our stars. Little fat Miss Elphick, too, must play her part.
She had gradually abandoned the strict disciplinarian
style, and had become in many respects as latitudinarian
as her Celtick nurtured pupils could desire. In this case,
moreover, personal vanity had a large share in her gracious
demeanour. She imagined herself handsome, graceful,
and an actress—Mrs Jordan[1] beautified, and from having
heard *her* read she had caught, my mother said, some

1. See p. 213.

of the tone of that wonderful woman's style. The part she chose for herself in 'As you like it' was Rosalind, and a vulgar Rosalind she made, exaggerating the very points an elegant mind would have softened, for Rosalind is somewhat more pert than even a 'saucy lacquey'[1] need have been, a little forward, and not over delicate. Mrs Harry Siddons[2] refined her into the most exquisite piece of gay impulsive woman-hood, a very Princess of romance. Poor Miss Elphick brought her up from the servants' hall. We thought her queer looking in her doublet and hose, but Belleville, who was a good judge of such matters, having finished his education behind the scenes in the theatres, declared that she was finely limbed, had a leg fit for the buskin, with an eye and a voice that would have made her fortune had she followed the profession. She was very much pleased with herself, took a deal of trouble about her dress and her hair—a crop—and the proper placing of her hat and feather, and she knew her part perfectly.

Jane was a very gentlemanly Orlando, William a first rate Jaques; there never was a better, he looked the character, felt it, for in his young days William was cynical, turned his nose up habitually, very different from his pleased tranquillity now. I did both the Duke and Celia, was a stiff Duke and a lively Celia, roused her up a bit although we gave her no lover, left out all that. But *the* Actor in this pretty Comedy was Mary—dull, listless Mary. She chose the part herself, and would have no other, and any thing equal to her Touchstone my father and Belleville solemnly declared they had never seen. Her humour, her voice, her manner, her air, her respectful fun to her ladies, her loving patronage of her Audrey, Anne Cameron, a very nice looking girl, the whole conception of the character was marvellous in a child of ten years of age. And she broke upon us suddenly, for in all our rehearsals her stupidity had been remarkable. She acted like a lump of lead. She never knew her part, every other word she was prompted, and when my father tried to put some life

1. *As You Like It*, III, ii, 277.
2. Henry Siddons, Sarah's eldest son, took a 21 year lease of the Theatre Royal in Edinburgh in 1809; his wife Harriet acted there too.

into her by reading to her as he wished her to speak, he made little of it; but how well she remembered. On the night of the play her acting was perfect. Johnny said it was the port wine, a large jug of which mixed with water stood in our green room, the upper part of the thrashing mill, and was dispensed in proper quantities by Miss Elphick between the Acts. Johnny affirmed that to this jug Touchstone applied at sundry unauthorised times, as he, in his capacity of third Lord, a very small one, attending on the forest Duke, had opportunities of discovering during his retirement behind the fanners, as he was seldom required upon the stage. The other Lords were represented by Jane McIntosh, and James and Eneas Cameron, and Caroline the french girl; by the help of caps and feathers and famous long boar spears they grouped remarkably well.

We grew so fond of our Comedy, Macbeth was thought less of. We acted it first, Jane and William surpassing themselves. Mary was Banquo, Miss Elphick the King, Mary was Hecate, and the witches and the Company at the Banquet were the same as did the Forest Lords, for we had each to play many parts. They were obliged to make me Lady Macbeth, a part I don't think it possible I could have done well, though my father took infinite pains with me. I was told I looked extremely handsome in black velvet and point lace, a dress the real Lady Macbeth would have opened her eyes at. All the people called out 'Preach, preach,' pronounced pree-ak, when, thus arrayed and with a long train, the Thane's wife came forward with her letter; a very gratifying sound to one, who had been hitherto considered the plainest of the family. Even Grace Baillie, the most obliging creature in the world, could only force herself to say, when contemplating the pale thin object presented to her, 'Eliza will be very lady like.' This was during the milk breakfast season. It is astonishing what a difference a fitter dish made. Grace Baillie was more polite to me than the great Joanna Baillie's[1] little old sister was to my cousin Anne Frere at Hampstead. Some one remarking how like Anne was to my Aunt, her

1. No relation; Joanna Baillie (1762–1851) was well known for her 'Plays on the Passions'.

mother, 'never mind my dear,' said this kind meaning old lady, 'it is better to be good than to be handsome'—and my Aunt sitting there, excellent as that dear good Aunt was, she did not quite like that story. While I was extremely vain of my 'pre-ach,' 'bonnie,' and they were judges of both beauty and merit, our highlanders, they were charmed with William's Macduff, applauded him after their fashion vehemently, many of the women bursting into tears; Jenny Dairy wetted her apron through 'to see puir Mr William greeting for his wife and family.'

We had a large audience. All our particular friends, Belle-ville, Mrs and Miss Macpherson, Camerons from the Croft, McIntoshes from the Dell, and Mr Alexander Grant from Garmouth. These were the select, on the front benches. Behind were John and Betty Campbell from the Dell of Killi-huntly up in Badenoch—the farm they had taken on leaving our service—McKenzie and Mrs McKenzie, once Mrs Lynch, from their inn at Aviemore, and all our own servants. Our theatre was part of the granary, decorated by ourselves with old carpets, old curtains, green boughs, and plenty of candles. We made all our own dresses, Anne Cameron and Jane McIntosh assisting; and as the old black trunk in the long garret was made over to us, we had my grandmother's blue and silver, and yellow satin, and flowered silks, and heaps of embroidered waistcoats, scarfs and handkerchiefs, all of which we turned to account.

One peculiarity of this acting was that we became so attached to the characters we could not bear to think ill of them. We excused every body for every act, with the exception of Lady Macbeth; we could in no way get her out of the scrape of the murder, till we stumbled in Holinshed's chronicles[1] on the story as told in his times. Even then we could not approve of her, but judging of her by the morals of her age, we almost justified her for getting rid of a wicked

1. Raphael Holinshed's *Chronicles of England, Scotland and Ireland* (1578), which for the Scottish section relied heavily on Hector Boece's *Historia Gentis Scotorum*, and thus provided Shakespeare with some dramatic but unhistorical possibilities.

cruel king, whose conduct to her and hers had been so ferocious. We quite forgot we were only shifting the saddle. We were like the biographers who always become so enamoured of their subjects they can never see their faults. We had also to make out the locality of the forest of Ardennes, and we settled it to our perfect satisfaction near Hainault; the principality or duchy from which the two Dukes came eluded our researches.

The next stirring event was another alteration, a final one it proved, of the principal Staircase, the painting and papering of all that new part of the house, and the fitting up of the drawing room as a Library. We had lived so long with doors and shutters of plain deal, cane backed chairs and sofas, common Scotch carpeting, etc., that the chilly atmosphere of our half furnished apartments never struck us as requiring improvement. My mother had long wished for a little more comfort round her, and the books having accumulated quite beyond the study shelves my father determined on removing them; he gave himself great credit for his tact in the choice of his bookcases; they were all made of the fir from his forest, picked pieces of course, highly varnished so as to resemble satinwood and relieved by black mouldings. The room was large, very lofty, and really looked well when finished, but it was a work of time. All summer and all autumn and part of the winter the various jobs were going on, and in the middle of the bustle we caught the measles, sickened one after the other, we four who had hitherto escaped—and no Doctor in the country, for tall Mr Stuart from Grantown, eighteen miles off, who used to attend every one on Speyside, was dead. He was a retired Army Surgeon who had settled in Strathspey on the chance of practice, skilful enough for ordinary cases in his line, medical aid being little wanted. Herbs and such simples cured the generality, and *we* had my grandfather's medicine chest administered very sagaciously by my father. He did not like undertaking the measles, then considered a serious complaint, so he sent to Inverness for Dr Ponton. He paid two very expensive visits, and we all got well.

Just at this time there dropped from the moon into the village of Kingussie a miserable looking man in a well worn tartan jacket, with a handsome wife, somewhat older than himself, and several children. They arrived from Lochaber in an old gig, a small cart following with luggage and a short supply of furniture and they hired the room over Peter McPherson's new shop. This man announced himself as Dr Smith, brother to a clever man of the same name in the west, near Fort William. He had been some weeks there, creeping into a little practice among the neighbours, before we heard of him. A poor woman in Rothiemurchus died in childbed, her case was one of difficulty and there being no skilful aid at hand, she died. The woman usually employed on these occasions had no way failed in attention but she had not been equal to the circumstances. This unhappy event determined my father to look out for a Doctor, and he went up to speak to Belleville about it. They also held an inquiry into the causes of the accident, and Dr Smith was brought forward to give his professional testimony, Belleville having heard him spoken of. His knowledge, his intelligence, his general information amazed them; here was the very man they wanted. Accordingly it was resolved to try him for a year. The Marquis of Huntly, the Duke of Gordon, and Ballindalloch were written to. Poor Balnespick was away; he had gone ill to Cheltenham, where he died. And the regular subscription for the care of the poor being immediately provided, this poor clever man was at once relieved from the fear of starvation, and had the hope besides of illness among the upper classes that would pay him better. He began with us, for we all took ill again, an illness no one could make any thing of; all the symptoms of measles, and measles we had just recovered from; yet measles it was and Mary and I had them very severely; her cough gave us great anxiety with winter approaching. Dr Ponton was again sent for, on her account, but his grave pomposity suggested no change from Dr Smith's treatment, and so with another heavy fee he took leave of us.

After the measles Dr Smith appeared no more in the old tartan jacket. A neat cloth coat and a pair of serviceable trowsers replaced the very shabby suit and though he still preferred walking to any other exercise, twenty or even thirty miles a day being a common thing with him, he neither looked so pale nor so worn as when he had first shewn himself at the Inquest. This it was his nature to be, no amount of good living could put any flesh on him, but good society in a wonderfully short time improved his manners. He was '*quick at the uptak*,' fond of reading, a good listener, and a pleasant talker. If we all improved him, he was himself a most agreeable addition to all of us. Even Belleville's well stored memory seldom found a quotation thrown away. The Doctor had been meant for something better; a cloud hung over his early history.

When my father had set all his various hands to work— Donald Maclean and his half dozen men to the Staircase, a cabinet maker from Perth with assistants, to the new Library, Grant the painter from Elgin with his men to their papering and oil brushes—he set off himself to be re-elected for Great Grimsby, a Dissolution of Parliament having made this necessary. An immensity of money was spent there on this occasion, another Candidate having been got to start, the rich Mr Fazakerley.[1] Out of four two only could succeed, and my unfortunate father was one of them. While he was away we had no room to sit in but the old gloomy study. My Mother made it as neat as she could, and as we could pop in and out of the shrubbery by the low windows we got reconciled to its other defects, yet were glad when the painters having finished the bowwindowed bedroom over the dining room, she was able to fit that up as her drawing room for the autumn company— Quite ready she got it against my father's return, with the finest man ever was seen for a valet, whom he had picked up in London; a Norfolk giant, six foot one, magnificent in shirt frill. It was well Bell did not work for him, she would never have stood that small plaiting. The poor girl who did, a Jenny Barron the dyer's daughter, that washed for all the men servants, got many a lecture for inefficiency, Mr Gouard making more fuss than enough about himself in all ways.

My mother had had all the bedrooms in the new part of the house painted and papered to please herself. In the old part

1. E.G. is wrong; her father was elected in 1812 and sought re-election in 1818 when he came third to Charles Tennyson (who spent £5,500 in the process) and J. N. Fazakerley.

she had painted, but had not ventured on papering, the old walls not having been studded; they were therefore done in distemper, as were those of the dining room. The colours were not happily chosen, buff and grey, and the dining room peagreen; all the wood work white, very cold looking. The dining room peagreen was relieved by the gilt frames of the Thorley pictures, mostly by Dutch or Flemish Artists, a small well chosen selection. There was a Berghem, two Boths, a Watteau, a Jan Stein, a small Wouverman, and several more undoubted originals, though by painters of less note.[1] One *we* admired much was one of the three authorised copies of Raphael's 'Giardiniera' the Virgin and child and little dark St John beside her, made by a favourite pupil. Castle Howard has another, Russborough claims the third.[2] The subject, however, was so in favour that many pencils were tried on it, all the possessors claiming of course to hold one of the three valuables. There were two coloured chalk sketches by Rembrandt of himself and a friend; a piece of fruit, fish, and game considered very fine;—in all about fifteen paintings, including two nearly full length portraits, a Raper ancestor and his friend Sir Christopher Wren. A court beauty by Sir Peter Lely[3] was sent up to a bedroom, she really was not dressed enough to be downstairs; and a James the 6th

1. Not all of their reputations were to stand so high, although Philip Wouverman (1614–68) is remembered as a prolific Haarlem painter, Jan Steen (1626–79) has seldom been out of favour as a genre artist, and Antoine Watteau (1626–79) came back after the French Revolution to enjoy a great reputation.

2. Russborough was the house of E.G.'s Co. Wicklow neighbour, the fourth Earl of Milltown. Raphael's masterpiece is more commonly known as 'La Belle Jardinière.' It is in the Louvre and although there are further copies it is doubtful if one of them ended up at Rothiemurchus.

3. Lely (1618–80), whose real name was van der Faes, succeeded van Dyke as principal painter to Charles II. The most influential of Restoration portraitists, he is famous for his voluptuous *Beauties* at Court, and for his patriotic studies of Charles's Admirals.

style of man was promoted to the Library, the only picture allowed to be in the room. We neither know the man nor the painter but it was always judged to have been done by a masterly hand. A few other old landscapes, not so well preserved, were hung about in the bedrooms. One portrait, unframed, in bad preservation too, always riveted my eyes. We called it the dying nun, because of the style of the accessories. It was awfully true to deputing nature and must, I think, have been the work of no pretender, whether his name be known to fame or not. Our Grant ancestors were spread over the walls of the Staircase. The Spreckled Laird and some of his family, Himself in armour, his brother Corrour in ditto, his wife the Lady Jean in a very low cut red velvet gown, with her yellow hair flowing all down over her shoulders, their little boys, my Uncle Rothy and one who died young, of whom my brother Johnny was the image, in court like suits, holding out birds and nosegays; Lord Elchies in his ermine, some others unknown. They made a better show after they were framed by my brother John when he was home on leave from India.

The Library was long in being completed; there was a good deal of work in the bookcases, as they entirely surrounded the room. My Mother had made the upstairs drawing room so pretty, and the view from its three windows was so very beautiful, no one entering it could wish for any other. We looked up the Spey to the Quaich range of mountains, Tor Alvie on the one hand, the Ord Ban on the other, and the broom island, now a pretty lawn covered by sheep, just in front between us and the river. The Grand piano forte was there, and the harp and a writing table, the fire place filled with balsams, other green house plants in the small light closets opening out of the room, and sofas and chairs in plenty. Angelica Koffman's prints were pinned on the walls.[1] Altogether it was very cheerful and summery, and many a pleasant hour was spent in this pretty apartment. Amongst other visitors there came 'Tom Lauder' and his friend, from henceforward our dear friend, Dr Gordon. My

1. Angelica Kaufmann (1741–1807) was one of the 36 original members of the Royal Academy.

father and Mother had known him before, but to us young people he was a stranger.

Dr Gordon was hardly handsome, and yet his friends all thought him so; not very tall, slight, fair. It was the expression of his countenance that was charming, and the manner, so gay, so simple, so attractive. He was very clever, had made his own way and was getting on rapidly. He had married, not well, I think, though he was very happy, and it had been a long attachment. It was a bad connexion, and she, to my mind, was not an agreeable woman—dawdling, untidy, grave. She was very useful to him, however, translating German for him and such like, having a good head for languages. Among his accomplishments was a most exquisite voice and style of singing; there was no greater treat than to hear his 'Banks and Braes o' bonnie Doon,' 'Scots wha hae wi Wallace bled' or 'Low down in the Broom,' etc., etc., for his fund was inexhaustible and whether the strain were tender or lively, spirited or sad, he gave musick and words as if inspired. He got up a great many duets with me and recommended the cultivation of both my voice and William's, but we really could not admire ourselves, it was such perfect delight listening to him. Mr Lauder sang too, but not well. He delighted in the 'Red Cross Knight'; his Wife, who had the voice of a Clarion trumpet, much admired by some, though rather louder toned than pleased refined ears, joined him in a great number of catches and glees of this sort. When she was not with him he sang them by himself with the greatest good nature. He shone much more in his drawings,[1] his sketches were very pretty, very faithful. We had holiday during the whole of his happy visit, accompanying him to all his favourite views in the mornings, and giving ourselves up to Dr Gordon and musick in the evenings.

There were two results followed our new friendship. Dr Gordon explained to my father the evil of our early rising and late breakfasting. It was often ten and after ten before my Mother appeared in the breakfast room. He also assured him that those stomachs that disliked milk, milk was not good

1. It was his drawings that illustrated his popular book on the Moray floods of 1829.

for. The consequence was that we went back in rising to my Mother's hour of seven, and that I had orders to make breakfast every morning at nine, and poor Mary partook of it; Caroline preferred remaining attached to 'Jacques Cameron,' Lachlan, and Johnny, who all throve on porridge or bread and milk. The other was that William, who was now fifteen, was to return no more to Eton. He was to remain at home till the College met in Edinburgh in October, when Dr Gordon consented to take charge of him. Great rejoicings followed this decision; England was so far away, the south of England, letters were long on the road; and though we had franks at command, so could write as often as we pleased,[1] that did not shorten the distance, for the post used to go all the way round by Aberdeen to Inverness and on to Grantown by a runner, where another runner received our bag, a little *foot* page, and brought it three times a week to the Doune.

This summer a very great improvement took place in our postal regulations. A stage coach was started to run three times a week over the hill between Perth and Inverness. Our bag was made up at Perth and dropped at Lynwilg at Robbie Cumming's, whose little shop soon became a receiving house for more bags than ours. It was quite an event. We used to listen for the horn; on still days or when the wind set that way we could hear it distinctly, when walking on the flowdyke round the farm. At one or two breaks in the wooding we could see the coach, a novel sight that made us clap our hands, and set poor Miss Elphick a crying. She took to walking in that direction, it was so gay, so like what she remembered. The Bridge of Alvie was passed by the new coach about five o'clock, and we had to hurry home to dress for dinner. During the second course, or later on a bad evening, the boy sent for the bag returned. The Butler brought it in, unlocked it, and delivered the contents. It came, one evening in autumn, late. It had been a stormy day. We had done dinner, I dined downstairs now, I and Miss Elphick. We were sitting round the fire on which fresh logs had just been thrown, the dessert and wine were on the horse shoe table, when the bag came in. Such startling news—the

1. As an M.P. her father would enjoy this privilege.

Dutch revolt, the signal for rousing Europe. There had been a dearth of warlike news after the Spanish campaigns were over, and this unexpected turn of affairs in Holland excited every one.[1] How very eagerly the papers were watched for many a day after.

I do not recollect any other matter of importance happening during the remainder of this year. Lord Huntly and a set of grouse shooting friends came to Kinrara, but we did not see much of them. Some of them dined with us once or twice; Lord Huntly often came over in the morning, and he had William with him a great deal more than was good for an idle boy of his age, inclined by nature to follow a leader.[2] I never like to think of the style of education given by the Aristocracy to their sons; home indulgence, School liberty, College license, and no enobling pursuits. We are then surprised that the low gratifications of the senses should during the season of the passions almost entirely supercede with our young men the higher pleasures of an exercised intellect. In one very important particular, the management of themselves, they are never in the very least instructed. At the schools it is a sort of catch who can system, get all you can, deceive all you can, conceal all you can, and for money. At Eton the boys had a great deal too much, not to be laid out by themselves for themselves, in necessaries first and indulgences afterwards; but all they could possibly want being provided for them at a cost of which they knew not one item, their 'pouches' were extra, to be wasted on nonsense, or worse. Some of these pouches were very heavy, great men's sons carrying back with them from ten guineas upwards according to the number of rich friends they had seen in the holidays, every body 'pouching' an Eton boy. This drove the less well supplied to various expedients for raising the 'ready,' the private expenses of the Upper boys being very great. Supper parties with plenty of wine, punch, and cards, trips on the

1. The Peninsular War effectively ended with the battle of Vittoria in June 1813; the Dutch revolted in November.
2. Lord Huntly himself had been at Eton between 1780 and 1786; he was 28 years older than her brother.

sly, hunting etc., bribes and so forth. One way of getting cash for all this was through the provision dealers. The boys bought their own breakfasts, that is they ordered them from these provision shops where they ran up accounts sent in every half year to the parents with the other charges. It was easy to have more rolls, more butter, more sugar etc. entered than were actually used, the accommodating dealer giving money instead of goods. Of course had this been known there would have been an end to it. When suspected all parties were well watched. As far as pounds, shillings and pence went, no great harm could be done. It was the principle that was so frightful, the breaking down of principle, the first step into the wrong, involving perhaps a lifetime of errour. There were other obliging persons at Eton who lent these children large sums, hung millstones round the necks of lads of fifteen that in many cases crushed them to the earth before they could set themselves free. William had Eton debts which he did not dare to tell of and with these weighing on his spirits, he departed for Edinburgh, where his Bond, washing and College expenses being paid, he was to be allowed a hundred a year for clothes and pocket money.

The first quarter was paid and most of it went faithfully to Eton. I don't know that he ever got another pound but he had credit and on that he drew, really, as ignorant as his little brother of how far his allowance would go, or what it would be wisest to do with it.

# CHAPTER FIFTEEN

# 1813–1814

THE winter of 1814 set in extremely cold; we had the Spey frozen over early in January. The whole country was hung with frost, the trees looking like so many feathers sparkling with diamonds in the sunshine. The harvest homes and the forest ball, and the Xmas at Belleville, and the Xmas at the Doune had all taken place in due order. Our fête being remarkable by the opening of the Library, now at last completed. The walls were distempered in french gray relieved by panelling in black. The bookcases, finished by handsome cornices, and very high, looked, when quite filled with books, very comfortable. All along upon the top were busts, vases, Indian arrows, old warlike weapons, curious horns, any objects indeed that were suited to the situation. The old puritan in the ruff was over the mantel piece, plenty of easy chairs, little tables, a sofa, a large writing table, a cosy tea table, all the Thorley telescope, microscope, theodolyte, and other instruments of scientifick value. A large atlas, portfolios of prints, ditto of caricatures, and a very fair collection of useful books amounting to three or four thousand volumes. There was not a subject on which sufficient information could not be gathered from amongst them. There were some little old Elzevirs, Aldines, Baskervilles,[1] and a Field Bible, to rank as Curiosities. A valuable shelf of huge folios, the Architecture of Italy, Balbec, Palmyra, and other engravings, as I may well know, for I wrote the catalogue. My father and I were months at this pleasant work,

1. Printers and publishers names: Elzevir is the famous Dutch publisher; Aldines stems from Aldus Manutius of Venice; John Baskerville (1706–75) was printer to the University of Cambridge.

during the progress of which I really think my somewhat frivolous mind learned more of actual worth to me than it had taken in, in all the former years of my young life.

The first point he insisted on, preparatory to my new employment, was that I should write a hand that could be read. On giving up half text on lines, I had got into the wavy unmeaning scribble then in fashion, pretty enough to look at, but extremely difficult to decipher, none of the letters being accurately formed, the c, the e, the legs of the m and the n, and the w and the u were all so like that except for the pop over the i, and the connexion of the sentences, it was quite impossible to say which was which. He therefore recommended an hour or so a day spent in forming letters that could not be mistaken. I was to write large, and slow, and carefully, gradually quicken the movement of the pen but not diminish the size of the writing. I was making an abstract of English history for him, and long before we got to the Crusades a very legible hand was formed, some what stiff perhaps, but easily read. The catalogue was written on folio paper, ruled for the proper headings; the books were classed, the size, edition, place of printing, number of volumes all mentioned; a column left for occasional remarks, and the place in the Library indicated by letters referring to the Divisions of the bookcases, and by numbers referring to the shelves, for the books were arranged according to size. When we came to putting them up we had to get Jane to help us; indeed she would have been the fitter assistant all through, her very decidedly studious turn of mind peculiarly qualifying her for the kind of work. That was I believe the reason my father did not employ her. She did not require sitting at any one's feet to acquire knowledge; I did.

James Craig,[1] who at the sale bought some of the books, has now I believe our poor old Catalogue. It was bound in blue morocco, with gilt leaves, and lay always for reference on the large oval table. Beside it was a little marble covered volume, in which I entered the names of all who borrowed, the name of the work lent, and the number of volumes that

1. Sir James Gibson Craig of Riccarton (E.G.'s sister Jane's father-in-law).

were taken away, with the date of the loan. My father thought a Library kept for self was only the talent hid in a napkin, and that any loss or damage, rarely occurring, was to be balanced against the amount of good distributed. His books were a blessing, far and near. How curiously we get attached to what we have the care of. I was actually as proud of all those books as if I had written them. I missed one from its place in a moment. I could now, I think, almost put them all back where I used to see them. I have the Library as a whole perfectly before me; I think I could very nearly make that catalogue again from memory. Individually I knew and loved each volume and bitter tears I shed when that useful collection was dispersed. The Biblical knowledge gained during the progress of this labour of love has often since been of infinite use to me.

We were still in the middle of our books when the poor old Captain died. He had been subject for many years to violent attacks of the tic in some of the nerves of the face. He had had teeth drawn, been up to Edinburgh to have a nerve cut, undergone treatment both surgical and medical, to no purpose. Twice a year, in the spring and fall, violent paroxysms of pain came on, lasting with intervals of care for many weeks. The only relief he got was from heat; he had to live in a room like an oven carefully stopped from every breath of air. During the fit he could not bear to see any one, the pain at times being so excruciating as to force him to cry out, a failing he considered unmanly. It once or twice happened that either before he took ill, or after he thought he was well, he felt a twinge approaching while we young people were with him. He turned us out in a hurry, quick march in a minute. His good wife was so tender of him at these times; what a mass of comforts she collected round him. He had been longer than usual without an attack. We were in hopes he was to be relieved during his decline from such agony as was scarce endurable and so he was, but how, by a stroke of paralysis. It took him in the night, affected one whole side, including his countenance and his speech. He never even partially recovered, and was a truly piteous spectacle sitting there helpless, well nigh senseless, knowing no one but his wife, and not her always, pleased with the warmth of the fire and sugar candy; the state of all others he had had the greatest horrour of ever falling into. He always prayed to preserve his faculties of mind whatever befell the failing body, and he lost them completely; not a gleam of reason ever more shot across his dimmed intellect, fortunately. This melancholy condition lasted eight months, and then the old man died quietly in the night, either 84 or 86 years of age.

The news was brought early to the Doune in the morning, and my father and mother immediately set out for Inverdruie. They remained there the greater part of the day, and in the evening my father and I were occupied in writing the funeral letters, and then the orders to Inverness for mourning.

Next day Jane and I were taken to Inverdruie. We had never seen a corpse, and the Captain had died so serenely, his vacant expression had so entirely disappeared, giving place to a placidity amounting to beauty, there was his old sweet smile about the mouth even; he lay there, so as if sleeping, that it was judged no less startling first view of death could be offered to young people. But the impression was fearful; for days I did not recover from it. Jane, who always cried abundantly when excited, got over it more easily. The colour, the indescribable want of colour, rather, the rigidity, the sharp outline of the high nose (he had piqued himself on *the* size and shape of this aristocratick feature), the total absence of flexibility. It was all horrour, him and not him. I longed to cry like Jane, but there only came a pain in my chest and head. My father preached a little sermon on the text before us. I am sure it was very good, but I did not hear it. He always spoke well, feelingly, and the people around seemed much affected; all my senses were absorbed by the awful image on that bed. We were led away, and then, while conversation was going on in the chamber of the Widow, my mind's eye went back to the scene we had left, and things I had not thought I noticed appeared as I must have seen them.

The body lay on the bed in the best room; it had on a shirt well ruffled, a night cap, and the hands were crossed over the breast. A white sheet was spread over all, white napkins were pinned on all the chair cushions, spread over the chest of drawers and the tables, and pinned over the few prints hung on the walls. Two bottles of wine and a plate of seed cake were on one small table, bread, cheese, butter, and whiskey on another, offered according to the rank of the numerous visitors by the one solitary watcher beside the corpse, a decent comely woman, a natural daughter of the poor Captain's who was respectably married to a farmer in Strathspey. A great crowd was gathered in and about the house; the name of each new arrival was carried up immediately to Mrs Grant, who bowed her head in approbation; the more that came the higher the compliment. She said nothing, however, she had a serious part to play—the highland Widow, and most decorously she went through it. Every body expected it from her, for when had she ever failed in any duty; and every body must have been gratified, for this performance was faultless. She sat on the Captain's cornered arm chair in a spare bedroom, dressed in a black gown, and with a white handkerchief pinned on her head, one *side* pinned round the head, and then all the rest hanging over it like, I must repeat myself, 'the kerchief on the head of some of the prints of our Henry of Bolingbroke.' Motionless the Widow sat during the whole length of the day, silent and motionless. If addressed, she either slowly nodded or waved her head, or, if an answer were indispensible, whispered it. Her insignia of office, the big bright bunch of large house keys, lay beside her, and if required, a lady friend, first begging permission, and ascertaining by the nod or the wave which key was the proper one, carried off the bunch, gave out what was wanted, and then replaced it. All the directions for the funeral were taken from herself in the same solemn manner. We were quite awe struck, the room was full, crowded up by comers and goers, and yet a pin could have been heard to drop in it. The short question solemnly asked in the lowest tone audible, the dignified sign in reply, alone broke the stillness of the scene—for scene it was. Early in the morning, before company hours, who had been so busy as the Widow. Streaking the corpse,[1] dressing its chamber, settling her own, giving out every bit and every drop that was to be used upstairs and down by gentle and simple, preparing

1. To lay out or compose a dead body.

the additional supplies in case of need afterwards so quietly applied for by the friendly young lady, there was nothing, from the merest trifle to the matter of most importance, that she had not, her own active self, seen to.

I shall never forget her on the day of the funeral, the fifth day from the death. Her weeds had arrived, and remarkably well she looked in them. She, a very plain woman in her ordinary somewhat shabby attire, came out in her 'new mournings' really like an elderly gentlewoman. She sat in the same room, in the same chair, with the addition of just a little more dignity, and a large white pocket handkerchief. All her lady friends were round her, Miss Mary and Mrs William from the Croft, Mrs McIntosh from the Dell, Mrs Stewart from Pityoulish, two of the Miss Grants, Kinchurdy. Her own sister Miss Anne from Burnside, Miss Bell Macpherson from Invereschie. My Mother, Jane, and I. There was very little said; every gig or horse arriving caused a little stir for a moment, hushed instantly. The noise without was incessant, for a great concourse had assembled to convoy the last of McAlpine's sons to his long home. A substantial Collation had been set out in the parlour, and another, unlimited in extent, in the kitchen. People coming from so far, waiting for so long, required abundance of refreshment. They were by no means so decorous below as we were above in the lady's chamber, though we had our table of good things too; but we helped ourselves sparingly and very quietly. At length my father entered with a paper in his hand; it was the list of the pall bearers. He read it over to Mrs Grant, and then gave it to her to read herself. She went over the names without a muscle moving, and then, putting her finger upon one, I don't know whose it was, she said in a low but very distinct voice, 'I would rather Ballintomb, they were brothers in arms.' My father bowed, and then offered her his hand, on which she rose, and every one making way they went out together, a few following. They passed along the passage to the death chamber, where on trestles stood the Coffin, uncovered as yet, and with the face exposed. The Widow took her calm last look, she then raised a small square bit of linen, probably put there by herself for the purpose, and dropping it over the countenance, turned and walked away. It was never to be raised again. Though Jane and I had been spared this solemnity, there was something in the whole proceedings that quite frightened us and when Mrs Grant returned to her arm chair and lay back in it, her own face covered by her handkerchief, and when my father's step sounded on the stairs as he descended, and the screws were heard as one by one they fastened down the coffin lid, and then the heavy tramp of the feet along the passage as the men moved with their burden, we drew closer to each other and to good Mrs McKenzie from Aviemore, who was among the company.

Hundreds attended the funeral. A young girl in her usual best attire walked first, then the Coffin borne by four sets of broad shoulders, extra bearers grouping round, as the distance was a couple of miles at least to the kirkyard. Next came the near of kin, and then all friends fell in according to their rank without being marshalled—highlanders never presume, their innate good breeding never subjecting them to a forced descent from too honourable a place; there is even a deal of fuss at times to get them to accept one due to them. Like the Bishops, etiquette requires them to refuse at first the proffered dignity. What would either say if taken at their word.

The presbyterian Church has no burial ceremony. It is the custom, however, for the minister to attend, generally speaking, to give a somewhat lengthy blessing before the feast, and a short prayer at the grave. Mr Grant of Duthil did his part better than was expected; no one, from the style of his sermons, expected the touching eulogy pronounced over the remains of the good old Captain—not undeserved, for our great grand Uncle had died in peace with all the world, as little burdened by sin of any sort as any poor frail humanity than ever ran through life. He was long regretted, many a kind action he had done, and never a harsh word had he said of or to any one.

My father gave the funeral feast at the Doune. Most of the friends of fit degree accompanied him home to dinner, upwards of twenty there must have been and very merry they were. All sorts of pleasant stories went the round with the wine bottles, clergy and all, and the Parsons of Alvie and

Abernethy were both there, as well as our own Minister of Duthill, coming in to the Library to tea in high good humour. The rest of the people, who had been abundantly refreshed at Inverdruie, dispersed.

The Captain had made a Will. Small as his income must have been, he left his Widow comfortably provided for, his sword, pistols and snuff box to William, £500 to us younger children and my father his residuary legatee. We three girls were each to have £100 for Wedding clothes, Johnny who was his Godson the remaining £200. Where it all went to who can tell. I only know I never got my share nor any of it. I never got any Wedding clothes, except a habit from my father which he had bought from Mary who never rode, and a hat and feathers from my Mother that came out for herself and she thought too youthful. I never wore this hat but once either, the Colonel made me take it off, he could not bear it and the insects ate it all up at Poona. Mary had the wit to order for herself such extras to her outfit as she thought necessary and she gave the bills to Masserwanjee so she did get an instalment—Jane must have got all the rest, her trousseau was very handsome and very expensive. Perhaps we might have been answered as the Lady Logie answered May Anne. Miss Brodie of Lethan left May Anne a legacy, I forget the amount, not large, but enough to be grateful for at any rate, and when May Anne on growing up enquired after it, 'your legacy, indeed,' said her astonished Mother, 'little legacy you're like to find at this time of day—you ate it, and you drank it, and you wore it, and what better would you do with it.'

The funeral over, there came on a marriage. Lord Huntly, now in the decline of his racketty life, overwhelmed with debts, sated with pleasure, tired of fashion, the last male heir of the Gordon line, married.[1] What would the mother who adored him have given to have seen his wedding day. All the regrets that she caused to herself and him for preventing the love of his youth from becoming her daughter in law. She actually carried this beautiful girl away with her to Paris and

1. George, thirteenth Earl, eighth Marquess, fifth and last Duke of Gordon (1770–1836). He and his family were Highland neighbours and close friends.

married her to an old merchant, while her son was away with his regiment.[1] His bride was young, and rich, and good, and *fair*, but neither clever nor handsome. She made him, however, very happy, and paid his most pressing debts, that is her father did, old Mr Brodie of the Burn, brother to Brodie of Brodie, who either himself or somebody for him had had the good sense to send him with a pen to a counting house instead of with a sword to the battle field, where he made a really large fortune; he gave with his daughter, his only child, £100,000 down, and left her more than another at his death—and really to her husband her large fortune in money was the least part of her value. She possessed upright principles, good clear common sense, and when by and by she began to feel her powers and took the management of his affairs, she turned out a first rate woman of business. She has got into the cant of the Methodists of late years, which sort of aberration, like any other, indeed, is a pity. She was very young at the time of her marriage, too unformed to be shewn as the fastidious Marquis' Bride, so while all the north was a blaze of bonfires in honour of the happy event, her Lord carried her off abroad.[2] The Minister of Alvie made what was thought a very indelicate allusion to 'coming rejoicings closely connected with the present' in a speech to the gathering round the blazing pile on Tor Alvie; and as no after events ever justified the prophecy, this incorrect allusion was never forgotten. The marriage was childless. Lord Huntly was the last Duke of Gordon.

1. He was Colonel of the 92nd. (Gordon) Highlanders from 1796 and of the 42nd. Highlanders (Black Watch) from 1806; he had seen active service during the Irish rebellion 1798, in Holland 1799 and Walcheren 1809; he commanded the army in Scotland between 1803 and 1806.
2. His wife was Elizabeth, daughter of Alexander Brodie of Arnhall and they were married in December 1813. According to the *Scots Peerage*, which also describes her father as 'a wealthy India merchant', it was not Methodism she turned towards; 'she became a leading adherent of the Free Church when that body seceded in 1843.'

A very unpleasant but unfortunately not a very rare occurrence in our part of the highlands about this time necessitated great changes in the family. My Mother's maid, poor Peggy Davidson, whom we all found much changed in temper of late, asked leave to go to Inverness for a week on a visit to the Aunt who had brought her up. The week passed and Peggy not returning my Mother was annoyed. She never liked advantage being taken of her good nature. A second week going by, Peggy was written to and after some delay an answer was returned that she was unable to resume her place, that the reason of this Simon Ross the Butler would give, for he 'had ruined her for ever.'

It was a regular thunder clap. We all much liked poor Peggy. She was very obliging, very useful, a remarkably neat dress maker and plain worker and a good hair dresser and we always fancied she would remain with us for ever, as besides being exceedingly plain in face, she was slightly deformed in figure, lame in her left leg and in her right arm, the leg was a contraction that kept the heel up several inches from the ground so that she only walked on the toes of that foot and even then she halted. The arm had been broken and also dislocated at the elbow joint, which stiffened so that she never afterwards got the full use of it. As this accident happened in our service, the rumble falling off the carriage while she was in it, and throwing her away on some stones by the side of the road in the hill of Drumochter, my father and Mother considered her as a sort of charge whom they were bound to provide for. Altogether the affair happening among the upper servants was very vexatious. Ross was the gardener's eldest son, a very superiour man, he had lived with us many years having come to us at Twyford, he had given us lessons in writing and ciphering during the summer when we had no governess. He had a good library up in his own room, often borrowed my father's books, played extremely well on the violin and though lame from a stiff knee joint was a handsome man, had a particularly fine head. What had bewitched him so to misconduct himself and to choose such an object for his love my Mother declared herself utterly unable to comprehend. She was very much irritated and insisted on his marriage or dismissal. My father we thought inclined to be more lenient but he was over ruled. My Mother, a quiet woman in general, was not roused with impunity. This affair roused her thoroughly and she would admit of no compromise. Ross was a good servant, a good son, a clever man, a nice looking man. To these and many other perfections she assented but he was an immoral man and he had outraged decency in her house and he should not remain in it unless he made Peggy in highland fashion 'an honest woman.' We were constantly patching up marriages all over the place a few months after the harvest homes. It was so common a matter no one thought much about it. Betty Ross the housemaid and John Fyffe the handsome Smith had been very quickly made man and wife after the great forest ball. *Their* wedding necessitated two or three more by the help of the Laird's authority, and at the farm kitchen the 'lass' who cooked for the 'lads' was changed regularly every half year, the late incumbent moving not much too soon into a house of her own. At that distance our eyes could be pardoned for not seeing too clearly, but in this case it was very different and as Ross stoutly refused to marry this unfortunate woman, he had to leave us. This makes me recollect that I have antedated the arrival of the magnificent Gouard—he did not come back with my father till this summer now approaching, to replace Ross who was parted with immediately. My Mother requiring only the footman to attend upon her during my father's absence, he was going as usual in the spring to London.

Miss Elphick's mother, an old woman, having had a serious illness during the winter, and wishing to see her daughter, it was determined that we should have holiday for six weeks, and that our Governess should travel under my father's escort to town, Caroline the French girl going with them to preserve the 'propers.' She was not to return, my Mother disapproving of her grimaces with Jacques Cameron, and also believing she knew more of the late nursery business than so young a person ought to have been acquainted with. Caroline was misjudged. She was very innocent and very timid, this prevented her understanding or speaking and as for her flirtation with our most loutish cousin, it was the mere manner of her country women—was exercising her little talent of coquetry on the only object within her reach. She had been very useful to us in the way of naturalizing her language among us. People may read a foreign language well, understand it as read, sufficiently, even write it well, idiom and all. But speak it, carry on the affairs of every day life from mere grammar and dictionary learning, I really do not believe to be possible. A needlefull of thread was my first example in point. We were all at work, and I asked for '*du fil pour mon aiguille.*' '*Ah, hah,*' said Caroline, '*une aiguillée de fil; tenez, Mademoiselle;*' and so on with a thousand other instances, never forgotten, for those eighteen months during which her Parisian french was our colloquial medium the greater part of the day made us all thoroughly at home in the language; and though rusted by years of disuse, a week in France brought it back so familiarly both to your Aunt Mary and me that the natives, as you may remember, could not believe we had not been brought up in their country. My father was much pleased at his plan succeeding so well; he however forbade any mixture of tongues. When we wrote and spoke french no English was to be interlarded. When we spoke or wrote English, there were to be no French words introduced. English was rich in expletives, he said, there could be no difficulty in finding fit expressions in it, able to convey any meaning, and he would send us to Dryden, Milton, Bolingbroke and Addison in proof of this.[1] Were we to alter any sentences of theirs by changing an English for a French word we should enfeeble the style, probably alter the signification.

One of his favourite exercises for us was the making us read aloud passages from his favourite Authours to impress them on our memories, besides giving us a just style of declamation; he himself had been taught by Stephen Kemble, and he certainly read beautifully. Jane was an apt pupil. She sometimes mouthed a little, only sometimes in general she in her round clear voice gave the musick, as it were, to the subject, expressed so perfectly by the gentle emphasis she employed. William was not bad either, by no means. I was

1. Noted historian, orator and friend of Alexander Pope, Viscount Bolingbroke was impeached over his attempt to restore the Stuart dynasty. As an extreme Tory, he keeps odd company in this list especially because E.G.'s father was such a dedicated Whig.

wretched, they did nothing but make fun of me. I don't think I was then capable of feeling much so could not *interpret* any, my mind being in some respects uncommonly slow of coming to maturity. They told an abominable story of me, at least half a dozen times a year, how that Jane, having got grandly through the mustering of all the devils in hell, alias fallen angels, and ended magnificently with 'He called so loud that all the hollow deep of hell resounded,' as did our library, I began in what William called my 'childish treble,' 'Princes, Potentates,' in a voice a mouse at the fireside could have imitated! Milton did not suit me, but Sterne was worse; nobody ever could read Sterne, I am certain—my father couldn't. That ass, and the Lieutenant's death, and the prisoner,—who could read them aloud, or without tears, in any way.[1]

To finish the tale of poor Peggy. Her stern Aunt at Inverness declined to keep her after the scandal she had brought on a decent name. So she was boarded in the neighbourhood till she weaned her baby, Ross being made to leave funds for her support. He then placed the child with one of his sisters at Kincairn. The Mother never saw him more. She went to London by the help of friends and staid there with our old Coachman William Bird and his nice wife who had set up hackney coaches. My father having told her story to Alderman Atkins, she was taken into that good man's family to attend upon his invalid wife, a service she faithfully performed and remained in till her own death. She died of consumption some years after this, most carefully nursed, poor thing, by those kind people who had become quite attached to her. My Mother promoted the housemaid, Christy Eason, to be her own maid. A Kingussie girl who began life as the attendant of one of the Montague children, their Grandmother the Duchess of Gordon, happened to have with her at Kinrara. Lord Francis, a delicate boy, became so fond of her and throve so well under her care that she was sent back with him to Kimbolton, and when he went to school she was made stillroom maid there till the

---

1. *Paradise Lost*, I, 314; *Tristram Shandy*, VI, ch. 6, recounts Le Fever's death.

Establishment was broken up on the Duke of Manchester going out as Governour to Jamaica. She came back to Badenoch an unspoiled pretty brunette and was glad after a while to leave an uncomfortable home for harder work at the Doune. She was a general favourite in the house, her promotion therefore pleased every one. She was much attached to us all, especially to my Mother, who liked her in turn. After some years, love led Christy far away from us, the love did not prosper, though she herself did, and curiously enough in the old age of both she returned to my Mother's service in Jane's house in Edinburgh and there she is now waiting on her faithfully.

Simon Ross got a good place with Colonel and Lady Charlotte Drummond. He left them to push his fortunes in London, from which time he ceased to hold any communication with his family. At long last came a letter to an elder sister married near Kilravock to say that she would receive in a few days a trunk containing some articles of value he would trust to her disposing of for the benefit of his son, that he bade her and all the rest of his relations farewell for of him no one would ever hear more. Not one trunk but two arrived filled with quite handsome wearing apparel, books, the gold watch with the chain and enormous bunch of seals we used so to admire as children, a fine breastpin and a few other trinkets, evidently the man's whole possessions. What had become of him remains to this day a mystery, no trace of him was ever recovered. Had he emigrated he would have required his wardrobe, had he been in distress he must have parted with it, had he died a felon's death it would have escheated to the crown. The only remaining probability was that he had contemplated and committed suicide. Why or wherefore no one will ever know. It was all a very melancholy story and had it come on at once would have excited more distressing feelings than it did when we heard it after a lapse of years. None of that old gardener's children turned out well. There must have been something wrong in the rearing of them. To return from this episode. My father, Miss Elphick, and Caroline happily off, we bade adieu to the restraints of the School-room. We did not neglect our studies, but we shoved them aside sometimes, and we led an easy sort of half busy, whole merry life, more out of doors than in, all the fine bright weather of the springtide. Jane looked after Mary's lessons, I carried Johnny on through his. We all four agreed that the Governess was quite a supernumerary—yet we owed her much. She was tidiness itself, a beautiful needlewoman, mended old things, like Burns's Cottar's Wife,[1] to look like new, and taught her art to us. She never allowed one atom to be put off till to-morrow that ought to be done to-day. She made us obedient to rule, careful of time, steady to business. Really with Mary she had done wonders; not much at first, very little at a time but by methodical perseverance she had roused her mind to exertion; Touchstone had been a great help. Jane and I were quite surprised to find the child who a year before would not count to ten, able to work any sum in the simple rules. She played neatly on the pianoforte giving great expression to the easy airs she had learned. She had waked up to ask questions and to be interested in the answers, could laugh and be merry and enjoy her walks, and though, from her great size for her age, her intellect remained slow till her growth of body was over, she was never again the stupid thing Miss Elphick found her. Jane and she got on very lovingly. Johnny was so easy to teach he and I worked in the sunshine. He was the dearest little fellow ever was in the world, not pretty, rather plain, except for fine eyes, small, slight, very quiet and silent, but full of fun, full of spirit, clever in seeing and hearing and observing and understanding all going on around, preferring to learn in this practical way rather than from books. He grew to be fond of reading, but he had found the mastering of the mere mechanical part so difficult that he had rather a distaste for the labour then. Jack dear,[2] you often put me in mind of Uncle John.

We had two ponies at our command, William's very pretty and rather headstrong and very spirited little black Sally, and the old gray my mother used to ride to the reviews, now

1. 'The Mother, wi' her needle and her sheers
   Gars ould claes look amaist as weel's the new'
   (*The Cottar's Saturday Night* verse 6)
2. E.G.'s youngest child and only son.

grown milk white—he was a large size but so quiet that Mary, who was a coward always, was mounted on him. She never liked riding, so went out but seldom. Johnny, besides being so little, was much of her mind; Jane and I therefore had our stud to ourselves, and plenty of use we made of it. We rode to Belleville and back, sixteen miles, to the Dell of Killiehuntly and back about the same distance, and all over the country up and down the Spey, a very fat coachman on one of the carriage horses behind us. At the Dell of Killiehuntly lived John and Betty Campbell, doing well, but alas! not happy. His brother shared the farm, a good managing man with whom it was easy to live, but he had a wife with whom it was not easy to live. The two ladies soon disagreed, and though they parted household, John and Betty living in the farm house, Donald and Mary in rooms they fitted up in the Offices, perfect harmony never substituted until sorrow came to both.

Donald and Mary had a fine son drowned in the Spey and John and Betty lost their only child, my Goddaughter, Eliza, in the measles. Neither bereaved Mother ever 'faulted' the other after these events; each had shewn so much heart on the occasion of the grief of the other, that some bond of kindness, at least of forbearance, existed evermore between them. Betty never got over her 'puir Eliza's' death. She never alluded to her, never replied when any one else did, nor did she outwardly appear to be any way altered, yet it had changed her. Her hair turned gray, her manner became restless, and she never called me from that time any thing but Miss Grant, my Christian name she never uttered, nor the pet name 'burdie' by which she had oftenest called us both. It altered John Campbell too, wore him down somehow. What had ever brought that pair together was a problem never to be solved. John Campbell had very few words of English, it was very difficult to make out his meaning when he tried to explain himself in that foreign language, and he certainly did not understand it when spoken to him. To the end of his life he never got one bit beyond the smattering he began with. Betty, a Forres woman, spoke broad, low country Scotch, pure Morayshire, and never any thing else to her husband nor any one; she never tried the gaelick nor attempted to try it. The language she did speak was incomprehensible, any English the highlanders acquire being real good English such as they were taught by books at school, and in conversation with the Upper classes the accent being Highland enough, certainly, but the words were fit for Cockney land. Betty's was another tongue, the low Dutch would have comprehended it as easily as did the Highlander, yet did she and John Campbell managed to understand each other and to get on together lovingly, the gray mare taking the lead, as was seemly. Both husband and wife dearly loved us; few events made either of them happier than the sight of our ponies cannily picking their steps down the brae a little piece away from their good farm house. All they had of the best was brought out for us, our steeds and our fat attendant faring equally well for our sakes; and then Betty would promise to return the visit, and she would not forget her promise either, but walk her eight or nine miles some fine day, and pay her respects all through the Duchus.

She always reminded me of Meg Merrilies, a tall, large framed, powerfully made woman, with dark flashing eyes and raven hair, eminently handsome, though somewhat resolute looking. Her dress, though in a very different style from the gypsy's, was extremely picturesque; a linsey gown, white handkerchief, white apron, a clear close fitting cap with a plaited lace edged border, and a bright satin ribbon to bind it on the head, and over this a high steeple cap of clearer muslin, set further back than the underneath one so that the borders did not interfere. A red plaid of the Campbell tartan, spun and dyed by herself, was thrown round her when she went out.

She spun the wool for stockings too, and knitted them; but at fine needle works she was not expert. Indeed she was too active to sit to them. She was a stirring wife, in and out, but and ben, cooking, washing, cleaning, keeping a quick eye over all, warm tempered, and kind hearted. Every one liked her, even the silly servant lasses who got so frequent a scold from her. In her old age, when husband and child were gone, Betty got fond of money. She was free handed in happier days.

It was a shorter ride to Aviemore, in quite the other

direction, down the water; by no means so pleasant a visit. The old servants there had for some years after their marriage gone on most comfortably. There was no such inn upon the road; fully furnished, neatly kept, excellent cooking, the most attentive of Landlords, all combined to raise the fame of Aviemore. Travellers pushed on from the one side, stopped short on the other, to sleep at this excellent inn. Poor Lynch! how hard she worked, how much she bore, to keep it up to its reputation. She dearly loved her husband, and after his failing became apparent, what she at first concealed she continued to excuse, and after disease set in, the consequence of perpetual drunkenness, she caught at it as the cause rather than the effect, and watched him and tended him, and did his work as well as her own, and never once was heard to reflect upon him. All the years he had been with us, for he had been my father's servant before my Mother's marriage, McKenzie had never even been suspected of want of sobriety; he took his drams and his punch like the rest, too much whiskey was going among them, but his steadiness had never been affected. At Aviemore the poor man breathed whiskey, so many travellers, drovers, and others of that class must have the welcome cup and the parting cup and the stirrup cup. Those that staid the night required the cheerful glass or bowl, the Landlord as of course partaking with every one, so that in an unfortunately short space of time the Landlord learned to love the bite as the child did on the Milltown muir. Quickly this dreadful craving increased, till he lost all care for all else. We used to see him staggering about the stable yard when his good wife would tell us he was too busy to come in to ask us how we did. Then when he got worse, and she could not keep him away, he would talk nonsense that frightened us and grieved her, as we saw by her pale face though she never said a word. Latterly, when epileptick fits and delirium tremens came on, she seemed relieved to be able to talk of his bad health and the effect this had produced upon his intellect. She was a good creature that dear little Mrs McKenzie, a proof of what a woman with a heart can turn herself to. Her father had kept a china shop in London. She was born and bred in the City, apprenticed to a dress maker and sent out as a Lady's maid. Her first place was with a rich merchant's wife, my Mother's was her second. Here she was at one end of the long moor stretching for miles from the foot of Craigellachie across the wild mountain range towards Inverness. The business of her inn sometimes overwhelming, often slack, her stores to be calculated and ordered from a distance, her fuel, not coals, but peats which she had to go to the Moss to see prepared in immense quantity; her plentiful housekeeping depending on the farm requiring her watchful management, her linen, her blanketing, most of her clothing made at home. Her nearest neighbour in Rothiemurchus three miles off. Children to educate, and that affliction of a husband to disturb all. Talk of the backwoods to a gentlewoman. Here was worse than the backwoods and the woman to go through the toil without help, taken from a class ignorant in the extreme of every practical detail, and used to every comfort. If ever I wrote a novel for the humble born, Mrs McKenzie shall be my heroine—few have had such trials, none ever bore them more cheerfully. Even during the long highland winter, her spirits never failed. She had always plenty to do—and so much to learn, she said. While her children were infants she had an old, nearly blind sister of her husband's to take care of them; on the death of old Auntie she got a Governess for them, an excellent little woman not too fine for her place, and though there were those that thought her 'set up wi a Governess indeed,' even they admitted before long that a better plan for herself or for them, and a cheaper, could not have been hit on. In her little odd way, with her Cockney English and her very dressy bonnets, she had sometimes feathers in them, how much good sense her conduct shewed. She was so respected that she was admitted on equal terms into society quite above her station. She dined at the Dell, the Croft, Lynwilg etc. Latterly at the table at the Doune. When my dear Mother got into bad health, long after this time though, she liked no one to have about her so much as Lynch.

Miss Elphick returned before my father. She came by sea to Inverness, remained a day or two with the Coopers, and then came on in the gig with Mr Cooper, who had other business with William Cameron and such a dose of North Country scandal for my Mother. She liked a little bit of gossip, and she got abundance. I like gossip too, I suppose we all do, clever gossip, not Mr Cooper's, that was unendurable: 'The laird of *this*, his Bills flying about like waste paper. The lady of *that*, too sharp a tongue to keep a servant. Every thing under lock and key at Glen *here*; and open house to allcomers at Rath *there*, with fish bought when extravagantly high by Mrs *So-and-So* of New Street, while the children of *Some-one* in Church Lane often came in to Mrs Cooper for a "piece".' He had got fat by this time. The face had turned red, the hair was always red, he crossed his rather short arms before him, gave a cough to untie the string of the bag, as it were, and then out came all this rubbish. Miss Elphick extremely admired him, he was a kind, good natured man, his home was so happy and his coats fitted so beautifully. She had brought for her own wear from London a bottle green cloth surcoat, abundantly braided, quite military looking, and a regular hat, a man's hat, a Welsh style of dress she fancied particularly becoming and suited to her, as tartans were to us, her mother being a Welshwoman. In this guise she went in the month of May, or June indeed, to pay her visit of condolence to the Widow at Inverdruie; a farewell on our part, Mrs Grant having determined to give up her farm and return to Burnside to keep house with her very old mother and her bachelour brother. We were coming back, and had reached the turn in the road under the bank of fire trees near James MacGregor's, when a very disastrous piece of news reached us. What we called the Widows' house at Loch an Eilein was burned to the ground.

My father had always had a turn for beautifying Rothie-murchus with cottages; it was more that, at first the effect of the picture in the scenery, than the wish to improve the dwellings of his people, consequently his first attempts were guiltless of any addition to family comfort. A single room, thatched, with a gable end battened down at top, like a snub nose, had been stuck on the hill at the Polchar for the Gamekeeper, on the bank at the ferry for the boatman, at the end of the West gate as a lodge. They were all inconvenient as an old turf hut, and a great deal more ugly, because more pretending. Searching through our drawing books for a model for the Croft amazingly improved his ideas of cottage architecture; also, he now better understood the wants of a household. He picked out a great many pretty elevations, suggested the necessary changes, and left it to Jane and me to make correct drawings and working plans. Our first attempts were usually so full of faults, we had to try perhaps a dozen times before a sketch was sufficiently perfect to be accepted. We really became attached to the subjects. It was no wonder that all the new cottages became of such importance to us.

The West gate was the first improved. It was lengthened by a room, heightened sufficiently to allow of a store loft under the steep roof, the snub nose disappeared, the heather thatch was extended over the wall by means of supporting brackets, and a neat verandah ran along the side next the road and round the gable end. We trained Ayrshire roses on the Walls, honeysuckle on the verandah, and we put all sorts of common flowers in a border between the cottage and the road. It was a very pretty cottage, particularly suited to the scenery, and when neatly kept as it was by the next occupant, was quite one of the Shows of the place. The first tenant, Sandy Cameron the tailor, brother to Jenny Dairy, should never have been put there, he had no taste for any thing he had not been used to.

The next attempt was the Polchar, a more ambitious one, for there were a front and a back door, a long passage, staircase, pantry, kitchen, parlour, and two bedrooms above. It had a very picturesque look with its over hanging heather thatched roof, its tall chimneys, and its wide latticed windows. There was no border of flowers, only a small grass plot and a gravel walk, but there was an enclosed yard fronted by the dog kennels. A path led to a good kitchen garden laid out in a hollow close by. Another path went down to the edge of the first of the chain of the Lochans, and so on through the birch wood towards the Croft. Another path skirted the 'little lakes' by James MacGregor's to the fir forest—Aunt Mary's walk. It was truly a model for the dwelling of a highland Gamekeeper.

Next came a cottage for four aged widows. They had been living apparently in discomfort, either alone in miserable sheilings, far away from aid in case of sickness, and on such dole as kind neighbours gave helped by a share of the poor's box, or in families weary enough of the burthen of supporting them. My father thought that by putting them all together he could lodge them cheaply, that they might be of use to one another in many ways, and that the help given to them would go farther when less subdivided. It was really a beautiful home he built for them. Like all he later erected, there were the cantalivre roof of heather, the wide latticed windows, the tall chimneys, but he made it two storeys high, and he put the staircase leading to the upper rooms outside. It had quite a Swiss look about it. Sociable as were his intentions regarding the widows, he knew too well to make them live together except when they were inclined. Each was to have a room and a closet for herself. Two of them were to live on the ground floor with a separate entrance to their apartments, one door opening from the front of the house, the other from the back. The two above reached their abode by the hanging stairs, a balcony landing them before their several door windows. We were charmed with this creation of our united fancies, and had grand plans in our heads for suitable fittings, creeping plants, flower borders, rustick seats, and even furniture. The Lake was on one hand; the meal mill at the foot of the Ord, with the burnie, the mill race, a few cottages and small fields, on the other. The gray mountains and the forest behind; all was 'divine' but the spirit of *wo*man.[1] The widows rebelled; old, smoke dried, shrivelled up witches with pipes in their mouths, and blankets on their backs, preferred the ingle nook in their dark, dirty, smoke filled huts to this picture of comfort.

Stone walls were cold, light hurt the eyes, deal floors got dirty unless they were scrubbed! The front door complained of the outside stair, it was so in the way and noisy. The back door objected to entering behind, she had as good a right to the exit of honour as her neighbour; her windows too looked on the burn, there was no road that way, she knew nothing that was doing. She equally detested the stairs, though they were not near her, people going up them and coming down

1. Where the virgins are soft as the roses they twine.
   And all, save the spirit of man, is divine.
      Byron, *The Bride of Abydos* (1, i)

them for ever, crossing them in all ways, both ground floors said, forcing them to spend a great deal of valuable time at the foot of this annoyance, expostulating with the upper windows for the ceaseless din they made.

These more exalted ladies felt themselves quite as ill used as those beneath them. Their backs were broken carrying burdens up those weary stairs; no one could come to see them without being watched from below; they could neither go out nor come in themselves without every movement being registered. In short, they were all in despair, agreeing in nothing but hatred of their beautiful home. The fact was they were not ready for it, fit for it; it's not at three score and ten that we can alter the habits and the feelings grown out of them. Our benevolent schemes failed in more than this one instance from our own ignorance. It was very little understood then where to begin, and how very slowly it was necessary to go on in order to reach even the first of the many resting places on the road to better ways.

The poor Captain sealed the fate of the Widows' house. One day after coming in from his drive in the old low pony phaeton with the long tailed black mare, somebody asking him which way he had been, he replied, 'By Rothy's poor house at Loch an Eilein.' Of all things on earth the most repugnant of all names to the feelings of the highlanders. 'Any form but that' charity might be tolerated in, assistance being very thankfully received when more delicately proferred, but to be paraded as a recognised almshouse inmate was more than the pride of any clanswoman could bear, and so it fell out that by accident the heather thatch took fire, and that although neighbours were near, and a stream ran past the door, and the widows all alive during the burning, were active as bees removing their effects, the stairs being no hindrance, the flames raged on. Only blackened walls remained in the morning. We could not help being so far uncharitable as to believe that whether or no they had lit the spark that threw them homeless on the world, they had at least taken no trouble to extinguish it.

My father was very much annoyed at this misfortune; he would do nothing towards any further arrangements for the comfort of these old bodies—perhaps they lived to repent their folly. He did not give up his building, however. The next cottage he undertook was given to much more grateful occupants. He had intended it as a toy for my Mother, but the sort of amusement of fitting it up not suiting her tastes, it was eventually made over to us, and became one of the principal delights of our happy Rothiemurchus life. We will *pause* before describing it. Dalachapple once conversing with my Mother concerning some firm in Glasgow the partners of which she had been acquainted with in her dancing days, 'They failed, didn't they,' said she. 'They *paused*,' said he. So will we. It was a very expressive term.

# CHAPTER SIXTEEN

# 1814

IN years long gone by a certain William Grant, who I believe claimed some sort of kin with the family, had listed for a soldier and gone off to foreign parts, never to return in his former station among his people. He rose early from the ranks, and during a very prosperous career in India won for himself fame, and rupees to balance it. A curious kind of narrow minded man, he had, however, the common virtue of his race—he never forgot his relations; in his advancement he remembered father, mother, brothers, sisters, Uncles, Aunts, and cousins, none were neglected. There was a deal of good sense, too, in the ways he took to provide for them. One brother was never more nor less than a common soldier. We knew him always as Peter the Pensioner, on account of sixpence a day my father got him from Greenwich, in lieu of an eye he had lost in some engagement. He lived in one of a row of cottages on the Milltown moor, with a very decent wife and a large family of children, all of whom earned their bread by labour. We had a son in the wood work and a daughter as kitchenmaid during the time their uncle the General was paying a visit to us.

The next brother rose to be a major, and retiring from the Army in middle life, settled on the farm of Craggan some miles down Speyside. His two sons, educated by the Uncle, were both of them Lieutenant Colonels before their death. The daughter, to whom he was equally kind, he took out to India, where she married a Civilian high up in the service.[1] He left the rest of his relations in their own place, merely befriending them occasionally; but for his mother, when she

1. One of the covenanted European servants of the East
   India Company, not in military employment.

became a widow and wished to return to Rothiemurchus, where she was born, he built a cottage in a situation chosen by herself, at the foot of the Ord Ban, surrounded by birch trees, just in front of the old Castle on the lake. Here she lived many years very happy in her own humble way on a little pension he regularly transmitted to her, neither 'lifted up' herself by the fortunate career of her son, nor more considered by the neighbours in consequence. She was just the Widow Grant to her death. After she was gone, no one caring to dwell in so lonely a spot, the little cottage fell to ruin; only the walls were standing when my father took a fancy to restore it, add to it, and make it a picture of an English home. He gave it high chimneys, two or three gable ends, and very wide windows. It was a very pretty outside. Within were three rooms, a parlour, a front kitchen boarded, a back kitchen bricked. He hoped my mother would have fitted it up like to her Houghton recollections of peasant comfort, but it was not her turn. She began indeed by putting six green painted Windsor chairs into the front kitchen, and hanging a spare warming pan she had on the wall, there being by the bye no bedroom in the cottage; here her labours ended. The shutters of these pretty, little, neatly finished cheerful rooms were seldom opened, moss, stones and heather lay undisturbed around its white washed walls, no one almost ever entered the door. But it had a good effect in the scenery. Coming out of the birch wood it struck every eye, and seen from the water when we were in the boat rowing over the lake, that single habitation amid the solitude quite enlivened the landscape. We young people had the key, for it was our business to go there on fine days to open the windows, and sometimes when we walked that way we went in to rest. How often we had wished it were our own, that we might fit it up to our fancy.

This spring I was furnished with a new occupation. My Mother told me that my childhood has passed away; I was now seventeen, and must for the future be dressed suitably to the Class young lady into which I had passed. Correct measures were taken of my size and height by the help of Mrs McKenzie who was not entirely rusted in her old art, and these were sent to the Miss Grants of Kinchurdy at Inverness, and to Aunt Leitch at Glasgow. I was so extremely pleased; I was always fond of being nicely dressed, but when the various things ordered arrived, my feelings rose to delight. We had hitherto, my sisters and myself, been all suited alike. In the summers we wore pink gingham or nankin frocks in the morning, white in the afternoon. Our common bonnets were of coarse straw lined and trimmed with green, and we had tippets to all our frocks. The best bonnets were of finer straw, lined and trimmed with white, and we had silk spencers of any colour that suited my Mother's eye. In the winter we wore dark stuff frocks, black and red for a while—the intended mourning for the king. At night always scarlet stuff with bodices of black velvet and tucks of the same at the bottom of the petticoat. While in England our wraps were in the pelisse form and made of cloth, with beaver bonnets; the bonnets did in the highlands, but on outgrowing the pelisses they were replaced by clokes with hoods, very comfortable in our harsh climate, made of tartan spun and dyed by Jenny Dairy, the red dressed tartan of our clan, the set[1] anciently belonging to the Grants. Our habits were of the green tartan, now commonly known by our name, first adopted by us when the Chief raised the 42nd regiment; it was originally Rifle corps, and the bright red of the belted plaid being too conspicuous, that colour was left out in the tartan wove for the soldiers; thus it gradually got into use in the Clan, and goes still by the name of the Grant or 42nd tartan. I retained none of my old attire but my bonnets, my cloke and my habits. All the rest was divided between my sisters and I now burst out full blown into the following wardrobe.

Two or three gingham dresses of different colours very neatly made with frills, tucks, flounces, etc. Two or three cambrick muslins in the same style with embroidery upon them, and one pale lilack silk, pattern a very small check, to be worn on very grand occasions. My first silk gown, answering to the *boots* of the brothers, then, not now—chits of any age are silked and booted long before they ought to be much to their own loss, as they will come to think when in their turn they will be called on to provide the same. A pink

1. The pattern of tartan associated with a particular clan.

muslin and a blue muslin for dinner, both prettily trimmed, and some clear and some soft muslins, white of course, with sashes of different colours tyed at one side in two small bows with two very long ends. In the bright, glossy, pale auburn hair no ornament was allowed but natural flowers. The gowns, very much flounced some of them, were not unlike what we wear now, only, the petticoats were scanty and the waists short, so short as to be most extremely disfiguring. The best bonnet was white chip trimmed with white satin and very small, very pale, blush roses, and the new spencer was of blush rose pink. Then there were pretty gloves, neat shoes, silk neckerchiefs, and a parasol—just fancy my happiness, I that had been kept so completely as a child, was in fact so childish, so young of my age in every respect, all at once to come out in this style, it was enough to turn my head and so perhaps it would have done but for two or three circumstances. The drawing room was so dull that, after a few stately days spent there in my new dignity, I slid back again to my sisters in the Schoolroom, undeterred from pursuing such studies as I liked and walking out as before by the foolish sneers and taunts of poor Miss Elphick, who, with the weak jealousy of an inferiour mind, chafed extremely at losing a pupil; and after all, it was only losing unlimited authority over the pupils. Next, it was not very easy to dress myself in my finery up in my corner of the barrack room, where at my toilette table I could hardly stand upright, and it was very difficult to carry my flounces and myself in safety down the narrow turning trap stair leading to the passage opening onto the principal staircase. Also, having no wardrobe, no hanging wardrobe, my dresses were kept in a trunk; the one I wanted generally somehow being at the bottom, and so troublesome to get at. Besides all this, my father had taken the opportunity of a quiet opening of the summer to take me through a short course of mathematicks. We went regularly over the first three books of Euclid, applying all the rules and some of the problems as we went on. The reason of his adding this then unusual science, or an idea of it, to his daughter's acquirements was this.

I could never either in conversation or by letter interest my Aunt Frere in the improvements at Rothiemurchus. She said it was all very proper, very necessary, very inevitable, but not agreeable. She liked the highlands as she had known them—primitive, when nobody spoke English, when all young men wore the kilt, when printed calicoes had never been seen, when there was no wheaten bread to be got, when she and Aunt Mary slept in two little closets in the old part of the house just big enough to hold them, and not big enough to hold any of their property, imperials[1] in the long garret acting as their wardrobes, when there was no tidy kitchen range, no kitchen even beyond the black hut, no neat lawn, but all the work going forward about the house, the maids in the broom island with kilted coats dancing in the tubs upon the linen, and the Laird worshipped as a divinity by every human being in the place. It was all very correct, the encrease of comfort and the gradual enlightenment etc., but it was not the highlands. Old feudal affection would die out with the old customs and the old prejudices, and that picturesque district would just become as prosaic as her meadows in Hertford-shire. To prove to her that life could still be happier among our mountains than elsewhere, progress notwithstanding, I thought I would keep a journal for a while with a regular history of our doings, great and small, and send it to her, partly to convince her of errour, partly to exercise my own love of scribbling, my pleasure in recurring thus to all I had noted with my quick eyes and ears. We of this sort of temperament cannot help noting down our sensations; it is meat and drink to our busy minds, a safety valve to the brain, I really believe, essential to its well being. Our descendants can very easily put our observations in the fire should they be too dull to comprehend the value of them.

Well, I had sent my journal to Aunt Lissy, and she had read it with great pleasure, and so had Uncle George and Uncle Bartle, we called them all Uncles and so had my father one afternoon at Hampstead, and he thought the little lady's wings wanted clipping. A walk along the flowdyke, where the plantation on either hand three feet high had grown up during my march, arched overhead, concealed the sun's rays, and only here and there revealed the opposite banks, was,

1. A trunk, fitted onto the roof of the carriage.

though an acknowledged prevision, rather a flight. And a salmon fishing taking up several pages with the river and its ripples, the leaps and pulls and darts of the fish, the wonderful skill of the fisherman with his rod made of the handle of a sweeping broom added to by himself; the crowd around, the sky overhead, a breeze of course, cattle, nut trees, and what not, so bewildered him, unused to that poetick or portraitick style of writing, it was not known at that period, that he judged the wisest thing to be done with so imaginative a brain was to square it a bit by rule and compass. The necessity of proving all that was advanced, of proving step by step, too, as we went along, would he believed strengthen the understanding sufficiently to give it power over the fancy. I don't think he was wrong, and what an entrancing study, I grieved to the heart when the arrival of the Autumn Company put a stop to our happy hour of mathematicks.

Shirt making is a good substitute for Euclid, shirt making as my Mother taught the art, cutting with such accuracy, fitting to a nicety, all methodically prepared, placed, finished, in a regular order—it was a lesson in itself.

A good deal of quiet gaiety took place this autumn. We had our usual relay; Sandy Grant from Garmouth, lame James Grant, Glenmoriston's uncle, Mr and Mrs Lauder, some of the Cumming Gordons, in great glee at Edwina's marriage to Mr Miller, Lord Glenlee's[1] son, a perfect fool, and we had Anne Grant, Glen's sister, and her husband Roderick McKenzie of Flowerburn, rather a good looking man, but stupid, quite as silent as his wife; during the two days they spent with us we hardly ever heard the sound of either voice, I think. Glen himself married this same year—very unfortunately—a cousin—rather pretty—very silly—of late years very eccentrick—never a fit companion for him. My father and mother were exceedingly grieved at this connexion. He was too young, at any rate, just of age and had he waited a while would probably have chosen very differently. They were near a week with us on their way home to Invermoriston

1. Sir William Miller (1755–1846) who was a judge from
   1795 to 1840 and was to be called upon to persuade
   E.G. to break off her engagement the following year.

after the wedding. Logie and Mrs Cumming were not with us; Alexander was for some time; he rode up on his pony, a fine handsome boy, in deep mourning for his father, who had died suddenly under painful circumstances. A publick meeting on some kind of County business had been held at Nairn, to be followed as a matter of course by a dinner; Logie was expected, and not arriving, the meeting had to proceed without him, and so had the dinner. The master of the hotel was a capital cook, famous above all things for dressing mushrooms well. This was a favourite dish of Logie's, and Logie being a favourite himself, the Landlord reserved some portion for him, keeping it hot in the brass or copper skillet he had cooked it in. Logie did come, accounting in some manner for his delay, and he ate the mushrooms, was taken ill shortly after, every symptom was that of poison, and he died in great agony before the morning. His head was no loss, but his heart was, for he was kind to everybody, and was long regretted by his neighbourhood. His very clever wife deluded herself with the idea of his great good sense, not a brilliant man she would say but excellent judgement, just the very quality she wanted for he could say a smart word occasionally and never was known to act wisely, yet when some opinion she advanced was contraverted, she has been known to imagine she silenced all argument by 'Mr Cumming thinks so, I assure you!'

Mr and Mrs Dunbar Brodie came as usual from Coulmonie, she riding on her gray pony, he driving all the luggage in a gig, flageolet included; and we went to the lake and rowed on the water and played to the echo, and then she measured all the rooms. Mr and Mrs Cooper paid their yearly visit; we all liked her and the Bellevilles came often; I don't know how many more, Dr Gordon, William, much improved we thought, Sir Robert Ainslie and so on; also Mrs Gillio, with her pretty little dark daughter and her Hindoo maid. She was the daughter of Major Grant of Craggan, whom the fortunate General William had educated and sent for to India. She had come home with her children, and had thought it right to visit the north. She was an excellent, unpretending, sensible woman, must have been very pretty, too, though at this time that was passed. She went to see all her poor relations more than once, had brought useful presents for them, and left a little money with them. Her Indian attendant was a great amusement to us. We made her describe her country in her broken English, and shew us how she put on her curious dress, the poor woman felt the cold badly and soon went back to her own warm climate. Our people all thought Mrs Gillio's husband must be black too, as she had married him in India.

Before Mrs Gillio had left the Doune, the Marquis and Marchioness of Huntly reached Kinrara. We gave them a few days to settle before calling, but might have spared our delicacy, for the following morning a great racket was heard at the ferry close to the house, and presently the very peculiar laugh of the Marquis. Soon he appeared at the window in his old shabby shooting dress and one of his queer hats, without gloves, calling, in the voice we knew well upon my father and mother to come out, he had brought his wife to visit them. And there she was, like another Cinderella, in a beautiful baby phaeton drawn by four goats. The pretty animals were harnessed with red ribbons, and at every hornèd head there ran a little footpage, these fairy steeds being rather unruly. The whole equipage had been brought over in our small passenger boat. No sylph stepped out of this frail machine, but a stout bouncing girl, not tastefully attired, and with a pale broad flat unmeaning face, fair, which he never liked, and stiff—which he could never endure. He got very fond of her, and so did I; the rest of the family never took to her, and my father and mother remembering her predecessor, the beautiful brilliant Duchess, could not avoid making disadvantageous comparisons. Kinrara too was so different, a more elevated and a very stupid society, dull propriety, regularity, ceremony. There was a feast of food, but not of reason; a flow of wine, but not of soul. I cannot wonder that they sighed over the change and thought with regret over the bright spirits departed.

They came and dined with us, Lord and Lady Huntly, alone, there was no one with them and we were alone. She was extremely timid, just out of the schoolroom when she married and quite unfashioned and though he had taken her abroad to accustom her to her new situation before shewing her at home in it, her shyness still remained. She never had the gift of conversation; she could talk and well, on a subject that interested her, with a person she liked, otherwise she was silent, not at ease herself, she could set no one else at ease. Buonaparte would not have chosen her for the wife of one of his *Maréchals*; she did not shine in her reception rooms. We therefore did not get on well at this dinner, we ladies by ourselves in the drawing room. I was of no use, having only just been brought out of the Schoolroom myself, besides, it was not then the custom for young persons to speak unless spoken to. At last Lady Huntly proposed musick, and on the fine, grand pianoforte being opened she sat down to it herself to let us hear some Swiss airs she had picked up in her travels. The first chord was sufficient, the touch was masterly. In every style she played well, but her Scotch musick, tender or lively, was perfection. Sir Walter Scott immortalised this delightful talent of hers in his Halidon Hill,[1] and she fully merited his highest praise. I have never heard her surpassed nor even equalled, as I don't reckon all that wonderful finger work now in fashion as worth listening to. Her Lord, who was very little sensible of the power of harmony, was always pleased with her musick, listening to it with evident pleasure and extreme pride, particularly when she gave him the reels and strathspeys he danced so well, when he would jump up gaily and crack his fingers like a pair of castagnets and ask did ever any one hear better playing than that. Then if she went on to the marches and quick steps of the highland regiments, which she certainly did give in the most inspiring manner, he would get quite excited and declare no bard could equal her. This enchanting playing of hers rather redeemed her character with my father. My Mother could never get over her unmeaning countenance and her formality, they never suited.

1. Sir Adam Gordon thus describes the musical skills of
    his love, Elizabeth (the name of Huntly's bride):
                            Her gift creative,
    New measures adds to every air she wakes;
    Varying and gracing it with liquid sweetness,
    Like the wild modulations of the lark;
        (*Halidon Hill*, Act II, ii)

Of course we were to dine at Kinrara, a visit the idea of which frightened me out of my wits. I was not afraid of Lord Huntly, I knew him well and he was my cousin besides. But she was so stiff, and I knew there would be company, strangers, and I had never dined out in my life. Young people did not slide into society then as they do now. They strode at once from pinafores, bread and butter, and the Governess, into long petticoats and their silent, young lady place. They did not add to the general sociability, most of them could not—all unpractised as they were in what was doing, going, saying, their little word would most likely have been put in out of season. In the ordinary run of houses, Company was any thing but pleasant. Every body seemed to assume an unnatural manner; nobody followed their customary employments; the books and the needleworks and the drawings of every day's occupation were all carefully put out of sight and we all either sat idle or busied ourselves with a bit of fine embroidery. All were put out of their way too by a grand fatigue day of best glass, best china, best linen, wax candles, plate, furniture uncovered, etc., making every thing look and feel as unlike home as possible. It was not a welcome we gave our friends, but a worry they gave us. In great houses there were skilful servants to take all this trouble and to prevent any mistakes or any fuss; in lesser establishments it was very annoying, I must say. There was very little of this sort of troublesome preparation in our house, but there was a certain degree of formality, it was the manner of the day; and happily and easily as we lived with our parents when alone, or when only very intimate friends were with them, we knew we were to keep at a respectful distance from *Company*.

It was a distasteful word, and the having to encounter all it meant in a strange house among strangers was far from agreeable. I went in the blue muslin frock, the first artificial flowers I had ever worn in my hair, wild roses, and I should have been more at my ease had I been let alone after dressing, but my own anxious Mother thought it necessary to read me a long lecture on proper behaviour, so the fear of transgressing in any particular deprived me of all self possession. I was thoroughly uncomfortable during an evening that might otherwise have afforded me pleasure. Lord Huntly, too, encreased this agitation by calling attention to me most unpleasantly. It was during dinner, that great long table filled with guests, covered with plate, brilliantly lighted, and a servant behind every chair. He was the greatest fidget on earth. All military men and naval too, for that matter, appear unable to resist acquiring a sort of unceasing nervous attention to trifling things. It is to be hoped they are equally occupied with particulars of importance—probably the one involves the other, is a necessity, a duty, a virtue, a profession of principle, but they might leave it there for these very minute interferences are really annoying in every day life. He had a set of rules for his household, any infringement of which was visited by rigorous punishment, certain penances for first and second offence, dismissal for the third without hope of forgiveness. He used to be up himself to call the maids in the morning, in the kitchen at odd times to see what was doing; at no hour of the day, or the night indeed, was the family safe from the bright, very bright, eyes of my Lord, peering here, there, and everywhere. A thread on the carpet would make him ring the bell. A messenger left in the hall would cause a ferment. So during the dinner he was glancing about all round the room, talking, laughing, apparently only intent on being agreeable; yet he knew all that was going on at the sideboard behind him better than Wagstaffe who presided there. The gentlemen sportsmen between whom I was placed found very little to interest them in the shy replies made by a young girl, hardly beyond childhood, to their few civil speeches. They busied themselves elsewhere and left me to the use of my eyes, and for them there was abundant amusement. I was accustomed to long dinners with all their tiresome courses, therefore bore the tedium of this very patiently. At last we reached the 'sweets,' and I took some jelly; not finding a fork beside my plate I asked my attendant for one, very gently too—I hardly heard my own voice. But Lord Huntly heard it right well—out he burst: 'No fork for Miss Grant! A fork for Miss Grant Rothiemurchus! Directly! Wagstaffe, pray who attends to these things. Who sees the covers laid. Great inattention somewhere. This must not happen again. Lizzy, have you got your fork, ha, ha, ha (that extraordinary laugh of his as if shook out through a comb).

Now for the jelly, ha, ha, ha! Extremely careless.' How I wished I had made shift with the spoon. I would gladly have sunk under the table, for the storm had pushed every voice and turned every eye on poor me. I hardly ever remember feeling more miserable. Certainly bashfulness is very near akin to vanity. Jane would have gone through the whole unmoved, and would have thought Wagstaffe and suite fully deserving of the reproof they got. I was not often troubled afterwards with such a degree of shyness. It wore away like other feelings as soon as I came to understand my own position. I should not have been half as awkward from the very first if my Mother had let me alone. We nervous tempers can only be strengthened by ourselves.

My next public appearance was much happier. It was the housewarming at the Croft. The family had already taken possession of the pretty new Cottage, and the old had been turned into offices and Mr Cameron had promised us a dance at the harvest home to commemorate the change; he now determined to give a dinner first, a dinner superintended by Mrs William, who had just been invested by her father in law with all power over the new premises. The great bunch of keys was made over to her, and poor Miss Mary, after so many years of rule, was displaced. Most surely the comfort of the whole family was much improved by this alteration. Mrs William was a most admirable housekeeper, active herself, very skilful, very managing, clean to a nicety, and economical without being stingy. She had found her vocation, and her temper, naturally none of the best, now less chafed since she had plenty to do and could take her own way to do it, became very much easier to live with. She paid a degree of respect to the old people she had never hitherto shewn them, exerting herself particularly to render the old lady comfortable, and though Miss Mary, piqued of course, would wonder sometimes at the *wastry* when she saw the table day after day so bountifully spread, Mr Cameron, finding his outgoings no larger, while his incomings were increased, and a warm look of plenty surrounded him, soon silenced rebellious murmurings.

My father and mother and William went up to the dinner, the rest of us followed to tea in our favourite equipage, a cart filled with hay. We always went in a cart to the Dell when we could manage it because of the seven streams of Druie we had to ford; it was so charming to be so near the water and to hear ourselves rumble over the stones; the hay prevented our being hurt by the jolting, and plenty of plaids kept us warm. Even Miss Elphick enjoyed this manner of visiting. We generally sang all the way, bursting into screams of laughter when a big stone under the wheel cut short a holding note. We had a rough enough way to the Croft, turning off the Loch an Eilein road, a mere cart track past the fairy's knowe to the Moss of Riachan, and so into the birchwood. William Cameron afterwards made a good approach to his house by this route, admired by every one but me; I had something of my Aunt Lissy in me, and liked it all in the wild state. The gates were all open for us—a lucky thought, as they had no hinges; they were merely tyed by two withes[1] on one side and one on the other, and had to be pulled back by a strong arm.

My sisters were dressed in their best white frocks, the two largest of those got for the Persian Ambassador. I had a blue satin body to mine made by myself, and a number of frills at the bottom of the skirt. The bunch of roses in my hair. None of the expensive dresses ordered for me afterwards in London gave me more pleasure than I felt in wearing this, nor do I know whether any real ball ever saw me happier. Between parlour, kitchen, and barn we had nearly all Rothiemurchus at the Croft house warming; Duncan McIntosh playing his best, his son Johnny in tartan, and our Johnny in his frightful shortwaisted nankin frock and trowsers, dancing the fling with all their hearts and cracking their small fingers. Old Mr Cameron danced too, and called for his tune *The Auld wife ayont the fire*, and went up and kissed the old lady instead of his partner, where she sat by the side of the hearth in the old chair, and in the bonnet and shawl and the green shade as usual, neither graver nor gayer than was her wont. We were all so merry except her. Even Miss Mary reeled away after her fashion.

My father in laying out the new cottage had been careful of the habits of the dear old people; a door from the common

1. Willow or osier bands.

parlour opened to the kitchen and to the family bedroom. They had no farther to go to either apartment than they had been used to. The best parlour was quite distinct, no visitor could 'get their ways ben' without permission. The young people and their children, and the strangers' room, were all upstairs, with such views from the windows! Of the sort, I don't think in the world I know a prettier place then the Croft; so peculiar in its beauty too, very wild, yet so very lovely, the solitude around being so peaceful.

This merry dance there was the end of the old times. Whether the old lady had caught cold the time she moved, or whether her ailing frame had simply been worn out, she never seemed to thrive after leaving the little but and ben she had so long lived in. Before the winter set in Mrs Cameron died without any encrease of illness or any suffering. She was buried with the rest of us in the small enclosure in the kirk yard, her husband attended the funeral, appearing in the house, and at the refreshment table, and walking after the corpse just as if it had been any other person's departure. He came in to visitors afterwards with his calm manner unaltered; there was no change in him to common eyes, nor in the proceedings of the family. There was only her empty chair, and a shade over his benignant countenance never left it. Before the Spring he was laid beside her. The immediate cause of his death was a fall he got, a broken shin never rightly healed, but this accident merely hastened his end, he never could have lived the twelve month out with that subdued manner, telling plainly of a broken heart. We were far away when we lost him. Many many years have passed since I last heard him try Crochallan, he never touched the 'trump' after his widowerhood, but I shall never forget Mr Cameron, a real highland gentleman. Loving us with the love of kin, teaching us all wisdom, piety and a lively fancy glowing through his clear, sound sense. His son, a good man, was of a different species.

Before these melancholy events took place we proceeded this pleasant Autumn with the usual merry makings. There was more company at the Doune, though I cannot remember who they all were, and there were more dinners at Kinrara, no longer formidable, and there was a party at Belleville

remaining there some days, when for the first time to my
recollection I saw him whom by courtesy for many years we
continued to call young Charles Grant. Writing that once
familiar name again is pleasant to me, recalling so much that
was so enjoyable, and some little that awakes regret. He was
no ordinary man, with all his weaknesses, and to be so
thoroughly estranged from one who had been quite a son of
the house, a dear elder brother, is cause for grief in a world
where few of us ever suit sufficiently for intimacy. There was
no fault on either part. It was merely our paths through life
lay differently. The father had been with us most summers;
he was our County member, so had to come to look after
political interests. He was now intending to introduce his son
to the Electors against the time when he should himself, from
age or weariness, disincline to continue in parliament. The
north country owed him much; we got canals, roads,
bridges, cadetships, and writerships in almost undue proportion. My father, his firm friend, his most useful supporter,
seldom applied in vain for any thing in the old Director's
power to give. We have reason to be grateful for all his many
kindnesses, but he was never to any of us the delightful
companion that we found his son.[1]

Young Charles was at this time deeply in love with Emilia
Cumming. She was a lovely looking woman—not a regular
beauty by any means but much more attractive than many
handsome persons. Old Charles Grant had reasons for forbid-
ding a marriage between them, and they were good ones,
acquiesced in by his son, yet he had not the resolution to
avoid her society, strength of character was not one of his
characteristicks. Year after year he dangled about her till her
youth and her beauty went, and he found absence no longer a
difficulty. Neither of them ever married though he did not
remain single for love of her. Mrs Macpherson, who really

1. Charles Grant of Glenelg (1778–1866) was M.P. for
   Inverness 1811–18 and Inverness-shire 1818–35; the
   source of his patronage at home came partly from his
   spell as President of the Board of Trade, whilst he was
   so influential in Indian matters because, as President of
   the Board of Control 1830–34, he had to organise a new
   charter for the East India Company.

was absurdly attached to him, she had known him from childhood, was extremely anxious we should make an agreeable impression on one another. I don't remember that he spoke ten words to me, not more certainly nor looked a second time at the childish girl quite overpraised to him. On my part, half a look was enough for me; I thought him hideous, tall, thin, yellow, grave, with sandy hair and small light eyes, and a shy awkward manner, though very nearly as old as my father and already of some note among clever men. These were the dear friends of after days. We have often laughed over our introduction, he positively forgot he had ever met me this autumn at Belleville.

Then came the Pitmain Tryst. It was an old custom in our district to hold a cattle market yearly in the month of September on a moor between Kingussie and Pitmain. Our highland cattle dealing is so different from what you have all been accustomed to see in this grazing country that it may be well to tell you about it. Instead of the gentlemen flying about on cars to fairs, dressed in old dirty clothes and with an inside pocket full of bank notes to buy a lot of beasts from the small rearing farmers, choosing them here and there according to their fitness for the quality of grass they are destined to be fatted on, our Highland proprietors *rear* large stocks of young cattle, regularly disposed of once a year at the current price. The Lairds would think that jobbing style of business quite unsuitable to their dignity. Belleville had 100 cows, every year 100 stots, or two year olds sold generally for from 7 to 8 £ apiece. If any died on his fine stretch of meadows along the Spey during their period of growth he made his number up again by buying from the cotter farmers, the only way these little bodies had of disposing of their single beast. Balnespick kept up 50 store cows, my father 30. There was great emulation among them as to which reared the finer cattle. I must say again though we boasted of our superiour breeding, great pains having been taken to improve the stock, Belleville generally got the top price for his at the Tryst. The buyers were the Drovers, such men as Walter Scott most faithfully describes in Rob Roy. It was a separate trade. The Drovers bought, and paid, and carried off their purchase in large herds to the South, either to be privately disposed of or resold at Falkirk for the English market. A few substantial yeomen farmers were gradually establishing themselves in the country, some of whom were also Drovers, or connected with Drovers and who tried hard by patient industry to rival the produce of the Laird's fuller purse. They probably made more of the business in the end. Our fine Staffa bull that was choked by an uncut turnip cost fifty guineas at three years old, his price swallowed up a deal of profit. Those who bought his yearling calves at six or eight, and waited, improved their stock at less expense in time.

After the market in the morning, there was a dinner in the evening, Drovers, farmers, and lairds all meeting in the large room at Pitmain to enjoy the best good cheer the country afforded. Lord Huntly always presided, and sent a stag from Guaick forest. My father was Croupier,[1] and very grand speeches he and others made after the punch began to circulate. This year it was proposed that the Ladies should be invited to shine on the assemblage—not to join the dinner, but to prepare tea in another room, which would break up the punch party earlier, and allow of the larger apartment being meanwhile prepared for dancing. Both my father and Lord Huntly were promoters of these sort of mixed meetings, so consonant to the spirit of feudalism still cherished throughout our mountains. They were themselves the life and soul of such assemblages, courteous to all, gay in manner, and very gallant to the fair. The Ball was received with much favour, and in future always followed the Tryst, doing a deal more in the way of improving the country than any one at first sight would suppose. Besides the renewal of intercourse between the ranks, leading to a continuance of kind feelings, a sort of stimulus was given to the spirits of those whom Belleville called 'the bodies.' They had hardly finished talking over the pleasure of the one Meeting before the preparations had to be begun for the next. Husbands were proud of producing handsome wives nicely dressed at this general gathering. Mothers looked forward to bringing pretty modest daughters to be introduced to grander friends. The dress and the manners of the higher portion of the Company had a sensible

1. Assistant Chairman at the lower end of the table.

effect on the lower. Mrs John Macnab's first cap was greatly moderated on her second appearance, and Janet Mitchell's very boisterous dancing fined down into a very sprightliness of movement not unbecoming.

All this is over now. The few Grandees in our part of the country shut themselves rigorously up in their proud exclusiveness. Those who could have perpetuated a better tone in our small society are gone, their places know them no more. Our former wise occasional reunions are matters of history; each section appears now to keep apart, unnoticed by the class above, and in turn not noticing the class below. The change struck me much, made me melancholy, altered the whole condition of our once united district. The highlands is not the highlands now.

Lady Huntly did not do her part with all the charming kindness of her Lord. She kept up at the head of the room among her own Kinrara guests, laughing frequently and so long her fits were and so loud nothing could ever persuade the Laggan and Badenoch farmers that she was not ridiculing them. Her dancing did not quite redeem her character, though it was really good, in the old reel and strathspey style—the sort of thing did not suit her. She was not fit for it with her formal ways and stiff manners, it was plain her being there at all was an effort. Her first appearance did not add to her popularity. The Lady Belleville was known of old to keep herself very distant, but she had been long enough among us to be valued for her kindness—besides she was a Southron, and little was expected from her. She sat up in her big red turban amid the great, and there as the fun encreased she, and such as she, were let to sit; all the rest of the room were in high glee, dancing, old and young, without a rest almost.

One of the ladies most in repute as a partner was an old, very old, Mrs McIntosh of Borlam, who lived in the village of Kingussie with her daughter, the Widow of a Major Macpherson, and a comely Widow too. The *Leddy* Borlam was said to be not far from ninety years of age, upright, active, slender, richly dressed for her station, and with a pleasant countenance. Her handsome silks caused many a sly remark. She was the widow of a celebrated freebooter whom Sir

Thomas Lauder endeavoured to portray as Lochandhu.[1] There are as many tales current of his doings in our part of the country as would fill more than one romance. A cave he hid his treasures in is still open on the hill at Belleville, for he did not deal in black cattle only; no traveller was safe when Borlam wanted. His wife and daughter were known to have been frequently occupied in picking out the marks in the fine ruffled hollands shirts it was his especial coxcombry always to appear in, and it was more than whispered that however he came by them he had given her 'braws' enough to last beyond a lifetime; seemingly a true suspicion, for the Lady Borlam's silks would stand alone, and she had plenty of them. With them she wore the Highland mutch, the high clear cap of fine muslin, trimmed, in her case with Flanders lace, and then, calm as a princess, she moved about in her ill gotten gear, with the stateliness of a Chieftain's Lady. She was a wonderful old woman, keen, merry, and kindly, and as 'cute' as an Irishwoman, never tripping in her talk, or giving the remotest hint of the true character of her lamented husband.

I found amongst the Kinrara guests at the Pitmain Tryst our old Arklow Place friend Colonel Thornton, he who had taught us all waltzing, and Mr Orby Hunter, and Mr Lane Fox, names afterwards brought more prominently before the public.

The Northern Meeting was to all of our degree as important a gathering as was the Badenoch Tryst to our humbler acquaintance. It had been set agoing soon after my birth by her who was the Life of all circles she entered, the Duchess of Gordon. She had persuaded all the northern Counties to come together once a year about the middle of October, and spend the better part of a week at Inverness. There were dinners and balls in the evenings; the mornings were devoted to visiting neighbouring friends and the beautiful scenery abounding on all sides. She had always taken a large party there herself, and done her utmost to induce her friends to do likewise—stray English being particularly acceptable, as supposed Admirers of our national beauties! while enacting the part of Lion themselves. No one with equal energy had

1. In his first novel, published 1825.

replaced her; still, the annual meeting went on pleasantly enough bringing many together who otherwise might never have become acquainted, renewing old intimacies, and sometimes obliterating old grudges.

New dresses had come for my decoration, and beautiful flowers my father had brought me, chosen by dear Annie Grant, her last kind office for a while for any of us. There was white muslin with blue trimmings, shoes to match, and roses; white gauze, pink shoes and trimmings, and hyacinths; pearlgray gauze and pink, and a bacchus wreath of grapes and vine leaves, for we had three balls, dinners before the first two, and a supper after the last. With what delight I stept into the Barouche and four which was to carry us to this scene of pleasure. I had no fears about partners, Pitmain had set me quite at ease on that score. We went through the ford at Inverdruie, every one we met bidding us Godspeed, and looking after us affectionately, for it was an era in the annals of the family, this coming out of Miss Grant, and we stopt at Aviemore to have a few pleasant words with Mrs McKenzie. It had been a beautiful drive so far, all along by the banks of the Spey, under the shade of the graceful birch trees, the well wooded rock of Craigellachie rising high above us to the left after we had crossed the river. Just at the foot of this, our beacon hill, there lies, quite close to Aviemore, a little Loch shrouded in the wood, and full of small sweet trout, which during the earthquake at Lisbon[1] was strangely agitated, sending up a column of water dashing about in its small basin in a way not soon to be forgotten. It is the last bit of beauty on the road for many a long mile. A bare moor, with little to mark on it or near it, leads on to the lonely inn at Freeburn, a desolate dirty inn, where never yet was found a fire, or any thing in any way comfortable. A short way from this abode of despair, a fine valley far below opens on the view, containing a lake of some extent, the banks artificially wooded, a good stretch of meadow land, and a very ugly box of a new house built by the Laird of McIntosh, the Chief of his Clan, 'my uncle Sir Eneas.' The planting was

1. The catastrophe of 1755 (which for Voltaire proved God did not exist).

then so young and there was so little taste shewn in the laying out of the grounds that even in that wilderness this solitary tract of cultivation was hardly worthy of much praise, but when we passed it lately it was really a fine place—roads were made, and shrubberies and gardens, and the trees were grown to a goodly size, but the present McIntosh did not live there; he preferred Divie Castle near Inverness, and Moy, the ancient residence of his ancient family, was let to sportsmen.

From Freeburn the moor extends again, another dreary waste till we reached a wild scene I always admired. The Findhorn, an unsheltered, very rocky stream, rises some where beyond the ken of travellers here, and tumbles on through a gully whose high banks give only an occasional glimpse of fair plains far off. A new road had been engineered along the sides of this 'pass of the wild boars,' Slough Mouich, thought a wonder of skill when viewed beside the frightful narrow precipitous pathway tracked out by General Wade, up and down which one could scarcely be made to believe a carriage, with people sitting in it! had ever attempted to pass. My mother had always walked those two or three miles, or the greater part of them, the new route not having been completed till some years after her marriage. A third we have just passed over puts to shame that much praised second, and the planting, and the cottages with gardens, and the roadside inns have all given a different character to this once bare region. There is no change, however, near Inverness; there could be no improvement. It breaks upon the eye weary of the monotony of the journey as a fairy scene on drawing up a curtain. On rising the hill at the Kirk of Divie, where the curious belfry is ever so far from this desolate looking place of worship, the whole of the Moray Firth, with the bounding Ross-shire hills, the great plain of Culloden, Loch Ness, the mountains beyond that fine sheet of water, the broad river, and one of the prettiest of towns scattered about its banks just as it meets the sea, open before wondering eyes. That vale of beauty must have been a surprise to the first discoverer—no Roman; their legions crept along the coast to reach their fort at Euchlass, they never tried the Grampians.

We put up at Mr Cooper's good house in Church Street,

where we were made very welcome and felt ourselves very comfortable; and being tired with our day's work, we much enjoyed a quiet evening with Mrs Cooper and her girls. We had come the day before the first ball purposely for the rest. Next morning I was sent up with some of the children to Castle Hill, a very pretty farm of Mr Cooper's about three miles from Inverness where there were quantities of country matters to be looked at. We came back in time for me to get my toilette laid out ready, and my Mother's too, with help, and to have my hair dressed by Mr Urquhart.

Probably all young persons have felt once in their lives, at least, as I felt on mounting the broad, handsome staircase of the Northern Meeting rooms on my father's arm. The hall was well lit, the musick from above sounded joyously, and my heart beat so quick, so full, it might have been seen to palpitate. My Mother and I passed into a suite of waiting rooms, where poor Peggy Davidson's Aunt attended to take care of wraps, then rejoining my father we entered, through the large folding doors, our really fine Assembly room. It was all noise and blaze and mob. I could neither hear nor see distinctly. A pleasant voice sounded near, it was Glenmoriston's; he was there with his wife, and his sisters, and her sisters, and their husbands and Cousins, a whole generation of us. A little further on we encountered relations new to me, Colonel and Mrs Rose of Holm, just returned from India; she was a little, ugly, crooked woman over loaded with diamonds; he was delightful, although he introduced me to a very plain small, pock marked man, the Captain of the Indiaman who brought them home, Captain Simpson and with this remarkable partner I joined the long country dance then forming. My Captain danced well; he was very pleasant too, and much amused at all the shaking hands that took place between me and half the room. We were really acquainted with almost every body, and of kin to a great number.

Lord and Lady Huntly were there with a large party. Old Lady Saltoun[1] ditto, dancing away in an open frock almost

---

1.  Margery, daughter of another East India Company
    Director, Simon Fraser; she married the eighteenth
    Lord Saltoun of Abernethy.

as lightly as her pretty daughter Eleanor, who afterwards married young Mr Donall Grant of Arndilly—and she near eighty. Charlotte Rose, now Lady Burgoyne,[1] was very pretty then, danced beautifully, dressed her fine hair well. But the beauties of the room, I thought, were the two Miss Duffs of Muirtown—tall, graceful girls with a pensive air that made them very attractive. My next partner was Culduthel, poor Culduthel, fine, gay, good natured, rattling young man. Then Lord Huntly in a reel vis a vis to his wife, then Sir Francis McKenzie of Gairloch, then one or two of the Kinrara gentlemen, and all the rest of the evening Applecross—poor McKenzie of Applecross, the last of his clever line. He was *the* catch of the north country from the extent of his property, and though very plain, very sickly, and no great use as a dancing partner, he would have been, without a penny, a catch for any one worthy of him. Had he lived, he would have ably filled his position, but he and his only sister both died of consumption a few years after this, and before their parents and a Writer in Edinburgh, with a large family, succeeded to that fine Ross-shire property.[2]

Mr Cooper informed us next morning at breakfast that my début had been a most decided success. I was perfectly aware of it, and not one bit elated, though my Mother was, her maternal anxieties had gone further than mine; I had stopped at abundance of dancing. This evening's ball was pleasanter than the first and the third and last, with the supper, was best of all, even in spite of a draw back. Every joy has its attendant sorrow, every rose its thorn, and I had the persevering assiduities of a very good natured and thoroughly vulgar Mr McIntosh of Farr quite unable to see that his company was disagreeable. In no way could I escape two or three dances with this forward young man, to my most extreme annoyance, and, as it seemed to me, the very unreasonable delight of my new friend, Mr McKenzie of Applecross.

1. She was the wife of General Sir John Burgoyne, cousin to the Field Marshal of the same name (1782–1811), and herself a cousin on the Grant side.

2. This was another Thomas McKenzie w.s. (1793–1856) who was to be M.P. for Ross and Cromartyshire between 1837 and 1847.

The mornings had hung heavy to many, but not to me. Most people merely lounged about the narrow ill paved streets of Inverness, paid each other visits, or congregated in our northern emporium of fashion, Mr Urquhart the hairdresser's shop. My father took my Mother, Mrs Cooper, one of her girls, and me charming drives in several directions; it was impossible to turn amiss, the whole surrounding scenery is so enchanting. The rapid change of air together with the pleasurable excitement freshened us up nicely for the evening. We had visitors too, people calling early, before luncheon; Mrs Rose of Kilravock, the Dowager, was one of them. An extraordinary woman, once a beauty and still a wit, who was now matronising two elderly young ladies, West Indians of large fortunes, and amusing them and every body else with their clever eccentricities and tales of her brilliant youth. She had been with Jacky Gordon, the particular friend of the Duchess, often at Kinrara in former days. It was indeed a happy week. I wonder whether other girls come out often under such pleasant auspices.

*Elizabeth Grant of Rothiemurchus*

# MEMOIRS OF A
# HIGHLAND
# LADY

*Edited by Andrew Tod*

⟨ TWO ⟩

# Contents

Volume I of Elizabeth Grant's *Memoirs of a Highland Lady* describes her recollections of early childhood in Rothiemurchus and London, painting a vivid picture of the life led by this landed highland family as her father's political and legal ambitions carried them to Edinburgh, London and back to Speyside.

The first volume ends in 1814 with the move to Edinburgh where John Peter Grant of Rothiemurchus, after spending more money than was wise in becoming Member of Parliament for the 'rotten borough' of Great Grimsby, was required to resume his career as an Advocate at the Scottish Bar. And this was to be the appropriate setting for his daughter, the seventeen-year-old Elizabeth Grant, to enter society and, as she wrote, 'commence life on her own account'.

# CHAPTER SEVENTEEN

## 1814–1815

I HAVE always looked on our appearance at this Inverness Meeting as the second great era in my life. Although it so closely followed the first remarkable change, it more completely changed me myself although at the time I was hardly aware of it, reflexion being no part of my character. Our removal to the highlands, our regular break-in under the governess, the partial opening of young minds, had all gone on in company with Jane, who was in many respects much more of a woman than I was, by three years her elder. I was now to be alone. From henceforward, my occupations, pursuits, habits, ideas were all to be perfectly different from, indeed repudiated by, the Schoolroom. Miss Elphick thought, and she was not wrong, that I was a year too young for the trials awaiting me, and for which I had been in no way prepared. She was annoyed too at not having been consulted on the fitness of her pupil for commencing life on her own account, and so, she would neither help my inexperience nor allow me to take shelter under my usual employments. A head filled with nonsense, dress balls, beaux, was very unfit to be trusted near the still innocent brains of my sister.

I felt very lonely wandering about by myself, or seated in state in the library, with no one to speak to. There was no Company in the house. My Mother was little with me. Her hours were late, her habits indolent; besides, she never much cared for me, and she was busily engaged with my father revolving several serious projects for the good of the family, none of them proper for us to be made acquainted with till they were decided on. His Scotch friends were anxious that my father should return to their Bar. There was a want of just such an Advocate as it was expected he would prove and the state of his affairs, though none of us young people knew it,

3

rendered some such step as this very desirable. Also my brother William had a home to look for while he continued in College. Mrs Gordon had had another baby, and in her small house, a flat in Buccleugh Place, there was no longer room for a lodger. Then there was the beautiful daughter! The pale thin girl had blossomed into a, let us tell the truth, why not, into a very lovely flower and fluttering hopes were raised of the consequences of her blushes being seen beyond the wilderness she had hitherto bloomed in. So Edinburgh was decided on, and Grace Baillie was written to, to engage us a house.

At this time Mrs Cameron died and was buried in our sacred corner of the kirk yard, her husband attending the funeral. He received the guests at his own house himself, walked as chief mourner, stood at the grave, returned home quietly with his son and grandsons and when the visits of condolence were paid, he appeared with the rest of the family. His manner had always been very calm, there was no difference perceptible in it. The faded eye alone and a certain drawn look about the mouth, evident only to a close observor, told the tale of the worn out heart. Yet, resigned, patient, Christian as he truly was, he might have survived the cherished wife of his youth, the companion of his age and many sorrows had not an accident shortened his life. He fell over a tub a few days before we left home, none of us thinking much of it but the blow, or cut indeed, was on the shin and it never healed. During the winter he died upwards of 78—young for a highlander, the last of his generation saving Miss Mary. When we went to take leave, he followed us down to the gate at the Lochan Mór; and there laying a hand on each young head, he bade God bless us with a fervour we recollected afterwards, and felt that he must have considered it as a final parting. Then wrapping his plaid round him and drawing his bonnet down over his eyes, he turned and moved away through the birch wood, our last sight of that dear, kind, worthy cousin from whom we had never heard but good. Rothiemurchus altered after all that old set were gone.

Our mourning did not interrupt our packing. We were all in great glee making our Edinburgh preparations, when late one night we got a fright. One of the chimneys in the old part of the house took fire, a common occurrence—it was the way they were frequently cleaned!—but on this occasion the flames communicated some sparks to a beam in the nearest ceiling, and very soon part of the roof was burning. None of us being in bed the house was soon roused, the masons sent for, and a plentiful supply of water being at hand all danger was soon over. My mother was however exceedingly frightened, could hardly be persuaded to retire to her room, and kept us all near her to be ready for whatever might befall. At last, when calmer, we missed Miss Elphick; she was no where to be found, and we really feared some mischance had happened to her. After a good search she was discovered as far from the house as she could well get, dancing about on the lawn in her night dress, without either a shoe or a stocking on her; by which crazy proceeding she caught so severe a cold as was nearly the death of her. The whole scene made a beautiful picture, Jane said, and while the rest of us were rather trembling for the fate of the poor old house, she was actually studying the various groups as they moved about under the flickering light of the blazing chimney.

We had no more adventures till we started on our journey, nor any incidents deserving of notice during our three days' travel, save indeed one, the most splendid bow with hat off from my odiously persevering partner, who, from the top of the Perth Coach as it passed us near Kinross, almost prostrated himself before the barouche. It was cold wretched weather, snow in the hills, frost in the plains, a fog over the ferry. We were none of us sorry to find ourselves within the warm cheerful house Miss Baillie had taken for us, at No. 4 Heriot Row. It was not a large house having no upper storey. One floor only over the drawing room, but there were four rooms on each floor and they were all of a good size. The situation was pleasant, though not at all what it is now. There were no prettily laid out gardens then between Heriot Row and Queen Street, only a long slope of unsightly grass, a green, fenced by an extremely untidy wall and abandoned to the use of the washerwomen. It was an ugly prospect, and we were daily indulged with it, the cleanliness of the inhabitants being so excessive that, except on Sundays and the 'Saturdays at e'en,' squares of bleaching linens and lines of drying ditto were ever before our eyes. Our arrival was notified to our acquaintance by what my father's brethren in the law called his advertisement, a large brass plate, really very little less than a page of this paper, on which in letters of suitable size were engraved the words—Mr Grant, Advocate.

We began our Edinburgh life in regular business fashion. My father established himself with a clerk and a quantity of law books in a study, where he really soon had a good deal of work to do. He went every morning to the parliament house, breakfasting rather before nine to suit William, who was to be at Dr Hope's chemistry class at that hour, and from thence proceed to Dr Brown's Moral Philosophy, and then to Mr Playfair's Natural Philosophy.[1] A Tutor for Greek and Latin awaited him at home, and in the evenings he had a good three hours' employment making notes and reading up, etc. Six masters were engaged for we three girls, three every day; Mr Penson for the pianoforte, M. Elouis for the Harp, M. L'Espinasse for French, Signor Something for Italian, and Mr I forget who for Drawing, Mr Scott for writing and cyphering. And oh, a seventh! I was near forgetting, the most important of all! Mr Smart for Dancing. I was occasionally to accompany my father and mother to a few select parties, provided I promised attention to this phalanx of instructors, and never omitted being up in the morning to make the breakfast in proper time. It was hoped that with Miss Elphick to look after us, such progress would be made and such order observed as would make this a profitable winter for every body. An eye over all was certainly wanted. My mother never left her room till mid day, she breakfasted in bed and took a good sleep afterwards, the marketing being made by Gouard, all the orders given the day before.

1. Thomas Charles Hope (1766–1844) was joint Professor of Chemistry with the celebrated Joseph Black; he
   is particularly remembered for his work on the newly
   discovered element, strontium. Thomas Brown
   (1778–1820), metaphysician, was awarded his chair in
   1810. John Playfair (1748–1819), one of the leaders of
   the Scottish Enlightenment, was successively Professor of Maths from 1785 and Natural Philosophy, 1805.

On the same floor with the Drawing rooms which communicated with each other by means of folding doors, were
my brother William's room and the Schoolroom. As I was
never welcome in the Schoolroom, my studies were all
carried on in the Drawing rooms, between the hours of ten,
when breakfast was over, and one, when people began to call.
It was just an hour apiece for each master, and very little
spare time at any other period of the day for practising for
them, invitations flowing in quick, and my occasional
visiting resulting in an eternal round of gaieties that never left
us one quiet evening except Sunday.

About two every day my mother went out to make calls or
shop either on foot or most commonly in the carriage, taking
me with her. On our return about four or maybe later the
drawing room filled with men, who at about that time were at
liberty from their different avocations to indulge themselves
with a pleasant hour of gossip before dinner. After the first
week or two, therefore, I gave up attempting to prepare for
the masters, and when the Balls began I had frequently to
miss their lessons, as the late hours coupled with the fatigue
of frequently uninterrupted dancing exhausted me too much
to make it possible for me to attend to their instructions
regularly. The only lessons I never neglected were Mr
Penson's. He brought his violin to accompany us, and
sometimes a violincello, so that we got up trios occasionally,
a very delightful treat to me without trouble, for I had no
leisure for practising, just played at sight with him what ever
he brought. Jane and Mary were kept more systematically to
their business, yet Jane having to make breakfast after a
while, and Mary having to wait on my Mother at that meal
and afterwards assist at her toilette, rather interrupted the
studies and extremely annoyed Miss Elphick. She found her
evenings dull too without the Drawing room party and she
could not bear dining early with the children when we either
went out or had Company at home. She was ill too, a teasing
cough and other bad symptoms from the effects of the cold
she caught during her half naked dance upon the lawn. So
cross and uncomfortable and disagreeable she became, the
whole house was quite relieved when she announced her
determination to take a holiday. She could be well spared,

she said, when there were such excellent masters to replace her, and so she set off on a visit to her mother and sister.

On her departure my Mother's maid was deputed to walk out once a day with Jane, Mary, and Johnny, all the exercise they got. Jane taught Johnny, and she and Mary continued their own employments I really believe conscientiously. They said, at first, they found their days long and the evenings dull, but these complaints ceased when, as my Mother supposed, they became accustomed to live alone, and then they had to make tea for William, who was always a kind and cheerful companion for them. The real fact was, that whenever my father was out with my Mother and me, William had a very pleasant party at home—young College friends, and M. L'Espinasse the French Master. Every visitor brought a small supply of fruit and cakes, and Jane had plenty of tea, sugar, bread and butter for the substantial part of the feast. Conscientious as she was, she kept this secret faithfully and the servants who were all engaged in their own amusements were equally honourable. There were two very good rules observed by this pretty assemblage, no intoxicating liquors were allowed, and the company separated before eleven o'clock. No wonder Miss Elphick's absence was agreeable. William certainly must have neglected his studies—he was out riding for two or three hours daily on pretty little Fairy, a thorough bred by way of for which he had given rather a long price and had my father's permission to keep in the Stables.

Our visiting began with dinners from the heads of the Bar, the judges, some of the Professors, and a few others, all Whigs nearly, for the two political parties mixed very little in those days. The hour was six, the company generally numbered sixteen, plate, fine wines, middling cookery, bad attendance and beautiful rooms. One or two young people generally enlivened them. They were mostly got through before the Christmas vacation. In January began the routs and balls; they were over by Easter, and then a few more sociable meetings were thinly spread over the remainder of the Spring, when, having little else to do, I really began to profit by the lessons of our Masters. My career of dissipation was therefore but a four months thrown away. It left me a wreck, however, in more ways than one; I was never strong, and I was quite unequal to all we went through. Mrs Macpherson, who came up with Belleville in March for a week or two, started when she saw me. She thought me in a galloping consumption and very properly frightened my mother about me, who had observed no change, as of course it had come on imperceptibly. She had been extremely flattered and I believe a little surprised by my extraordinary success in our small world of fashion. I was high on the list of beauties, no ball could go on without me, ladies intending to open up their houses for dancing, solicited introductions to the mother for the sake of ensuring the daughter's presence. Crowds of beaux surrounded us when we walked out, filled our drawing rooms when we staid within. It was very intoxicating, but it did not intoxicate me, young and unformed as I was, and unused to admiration, personal beauty being little spoken of in the family. I owed my steadiness to neither good sense nor wise counsel, for neither of these were watching over me. A simple happy temper, a genuine love of dancing, a little highland pride that took every attention as the due of one of Grant blood, these were my safeguards, these and the one all absorbing feeling which early took possession of the young heart to the exclusion of other ideas.

The intimate friends of my father were among the cleverest of the Whigs. Lord Gillies and his charming wife, John Clerk and his sister, Sir David and Lady Brewster—more than suspected of Toryism, yet admitted on account of the Belleville connexion and his great reputation—Mr and Mrs Jeffrey, John Murray, Tommy Thomson, William Clerk. There were others attached to these brighter stars, who, judiciously mixed among them, improved the agreeableness of the dinner parties. My Mother's new and gay acquaintance were of all parties. Lady Molesworth, her handsome sister, Mrs Munro, Mrs Stein, Lady Arbuthnot, Mrs Grant of Kilgraston, etc. We had had the wisdom to begin the season with a Ball ourselves, before Balls were plenty. All the Beaux strove for tickets, because all the Belles of the season made their first appearance there. It was a decided hit, my Mother shining in the style of her preparations, and in her manner of receiving her company. The dancing was kept up till near the day dawn and every one departed pleased with the degree of attention paid to each individually. It struck me afterwards, in more reflecting days, that this Ball and my father's fir forest had no small share in my successful campaign, for my sister beauties were many of them so far beyond any loveliness I could pretend to. There were the two unmarried Dennistouns, afterwards Lady Campbell and Lady Baillie, Miss Farquhar Gray who became Mrs Ashburner, poor Betty Brown. Above all that really beautiful Miss Logan, the quite splendid Miss Dewar of Vogrie, Mrs Hastings Anderson, and several more pretty pleasing girls, who as usual married better than the more admired. Yet we none of us wanted for lovers, earnest, honest lovers, men that a few years later might have been listened to by the scornful fair who in the height of their pride considered them as just good enough to dance with. It is a great mistake sometimes to speak too soon.

The return to the Bar had answered pretty well; fees came in I know usefully, though certainly not in sufficient quantity to authorise our expensive way of living. We gave dinners of course, very pleasant ones, the dishes so well dressed, the wines so choice, and the company well selected that the parties always appeared to be more thoroughly at ease with us than elsewhere. My dress and my Mother's must have cost a fortune, it all came from London, from the *little* Miss Steuarts, who covered my mother with velvet, satin, rich silks, costly furs and loads of expensive lace while the variety of my nets, gauzes, Roman pearl trimmings and French wreaths, with a few more substantial morning and dinner dresses must have helped to swell up the bills to some very large amount. Some of the fashions were curious. I walked out like a hussar in a dark cloth pelisse trimmed with fur and braided like the coat of a Staff officer, boots to match, and a fur cap set on one side, and kept on the head by means of a cord with very long tassels. This equipment was copied by half the town, it was thought so exquisite. We wound up our gaieties too by a large evening party, so that all received civilities were fully repaid to the entire satisfaction of every body. This *Rout*, for so these mere card and conversation parties were called, made more stir than was at all intended.

It was given in the Easter holidays, or about that time, for my father was back with us after having been in London. He had gone up on some Appeal Cases, and took the opportunity of appearing in his place in the House of Commons, speaking a little, and voting on several occasions, particularly on the Corn Law Bill,[1] his opinion on which made him extremely unpopular with the Radical section of his own party, and with the lower orders throughout the country, who kept clamouring for cheap bread, while he supported the producer, the agriculturist. His name as a protectionist was very quickly remarked in Edinburgh where there was hardly another Member of Parliament to be had, and the mob being in its first fresh excitement the very evening of my Mother's rout, she and her acquaintance came in for a very unpleasant demonstration of its anger against their former favourite.

Our first intimation of danger was from a volley of stones rattling through the windows, which had been left without closed shutters on account of the heat of the crowded rooms. A great mob had collected unknown to us, as we had musick within, and much noise from the buzz of the crowd. A score of ladies fainted by way of improving matters. Lady Matilda Wynyard, who had always all her senses about her, came up to my mother and told her she need be under no alarm. The General, who had had some hint of what was preparing, had given the necessary orders, and one of the Company, a highland Captain Macpherson, had been despatched some time since for the military. A violent ringing of the door bell, and then the heavy tread of soldiers' feet announced to us our guard had come. Then followed voices of command outside, ironical cheers, groans, hisses, a sad confusion. At last came the tramp of dragoons, under whose polite attentions the company in some haste departed. Our Guard remained with us all night and ate up all the refreshments provided for our dismayed guests, with the addition of a cold round of beef which most fortunately was found in the larder. Next day quiet was perfectly restored, the mob molested us no more, and the incident served as conversation very usefully for a week or more. It also brought us better acquainted with

1. See *Hansard*, XXIX (1815), pp. 1026, 1123.

those excellent people, General and Lady Matilda Wynyard, whose English reserve had hitherto kept them merely on civil visiting terms with us. From her conduct, with a little help from a side remark or two of my father's, I got a good lesson in some of the trials of life.

There was a flirting, singing, not very wise Widow, rather in fashion in Edinburgh, a good natured Mrs General Anstruther whose principal merit was the having had her husband, a man of good Fifeshire family, killed in Egypt while serving under General Abercromby. She was far from handsome yet many men were much taken by her, amongst others General Wynyard, whose admiration was so very undisguised and all of whose spare time was so entirely occupied in attending on her, that his devotion was really the talk of the town and could not possibly have escaped the notice of Lady Matilda and yet she never seemed to observe it. She behaved with the same politeness to this illbehaved trifling woman as she did to her other acquaintance, invited her in her turn, spoke to her when necessary just as if she were neither more or less to her than any other of their society, always however in some unaccountable way throwing Mrs Anstruther back, as it were, putting herself and her requirements first, without effort either, when she and her husband were together so that in the end the General wearied of his unapproved flirtation and came to look upon this foolish woman with the same indifference he fancied his wife did. That Lady Matilda suffered, clear sighted bystanders could not but observe. And when her calmness had triumphed, every one most sincerely rejoiced.

A second lesson was on this wise. We had a party of rather noted people coming to dine with us. William Cameron, after his good father's death, and Mr Cooper arrived on some business in town. In Highland fashion they announced having merely ordered beds at an hotel, sure of a welcome at all meals with us. My mother wanted to tell them we had company and the table full; my father said no; he would hurt no one's feelings, they were fully entitled to a place at his board, let who would be invited to it. So a leaf was added; they were made extremely happy by eating on terms of equality with men whose names were before the world, and the celebrated guests were so charmed with new listeners to their witticisms that their conversation sparkled with unusual brilliancy. No dinner ever went off better, and though Mr Cooper added no lustre to the company, Mr Cameron in spectacles looked the quiet country gentleman to perfection. My Mother was perfectly satisfied.

The last large party of the season was given by Grace Baillie in her curious apartment on the ground floor of an old fashioned corner house in Queen Street. The rooms being small and ill furnished, she hit upon a curious way of arranging them. All the doors were taken away, all the movables carried off, the walls were covered with evergreens, through the leaves of which peeped the light of coloured lamps festooned about with garlands of coarse paper flowers. Her passages, parlours, bedrooms, closets, were all adorned *en suite*, and in odd corners were various surprises intended for the amusement of the visitors; a cage of birds here, a stuffed figure in a bower there, water trickling over mossy stones into an ivy covered basin, a shepherdess, in white muslin, a wreath of roses and a crook, offering ices, a highland laddie well-kilted presenting lemonade, a cupid with cake, a gypsey with fruit, intricacies purposefully contrived that no one might easily find a way through them, while a french horn, or a flute, or a harp at intervals from different directions served rather to delude than to guide the steps 'in wandering mazes lost.'[1] It was extremely ridiculous, and yet the effect was pretty, and the town so amused by the affair that the wits did it all into rhyme, and half a dozen poems were made upon this Arcadian entertainment, describing the scene and the Actors in it in every variety of style. Sir Alexander Boswell's production was the cleverest, because so very neatly sarcastick. My brother's most particular friend wrote the prettiest. In all, we beauties were enumerated with most flattering commendation, but in *the friend's* the encomium on me was so marked that it drew the attention of all our acquaintance, and most unluckily for me opened my Mother's eyes.

She knew enough of my father's embarrassments to feel

1. Milton, *Paradise Lost*, I, 555.

that my 'early establishment,' as the cant phrase went, was of importance to the future well being of the rest of us. She was not sure of the Bar and the House of Commons answering together. She feared another winter in Edinburgh might not come, or might not be a gay one, newer faces might supersede old favourites, a second season be less glorious than the first. She had been quite delighted with the crowd of admirers, but she had begun to be annoyed at no serious result following all these attentions. She counted the lovers, there was no scarcity of them, there were eligibles among them, some of whom she had believed prepared. How had it come that they had all slipt away. Poor dear mother, while you were straining your eyes abroad, it never struck you to use them at home. While you slept so quietly in the mornings you were unaware that others were broad awake. While you dreamed of Sheffield gold, and Perthshire acres, and Ross-shire principalities, my father and Miss Elphick both away, the daughter you intended disposing of for the benefit of the family had been left to enter upon a series of sorrows she never during the whole of her after life recovered from the effects of.

It is with pain, the most extreme pain, that I even now in my old age revert to this unhappy passage of my youth. I was wrong; my own version of my tale will prove my errours; but at the same time I was wronged—ay, and more sinned against than sinning. I would pass the matter over if I could, but unless I related it you would hardly understand my altered character; you would see no reason for my doing and not doing much that had been better either undone or done differently. You would wonder without comprehending, accuse without excusing; in short, you would know me not. Therefore, with as much fairness as can be expected from feelings deeply wounded and ill understood, I will recall the short romance which changed all things in life to me.

The first year my brother was at College he made acquaintance with a young man a few years older than himself, the son of one of the Professors. His friend was tall, dark, handsome, very engaging in his manners, very agreeable in his conversation, and considered by all who had been employed in his education to possess abilities quite worthy of the talented race he belonged to. The Bar was to be his profession, more by way of occupation for him in the meanwhile than for any need he would ever have to practise Law for a livelihood. He was an only son. His father was rich, his mother had been an heiress, and he was the heir of an old, nearly bedrid bachelour Uncle who possessed a very large landed property on the banks of the Tweed. Was it fair, when a marriage was impossible, to let two young people as him and me pass day after day for months familiarly together. My brother, introduced by his friend to the Professor's family during the first year he was at College, soon became extremely intimate in the house. The father was very attentive to him, the mother particularly liked him, the three sisters, none of them quite young, all treated him as a new found relation. William wrote constantly about them, and talked so much of them when at home at the Doune for the summer vacation that we rallied him perpetually on his excessive partiality, my mother frequently joining in our good humoured quizzing. It never struck us that on these occasions my father never by any chance entered into our pleasantry.

When we all removed to Edinburgh William lost no time in introducing his friend to us; all took to him amazingly; he was my constant partner, joined us in our walks, sat with us every morning, was invited frequently as company and was several times asked to stay and partake of the family dinner. It never entered my head that his serious attentions would be disagreeable, nor my Mother's, I really believe, that such would ever grow out of our brother and sister intimacy. I made acquaintance with the sisters at the houses of mutual friends. We visited and exchanged calls as young ladies did then in Edinburgh; and then I first thought it odd that the seniors of each family, so particularly obliging as they were to the junior members of each other's households, made no move towards an acquaintance on their own parts. The gentlemen, as much occupied with their affairs, were excusable, but the ladies, what could prevent the common forms of civility passing between them. I had by this time become shy of making any remarks on them, but Jane, who had marvelled too, one day asked my mother why she did not cultivate the society of such agreeable persons. My Mother's answer was quite satisfactory. She was the last comer, it was not her place to call first on old residents. I had no way of arriving at the reasons of the other side, but the fact of the non intercourse, the avoidance of intercourse, annoyed me, and frequently caused me a few minutes more of thought than I had ever before been conscious of indulging in.

Then came Miss Baillie's *fête*, and the poem in which I figured so gracefully. It was in every mouth, for in itself it was a gem, and I was so completely the genius of it, none but a lover could have mingled so much tenderness with his admiration. On the poet's next visit my Mother received him very coldly. At our next meeting she declined his now regular attendance. At the next party she forbade my dancing with him : after the indelicate manner in which he had brought my name before the publick in connexion with his own, it was necessary to meet so much forwardness by a reserve that would keep such presumption at a proper distance. I listened in silence, utterly amazed, and might in such perfectly submissive habits of obedience had we been brought up, have submitted sorrowfully and patiently, but she went too far. She added that she was not asking much of me, for this disagreeable young man had no attaching qualities; he was neither good looking, nor well bred, nor clever, nor much considered by persons of judgment, and certainly by birth no way the equal of a Grant of Rothiemurchus.

I left the room, flew to my own little attick, what a comfort that corner all to myself was then and often afterwards to me. I laid my head upon my bed, and covering my face with my hands, vainly trying to keep back the tears. The words darted through my brain, 'all false, quite false—what can it be, what will become of us,' for I had reached that turning point, though till this bitter moment unconsciously. Long I staid there, half thinking, half dreaming, till a new turn took me, the turn of unmitigated anger. Were we puppets, to be moved about with strings. Were we supposed to have neither sense nor feeling. Was I so poor in heart as to be able to like today, and loathe tomorrow, so deficient in understanding as to be incapable of seeing with my eyes, hearing with my ears, judging with my own perceptions. This long familiar intimacy permitted, then suddenly broken upon *false* pretences. They don't know me, thought I; alas, I did not know myself. To my mother throughout that memorable day I never articulated one syllable. My father was in London.

My first determination was to see my poet and inquire of him whether he were aware of any private enmity between our houses. Fortunately he also had determined on seeking an interview with me in order to find out what it was my mother had so suddenly taken amiss in him. Both so resolved, we made our Meeting out, and a pretty Romeo and Juliet business it ended in. There *was* an ancient feud, a College quarrel between our fathers which neither of them had ever made a movement to forgive. It was more guessed at from some words his mother had dropt than clearly ascertained, but so much he had too late discovered, that a more intimate connexion would be as distasteful to the one side as the other.

We were very young, we were very much in love, we were very hopeful. Life looked so fair, it had been latterly so happy. We could conceive of no old resentments between parents that would not yield to the welfare of their children. He remembered that his father's own marriage was an elopement followed by forgiveness and a long lifetime of perfect conjugal felicity. I recollected my mother telling me of the Montague and Capulet feud between the Neshams and the Ironsides, how my grandfather had sped so ill for years in his wooing, and how my grandmother's constancy had carried the day, and how all parties had 'as usual' been reconciled. Also when my father had been reading some of the old comedies to us, and hit upon the Clandestine marriage,[1] though he affected to reprobate the conduct of Miss Fanny, his whole sympathy was with her and her friend Lord Ogleby, so that he leaned very lightly on her errour. He would laugh so merrily too at the old ballads, Whistle and I'll

1. The best-known play (1766) of George Colman the Elder (1732–94); its most familiar lines ('Love and a cottage! Eh, Fanny! Ah, give me indifference and a coach and six.' II, ii) might also have come to mind.

come to ye, my lad, Low down in the broom,[1] and the girl who sent her love away deceived by a blink of the morn etc. These lessons had made quite as much impression as more moral ones. So, reassured by these arguments, we agreed to wait, to keep up our spirits, to give time to be true and faithful to each other, and to trust to the Chapter of accidents.

In all this there was nothing wrong, but a secret correspondence in which we indulged ourselves was a step into the wrong, certainly. We knew we should seldom meet, never without witnesses, and I had not the resolution to refuse the only method left us of softening our separation. One of these stray notes from him to me was intercepted by my mother, and some of the expressions employed were so startling to her that in a country like Scotland, where so little constitutes a marriage, she almost feared we had bound ourselves by ties sufficiently binding to cause considerable annoyance, to say the least of it. She therefore consulted Lord Gillies as her confidential adviser, and he had a conference with Lord Glenlee, the trusted lawyer on the other side, and then the young people were spoken to, to very little purpose.

What passed in the other house I could only guess at from after circumstances. In ours, Lord Gillies was left by my Mother in the room with me; he was always gruff, cold, short in manner, the reverse of agreeable and no favourite with me, he was ill selected therefore for the task of inducing a young lady to give up her lover. I heard him, of course, respectfully, the more so as he avoided all blame of either of us, neither did he attempt to approve of the conduct of our seniors; he restricted his arguments to the inexperience of youth, the unsurmountable aversion of the two fathers, the cruelty of

1. There is a poignancy about a couplet from Burns' song
    O, whistle an' I'll come to ye, my lad!
    Tho' father an' mother an' a' should gae mad,
and the chorus of the other favourite ballad of E.G.'s father
    For he's low doun, he's in the brume,
    That's waitin' on me,
    Waiting on me, my love,
    He's waiting on me.
            (Alexander Whitelaw, *Songs of Scotland*).

separating family ties, dividing those hitherto living lovingly together, the indecorum of a woman entering a family which not only would not welcome her, but the head of which repudiated her. He counselled me, by every consideration of propriety, affection, and duty, to give 'this foolish matter up.' Ah, Lord Gillies, thought I, did you give up Elizabeth Carnegie? did she give up you. When you dared not meet openly, what friend abetted you secretly. I wish I had had the courage to say this, but I was so nervous at his knowing my story, so abashed at our conversation that words would not come, and I was silent. To my mother I found courage to say that I had yet heard no reasons which would move me to break the word solemnly given, the troth plighted, and could only repeat what I had said at the beginning that we were resigned to wait.

Lord Glenlee had made as little progress; he had had more of a storm to encounter, indignation having produced a flow of eloquence. Affairs therefore remained at a stand still. The fathers kept aloof—mine indeed was still in London; but the mothers agreed to meet and see what could be managed through their agency. Nothing very satisfactory. I would promise nothing, sign nothing, change nothing, without an interview with my betrothed to hear from his own lips his wishes. As if my mind had flown to meet his, he made exactly the same reply to similar importunities. No interview would be granted, so there we stopt again. A *growing* fancy early perceived might have been easily diverted. It was a matter of more difficulty to tear asunder two hearts too long united.

At length his mother proposed to come and see me, and to bring with her a letter from him, which I was to burn in her presence after reading, and might answer, and she would carry the answer back on the same terms. I knew her well, for she had been always kind to me and had encouraged my intimacy with her daughters; she knew nothing of my more intimate relations with her son. The letter was very lover like, very tender to me, very indignant with every one else, very undutiful and very devoted, less patient than we had agreed on being, more audacious than I dared to be. I read it in much agitation—read it, and then laid it on the fire. 'and now before you answer it, my poor dear child,' said this most excellent and most sensible woman, 'listen to the very words I must say to you,' and then in the gentlest manner, as a tender surgeon might cautiously touch a wound, rationally and truthfully, she laid all the circumstances of our unhappy case before me, and bade me judge for my self on what was fitting for me to do. She indeed altered all my high resolves, annihilated all my hopes, yet she soothed while she probed, she roused while seeming to crush and she called forth feelings of duty, of self respect, of proper self sacrifice, in the place of the mere passion that had hitherto governed me. She told me that although she considered my education to have been in many respects faulty, the life I led frivolous and that there was much in my own unformed character to condemn, she would have taken me to her heart as her daughter, for the pure, simple nature that shone through all imperfections, and for the true love I bore her son. She knew there was a noble disposition beneath the little follies, but her husband she said would never think so, never ever endure an alliance with my father's child. They had been friends, intimate friends, in their School and College days; they quarrelled, on what grounds neither of them ever had been known to give to any human being the most distant hint, but in proportion to their former affection was the inveteracy of their after dislike. All communication was over between them, they met as strangers, and were never known to allude to each other, nor to name either fine old name. My father had written to my mother that he would rather see me in the grave than the wife of that man's son. Her husband had said to her that if that marriage took place he would never speak to his son again, never notice him, nor allow of his being noticed by the family. She told me her husband had a vindictive as well as a violent and a positive temper, and that she suspected there must be a touch of the same evil dispositions in my father, or so determined an enmity could not have existed; they were, she thought, aware of what might be the consequences of such unchristian feelings, for they had swore never to have any intercourse and they felt that they were wrong, as was evidenced by the extra attention each had paid the other's children. At their age she feared there was no cure. She plainly shewed she had no hope of shaking any of the resolve in her house. She came then she added, to confide in me, to tell me the whole truth, as it would be safe with me, to shew me that, with such feelings active against us, nothing but serious unhappiness lay before us, in which distress all connexions must expect to share. She said we had been cruelly used, most undesignedly; she blamed neither so far, but she had satisfied her judgment that the peculiar situation of the families now demanded from me this sacrifice; I must set free her son, he could not give me up honourably. She added very, very kindly that great trials produced great characters, that fine natures rose up above difficulties, that few women, or men either, wedded their first love, that these disappointments were salutary. She said what she liked, for I seldom answered her; my doom was sealed; I was not going to bring misery in my train to any family, to divide it and humiliate myself, destroy perhaps the future of the man I loved, rather than give him or myself some present pain. The picture of the old gentleman too was far from pleasing, and perhaps affected, though unconsciously, the very timid nature that was now so crushed.

I told her I would write what she dictated, sign Lord Glenlee's 'renunciation,' promise to hold no secret communication with her son. I kept my word; she took back a short note in which, for the reasons his mother would explain to him, I gave him back his troth. He wrote, and I never opened his letter; he came and I would not speak, but as a cold acquaintance. What pain it was to me those who have gone through the same ordeal alone could comprehend. His angry disappointment was the worst to bear; I felt it was unjust, and yet it could not be explained away, and pacified. I caught a cold luckily, and kept my room awhile. I think I should have died if I had not been left to rest a bit.

My father on his return from London never once alluded to this heart breaking subject; I think he felt for me, for he was more considerate than usual, bought a nice little pony and took me rides, sent me twice a week to Seafield for warm baths, and used to beg me off the parties, saying I had been racketted to death, when she, my mother, would get angry and say such affectation was unendurable—girls in her day did as they were bid without fancying themselves heroines.

She was very hard upon me, and I am sure I provoked her not; I was utterly stricken down and to have lifted up my voice in any way was quite beyond me. What weary days dragged on till the month of July brought the change to the highlands.

# CHAPTER EIGHTEEN

# 1815 – 1816

HAD I been left in quiet, to time—my own sense of duty, my conviction of having acted rightly, a natural spring of cheerfulness, with occupation, change, etc., all would have acted together to restore lost peace of mind, and the lesson, severe as it was, would have certainly worked for good, had it even done no more than to have sobered a too sanguine disposition. Had my father's judicious silence been observed by all, how much happier would it have been for every one. Miss Elphick returned to us in June, and I fancy received from my Mother her version of my delinquencies, for what I had to endure in the shape of rubs, snubs, and sneers and other impertinences, no impulsive temper such as mine could possibly have put up with. My poor Mother dealt too much in the hard hit line herself, and she worried me with another odious lover. Defenceless from being blameable, for I should have entered into no engagement unsanctioned, I had only to bear in silence this never ending series of irritations. Between them, I do think they crazed me. My own faults slid into the shade comfortably shrouded behind the cruelties of which I was the victim, and all my corruption rising, I actually in sober earnest formed a deliberate plan to punish my principal oppressor—not Miss Elphick, she could get a slap or two very well by the way. My resolve was to wound my Mother where she was most vulnerable, to tantalise her with the hope of what she most wished for, and then to disappoint her. I am ashamed now to think of the state of mind I was in; I was astray indeed, with none to guide me, and I suffered for it; but I caused suffering, and that satisfied me. It was many a year yet before my rebellious spirit learned to kiss the rod.

In journeying to the highlands we were to sleep at Perth.

We reached this pretty town early, and were surprised by a visit from Mr Anderson Blair, a young gentleman possessing property in the Carse of Gowrie, with whom our family had got very intimate during the winter. William was not with us, he had gone on a tour through the west highlands with a very nice person, a College friend, an Englishman. He came to Edinburgh as Mr Shore, rather later than was customary, for he was by no means so young as William and others attending the Classes, but being rich, having no profession, and not College bred, he thought a term or two under our Professors, our University was then deservedly celebrated,[1] would be a very profitable way of passing idle time. Just before he and my brother set out in their tandem with their servants, a second large fortune was left to this favoured son of a mercantile race, for which, however, he had to take the ridiculous name of Nightingale. Mr Blair owed this well sounding addition to the more humble Anderson, borne by all the other branches of his large and prosperous family, to the bequest of an old relation. Her legacy was very inferiour in amount to the one left to Mr Nightingale, but the pretty estate of Inchyra with a good modern house overlooking the Tay, was part of it, and old Mr John Anderson, the father, was supposed to have died rich. He was therefore a charming escort for my Mother about the town. We had none of us ever seen so much of Perth before. We were taken to sights of all kinds, to shops among the rest, and Perth being famous for whips and gloves, while we admired, Mr Blair bought, and Jane and I were desired to accept a very pretty riding whip each, and a packet of gloves was divided between us. Of course our gallant acquaintance was invited to dinner.

The walk had been so agreeable, the weather was so extremely beautiful, it was proposed, I can hardly tell by who, to drive no farther than to Dunkeld next morning, and spend the remainder of the day in wandering through all the beautiful grounds along the miles and miles of walks conducted by the riverside through the woods and up the

1. Two near contemporaries who led the way were
   the future Prime Ministers, Lord Palmerston
   (1800–03) and Lord John Russell (1809–12),
   who lodged with Professor Playfair.

mountains. 'Have you any objection to such an arrangement, Eli,' said my father to me. 'I, papa! none in the world.'
It suited my tacticks exactly. Accordingly so it was settled,
and a very enjoyable day we spent. The scenery is exquisite, every step leads to new beauties, and after the wanderings of the morning it was but a change of pleasure to return
to the quiet inn at Inver to dine and rest, and have Neil Gow
[the younger] in the evening to play the violin. It was the
last time we were ever there. The next time we travelled the
road the new bridge over the Tay at Dunkeld was finished,
the new inn, the Duke's Arms, opened, the ferry and the
quiet inn at Inver done up, and Neil Gow dead.

Apropros of the Duke's Arms, ages after, when our dear
amusing Uncle Ralph was visiting us in the highlands, he
made a large party laugh, as indeed he did frequently, by his
comical way of turning dry facts into fun. A coach was
started by some enterprising individual to run between
Dunkeld and Blair during the summer season, which
announcement my Uncle read as if from the advertisement
in the newspaper as follows: 'Pleasing intelligence. The
Duchess of Athole starts every morning from the Duke's
Arms at eight o'clock . . .' There was no need to manufacture any more of the sentence.

The day had passed so agreeably at Dunkeld, it was
decided on proceeding in the same way to Blair, a longer
drive by a few miles, and through that most beautiful of all
bits of mountain scenery, the pass of Killiecrankie. We did
not spend our time near the Castle, we walked to the falls of
the Bruar, first brought into notice by Burns, and then too
much made of; as besides planting the banks and conducting
a path up the stream,¹ so many summer houses and
hermitages and peep bo places of one sort or another had

1. Burns' poem written about this tributary of the river
   Garry in 1787, took the form of a plea to the Duke of
   Athole for just this sort of development:
       Let lofty firs, and ashes cool,
           My lowly banks o'erspread . . .
       Let fragrant birks, in woodbines drest,
           My craggy cliffs adorn,
               ('The Humble Petition of Bruar Water').

been perched on favourite situations, that the proper character of the wild torrent was completely lost—nature was much
disturbed, but no ill taste could destroy so grand a scene. We
were fortunate in finding plenty of water leaping in wide
cascades over rocks of every size and shape, for there had
been rain a few days before.

Our obliging friend left us next morning with the consola-
tory information that we should meet again before the 12th of
August, as a letter from Mr Nightingale had brought his
agreement to a plan for them to spend the autumn in the
highlands. They had taken the Invereschie Shootings, and
were to lodge at the Dell of Killiehuntly with John and Betty
Campbell.

We had hardly got settled at the Doune before a note from
Mr Blair, a very nice pony, and a basket of most delicious
fruit, hothouse fruit, arrived from Inchyra; the fruit we ate
with the greatest pleasure, the pony had been sent to be
acclimatised as it would be used hereafter on the hill, and the
note said it would be conferring the greatest favour if the
young ladies would be so very kind as to ride and help to train
it. We were all perfectly willing to accept all civilities, and
Jane and I henceforth were able to ride out together, and
found our chief happiness in resuming our old wanderings,
which the encreasing stiffness of the poor old white pony had
made us fear must for the future have been undertaken
singly. Our excursions, however, were far from being as
enjoyable as formerly. Inverdruie was shut up. The attraction of the Croft was gone; Duncan McIntosh, broken by ill
health and distress of mind owing to the misconduct of his
eldest son, was no longer the animated companion of former
days. Aviemore was a painful visit. We had only Belleville
and Kinrara and the scenery. Belleville was almost always
our great resource. We young people were much liked there,
and we ourselves liked going there. Kinrara, it must be
confessed, was dull, too stiff, too constrained, although
kindness was never wanting; but the Marquis and Marchioness were not to arrive till the famous 12th of August. Our
first three weeks at home were very quiet, no company
arriving, and my father being absent at Inverness, Forres,
Garmouth, etc., on business. We had all our humble friends

to see, all our favourite spots to visit. To me the repose was delightful, and had I been spared all those unkind jibes, my irritated feelings might have calmed down and softened my temper; exasperated as they continually were by the most cutting allusions, the persuasion that I had been most unjustly treated and was now suffering unjustly for the faults of others, grew day by day stronger and stronger, and estranged me completely from those of the family who so perpetually annoyed me. Enough of this. So it was, so it ever was, blame me who will.

After this quiet beginning our highland autumn set in gaily. The 10th of August filled every house in the country in preparation for the 12th. Kinrara was full, though Lord Huntly had not come with the Marchioness; some family business detained him in the south, or he made pretence of it, in order that his very shy wife might have no assistance in doing the honours, and so rub off some of the awkward reserve which so very much annoyed him. Belleville was full, the inns were full, the farm houses attached to the shootings let were full, the whole country was alive, and Mr Nightingale, Mr Blair and my brother arrived at the Doune. Other guests succeeded them, and what with rides and walks in the mornings, dinners and dances in the evenings, expeditions to distant lakes or glens or other picturesque localities, the Pitmain tryst and the Inverness Meeting, a merrier shooting season was never passed. So every one said. I don't particularly remember any one person as very prominent among the crowd, nor any thing very interesting by way of conversation. The Battle of Waterloo and its heroes did duty for all else, our highlanders having had their full share of its glories.

We ladies went up for the first time this year to Glen Einich, our shooting friends with us. The way lay through the birch wood to Tullochgrue, past McAlpine's well and a corner of the fir forest and wide heath, till we reached the banks of the Luinach, up the rapid course of which we went till the heath narrowed to a Glen, rocks and hills closed in upon us, and we came upon a sheet of water terminating the *cul de sac*, fed by a cataract tumbling down for ever over the face of the precipice at the end of it. All the party rode on ponies caught about the country, each rider attended by a man at the bridle head. Jane and I were better mounted, for the Inchyra pony had never been reclaimed; it was not wanted, so she and I had it by turns on all occasions. The Edinburgh pony, poor Toper, so called from its love of porter, carried the one that was not honoured with *Paddle*. A very pleasant day we passed, many merry adventures of course taking place in so singular a cavalcade. We halted at a fine spring to pass round a refreshing drink of whiskey and water, but did not unload our sumpter horses¹ till we reached the granite pebbled shore of the lake. Fairy tales belong to this beautiful wilderness; the steep rock on the one hand is the dwelling of the Bodach² of the Scarigour, and the Castle like row of precipitous banks on the other is the domain of the Bodach of the Corriegowanthill—titles of honour these in fairy land, whose high condition did not however prevent their owners from quarrelling, for no mortal ever gained the good graces of the one without offending the other, loud laughing mockery ever filling the Glen from one potentate or the other, whenever their territories were invaded after certain hours. Good Mr Stalker the Dominie had been prevented continuing his fishing there by the extreme rudeness of the Corriegowanthill, although encouraged by his opposite neighbour and fortified by several glasses of stiff grog. We met with no opposition from either; probably the Laird and all belonging to him were unassailable. We had a stroll and our luncheon, and we filled our baskets with those delicious delicate char which abound in Loch Einich, and returned gaily home in safety.

Another much more adventurous expedition we made to the parallel roads, attended as usual. Our shooting friends did not thin their own moors too much. A tenant of the Duke of Gordon's who lived near Kingussie, a most excellent oddity of a little old man, had a large sheep farm up in Laggan with a better sort of bothie in a pretty glen, where he and Mrs Mitchell frequently remained a day or two at shearing time. The poor Captain's phaeton carried my Mother, Miss Elphick, and the carpet bags; the rest of us rode, and we

1. Pack or baggage horse.
2. An 'old man' or a 'hobgoblin'.

came up with Mr and Mrs Mitchell by the way, travelling in their gig, a cart following them containing one of their pretty daughters and plenty of provisions. The bothie had but two rooms, a parlour and a kitchen; the gentlemen occupied the kitchen, the ladies the parlour, all sleeping at night on beds of heather thickly strewed over the floor. The cooking kitchen was outside in the open air, near an old wall under a tree. We took all our meals out of doors, and so merry were we, so happy in this gypsy life, we could have enjoyed a good week of it instead of the two days my mother limited our visit to, out of consideration for the resources of Mrs Mitchell; particularly as two fiddlers were of the party, and after walking miles all day we danced for hours at night in the gentlemen's larger apartment. Our English friend, Mr Nightingale, was no great walker, nine miles there and back to fish for dinner in a beautiful little loch at the head of the Glen, where the trout actually leaped up by dozens to the hook, wore him and a fine pair of boots completely out, as he had the honesty to confess, and so declined a walk of sixteen miles on the morrow to the parallel roads in Glenroy. We suspected that our Scotch Mr Anderson Blair was little better able for such a highland amount of exercise, but this he would by no means allow, so he and William set out with a guide for the object of our enterprise, and lost their way, and returned very weary in the evening.

Some dinners at Kinrara were rather dull, pleasanter at Belleville, very agreeable at home, so they all said. The Pitmain Tryst was a very good one. My principal partner was old Mr Mitchell, with whom I finished off in the Haymakers, he, short and fat and no great dancer, doing his part so lovingly, the spectators were all in convulsions of laughter. Jane, though only fifteen, was taken to this country gathering and to all the dinners at Belleville. At one party there we met the two Charles Grants, father and son, and brought them back with us to Rothiemurchus.

At this time Mr Blair took leave, as he was one of the Stewards of the Perth Hunt, and their yearly Ball was approaching. He left us Paddle, and he sent us fruit and musick, and seemed much more to regret his going than some of us did to see him go. My Mother was consoled by retaining Mr Nightingale, whom really everybody liked–he staid, and went with us to the Inverness Meeting. It was a very bad one, I recollect, no new beauties, a failure of old friends, and a dearth of the family connexions. Having a party with us we went to Grant's hotel, much more in the midst of the fun than Mr Cooper's quiet house in Church Street. Chisholm and Mrs Chisholm were in rooms next ours, once such dear friends of my father and mother's. The connexion had long ceased, in spite of untiring efforts on the Chisholm part to renew it. She, in anticipation of the Meeting, had brought for me a french enamelled watch set with pearls, a venetian chain to hang it on, a large packet of french gloves, and a whole suit of embroidery. There was a great consultation about the propriety of my keeping them. No reason could be assigned for a refusal, so I, at any rate, gained by the civility. My last year's friend, the new Member for Ross-shire, Mr McKenzie of Applecross,[1] was at this Meeting, more agreeable than ever, but looking extremely ill. I introduced him by desire to my Cousin Charlotte Rose, who got on with him capitally. He was a plain man, and he had a buck tooth to which some one had called attention, and it was soon the only topick spoken of, for an old prophecy[2] ran that whenever a mad Lovat, a childless Chisholm, and an Applecross with a buck tooth met, there would be an end of Seaforth. The buck tooth all could see, the mad Lovat was equally conspicuous, and though Mrs Chisholm had two handsome sons born after several years of childless wedlock, nobody ever thought of fathering them on her husband. In the beginning of this year Seaforth, the Chief of the McKenzies, boasted of two promising sons; both were gone, died within a few months of each other. The Chieftainship went into another branch, but the lands and the old Castle of Brahan would descend after Lord Seaforth's death to his daughter, Lady Hood—an end of

1. Thomas McKenzie of Applecross was M.P. for Ross-shire, 1818–22.
2. One of the best-known of the prophesies of Coinneach Odhar, the seventeenth century 'Brahan Seer' from Lewis.

Caber-Feigh.[1] This made every one melancholy, and the deaths had of course kept many away from the Meeting.

Mr Nightingale left us soon after our return home to pay a visit to Mr Blair and his mother and sisters at Inchyra. We put all our home affairs in order for our long absence, and then we set out for Edinburgh. My father had taken there the most disagreeable house possible; a large gloomy No. 11 in Queen Street, on the front of which the sun never shone, and which was so built against behind there was no free circulation of air through it. It belonged to Lady Augusta Claverhouse, once Campbell, one of the handsome sisters of the handsome Duke of Argyll, who had run off from a masquerade with a lover who made her bitterly repent she ever took him for a husband.[2] It was comfortable within, plenty of rooms in it, four good ones on a floor, but they did not communicate. The drawing room was very large, four windows along the side of it. There were, however, no convenient rooms for refreshments for evening parties, so during our stay in it nothing could be given but dinners, and very few of them either, for none of us were in very good humour. It was well for me that my little bedroom was to the sunny and quiet back of the house, and on the Drawing room floor, for I had to spend many a week in it. A long illness beginning with a cold confined me there during the early part of the winter, and when I began to recover I was so weakened dear and kind Dr Gordon, who had attended me with the affection of a brother, positively forbade all hot rooms and late hours. It was a sentence I would have bribed him to pronounce, for I was sick of those everlasting gaieties, and with his encouragement and the assistance of a few other friends I was making for my self, I was able to find employment for my time infinitely more agreeable than that

1. The twenty-first Caber Feidh (the hereditary chief of the Clan McKenzie) had four sons, the last of whom died in 1814; the chief died of a broken heart the following year. The title went to Mackenzie of Allen-grange and the estates to his eldest daughter, who had married Admiral Sir Samuel Hood.
2. Lady Augusta (1760–1831) married Colonel Henry Clavering; she was the sister of the sixth Duke.

round of frivolous company. We were spared the train of masters. Harp and Italian alone were given to us this winter, a new Italian master, a fop and an oddity, very much superiour as a Teacher to the other poor old creature. M. L'Espinasse visited as a friend, and spent many pleasant evenings with us. My Mother did not at all approve of this secluded life. In heart she loved both dress and visiting; besides, she did not wish it to be thought that I was breaking my heart, or had had it broken by cruel parents. Spectre as I was, she really believed half my illness feigned. The Roses of Holm, too, had come to town, and Charlotte was dancing every where with Mr McKenzie. I am sure my ghostlike appearance would not have brought him back to his first fancy. Still, with her peculiar hopes and fears and wishes, it was rather hard upon her, but Dr Gordon was peremptory. My father supported him, and so he, that is my father, and my mother went out to the dinners together, and declined the evening parties till I was fit to accompany them. How I enjoyed our home tea circle. M. L'Espinasse generally with us, keeping Miss Elphick in good humour, but no College friends; those little domestick scenes were over.

Mr McKenzie and my father went up by the mail after Christmas together to attend their duties in Parliament. He had called frequently in the mornings after I was well enough to sit in the drawing room, and had once or twice dined with us. He and I were on the most friendly terms; my Mother could not understand us. We parted with the cordially expressed hope on both sides to meet soon again, I promising to cheer my cousin Charlotte's spirits during his absence—he really admired her, she was clever, pretty, and lively, though too flippant to secure the heart of a man like him. Mr Blair and Mr Nightingale then suddenly announced their intention of making a tour on the Continent of some duration. They just remained for Mr Nightingale to get possession of a set of shirts my Mother had very obligingly offered that I should cut out for him, and then they set out, thus quite breaking up our home party.

We had two pieces of family news to raise our spirits after all these disappointments. Uncle Edward and Annie Grant were married—not to each other! He in Bombay, now a

Judge of the Sudder,[1] had married a Miss Rawlings, the daughter of an old Madras Civilian, a highly respectable connexion; and she in Bengal, had become the wife of Major General Need, commanding at Cawnpore, a King's Cavalry Officer.[2] I have quite forgot, I see, to mention that when we left London she had gone on a visit to Mrs Drury, the sister of Mr Hunter, the husband of one of the Malings. Mrs Drury took such a fancy to her that she would not part with her, at least not to a house of business. She proposed to my father to equip her for India. She went out with Miss Stairs, sister to Lady Bury and Mrs Vine, and she was received by Mrs Irwine Maling, from whose house she married. The Needs belonged to Arkwright, Need, and Strutt, names we British have cause to remember.[3]

By the end of February, this winter of 1816, I was able to indulge my Mother with my company even to a Ball or two. Though received by the world with as much indulgence as before, I had the prudence to dance little, generally sitting by Mrs Rose, or walking about with my steadiest of Admirers, the Colonel; my mother having the gratification of interrupting us frequently by bearing petitions from numerous partners for just one dance before the early hour at which we now retired. There was one I seldom refused—no lover, but a most true and agreeable friend, the best dancer in Edinburgh, Campbell Riddell, who, tho' a younger son and very little likely to make a living at the Bar, a profession quite unsuitable to him, was the favourite of all the belles, and more than tolerated by the mothers. We were very happy, he and I, together, I was hardly so intimate with any other young man, and long years after when we met in Ceylon we both recollected with equal pleasure the days of our innocent flirtation. The Roses were a great addition to us; we saw a great deal of them; she was kind, and clever, he was

1. Anglo-Indian for Chief or Supreme.
2. See II, pp. 175–7.
3. Jebediah Strutt and Need had a successful partnership joined by Richard Arkwright in 1768; their development of his water-frame played an important part in the Industrial Revolution.

charming, and I liked both the girls, tho' they were coheiresses and far from faultless. Old Miss Lawrence, who had just given herself brevet rank, and was to be Mrs Lawrence in future, came on a visit this year to the Man of Feeling.[1] I saw her for the first time, and thought her most extraordinary. She was greatly taken up with a poem old Mr McKenzie had made on me, and reminded me of it afterwards at Studley. Dr Ogle, of Oxford, an old Etonian, also made us out—he brought with him a very fine musical box he had bought at Geneva, a toy not common then.

A very singular set of persons, Nesham cousins, appeared to us about this time; Mr and Mrs Goodchild, and their son Jack. My mother's cousins in Durham were really innumerable. In one family, her Uncle John Nesham's, there had been nine handsome daughters, all married, and two sons. Mrs Goodchild was, I think, the third daughter. Her husband was a man of great wealth, deriving his income principally from the valuable lime quarries on his estates. He was rude, boisterous, and strangely ignorant of every gentlemanly acquisition, yet there was a natural frankness and kindness and clever fun, very redeeming, particularly when we knew him better. The wife was a very noisy, underbred, overdressed woman, evidently imbued with the idea that her money lifted her over the heads of almost every body. The son was worse than Tony Lumpkin[2], worse than Miss Jenny's booby of a brother, for to their ignorance and coarseness and loutishness he added a self sufficiency that kept him completely at his ease, while he was shocking all listeners. 'Well, *coosin*,' said he to me after sitting a while, 'got any prog? my stomach's been crying cupboard this hour.' We were delighted to shut such a mouth so easily. My Mother said these Goodchilds had always been remarkable for an affectation of vulgarity; from long practice it seemed to me to

1. Henry Mackenzie (1745–1831), Scott's 'Northern Addison', published his *Man of Feeling* in 1771; James Ogle (1792–1857) was appointed Professor of Medicine at Oxford in 1824.
2. An insensitive youth in Oliver Goldsmith's boor in *She Stoops to Conquer* (1773).

have become natural. They were only passing through, so we saw no more of them at this time.

We were inundated this whole winter with a deluge of a dull ugly colour called Waterloo bleu, copied from the dye used in Flanders for the calico of which the peasantry make their smock frocks or blouses. Every thing new was Waterloo, not unreasonably, it had been such a victory, such an event, after so many years of exhausting suffering. And as a surname to hats, coats, trowsers, instruments, furniture, it was very well—a very fair way of trying to perpetuate the return of tranquillity; but to deluge us with that vile indigo, so unbecoming even to the fairest! It was really a punishment. Our *Albert* blue of this day is worth the wearing but that Waterloo was an infliction, none of us were sufficiently patriotick to deform ourselves by trying it. The fashions were remarkably ugly this season. I got nothing new, as I went out so little, till the spring, when white muslin frocks were the most suitable dress for the small parties then given. There was a dearth of news, too, a lull after the war excitement; or my feeling stupid might make all seem stupid. I know my memory recollects this as a disagreeable winter. The Lawyers were busy with a contemplated change in the Jury Court. Trial by jury in Civil cases had not, up to this date, been the custom in Scotland. In penal Cases the Scotch Jury law so far differed from the English that a majority of voices convicted the prisoner; unanimity was unnecessary; and this, which many very sagacious lawyers considered as the better rule, was not to be interfered with, it was only to be extended to Civil cases. The machinery of the Courts of Justice had of course to be slightly altered for this change of system. If I remember rightly, two new Barons were required, and a Chief Baron, whom we had never had before. Sir William Shepherd, from the London Bar, was sent in this capacity to set it all agoing. His very English wife came with him, and amused us more than I can tell with her Cockneyisms. He was very agreeable.

It may seem beyond the range of a girl of my then age to have entered into so grave a subject, but these sort of topicks were becoming my business. I wrote quick and clearly, and seldom made mistakes; my father, though he had a Clerk, frequently found it suit him to employ me as his more private Secretary. I even helped him to correct the press for some of his pamphlets,[1] sought out and marked his references, and could be trusted to make necessary notes. I delighted in this occupation, and was frequently indulged in it both in town and country at such odd times as help was wanted. Indeed from henceforward I was his assistant in almost all employments—work much more to my mind than that eternal 'outing.'

In July we returned again to the Doune. We had not many visitors, so far as I recollect : Miss Baillie on her way to Logie, Alexander so far with her on her return. Two brothers of the name of Davies, friends of Mrs Cumming's, one a merchant, the other a barrister, recreating themselves by a tour in the highlands, with the hope of a day or two's shooting here and there. Their first essay of the moors was with us, and a failure, for they waited for the late breakfast, came in dress coats to it, and were so long afterwards fitting on all the astonishing variety of their sportsman accoutrements, the day was too far advanced by the time they were completely equipped for the keepers to be able to take them to the best ground, although they rode ponies for the first half dozen miles. They were stupid specimens, and an elder brother whom we knew afterwards, a Colonel and an M.P., was positively disagreeable. The country was filled with half pay Officers, many of them returned wounded to very humble homes in search of a renewal of the health they had bartered for glory. A few of these had been raised to a rank they were certainly far from adorning; very unfit claimants got commissions occasionally in those war days. Lord Huntly had most improperly so advanced one or two of his servants and several of his servants' sons, and in the German legion there had been two lieutenants who began life as carpenters' apprentices to Donald Mclean. One of these, Sandy McBean, who lived the rest of his days at Guislich under the title of the *Offisher*, attended the church very smart, and dined once every season at our table, as was now his due, had helped to

1. He published in 1812 *Essays towards illustrating some Elementary Principles relating to Wealth and Currency.*

alter the staircase with the same hands that afterwards held his sword. Wagstaffe's son rose to be a Major. When he got his Company the father resigned his Stewardship, and received some situation from the Marquis more suited to the son's position.

Kinrara was very full this season, and very pleasant. The charming Duchess, whose heart was in the highlands, had left orders to be buried on the banks of the Spey in a field she had herself pointed out. Lord Huntly planted a few larch around the enclosure, but Lady Huntly laid out a beautiful shrubbery and extended the plantation, making paths through it. The grave was covered by a plain marble slab, but behind this rose a stunted obelisk of granite, bearing on its front by way of inscription the names of all her children with their marriages; this was by her own desire. Her youngest son, Alexander, died unmarried before herself; Lord Huntly she left a bachelour—her four younger daughters had all made distinguished connexions. The eldest, and the best bred amongst them, shewed to less effect among the list of great names, but then she had two husbands to make up for their being commoners. The first, Sir John Sinclair of Murkle, was a cousin of her own; they had one child only, the merry sailor son whom every one was fond of. The second husband, a Mr Palmer of Bedfordshire, it was supposed took her for the connexion as she was very oddly spoken of. The second daughter was Duchess of Richmond,[1] the third the Duchess of Manchester, the fourth the Marchioness of Cornwallis, the fifth the Duchess of Bedford. When the Duchess of Manchester was driven from the house of the husband she had disgraced, she left behind her two sons, and six daughters placed by their father under the care of a governess to be superintended by the Dowager Duchess; the boys were at Eton. The eldest of these girls, however, Lady Jane Montague, had almost always lived with her other

1. It was her second daughter, Madelina, who married twice and the eldest, Charlotte, who married Charles, the fourth Duke of Richmond and Lennox (it was she who gave the Ball before Waterloo—'There was a sound of revelry by night,' Byron, *Childe Harold's Pilgrimage*, III, xxi).

Grandmother, the Duchess of Gordon. She it was who danced the chantreuse, and trotted over to the Doune on her poney, as often nearly as she staid at home. My father and mother were dotingly fond of her, for she was a fine natural handsome creature, quite unspoiled. When our Duchess, as we always called her, died, Lady Jane was not happy at home with her younger sisters and their governess. She went to live with her aunt the Duchess of Bedford, and was shortly announced to be on the point of marriage with the second of the Duke's three sons by his first wife, Lord William Russell. Next we heard she was very ill, consumptive—dying—and that kind aunt of hers took her to Nice, and attended her like a mother till she laid her in her grave. It was a real grief to every one that knew her, particularly those who had watched the fair show of her childhood.

The second of these deserted girls was now of an age to be introduced into society, and Lord and Lady Huntly brought her with them to Kinrara. No, it was the third, Lady Susan, a beautiful creature; the second, Lady Elizabeth, was just married to a handsome Colonel Steele, whom she had become acquainted with through her Governess. It was on Lady Susan's account Kinrara was made so particularly agreeable. There were plenty of morning strolls and evening dances, a little tour of visits afterwards, all ending in her engagement to the Marquis of Tweeddale, a man liked I believe by men, and it was said by some women—of extraordinary taste, to my mind; for, thick set and square built and coarse mannered, with that flat Maitland face which when it once gets into a family never can be got out of it, he was altogether the ugliest boxer or bruiser looking sort of common order of prize fighter that ever was seen in or out of a ring. Yet he had a kind manner and a pleasant smile, and he made a tender husband to this sweet gentle creature, who accepted him of her own free will and never regretted the union.

Neither house went to the Tryst this year, nor to the Meeting. Lady Susan's approaching marriage prevented any publick displays from Kinrara, and my father having been called to a distance on business the Doune did not care to exhibit without him.

We had had some troubles in our usually quiet Duchus

this autumn. Urquhart Gale, the principal Saw miller, and George McIntosh, one of the returned officers, had each got into an unpleasant scrape. Urquhart Gale's backsliding was only suspected as yet, but George McIntosh's was a most miserable business; the young man was in the jail of Inverness for murder. Mrs McIntosh, as I am sure I must have mentioned[1] was one of the two very pretty daughters of Steuart of Pityoulish, an old tacksman on the Gordon property, very superiour in station to his forester son in law. He was devotedly attached to all of Gordon blood, but particularly so to the family of his Grace, and he insisted on his first grand child, a boy, being called after our Prince of Wales of the north, the Marquis of Huntly. At a proper age this piece of respect got George McIntosh a Commission. He had never joined his regiment in the field, but he had been away and come home, and finding other young officers in the country they one unlucky day entered the publick house at the Boat of Inverdruie, and ordering whiskey drank to one another till they fell to quarrelling. Very hard words passed between George McIntosh and one of the company; the rest took part against poor George, and Duncan Cameron the Landlord, fearing for unpleasant consequences, rushed amongst these half mad boys, as he said, to prevent mischief. A frightful scuffle ensued, at the end of which George McIntosh's first opponent was picked up senseless. Nor did he ever speak again. He died in a few hours without apparent injury except a small triangular wound near the temple, which, on the Doctor probing, was found to run deep into the brain. The whole party were taken up, lodged in prison, and indicted for murder; they could not, however, be tried till the Spring circuit, and the connexions had all to wear away the winter in this dreadful anxiety. Mr and Mrs McIntosh were completely overwhelmed by this calamity, the end of which I may as well tell now as keep it over to its proper season.

My father, feeling quite unable to conduct such a cause himself, engaged George Joseph Bell[2] to defend George

1. See I, pp. 233–4.
2. Bell (1770–1843) was six years later appointed to the Chair of Scots Law in Edinburgh.

McIntosh and Duncan Cameron, and he sent a very clever writer body, a regular rogue of the name of Lyon, to assist Mr Cooper in preparing the evidence. The friends of the other young men spared no means of assisting them, and they all got off easily, having been on the side of the poor murdered lad; his opponent and the Rothiemurchus man who had rushed in to help him were in a very different position. Nothing, however, transpired to criminate George McIntosh; he was acquitted; but the Landlord—he was by trade a tailor, and the wound had the appearance of having been made by closed scissors; this persuasion saved him; it was proved that it could not be scissors; neither was it—he had done it with the snuffers. The verdict was manslaughter, and he was transported for life. We all felt the whole affair as a disgrace to Rothiemurchus. My father was quite depressed by such an occurrence happening. Jane and I talking it over a year afterwards with Belleville, he said the fault lay with those who had put young men who were not gentlemen into a position only fit for gentlemen; had these lowly born, uneducated youths been at the plough, they would neither have had time nor inclination for such a scandal.

My father actually got a Cadetship for George McIntosh after this, and sent him to India.

# CHAPTER NINETEEN

# 1816–1817

In November 1816 we travelled back to Edinburgh to take possession of Sir John Hay's house in George Street, an infinitely more agreeable winter residence than Lady Augusta Clavering's very gloomy old barrack in Queen Street. It was an excellent family house, warm, cheerful, aery, with abundant accommodation for a larger party than ours; but there was the same fault of but one drawing room and a small study off of it. Perhaps my father wanted no space for a Ball. The town was much fuller than it had been before, of course gayer, many very pleasant people were added to our society. War was over. All its anxieties, all its sorrows had passed away, and though there must have been many sad homes made for ever, in a degree, desolate, these individual griefs did not affect the surface of our cheerful world. The bitterness of party still prevailed too much in the town, estranging many who would have been improved by mixing more with one another. Also it was a bad system that divided us all into small côteries; the bounds were not strictly defined, and far from strictly kept; still, the various little sections were all there, apart, each small set overvaluing itself and undervaluing its neighbours.

There was the fashionable set, headed by Lady Gray of Kinfauns, Lady Molesworth unwillingly admitted, her sister Mrs Munro, and several other regular party giving women, seeming to live for crowds at home and abroad. Lady Molesworth, the fast daughter of a managing manoeuvring mother, very clever, no longer young, ran off with a boy at College of old Cornish family and large fortune, and made him an admirable wife—for he was little beyond a fool—and gave him a clever son, the present Sir William

Molesworth.[1] Within, or beyond this, was an exclusive set, the McLeods of McLeod, Cumming Gordons, Shaw Steuarts, Murrays of Ochtertyre, etc. Then there was a card playing set, of which old Mrs Oliphant of Rossie was the principal support, assisted by her daughters Mrs Grant of Kilgraston and Mrs Veitch, Mr and Mrs Massie, Mr and Mrs Richmond, she was sister to Sir Thomas Liddell, Lord Ravensworth, Miss Sinclair of Murkle the Duchess of Gordon's first cousin and the image of her, though a plain likeness, Sam Anderson and others. By the bye, Mrs Richmond was the heroine of the queer story in Mr Ward's Tremaine,[2] and she actually did wear the breeches. And there was a quiet country gentleman set, Lord and Lady Wemyss, all the Campbells, Lord and Lady Murray, Sir James and Lady Helen Hall, Sir John and Lady Steuart, Graemes, Hays, and so forth. A literary set, including College professors, Authours, and others pleased thus to represent themselves. A clever set with Mrs Fletcher. The law set. Strangers, and inferiours. All shook up together they would have done very well. Even when partially mingled they were very agreeable. When primmed up, each phalanx apart, on two sides of the turbulent stream of politicks, arrayed as if for battle, there was really some fear of a clash at times. We were so fortunate as to skim the cream, I think, off all varieties; though my father publickly was violent enough in his Whiggism he never let it interfere with the amenities of private life, and my Mother kept herself quite aloof from all party work.

The Lord Provöst of Edinburgh was seldom in any of these sets; he was generally a tradesman of repute among his equals, and in their society he was content to abide. This winter the choice happened to fall on a little man of good family, highly connected in the mercantile world, married to

---

1. Sir William Molesworth, the politician (1810–55). His mother Mary Brown from Edinburgh married Sir Arscott-Ourry Molesworth, the seventh baronet, whose family had been of influence in Cornwall since the reign of Queen Elizabeth.

2. Robert Plumer Ward's *Tremaine, or the Man of Refinement* was to be published in 1825.

an Inverness Alves, and much liked. I don't remember what his pursuit was, whether he was a Banker, or Agent for the great Madras house his brother George was the head of,[1] but he was a kind hospitable man, his wife Mrs Arbuthnot very Highland, and though neither the one nor the other had the least pretensions to good manners, they were general favourites. He was chosen provost again when his three years were out, so he received the king, George IV., on his memorable visit, and was made a Baronet.[2] Just before him we had had Sir John Marjoribanks of Lees, mercantile too.[3] After him, the town Council went back to their own degree. The name amongst us for Sir William Arbuthnot, I call him by the name we knew him best by, was *Dicky Gossip*, and richly he deserved it, for he knew all that was doing every where to every body, all that was pleasant to know; a bit of illnature or a bit of ill news he never uttered. After a visit from him and his excellent wife, they were fond of going about together, a deal of what was going on seemed to have suddenly enlightened their listeners, and most agreeably. A tale of scandal never spread from them, nor yet a sarcasm. They, from their situation, saw a great deal of company, and no parties could be pleasanter than those they gave. They were much enlivened this year by the arrival of a sister from Spain, the Widow of Sir John Hunter, the late Consul general at Madrid. Lady Hunter, still in weeds, she did not shew herself; her two very nice daughters appeared at home, though they went out only to small gatherings of relations till the spring. They were just sufficiently foreign to be the more interesting, and they were so ladylike we took greatly to them, became quite intimate, and never were

1. George Arbuthnot (1772–1843) founded this famous merchant company.
2. He was Provost from 1815–17 (when he was praised for setting up public works, such as the construction of a road round the King's Park, to help relieve distress) and then again from 1821 to 1823; George IV knighted him after the Town Council banquet in Parliament House.
3. His father had been a wine merchant in Bordeaux.

estranged although widely separated. Jane Hunter and Jane Grant more particularly remained faithful to their early friendship even after their names were changed, even to this day.

Locality has a good deal to do with intimacies. In Heriot Row and in Queen Street we had no acquaintance very near us. In Heriot Row the Cathcarts were next door, and Lord Alloway, who was a Widower, seemed anxious that his daughters should be a good deal with us; they were,—but that was all, for Agnes was merely gentle and pleasing, Mary very pretty, the brothers quite cloddish, so that we never got on very far, although we were much together. In George Street we were in the midst of agreeable neighbours. Near the Arbuthnots in Charlotte Square were the Cumming Gordons, the old Lady and her four unmarried daughters, Charles, and Sir William and his Bride on a visit to them. Young Lady Gordon Cumming, as she called herself for distinction, was not handsome, very tall—five feet ten and a half—thin, not well made, neither were her features good, yet all together, when well dressed, I have seen her look magnificent. The whole connexion was in a dream of joy at Sir Willie's wife being the daughter of Lady Charlotte Campbell, niece to the Duke of Argylle. It was Eliza here, and Eliza there, and Eliza only; they were awakened by and bye, and rather rudely, but this winter it was all an intoxication of happiness. Old Lady Cumming never went out, but every evening, when the rest of the family were in, the shutters were left open to shew the drawing rooms lighted up, and a general invitation was given to certain familiar friends on such occasions to enter if agreeable. There was a card table, always musick, for Sophy Cumming played delightfully, Charles very well on the violincello, Sir James Riddell, my friend Campbell's elder brother, equally well on the violin; there was a flute too sometimes, and in the flute's absence, a man whose name I can't remember *whistled* like a sweet double flageolet. When Sophy was out of the way I have taken the pianoforte for her—a very miserable substitute. Young Lady Cumming sang ballads neatly, all she had voice for. One of the married daughters, Mrs John Forbes, was observed by the old Lady to shirk these pleasant evenings rather, so the four sisters remonstrated. Mrs Forbes frankly acknowledged that she had not time, a houseful of children and an advocate's income left her little leisure for gadding; the sisters begged however she would come, as their mother liked to have as many of her family as she could gather round her, and they told her to bring her work, that would prevent her loss of time. So she did; I saw her there busy with a pair of coarse sheets, seaming down the long seam with a long thread, stitching and stretching, dragging this web bit by bit out of a great canvas bag as she wanted it; and yet she did not look unladylike. All the Cummings were queer, queerer than one ever sees people now, but the good blood kept order to a certain degree.

Lady Charlotte *Bury*, she had become, passed a few days in Edinburgh this season without the husband; her second daughter Eleanor, afterwards Lady Uxbridge, was with her, a pretty creature, the image of me! It was really curious the extraordinary likeness to us that ran through this whole Campbell connexion, and no relationship between us. Some two hundred years back or more an Argylle Campbell had married a Grant of Grant, and her daughter had married a Grant of Rothiemurchus, but that was too remote descent; besides, 'twas in the Gunning and the Ironside the likeness lay. My mother was so like Lady Wemyss they were frequently mistaken. Uncle Ralph and Walter Campbell the Uncle, the sailor, were like as two brothers. Lady Eleanor Charteris—afterwards Campbell, for she married her cousin Walter—was asked to dance for me, and I was congratulated on my approaching marriage for her. Lady Uxbridge and I were more alike. Even Charlotte Clavering, Lady Augusta's daughter, had a look of me after she dressed quietly as the wife of Miles Fletcher. Emma Campbell could hardly be known from my sister Mary, William and Walter Campbell ditto, Johnny and Johnny Campbell; and Mary and I were both so like the Miss Gunning, Duchess of Hamilton and Argylle, that they used at Altyre to dress us up and set us underneath her picture as a show and Mary certainly was as beautiful. After all, perhaps the surprise is that with so few features to work with nature is able to vary us all so much; that really is more wonderful than that some few of us should be alike. Where there is such near resemblance, character must have something to do with it.

Lady Ashburton's was another pleasant house; she was a Cuninghame of Lainshaw, niece to Lord Cranstoun[1] and to Dugald Stewart, one of the College professors.[2] He took pupils, and had among them this very eccentric son of the Speaker, Mr Dunning, Lord Ashburton,[3] he was ungainly in person, disagreeable in habits, some years younger than Miss Cunninghame, who would have him, despight both uncles; Lord Cranston felt it was a throwing away of a fine girl, Dugald Stewart took it a reflexion on himself that in his house, while under his care, a very wealthy nobleman should be while so young engaged to his niece. The niece did not care; she was cold and she was ambitious, so she married her Lord, and they had a fine country house and a beautiful town house—two houses thrown into one, which gave her a splendid suite of apartments for the grave style of receiving company that suited her taste; a dinner party every week, and in the evening her rooms thrown open to an assemblage that filled them. Her intimate acquaintance had cards for the season. Others she asked when she liked—there was no amusement provided, neither dancing nor musick nor cards, and yet it was always agreeable. In one of the many rooms was a counter spread with a variety of refreshments. In another were a number of small round tables where groups of any desired size were served with tea. Lord Ashburton delighted in company, and in people that were fat; like Julius Caesar he objected to all who had a lean and hungry look! He went about smiling, though saying little except to himself; he had a trick of soliloquising, so very oddly. We dined there

1. George Cranstoun became a judge in 1826; one sister, Jane Anne, did marry the Count of Purgstall, and the other, Helen D'Arcy, married Professor Dugald Stewart. See Cockburn's *Memorials* for an interesting portrait.
2. Dugald Stewart (the distinguished figure of the Scottish Enlightenment, 1753–1828) was appointed to the Chair of Moral Philosophy in 1785.
3. John Dunning, first Lord Ashburton (1731–83); his son Richard married Ann Cunningham; the title died with him in 1823.

one day, and it so happened that I sat next to him; he looked at me, after a while he looked again: 'That's a pretty girl—Miss Grant, I fancy; not fat enough. I must ask her to take wine.' All this was to himself, then aloud: 'Miss Grant, a glass of wine with me?' It was the fashion then to pay this civility to all ladies, who could not have got any otherwise, and who, some of them, liked a good deal. 'It's a pity she's so thin. What shall I say next to her?' He could not talk, converse, I mean, merely start out a few words thus, always however to the purpose. One of Lady Ashburton's sisters was married to McLeod of Cadboll, a Ross-shire laird, and an aunt was the Baroness Purgstall in Germany. This German aunt had given to two of her country men letters of introduction to her old friends in Edinburgh. Lady Ashburton presented them to my Mother. My Mother, who always liked foreigners, paid them a great deal of attention. The Styrian Baron Gudenus and the Saxon Chevalier Thinnfeldt were soon made free of our house, and very much indeed they enlivened it. They were well bred, well educated, sensible young men, great additions to our society. The Baron, the only son of an old Gratz family, was travelling for pleasure, or perhaps for health—he looked sickly. The Chevalier had a large property in mines, and came to our country to get some insight into a better method of working them.

There were very few large balls given this winter. Lady Gray, Mrs Grant of Kilgraston, Mrs McLeod, and a few others retained this old method of entertaining. A much pleasanter style of smaller parties had come into fashion with the new style of dancing. It was the first season of quadrilles, against the introduction of which there had been a great stand made by old fashioned respectables. Many resisted the new french figures altogether, and it was a pity so entirely to give up the merry country dance, in which the warfare between the two opinions resulted; but we were all the young people bit by the quadrille mania, and I was one of the set that brought them first into notice. We practised privately by the aid of a very much better master than Mr Smart. Finlay Dunn had been abroad, imported all the most graceful steps from Paris; and having kept our secret well, we burst upon the world at a select reunion at the White Melvilles', the

Spectators standing up the chairs and sofas to admire us. People danced in those days; we did not merely stand and talk, look about bewildered for our vis a vis, return to our partners either too soon or too late, without any regard to the completion of the figure, the conclusion of the measure, or the step belonging to it; we attended to our business, we moved in cadence, easily and quietly, embarrassing no one and appearing to considerable advantage ourselves. We were only eight; Mr White Melville and Nancy McLeod opposite to Charles Cochrane and me, Johnny Melville and Charles McLeod with Fanny Hall and Miss Melville. So well did we all perform, that our Exhibition was called for and repeated several times in the course of the evening. We had no trouble in enlisting cooperators, the rage for Cotillons[1] spread, the dancing master was in every house, and every other style discarded. Room being required for the display, much smaller numbers were invited to the quadrille parties. Two, or at the most three, instruments sufficed for band, refreshments suited us better than suppers, an economy that enabled the Inviters to give three or four of these little sociable dances at less cost than one ball; it was every way an improvement. My Mother gave several of these little parties so well suited to the accommodations of our house, and at no cost to my father, Uncle Edward having sent her for the purpose of being spent in any way she liked upon her daughter, a hundred pounds.

Of our first Edinburgh quadrille who are left. The White Melvilles were a family of two bachelour brothers and two unmarried sisters, protected by a married sister and her handsome Irish husband, Mr Jackson. Of the women I have never heard more; they were plain, well brought up, and had good fortunes. Robert the laird was a man of large property and very likeable, but he died, and Johnny, his brother, a very nice person, little thought of by the managing Committees, and small and plain, grew wonderfully in all ways on becoming great. But he remembered his younger brother days, and sought his Bride from afar; he married Lady

1. The name given to several French dances, including the quadrille.

Catherine Osborne, sister, half-sister rather, to the present Duke of Leeds; both are dead, and their children are married. Charles Cochrane, very handsome, a most perfect dancer, and always a great friend of mine, for I like all sailors, is still living, I think. He has been a great traveller, *walking* all over the world, is an authour,[1] a philanthropist, eccentrick but kindly. All the Cochranes are maddish. Charles had a brother Andrew, madly in love with one of the Ladies Charteris. He disguised himself first as a lamp lighter that he might look on her as she sat at dinner, and then as a gardener that he might watch her in her walks, Lord Wemyss having a large garden belonging to his house in Queen Street. Charles McLeod was brother to Harris, no way *nearly* related to Nancy. She was sister to *the* McLeod, as plain a man as she was a handsome girl; her brother's wife was a very underbred woman, City reared, daughter of a merchant, and sister to the Banker Stephenson, almost another Fauntleroy. Nancy McLeod married Spencer Percival, an old Italian love.[2] I met her afterwards at Cheltenham with nine not pretty daughters and two sons. I liked her much.

At our little parties Jane came out amazingly; she was never shy, always natural and gay and clever, and though not strictly handsome, she looked so bright, so well, with her fine eyes and her rosy mouth, she was in extreme request with all our Beaux. To the old set of the two former winters I had added considerably during the course of this more sociable one, and Jane went shares whenever she was seen. She carried one altogether away from me, the celebrated Basil Hall. He had just this very year returned from Loo Choo, had

1. *Journal of a Residence and Travels in Columbia during the years 1823 and 1824* by Captain Charles Stuart Cochrane of the Royal Navy (1825). Columbia, he wrote 'presents the gratifying spectacle of a nation successful in the vindication of its rights, and triumphant over the mean and mistaken policy that would have condemned it to a perpetuity of sloth, ignorance, bigoted superstition and slavery'. It was dedicated to Simon Bolivar.
2. This seems to be an uncharacteristic error as, according to the D.N.B., he married Jane Spencer-Wilson.

published his book,[1] brought home flat needles, and cloth made from wood, and a funny cap which he put on very good humouredly, and chop sticks which he ate with very obligingly; in short, he did the polite voyager to no end. Jane was quite taken with him, so was Jane Hunter; *Margaret* Hunter[2] and I used to be quite amused with them and him, and wonder how they could wait on the Lion so perseveringly. He was the second son of Sir James Hall, a man not actually crazy, but not far from it; so given up to scientifick pursuits as to be incapable of attending to his private affairs. They were in consequence much disordered, and they would have been entirely deranged but for the care of his wife, Lady Helen. Sir James had very lately published a truly ingenious work,[3] an attempt to deduce gothick architecture from the original wigwams made of reeds. The drawings were beautifully executed, not by himself, I fancy, and by them he clearly shewed the fluted pillars of stone copied from faggots of osier, groined arches from the slender shoots bent over and tyed together, buds originating ornaments; a fanciful theory may be, yet with some shew of reason in it. Lady Helen, a great friend of my Mother's, was sister to the Lord Selkirk[4] who went to colonise in America. How could the children of such a pair escape. Their eldest son was a fool merely; Basil, flighty, and his end miserable; a third, Jamie, used to cry unless Jane or I danced with him—nobody else would. Three or four beautiful girls died of consumption, Fanny

1. Basil Hall (1788–1844) published his book *Account of a Voyage of Discovery to the West Coast of Corea and the Great Loo-Choo Islands* in 1818 not 1817.
2. In fact Margaret married Basil Hall in 1825; she was the daughter of Sir John Hunter, a diplomat.
3. Sir James Hall, Bart. (1761–1832), made many contributions to geological studies; this book, entitled *Essay on the Origin, History and Principles of Gothic Architecture*, was published in 1813.
4. Thomas Douglas, fifth Earl of Selkirk (he succeeded after the deaths of six elder brothers) organised a successful colonising expedition to Prince Edward's Island and one, fraught with controversy, to Red River in Manitoba.

among them, two were idiots out at nurse some where in the country, and one had neither hands nor feet, only stumps. I used to wonder how Lady Helen[1] kept her senses; calm she always looked, very kind, she always was, wrapt up her affections were in Basil and the two daughters who lived and married—Magdalen, first Lady de Lancey and then Mrs Harvey, and Emily, the wife of an English clergyman. The eldest son married too, Julia Walker, Dr Hope's niece and heiress.

Dr Hope was the Professor of chemistry,[2] an old Admirer, nay I believe more, of my Aunt Mary's, and still the flutterer round every new beauty that appeared. I preferred him to Professor Leslie[3] because he was clean, but not to Professor Playfair; *he*, old, and ugly, and absent, was charming, fond of the young who none of them feared him, glad to be drawn away from his mathematical difficulties to laugh over a tea table with such as Jane and me. We were favourites too with Dr Brewster, who was particularly agreeable, and with John Clerk, who called Jane, Euphrosyne, and with Mr Jeffrey with whom we gradually came to spend a great deal of our time.[4] I had Lord Buchan all to myself though, he cared for no one else in the house. He lived very near us, and came

1. Helen, daughter of the fourth Earl of Selkirk, had, in fact, three sons and three daughters; the eldest son may have been 'a fool merely' but he was also according to the D.N.B. a F.R.S.; Basil, the second son's end was indeed 'miserable' for he became insane in 1842 and died two years later in Haslar Hospital.
2. See II, p. 6.
3. Sir John Leslie (1766–1832): with the versatility of the Enlightenment, he succeeded Playfair to the Chair of Mathematics in 1805 when he moved to that of Natural Philosophy; and he in turn followed Playfair to that Chair on his death in 1819; Sir John was to be knighted in the year of his death.
4. Although Sir David Brewster was clearly suspected of Tory sympathies, he with Jeffrey and Clerk were 'the intimate friends of my father', and 'among the cleverest of the Whigs' (see II, p. 2), Euphrosyne was one of the Three Graces.

in most mornings in his shepherd's plaid, with his long white hair flowing over his shoulders, to give me lessons in behaviour. He was particularly uneasy at my biting my nails, rated me well, examined the fingers and would give a smart rap where necessary. If he were pleased he would bring out some curiosity from his pockets—a tooth of Queen Mary's, a bone of James the 5th, imaginary relicks he set great store by. How many flighty people there were in Scotland—neither of his extraordinary brothers quite escaped the taint. Lord Erskine and Harry Erskine[1] were both of them at times excited. At a certain point judgment seems to desert genius. Another friend I made this year who remembered to ask about me very lately, Adam Hay, now Sir Adam. He was Sir John Hay's third son when I knew him. John died, Robert the very handsome sailor was drowned, so the Baronetcy fell to Adam. Are not the Memoirs of the old a catalogue of the deaths of all who were young with them. Adam Hay tried to shake my integrity; he advocated, as he thought, the cause of his dearest friend, whose mother, dear excellent woman, having died, their sophistry persuaded them so had my promise. We had many grave conversations on a sad subject, while people thought we were arranging our matrimonial excursion.[2] He told me I was blamed, and I told him I must bear it; I did add one day, it was no easy burden, he should not seek to make it heavier. His own sister, some time after this, succeeded to my place; lovely and most loveable she was, and truly loved I do believe. Adam Hay told me of it when he first knew it, long afterwards, and I said, so best; yet the end was not yet. I had never female friends, I don't know why; I never took to them unless they were quite elderly. I had only Jane, but she was a host.

Poor Jane—this very spring she sprained her ankle, that very ankle that never strengthened again. My Uncle William suddenly arrived from Houghton, and all of us running

1. See I, p. 143.
2. Sir Adam Hay (1795–1867) was M.P. for Linlithgow burghs (1826–30). This tantalising hint as to the identity of E.G's lover (see II, pp. 14–22), alas, does not appear to fit any of his four married sisters.

quickly down to welcome him, Jane slipt her left foot, turned it under her, and fell from the pain, tumbling on over the whole flight of the stairs. All that was proper was done for it, and we thought lightly of the accident, as she was only laid up three weeks or so. She felt it better not to use it much, and so for the present the matter rested. Our Uncle remained with us a few days only; he had come to consult my father on some business, and my Mother on an invitation he had received for his eldest daughter Kate to join Uncle Edward and his lately married wife in India. Soon after he went Aunt Leitch arrived—not to us. She liked being independant. She had taken lodgings at Leith for the purpose of sea bathing for Mary and Charlotte, two other daughters of Uncle William's, who had lived with her for some years. Charlotte had not been well and had been ordered to the sea, so on our account my Aunt thought she would try the East coast. Every second day they dined with us, at least, walking up that mile long Leith Walk[1] and our long street, and back again in the cool April evenings; fatigue enough to do away with all the good of the sea bathing. Charlotte was a mere rather pretty girl, nothing particular; Mary was most extremely beautiful. What a fate was hers! but I must not anticipate [see II 186].

Aunt Leitch told us of Durham cousins living, poor people, very near us, within the rules of the Abbey,[2] on account of debt. Misfortunes had overtaken some of the husbands of the nine Miss Neshams. The Goodchilds were bankrupt, as were such of the connexions who had been engaged in business with them. Mr Carr, the husband of the eldest sister, had lost all; they had to fly with a very small portion of their personal property from their comfortable house at Stockton, and take refuge in a very sorry lodging inside the kennel at Holyrood. We found them out immediately, and from that time forward very much lightened their

1. Leith Walk was formed in 1774 and tolls were only abolished in 1835.
2. The Palace, its precincts and the Park were (until the ending of imprisonment for debt) a sanctuary for debtors so long so they only ventured out on Sunday; the peak numbers were 116 in 1816 (John Harrison, *History of Holyrood*).

banishment. At first there were only the poor silly old man and his wife, and two Stockton maidservants, not yet done with untiring efforts to clean up indifferent furniture. By and bye came George, their youngest son, not long from School, clever enough and the best of good creatures, but so unmitigably vulgar his company was frequently distressing. My Mother was quite disturbed by his conduct, and the roars of laughter it elicited from my father. They generally dined with us on Sunday, the only day the old man could go out, the carriage going for them and taking them home, George calling out 'my eye' and making faces at the coachman. He was a fit beau for a belle lately arrived amongst us.

Mrs Gillio, once Miss Peggy Grant of Craggan, niece to the old General and to Peter the Pensioner, had settled at Bath after her visit to the highlands. She intended leaving her youngest daughter and her son at good schools in England, and was preparing to return to Bombay with her two eldest girls when she heard of her husband's death. Her circumstances being much changed by this calamity, she thought of Edinburgh as uniting many advantages for all her children at a cheaper rate than she could procure them else where. We took lodgings for them which, by the bye, they changed; the boy was to attend the high School, the two younger girls the classes, and the elder ones to go a little out if they made desirable acquaintance. Amelia Gillio, with her brilliant eyes, was not a plain girl; she was worse, she was an impudent one, and many and many a time I should liked to have shipped her off to the antipodes for the annoyance she caused us. After a walk with Nancy McLeod, or a visit to Agnes Cathcart, or the Hunters, how this fourth rate young lady's tones grated rather on the ears all unaccustomed to them. It was the time of short waists and short petticoats, and the Bath, or Miss Amelia's, fashions were so extra short at both extremities, we were really ashamed of being seen with her; the black frock reached very little below the knee—she had certainly irreproachable feet and ankles. George Carr attracted equal attention by wearing his hat on the back of his head, never having a glove on, and besides talking very loudly, he snatched up all the notices of sales and such like carried about the streets by hawkers, and stuffed them with a meaning laugh into his pockets, saying they would do for 'summat,' he was very intolerable.

We had a visitor this spring of a different grade, Colonel d'Este, whom we had not seen since the old Prince Augustus days. He was just as natural as ever, asked himself to dinner, and talked of Ramsgate. He had not then given up his claim to Royalty,[1] therefore there was a little skilful arrangement on his part to avoid either assumption or renunciation. He entered unannounced, my father meeting him at the door and ushering him into the room, my mother, and all the ladies on her hint, rising till he begged them to be seated and on going to dinner he bowed all out, remaining beside my Mother as her escort. Other wise he conformed to common usage, let the servants wait on him, and perhaps did not observe that we had no finger glasses; which reminds me that a year or two after when Prince Leopold was at Kinrara, Lord Huntly, precise as he was, had forgotten to mention to his servants that nobody ever washed before royalty, and from the moment this omission struck him, he sat in such an agony as to be incapable of his usual happy knack of keeping the ball going. Very luckily some of the Prince's attendants had an eye to all, and stopt the offending chrystals on their way. I don't know what brought Colonel D'Este to Scotland at that season of year, he was probably going to some of his Mother's relations in the West.[2] I remember Lord Abercromby being asked to meet him, and after accepting, he sent an apology; 'an unavoidable accident which happily would never be repeated' set us all off on a train of conjectures wide of the truth, the newspapers next day announcing the marriage of this grave elderly friend of my father's.

We left Sir John Hay's house in May; he was coming to live in it himself with his pretty daughters; and we went for three months to the house of Mr Allan the Banker, in Charlotte Square, just while we should be considering where to fix for a permanency. Mrs Allan was ill, and was going to some

1. See I, pp. 182–3; as late as 1831 he is reported as filing a Bill in chancery to prove the validity of his parents' marriage.
2. His mother's family were the Earls of Dunmore and Galloway.

watering place, and they were glad to have their house occupied. Before we moved we paid two country visits, my father, my mother and I.

Our first visit was to Dunbar, Lord Lauderdale's,[1] a mere family party, to last the two or three days my Lord and my father were arranging some political matters. They were always brimfull of party mysteries, having a constant correspondence on these subjects. My mother had so lectured me on the necessity of being any thing but myself on this startling occasion that in spite of all my experience a fit of *Kinrara feel* came over me for the first evening. I was so busy with the proper way to sit, and the proper mode to speak the few words I was to be allowed to say, and the attention I was to pay to all the nods and winks she was to give me, that a fit of shyness actually came on, and my spirits were quite crushed by these preliminaries and the curious state of household we fell upon. In the very large drawing room the family sat in there was plenty of comfortable furniture, including an abundance of easy chairs set in a wide circle around the fire. Before each easy chair was placed a stool rather higher than would have been agreeable for feet to rest on, but quite suited to the purpose it was prepared for—the kennel of a dog. I don't know how many of these pets the Ladies Maitland and their mother were provided with, but a black nose peeped out of an opening in the side of every stool immediately on the entrance of a visitor, and the barking was incessant. At this time four daughters were at home unmarried, and two or three sons. One daughter was dead, and one had disposed of herself some years before by running away with poor, very silly, and not wealthy Fraser of Torbreck, then quartered at Dunbar with the regiment of Militia in which he was a Captain. This proceeding of the Lady Anne quite changed the face of affairs in her father's family. Lord Lauderdale had rather late in his man of fashion life married the only child of one Mr Antony Tod, Citizen of London.[2] Pretty she had been never; she was a mere little painted doll when we knew

1. This visit to the eighth Earl ( 1759–1839 ) might be
   explained by Cockburn's description of him as 'the
   chief of the Whig party in Scotland.'
2. 'Secretary to the G.P.O.' (*Scots Peerage*).

her, a cypher as to intellect, but her fortune had been very large, and she was amiable and obedient, and her Lord, they said, really became fond of her and of all the many children she brought him. He was not vain, however, either of her or of them, he had no reason; so he kept them all greatly living in great retirement at Dunbar, never taking any of them with him to town, nor allowing them to visit either in Edinburgh or in their own neighbourhood, till the elopement of Lady Anne, the only beauty. From that sore time Lady Lauderdale and her remaining daughters lived much more in society. They had begun too to feel their own importance, and to venture on opposing my Lord, for Mr Tod was dead, and had left to each of his grandchildren, sons and daughters alike, £15,000. The rest to his daughter for her life, with remainder to her eldest son, Lord Maitland. To his son in law the Earl Mr Tod left nothing. Here was power to the weaker side, exerted, it was said, occasionally, but they were an united happy family, fondly attached to each other.[1]

The square Maitland face was not improved by the Tod connexion, though the family finances so greatly benefited by it. Sons and daughters of the house were alike plain in face and short in person, even Lady Anne, with her really lovely countenance, was a dwarf in size and ill proportioned; but there was a very redeeming expression generally thrown over the flat features, and they had all pleasant manners. The second day went off much more agreeably than the first, although I had to bear some quizzing on my horrour of gambling. In the morning the young people drove, or rode, and walked; before dinner the ladies worked a little, netting purses and knotting bags; the gentlemen played with the dogs. All the evenings were spent at cards, and such high play, Brag and Loo[2] unlimited. It was nothing for fifty or an hundred pounds to change hands among them. I was quite terrified. My few shillings, the first I had called my own for ages, given me for the occasion in a new purse bought to hold

1. After Lady Anne's marriage, three of the four remaining daughters were to marry.
2. Brag is an early form of poker; Loo was a version of whist where any player failing to take a trick pays an agreed sum or 'loo' to the pool.

them, were soon gone at Brag, under the management of Captain Antony Maitland, R.N. He had undertaken to teach me the game, of which I had acknowledged I knew nothing, for we never saw cards at home except when a whist table was made up for Belleville; and as the eternal cry 'Anty Anty' did not repair my losses, and I sturdily refused to borrow, declining therefore to play, and composing myself gravely to look on, they could hardly keep their countenances; my whole poor fortune was such a trifle to them. It was not however my loss so much as what my Mother would say to it that disturbed me. She was very economical in those little ways, and her unwonted liberality upon this occasion would, I knew, be referred to ever after as a bar to any further supplies, the sum now given having been so squandered. I sought her in her room before we went to bed to make the confession, fully believing it had been a crime. The thoughts of the whole scene make me laugh now, though I certainly slept all the better then on being graciously forgiven 'under the circumstances.'

There was no company, only sir Philip Dirom, arranging his marriage settlements with Lord Lauderdale, the guardian of the Bride, the heiress Miss Henderson. He was a handsome man, gentlemanly, and rather agreeable, not clever in the least, and very vain. He had won honours in his profession, the navy, and his latest acquisition, a diamond star of some order, was the single object of his thoughts, after Miss Henderson's acres. Lord Lauderdale laid a bet that Sir Philip would not be two hours in the house without producing it; nor was he. In the middle of dinner, having dexterously turned the conversation on the orders of knighthood, he sent his servant for it, sure, he said, that some of the ladies would like to see the pretty bauble—one of the principal insignia of the *Bath* I suppose it was. Lord Maitland received and handed the little red case round with a mock gravity that nearly overset the decorum of the company. How little, when laughing at these foibles, did we foresee that the vain knight's great niece was to be my cousin Edmund [Ironside]'s wife, or fancy that he would be so kind, so generous, to that thoughtless pair.

The other visit was only for the day. We did not even sleep

from home, but returned very late at night, for Almondell was twelve miles good from Edinburgh. Henry Erskine had added to a small cottage prettily situated on the river from which he named his retirement, and there, tired of politicks, he wore away time that I believed sometimes lagged with him, in such country pursuits as he could follow on an income that gave him little beyond the necessaries of life. He and Mrs Erskine had no greater pleasure than to receive a few friends to an early dinner; they had a large connexion, a choice acquaintance, and were in themselves so particularly agreeable that, company or no, a few hours passed with them were always a treat. Each had been twice married; his first wife I never heard more of than that she had left him children, two sons no way worthy of him, Mrs Callander, and another married daughter. The last wife had no children, either Erskines or Turnbulls, and her father, Mr Munro, a merchant in Glasgow, having failed, her youth was a struggling one. She had even had to draw patterns for tambour work for her bread. Her sister Meg Munro, afterwards Mrs Harley Drummond, was a much more conspicuous person than Mrs Erskine. Their brothers were Sir Thomas Munro and Mr Alexander Munro, the husband of Lady Molesworth's handsome sister. Mrs Cumming and Grace Baillie had an old intimacy with these Munros; they were all from Ayrshire, and that is a bond in Scotland.

In May we removed to Charlotte Square, a house I found the most agreeable of any we had ever lived in in Edinburgh. The shrubbery in front, and the peep from the upper windows behind, of the Firth of Forth with its wooded shores and distant hills, made the look out each way so very cheerful. We were in the midst, too, of our friends. We made two new acquaintances, the Wolfe Murrays next door, and Sir James and Lady Henrietta Ferguson in my father's old house, in which Jane and I were born. Nothing could be pleasanter than our sociable life. The gaiety was over, but every day some meeting took place among us young people. My Mother's tea table was, I think, the general gathering point. The two Hunters were almost always with us in the evenings; they danced their Spanish dances, fandangoes and boleros, striking the castagnettes so prettily in time to the musick, Agnes Cathcart often; and for Beaux our German friends, George and Henry Lindsay, at College then, Basil Hall, and sometimes a class fellow of my brother's. In the mornings we made walking parties, and one day we went to Roslin and Lasswade, a merry company. Another day we spent at sea.

The Captain of the frigate lying in the roads gallantly determined to make a return to Edinburgh for all the attention Edinburgh had paid him. He invited all left of his winter acquaintance to a breakfast and a dance on board. We all drove down to the pier at Newhaven in large merry parties, where now the splendid Granton pier shames its predecessors,[1] and there found boats awaiting us, manned by the merry sailors in their best suits, and we were quickly rowed across the sparkling water, for it was a beautiful day, such a gay little fleet, and hoisted up on the deck. There an awning was spread, flags, etc., waving, a quadrille and a military Band all ready, and Jane, who was in high good looks, soon took her place among the dancers, having been engaged by the little monkey of a Middy who had piloted us over. The collation was below, all along the lower deck. We sat down to it at four o'clock, and then danced on again till near midnight, plentifully served with refreshments, most hospitably pressed upon us by our entertainers. Sailors are so hearty, and every Officer of the ship seemed to feel he had the part of host to play. There never was a merrier *fête*.

Jane always considered this her *début*. She was nicely dressed, was very happy, much admired, and danced so well. She and I were never dressed alike; indeed there was so little resemblance then between us that probably the same style of dress would not have become us. Her figure was not good, yet when any one with better taste than herself presided at her toilette, it could be made to look light and pleasing; her complexion was not good either, at least the skin was far from fair, but there was such a bright healthy colour in her rounded cheek, and such a pair of deep blue brilliant eyes,

1. Newhaven pier was destroyed by a storm in 1797 and replaced in 1812 by a slip; the new Granton pier was where Queen Victoria landed in 1842.

and such a rosy mouth which laughter suited, two such rows of even pearls for teeth, she well deserved her names, Euphrosyne and Hebe;[1] and she was such a clever creature, had such a power of conversation, without pedantry or blueism, it all flowed so naturally from a well stored head and warm honest heart. The little Middy's fancy was not the only one she touched that day. We were, like the best bred of the company, in half dress, white frocks made half high and with long sleeves. Jane's frock was abundantly flounced, but it had no other trimming; she wore a white belt, and had a hanging bunch of lilacks with a number of green leaves in her hair. My frock was white too, but all its flounces were headed with pink ribbon run through muslin, a pink sash, and all my load of hair quite plain. A few unhappy girls were in full dress, short sleeves, low necks, white shoes. Miss Cochrane, the Admiral's daughter,[2] was the most properly dressed amongst us; she was more accustomed to the sort of thing. She wore a white well frilled petticoat, an open silk spenser, and a little Swiss hat, from one side of which hung a bunch of roses. She and the dress together conquered Captain Darling; they were married a few months after.

Just before we left Charlotte Square we had a visit from the whole family of Goodchild. They were on their way from their handsome old home of High Pallion to a cottage in Perthshire, very cheap, with a good garden, and quite out of the way of expense of any kind. Mr Goodchild shipped a good deal of his lime to Dundee and thereabouts, it was therefore a good situation for him. Mrs Goodchild was glad to leave her old neighbourhood. Since their misfortunes she had come out quite in a new character. All her harshness, all her sarcasms, all her follies indeed, were gone. She had put her shoulder to the wheel in earnest, and tho' she could never make herself agreeable, she had become respectable. Still we were not prepared for the storming party by which we were assaulted; six daughters, I think, the father, mother, and two sons. The girls, all in coloured cotton frocks, close coarse

1. Hebe was a daughter of Zeus, seen as the personification of Youth.
2. See I, p. 187.

cottage bonnets, thick shoes, talking loud in sharp Durham voices, chose to walk about to see the town, with the brothers and George Carr attending. They were quite at their ease in the streets, gloves off or on, bonnets untied for the heat, shop windows inspected, remarks of all sorts made, George Carr perpetrating his usual series of misdemeanours with a gay effrontery unparalleled. Jane and I deputed to escort this assemblage, rejoiced we had so few acquaintances left in town, the lawyers only remaining for the summer. I was more remarkable myself if I had but known it! My walking dress was a white gown, a pink spenser, yellow tan boots with tassels dangling, and a fine straw, high crowned, deep poked bonnet, trimmed with white satin, in the front of which were stuck up there three white tall Ostrich feathers in a Prince's plume, nodding their tops forward with every step, unless the wind held them straight up like poplar trees. 'Fair and feathery Artizan' must have brought up this fashion; it was very ungraceful.

Mrs Goodchild and her younger children proceeded almost immediately on their journey. Mr Goodchild had to remain a short time on account of business. After this time he was frequently with us on his way backwards and forwards, and became quite a favourite in spite of his very strange manners, he was so cleverly original and so good natured. He took amazingly to our Germans, particularly to the Cheva*leer*, as he called him, and the Chevalier to him, and more especially to Bessy, the eldest daughter, whom my Mother had consented to receive for a week or so as she had occasion to see a dentist, and wished besides to remain to travel home with her father. She was a pleasant person, very amusing, but not to my mind likeable. I was forced to admire her very pretty feet, but M. Thinnfeldt could not get me any farther. To be rid of *Jack* was such a blessing, we cheerfully put up with his rather too lively sister. She was an addition too to the tea table and dancing, making her way with every body. Early in July we moved to a large house in Picardy Place, No. 8, with four windows in front, a great many rooms all of handsome size, and every accommodation, as the advertisements say, for a family of distinction. My father took a lease of it for three years, hiring the furniture from Mr

Trotter.[1] It was a sad change to us young people, down in the fogs of Leith, far from any country walk, quite away from all *our* friends, and an additional mile from Craigcrook too, reckoning both ways. We had got very intimate with Mr and Mrs Jeffrey, Jane and I, and we had frequently from Charlotte Square walked out to their beautiful old place on Corstorphine hill, spent the day there, and returned late when any one was with us, earlier when alone. Mr Jeffrey was enchanted with Jane, he had never seen any girl at all like her; he liked me too, but he did not find me out till long after. He left me now more to Mrs Jeffrey and their little Charlotte, a pretty child in those days.[2]

We had been at Craigcrook on a visit of some days, and William had come out to walk home to Picardy Place with us, looking strangely sad; and on the road he told us there was very little hope of the life of Dr Gordon. What a shock it was. Our intimacy had continued unbroken from the hour of our first acquaintance, William and I more particularly having been very much with him. He had got on in his profession as he deserved to do, and had lately got a Chair in the University[3] and a very full class, and they had left the old flat in Buccleuch Place in the old town off by the meadows, and lived in a nice house in Castle Street. All was prospering with them, but he died. It was some kind of fever he had neglected the first symptoms of, and I believe he had injured himself by too exclusive a meat diet. He was the first physician who had ever tried checking a certain sort of consumptive tendency by high feeding; he had succeeded so well with patients requiring this extra stimulus that he tried the plan on

1. The Trotter family were well-known for the quality of the furniture they supplied to the houses of this early stage of the development of the New Town of Edinburgh; Picardy Place, on the edge of one of its most fashionable areas, is scarcely in 'the fogs of Leith'.
2. For Lord Jeffrey see I, p. 76; the D.N.B. commented he was 'chivalrous to women, with whom he liked to cultivate little flirtations'.
3. Dr Gordon (see I, p. 298), whose Chair was Anatomy, died in June 1818; for Henry Cockburn his death 'clouded our city'.

himself, he who overstudying and under exercising should have given his system rest. Deeply we lamented him; William felt the lost most sincerely, nor did any other friend, I think, ever replace him. Mrs Gordon was left with three children, and only tolerably well off. She was unable to remain in Castle Street. She therefore removed soon to some place in Ayrshire, where there was good and cheap education to be had for her boys. Gogar, or some such name—her little boy, died; so, I think, did her pretty Jane. John only lived and was hardly a comfort to her. He has got steadier since his marriage but he is not what his father's son should have been.

We went late to the highlands and staid very quietly there. Kinrara was deserted this season, Belleville less gay than usual, and we did not go to the Meeting. My mother was not in spirits, my father was away; he went to Ireland to defend some rebels, trials that made a great stir at the time, being made quite a political battle field. The junior Counsel was little Erskine Sandford, the Bishop's son,[1] who went with us by the name of Portia, as it was his gown Mrs Henry Siddons[2] borrowed when she acted that character; it fitted her well, for he was only about her size, and she did not look unlike him, for he was handsome, though so small. They were some weeks absent. While in the north of Ireland my father took up his quarters in the house of an old acquaintance, the Marquis of Donegal, whose brother, Lord Spenser Chichester, my mother was once expected to marry. The Marquis was in some perplexity about his own marriage; he was ultimately obliged to go to the serious expense of having an act of parliament passed to legalise it, the Marchioness having been under age at the time it was celebrated. She was a natural child, so without a parent, consequently the Chancellor was her guardian. She had been brought up, indeed adopted, by a worthy couple somewhere in Wales; they supposed their consent sufficient, but it was not.[3]

1. Erskine Sandford (1793–1861), son of the bishop of Edinburgh, was to become Sheriff of Galloway.
2. Daughter-in-law to Sarah Siddons.
3. George Augustus, second Marquess and sixth Earl of Donegal (1769–1844), married Anna May, illegitimate daughter of Sir Edmund May, Bart., in 1795. Until the act of Parliament, this brother was the rightful heir.

I spent most of the Autumn rubbing dear Jane's ankle, on the Oxford Mr Grosvenor's plan.¹ We sat under the large ash tree, while I rubbed and she read aloud to me. We got through many interesting books this way. She had hurt herself dancing so very much on board the frigate. We rode too; Paddle was gone back to Inchyra, but a big Bogtrotter was there instead, on which Jane, who knew not fear, was mounted. Mr Blair had returned from abroad, and had not come near us, and my Mother bore it well, for after hearing that he had asked the Duc de Berri to drink wine with him, she had given him quite up. At a publick dinner in Paris this Prince had paid an unusual compliment to some of the English by proposing to 'troquer' with them in their fashion; he was certainly unprepared for the civility being returned.² Mr Nightingale could not get over this and a few other such instances, so they parted company. Mr Nightingale had come home too; we heard from him once or twice, and then we heard of him. He was married to his old love, Fanny Smith.

1. John Grosvenor (1742–1823): 'for long the most noted practical surgeon in Oxford . . . he was specially successful in his treatment of stiff and diseased joints by friction.' (D.N.B.)

2. If E.G.'s mother shared her husband's Whig principles then she would not have cared for the Duc de Berry, nephew to Louis XVIII and great hope of the 'ultra', legitimist faction in restoration France; he was assassinated in 1820. The verb 'troquer' (to barter) should be 'triquer' (to toast) . . . a rare error for E.G.

# CHAPTER TWENTY

## 1817–1818

AFTER a very short stay in the highlands we all came up to Picardy Place the end of October 1817, to meet my father on his return from Ireland. We soon settled ourselves in our spacious house, making ourselves more really at home than we had hitherto felt ourselves to be in town, having the certainty of no removal for three years. Still we younger ones were not soon reconciled to the situation, all our habits being disturbed by the separation from the West End! Three winters we spent here, none of them worthy of particular note, neither indeed can I at this distance of time separate the occurrences of each from the others. The usual routine seemed to be followed in all. My father and his new, very queer clerk, Mr Caw, worked away in their law chambers till my father went up to London late in Spring. The second winter he lost his seat for Grimsby, a richer competitor carried all votes, and for a few months he was out of Parliament. How much better it would have been for him had he remained out, stuck to the Bar, at which he really would have done well had he not left ever so many cases in the lurch when attending the 'House,' where he made no figure—he seldom spoke, said little when he did speak, and never in any way made himself of consequence. Only once, when all his party censured the Speaker, he made a little reputation by the polite severity of his few words, called by Sir Alexander Boswell his bit of brimstone and butter, a witticism that ran through all *côteries*, almost turning the laugh against the really clever speech.[1] He dined out every where with my

1. E.G. does her father less than justice; during these years
   he spoke regularly on Ireland, the Corn trade, Army
   expenditure, banking and, of course, Scots Law.
   Boswell himself was an M.P. 1816–21.

Mother while he was in Edinburgh, but hardly ever went out in an evening. He seemed, from his daily letters to my Mother, to go a good deal into society while he was in London, dining at Holland House, Lord Lansdowne's, Lord Grey's, all the Whigs in fact, for he got into Parliament again. The Duke of Bedford gave him Tavistock till one of his own sons should be ready for it.

Five or six dinners, two small evening parties, and one large one, a regular rout, paid my mother's debts in the visiting line each winter. She understood the management of company so well, every assembly of whatever kind always went off admirably at her house. In particular she lighted her rooms brilliantly, had plenty of refreshments, abundance of attendants, always a piece of matting spread from the carriage steps to the house door, and two dressing rooms with toilettes, good fires, hot water, and in the one prepared for the ladies stood a maid with thread and needle in case of accident. Every body praised, though few imitated; such preparations involved a little trouble, besides requiring more rooms than many people had to dispose of. We dined out a great deal, Jane and I taking the dinners in turns. We both went out in the evenings except when I could manage an escape, which was easier than formerly, my Mother having given me up as a matrimonial speculation, and Jane really delighting in Society. We got into rather a graver set than we had belonged to while in the sunshine of George Street and Charlotte Square, not quite giving up our gayer companions, but the distance from them was so great our easy sociable intercourse was very much broken. In our own short street we knew only John Clerk, not then a judge, and his truly agreeable sister Miss Bessy. We half lived in their house, William, Jane and I. They never gave a dinner without one of us being wanted to fill the place of an apology, and none of us ever shirked the summons feeling so at home, and meeting always such pleasant people. All the Law set of course, judges, barristers, and Writers; some of the literary, some of the scientifick, and a great many country families. The drawing rooms, four of them, were just a picture gallery, hung with paintings by the 'ancient masters,' some of them genuine! There were besides portfolios of prints, clever caricatures, and original sketches, these last undoubted and very valuable. John Clerk was a Collector; a thousand curiosities were spread about. He made more of his profession than any man at the Bar, and with his ready money commanded the market to a certain extent. The last purchase was the favourite always, indeed the only one worth possessing, so that it almost seemed as if the enjoyment was in the acquisition, not in the intrinsick merit of the object. A hideous daub called a Rubens, a crowd of fat lumps of children miscalled angels, with as much to spare of 'de quoi' as would have supplied the deficiencies of the whole cherubim, was the wonder of the world for ever so long; my wonder too, for if it was a Rubens it must have been a mere sketch, and never finished. I think I have heard that at the sale of this museum on Lord Eldin's death, a great many of his best loved pictures were acknowledged to be trash.[1]

I did not like him; the immorality of his private life was very discreditable; he was cynical too, severe, very, when offended, though of a kindly nature in the main. His talents there was no dispute about, though his reputation certainly was enhanced by his eccentricities and by his personal appearance, which was truly hideous. He was very lame, one leg being many inches shorter than the other, and his countenance, harsh and heavy when composed, became demoniack when illumined by the mocking smile that sometimes relaxed it. I always thought him the personification of the devil on two sticks, a living, actual Mephistopheles. He spoke but little to his guests, uttering some caustick remark, cruelly applicable, at rare intervals, treasured up by every body around as another saying of the Wise man's deserving of being written in gold, eastern fashion. When he did rouse up beyond this, his exposition of any subject he warmed on was really luminous, masterly, carried one away. The young men were all frightened to death of him; he did look as if he could bite, and as if the bite would be deadly. The young

1. John Clerk, who took the title Lord Eldin, died in 1832. The sale of his principal pictures, held in Picardy House, was remembered because a floor of the house fell in. His natural daughter became the Smith family governess.

ladies played with the monster, for he was very gentle to us.

In the parliament house, as the Courts of Justice are called in Scotland, he was a very tiger, seizing on his adversary with tooth and nail, and demolishing him without mercy, often without justice, for he was a true Advocate, heart and soul, right or wrong, in his client's cause. Standing very upright on the long leg, half a dozen pair of spectacles shoved up over his forehead, his wickedest countenance on, beaming with energy, he poured forth in his broad scotch a torrent of flaming rhetorick too bewildering to be often very successfully opposed. There was a story went of his once having mistaken a case, and so in his most vehement manner pleading on the wrong side, the Attorneys, called writers with us, in vain whispering and touching and pulling, trying in their agony every possible means of recalling his attention. At last he was made to comprehend the mischief he was doing. So he paused—for breath, readjusted his notes, probably never before looked at, held out his hand for the spectacles his old fat clerk Mr George had always a packet of ready, put them on, shoved them up over all the series sent up before, and then turning to the Judge resumed his address thus, 'Having now, my lord, to the best of my ability stated my opponent's case as strongly as it is possible for even my learned brother'—bowing to the opposite Counsel with a peculiar swing of the short leg—'to argue it, I shall proceed point by point to refute every plea advanced, etc. etc.'; and he did, amid a convulsion of laughter. As a consulting lawyer he was calm and clear, a favourite Arbitrator, making indeed most of his heavy fees by chamber practice.[1]

The sort of tart things he said at dinner were like this. Some one having died, a man of birth and fortune in the West country, rather celebrated during his life for drawing pretty freely with the long bow in conversation, it was remarked that the heir had buried him with much pomp, and had ordered for his remains a handsome monument: 'wi' an epitaph,' said John Clerk in his broadest border dialect; 'he must hae an epitaph, an appropriate epitaph, an' we'll

1. For a contemporary assessment of his legal reputation,
   see Cockburn.

change the exordium out o' respect. Instead o' the usual *Here lies*, we'll begin his epitaph wi' *Here* continues *to lie* . . . I wish I could remember more of them; they were scattered broadcast, and too many fell by the wayside. The sister who lived with him and kept his house must in her youth have been a beauty. Indeed she acknowledged this, and told how to enhance it, she had when about fifteen possessed herself of her mother's patch box, and not content with one or two black spots to brighten her complexion, had stuck on a whole shower, and thus speckled had set out on a very satisfactory walk, every one she met staring at her admiringly. A deal of such quiet fun enlivened her conversation, adding considerably to the attraction of a thoroughly well bred manner. She painted a little, modelled in clay beautifully, sometimes finishing her small groups in ivory, and her busts in stone or marble. She was well read in French and English Classicks, had seen much, suffered some, reflected a good deal. She was a most charming companion, saying often in few words what one could think over at good length. She was very proud—the Clerks of Eldin had every right so to be—and the patronising pity with which she folded up her ancient skirts from contact with the *snobs*, as we call them now,[1] whom she met and visited and was studiously polite to, was often my amusement to watch. She never disparaged them by a syllable individually, but she would describe a rather *fast* family as 'the sort of people you never see in mourning,' 'persons likely to make the mistake of being in advance of the fashion—so busy trying to push themselves into a place and not succeeding,' added with a smile a trifle akin to her brother's.

There was a younger brother William who, likewise a bachelour, had some office with a small salary and lived in lodgings, dining out every day, for no party was complete without him. He was less kindly than John, but his manner concealed this. He was as clever, if not cleverer, but too indolent to make any use of his great natural abilities. He had never practised at the Bar, and was quite content with his small income and his large reputation, though I have heard

1. Thackery's *The Snobs of England by One of Themselves* appeared in *Punch* the year after E.G. began her *Memoirs*.

say, when wondering at the extent of his information, that his memory was regularly refreshed for society, it being his habit to read up in the morning for his display in the evening, and then dexterously turn the Conversation into the prepared channel. He told a story better than any one in the world, except his friend Sir Adam Ferguson. He one dark winter's evening over the fire gave us a whole murder case so graphically that when he seized me to illustrate the manner of the strangling, I and the whole of the rest of us shrieked. I never trembled so much in my life.

Sir Adam Ferguson was the son of the 'Roman Antiquities';[1] another idler. He was fond in the summer of walking excursions in two or three localities where he had friends, in the Perthshire highlands, along the coasts of Fife and Forfar, and in the border country, the heights along the Tweed, etc. Mark the points well. His acquaintance were of all ranks. He had eyes, ears, observation of all kinds, a wonderful memory, extraordinary powers of imitation, a pleasure in detailing—acting, in fact, all that occurred to him. He was the bosom friend of Walter Scott; he and William Clerk lived half their time with the 'great novelist,' and it was very ungenerous in him and Mr Lockhart to have made so little mention of them in the biography, for most undoubtedly Sir Adam Ferguson was the 'nature' from which many of these lifelike pictures were drawn.[2] We, who

1. He was Scott's staunchest friend from school and college; his father during his long life (1723–1816) was successively Professor of Natural and Moral Philosophy at the University of Edinburgh—the book referred to is his *History of the Progress and Termination of the Roman Republic* (1782).
2. John Gibson Lockhart's biography of his father-in-law was published in 1837–8; he *was* generous enough to write that Scott's 'intimacy with Adam was thus his first means of introduction to the higher literary society of Edinburgh'. (I, p. 153). Ferguson's long and eventful life (1771–1855) saw him Secretary to the Governor of the Channel Islands, Captain in Portugal during the Peninsular War, a prisoner of war for two years in France and, thanks to Sir Walter, Custodian of the Crown Jewels of Scotland.

knew all, recognised our old familiar stories, nay, characters, and afterwards accounted for the silence on the subject of the friends from the desire to avoid acknowledging the rich source that had been so constantly drawn on. Walter Scott had never crossed the Firth of Forth as far as I know.[1]

*Waverley* came out, I think it must have been in the autumn of 1814, just before we went first to Edinburgh. It was brought to us to the Doune, I know, by 'little Jemmy Simpson,' as that good man, since so famous, was then most irreverently called. Some liked the book, he said; he thought himself it was in parts quite beyond the common run, and the determined mystery as to the Authour added much to its vogue. I did not like it. The opening English scenes were to me intolerably dull, so lengthy, and so prosy, and the persons introduced so uninteresting, the hero contemptible, the two heroines unnatural and disagreeable, and the whole idea given of the highlands so utterly at variance with truth. I read it again long afterwards, and remained of the same mind. Then burst out *Guy Mannering*, carrying all the world before it, in spite of the very pitiful setting, the gipsies, the smugglers, and Dandie Dinmont are surrounded by. Here again is the copyist, the scenery Dumfries and Galloway, the dialect Forfar. People now began to feel these works could come but from one Authour, particularly as a few acres began to be added to the recent purchase of the old tower of Abbotsford, and Mrs Scott set up a carriage, a Barouche landau built in London, and which from the time she got it she was seldom out of, appearing indeed to spend her life in driving about the streets all day. I forget which came next, the Baronetcy or *the Antiquary*—the one was very quickly succeeded by the other[2]—and were followed by the *Castle* at

1. This increasingly uncharitable portrait is here quite wrong. Scott and Ferguson had travelled through the territory of *The Lady of the Lake* (1810), for example, and four years later he joined the Commissioners for the Northern Lights in a circumnavigation of Scotland, that provided material for his Orcadian novel *The Pirate* (1822).

2. *The Antiquary* was published in 1816 and George IV conferred the baronetcy four years later.

Abbotsford, that monument of vanity, human absurdity, or madness, William Clerk used to speak of this most melancholy act of folly almost with tears.

I was never in company with Walter Scott; he went very little out, and when he did go he was not agreeable, generally sitting very silent, looking dull and listless, unless an occasional flash lighted up his heavy countenance. In his own house he was another character, especially if he liked his guests. His family were all inferiour. I have often thought that this was the reason of the insipidity of his ideal gentlemen and ladies—he knew none better. Lady Scott,[1] a natural daughter of a Marquis of Downshire, her mother French of low degree, herself half educated in Paris, very silly and very foolish, was a most unfortunate mate for such a man. When I saw her she had no remains of beauty, dressed fantastically, spoke the greatest nonsense in her broken English—and very frequently had taken too much wine. I recollect one evening at the Miss Pringles', she was actually unconscious of her actions, poor Anne Scott vainly trying to conceal her condition, till catching sight of William Clerk they got her to go away. The excuse was Asthma, a particular Asthmatick affection, which a glass or more of Madeira relieved. Such a Mother could scarcely do much for or with her children. The eldest son, Walter, was a mere good-natured goose forced into a marriage he hated and never able to get over the annoyance his unsuitable partner gave him. The younger, Charles, was thought more of, he died on his travels before being in any way brought to notice. Sophy,

1. The mysterious circumstances of the early years of Charlotte Charpentier (Carpenter) are described in Edgar Johnson *Sir Walter Scott: The Great Unknown*. The second Marquis of Downshire was certainly her guardian from as early as 1786, but at the time she was conceived he was a sixteen year old at Eton. Her mother was far from being 'of low degree'; M. Charpentier had worked in the French Embassy in Constantinople and became Master of the Military Academy at Lyons. The explanation for this hostile portrait probably lies in E.G.'s distaste for Scott's Tory politics and social pretensions.

Mrs Lockhart, was an awkward, very ignorant girl, not exactly plain yet scarcely otherwise, her husband did a great deal with her. She was liked in London, her manner remaining simple after it was softened. Anne was odious— very ugly and very pretending and very unpopular, which she should not have been, would not, had she been less exacting, less irritable, for she was a good daughter in different ways to both parents.[1] It was odd, but Sir Walter never had the reputation in Edinburgh he had elsewhere— was not the Lion, I mean. His wonderful works were looked for, read with avidity, praised on all hands, still the Authour made far less noise at home than he did abroad. The fat, very vulgar Mrs Jobson, whose low husband had made his large fortune at Dundee by pickling herrings, on being congratulated at the approaching marriage of her daughter to Sir Walter's son, said the young people were attached, which was not true, otherwise her Jane might have looked higher. It was only a baronetcy, and quite a late creation.[2]

Another family in the Clerk set and ours were the Dalzels; they lived in a small house just behind Picardy Place, in Albany or Forth Street. They were a Professor's Widow,[3] her sister, and her sons and daughters, reduced in the short space of a few years to the one son and one daughter who still survive. Mary Dalzel played well on the piano forte; there was no other talent among them. The Professor had been a learned but a singularly simple man.

1. The eldest son Walter (1801–47) married Jane Jobson, a match which was set up by the joint efforts of his father and Sir Adam Ferguson; Charlotte Sophia (1799–1837) married John Gibson Lockhart whose biography of his father-in-law was the cause of his literary success in London; Anne (1803–33) and Charles (1805–41) both died unmarried.
2. Mrs Jobson was an Athole Stewart, descending from Robert II through Alexander, the 'Wolf of Badenoch' (see I 265); another attraction for the Scotts was that the prospective bride, Jane, was heiress to the estate of Lochore in Fife.
3. Andrew Dalzel was Professor of Greek at the University of Edinburgh between 1772 and 1806.

He had been tutor to either Lord Lauderdale or to his eldest
son, and they had a story of him which Lady Mary told us,
that at dinner at Dunbar—a large party—a guest alluding
to the profligacy of some prominent political character, Mr
Dalzel burst in with, 'There has not been such a rogue
unhanged since the days of the wicked Duke of
Lauderdale.' John Dalzel was a great companion of my
brother William's; they had gone through College, and were
now studying for their Civil Law trials together. He was dull
but persevering, and might have risen to respectability at
least in his profession had he lived.

In York Place we had only the old Miss Pringles, chiefly
remarkable for never in the morning going out together—
always different ways, that when they met at dinner there
might be the more to say; and Miss Kate Sinclair; and two
families which, all unguessed by us, were destined to have
such close connexion with us hereafter, Mrs Henry Siddons
and the Gibson Craigs.[1] Mrs Siddons was now a Widow living
with her two very nice daughters and her two charming little
boys, quietly as became her circumstances. She acted regularly, as the main prop of the Theatre on which the principal
part of her income depended. She went a little into society.
She had pleasure in seeing her friends in a morning in her
own house, and the friends were always delighted to go to see
her, she was so very agreeable. The girls were great friends of
my sister Mary's. The little boys were my Mother's passion,
they were with us for ever, quite little pets. The Gibsons, who
were not Craigs then, we got more intimate with after they
moved to a fine large house Mr Gibson was building in [24]
Picardy Place when we went there. There were two sons, and
seven daughters of every age, all of them younger than the
brothers. Mr Shannon, the Irish chaplain of the Episcopal
chapel we attended, the fashionable one, lived in York Place,
and the Gillies's, with whom we were as intimate as with the
Clerks, and on the same easy terms; we young people being
called on when wanted, and never loth to answer the call, Lord

1. E.G.'s brother William married her daughter Sally; sister
   Jane took as her second husband James Thomson Gibson
   Craig, lawyer and bibliophile.

Gillies being kind in his rough way, and Mrs Gillies then, as now, delightful. Their nieces Mary and Margaret at this time lived with them.

Jane and I added to our private list of so called friends Mr Kennedy of Dunure, whose sister wrote *Father Clement*, whose Mother, beautiful at eighty, was sister to the Mother of Lord Brougham, who himself married Sir Samuel Romilly's daughter [Sophie] and held for many years a high situation here in Ireland.[1] Archy Alison, now Sir Archibald, heavy, awkward, plain, and yet foredoomed to greatness by the united testimony of every one sufficiently acquainted with him. His father, one of the Episcopal Chaplains and author of a work on Taste, had married Mrs Montague's Miss Gregory, so there was celebrity on all sides.[2] Willy and Walter Campbell, Uncle and nephew the same age. Willy Campbell of Winton was really a favourite with all the world, and most certainly would have shone in it had he been spared; he died in Greece, bequeathing his immense fortune equally between his two sisters, Lady Ruthven and Lady Belhaven; they were all three the children of a second marriage of old Campbell of Shawfield's with the heiress of Winton. Robert Hay, Captain Dalzel who lent us the whole of M. Jouy's then published works beginning with L'hermite de la Chaussée d'Antin, and the *Scots Greys*, completed our first winter's List. There was always a Cavalry regiment at the barracks at Piers Hill, and in this fine corps was a nephew

1. Thomas Francis Kennedy of Dunure and Dalquarran Castle (1788–1871), and M.P. for Ayr, was appointed by Melbourne's Whig government to be Paymaster of the Civil Service in Ireland in 1837, a post he held until 1856. His sister Grace (1782–1825) was well known for her religious tales. For once E.G.'s memory has let her down, for Kennedy's mother was in fact Jane Adam, a daughter of the eldest of the famous architect brothers.
2. This was Sir Archibald Alison (1797–1867) the historian, whose father had published an *Essay on the Nature and Principles of Taste* in 1790. His mother was Dorothea, daughter of Dr John Gregory, author of *A Father's Legacy to his Daughters*.

of General Need's, Tom Walker, who was the means of introducing us to the rest of the Officers.

The gay set in Edinburgh was increased by the advent of Mr and Mrs Inglis, Mr and Mrs Horrocks, the McLeods of Harris, and others. Mr Inglis was but a Writer to the Signet, but a hospitable man reputed to be thriving in business; his Wife, sister to Mr Stein, the rich distiller, with a sister married to General Duff, Lord Fife's brother, kept a sort of open dancing house, thus, as she fancied, ushering her two very pretty little daughters, really nice natural girls, into the world with every advantage. Her aim was to marry them well, that is, highly or wealthily. She fixed on McLeod of Harris for the younger, and got him; the elder fixed on Davidson of Tulloch for herself, and lost him. Did I forget to name Duncan Davidson among our peculiar friends. A finer, simpler, handsomer, more attractive young man was never ruined. Spoiled by flattery, and not very judiciously managed at home, year by year with sorrow we saw him falling from the better road, till at last no one named him. He was much in love with Catherine Inglis, and there was no doubt meant to marry her. He might perhaps have turned out better had his early inclinations not been thwarted. The old stock broker was as ambitious as Mrs Inglis, and expected a very much superiour connexion for his eldest son. Harris, having no father, could choose his own wife, too blind to see how very distasteful he was to her. This miserable beginning had a wretched ending hereafter. Charles McLeod, the brother, would have been more likely to take a young girl's fancy. The McLeod sisters were nothing particular. Mr Horrocks was the very rich and extremely under bred son of a Liverpool merchant, a handsome little man married to a Glasgow beauty, a cold, reserved woman, who did not care for him a bit. They could do nothing better than give balls.

Of course Miss Baillie gave her annual *fête*, no longer an amusing one. An Ayrshire aunt had died and left her and Mrs Cumming handsome legacies, upon the strength of which the Lady Logie came up to live in Edinburgh, and Grace Baillie bought a good house, furnished it neatly, and became quite humdrum. She had taken charge of a 'decent man,' for whom she wanted a proper wife—Sir Ewan Cameron of

Fassiefern, made a Baronet as a mark of honour to the reputation of two, if not three, elder brothers all killed in the battlefield, leaving this poor body the only representative of the old family. She offered him both to Jane and me, and that we might not buy a pig in a poke, she paraded him several times before our windows on the opposite side of the street. These old kind of men were beginning to fancy us. I suppose we were considered, like them, on the decline. Mr Crawford, of Japan reputation, was seriously attracted first by one and then the other, but Jane carried the day, got all the languishing looks from such bilious eyes, an ivory fan, and the two heavy volumes of his Eastern history.[1] A year or two after, he married Miss Perry, the Morning Chronicle,[2] she being referred to me for his character, like a servant, and getting Mary Gillies to write to me to beg for a candid opinion of her elderly lover. When ladies arrive at asking for such opinions, one only answer can be given. Mine was highly satisfactory. We really knew no ill of the man; his appearance was the worst of him, and there was a drowned wife too, lost on her voyage home. She might have been saved on a desert island, and so start up some day like the old woman in the farce, to destroy the happiness of the younger bride and the bridegroom.

But I had an old lover all to myself, unshared with any rival, won, not by my bright eyes, but by my spirited fingers, from playing the highland marches as Lady Huntly had taught me them. Old Colonel Steuart of Garth, seventy, I should think, always in a green coat, and silver broad rimmed spectacles, was writing the history of the 42nd Regiment, and the slow Black Watch, and the quickstep of the Highland Laddie, given better, he said, than by the band of his old love, so over excited or over enchanted him that he hardly

1. A later mention of this learned orientalist suggests he was John Crawford (1783–1868), author of *History of the Indian Archipelago*, written in three volumes by 1820.
2. James Perry (1756–1821) purchased the *Morning Chronicle* in 1789; it became a leading Whig party journal.

ever quitted my side, and he gave me his precious work on its publication. I had my two thick volumes too, but they were not heavy ones. He was a fine old soldier, though a little of a bore sometimes, so very enthusiastick about the deeds of his warrior country men.[1] He never went further in his love making than to wish he were a young man for my sake, so that Jane had the advantage over me of a real offer. As for poor little Sir Ewan, we left him to Grace Baillie.

It was a great addition to the quiet home society we were beginning to prefer to the regular gaiety, the having Mrs Cumming settled near us. Her two elder sons had already gone out to India, Alexander in the Civil Service, Robert in the Artillery, both to Bengal. The three younger it was necessary to educate better, as it was gradually becoming more difficult to get passed through the examinations, and all were destined for the East. Besides, there was May Anne, who had hitherto, happy child, been let to run wild on the beautiful banks of the Findhorn, and who was now declared to be of an age requiring taming and training. John Peter, the third son, whom you know best as the Colonel, soon got his Cadetship and sailed away to Bombay. George and Willie, intended for army surgeons, were to study medicine, and were also to have their manners formed by appearing occasionally in society. Willie made his entrance into fashionable life at a large evening party of my mother's. He was a handsome lad, very desirous of being thought a Beau, so he dressed himself in his best carefully, and noticing that all the fine young men were scented, he provided himself with a large white cotton pockethandkerchief of his mother's which he steeped in peppermint water, a large bottle of this useful corrective always standing on the chimney piece in her room. Thus perfumed, and hair and whiskers oiled and curled, Willie, in a flutter of shyness and happiness, entered our

1. David Stewart published his *Sketches of the Character, Manners and Present State of the Highlanders of Scotland, with details of the Military Service of the Highland Regiments* in two volumes in 1822, written as propaganda against emigration; he became governor of St Lucia in 1825.

brilliant drawing rooms, when he was pounced on by Miss Shearer, the very plain sister of Mrs James Grant, an oldish woman of no sort of fashion and cruelly marked with the small pox. 'We'll keep together, Willie,' said Miss Shearer, at every attempt of poor Willie's to shake himself clear of such an encumbrance in the crowd. How Dr Cumming laughed at these recollections when he and I met again after a lifetime's separation. Up and down this ill assorted pair paraded, Miss Shearer seeming determined to shew off her beau. 'There's an extraordinary smell of peppermint here,' said Lord Erskine to Mrs Henry Siddons, as the couple turned and twirled round to pass them, Willie flourishing the large pockethandkerchief in most approved style. It was really overpowering, nor could we contrive to get rid of it, nor to detect the offending distributor of such pharmaceutical perfume, till next day, talking over the party with the Lady Logie, she enlightened us, more amused herself by the incident than almost any of the rest of us.

She was right to keep the bottle of peppermint where it could easily be found, as the sort of housekeeping she practised must have made a frequent appeal to it necessary. She bought every Saturday a leg of mutton and a round of beef; when the one was finished, the other was begun; the leg was roasted, the round was boiled, and after the first day they were eaten cold, and served herself, her daughter, her two sons, and her two maid servants the week. There were potatoes, and in summer cabbage, and peas that rattled, in winter oranges, and by the help of the peppermint the family throve. We never heard of illness among them; the minds expanded too, after their own queer fashion, even George, the most eccentrick of human beings, doing credit to the rearing. He was so very singular in his ways, his Mother was really uncertain about his getting through the College of surgeons. She made cautious enquiries now and then as to his studies, attention to lectures, notes of them, visits to the hospital, preparation for his thesis and so on, and getting very unsatisfactory replies, grew very fidgetty. One day one of the Medical Examiners stopt her in the street to congratulate her on the admirable appearance made by her son George when he was passed at Surgeon's hall; his answers had been remarkable, and his thesis, dedicated to my father, had been No. 2 or No. 3 out of fifty. She was really amazed. 'George,' said she, when they met, 'when did you get your degree?' When did you pass your trials?' 'Eh!' said George, looking up with his most vacant expression. 'Oh! just when I was ready for them.' 'You never told me a word about it?' 'No? Humph! you'd have heard fast enough if I'd failed.' That was all she could get out of him; but he told us, that seeing the door of the Surgeon's hall open and finding it was an examining day, it just struck him that he would go in and get the job over; it was very easy to pass, he added. He has since at Madras risen high in his profession, been twice publickly thanked for the care of the troops, made money, married a wife; yet when he was at home on furlough he acted more like Dominie Sampson[1] than any other character ever heard of.

George Carr was also a medical student, a very attentive one, making up by diligence for no great natural capacity; he was kept in order by his sister, a young lady lately from Bath, as we were without ceasing reminded. She was a ladylike, rather nice looking person, without being at all handsome; beautifully neat and neat handed, and amiable, I believe, in her home, though dreadfully tiresome in ours; for when asked for a day, she staid a week, sharing my small room and civilly begging the loan of pins, oils, gloves, ribbons, handkerchiefs, and other small articles with none of which I was particularly well provided, and yet none were ever returned. We were not comfortably managed with regard to our private expenses, Jane and I. My Mother bought for us what she judged necessary, and she was apt to lay out more on handsome gowns than left her sufficient for clean gloves, neat shoes, fresh flowers; a way of proceeding that greatly distressed us—distressed me at least, for I was by nature tidy, had all the Raper methodically pricknickity ways, and a five guinea blonde trimmed dress, with calico or dirty gloves and ill made shoes, made me wretched; besides, there was no pleasure in managing a wardrobe not under my own controul. Out of economy I made most of my own clothes, many of my mother's and Jane's, yet reaped no benefit from this diligence, as what I disliked was often chosen for me, and

1. The learned but gauche tutor in Scott's *Guy Mannering*.

what I hated I had to wear. The extreme neatness of Miss Carr exactly suited me; all her under clothes, made by herself, were perfection; her dresses of simple materials, except such as had been presents, were well fitting and fresh, so that she looked always nicer in a room than many much more expensively attired. She had the fault of hinting for presents, but then she loved dress, she loved company, she was not very wise, and her purse was very scanty. She amused us another way. She had such a string of lovers—had had; it was poor Miss Elphick and her early adorers over again; and if any one danced twice with her, she wriggled about like an eel when his name was mentioned. Every now and then we were informed in confidence that she was going to be married, or to try make up her mind to marry—that was the form. However, these affairs never progressed. A Mr Lloyd did 'make his offer'; mother and daughter walked up in pleased agitation to tell us. He was an ugly, little, shabby old man, a friend of Mr Massie's, who wanted a wife and was taken with her, but when they came to particulars, there was not money enough on either side to make the connexion prudent. It was a great feather though in Miss Carr's thirty year cap, and she shook it out on all occasions with much complacency.

Bessie Goodchild likewise favoured us with another visit; her teeth again required attention. She did not trust to a request and a favourable answer, but very sagaciously made sure she would be welcome for three days, and then contrived one way or another to stay above a month. She was very entertaining, and made herself very agreeable to my Mother with funny gossip about all the old Durham relations. She was no plague in the house, but we had been brought up too honestly to approve of her carrying tales from family to family, and mimicking the oddities of persons from whom she had received kindness. We had an odd family party sometimes—a Carr, a Goodchild, a Gillio, and Grace Baillie who thrice a week at least walked in at dinner time. My brother's young men friends continued popping in morning and evening, when it suited them. He brought us most frequently William Gibson, Germaine Lavie, Robert Ferguson, now the superfine colonel, Mr Beauclerk, grandson of

Topham's[1] John Dalzel, and the two Lindsays while they remained at College. Mary, now grown into a very handsome girl, did her part well in all home company. Johnny also was made a little man of; he had a Tutor for Latin, attended the French and dancing classes, and read English history with Jane. We had given up all masters except the Italian and the harp, which last taught us in classes, and thereby hangs a tale.

Monsieur Elouis, the Harp master, charged so high for his private lessons, that my Mother suggested to him to follow the Edinburgh fashion of Classes at so much a quarter, three lessons a week. He made quite a fortune. There were eight pupils in a Class, the lessons lasting two hours. We three, the two Hunters, Grace Stein, afterwards Lady Don, Amelia Gillio and Catherine Inglis were his best scholars. We played concerted pieces doubling the parts. Chorus's arranged by him, and sometimes duetts or solos, practising in other rooms. The fame of our execution spread over the town, and many persons entreated permission to mount up the long Common Stair to the poor frenchman's garret to listen to such a number of harps played by such handsome girls. One or two of the Mamas would have had no objection, but my mother and Lady Hunter would not hear of their daughters being part of an exhibition. We went there to learn, not to shew off. Miss Elphick, too, had her own ideas upon the subject. She always went with us, and was extremely annoyed by the group of young men so frequently happening to pass down the street just at the time our Class dispersed, some of them our dancing partners, so that there were bows and speeches and attendance home, much to her disgust. She waited once or twice till the Second Class assembled, but the Beaux waited too. So then she carried *us* all of a quarter of an hour too soon, leaving our five companions to their fate; and this not answering long, she set to scold Monsieur Elouis, and called the Edinburgh gentlemen all sorts of vile names. In the midst of her season of wrath the door of our musick room opened one day, and a

1. Topham Beauclerk (1739–80) was a member of Dr Johnson's circle.

very large fine looking military man, braided and belted and moustached, entered and was invited to be seated. Every harp was silent. 'Mesdemoiselles,' said Monsieur Elouis with his most polished air of command, 'recommence if you please; this gentleman is my most particular friend, a musical amateur, etc.' Miss Elphick was all in a flame; up she rose, up she made us rise, gather our musick together, and driving us and Amelia Gillio before her, we were shawled and bonnetted in less time than I am writing of it, and on our way down stairs before poor Monsieur had finished his apologies to the officer and the other young ladies. Never was little woman in such a fury. We never returned to the Harp Classes, neither did the Hunters, and very soon they were given up. It was certainly an unwarrantable liberty, an impertinence, and the man must either have been totally unaware of the sort of pupils he was to find, or else an illbred ignorant person. Poor Elouis never recovered the mistake; he had to leave for want of business.

Margaret Gillio and I went shares in another master, mistress rather. She had a sweet, flexible, bird like voice and sang her little English ballads very prettily. I tried higher flights, but my singing was very so so till we had some lessons from Mrs Bianchi Lacey. She came with her husband and her apprentice, a Miss Simmons, to give a Concert or two and take a few pupils by the way. The concerts were delightful, the three sang so well together, the musick they gave us was so good, and it was all so simply done; her pianoforte the only accompaniment, and in the small Assembly room so that they were perfectly heard. It was a style of singing, hers, that we may call peculiarly ladylike; no very powerful voice, and it was now going, for she was no longer young; still it was round and true and sweet in the upper notes, and the finish of her whole song, the neatness of every passage, the perfect expression she gave both to musick and words, was all new to me. I could now understand it, and it gave to me a different notion of the *art* from any that had ever entered into my head before. The first Concert she gave we were so much amused with old Sir John Hay, one of the Directors, squiring her about, bringing her negus,[1] a shawl, a chair, and what not,

1. Spiced wine or sherry with hot water.

and my brother William doing ditto by Miss Simmons, that the first song by that young lady, '*H*angels ever bright and fair,'[1] she was Birmingham, made less impression than it should have done, for her voice was splendid. We never heard what became of her; she was pretty, so perhaps she married a pinmaker and led a private, instead of a hazardous publick, life. But the moment Mr Lacey and his Wife began their delightful duetts we had ears for none else. My father offered me a dozen lessons. We had time for only ten—all, I may say, I ever got—but we went to her three concerts. They dined with us twice, and sang as much as we liked, and my mother gave an evening party for them at which their singing enchanted every body. It was essentially suited to the Drawing room. She was taught by old Bianchi, who made her a perfect musician. She played admirably and had a thorough knowledge of the Science. She was his apprentice and he married her. After a short widowhood she rather threw herself away on too young a husband,[2] a very vulgar man with so much presumption of manner as to keep one in a fright lest he should commit some atrocity. It was like sitting on needles and pins, that young monkey our brother Johnny said, to sit in company with him. However, he never offended, and if he had, his fine voice would have secured his pardon.

Mrs Lacey took a fancy to me, gave me extra long lessons, and the kindest directions for the management of my voice in her absence. She was very particular about the erect position of the head and chest, the smile with which the mouth was to be opened, the clear pronunciation of every word. She gave me a set of exercises to develop the powers of the voice, every tone, every half tone being brought out in every one of them; the inequalities were to be carefully marked and carefully improved. When we came to songs, she made me study one. First the poet's meaning; his intentions were to be accurately ascertained, as accurately expressed *aided* by the musick,

1. An aria from Handel's oratorio, *Theodora* (1755).
2. Francesco Bianchi committed suicide in 1810; his widow married another singer, John Lacey, two years later.

which was to accompany the words and follow out the idea. In fact the song was to be acted. Next it was to be embellished with a *few* occasional graces, very neatly executed, applied in fit pauses, the whole got up so perfectly as to be poured forth with ease, any effort, such as straining or forcing the voice or unduly emphasising a passage, being altogether so much out of taste as to produce pain instead of pleasure. Lastly she bid me practise what I liked, but never inflict on other ears what was not completely *within* my compass—no effort to myself. I owed her much, very much, and yet she did not teach me singing, at least not altogether. Her valuable advice, and her care of the form of the mouth, were the foundation of my after fame. My finishing instructress was Mrs Robert Campbell. She and her sister Mrs James Hamilton were two little Jewesses four feet high, whose father had been Consul at some of the Italian ports. One evening, at a small party at Mrs Munro's, Mrs Robert Campbell sang a simple Italian ballad so beautifully, so exactly according to Mrs Lacey's rules, it was all so easy, so satisfying, my lesson in singing was then, I felt, given me. She was encored by acclamation; this enabled me to follow every note. On going home I sat down to the piano forte, sang the ballad myself with every little grace that she had given it, next day repeated it, took another from a store sent us by Eliza Cottam, Ironside, then decorated it after my own taste, got every little turn to flow as from a flute, and in the evening treated my father to both. His surprise was only equalled by his extreme pleasure. It seemed to be the height of his musical expectations. However, we did more for him than that. He really loved musick, he loved us and was proud of us, and though he could sternly express his dissatisfaction, he was no niggard of praise when praise was due. We worked with a heart for a person so discriminating.

Mr Loder[1] brought an Opera company with him, and gave, not whole Operas, he had not strength enough for that, but very well got up scenes from several most in favour. It was a most agreeable variety in a place where publick

1. John David Loder (1788–1846), violinist and musical publisher.

amusements were but scantily supplied to the inhabitants. We had de Begnis and his wife,[1] and scenes from Figaro, Don Giovanni, etc.; the rest of the artistes were very fair, but I forget their names. Going into a musick shop we saw on the Counter two numbers of a new work—the opera of Don Juan arranged for two performers on the pianoforte; the first attempt in a kind that had such success, and that brought real good musick within the power of the family circle. We secured our prize, Jane and I, hurried home, tried the first Scena, were delighted, gave a week to private, very diligent study, and when we had it all by heart, the first afternoon my father came up to spend the *gloaming* napping in an easy chair, we arrested his sleepy fit by 'notte e giorno,' to his amazement.[2] He liked our Opera better, I think, than 'Sul margine dun rio' or 'Ninetta cara,'[3] for we had so lately heard all the airs we played that we were quite up to the proper style, and had ourselves all the desire in the world to give the musick we loved the expression intended by our then favourite composer, Mozart. William also began to try a few tenor duetts with me. Mrs Lacey had taken the trouble to teach him half a dozen for love. It is surprising how well he could do both tender and buffo. His ear either was slightly defective naturally, or from want of early exercise; this made it difficult to keep his voice in order, otherwise he was a most agreeable singer, and once set out kept the key well, but after a pause *might* begin flat again, never sharp luckily. Really our home concerts, with Mary Dalzel's help, were very much applauded by our partial audience.

Edinburgh did not afford much publick amusement. Except these Operas which were a chance, a stray Concert now and then, catches and glees being the most popular, and the six Assemblies, there were none other. The Assemblies

1. The bass Guiseppi de Begnis married the soprano Giusepina Roazi in 1816.
2. Leporello's opening aria in *Don Giovanni*.
3. The first, an Italian Arietta, was written by Vincenzo Pucitta (1778–1861) around this year 1818; the second is probably based on one of Ninette's arias from *La gazza ludra* (*Thieving Magpie*) which Rossini had completed the year before.

were very ill attended, the small room never half full, the large, which held with ease twelve hundred people, was never entered except upon occasion of the Caledonian Hunt Ball, when the Members presented the tickets, and their friends graciously accepted the free entertainment. The very crowded dances at home, inconvenient, and troublesome and expensive as they were, seemed to be more popular than those easy balls, where for five shillings we had space, spring, a full orchestra, and plenty of slight refreshments. I heard afterwards that as private houses became more fully and handsomely furnished, the fashion of attending the Assemblies revived. McLeod of Harris did a very sensible thing the winter he married poor, pretty little Richmond Inglis. They were living with her father and mother, and so very much invited out that he did not think Mrs Inglis' perpetual entertainments sufficient return for the many civilities he and his young wife had received. He therefore hired Smart's rooms where the dancing master had his Academy, asked every one he knew far and near, contracted for a supper, and gave the best ball I was ever at in my young days; a ball that finally established waltzing among us. This much persecuted dance had been struggling on for a season, gaining far less ground than the quadrilles; but a strong band mustering on this occasion, the very 'propers' gave in as by magick touch, and the whole large room was one whirligig. Harris himself danced for the first time at his own ball, and beautifully; his brother Charles was the Vestris[1] of our Society—acknowledged. The Laird was even more graceful in his movements. 'Ah!' said poor Richmond, 'if I had ever seen my husband dance, Mama would not have found it so difficult to get me to marry him.' She saw his perfections too late, I fancy, for she left him and seven children afterwards.

1. Born Lucia Elizabeth Mathews, Madame Vestris (1797–1856), was a well-known actress.

# CHAPTER TWENTY-ONE

# 1818–1819

THE first summer we were in Picardy Place, 1818, we younger ones, or rather we girls remained there protected by Miss Elphick during the whole of it. When the fine weather came on in Spring we had resumed our excursions to Craig Crook, and it was then we got so intimate with Basil Hall. We could not have been acquainted with him while we lived in George Street, because he only returned from his Loo Choo cruise late in the Autumn of 1817. During the following winter we saw a good deal of him both before he went to London, and after they had tried to spoil him there, for he was made such a wonder of there, it was a miracle his head kept steady; but it was at Craig Crook that we became such friends. Cruel Lord Jeffrey limited his two young favourites to friendship; the Halls and the Selkirks were all so crazy that he forbid any warmer feelings, closetting Jane in his pretty Cabinet, and under the shades of the wood on Corstorphine Hill, to explain all the melancholy particulars. And then Basil went off to sea. The Jeffreys generally went out on Friday evenings, or, at any rate, on Saturdays, to a late dinner at Craig Crook, and came back to town on Monday morning, till the 12th of July released him from law labours. Jane and I frequently went with them, sometimes only to them for one day, returning in the evening. We never met any lady there but Mrs George Russell occasionally; a clever woman, not to my mind agreeable. The men were John Murray, now and then his elder brother, Tommy Thomson, Robert Graeme, Mr Fullerton till he married, James Keay till he married, William Clerk very seldom, Mr Cockburn always, John Jeffrey, the Moreheads now and then, chance celebrities, and a London friend at intervals. It was not a big wig set at all.[1] My father, Lord Gillies, and such like dignitaries would have been quite out of place in this rather riotous crew; indeed, the prevailing free and easy tone did not altogether suit *me*. Individually, almost all of our party were agreeable, cleverly amusing. Collectively, there was far too much boisterous mirth for my taste. I preferred being with Mrs Jeffrey, that *naturally* charming woman, not then by any means sufficiently appreciated by those so much her inferiours. She and I spent our time gardening, she was a perfect florist, playing with little Charlotte, to whom all my old nursery tales and songs were new, preparing for the company, and chattering to one another. My gentleman friends were William Murray of Henderland, and Robert Graeme of Lynedoch; they used to find Mrs Jeffrey, chatty and stout, where we were weeding our borders, and often carry us off up the hill, Jane remaining queen of the bowling green. How much she was admired by all those clever heads.

The dinners were delightful, so little form, so much fun, real wit sometimes, and always cheerfulness. The windows open to the garden, the sight and the scent of the flowers heightening the flavour of repasts unequalled for excellence. Wines, all our set were famous for having of the best and in startling variety—it was a mania; their cellars and their books divided the attention of the husband; the wife, alas, was more easily satisfied with the cookery. Except in a real old fashioned Scotch house, where no dish was attempted that was not national, the various abominations served up in corner dishes under French names were merely libels upon housekeeping. Mrs Jeffrey presented nothing upon her table but what her Cook could dress; her home fed fowl and home made bread, and fine cream and sweet butter, and juicy vegetables, all so good, served so well, the hot things *hot*, the fruits, creams, and butter so cold, gave such a feeling of comfort every one got good humoured, even cranky William Clerk. They were bright days, those happy summer days at Craig Crook.

Another country house we were very much in was one the

1. This is the only mention of Henry Cockburn, author of the indispensable *Memorials of his Time*.

Gibsons had a lease of, Woodside. It was six miles from town, a good ride. We went out early, staid all day, and came back in the cool of the summer evening. They were kind people, the father and mother very little in our way, the sons not much, the seven daughters of all ages our great friends. Mrs Kaye and Jane drew most together, Cecilia and I; the little ones were pets, and very pretty ones. We rode a good deal, one at a time, with the Coachman attending. We had struck up a friendship with a Captain and Mrs Bingham through the medium of their three fine little boys. He commanded the frigate in the Roads, had succeeded Captain Dalling. In winter, they lived in lodgings in the town; in summer, took a small house close to the sea at Newhaven. They gave a very pretty party in town, towards the end of a winter, inviting people simply to spend the evening. We found tea, and a good many friends, and a very hearty Sailor's welcome. After tea, said the Captain, 'Couldn't we get up a dance, don't you think, for the young people,' and pulling out a whistle gave a shrill call, on which in skipt half a dozen smart young sailors in their best, who wheeled out the tables, lifted up the carpet, settled the seats round the room, and then ushered in a Band. It had all been prepared before, but it was nicely done and a surprise, and put us all in high spirits. The sailors brought in supper at the proper time, and whilst we were enjoying our refreshments in the one room, they danced us a hornpipe in the other. When we *rode* to see them at Newhaven our luncheon was strawberries and cream. More than once we afterwards *rowed* to the frigate, and they gave us one little *fête* there on board; a dozen friends and a collation; the boats took us up the Forth for an hour instead of any dancing.

Captain Bingham's 'impromptu fait à loisir' party puts me in mind of Johnny Bell's. He was the celebrated Surgeon,[1] a morsel of a man married to a Wife as small, and they lived in rooms proportioned to their size, in a flat in George Street. He was extremely musical, of course collected a musical society about him; his instrument, the bass viol or double bass, bigger a great deal than himself; his hands could just

1. He was 'the best surgeon that Scotland had then produced' (Cockburn); he died in 1820 aged 57.

meet on it, the bow producing sounds from those thick strings a giant could only have emulated. It was a Grace Baillie affair, their single Concert, the return for all they went to; their whole apartment thrown open, kitchen and bedroom and all, made to communicate not only by doors but by windows, oval windows cut in the walls, filled by book shelves at ordinary times and opened on this state occasion, having all the effect of mirrours, spectators fancying at first that the moving mob seen through these openings was a reflexion. The many tiny rooms were by this means really made into one large enough for the company, nearly all of whom met the eye at any spot, by turning round the head. Some one wondering where the little couple slept on this gala night, Lord Jeffrey gravely answered, 'In the case of the bass viol.' A brother, George Bell, a barrister, was a great friend of my father's, a very first rate man; it was he who helped poor Duncan Cameron so well out of his scrape.

In August my father and Mother and William went to the highlands. Johnny accompanied M. L'Espinasse to France. The little monkey had a turn for languages, was making good progress in French, so as a reward this pleasant trip was arranged for him. We three young ladies were left to amuse ourselves—and Miss Elphick. John Dalzel was good enough to take us long walks frequently, sometimes as far as Portobello, where Mrs Gillio had taken lodgings for sea bathing. She had been in considerable difficulties, poor woman, on account of her children. Amelia was very unmanageable, a forward flirting girl, by no means pleased when found fault with. George, her only son, had run away; after a search of some days he was discovered on board a collier, bent on going to sea. He made stipulations before consenting to return home, one of which was that he should no more attend the High School. One of her Indian friends placed him some where in England under a Tutor, who prepared young men for Cadetships; he got his appointment in proper time, and went out to Bombay, where he died. Just as he left Edinburgh the mother broke her leg, and it was to recover her strength that she was sent to the seaside. Nobody could be kinder than she ever was to us, and in every way by attention on our part we tried to repay her warmth of feeling, but we could not go the length of having Amelia much with us, or of at all forming part of Amelia's own society. She had picked up a very under set of girl acquaintance, with Beaux of manners agreeable to them, principally young medical students, as a Class, the lowest of all at college. She had a 'Morris' and a 'Turnbull' she called them all thus by their plain surnames, and 'two Goldwires,' and I really forget how many more, with whom she seemed to be equally intimate; for, by her account, extraordinary personal liberties seemed to be taken by these young men with those young ladies without much offence, though she confessed she did not approve of all proceedings. She 'hated,' she said, 'pawing men.' 'Morris was not a pawing man, nor one of the Goldwires's, but the other was, and so was Hogg, and it was quite unpleasant,' she thought, 'to have a great hot hand feeling all over one.' We used to wonder at what School in Bath this girl could possibly have been educated.

We were obliged to offend poor Mrs Gillio about a trip to Roslin. She had hired a carriage, and made sure of our delighted acceptance of seats in it. We were to have cold meat and strawberries and cream at Lasswade, a day of thorough enjoyment; but as Amelia's Beaux were to have joined the party, Miss Elphick took it upon herself to say that she could not sanction the excursion. Amelia gave us a very lively description of the pleasures we had lost, concluding by a fine trick she had played her Mother. Going, Mrs Gillio had packed up all her young ladies inside the carriage with herself; two gentlemen going on the box, the rest in a gig. Returning Miss Amelia had no intention of a continuance of 'such old fudge'; so forming a respectable league with a 'Goldwire,' not the 'pawing one' it was to be hoped, 'off him and me set, and jumped upon the dickey box.' Dislodgement was stoutly resisted, and so there was rather a riotous journey home. Margaret, a pretty, gentle girl, was quite innocent of all these illbreedings. She occupied herself with her masters, her needleworks and her birds, and as a child, a companion for Mary, was very much with us, improving herself in every way with Mary in the schoolroom. A little spoiled Isabella, once so pretty, growing plain, was the plague of every body.

We did not neglect our unfortunate Cousins in the Abbey.

We never failed to visit them as when my Mother ordered the visit. Miss Carr, however, did not so much care to come to us, our ways were rather dull for her; Jane spent most of her time drawing, I worked a robe in imitation point, appliquée, intended for Mary's first Northern Meeting. We were so quiet, so orderly, so very correct in our whole conduct during the absence of the Heads of the family, that on their return my father was addressed in the Parliament House by our opposite neighbour, a Writer who lived on a flat, a second storey, high enough for good observation, and assured by him of the perfect propriety of our behaviour.

Jane's turn for drawing had been considerably increased by some lessons from Mr Wilson, the head of the Academy of painting, to whom Lord Eldin had most especially recommended her. She went twice a week to his painting rooms, where she worked away in earnest with several clever companions, among them poor Marianne Grant of Kilgraston, who very soon married James Lindsay, and Grace Fletcher, both of them good painters in oils. Mr Wilson sometimes read a picture or a drawing or a print with his pupils, and as I sometimes took my work and went with Jane, I came in for the lecture. He began with the general effect, went on to the grouping, the shading, the light, the distance, the peculiar propriety of certain objects in certain situations, directing our attention to an apparent trifle on which perhaps the whole beauty depended. Always afterwards, whether viewing fine scenery or examining paintings, we applied these explanations to our pictures, and found our pleasure in them heightened beyond any previous idea. It was like opening another eye, an eye with brains behind it; and we had ample opportunity for exercising our newly perceived faculty, for not only was the surrounding sea and land and our own town beautiful as art and nature could make them, but we had access to an admirable collection of paintings by the best Ancient and modern Artists, gathered from all quarters early the following winter, and exhibited at small cost to all who chose to buy a ticket. An empty house in York Place was hired for the purpose, and open every morning to the publick. Once a week in the evening the holders of season tickets were admitted; the rooms were well warmed, well lighted, and there were plenty of seats and it really was the most agreeable of assemblies, there being a paramount object to engage the attention and furnish an unfailing subject of discourse. All the possessors of good paintings had contributed to this Collection. We used to know the owners of particular gems by the air of triumph with which they stood contemplating what they were thoroughly acquainted with, instead of searching out stranger beauties. Mr Wilson frequently called us to him there, when surrounded by eager listeners to his criticisms. He and I did not always agree! I never would at any time surrender my private judgment, tho' I had sense enough to keep my free rights to myself.

Before my father and Mother went north, Jane and I had spent a week with them at Hermandstone, an ugly but comfortable place which Lord Gillies rented of Lord St Clair. I had been there before, and we were often there again, and when they were quietly leading a country life with only a few intimate friends visiting them, it was very pleasant. But when they had all their rich, grand, formal East Lothian neighbours, we young people hated going there. Lord Gillies was extremely fond of aristocratick company; the more grandees he could seat together at his very splendidly furnished table the better pleased he seemed to be. How often we see this in those of humble birth, as if the having risen to a place in that 'charmed circle' did not add a lustre to it, when talents and probity such as his had been the passport. Mrs Gillies, well born and highly bred, took her position naturally, content with what contented him. Neither of them, for all this, ever neglected the poor relations. His one prosperous brother, the doctor and authour,[1] was never as kindly welcomed as poor William, and poorer, more primitive Colin. At this very time William Gillies' three children found their home with their uncle Adam; for years they had had no other, the two girls going to the different classes while in Edinburgh, the boy placed first at the High School and then sent to the Charter House; and every Saturday when in town there was a dinner

1. John Gillies (1747-1836) was, in fact, not a M.D.; he was an historian who succeeded Principal Robertson as Historiographer Royal for Scotland.

for the young family connexions, school boys and girls, and College boys, all made as welcome as the grandees, and appearing a good deal happier. Miss Bessy Clerk and others used to fear that young people like William Gillies' children, brought up in such society, in a house so luxurious, would be spoiled for a ruder life, should such a change, as was most likely, come to them. But it did not so turn out; the change did come, and they bore it perfectly. Robert the corn factor, Mary the Authouress, and Margaret the professional painter, have followed their different employments better than if they had never had their intellects improved by their superiour education. The Authouress and the painter in particular benefited by the early cultivation of their taste, neither did I ever hear that Robert did less in Mark Lane because he was capable of enjoying in his Villa at Kensington the refinements of a gentleman's leisure. Margaret was never agreeable, but she was very clever. She did not wait to be turned out of Lord Gillies' house by his death or any accident. 'Uncle Adam,' said she one day, 'do you mean to leave Mary and me any thing in your Will?' 'Perhaps a trifle,' answered the Uncle. 'Not an independance?' pursued the niece. 'Certainly not, by no means; these are strange questions, Margaret.' 'Necessary ones, Uncle. My father has nothing to give us; he has married a second wife. We shall have then to work for our bread some time; we had better begin now while we are young, have health, activity, and friends to help us. I go to London next week.' She did, to her father's, where she was not welcome; so she hired two rooms, sent for Mary, began painting dauby portraits while learning her art more thoroughly; and when I saw them in their pretty home at Highgate they told me they had never been in want, nor ever regretted the decisive step they had taken.[1] The friends were at first seriously displeased; but the success of the nieces in time appeased the Uncles, and both the doctor and Lord Gillies left them legacies.

1. Margaret Gillies (1803–87) earned a reputation as a
   miniaturist and water-colour painter. Her sister Mary,
   the author of many books for children (often using the
   pseudonym Harriet Myrtle), died in 1860.

In the early part of the Edinburgh summers a good many very pleasant, quiet parties went on among such of us as had to remain in town till the Courts rose in July. I remember several very agreeable dinners at this season at the Arbuthnots, foreigners generally bringing their introductions about this time of year. At the Brewsters they had foreigners sent to them too, and they entertained them now, not in the flat where we first found them, but in their own house in Athole Crescent newly built out of the profits of the Kaleidoscope,[1] a toy that was ridiculously the rage from its humble beginning in the tin tube with a perforated card in the end, to the fine brass instrument set on a stand, that was quite an ornament to a drawing room. Had Sir David managed matters well, this would have turned out quite a fortune to him; he missed the moment and only made a few thousand pounds; still they gave him ease, and that was a blessing. The little dinners at his house were always pleasant. *She* was charming, and they selected their guests so well and were so particularly agreeable themselves, I don't remember any where passing more thoroughly enjoyable evenings than at their house. He was then, and is still, not only among the first of scientifick men, but in manners and in conversation utterly delightful; no such favourite every where as Sir David Brewster, except at home or with anyone engaged with him in business. Irritable as a husband, careless of his wife, thankless for her unceasing attentions, tyrannical and penurious, her life was rendered miserable; harsh, even cruel, as a father, his children were terrified by him. Nobody ever had dealings with him and escaped a quarrel. Whether he were ill, the brain overworked and the body thus overweighted, or whether his wife did not understand him, or did not know and exert himself, there is no saying. His temper has much improved since his sensible very patient daughter grew up, and since Lady Brewster died before her sister Miss Macpherson, and so put the succession to Belleville out of his head.[2] I have

1. Brewster's *Treatise on the Kaleidoscope* was published in 1819—he had invented it in 1816, but the patents were faulty so it was pirated.
2. This is explained on I, p. 258.

sometimes spent the greater part of a day with them, when he would leave all his calculations and devote himself to our amusement, keeping close by the side of our worktable for hours, without giving expression to one cross word, and at dinner he would be in high spirits. Holy days poor Lady Brewster called those bright gleams in her much vexed existence.

At one of their small dinners my father and I could not take our eyes off a Tweedside neighbour, Miss Cochrane Johnstone. The Kaleidoscope had bought a few acres near Galla Water and built a small house upon them, where the Brewsters for some years passed every summer. She was one of the loveliest creatures that ever inherited broad lands, and she became the prize of a tall, red haired, rough sailor, who did not make her happy. She had a round beautiful figure, beautiful complexion, regular features, finely formed head, and a pair of almond shaped, warm, hazel, sleepy eyes, that must have killed every man they glanced on—gently. When I was reintroduced, in 1842 was it, to the widowed Lady Napier, a little thin, prim looking body surrounded by unmistakeably their father's daughters, I could not recall a trace of her youthful beauty. It quite grieved me. Perhaps, if she remembered me, I may have struck her as as much changed.

Miss Cochrane Wishart was another heiress that was thought handsome in a masculine way. She married a pretty little ladylike Sir Thomas Trowbridge, a sailor. A real beauty who was no heiress was a Miss Maclean. She made a perfect hubbub, and it was so odd a story altogether, the rights of it, as they say, not known till long afterwards.

At a mess dinner the conversation turning on beauties, their varieties, their reputations, their fashion, their merits, etc., a young officer laid a bet that he would bring any pretty girl into notice and have her cried up as a wonder, by properly preparing for her reception by the publick. The bet was taken and the plot laid. The Barrack Master at Berwick had several pretty daughters; the handsomest was selected, and very soon a whisper grew to an inquiry, and the inquiry to a strong desire to see either herself, or some one who had seen the beautiful Miss Maclean. She was very judiciously kept just long enough in retirement to excite curiosity, and then she appeared on a visit to Mrs Major somebody. The accomplices praised her to the skies, her fame increased, the few that saw her reported in exstasies. Presently crowds followed her out goings and her in comings. She lived in a mob, and so interested everybody. Mrs Major became suddenly the rage, she had more invitations for herself and her friend than there was a possibility of accepting, and in a room the rudeness of Admirers quite blocked up the poor girl's position, every eye too fixed on her. She really was a pretty creature, with a fine clear skin, dark hair and eyes, and a modest manner. She was not to be named by the side of many who had been less noticed, however. What stamped her celebrity was the notice taken of her by the Count and Countess Flahault; they invited her to stay with them, and as they saw company in an easy way every evening, Miss Maclean was at once raised into our great world. The Countess, Miss Mercer Elphinstone by birth, Baroness Keith in expectancy, had fallen in love with this most attractive foreigner and would marry him.[1] An heir to her vast fortune was of consequence, and an heir did not come; all sorts of accidents preventing it. Little Dr Hamilton was consulted, and when the next occasion presented itself Madame de Flahault was condemned to her sofa; but as her mind was to be amused she was to pass her time cheerfully. There she lay, covered with a lace overlay lined with pink silk, her hair nicely arranged, chattering at a great rate to thirty or forty guests. She was a very ugly woman and not a clever one and very far from being generally agreeable. I do not think she would have continued to attract much company, men at least, whom she greatly preferred, without some such magnet as her new protégée. Miss Maclean's reign

1. Margaret Elphinstone, Viscountess Keith
   (1788–1867) married Auguste Charles Joseph,
   Comte de Flahault de la Billardrie, in Edinburgh in
   1817. A natural son of Tallyrand, he became aide-de-
   camp to Napoleon. He was exiled but returned to
   favour after the Restoration, becoming ambassador in
   Rome, Vienna and London.

was short, but like Miss Manie Dreghorn's long before, Oh!, it was glorious. She had to return to Berwick, where she married poorly enough, a lieutenant in a marching regiment, a Mr Clarke; went with him to Bombay and died; and the young Officer won his bet.

M. de Flahault was in manner perfection, a finished frenchman, than which one can go no further in describing a gentleman; very handsome too, of a lively conversation truly agreeable. One small trait much struck me and set me thinking too. Mrs Munro had a small party, a good many young people at it, so she wished to set them dancing. Who would play? Mrs This had not any musick, and Mrs That made some other excuse. My Mother desired me to go to the instrument, which of course I did. 'Oh, no,' said M. de Flahault, 'that would be too severe a punishment to the gentlemen; let me relieve you, I can keep good time.' He played particularly well, so that it was a treat to dance to him, but what I thought over was his putting himself and his playing out of the question; his intention was to assist the amusement of the evening, make everybody happy, and pay a neat compliment the while. It was all so high bred, so very un British. He behaved very well to his somewhat haughty wife, and she got on very well with him always. They had in time three daughters, one [Jane] married to Lord Shelburne, I think, and one dead, but no son ever.

Lady Wiseman came to Edinburgh this summer; she was staying with her mother's relations the old Miss Steuarts, Annie Need's old friends, or foes, who on retiring from business had settled in their native town. She and two sisters, Mrs Rich and Mrs Erskine, were Sir James Mackintosh's children by his first wife. She was a clever, flighty creature, very foolish in her conduct, plain in face, but very pleasant, and a great friend of Jane's in a short time. After parting they corresponded. Sir William Wiseman being at sea, she had been left at Hertford College with her father, where she had picked up an admirer with whom her proceedings went rather beyond discretion, and so she was sent out of his way. No heart break for she very soon replaced him, first by Basil Hall, and then by Sir James Ramsay. It is to be hoped she *then* found safety in numbers. Afterwards, when she joined her husband on the

Jamaica Station, she did not escape so well. She had two fine little boys: Willie, the present Baronet, who went to sea, and has come through life well, and dear little clever Jamie, who went all entirely wrong and shot himself in India. What has not a mother to answer for who deserts her children. How could she ever smile as Mrs Turnball. Above all, be saucy as she was at Grandville [*H.L. in France*, p. 148].

I think it was about the May or June of this year that old Mrs Siddons returned to the stage for twelve nights to act for the benefit of her grandchildren.[1] Henry Siddons was dead, leaving his affairs in much perplexity. He had purchased the theatre and never made it a paying concern, altho' his Wife acted perseveringly, and all the Kemble family came regularly and drew good houses. His ordinary company was not good; he was a dreadful stick himself, and he would keep the best parts for himself, and in every way managed badly. She did better after his death; her clever brother William Murray conducting affairs much more wisely for her, and certainly for himself in the end, slow as she was in perceiving this. Some pressing debts, however, required to be met, and Mrs Siddons came forward. We were all great play goers, often attending our own poor third rates, Mrs Harry redeeming all else in our eyes, and never missing the stars, John and Charles Kemble, Young, Liston, Matthews, Miss Stephens, etc. But to see the great queen again we had never dreamed of. She had taken leave of the stage before we left London. She was little changed, not at all in appearance, neither had her voice suffered; the limbs were just hardly stiffer, more slowly moved rather, therefore in the older characters she was the finest, most natural; they suited her age. Queen Catherine she took leave in. To my dying hour I never shall forget the trial scene; the silver tone of her severely cold 'My Lord Cardinal,' and then on the wrong one starting up, the

1. See 1, pp. 198–9 for the great Sarah Siddons' triumphant 'final' appearance as Lady Macbeth in 1812. After her son Henry's death in 1815, she returned ten times to the stage of the Theatre Royal in Edinburgh (on which he had taken a twenty-one year lease in 1809) in benefit performances for her grand-children.

scorn of her attitude, and the outraged dignity of the voice in which she uttered 'To *You* I speak.'[1] We were breathless. Her sick room was very fine too. Then her Lady Macbeth, Volumnia, Constance[2]—ah, no such acting since, for she was nature, on stilts in her private life. 'Bring me some beer, boy, and another plate,' is a true anecdote, blank verse and a tragick tone being her daily wear.

Once when Liston was down I longed to see him in Lubin Log; for some reason I could not manage it, and Mrs Harry let me go to her private box. He had been Tony Lumpkin in the Play, and we were talking him over, waiting for his appearance in the farce. 'I have heard,' said I, 'of his giving a look with that queer face of his, not uttering a word, yet sending people into convulsions of laughter not to be checked while he remained in sight.' 'Hush,' said Mrs Harry, 'here he comes.' Enter Lubin from the Coach with all his parcels. Between his first two inquiries for his 'numbrella' and his ''at,' he threw up at our hidden box, at *me, the* look—perfectly oversetting; there never could be such another grotesque expression of fun since the days of fauns and satyrs, and when composure in a degree returned, a sly twinkle of one squinting eye, or the buck tooth interrupting a smile, or some indescribable secret sign of intelligence, would reach us and set us off again. We were ill with laughing. He played that whole farce to us, to Mrs Harry and me, and not to the House, and every one agreed he had surpassed himself.[3]

The early part of the next summer, 1819, passed much in the same way as the one before; sociable small parties among our friends in town, and visits to those in the country. Messages to the Abbey of course, and we were always the messengers. My Mother was very careful of the servants;

1. *Henry VIII*, iv, 69.
2. Mother of *Coriolanus*; Arthur's mother in *King John*.
3. John Liston (1776?–1846) is described by the D.N.B. as the highest paid comic actor of his day; it adds he was 'unjustly charged with a mere power of grimace'.
   Lubin Log was a rôle he created in *Love, Law & Physic* (1812); Goldsmith's Tony Lumpkin appears in *She Stoops to Conquer*.

Johnny declared that one extremely rainy day when it was proper the Newcastle Chronicle should be returned to Mrs General Maxwell, my Mother called out to him, 'Johnny, my dear, I wish you would run to George Street with this; it's such a dreadful day I don't like sending out poor Richard'—a colossus of a footman, weighing heavier every day from having too little to do. Poor Johnny! I can't somehow separate him in boyhood, dear Jack, from you. My recollection of him is so like you while he was little, before he grew to six foot one. This very spring he, may be, thought with regret of even Mrs Maxwell's newspaper, for my father took him up to town with himself and sent him to Eton. They first paid a visit to the Electors of Tavistock, and on their way spent a day or two with Dugald Stewart, who lived then near the Duke of Bedford's cottage at Endsleigh. The old philosopher predicted the boy's future eminence, although we at home had not seen through his reserve. He was idle, slow, quiet, passing as almost stupid beside his brilliant brother. 'Take care of that boy, Grant,' said Dugald Stewart at their parting; 'he will make a great name for himself, or I am much mistaken.' And has he not? Quiet he has remained, indolent too, and eccentrick, but in his own field of action where is his parallel? My Mother and I thought of no honourable future when our pet left us. We watched him from the window, stepping into the travelling chariot after my father in the new great coat that had been made for him, the little tearful face not daring to venture a last glance back to us. He was small of his age, and from being the youngest he was childish. We did not see him for fifteen months. He came back to us an Eton boy; how much those three small words imply. My poor Mother, I can understand now the sob with which she threw herself back upon the sofa, exclaiming, as the carriage rolled away 'I have lost my Johnny!' His cousin John Frere went to Eton at the same time, and our John spent all short holidays at Hampstead, only coming home to the highlands once a year in the summer. The two cousins remained attached friends ever, and though widely separated, never lost sight of one another till poor John Frere died.

The next event was the arrival of Uncle Ralph, his wife, daughter Eliza, and sister Fanny, to have just a peep of us before settling again at Tennochside. They had tired of England and were glad to return home, leaving Edmund behind at School. Jane, who was a great favourite with Mrs Ralph, went to see them soon afterwards, and spent a very happy three weeks at that comfortable place. During her absence we had a visit from Aunt Leitch and our cousin Kate. Kate had been with us before, which I have neglected to mention. Uncle Edward, soon after his marriage, invited her out to India, funds were sent home for her equipment and passage, and it was decided by the family that Aunt Leitch should have the charge of all matters concerning her departure. She was to spend the winter in Glasgow, and the following spring proceed to London to be outfitted before embarking. She came direct from Houghton to us, and remained with us two months, going to any parties that offered, and very much admired. She was not pretty, in spite of fine eyes, but the expression of her countenance was very bright; she was clever and natural and lively, with modest, simple manners, and she was tall and her figure was good. She dressed very becomingly, scanty and plain as her wardrobe was when she arrived; it increased in size and value considerably during her stay at Picardy Place. We were all quite sorry when she left us, the more so that she sadly deteriorated during her visit to Glasgow. Aunt Leitch's temper ruffled Kate's, want of exercise destroyed her looks. She returned to us fat, and dark, and pert, and quite unlike herself. This all went off after she reached India, although Mrs Edward Ironside's humours tried her *im*patience sorely. She married very happily, and as Mrs Barnwall was one of the most agreeable women in all Bombay. Glasgow was not a place to improve in. We were there once, I forget in what year. My father went to collect evidence in some political business, my Mother and I with him, as a cloke I suppose. We were at Aunt Leitch's pretty new house in St Vincent Street, and she took a great deal of trouble for us in making up parties at home, engagements abroad, and even directed an Assembly. We were not very refined in manners in Edinburgh, some of us, but there were brains with us, abilities of a high order, turned to a more intellectual account than could be the general employment of them in a mere manufacturing seaport town, for into that had Glasgow sunk. Its College, as to renown, was gone; its merchants no longer the Cadets of the neighbouring old County families, but their clerks of low degree shot up into the high places. 'Some *did* remain who in vain mourned the *better* days when they were young,' but as a whole the Society was indescribably underbred. I should have been very much out of my element in that Assembly had it not been for an accidental meeting with the little merry sailor Houston Steuart, and Dick Honeyman, a son of Lord Armidale's.

About July the Scots Grays got the route for Ireland. Tom Walker was in despair. He was a fine looking young man, truly amiable, played the flute to Jane's pianoforte, a performance suitable in every respect and unimprovable, for in spite of daily very lengthened practisings neither artist made much progress. He had a handsome private fortune. Altogether, Annie Need had hoped this favourite nephew of her general's would have brought them a Scotch niece back; but his knowledge of history was so defective! It was not possible for a moment to think seriously of a companion for life with whom there could be no rational conversation! So the handsome Cavalry officer *walked* away—no, *rode*. I daresay the Band master was glad, for most of his spare time had been occupied copying out Waltzes. An Irish love soon replaced the 'bonnie Jean' so honestly wooed. A Miss Constantia Beresford made no educational difficulties. She caused a few, however, of many another kind, and poor Tom Walker bore them.

General Need had returned home very soon after his marriage to our dear Annie. They had settled amidst his rich manufacturing relations near Nottingham, who had all received her most kindly. We heard from her constantly and were always planning to meet, yet never managed it. My father had seen her with her two nice little boys, and found her perfectly happy; her General no genius, but an excellent man.

I cannot recollect much else that is worthy of note before our little tour upon the Continent. We set out in August, and were two months and a half away. My father was not inclined for such a movement at all, it was probably very inconvenient to the treasury, but my mother had so set her heart upon it, he, as usual, good naturedly gave way. Johnny was to spend his holidays with the Freres. Miss Elphick went to the Kirkman Finlays,[1] her parting was quite a dreadful scene, screams, convulsions, sobs, hystericks. The poor woman was attached to some of us, and had of late been much more agreeable to the rest; but she was a plague in the house, did a deal of mischief, and was no guide, no help. She had been seven years with us, so there was a chain of habit to loosen at any rate.

1. Kirkman Finlay (1773–1842) was a famous Glasgow merchant, who prospered in the difficult conditions after the American War to become Lord Provost in 1812 and one of the M.P.s for the city 1812–18.

# CHAPTER TWENTY-TWO

## 1819

IN the month of August, then, of this year 1819 we set out on our foreign travels, my father, my Mother, William, Jane, Mary and I; rather too large a party as we found when we had more experience, particularly as we were attended by a man, a maid, and a dog. The maid, a thoroughly stupid creature, and the dog, poor Dowran, went with us; the man, a black, and a deal too clever, joined us in Holland, for to the Netherlands we were bound. My father had always had a passion for Dutch and Flemish paintings, farming, buildings, and politicks; besides, he was so very kind as to wish to take me to the waters at Aix la Chapelle. I had been attacked in the Spring with the same sort of strange suffering that has fallen upon me several times since, at intervals often of years, after any disturbance of mind, a failure as it seemed of all powers of body, the whole system paralysed, as it were, without any apparent cause other than that reserve of disposition inherited from my Mother, which threw all grief back inwardly while the outward manner was unchanged. She never told me that anxiety for me made her anxious for the complete change of scene we were entering on. I only guessed it many years afterwards.

We embarked at Leith in a common trading vessel, a tub, with but moderate accommodation, the Van Egmont, bound for Rotterdam. Its very slow rate of sailing kept us nine days at sea; luckily the weather the whole time was beautiful, and our few fellow passengers accommodating, with the exception of one unhappy looking man, a merchant in some embarrassment with regard to his affairs. He used to watch the wind so nervously, it being of consequence to him to appear before a certain day in the Counting House of his Dutch Correspondent. We had some difficulty in sweetening the disturbed moments of this anxious minded poor man, but we succeeded in a degree, the wind, the last few days, aiding us. His father was a light hearted very old man, taking the voyage for pleasure, probably unaware of the full extent of his son's perplexities. A very grave Merchant's Clerk and two young Officers completed our party. One of the Officers, now Colonel Clunie, has been to India and back, found Jane out in Edinburgh, and has several times dined with her in York Place, recurring with delight to the happy nine days on board the Van Egmont. We all did our best to make them pass cheerfully. We watched the land, the sea, the sky, the day's work. Our skipper was extremely civil; his mate, a merry scapegrace, inventing all sorts of fun to amuse every body; the fare was good, the Cabin clean, and living out on deck in the open air even I regained an appetite.

On nearing the Dutch Coast the scene became very interesting. All at once we found ourselves amid a crowd of little fishing vessels, rigged with three cornered sails of a deep orange colour. We passed then a few larger boats, a merchantman or two, and then there suddenly rose upon us from the waves, steeples, treetops, towers and windmills, without any more stable foundation seemingly than the water. There was some delay in crossing the Bar, an accumulation of sand at the mouth of the Maas that can only be crossed at the full tide; once over that we sailed quietly on, the windmills and steeples closing in upon us, till the sedgy banks of the river appeared on either hand, with houses, gardens, small fields full of cattle, all as it seemed below the level of the water. It was a curious sight, and a pretty one; for as the river narrowed and so enabled us to distinguish the objects we were passing, the total difference they exhibited from any of the kind we had been accustomed to look on created the most lively feelings of surprise. The villages looked all like toys, little, formal, green, round topped trees in rows, small baby houses painted in such bright colours—red, and blue, and green, and yellow, and dazzling white—with window panes that shone like diamonds, door steps clean enough to dine on, neat gravel paths, and palings without a blemish. One could not fancy the large, heavy looking, heavily clothed men we saw in all the Craft on the river being allowed to enter such fairy premises. It now became a matter of nice piloting to get our heavy barge through the thickening throng of vessels of all sizes, but the big Dutchman in his big balloon breeches, and his big overcoat covered with great big dollars for buttons, and his red night Cap, whom we had taken on board below the Bar, carried us safe in and out and all round all obstacles, and brought us up easily to the quay in the heart of the busy and very beautiful City of Rotterdam.

The extent of the Bompjes I really don't remember. A row of fine elms runs all along the parapet by the river's edge.[1] A broad road, so clean, is beyond, then a narrow pavement in front of the street of irregularly built houses, some high, some low, some palaces, some cottages, some with a handsome façade, and others with picturesque gable ends, *portes cochères* every here and there admitting to the Court-yard and the ware rooms as well as the dwelling house of the Merchants, even cranes at intervals impending over head. A large, long, low building, a capital hotel, the Badthouse, was where we were bound, gladly availing ourselves of all its name promising hot water luxuries, to refresh bodies wearied by near a fortnight of a sea toilette.

We arrived in the very midst of the Kermess, the annual fair, the most favourable of all times for the visit of strangers. The wares of all the world were exposed for sale in streets of booths tastefully decorated, lighted up brilliantly at night, and crowded at all hours by purchasers from every province in the two united kingdoms,[2] all in their best and very handsome and perfectly distinct attire. Like Venice, Rotterdam is built in the water, long canals intersect it in every direction, on which the traffick is constant; there are mere footpaths on either side, with quantities of narrow bridges for

1. It was this avenue of elms that gave its name to the Boompjes, the quarter mile long quay in the heart of the city.
2. The former Austrian Netherlands had been joined to the Kingdom of Holland by the victorious allies four years earlier at Vienna; E.G. seemed well aware of this union's deficiencies.

the convenience of crossing. The tall houses forming the street must have been gloomy abodes, just looking over the narrow stream to one another. Outside they were gay enough from the excessive cleanliness observed, and the bright paint, and the shining brass knockers, and the old fashioned solidity of the building. It was quite amusement enough to wander all about this fine old City, every now and then getting back into the throng of the fair, where indeed I could have spent the day most agreeably, every object presented to the eye was so totally different from any ever seen at home. The people were of course the most dissimilar, national features varying as much as national dress. The men were merely sturdy, healthy, sailor like persons, enveloped in a great quantity of substantial clothing, each coat and pair of breeches containing stuff enough for two; the women were quite superiour, the younger ones beautiful, with the loveliest of fair clear skins; even the old were agreeable from the perfect cleanliness and good order of their appearance; a rag, a tatter, is never seen, nor a speck of dirt either, and the peculiarity of the costume of every province, all so befitting the station of the wearers, made every little group we fell in with a picture. Full stuff petticoats rather short, such clean white stockings, neat, very black, polished shoes, pretty ankles too, snow white handkerchiefs, smart aprons, clear muslin caps edged with the finest lace in good quantity, varying in shape according to the district that sent it forth, and often very valuable gold ornaments about the head, round the throat, and in the ears. The north Hollanders especially were remarkable for thus adorning themselves; their style of head was particularly becoming, or else they were so pretty that whatever they wore would have suited them.

After the people came the vehicles, the queerest assortment of strangely shaped post waagens not unlike our omnibus's with open sides, or some of the third class carriages on our railways. Quantities of these, of all sizes, were running through the paved streets all day, and for the narrow pathways by the canals there were very small carts drawn by dogs to convey such market produce as it was not worth while to send by water to every door; larger carts with or without tilts plied in the more accessible thoroughfares. It was a very busy scene, very cheerful, and very curious to us who had never been out of our own country before.

The excessive cleanliness was almost more to be admired than all else; it pervaded the habits of the nation throughout. The streets were daily swept, the pavements daily washed, the railings daily wiped, the windows daily rubbed, the brasses daily brightened. Within it was the same; no corner left unvisited by the busy maid, the very door keys were polished, like the small bunches we keep in our pockets, cupboards, closets, shelves, not only spotless but neatly ornamental; white paper with a cut fringe, or white linen frilled, laid along under the shining wares they were appropriated to hold. Yet nobody seemed overworked. In the afternoons all the women were spinning or knitting, as beautifully tidy in their own persons as was all the property around them. There were no dirty children, even no beggars. They are all early risers, and very active in their movements—regardless of consequences too! In our before breakfast walks we often got more from the whirl of the mop than we liked, while the regular splashing and dashing was going on during the hour all the houses were having their faces washed. A girl with long gold ear rings dangling, would be out in the street with her pail, too intent on the freshening up of her master's dwelling to think of the passers by. In Ireland here we can't get our maids to wash our doorsteps—must not propose such an indignity—some of the very particular ones object to kneel to wash the kitchen flags; and as for dusting, or bright rubbing! alas! damp as is our climate we must put up not only with rusty keys, but rusty fire irons, for a generation or two yet. Our lady wives not thinking the care of their families a duty, as does the comfortable Dutch *vrow*. The damp in Holland was the original cause of all this care, destruction would have followed carelessness, and does follow it here. The hotel was just as admirably kept as any private house. We had no sitting room, but the bedrooms were very large, and we took our meals in the saloon, breakfast at a small table at our own hour, dinner at the *table d'hôte*. The eating was very good, abundance of it, nice fruit, wine, beer, and most delicious tea; never before nor since nor any where else did

I ever drink any equal to it. The coffee was very strong of *chicorée*, but well made, and I believe the bitter made it more wholesome. The bread was either too heavy or too spongy for our taste.

The *table d'hôte* was very pleasant; many of the townspeople seemed to dine there, bachelours mostly, without homes, and travellers, all of whom spoke to those they happened to sit next, charitably acting to one another as if there were no convicts in the company. The Dutch are called a silent people, yet some of them at least had plenty to say, French being our medium of conversation—a foreign language both to them and us. We found the low Dutch commonly spoken by no means hard to learn a little of. Jane and I were very soon able to carry on all the business of our travelling party so as to be perfectly understood by servants and tradespeople. We were bargaining at the door steps with a flower girl, when a very smart English group, new arrivals, elbowed their way past us. Some of the faces were familiar to us, and a lady's loud, shrill, very English voice gave me quite a start I remembered it so well, but where, I could not puzzle out. When we were assembled at three o'clock to dinner a door opened and the party entered, the ladies in great dress, all in rich silks, one with a bare neck, all with the smartest heads, a turban, a blonde cap with flowers, ribbons, trinkets—making themselves in every way so conspicuous that we really felt ashamed of our compatriots. Imagine the feelings then with which *I* received the most gracious of bows from the turban, and heard the sharp provincial voice pronounce my name, adding that the owner of these two properties could give me a better than ordinary report of my 'poor dear Uncle at Oxford.' It was the President of Trinity and Mrs Lee! her sister and a soldier husband, Captain English by name, and two or three other Ipswich friends who had made a run across the Channel to see some of the wonders of Holland. Introductions all round followed of course as soon as we rose from the table, and we agreed to take tea together in one of our bedrooms. Very obliging they all were, and Mrs Lee did give my mother a more comfortable account of Dr Griffith's health than my Aunt Mary had latterly been able to send us. Still the case looked melancholy enough, and this kind hearted woman seemed to feel it so sincerely that even William forgave the midday turban. They were going on to Antwerp next day, so that we were saved another full dress daylight dinner. My father, who extremely enjoyed my Mother's discomfiture on this rather startling occasion, had behaved very ill by drawing Mrs English out, as he called it, and so he was banished after their departure to take a walk till his extraordinary paroxisms of laughter were over. I went with him along the Bompjes under the trees by the side of the water, and reaching the part at which the Harwich packet landed the passengers, who should step ashore but Mr Canning—the only time I ever saw him. He and my father seemed glad to meet,[1] and while they were conversing I had an opportunity of correcting all my imaginary impressions of the great man. He was not so tall and much more slender than I expected. His countenance was pale, anxious almost, and certainly no longer handsome; the high, well developed forehead alone reminded me of the prints of him. He was travelling with his sick son, a boy of seventeen or so, a cripple confined to a Merlin chair, and supported in that by many cushions. An elderly, very attentive servant never left the invalid's side, while another looked after the luggage and a carriage fitted up with a sort of sofa bed. They did not come to the Badthouse, so we saw no more of them; but I could not forget them, and often after, when the world was ringing with Mr Canning's fame, this scene of his private life returned to me, for he lost the son. It was Mr Burke and his son over again[2] as to many of the circumstances, only Mr Canning had another son, and one daughter whose marriage to Lord Clanricarde helped to kill him. Mrs Canning, the wife, was sister to the Duchess of Portland and the Countess of Moray. They were co-heiresses with very large fortunes,

1. Although of different parties, they knew each other well. Canning was Prime Minister for a few months before his death in 1827.
2. His eldest son died next year aged 19; Edmund Burke's son, Christopher, had died in childhood; a Merlin chair was an invalid wheel chair named after its inventor.

something like a hundred thousand pounds apiece; indeed I believe the eldest sister had more. It was all made by whist, their father, General Scott, being the most accomplished player of his day. He pursued it as a business, ate an early dinner of mutton or chicken with a glass of wine, no more, and then encountered any body, every body, *full* or fasting, taking good care however of who was his partner. He was never accused of the slightest approach to any incorrect practices, he merely took the advantage of a sober man over those who had dined well; it was not called dishonourable, this!, his opponents were free Agents. He left a curious will. He ordered his daughters to marry into the peerage under the penalty of forfeiting all share of their inheritance should any of them give herself to a Commoner. How absurd are these meddlers with the future. Mrs Canning, of course, lost her fortune, but her ennobled sisters each presented her with fifty thousand pounds as a wedding present.

We remained above a week in Rotterdam. Besides that this first specimen of foreign lands extremely interested us, we had made acquaintance with a very agreeable family long residents in the town, Mr Ferrier's our consul, a native of Brechin, not then knighted, to whom Lord Gillies had given us an introduction. They had been schoolfellows and friends; for the civilities we received could hardly, at first at least, have been paid us on our own account. The handsomest house on the Bompjes was Sir Alexander Ferrier's; it was quite a palace, far too splendid for a private family, having belonged to some great functionary during the reign of Louis Buonaparte.[1] The principal Staircase and the pavement of the hall and the door steps were of polished marble. One room was of such large dimensions it had never been furnished by Lady Ferrier; it occupied the height of two storeys, and was opened only on occasion of the Consul's annual ball. Even the dining room was much larger than any room at Russborough,[2] the daily parties of fourteen, sixteen, or so, were lost in it. They dined late for Holland, six

1. He ruled Holland for his brother, 1805–10.
2. The beautiful house of E.G.'s Co. Wicklow neighbour, the Earl of Milltown.

o'clock, and had musick and dancing among a large society of young people every evening. The daughters of the house were of all ages, and all of them were handsome, Amelia the eldest perhaps the least so; neither was she clever; she was amiable, gentle, and most obliging in manner to every one, and soon became quite a favourite with us. We suspected her of a little tender interest in the handsome son of her father's Dutch partner, young Mr Blankenhelm, for she certainly looked grave when he chose any other lady to drive out with him in his pea green gig on either of the only two roads available for carriage exercise, the one to Dort and the one to the Hague. The second sister was in School in England, quite a beauty, young enough, yet old enough to be in love too, and engaged to Sir James Turing, a very old Aberdeenshire Baronet, whose father while a Cadet had settled in Holland. The third and fourth, very pretty girls, afterwards married well among their father's mercantile friends. One of them, Eliza, was the mother of Mrs George Lauder! There were only two sons, John, married to a tiresome little heiress who had been a ward of his father's, a Walter Scott story, I am afraid,[1] and little Alex, who with a little Georgy still younger, two beautiful children, was in the nursery. Sir James, or Sir *Robert* Turing, I believe he was, had a brother, a very small little man; he arrived with a ship full of valuables from Batavia while we were in Rotterdam. Much of the Merchandise had been a venture of Mr Ferrier's. We saw it arrive, enter the great gates, be unloaded from the trucks. Some of it was arranged in the extensive surrounding warerooms on the ground floor; some of it raised by the crane into the upper storeys, and one small bale left at the Counting house door. We saw all this from Amelia's apartments high up at the back of the house overlooking the yard. She had a bedroom and sitting room to herself beautifully furnished. 'Come,' said she, 'now's *our* time for the Indian curiosities,' and she led the way running lightly downstairs. The unpacking of the cases in the Office had begun. There were China crapes, and China silks, and India muslins, ivory, Japan, Bombay pretty

1. For Scott's securing an heiress for his eldest son,
   see II, pp. 73-4.

things, preserved fruits, an infinite variety. Some of these were commissions and would be sold well; some were for the general market, and some for presents. My share was a box of dates, and the black lacquer fan I gave to you, Annie, dear. Mrs Ferrier had pieces of damask for new drawing room curtains. We highly approved of the generosity of the Mercantile profession, though Mr Blankenhelm took care to repeat more than once that his partner was not usually so liberal; his heart had evidently warmed to his country folk.

Sir James Gambier was another visitor. He was the Consul General for the Netherlands, a very fine looking, most agreeable man, though the father of a grown up family. He lived at the Hague, but had business at Rotterdam during our stay which kept him with us almost the whole time. Mr Blankenhelm said these affairs were of that mysterious nature no one could form the least idea of them. He was a busy body evidently, that tall, slender, handsome, gentlemanly Dutchman. The father and mother were formed after the old squat type, as were one or two other native heads of firms; the ladies belonging to them we did not see; they were either at Schevening bathing, or at their pleasure houses in the country. We had Mr Anderson Blair however for a couple of days. He was on his road to the German Spas and wanted to engage us to extend our travels so far. He liked every thing and every body at Rotterdam, except the pea green gig and Mr Blankenhelm; however sunny were our morning drives, clouds obscured our return from that quarter.

At last we were to move, the quicker because the low fever common to the place had seized on me and change of air was the cure, assisted by a glass every morning of gin bitters the first thing, ordered peremptorily by Mr Ferrier, and sent in in a dumpy bottle bulging out on either side from a long neck, sometimes ages ago seen of alike shape and larger size in our own country, and called a tappit hen. How they were to get on without us, without Jane's highland fling and my rebel songs, they were afraid to think of in that palace house. We were quite grieved ourselves to leave them, they had made us so very happy. We settled to return and embark for home from thence, and that during the time we were at Brussels Mr Ferrier should bring Amelia to us and leave her there for the few weeks we intended remaining, and so bidding farewell overnight, we set out early next morning for the Hague, twelve miles only along a paved road by the side of the Canal. It was the same neatness, the same cleanliness, the same flatness and the same baby house prettiness of scenery the whole way. We were in two carriages: a large, long caravan sort of concern for ourselves; the servants, the luggage and Dowran in a smaller queer shaped machine behind us. Dowran, disliking his position cooped up at Ward's feet, took an opportunity to jump out, against all rules, no dogs allowed to be at large during the hot months. A frightful hubbub ensued. Men running, yelling, screaming, brandishing sticks, throwing stones. The terrified animal flying over the burning pavement, till with one thing and another he was very nearly driven mad. William, jumping from the carriage, had just time to save his favourite from an uplifted club, but in what a condition was the poor creature! A respectable bystander advised his being plunged and replunged into the canal till he was nearly insensible; he was then replaced at Ward's feet, and she and the courier turning round, retraced the road to Rotterdam, my father giving them a few pencil lines to deliver with the Dog to Mr Ferrier. So long as the poor beast lived we were content, for that he had not gone really mad we were certain. We reached the Hague in good time to order dinner in a private room, and to invite Sir James Gambier to partake of it.

The Hague is a beautiful town, a perfect contrast to Rotterdam, built on a plain of course, scattered over it, space being every where; large squares, wide streets, even gardens, and very little water. There were buildings to see, of course, of which I only remember the Stadt house, left with all its splendid furniture as Louis and Hortense[1] had lived in it. It contains one hall of Audience, said to be the largest room ever a flat roof had been ventured to be stretched over. The present King and Queen, though bound to live occasionally in Holland, were supposed by the jealous Dutch to prefer

1. Hortense, daughter of Napoleon's first wife by a
   former marriage, Josephine de Beauharnais, married
   his brother Louis.

Flanders, and when they did come to their ancient dominions they preferred the privacy of the House in the Wood to the grander Stadt house in the 'village.' We went out to see the House in the Wood, an extremely pretty, country gentleman's residence, interesting to us on account of our own Queen Mary, who lived there so long with her cross but adored Prince William in days when the Stadtholder was not allowed to affect much splendour. They could hardly have had a simpler household than the King William of this age. The apartments were all comfortable, but none of them too fine for daily use; there was quite an air of domestick repose about them. The little Princess Marianne's cribbed, poor thing, stood beside her mother's, and little chairs and little tables suited to her childish size were in the business like sitting room the queen always lived in. There were good paintings in both these Royal residences, and a great many valuable curiosities scattered about. An ormolu clock in every room, abundance of chandeliers and sconces, and the beds were all set upon platforms, raised a step, or even two, from the floor, it had a good effect—imposing.

Amsterdam, twenty miles on, was a regular town again, none of the free, villa like look of the Hague; high houses with quaint gable ends, narrow streets and canals through them, bridges innumerable, ships and bustle. Plenty of sights for travellers, just the very things I care least to see. A fine picture, a few fine pictures, I can enjoy, give me time to study them one by one when I'm in the humour to look at them, but a Collection of pictures weighs me down with the headache, and to run about from one gallery of paintings to another, then to a Museum, after that to a church or two to see monuments here and carvings there, is all, to my peculiar feelings, utterly wearisome. I would walk about all day with pleasure in a strange country, keep my senses awake, and take my leisure to examine any object that interested me as it met me; but to run about looking for lions was to me intolerable. I had, however, in general to follow the lead, and so have a confused idea of a Statue to Erasmus, a pulpit and skreen, perfect marvels of carving, a whole string of ships commemorating Van Tromp, no *broom* though, some fine marble momuments to the murdered Prince of Orange, and what remains with me beyond them all, the painting of the death of Abel in the Museum of Amsterdam.

Far more than all this sightseeing I enjoyed an excursion to North Holland across the Zuyder Zee. We went to see Brock and Saardam, and on the way, as there was nothing very remarkable in the surrounding scenery, my attention was drawn to some of the passengers in the boat; they were of all degrees, market people, traders, pleasure seekers and travellers, and less noise I suppose was never made by any such number of persons who had nothing else to do but talk and smoke. The smoking was incessant, but as for talking, a word was hardly spoken by any but ourselves.

Another of my peculiarities being the total want of discernment of any brilliant qualities in that lunatick barbarian Peter the Great, Saardam with his little hut, still existing, made small impression. Brock was enchanting, a perfect curiosity, really the fit capital of a Lilliputian fairy tale. It seemed unnatural to see human beings of the usual dimensions moving about this toy of a village. No carriage was allowed to pass through its tiny streets; indeed there would hardly have been room for any much wider than a wheelbarrow. The roads or paths rather, were all paved with coloured stones in patterns. No one ever entered the little, baby houses by the front door but a Bride, or left them thro' this honoured entrance till a corpse; the family only made use of the back door, opening on a little yard as scrupulously clean as our best kept kitchens. We were permitted to enter several of the houses; the people seemed to be accustomed to shew them, and to have the greatest pride in the display of their quantities of heavy handsome furniture, polished up by hard labour to rival the best French varnish. The parlours were never lived in, that was plain, and that any family labours ever went on in the kitchen almost seemed impossible; one could hardly fancy slop pails, dirty dishes, rubbers, brick bats and scrubbing brushes could have profaned for a moment precincts apparently just burnished up for an Exhibition. The inhabitants, though too big for their dwellings, were all as spotlessly clean. Whether any dirt ever made its way to Holland looked problematical. Cooking with stoves is certainly a means of cleanliness, pipkins[1] can be used instead of black pots, and there is no burning to coat the outsides of them with soot.

The great man of the village lived in a much larger baby house than any other person possessed; he had a larger court yard too, and more than an Acre of ground behind, which he had laid out as an English garden in the following style. A wood, a meadow, a labyrinth, a river, a lake, a shady lane, a grove, and a cottage residence. Meandering walks led to all these various beauties, and at different points, in appropriate attitudes, were placed stuffed figures of men, all supposed to be busy about different rural pursuits. At the edge of the wood was a stuffed image of a sportsman properly equipped with belts and bags and a real gun, accompanied by a stuffed dog pointing at a small covey of wooden partridges nestled under a shrub. On a pretty bridge that crossed the river, a stuffed fisher with a basket under his arm held a rod over the stream, while another image on the banks was taking a painted trout off the hook at the end of his line. Under a tree sat a stuffed elderly gentleman with a real book. On the lake were two large painted swans; and in the cottage down the shady lane there were seated by a fictitious kitchen fire an old couple properly dressed, the old man mending a net, the old woman spinning at her wheel, exact representations of the proprietor's parents, in their identical clothing and their own abode, for in this hut they had passed their humble lives, and were thus commemorated by their prosperous son. All the furniture was preserved as it had been left: the bed, the heavy wardrobe, table, chairs, down to the whole kitchen utensils. It was the great man's pleasure to visit this his birthplace constantly, and keep his parents and all around them in repair. The whole garden was the idol of Brock, spoke of with an exultation quite amusing; little nursery people three feet high might have had it for a play thing, but as a real honest pleasure ground to a man weighing fifteen stone, amply fitted out with broadcloth, the fact could hardly be realised.

After Amsterdam came Leyden, the same quaint style of town, where we slept in order to have time to walk over

1. Earthenware cooking pot.

ground trodden, when its University was more famous, by my Grandfather. Then we went on to Haarlem, its environs blooming in their sandy plain, the florists here being the best in all Holland, both the soil and the water particularly suiting the gardener's trade. The water of the famous mere, since partly drained, is equally prized by the laundress, the lime it contains whitening linen so perfectly trunks of clothes come from as far as Paris to undergo the good bleaching they get here. The banker, Mr Hope, has quite a noble villa near the mere, with wonderful gardens round it. Haarlem is a pretty open town, much more cheerful than the old cooped up Cities. It has a fine market place and a great Square, and a beautiful Cathedral, where we went to hear the Organ, once the boast of Europe; there are others, they say, modern ones, finer now, only I never heard them. The performing on this at Haarlem so exhausted the Organist, he requires a high bribe to play more than once a day. We thought he deserved whatever he chose to ask, his taste and his execution were so perfect, and the tones of the Organ, some of them, so exquisite. He told us the windows had been broken once when the full power of the instrument had been called out. Since then they blow more moderately, but a battle piece he gave us, and a storm, were really surprising, the trumpet stops glorious, and the vox humana actually from a Soprano chest.

We had much disturbed our host by choosing to arrive at his hôtel, English fashion, near midnight. Every one was in bed, and to have to get up, light the stove, air linen, prepare so many chambers during the hours of natural sleep, considerably deranged the establishment. Mynherr was very cross, but there were two pretty vrowleins who, though disturbed a bit, kept their tempers that night, and gave us good counsel in the morning. They came in when Jane and I were brushing our hair, and said to us with great civility that these unseasonable arrivals were not the custom of the country, that travellers arranged their movements so as least to inconvenience other parties, and that we should find ourselves more comfortable by conforming to the habits we found established; the meals were better prepared for the regular times than when a chance repast was dished up hurriedly.

After this they proposed to dress our hair. Mine, which reached to my Ankles and was too thick to hold in one hand, they admired in an extasy; and when it had been plaited in strands and wound about my head in their own beautiful fashion, a few ringlets only allowed to hang low upon the cheek and fall still lower behind the ear, I admired it myself abundantly; and so becoming was it thought to be, and so much more easily manageable did I find it, that till I took to caps some years after my marriage, fashion or no fashion, I never altered this most classical arrangement of my golden hair. We very faithfully reported the good advice of our obliging attendants, and found considerable advantage in ever after abiding by it.

Somewhere here we got to Zeist, and then to Utrecht, and so by some means to Arnheim. My recollections of the order of our progress are indistinct. I remember the places we passed through and what we saw in them, and I remember the queer Cabriolets we sometimes travelled in, and the tiresomely slow *trekshuyts* we were condemned to at others, and that is all at this distance of time I can bring to mind: a sort of generalising of the journey. Zeist was pretty, fields and wood, a village, a good inn, and the curious establishment of the Herrnhuters or Moravians within a walking distance. One of the Laboucheres, with a pretty French wife, was living at the inn. The air hereabouts is thought to be particularly salubrious, and she was established here to recover her health after a long illness. We were amused at her *English* shyness about making the slightest approach to acquaintance with us till the two M.P.s mutually recognised one another.[1] My Mother thought it was finery, as we had arrived in two extraordinary post waggons, the horses harnessed with ropes, and we ourselves very dusty. It went off, whichever it was, and we found her both pleasant and useful. She directed us to what was best worth seeing at the Moravian Mission House, namely, their very ingeniously made toys; a whole country exhibited upon a table by means of miniature facsmiles of every article used

1. Actually, the radical Henry Labouchere (1798–1869) was not elected until 1826.

in it, and the people in their national costume besides. We sent a large box full of Dutch representations to the Freres, unknowing of the heavy duty which made it an expensive although an amusing present.

The establishment was a sort of Mr Owen sociable affair;[1] all goods in common, no private property, no homes. Buildings for all purposes were erected round spacious yards. There was a great hall where all assembled for every meal. A Chapel, Workshops, Storerooms, Bedrooms, Schoolrooms. At a certain age the young people were married, at proper time their children entered the School; they had no choice in matrimony, nor any power to bring up their offspring by their own sides; indeed the parents were otherwise employed in this true commonwealth, each person being at some work for a certain number of hours. The premises were scrupulously clean, but very plain, a sort of total abstinence system denying the beautiful and the agreeable. The married men had a peculiar dress all alike, so had the married women, and the old people of each sex, and the young, and the children; and all the private rooms were furnished alike, nothing in them that was not absolutely requisite. I don't think the community were happy, certainly not cheerful, merely contented, and it was an uninteresting, unnatural whim altogether. They would be dull enough were they not kept constantly busy, they make every thing they use, spin, knit, weave, bake, etc., and have a large farm in high order.

Utrecht I forget. A large town with pleasant environs, I think. We took the boat there to Arnheim, and were amused for some miles by the neatness of the villas thickly succeeding each other along the level banks of the Canal. They were all very much alike, long houses with steep roofs, very brightly painted, tiles one colour, walls another, windows and doors a third. They all stand in pretty gardens, with a broad gravel

1. Robert Owen (1771–1858) used his wealth as an industri-
alist to found two communities, New Lanark in Scotland
and New Harmony in the u.s.a., based on the idealistic
principles of his *New View of Society*; for the D.N.B. he was
'an intolerable bore who was the salt of the earth'.

walk leading to a summer house overhanging the water. In this summer house, as the day advanced, we saw many parties smoking and drinking beer out of tall glasses, with the gravity of red Indians—pictures of Dutch enjoyment. Conversation, most surely they never thought of, even a stray remark was rare among them. Words are not wasted in Holland. In our own boat a heavy looking man stood on the deck smoking; he puffed away in a comfortable, composed manner, regardless of all around. Another heavy looking man came up to him with a countenance of exactly the same stolid cast: it was as if a thought of any kind had never crossed the mind of either; he had a pipe in his hand, too, but it was not lighted. The second heavy man approached the first, stood for a moment, not a word, not a sign passed between them; the cold pipe was raised, advanced towards the hot one—they touched—puff, puff, puff at both ends in grave silence. When the cold pipe had lighted, the owner moved away without even a bow passing between the smokers. How much this pair amused us.

Arnheim is beautiful, a pretty town in a very picturesque situation. Nimeguen still more striking; the journey between the two did not strike me sufficiently to be remembered. I recalled the bridge of boats though, by means of which we crossed the Maes, and so entered Flanders. Liège was our next stage, quite a fine city, full of handsome streets and squares and buildings, shops rivalling our own, and hotels very superiour to any we had yet met with. It is the Birmingham of Belgium, a busy manufacturing town, and thriving. I should have liked much to have visited some of the iron works, and we had time enough, for my Mother had caught a feverish cold and had to stay here three days to nurse herself; but none of the rest having my turn for details, they went on as usual hunting out the Hôtel de Ville, the churches and pictures. There is an old Cathedral at Liège worth a visit, otherwise a walk about the town is all that need be attempted. We were returning home from rather a hot one when we found several Carriages crowding the yard, and were told a great English *Milor* had just arrived. It was the Duke and Duchess of Bedford on their way to one of the German Spas for his health, without any of their children, but with Upper

Servants and Under Servants, and their Doctor, good Mr
Wolridge. I had gone up to my Mother and did not see them,
but the rest were glad to meet—at least there was great
chattering.

Nothing could equal the dreariness of the drive the greater
part of the way from Liège to Aix la Chapelle. A wild, barren
heath after the first few miles, on which, at long intervals, we
saw a few poor wretched creatures gathering the manure
from the road to mix with clay and coal dust for fuel. They
formed this composition into neat enough cakes the size of
bricks, and said it made a good strong fire, but the perfume
was the reverse of agreeable. About the middle of our journey
we stopt to rest the horses at a more desolate inn than either
Freeburn or Moulinearn in their worst days. We could get
nothing for ourselves save a very greasy omelette fried in a
bacon pan with lard, and not made of very fresh eggs; there
was some horrible cake of rye flour, and schnapps, for this
was Germany—Prussian Germany. Black eagles with two
heads stuck up every where, and little round sticks girt with
the three colours to mark the boundaries. The postillions were
in long boots, queer hats, the orthodox colours, and they
cracked for ever their thick handled whips, and kept in their
mouths the amber head of the immense pipe they never
ceased smoking. They fed their horses every now and then
with slices of the same rye bread they ate themselves, and
they were fine, tall, handsome men into the bargain. The
gloom of Aix was excessive, ''twas like some vast City of the
dead,' hardly a stir in it. Well built streets, broad, with
handsome houses, all, as it were, shut up, for we never saw
either exits or entrances, and, except the old Cathedral and
the little chair in it on which the corpse of Charlemagne had
been found seated, there was hardly any object of curiosity
in the whole large town. The neighbourhood was equally
uninteresting, there was nothing to recommend the place
but the waters; they rise warm from the Springs, and are
nauseous enough to drink; to bathe in they are delightful
leaving a softness upon the skin and a suppleness among the
bones that invigorate the whole frame. My third bath told
upon my looks quite magically, and I felt so comfortably alive
and alert, that dull as this odious place was, I should have

liked to make the week out; but nobody else could have endured the monotony of fine summer days so lost behind those walls, so we moved again back to Liège, and on to Maestricht, and then to Spa, which pretty place suited us so well we remained there for ten days. It is a hilly country, not unlike Tunbridge Wells, great variety in the scenery, the town clean and cheerful, its one steep street filled with good houses, plenty of them being hotels.

We put up at the best, where we got excellent apartments, and we diverted ourselves by walking, driving, shopping, and drinking the waters, meeting very few of the numerous visitors except early in the morning at the fountains, the *ladies* and gentlemen mostly spending their day round the rouge et noir tables. It was frightful to see them, all pale and anxious except the few who were flushed from excitement, gathered for such an unholy purpose in the lovely Autumn weather. Dupes, sharpers, swindlers, all fermenting together. A son of old Blucher's was undergoing the process of being ruined, and though he had no good looks to recommend him, his youth made one incline to pity him. There were gaming rooms in our hotel. I declare I never passed the green door leading to them without a shudder. As it swung noiselessly to and fro when pushed on either side, it seemed to me to be the barrier Dante sang of, cutting off every hope from all the doomed admitted beyond it.[1] Peace brought all this vice, and how much more, to England. There was evil enough in our country before, but not the open familiarity with degrading pursuits our Continental neighbours habitually indulge. It was then such a curse; it is only perhaps another phase of the guilt of ignorance, for in ignorance we may ascribe all the errours of our imperfect nature, errours that keep us morally and physically beneath what we might be, too frequently rendering an existence miserable that was intended to be all enjoyment. Little as I had accustomed myself to reflect at this time, those dreadful fables forced thought on me. I have ever had such an horrour of swerving from the right path.

We had a much more agreeable subject of contemplation

1. *Divina Commedia:* 'Inferno' I, ii.

across the street. From our sitting room windows, a rather lofty premier, we looked down into the quiet ménage in a lower entresol of an elderly French gentleman and his much younger wife. As their curtains were generally drawn aside, their windows frequently opened, we had by good management the opportunity of investigating all details of their daily life. Madame got up first, rather early, threw on a wrapper, covered herself further with a shawl, slipt her bare feet into *shufflers*, and leaving her plain, unbordered skull night cap over her curl papers, without further ado began to prepare the coffee. When this was ready Monsieur rose, popt on a flowered robe de chambre, tossed away his night cap, stept into his slippers, and then sat down to his coffee. Madame opened the door, evidently to a knock; it was the gazette, which she received and handed to Monsieur. While he read she busied herself in clearing away the coffee tray and setting the room to rights. The beds were soon plumped up into sofas, the draperies drawn back, the chairs and tables put in order, and then the work seemed done. Another tap at the door, the gazette was handed out again, the window curtain was let down, and we were left to imagine the toilet of Monsieur. His appearance at the conclusion of his labours, in about an hour, was perfect; we knew him quite well under his metamorphosis issuing from the door of the house with shining hat, smart redingote,[1] shirt front, cane, moustache, all in high order, and we watched him sauntering off to the Café with an air of easy negligence, quite an amusing contrast to the bustle of Madame. She, after one long look at the retiring form of her beloved, we supposed that they had been but lately married, and she was very pretty, pulled back her curtain and commenced her morning works. Sometimes she sewed, sometimes she clear starched, sometimes she ironed, folded, brushed the clothes. She was never idle. Towards the dinner hour her window was darkened for a while, and when she unveiled her chamber, Monsieur was already within sight, sauntering down the street again to receive a Lady worthy of him. The neatest little figure in the prettiest half dress tripped along the floor to meet him, and away they went

1. Double-breasted French gentleman's coat.

together, as nice looking and as quiet and as happy a pair as could well be seen at the Spa. We could never detect the time of their return home in the evening. The casement, left open by Madame, was always closed at dusk by the maid of the lodging house; no light ever seemed to gleam from within, yet we never failed in the early morning to see the fair lady in her wrapper and her curl papers, looking out for a breath of fresh air before preparing her coffee.

We went from Spa to Maestricht, a large garrison town of most agreeable aspect, and there we waited a couple of days, nothing loth, for letters. The Landlady of an excellent hotel kept a capital table d'hôte. Many of the Officers dined with her, lawyers, merchants, and a few others, her husband among them; he was a notary, with an office at a little distance, and quite as much a guest in his Wife's salon as any of the rest of the company. Madame, short and fat and well dressed, and very obliging, sat at the head of the table, her pretty daughters dispersed along each side; one made the salad, another, who spoke a little English, attended to the travellers; a third, quite a child, seemed to be a pet with the acquaintance. It was quite a gay family party, and really very amusing to strangers; no very refined manners visible, but no ill breeding. Madame had been learning English from her schooltaught daughter, and had got very perfect two small words, which on every occasion she pronounced with a winning smile to my Mother—*Ros bif*—and next day we had two miserable ribs of lean beef at dinner, baked till quite black, out of compliment to our party. A Dutch naval Officer sat next to me, a very agreeable man, and so polite as to dress himself in his Uniform afterwards, because we had none of us seen what was worn by his countrymen. It was not very unlike our own, blue, but turned up, I think, with red. Two Dutch merchants I also got on with so well that the father gave my father his card with his address at Rotterdam, and begged we would let him know when we returned there, as he must give his family the advantage of an introduction to foreigners who had made two days pass so very agreeably to himself and his son. A Frenchman could not have made a neater speech.

Here we saw the last of a Mr Hare, a young Englishman

who had tormented Jane from the hour of our landing in Holland. They had met in some passage in the Badthouse at Rotterdam, and he had neglected no opportunity of throwing himself, ever after, in her way. He even addressed her, not rudely, not at all, but humbly, laid nosegays at her feet, sent her flowers by Ward the maid, stood in doorways and sighed, looked up at windows in languishing despair, followed her not only from street to street but from place to place. We found him at the Hague the morning after our arrival, at Amsterdam as soon as ourselves, at Liège immediately after us. We only escaped him at Spa from some misapprehension about our journey there, for he used to waylay Ward and try to bribe her with large sums of money to deliver notes and give him intelligence of our plans. He tried the courier too, and I am pretty sure made more of him than of little indignant Ward, who, after many minor repulses, at last made him a long speech in the style of Mrs Nickleby to the man with the vegetable marrow,[1] and with equal effect, for this poor Mr Hare was insane, had escaped from his friends, and was not recovered by them till he had reached Maestricht. Many years afterwards, when Jane was Mrs Pennington, she met him, also married, quite rational, and perfectly oblivious of his wanderings in the Netherlands.

Whereabouts could we have seen Cleves. We certainly passed through this most beautiful little Duchy. A little paradise it seemed to be, with its rich fields, its wooded hills and old Castles upon heights. All this German scenery was very pretty, and so was the part of Flanders we next proceeded to. We had to return to Liège, and then we travelled up the Maese, an enchanting journey; past Huy, such a perfect picture of beauty, to Namur, a large fortified town. Here, though I was never noted for a painter's eye, I recollect nothing so well as a large picture of the Crucifixion by Vandyke, *unrolled* for us to examine. With pride the priest told us it had never been to France. When Buonaparte carried off all the Spoils of all countries to embellish the Louvre, this gem was saved by being taken down from its place over the high altar of the Cathedral, removed out of its

1. Dickens, *Nicholas Nickleby*, Chapter XXIII.

frame, rolled up, and hid in a chimney. They were just going to replace it, there being no longer any fear of French invasions. The works of Vandyke always touch me, as do the few paintings I have seen of the Italian Masters. This consists but of two figures, the Christ on the Cross, his Mother beneath it. It has never gone out of my head. For many months after seeing it, it came back to me in my dreams, or when I was sitting quietly at work alone. I can't tell what it was that attracted me. I have no knowledge of colouring, or grouping, or even of correct outline, so that all the beauties of the painting could never be described by one so ignorant. I felt them though, and I rather think that would have satisfied the Artist himself nearly as well as the panegyrick of a connoisseur! They do talk such stuff with their technical round about phrases.[1]

The next point was Gemappes, the little rather bleak village on the hill near Quatre Bras. We dined in a room the walls of which still bore the marks of Cannon balls. The girl who waited on us had been in the house during the battle, saw the Highland regiments trot up in their peculiar fashion through the town, the people crowding out of their doors to offer them a snatch of refreshments as they quickly passed. She sang to us, in a loud, shrill voice, a few bars of some tune bearing a resemblance to the White Cockade, so that it must have been the 92nd, the gallant Gordons, that every one liked so much! those charming men with petticoats, who, when billeted on the inhabitants, helped to make the soup and rock the cradle for the half frightened mistress of the family. On the table where we had sat to eat, so many wounded Officers had lain under the Surgeon's knife. In the room overhead so many had died; the garden had been destroyed, the fields had been desolated, losses of all kinds had been suffered during those dreadful days, yet for this no one blamed Napoleon. We found his great name treasured in almost every heart, every where except in Holland proper, where neither he nor any of his dynasty were popular. Here in Flanders they made no secret of preferring any Sovereign to their present Dutch

1. *Baedeker's* first English edition (1869) suggests this
   picture is a copy.

one. The Flemings are half Spanish, half French; there is no similitude whatever between them and the nation they have been ill advisedly joined to; *had been*, I should say, for the forced union did not last long.[1]

On reaching Brussels we put up at the Hôtel de Bellevue in the Place Royale, just for a couple of days while we looked about us, for the whole aspect of this particularly pretty town was so agreeable to my Mother, now quite tired of travelling, that it was determined to take a house here for a month, and send for our friend Amelia Ferrier. We spent two mornings, my father and I, walking about the high and new town, looking for lodgings, and all over the low and old town, admiring both, so beautiful they are in different ways. The Place Royale in the high town is the fashionable residence of the Court, some of the nobles, most of the strangers; the houses are like palaces, three fine rows enclosing a large oblong park, very agreeably laid out in shady walks. A steep street, the Montagne de la cour, leads from this to the low town, where all the publick buildings are to be found; and there are the ramparts, a broad causeway with neat houses on one side, and fine trees in a row upon the other. A good many handsome equipages rolled about during the middle of the day; there was plenty of traffick going forward, plenty of handsome well filled shops, foot passengers in constant variety, all well dressed, and the women mostly wearing very coquettishly the becoming Spanish Mantilla instead of shawl and bonnet, so disposed as by no means to conceal the features. The whole scene was gay, it was quite a place to fall in love with. Cheap, too, as we found Flanders generally; nearly half as cheap again as Holland, and about a third cheaper than the short experience we had of Germany.

The people spoke French in Brussels so well that we got on most easily with them, and very soon settled all our business. We fixed on apartments in a fine house in the Place Royale belonging to a Cotton manufacturer whose principal residence was close to his Mill in the country. He only used the ground floor of his town house during occasional visits to the

1. It ended with the outbreak of the Belgian revolution in 1830.

City and let all the upper part. We had on the first floor a dining and a drawing room and my Mother's bedroom, all communicating; on the second floor four good bedrooms, and there were rooms in a back wing for the servants. We required no additional plagues, the Courier dusting, and the porter's daughter helping Ward upstairs; for our dinner came from a traiteur in a tray on a boy's head, cheaper than we could have cooked it at home, and very much better. We ordered it for *six*, and there was always more left than the servants wanted. Breakfast and tea the Courier managed, our obliging landlord allowing us to boil our kettle on his stove. The entrance to our 'palace home' was through a *porte cochère* into a yard surrounded by low buildings used for warehouses. A staircase, broad and handsome, led up to our apartments; they were neatly finished, the drawing room indeed handsomely, and with its cheerful look out on the Parc, it was a very pleasant sitting room, particularly after we had put a harp and a pianoforte into it. Unpacking was a short business, for we travelled light, so soon felt at home in our new situation.

# CHAPTER TWENTY-THREE

## 1819–1820

THE day we moved from the hotel, just before despatching our last truck full of luggage, my father, who had gone out alone on some errand, returned accompanied by a country man, a gentleman he had known in his youth, Mr Pryse Gordon, a good looking, busy mannered person, with whom the world had not gone altogether well whoever had been to blame for it. He had been, he said, for some time settled in Brussels, and from a perfect knowledge of the place might be of some use to us, where so many were on the alert to take every advantage of strangers.[1] He very much regretted our precipitation in taking a house so entirely on chance, and unguardedly throwing ourselves quite into our Landlord's hands by employing all his tradespeople, the Belgians being rogues from top to bottom. He would take care in future to preserve us from this race of harpies by going with us himself to all shops as a protection, these crooked traders knowing him well, and knowing, too, that he would not suffer his friends to be imposed upon. Mrs Gordon, who was ill, or she would immediately have done herself the honour of waiting on my Mother, would introduce us to respectable milliners and dress makers; they would also shew us a little of Brussels society—do their best to make our sojourn agreeable. If we

1.  See *Personal Memoirs or Reminiscences of Men and Manners at Home and Abroad during the last half century, with occasional Sketches of the Author's Life*—being *Fragments from the Portfolio of Pryse Gordon Esquire*, which he published in 1830; four years later came his *Belgium and Holland, with a Sketch of the Revolution in the year 1830*—this included a chapter entitled 'Hints to English families settling in Brussels'.

had never read Gil Blas,[1] we might have been more grateful to him. There was something that jarred against our sympathies in some way in his many professions; that is, we young people fancied we could do just as well without him. My father and mother were quite delighted at meeting so zealous a friend. We therefore kept our own Counsel, but as far as I could manage if I prevented Mr Gordon's interference, the rather that in one or two trifling instances I found I had made better bargains for myself than he would have made for me. The black Courier detested him, I fancy their vocations clashed; neither did Monsieur François like me, as he required a watchful eye over his proceedings; he cheated us in spite of being looked after, but he would have made a much larger private purse had Mademoiselle not learned the value of the different moneys, and picked up useful words both in Dutch and German. One thing Mr Gordon certainly did well for us, he gave us the names of the best masters. Whether, poor people, he made them pay for the recommendation there is no saying. We lost not a franc, for their terms being known we paid them the customary fees, no more.

Education at Brussels was remarkably good at this time. Many English families were living there on account of the excellence and cheapness of the Masters. We took advantage of three, Henri Bertini for the pianoforte, a lesson from whom was worth at least half a dozen from an inferiour professor. His wife for the Harp, rather a so so teacher; and inimitable Monsieur Sacré for dancing. He was the Master of the Ceremonies at the palace, most particularly attentive to the *Deportment*, yet taking the greatest trouble with the most curiously minute incidents of every day life, as relating to the manners. He gave his pupils an ease of movement that very few inherited from nature. He must have been descended from Monsieur Jourdain's celebrated Teacher, for the importance of his art filled his whole understanding.[2] He used to give us long lectures upon simple elegance, act awkwardness before

1. *Histoire de Gil Blas de Santillane* by Alaine René le Sage (1734), translated by Smollet in 1761.
2. See Molière's *Le Bourgeois Gentilhomme* (1770).

us, and then triumphantly ask which style would have greatest effect on the sympathies of our neighbour in every circumstance of life. Amelia Ferrier listened to him so gravely, so with an air of fully appreciating his reasoning, that between them we could hardly keep the entertainment they gave us within the bounds of good breeding.

Mr Ferrier had not been able to accompany his daughter. He sent her with a friend, Mr Steuart, the Editor of the Courier, a most clever, amusing little man sadly in want of a few lessons from Monsieur Sacré, for he was so thoroughly vulgar as to be some times annoying, but very witty; so up to the times, too, acquainted with every thing and every body, and so shrewd in his remarks he quite enlivened us. He delighted in musick, so that every evening while he staid we had quite a Concert. Both Amelia and I were anxious to have had some singing lessons; a celebrity was therefore engaged, but my father, who superintended the first interview, took good care to preserve us from a second. My father was unable to endure the new system of the 'sons de tête', such an ease to the singer . . . all the notes must be formed in the chest, and those that could not be thus reached, had to be let alone. The chest notes certainly are fuller, more satisfactory to a musical ear than the head notes, unless these last are excellently well produced, which they were not always in the beginning from want of practice probably. In our present day, by careful study, there is really no knowing where the two voices join, or part, and our taste being now formed to this falsetto, its sweetness and its *truth*, for being easily reached, these upper notes are never flat, quite reconcile us to what was condemned as a serious fault in the days of our fathers. Even the Italians now teach in this mode.

Our early mornings being thus occupied in agreeable studies, we devoted the middle of every day to walks about the town, or drives in the environs; the evenings we occasionally spent in such society as was accessible to us, not the best by any means, Brussels being then the refuge for all the scum and dregs of Britain. It would have required a good introduction to get at all among the Belgian *noblesse*, the specimens within their view making them very difficult of access by our countrymen. The Prince of (I forget the name) alone, who laid himself out to entertain the English, invited my father and William twice or thrice to dine. The company they met they described as no way remarkable; but they both of them spoke french so badly they were quite unequal to judge of any one's conversational powers in that language. The banquet was like one in London, with two or three slight differences.

We ladies had to put up with Mr and Mrs James Conynghame and George—the married brother had been long done up and was living with his really nice wife on a small allowance granted to him by his creditors, to whom the father Sir James, made over his income. George was run out and was recruiting queer disagreeable odd pleasant ugly old Beau of mine—Mr and Mrs Wynne Aubrey, or in full as he was a younger son, Mr and Mrs Henry Harcourt Wynne Aubrey, precisely under the same delapidated circumstances. She, such a pretty woman, beautiful indeed, a great deal handsomer than Mrs Munro her sister. Two or three more there were of this same creditable description, and one very nice family who had certainly come to Brussels to economise while educating their many children; but then they had the sure prospect of a few years of prudent saving setting their affairs all right again. Mr Houlton had been building a very fine house. We may all know the cost of that amusement. Mrs Houlton, a fair specimen of a thoroughly English woman, handsome and pleasant, looked well after all under her control. The eldest son was in the Army, not with them; the second, a dear little George, was worth making a pet of. The two elder girls were beauties in different styles; the second, a Brunette, played the guitar in Spanish fashion, not picking at the strings, but sweeping them with the thumb, and she sang Spanish and Portuguese airs to this accompaniment so bewitchingly we were not at all surprised to hear afterwards that she had married well before she was 17. There was no danger of her marrying *ill* with that wide awake mother; and so the pretty Fanny never married at all. There were several clever younger sisters, but none of them possessed the remarkable good looks of the elder ones. We got extremely intimate with these Houltons, spent many walking or driving mornings, and happy musical evenings,

together. They were from the West of England, from somewhere near Bowood, Lord Lansdowne's, I visited there, I
forget the County.

All this time Mrs Gordon never came to call. He was with
us daily, and had managed to carry us to his hairdresser and
his shoemaker and his dressmaker, etc. I really believe they
were all the best in their line, and they may not have charged
us with the *douceur* given to our obliging friend—or they
may; there was no knowing. At this period of our acquaintance suspicion of the cause of all the trouble taken for us had
not entered into the heads of the most influential among us. A
stray word of Mr Steuart of the Courier first enlightened us.
Speaking of him once after his regular daily visit, when he
had been as usual all kindness and very cheerful and
agreeable, 'Ah,' said Mr Steuart, 'poor devil! I wonder how
the deuce the fellow gets on; never did a man throw
opportunities away as did that poor Pryse Gordon, clever,
very gentlemanly man, quite cleared out long before he had
to run for it, how on earth does he manage to live here? On
his countrymen? eh? a per centage on all wares perhaps
supplied by *his* tradesmen. He had not a penny left, nor has
he any way of earning one. Who was the wife? had *she*
money?' That bit of news it seemed as if we were not likely to
know. Mr Gordon made the civilest apologies for her non
appearance, but she never came; her cold remained so very
oppressive that she, being a delicate person, could not
venture out so late in the year, September or October, while
any cough continued. At length, the day after Mr Steuart
departed to resume his editorial duties in London, Mrs
Gordon's cough had sufficiently moderated and Mr Gordon
brought her to see us, literally brought her, for she was
evidently unwilling to come. She was very awkward, very
reserved in manner, extremely silent, and instead of the
slight delicate looking woman we expected, she was a great
rawboned giantess with a scorbutick face. She must have had
a fortune; that we were persuaded of. We found from George
Conyngham that it was a *jointure*, and that she had been
married for her beauty in very early youth.

The call was returned, and then came an invitation to an
Evening party; neither Mary nor I inclined to go, nor Amelia

Ferrier, most luckily as the affair turned out. The rest accepted this civility, and Jane gave us the following account of the entertainment. In a very handsome room, scantily furnished, about twenty of the British inhabitants of Brussels were assembled, tea and cakes and lemonade were the refreshments, cards the amusement—a whist table, and a party at Stop Commerce. Every one who played Commerce had a franc in the Pool. Jane won, and was preparing to receive from George Conyngham the contents of the Cup, when the large hand of Mr Pryse Gordon arrested the movement. 'Pardon me, my dear young lady, I thought I had mentioned it; in this house we always play for the poor.' So saying, he poured the money, fifteen or sixteen francs, into a bag he took from a table drawer. We commented among ourselves upon this charitable transaction, and our eyes opening wider by the help of Ward, who got her knowledge from the Courier, we began to make out the true character of our new acquaintance; the depth to which had fallen a man equal by birth and education to the best of the society into which he had been early introduced. We did not find out his whole delinquencies, *her* history, till we were on the point of leaving Brussels. John Ferrier and his young wife, who had been travelling on the Rhine, came to pick up his sister Amelia and carry her home; and he told my brother William that Mrs Gordon had more than one jointure although she had never been a wife before, and that Mr Gordon went twice a year to England to receive for her these different annuities. Fancy the family horrour. 'Such an ugly creature too,' said my Mother. It was a most disagreeable adventure, though in reality no harm came of it. It was worth something in the way of experience, teaching a prudent caution as to the admittance of our travelling compatriots to intimacy.

A much pleasanter visit was paid by us to the country house of our Landlord. We did not all go, being now, with the John Ferriers, a large party; but I was one of the selected, having become through the medium of our housekeeping transactions quite on the most friendly terms with our Landlady. Monsieur frequently remained in town a week or more at a time, when business was lively. Madame seldom staid above a day or two at a time, much preferring her very

pretty house at the Factory, where we were very kindly
pressed to pass a day. I was in hopes we should have gone out
early enough to have had time to go all over the Mills, where
the whole process of cotton cleaning, spinning, weaving,
dyeing, printing, was carried on by the largest number of
hands employed in one concern in Belgium. However, we
were only ready for the early dinner, the Master keeping the
Workmen's hours as he superintended all matters himself.
The family consisted of the round headed, plain mannered,
thoroughly business like father; a mother infinitely more
alive—a good, homely, managing housewife too, yet seeing
beyond the cotton; a quiet, pretty, married daughter, with
two fat children and a silent husband, the Manager of the
Factory; two unmarried daughters likely to turn out as well
as their elder sister; and one son, College bred, a little
inclined to keep the spinning jennies out of sight while
making abundant use of their produce. He was particularly
well dressed, spoke French well, aped the Frenchman
indeed, and not badly at all, which 'youthful extravagances'
the good mother smiled, assuring mine that this would all
subside by and bye, and that he would become reasonable as
years passed, and become as respectable a manufacturer as
his ancestors; for the Mill had been for some generations the
patrimony of the family. She was a dear sensible old lady,
looked up to by her whole household. The dinner she gave us
was quite in the old Fleming style, very long, oddly served,
dish by dish, not in the order we are accustomed to; soup
first, some sweet things, the bouilli, different dressed meats,
fish, more sweets, game and larks, and other little birds—mere
mouthfuls, some no bigger than a walnut—fruit and cheese
together, plenty of beer and wine handed round, and coffee
directly after in another room. A walk in the pleasure
grounds, and then the drive home before dark, in full time
for our own tea. Next morning Madame came in with her
husband in his gig, to make her marketings while he loaded
waggons with bales of his finished goods, a good store of
which he always kept steady in the spacious warerooms
round the yard. I quite liked these good people and they were
so obliging. I found her recommendations to tradespeople
much more effective than Mr Gordon's. Her silk mercer gave

us infinitely better bargains than were offered us by his. My father gave us each a silk dress to remember Brussels by, and my Mother got three, all of them neatly made up by a French mantua maker, and exceedingly admired after our return home, though really I could not see that they were any way superiour either in make or fabrick to what we could have procured in Edinburgh. They were certainly cheaper though.

One of the pleasures of Brussels was walking about the pretty, clean town. Besides the shopping, there was a great deal to see in the old low town, ancient buildings and other monuments, numerous fountains in open areas amongst the rest, always surrounded by amusing groups, for there was no supply of water through pipes to every house. Perhaps this was one cause of the indelicate manners of the people; nothing near so bad as the Dutch in this respect, who are positively indecent, openly so, unpleasantly so to strangers unaccustomed to the simplicity or the coarseness of such habits. The Flemings are a degree or two more refined, still there is room for great improvement. One fountain I never could pass in any comfort; it really was only fit for playing at a Hindù festival, and strange to say, Hindostanée virtues were ascribed to the use of it. A turn on the Ramparts of a fine afternoon was delightful. Any day, rain or no rain, we could stroll in the parc, the gravel there being kept in exact order. There we constantly met the two nice little boys of the Prince of Orange, who played out half the day with their balls and hoops and bats, etc., attended by a single footman in livery. The children were plainly dressed in nankin trowsers, round blue jackets, and white hats, and they kept quite aloof from the servant, though he managed to have them always in his eye. The Abbé Sieyès, too, walked regularly in these gardens, a small, thin, thoughtful man with gray hair, a grave smile, and courteous manner; he reminded us of Belleville, wearing his stick in the same style, held out from his hands crossed behind him.[1] Another 'silent Monitor,' as some one

1. Abbé Emmanuel Joseph Sieyès (1748–1836), who
   helped to draft no less than three constitutions during
   the Revolution, was exiled to Brussels as a regicide and
   only returned to France in 1830.

calls these marked objects on the stream of time, was the balcony before the windows of the Hôtel de Ville whence the Duke of Alva leaned to witness his massacres of the Huguenots.¹ We are better than our fathers. Somewhat less cruel at any rate.

We had a pleasant drive one morning to Louvaine, where the sight lovers inspected the curious Hôtel de Ville. I forget how many storeys of atticks it has in its steep roof, rows of storm windows one over the other. And then we went to Lacken, the country palace of the King, only a few miles out of town and hardly a very healthy situation, lying low, a great deal of water and too much wood near the house, but very pretty and very enjoyable as a private residence, every thing that is most agreeable to rural life being in profusion—gardens, a farm, a park, a lake, and a most convenient abode fitted up with taste quite unostentatiously. The Palace in the Place Royale, on the contrary, was furnished magnificently. If I remember right, felt slippers were put on over our shoes before any of us, ladies or gentlemen, were allowed to step over the highly polished inlaid floors, and where our eyes were quite dazzled with gold, silver, chrystal, velvet, and bijouterie.

And then we went to Waterloo. Oh, will there ever be another war! At first sight there was nothing, as it seemed, to look at. A wide plain under crop, a few rising grounds wooded, a hamlet or two, and the forest of Soigny. An old man of the name of Lacoste—an old cheat, I believe—in a blouse, striped night cap, and immense shoes, came up as a guide to all the different points of interest, and did his part well, although his pretension to having been the attendant of Buonaparte during the Battle and his director in his flight was a fable. He took us up to the ruins of Houguemont, to La Haie Sainte, to the hollow with the *paved* road in the bottom of it where the Guards felt themselves so at home, to the wide

1. The Duke of Alva, Governor of the Netherlands for Philip II of Spain between 1567 and 1573, tried to quell rebellion by executing twenty-five nobles (not *Huguenots*, who were French protestants) on 5 June 1568 in the market place in front of the Hôtel de Ville.

mound raised by the heaps of the slain, to the truncated column of black marble erected to the memory of an hero. At this distance of time I do not remember all we saw, and I did not attend to all he told, mistrusting his veracity. The scene was impressive enough gazed on silently; and then to think of the terrour in Brussels, of the despair in the neighbouring villages, of the two armies individually and collectively, of the two Commanders and all that hung upon the strife so lately ended! This was but the fourth year after the victory, the world was still full of the theme, but there was little trace of the struggle left upon the ground it had been fought on. Fine crops of corn had been this very Autumn waving there, though the plough still turned up relicks of the eventful day. Monsieur Lacoste had a sack full of trophies he said had been found upon the field.[1] The feeling of the people most certainly did not go with the victors. They hated the Union with the Dutch, they hated the Dutch King ruling over them; the habits and manners of the two ill cemented nations were totally dissimilar, and with the French they amalgamated readily. The Emperour really lived in their hearts, spite of the Conscription, spite of his defeat, spite of his crimes, as we may call the consequences of his ambition.

One day my father and I, walking out a good mile into the country, we came to a tidy looking farmhouse, which, as we stopt to examine, the owner of civilly asked us to enter. We crossed a yard and were ushered at once into the Cow stable, where at the Upper end, in a space separated by a latticed-partition from the long row of milch cattle, the family lived. The place was clean, all the dairy utensils hanging round the walls were bright, and the cows were very comfortably stalled, a neat pavement running up the whole length of the building with a drain between it and the animals. After we had made what observations we chose here, the farmer opened a door into the best room, where, French fashion,

1. *Baedeker* first edition in English (1869 but the eleventh in German) comments 'Genuine relics are still occasionally turned up by the plough, but it need hardly be observed that most of those which the traveller is importuned to purchase are spurious'.

was a bed with a canopy over it and all the good furniture: massive, highly polished and well carved presses, chests, chairs and tables. In one corner was the treasure of the family, a crucifix as large as life, the figure glaringly painted, always a distressing object to me and a sort of shock when represented thus coarsely. On the wall close to this hung not a bad print of Napoleon. I don't know which the old Fleming regarded with most veneration.

A Flemish farm is small generally, the fields small, dull looking from the absence of living beings, the cattle being mostly kept in the house. Their agriculture rather disappointed my father. A great many mouths are certainly fed for the acres, but no fortunes are made by the farmers, who are all mere peasants living in the most homely way on the produce of their industry, providing themselves with all necessaries as in more primitive times, going to market with what they can spare, giving a fixed proportion of the profits to the Landlord when the cultivators do not themselves own their little domains, and buying nothing that can by any possibility be made at home. They all seemed contented; there were few poor, no beggars, no rags. Notwithstanding the under current of discontent, the surface betrayed no approaching danger; it would have been difficult to suppose another revolution so near at hand as it proved to be. Very likely the priests had something to do with the deposition of the Presbyterian House of Orange.[1] The Flemings are much attached to their own superstitions. Little Virgins and other saints in Boxes stand in many conspicuous places; the Altars in all the churches were gaily decorated and seldom without kneeling figures round them; and shows went about of Mount Calvary and the holy family and the martyrs, etc., all figures on stages, as large as life, dressed up in real garments, before which unpleasant appearances crowds kneeled in mute devotion. There were quantities of images in the Churches, all very fine, silks, velvets, jewels, and some in wigs truly ridiculous. The worshippers as much in earnest as

1. The Belgian revolt broke out in 1830; E.G. (by then the wife of a protestant Irish landowner of Orange sympathies) was writing thirty years after this visit.

the Hindùs with their horrible figures. More so than many of us who from the heights of our spiritual simplicity pity what we think a mockery, and what is certainly a strange remains of barbarity to linger on for eighteen centuries after the truth was preached.

We were very sorry to leave Brussels. We had passed a very pleasant month there one way or another but the Autumn was advancing and we had the sea to cross and so we must begin our journey home. We returned by Valenciennes and Malines and gloomy Ghent, where of course we were shewn the house of Philip von Artevelde.[1] Other Friesland heroes were recalled many a time during our pleasant journey and then we rested a few days at Antwerp, John Ferrier having business there, and we besides the publick sight seeing, having a whole morning's work in viewing a private collection of paintings belonging to a Banker or a Merchant, who had spent a life time and a fortune very happily in forming this gallery. Mr Steuart had got tickets of admission for us, the *chapeau de paille* being the attraction, but many fine pictures deserved as much notice to the full. A few years after the Banker died, the Collection was dispersed, sold, and we saw the fair third wife of Rubens in a small room in Pall Mall, by herself, just before she became the property of Sir Robert Peel.[2]

Antwerp might be a noble town, perhaps it was once. Now, the wide streets are empty, the destruction of its harbour put an end to its commerce. All the fine buildings looked deserted, no new houses were rising anywhere. Very few vessels were in the river and those were of a small size. Buonaparte filled up the bed of the Scheldt in order to ruin the City and yet they like his memory. The docks are splendid but empty. It really was a melancholy place,

1. An authoritarian ruler who seized power in 1381 but died in battle two years later against Charles VI of France.
2. This famous portrait of Susanna Fourment (elder sister of Hélène, Ruben's second wife) was auctioned in Antwerp in 1822 and shown in London the following year when it was bought by Peel for the unprecedented sum of £3000.

although still there is a great deal to be seen in it. Pictures of course in plenty—the Descent from the Cross, with its two accessary wings over the high altar in the Cathedral being the *gem*. The Magdalen kneeling quite in front, her back to the Spectator, her long fair hair streaming down upon a peculiar coloured leghorn tinted gown,[1] was like a regality. Some where I saw a Madre dolorosa, whether it was here or not I cannot say. She was seated on the ground, with her son's body on her knees, there were no other figures in the picture.[2] I could have worshipped her myself, almost, her expression forbade piety. No wonder these creations added to the imposing effect of ceremonial processions and other means of exciting the imagination, take such hold of the feelings of sensitive and ignorant people, whose reasoning powers are of the weakest.

At the hôtel at Antwerp, an exceedingly comfortable one, we were waited on entirely by men. They called us in the mornings, entered our bedrooms with the jugs of hot water etc., made the beds even. We saw no maid servants—in any department. We went to Vespers in the Cathedral on the Sunday Evening, quite an Opera. An orchestra of all instruments and excellent choir, and next morning resumed our journey and soon found ourselves in an open boat on Holland's deep with a cold gale blowing and a good stiff shower meeting us when half way over. We passed Dort, saw piles of common crockery ware in stalls, on the pavements, in barges, and gladly resumed our pleasant quarters in the Badthouse at Rotterdam. Here we had a great deal to do. Every evening was spent at the Ferriers. All the mornings my father was packing his old China, quantities of which he had picked up here and there in the course of our wanderings, always despatching his purchases to Rotterdam to await our arrival. So heavy was then the duty upon foreign porcelaine, it would have cost a fortune to have sent all this Collection

1. Straw-coloured (straw-plaiting for hats came from Livorno in Tuscany).
2. This masterpiece was painted by Rubens between 1611 and 1614; it had only been returned to the Cathedral in 1814 after twenty years in Paris during the war.

home through the Custom House—it was therefore to reach us by degrees, a barrel of butter or herring or such commodities as these plates and dishes could be packed amongst was to be entrusted to our old friend the skipper of the Van Egmont every return journey he made, and positively most of these treasures in time reached us, the skipper not always taking the trouble to put them up as directed. There were private holes and corners in the Van Egmont, as the Master and Mate well knew, the mate *too* well knew, for on occasion of a quarrel between the two, the little merry mate who had been quite a favourite with us, imparted the secrets of the old tub to the Leith Custom house Officers and so half ruined his Captain. Dowran had been returned home in the same way. Mr Ferrier kept the unhappy creature till the moment for embarking, when he was taken on board in a sack and tied upon deck during the first part of his voyage. On his release he took possession of William's old bed and kept his chamber till he landed!

It was a sad leavetaking when we parted from the Ferriers. We embarked from their house for Harwich, not in the regular packet but in one which on this occasion carried the Mail. We had a stormy passage, a *pitchy* sea, the result of a storm just lulling, with a wind ahead. Even I who never suffer at sea, was ill enough for an hour or two. There were few passengers, only one at all remarkable, a little old Jew, very much frightened at the heaving of the troubled waters. He was a queer sort of dealer in odd knick knacks, pulling out quantities of valuable old fashioned jewellery from every part of his dress, for he had tucked it all away, here and there about his clothing, much after the fashion of Filch.[1] We could not help suspecting that, squally as it was, he had more to do than the wind with the difficulty of our little packet making the proper harbour. Instead of landing at Harwich, we were put ashore some few miles up the coast at a small village, where the Custom House Officer seldom expecting strangers, was certainly far from vigilant. Our inn was village like—clean beds its greatest luxury. After the palace hotels we had been accustomed to of late, the little ill furnished

1. A character in John Gay's *Beggar's Opera* (1728).

parlours, the closet bedrooms, and the inferiour style of establishment altogether in these English Country inns, made an unfavourable first impression. The hack post chaises were no worse than our cabriolets, and the horses were better, but then they were not open—there was the want of air. We saved the trouble of changing much luggage by having sent all we could spare by the Van Egmont.

It was an ugly journey all through the flats and the fens of the East Coast on to Newcastle, with but one remarkable object on the route, the Cathedral at Lincoln. The first church I saw abroad struck me as bare, so cold, with so much white washed wall and so very little ornament. The first I saw again at home seemed only like an aisle of the others, rich enough in carvings, pillars, stained glass, and so on, but so confined, so narrow, so small, all stuffed up with seats for dignatories. I missed the grand space that to the unaccustomed eye had seemed desolate. Has habit much to do with taste, after all. Do foreigners admire our florid gothick. I felt as if there were not room to move in the Cathedral, Lincoln, after being but a mite in the one at Antwerp.

At Newcastle we met Lord Grey[1] carrying some of his daughters home in a handsome travelling barouche, beside which our two hack chaises drew up, much to the annoyance of some of our party. Explanations, however, set all right, and we proceeded in our humble equipages with minds more at peace than under the circumstances could have been expected. We had all through travelled in two divisions. My father, my Mother and I and Ward. And William, Jane, Mary and the Courier. With him, however, we had parted at Brussels, where he had got a good engagement, to our relief. The people every where had taken us at first for two distinct families. My father and I they supposed to be man and wife, and my Mother was his Mother in law. William and Mary were the Monsieur and Madame of the other carriage, and Jane the sister in law; not bad guesses. My father looked like my Mother's son, and I looked far too old to be his daughter. William infinitely too old to be his son and Jane and William

1. Charles, second Earl Grey (1764–1845), was one of the leaders of her father's Whig party.

were so alike they could not be mistaken for brother and sister. We were quite amused at all these erroneous impressions, and the younger ones eager still further to mystify our hosts and hostesses and my father in the front of the fun, but we saw soon that it seriously annoyed my Mother. She had no idea of acting *Madame* mère to the whole party, so we had to restrain our mirth when she was by.

We reached Edinburgh late in the evening of the very last day in the month of October, welcomed back by the two highland maids, Mr Caw and poor old Dowran; the poor dog had been faithfully delivered over to Peggy and seemed glad to be at home and took kindly to his old quarters, generally lying contented by the kitchen fire, after having made a regular survey of every room in the house to satisfy himself there was really no one in it. He had once or twice set out for a walk but had never gone far, nor ever minded who came in or who went out or heeded the door bell. The night we arrived he was sleeping on the hearth. When the chaises stopt, he roused himself, pricked up his ears, got upon his feet and when the bell rang, he flew up the stairs, bounded along the passage, darted out of the door like a mad thing and passing our carriage, threw himself panting and barking up into William's arms as he was stepping out of his. There was combination in that dog's head, something far beyond instinct, quite akin to reason. *Fright* herself, clever as she is, is not more intelligent than was poor Dowran.

The length of time that has passed away since we made this pleasant little tour in the Netherlands has caused forgetfulness of a thousand details which always add so much to the interest of any account of the first impressions of a foreign country. In talking over our travels with our good friend Miss Bessy Clerk, we used to keep her laughing by the hour at several of our adventures, none of which can I now recall. My father discouraged much conversation on the subject, he having a great objection to any egotistical display of whatever kind; the less people obtruded themselves upon the rest of the world, the better, he thought, the world liked them; besides the check to individual vanity where a prudent reserve regarding the actions, feelings, and intentions of dear self was exercised. So we soon fell back upon local topicks.

It was our last winter in Edinburgh and a gloomy one. The Law point between my father and Ballindaloch concerning the navigation of the Spey, had been appealed to the House of Lords and was a very breathless anxiety— it was a very costly suit, had we lost it ruin would have overwhelmed us some years the sooner. It was gained but at great cost and while it was pending my Mother neither liked going out nor letting us go. Jane went sometimes to our intimate friends, with all of whom she was very popular and her lively descriptions much diverted us stay at homes. When she set off on her gaieties, my Mother read aloud to Mary and me as we sat at work beside her.

There were great riots in the West Country[1] during this winter, and the yeomanry called out to keep the quarrelsome in order. Our friend and neighbour, William Gibson, quite vain of his appearance in the handsome uniform, took several occasions of running in when dressed, as if accidentally, in order we supposed to be admired. He and I had fallen out before we went abroad and we never rightly fell in again, for there was an under current of ill breeding, which sometimes broke through the artificial manner that imposed on most persons, and shocked my 'gentle' highland blood. He was a little spoiled, known to be the heir of his wealthy father and still wealthier Cousin, Mr Craig of Riccarton; the idea, therefore, of his studying for the Bar struck us all as absurd. Of course he did not spend much time over his law books, and having besides a curious habit of falling in love with every girl, no, but women he met with, even plain, stupid, elderly women if none more attractive were at hand, his father determined to send him to travel. My father and mother were sorry to see him go; he was a favourite, and has turned out so as fully to justify their early partiality. Probably the going laid the foundation of that better style of manner and feeling which have made his middle age so every way superiour to his youth.[2]

1. Strikes and riots in Glasgow culminated in the *Radical War* of April 1820 when radical weavers were dispersed in a skirmish at Bonnymuir.
2. E.G.'s sister Jane married his brother James.

Uncle Ralph had brought his family to Edinburgh, let Tennochside, and taken an excellent house in the most out of the way part of the town, getting it for a trifle on account of its situation in St John's Street—a blind lane off the Cannongate. James Hamilton was with them, he and Edmund having a Tutor between them to prepare them for College. They came a very short time before we left, otherwise our winter would have been pleasanter. There were many publick rejoicings although private affairs had been gathering gloom. The old Queen Charlotte had died and George the 3rd ditto. The Princess Charlotte had married and had died in childbirth with her baby, and this had set all her royal Uncles upon marrying to provide heirs to the throne. One after the other German Princesses came over to them, and in this year began the births, to the supposed delight of a grateful country. We had long tiresome mournings and then the joy bells—the old tale. But there were other losses more felt. Madame de Staël died, to the regret of Europe.[1] We had heard so much of her through the Mackintoshs that we almost fancied her an acquaintance. I think the Duke of York must have died too, and Mrs Cumming—but may be this was later. I am confused about dates, having never made any memoranda to guide me. Altogether my recollection of these few last months in Edinburgh are rather confused and far from pleasant.

One morning my mother sent Jane and Mary with a message to the poor Carrs in the Abbey; William was out elsewhere; most of the servants were despatched on errands; and then, poor woman, she told me there was to be an Execution in the house, and that I must help her to ticket a few books and drawings as belonging to the friends that had lent them to us. We had hardly finished when two startling rings announced the arrival of a string of rude looking men, who proceeded at once to business however with perfect civility, although their visit could not have been satisfactory, inasmuch as nothing almost was personal property. The

1. (1776–1817) French author, essayist, critic and famous conversationalist, this brilliant lady was widely fêted in England during her visit in 1813.

furniture was all hired, there was no cellar, very little plate. The Law library and the pianoforte were the most valuable items of the short catalogue. I attended them with the keys, and certainly they were very courteous, not going up to the bedrooms at all, nor scrutinising any where closely. When they were gone we had a good fit of crying, my mother and I, and then she told me for the first time of our difficulties as far as she herself knew them, adding that her whole wish now was to retire to the highlands; for, disappointed as she had been in every way, she had no wish to remain before the publick eye nor to continue an expensive way of living evidently beyond their circumstances. How severely I reflected on myself for having added to her griefs, for I had considerably distressed her by my heartless flirtations, entered on purposely to end in disappointment. The guilt of such conduct now came upon me as a blow, meriting just as cruel punishment as my awakening conscience was giving me; for there was no help, no cure for the past, all remaining was a better line of conduct for the future, on which I fully determined, and, thank God, lived to carry out, and so in some small degree atone for that vile flippancy which had hurt my own character and my own reputation while it tortured my poor Mother. I don't now take all the blame upon myself; I had never been rightly guided. The relations between Mother and daughter were very different then from what they are now. Our mother was very reserved with us, not watchful of us, nor considerate, nor consistent. The Governess was an affliction. We had no rule of right and so deserve excuse for our many errours. Thought would have schooled us but I never thought till this sad day. Then it seemed as if a veil fell from between my giddy spirits and real life, and the lesson I read began my education.

Mary had also grieved my poor mother a little by refusing Uncle Edward's invitation to India; Jane, by declining what were called good marriages; William, by neglecting his Law studies. A little more openness with kindness might have done good to all; tart speeches and undue fault finding will put nothing straight, ever. We had all suffered from the fretful without knowing what had caused the ill humour. It was easy to bear and easy to soothe once it was understood.

We were all the happier after we knew more of the truth of our position.

It was easy to get leave to spend the summer in Rothiemurchus; it was impossible to persuade my father that he had lost his chance of succeeding at the Scotch Bar. He took another house in Great King Street, removing all the furniture and his law books into it, as our Lease of No. 8 Picardy Place was out. My Mother, who had charge of the packing, put up and carried north every atom that was our own. She had made up her mind to return no more, though she said nothing after the new house was taken. Had she been as resolute earlier it would have been better; perhaps she did not know the necessity of the case; and then she and we looked on the forest as inexhaustible, a growth of wealth that would last for ever and retrieve any passing difficulties, with proper management. This was our sunny gleam, always.

On reading over my travels, I find I have left out a good many little incidents that in their due place would have materially lightened the rather meagre narrative, but they are in themselves too trifling to stand alone in a list of omissions—excepting indeed two incidents which really should not be forgotten. Our dinner at the Dutch merchant's at Rotterdam, for he kept his word that chance acquaintance of ours of the table d'hôte at Maestricht, and the singular behaviour of two people who, one or the other of them, crossed our path in almost every direction, the queen of Sweden and the Duc de Richelieu.

She was the Wife of Bernadotte, once Mademoiselle Le Clerk of Marseilles. Monsieur de Richelieu had, "twas said, been her lover and *she* was constant still, age though detracting from her charms not having chilled her heart. *He* had tired of the business and he was now intent on flying, while she pursued. He had a light carriage and travelled post with small attendance and he must have had a staff of intelligence Agents all along the road besides, for frequently when he seemed quite settled comfortably in the same hotel with ourselves at different places, Aix, Liège, Spa, he would suddenly interrupt all his quiet arrangements, pack up and be off without leaving a trace behind and just get out of sight before the queen arrived in her more stately equipage, a well loaded Berline.[1] Her stay was always short, her manners hurried, the many imperials were no sooner unpacked and carried up to her apartment than they were down again and replaced upon the carriage, and her Majesty and suite hastening after them, when away they rolled upon their fruitless search. While we were in the habit of encountering them, he had always the start of her, always escaped her. She was a pretty little woman, no longer young but well preserved, beautifully dressed and had something attractive about her air though she was not in the least dignified. It was odd altogether such proceedings in a queen, for there seemed to be no attempt at any concealment of the object of her cross journeyings, the enquiries concerning the pursued being quite open and most minute. We set the whole affair down to the account of foreign manners.[2]

The dinner at the Dutch merchant's was very pleasant. He came with his wife, a very thin woman, to remind us of our promise and told us it would be quite a family party, his sons and their wives, his daughters and their husbands, and other near relations, in all we found about twenty. The hour was three and while we were waiting in the heavily furnished Drawing room, the ladies amused themselves in the windows looking at the passengers in the street below by means of small mirrours hung against the shutters for the purpose of reflecting the objects outside. The gentlemen drank madeira handed about in tall glasses on a tray. The first dish at dinner was oysters, a great quantity of which were eaten and more madeira was taken after them. Then a great number of dishes were set on the table together—the soup and the bouilli with pickles like France; several sorts of fish variously dressed; roast meat and baked meat and ragouts with vegetables.

1. A four-wheeled covered carriage, with a seat behind covered with a hood.
2. Jean Baptiste Jules Bernadotte, Napoleon's Marshal, was chosen King of Sweden in 1810, Karl XIV, and reigned for thirty-four years. His wife, Desirée Clary, daughter of a wealthy Marseilles merchant, had been Napoleon's first fiancée and was the sister of Joseph Buonaparte's wife, Julie. The Duc de Richelieu (1766–1822) became Prime Minister in February of this same year, 1820.

Wine, excellent wine, constantly going about and Bier. A course of pastry, game and sweet dishes, came next, then red herrings raw, dressed with oil and vinegar and cut in small pieces, then a very fine dessert and cheese of two or three kinds. We had coffee in the Drawing room and so came away. They were very friendly, mannered people, not particularly bright but they had plenty to say in their bad french. The naval officer, who turned out to be a nephew, was there and a great addition to the cheerfulness of the company. It was very civil of these perfect strangers to introduce us into their home circle, the thing of all other foreigners most wish for and so seldom accomplished.

We often talked over amongst ourselves all that befell us in our short wanderings—it was conversation for many an evening that might otherwise have been dull, as little was happening that we cared for. A marriage or two took place in our Circle, the most interesting of which to us was Jane Hunter's to Charles Guthrie, a London Russian Merchant, well to do and the son of a Fifeshire Laird. Some of the relations thought she might have done better, trade not being much in favour where Highland blood flows. She chose for herself, however, and never repented though she had to live for many years in Idol Lane in a set of rooms over the Warehouse. Lady Hunter was quite pleased with the connexion, wrote long notes to my Mother on the subject and coming to dine with us to meet Uncle Bartle, who was travelling for his health, she gave him such an overdose of Guthrie-ism that he declared nothing should tempt him within a hundred miles of her till the other daughter was safe off, married, and all over for months and the affair half forgotten. Uncle Bartle had lost the Spanish Wife whom he never married! and he really believed he was sorry for her.

# CHAPTER TWENTY-FOUR

1820–1823

IN July then, 1820, we returned to the highlands, which for seven years remained the only home of the family. My Mother resisted all arguments for a return to Edinburgh this first winter, and they were never again employed. She had begun to lose her brave heart, to find out how much more serious than she had ever dreamed of had become the difficulties in which my father was involved, though the full extent of his debts was concealed for some time longer from her and the world. Some sort of a Trust Deed was executed this summer, to which I know our Cousin lame James Grant, Glenmoriston's Uncle, was a party. William was to give up the Bar, and devote himself to the management of the property. Take the forest affairs into his own hands, Duncan McIntosh being quite invalided, and turn farmer as well, having qualified himself by a residence of some months in East Lothian at a first rate practical farmer's, for the care of the comparatively few acres round the Doune. My father was to proceed as usual; London and the House in Spring, and such improvements as amused him when at home.

My Mother did not enjoy a country life; she had therefore the more merit in suiting herself to it. She had no pleasure in gardening or in wandering through all that beautiful scenery, neither had she any turn for Schools, or 'cottage comforts,' or the general care of her husband's people, though in particular instances she was very kind; nor was she an active house-keeper. She ordered very good dinners, but as general overseer of expenditure she failed. She liked seeing her hanks of yarn come in and her webs come home; but whether she got back all she ought from what she sent, she never thought of. She had no extravagant habits, not one; yet for want of supervision the waste in all departments of the household was excessive. Indolently content with her book, her newspaper, or her work, late up and very late to bed, a walk to her poultry yard which was her only diversion was almost a bore to her, and a drive with my father in her pretty pony carriage quite a sacrifice. Her health was beginning to give way and her spirits with it.

William was quite pleased with the change in his destiny; he was extremely fond of commanding, very active in his habits, by no means studious, and he had never much fancied the Law. Farming he took to eagerly, and what a farmer he made. They were changed times to the highland idlers. The whole yard astir at five o'clock in the morning, himself perhaps the first to pull the bell, a certain task allotted to every one, hours fixed for this work, days set apart for that, method pursued, order enforced. It was hard, up hill work, but even to tidiness and cleanliness it was accomplished in time. He overturned the old system a little too quickly, a woman would have gone about the requisite changes with more delicacy; the result, however, justified the means. There was one stumbling block in his way, a clever rogue of a grieve, by name Aitchieson, a handsome well mannered man, a great favourite, who blinded even William by his adroit flatteries. He came from Ayrshire, highly recommended by I forget who, and having married Donald Maclean the Carpenter's pretty daughter, called Jane after my Mother, he had a strong back of connexions all disposed to be favourable to him. He was gardener as well as grieve, for George Ross was dead, and he was really skilful in both capacities, when properly guided.

The forest affairs were at least equally improved by such active superintendence, although the alterations came more by degrees. I must try and remember all that was done there, and in due order if possible. First, the general felling of timber at whatever spot the men so employed found it most convenient to them to use their axe on a marked tree, was put a stop to. William made a plan of the forest,[1] divided it into sections, and as far as was practicable allotted one portion to

1.  These meticulous plans are in the possession of the
    present generation of the Grant family.

be cleared immediately, enclosed by a stout fencing, and then left to nature, not to be touched again for fifty or sixty years. The ground was so rich in seed that no other care was requisite. By the following Spring a carpet of inch high plants would be struggling to rise above the heather, in a season or two more a thicket of young fir trees would be found there, thinning themselves as they grew, the larger destroying all the weaker. Had this plan been pursued from the beginning there would never have been an end to the wood of Rothiemurchus.

The dragging of the felled timber was next systematised. The horses required were kept at the Doune, sent out regularly to their work during the time of year they were wanted, and when their business was done employed in carting deals to Forres, returning with meal sufficient for the consumption of the whole place, or to Inverness to bring back coals and other stores for the house. The little bodies and idle boys with ponies were got rid of. The Mills also disappeared. One by one these picturesque objects fell into disuse. A large building was erected on the Druie near its junction with the Spey, where all the sawing was effected. A coarse upright saw for slabbing, that is, slicing off the outsides or backs of the logs, and several packs of saws which cut the whole log up at once into deals, were all arranged in the larger division of the Mill. A wide reservoir of water held all the wood floated or dragged to the inclined plane up which the logs were rolled as wanted. When cut up, the backs were thrown out through one window, the deals through another, into a yard at the back of the Mill, where the wood was all sorted and stacked. Very few men and as many boys got easily through the work of the day. It was always a busy scene and a very exciting one, the great Lion of the place, strangers delighting in a visit to it. The noise was frightful, but there was no confusion, no bustle, no hurry. Every one employed had his own particular task, and plenty of time and space to do it in.

The smaller compartment of the great Mill was fitted up with circular saws for the purpose of preparing the thinnings of the birch woods for herring barrel staves. It was a mere toy beside its gigantick neighbour, but a very pretty one and a very profitable one, above £1000 a year profit being cleared by this manufacture of what had hitherto been valueless except as fuel. This circular saw Mill had been the first erected. It was planned by my father and William the summer they went north with my Mother and left us girls in Edinburgh. The large Mill followed, and was but just finished as we arrived, so that it was not in the good working order I have described till some months later. An Urquhart Gale, an oddity imported a few years before, had entire charge of it, and Sandy McIntosh gave all his attention to the woods. He lived with his father at the Dell, and Urquhart Gale lived on one of the islands in the Druie, where he had built himself a wooden house surrounded by a strip of garden bounded by the water.

Having set the staple business of the place in more regular order than it ever had been conducted in before, William turned his attention to the farm, with less success however for a year or two. More work was done and all work was better done, but the management remained expensive till we got rid of Aitchieson. In time he was replaced by a head ploughman from the Lothians, when all the others having learnt their places required less supervision. William indeed was himself always at his post, this new profession of his being his passion. The order he got that farm into, the crops it yielded afterwards, the beauty of his fields, the improvement of the Stock, were the wonder of the Country. This first year I did not so much attend to his doings as I did the next, having little or nothing to do with his operations. Jane and I rode as usual. We all wandered about in the woods and spent long days in the garden, and then we had the usual Autumn Company to entertain at home and in the neighbourhood.

Our first guest was John. Our young brother John whom we had not seen since he went first to Eton. My Mother, whose anxiety to meet her pet was fully equal to my sisters' and mine, proposed our driving to Pitmain, thirteen miles off, where the Coach then stopt to dine. The Barouche and four was ordered accordingly and away we went. We had nearly reached Kingussie when we espied upon the road a tall figure walking with long strides, his hat on the back of his head, his hair blowing about in the wind, very short trowsers, and arms beyond his coat sleeves—in fact an object! and this was John! grown five inches! or indeed I believe six! for he had been sixteen months away. He had carried up very creditable breadth with all this height, looking strong enough, but so altered, so unlike our little plaything of a brother, we were rather discomfited. However, we found that the ways of old had lost no charms for the Eton boy; he was more our companion than ever, promoting and enjoying fun in his quiet way, and so long as no sort of trouble fell to him, objecting to none of our many schemes of amusement. Old as we elder ones were, we used to join in cat concerts after breakfast in the dining room. My mother always breakfasted in her room, my father frequently had a tray sent to him in the Study, or if he came to us, he ate hurriedly and soon departed. We each pretended we were playing on some instrument, the sound of which we endeavoured to imitate with the voice, taking parts as in a real orchestra, generally contriving to make harmony, and going through all our favourite overtures as well as innumerable melodies. Then we would act Scenes from different plays, substituting our own words when memory failed us, or sing bits of Operas in the same *improvisatori* style. Then we would rush out of doors, be off to fish, or to visit our thousand friends, or to the forest or to the Mill, or to take a row upon the lake, unmooring the boat ourselves, and Jane and I handling the oars just as well as our brothers. Sometimes we stopt short in the garden or went no further than the hill of the Doune, or may be would lounge on to the farm yard if any work we liked was going on there. Jane had taken to sketching from nature and to gardening. I had my green house plants indoors, and the linen press, made over to my case by my mother, as were the wardrobes of my brothers. We were so happy, so busy, we felt it an interruption when there came visitors, Jane excepted. She was only in her element when in company. She very soon took the whole charge of receiving and entertaining the guests. She quite shone in this capacity and certainly made the gay meetings of friends henceforward very different from the formal parties of former times. Our guests this autumn of 1820 were Charles and Robert Grant (names ever dear to me), Sir David and Lady Brewster, and Mrs Marcet the clever authoress,[1] brought to us by the Bellevilles. We gave her a luncheon in our Cottage at Loch an Eilein, which much pleased her. This cottage had been built by General Grant of the diamond ring for his old mother—on her death it had remained untenanted till it was bestowed on us. Our kind father repaired and improved it and built us a back kitchen and made us a flower garden and my mother gave us some furniture. Our cousin Edmund was with us this summer; he helped us to fit it up, whitewashing, staining, painting, etc. One of the woodmen's wives lived in it and kept it tidy. We had a pantry and a store room, well furnished both of them, and many a party we gave there, sometimes a boating and fishing party with a luncheon, sometimes a tea with cakes of our own making, and a merry walk home by moonlight. Doctor Hooker[2] also came to botanise and the Sportsmen to shoot. Kinrara filled, and Uncle Ralph and Eliza passed the whole summer with us. Mrs Ironside was at Oxford, watching with aunt Mary the last days of Dr Griffith. Uncle Ralph was the most delightful companion that ever dwelt in a country house. Never in the way, always up to every thing, the promoter of all enjoyment, full of fun, full of anecdote, charming by the fire on a wet day, charming out of doors in the sunshine, enthusiastick about scenery, unrivalled in weaving garlands of natural flowers for the hair, altogether such a prose poet as one almost never meets with; hardly handsome, yet very fine looking, tall and with the air and the manners of a prince of the blood. He had lived much in the best society and had adorned it. Eliza was clever, very obliging, and her playing on the pianoforte was delightful. She had an everlasting collection of old simple airs belonging to all countries, which she strung together with skill, and played with expression. We had great fun this Autumn;

1. Mrs Jane Marcet (1769–1858) wrote for the young; one of her most recent works had been *Conversations on Chemistry, intended more specifically for the Female Sex* (1816).
2. Sir William Jackson Hooker (1785–1868) was to become Director of Kew Gardens in 1841.

poney races at Kingussie and a ball at the cattle tryst, picnics in the woods, quantities of fine people at Kinrara, Lord Tweeddale and his beautiful Marchioness (Lady Susan Montague), the Ladies Cornwallis, kind merry girls, one of them, Lady Louisa, nearly killing uncle Ralph by making him dance twice down the Haymakers with her; Mrs Rawdon and her clever daughter, Lady William Russell, who I do not think much liked her little shabby looking Lord; Lord Lynedoch at 80 shooting with the young men; Colonel Ponsonby, who had gambled away a fine fortune or two and Lady Harriet Bathurst's heart, and being supposed to be killed at Waterloo, had had his body, when he had swooned, built up in a wall of corpses, as a breastwork before some regiment to shoot over. Mrs Rawdon, rather a handsome flirting widow, taking Uncle Ralph for a widower, paid him very tender attentions and invited Eliza to visit her in London.

This was the summer of Queen Caroline's trial;[1] the newspapers were of course forbidden to all us young people; a useless prohibition, for while we sat working or drawing, my Uncle and my Mother favoured us with full comments on these disgusting proceedings. 'Good God, Jane', said my Uncle, 'the woman must be a beast, just listen . . . did you ever hear of any thing so utterly abominable . . .'; 'Not near so bad Ralph as her exhibition before the Banker at . . .'; and so they would go on skimming the rich filth of the dirt the papers were polluted with. In September the poor creature died. None of the grandees in our neighbourhood would wear mourning for her. We had to put on black for our Uncle Griffith, and the good natured world said that my father, in his violent Whiggery, had dressed us in sables, when, in truth, he had always supported the king's right to exercise his

1. When George IV became King in June 1820, he was determined to exclude his wife, Caroline of Brunswick-Wolfenbättel (whom he had bigamously married 25 years before) from the throne. Unsavoury parliamentary inquiries were accordingly held, and for many Whigs Caroline was seen as a symbol of resistance to tyranny. Conveniently for the King, she died a month after his coronation, in August 1821.

own authority in his own family. So tales rise and spread. Mrs Ralph remained at Oxford to assist Aunt Mary in selecting furniture, packing up some, selling the rest, and giving up the lodgings to the new Master, Dr Rowley, our old friend of the pear tree days. The two ladies then set out for Tennochside, where Aunt Mary was to pass her year of Widowhood, Uncle Ralph and Eliza hurrying back to meet them as soon as we had returned from the Northern Meeting in October. We enjoyed it much, and brought Duncan Davidson back with us in his kilt, still a fine boy though much spoiled. He was quite in love with Jane, and she seemed for a while to respond, but they fell out one rainy day and he departed. We never could make out exactly what the disagreement had been, perhaps some historical subject—a failure as to dates or facts or something had caused her to dismiss a bold dragoon, Tom Walker of the Scots Greys, a nephew of General Need's, an excellent young man, good looking, rich and gentlemanly but not literary. She was hard to please, for Mr Crawfurd (*Archipelago*) was as learned as a professor, but sticking a fork into the potatoes, lost by his ill manners all that his learning had gained him.[1]

At the end of this year my sisters and I had to manage amongst us to replace wasteful servants and attend to my Mother's simple wants. The housekeeper went, in bad health, to the Spa at Strathpeffer, where she died; the fine cook married the Butler, and took the Inn at Dalwhinnie, which they partly furnished out of our lumber room! My Mother placed me in authority, and by patience, regularity, tact and resolution, the necessary reforms were silently made without annoying any one. It was the beginning of troubles the full extent of which I had indeed little idea of then, nor had I thought much of what I did know till one bright day, on one of our forest excursions, my rough pony was led through the moss above Auchnahartenich by honest old John Bain. We were looking over a wide, bare plain, which the last time I had seen it had been all wood. I believe I started. The good old man shook his gray head, and then, with more respect than usual in his affectionate highland manner, he told me all

1. See II, p. 78.

that was said, all that he feared, all that some one of us should know, and that he saw 'it was fixed' that Miss Lizzie should hear, for though she was 'lightsome' she would come to sense when it was wanted to keep her Mama easy, try to get her brothers on and not refuse a good match for herself, or her sisters should it come their way. Good, wise John Bain—'A match for me!' that was over, but the rest was easy, could at least be tried. 'A stout heart to a stiff brae' gets up the hill. I was ignorant of household matters. My kind friend the Lady Belleville was an admirable economist, she taught me much. Dairy and farmkitchen matters were picked up at the Dell and the Croft, and with books of reference, honest intentions, and untiring activity, less mistakes were made in this season of apprenticeship than could have been expected. And so passed the year of 1821. Few visitors that season, no Northern Meeting, a dinner or two at Kinrara, and a good many visits at Belleville. William busy with the forest and the farm.

1822 was more lively; William and I had got our departments into fair working order. Whether he had diminished expenses, I know not; I had, beyond my slightest idea, and we were fully more comfortable than we had ever been under the reign of the housekeepers. Sir David and Lady Brewster were with us for a while, and Dr Hooker, and the Grants of course, with their quaint fun and their oddities and their extra piety, which, I think, was wearing away. In the early part of the year 1822 Aunt Mary came to us from Tennochside, escorted by my father on his way home from London. She found me very ill. I had gone at Xmas on a visit to our Cousins the Roses of Holm, where I had not been since Charlotte's marriage to Sir John, then only Colonel Burgoyne. There had been no Company in the house for some time; I was put into a damp bed, which gave me such a cold, followed by such a cough that I had kept my room ever since; the dull unhealthy barrack room, very low in the roof, just under the slates, cold in winter, a furnace in summer, only one window in it. We three girls in it, my poor sisters disturbed all night with my incessant cough. Dr Smith, kind little man, took what care he could of me, and Jane, who succeeded to my 'situation,' was the best, the most untiring of nurses, but neither of them could manage my removal to a fitter apartment. Aunt Mary effected it at once. We were all brought down to the white room and its dressing room, the best in the house, so light, so very cheerful; I had the large room. The dear Miss Cumming Gordons sent up from Forres House a cuddy, whose milk, brought up to me warm every morning, soon softened the cough. Nourishing soups restored strength. In June I was on my poney; in August I was well. Weak enough, how much I owed to our dear, wise Aunt Mary. She never let us return to the barrack room. She prevailed on my father to have us settled in the old Schoolroom and the room through it, which we inhabited ever after; had we been there before I should not have been so ill, for my mother lived on the same floor, and would have been able to look after us. She was very ill herself, in the Doctor's hands, rose late, never got up the garret stairs, and was no great believer in the danger of a mere cold.

Aunt Mary amused us very much by her admiration of handsome young men. One of the Macphersons of Ralea, and the two Clarkes of Dalnavert, John and William, were very much with us; they were dangerous intimates, but they did us no harm; I do not know that they did themselves much good. Aunt Mary would have woven a romance about the Clarkes had she had time; nobodies on the father's side, but on the Mother's lineally descended from the Shawes of Rothiemurchus. It was hard on them to see their ancient foes in their inheritance. It is curious how those highland *laddies*, once introduced to the upper world, take their places in it as if born to fill them. No young man, School and College bred, could have more graceful manners than John Clarke; he entered the army from his humble home at Dalnavert, just taught a little by the kindness of Belleville. He was a first rate Officer, became A.D.C., married a Baronet's daughter, and became well the high position he won. The brother William, a gentlemanly sailor, married a woman of family and fortune, and settled in Hampshire. The sisters, after the death of their parents, went to an Aunt in South America, where most of them married well, the eldest to a nephew of the celebrated

General Greene.[1] All of them rose as no other race ever rises; there is no vulgarity for them to lose and there is the good blood and the old recollections to help them on. Then came John Dalzel, a good young man, said to be clever, known to be industrious, educated with all the care that clever parents, School, College, a good society in Lord Eldin's house, could command; who, grave, dull, awkward, looked of inferiour species to the 'gentle Celts.'

This Autumn King George the 4th, then, I think, only Regent, visited Scotland. The whole country went mad. Every body strained every point to get to Edinburgh to receive him. Sir Walter Scott and the town Council were overwhelming themselves with the preparations. My Mother did not feel well enough for the bustle, neither was I at all fit for it, so we staid at home with Aunt Mary. My father, my two sisters and William, with lace, feathers, pearls, the old landau, the old horses, and the old liveries, all went to add to the Show, which they said was delightful. The Countess of Lauderdale presented my two sisters and the two Miss Grants of Congalton, a group allowed to be the prettiest there. The Clan Grant had quite a triumph, no equipage was as handsome as that of Colonel Francis Grant, our acting Chief, in their red and green and gold. There were processions, a Review, a Levée, a Drawing room, and a Ball, at which last Jane was one of the young ladies selected to dance in the reel before the Regent, with, I think, poor Captain Murray of Abercairney, a young naval officer, for her partner.[2] A great mistake was made by the Stage Managers—one that offended all the southron Scots; the King wore at the Levée the highland dress. I daresay he

1. General Sir William Green (1725–1811), the engineer.
2. Mary and Jane Grant wrote a series of letters back to E.G. describing their experiences during this memorable visit. These were collected and privately printed in Dublin, presumably by E.G. after her marriage. They are an entertaining description of the King (Mary 'only saw a pair of thick lips, and a grave respectful-looking face bending towards me') and all the occasions he was publicly fêted.

thought the country all highland, expected no fertile plains, did not know the difference between the Saxon and the Celt.[1] However, all else went off well, this little slur on the Saxon was overlooked, and it gave occasion for a good laugh at one of Lady Saltoun's witty speeches. Some one objecting to this dress, particularly on so large a man, whose nudities were no longer attractive, 'Nay,' said she, 'we should take it very kind of him; since his stay will be so short, the more we see of him the better.' Sir William Curtis was kilted too, and standing near the King, many persons mistook them, amongst others John Hamilton Dundas, who kneeled to kiss the fat Alderman's hand, when, finding out his mistake, he called out, 'Wrong, by Jove,' and rising, moved on undaunted to the larger presence.

One incident connected with this bustling time made me very cross. Lord Conyngham, the Chamberlain, was looking every where for pure *Glenlivet* whiskey—the King drank nothing else—it was not to be had out of the highlands. My father sent word to me, I was the Cellarer, to empty my pet bin, where was whiskey long in wood, long in uncorked bottles, mild as milk, and the true contraband *goût* in it. Much as I grudged this treasure it made our fortunes afterwards, shewing on what trifles great events sometimes depend. The whiskey, and fifty brace of ptarmigan all shot by one man in one day, went up to Holyrood House, and were graciously received and made much of, and a reminder of this attention at a proper moment by the gentlemanly Chamberlain ensured to my father the Indian Judgeship.

While part of the family were thus royally or loyally occupied, passing away a gay ten days in Edinburgh, my dear, kind Aunt and I were strolling through the beautiful

1. In a letter to Rothiemurchus (11.8.1822), E.G.'s father also criticised 'the ludicrous state of bustle and expectation of the sedate and sober citizens of the Scottish Metropolis—and the whimsical affectation of a sort of highland costume, with about as much propriety in the conception and execution as if it had taken place in Paris or Brussels'.

scenery of Rothiemurchus. She loved to revisit all the places she had so admired in her youth. When attended by the train of retainers which then accompanied her progress, she had learned from her kilted suite more of the ancient doings of our race than I with all my research had been able to pick up even from dear old Mr Cameron. She was all highland, an enthusiast in her admiration of all that fed the romance of her nature, so different from the placid comfort of her early home. Our strolls were charming; she on foot, I on my poney. We went long distances, for we often stopt to rest beside some little sparkling burnie, and seated on the heather and beside the cranberries, we ate the luncheon we had brought with us in a basket that was hung on the crutch of my saddle. I was much more fitted to understand her fine mind at this time than I should have been the year before. My long illness, which had confined me for so many months to my room, where most of the time was passed in solitude, had thrown me for amusement on the treasures of my father's library. First I took to light reading, but finding there allusions to subjects of graver import of which I was nearly ignorant, I chalked out for myself really a plan of earnest study. The history of my own country, and all connected with it, in eras, taking in a sketch of other countries, consulting the references where we had them, studying the literature of each period, comparing the past with the present. It was this course faithfully pursued till it interested me beyond idea that made me acquainted with the worth of our small collection of books. There was no subject on which sufficient information could not be got. I divided my reading time into four short sittings, varying the subjects, by advice of good Dr Smith, to avoid fatigue, and as I slept little it was surprising how many volumes even in this way I got through. It was 'the making of me,' as we Irish say. Our real mission here on earth had never been hinted to me. We had no fixed aim in life, nor even an idea of 'wasted time.' To do good, and to avoid evil, we were certainly taught, and very happy we were while all was bright around us. When sorrow came I was not fit to bear it, I had to bear it all alone. We were brought up in Spartan fashion, to let the fox bite beneath the cloke. The utmost reserve was inculcated upon us whenever a disagreeable effect would be produced by an exhibition of our feelings. In this case, too, the subject had been prohibited, so the fox bit hard and the long illness was the result, but the after-consequences were good. The mind was brightened, as well as chastened and strengthened by this wise occupation, the disposition improved by the habit of reflexion.

It was new to me to think. I had never thought before. I often lay awake in the early summer morning looking from my bed through the large south window of that pretty 'White room,' thinking of the world beyond those fine old beech trees, taking into the picture the green gate, the undulating field, the bank of birch trees, and the Ord Bain, and on the other side the height of the Polchar, and the smoke from the gardener's cottage; wondering, dreaming, and not omitting self accusation, for discipline had been necessary to me, and I had not borne my cross meekly. My foolish, frivolous, careless career and its punishment came back upon me painfully, but no longer angrily; I learned to excuse as well as to submit, so kissed the rod in a brave spirit which met its reward. Poor, poor Lizzy Glass, my name sake, the very pretty under dairy maid, used to come to my bedside every morning with a frothy cup of Ass's milk, which I owed to the kindness of Jane and Emilia Cumming, and she always said in presenting it with her sweet, innocent smile—for she was innocent then, poor thing—in the only English she knew, 'Sleep well'; which I generally did for an hour or two. I was still confined to my room, but being able now to write and to work, no longer found the time so weary and my wise Aunt found me a new and most pleasant employment. She set me upon writing essays, short tales, and at length a novel. I don't suppose they were intrinsically worth much, and I am sure I do not know what has become of them, but the venture was invaluable. I tried higher flights afterwards with success when help was more wanted.

All this while, who was very near us, within a thought of coming on to find us out, had he more accurately known our whereabouts. He who hardly seven years after became my husband. He was an Officer of the Indian Army at home on furlough,[1] diverting his leisure by a tour through part of Scotland; he was sleeping quietly at Dunkeld while I was waking during the long night at the Doune. Uncle Edward, his particular friend, had so often talked of us to him that he knew us almost individually, but for want of a letter of introduction would not volunteer a better acquaintance. It was better for me as it was. I know well, had he come to Rothiemurchus, Jane would have won his heart. So handsome she was, so lively, so kind, a sickly invalid would have had no chance with her. Major Smith and Miss Jane would have ridden enthusiastically through the woods together, and I should have been unnoticed. All happens well, could we but think so; and so my future husband returned alone to India, and I had to go there after him!

At the close of this Autumn my Aunt was to leave us to spend the winter with her old friend Miss Lawrence at Studley. I was to go with her, Doctor Smith not thinking it would be safe for me to risk the cold frosts of the highlands. Miss Lawrence so very kindly wished me to remain with her during my Aunt's visit, but Annie Need had arranged with my father that I was to be her guest during this winter; it was a long promised treat, so I could only give a month to Studley on my way to Sherwood forest.

Before we left the Doune there had been a family Council held on Weighty affairs. Our cousin Kate Ironside, the eldest of the Houghton family, who had been sent for to Bombay by Uncle Edward in the year 1819, had married well; her husband, Colonel Barnewall, an excellent man, was then Resident at Kaira, much considered in the Service; he had permitted Kate to send for her two next sisters, Eliza and Mary, and Uncle Edward wished my sister Mary to accompany them. She had been his pet in her babyhood. My father and Mother were rather offended by the proposal, but left

1. An extended leave. Born in 1780, the second son of a Co. Wicklow landowner, Henry Smith had been admitted to King's Inn, after which he enrolled as a Cadet in the East India Company Cavalry. He was promoted Major in 1820 and was to be Lieutenant Colonel four years later.

the decision to Mary herself. She declined of course for the present, leaving the matter open for future consideration, with the caution for which she was so remarkable. 'There is no saying,' said she, 'but what Bombay might some day prove a Godsend. Life is dull enough here.' At this same time a Writership offered by old Charles Grant to my brother John was refused, to my Mother's grief, for she had set her heart upon it. She had a craze for India, and would have despatched every individual boy or girl over whom she had any influence to that land of the sun. My father and William, indeed our Aunt Mary too, thought that John's great abilities would ensure him employment at home. So this matter was postponed.

At the end of October my Aunt and I set out upon our travels, escorted by my brother William. We went in the travelling chariot with our own horses, sleeping two nights upon the road, and we staid a week in Edinburgh in our own house in Great King Street, which my father had lent to Uncle Ralph. His son Edmund, his nephew James Hamilton, and John Dundas were living with him and attending College. Very few people were in town, but Aunt Judy kindly brought these few of our old friends who were remaining there to see us, and gave two very pleasant little dinners to us. Miss Clerk, and Mary Dalzel of course, with her beautiful pianoforte musick, only equalled by poor Eliza's own, and William Clerk, the clever oddity who, it was said, read up in the mornings for conversational purposes, and at the dinners adroitly brought in the prepared subject; he made himself most agreeable any way with his shrewd mother wit. I remember one bit of sarcasm particularly well. He could not bear a pompous little man, who had married his cousin, Mr Wedderburn, the Solicitor-General. As this little body was parading the Parliament house one day with the air of a Socrates, he was thus weighed and valued by the Cynick—'Oh, gin I could buy you at my price and sell you at your own.'

We proceeded by Coach to Carlisle, the first time I had ever set foot in a publick carriage, and very disagreeable I found it, so fine was the upper world in those days. The country we passed through was delightful to us who were learned in Ballad lore; Ettrick Shawes and Galla water, the braes of Yarrow and the Cowdenknowes, all spoke to us though from a distance, as we passed on to merry Carlisle, which we reached too late and too sleepy to look at. Next day we passed on over the Wolds to Greta Bridge and Kirby, and so on to Studley, where I remained till close on Xmas. William found the life too dull, so he set off to Annie Need, with whom he remained visiting about till it was time to return for me.

At that season of the year old Miss Lawrence lived nearly alone; her open house style ended with the autumn. We found only a few intimate friends with her. Two middle aged Miss Johnstones, who seemed to make regular tours among rich acquaintances. A very underbred and very flirting Miss Glaister the old lady's goddaughter, the child of her Land Steward; Mr Charnock, her chaplain, a good kind of man in an humble way; his pupil, Mr Nares; Sir Tristram Ricketts, who romped with the younger Miss Johnstone and occasionally a Mr Newsam, a young clergyman to whom Miss Lawrence had given a good living, in expectation of his marriage with Miss Glaister.

Breakfast was early; the post, needle work, and musick occupied the morning, and a ride or a walk before luncheon; a drive in the afternoon, or another walk. Dinner, which was served in the small dining room, and was always pleasant, and then duetts on the pianoforte in the evenings. Miss Lawrence always played the bass, Miss Johnstone and I in turn the treble. I daresay the old lady had been a good musician in her day, according to the style of musick and limited execution then in fashion. It was rather a melancholy performance now. She was quite unaware of this, for when she went out to dinner she always took musick and Miss Johnstone with her. Poor Miss Johnstone, she used to look up with such a peculiar smile while selecting the pieces.

Miss Lawrence was very kind to me. She sent a pianoforte to my room that I might practise in quiet. She gave me a key to the bookcases in the library, and generally chose me as her companion in her morning rides. We rode two donkeys, she on Johnny, I on Jack. She rode first in a very old duffle cloke of a grey colour and a black gypsey hat, encouraging her somewhat slothful steed by a brisk 'Johnny, get on' every now and then. Jack required no stimulus, and thus we wandered for hours through the beautiful grounds of Studley Royal. It was one of the Lions of Harrogate, and certainly its extensive old fashioned gardens deserved a visit. There were lawns, thickets, laurel banks, lakes, grottoes, temples, statues, the beautiful old ruins of Fountains Abbey, kept most incorrectly clean and tidy as if washed and trimmed daily, and one old manor house near it—a gem—now the residence of the game keeper. The fruit gardens were large, the offices good, the house itself, though convenient, with many fine rooms in it, was hardly worthy of its surroundings. The pretty village of Ripon was within a couple of miles, a fine old Cathedral in it, which I was always to be sent to visit, but somehow never managed to get there. I did go one fine, sunny, frosty day on my donkey to Kirby Lonsdale, a pretty little bit of scenery in a tame country. It was Miss Lawrence's original inheritance, she was very fond of it. She succeeded to Studley and the large Leicestershire estates on the death of her only brother, and had passed an uneasy life since, lived on by a host of parasites who knew well how to make their own use of her. She would have been happier had she married, but she had early determined to remain single. Very plain in person, very awkward in manner, no man had ever found out her real worth during her brother's life. After his death proposals of marriage were showered on her, which so disgusted her that she made a resolution to refuse all. A sensible husband, though he could not have been a lover, would have been a true friend and would have managed her immense property, political interests and all, and kept the mean crew off.

Her chaplain, good Mr Charnock, did his best to prevent her being too shamelessly imposed upon, but he could not save her altogether; neither could her Auditor, Sir Launcelot Shadwell, whose visits were rare. She did not particularly like her heir, Lord Grantham, and she particularly disliked his very handsome Irish wife, whom she thought with reason to be rather worldly.

At this time the kind old lady was quite occupied with Miss Glaister's marriage. She had made the young pair many handsome presents, and had been deceived all through, both

she and poor Mr Newsam, by this artful girl; for one fine day
the young lady set out for the Border with that mere boy Mr
Nares, Mr Charnock's pupil, and such a fuss ensued as never
was—Doctor Nares accused Mr Charnock of inattention;
Lady Charlotte accused Mrs Lawrence with connivance, and
the Bride being of humble birth, only the Land Steward's
daughter, the *respectable* Churchill blood never could forgive
the misalliance. I never heard what became of the pair.

It was very cold during my stay at Studley, frost and snow
equal to the highlands. William and I had a very chilly
journey after being set down, I forget where, out of Miss
Lawrence's comfortable chariot. Dear Annie Need was
waiting for us at Doncaster, where poor William and I
parted; he went back to Edinburgh. Annie took me to the
pleasant jointure house of one of the Mrs Walkers, where we
spent the night, and were amused and amazed at the Xmas
Storeroom; it was as full as Mrs Lawrence's. Blankets,
flannels, great coats, clokes, petticoats, stockings, all the
warmth that the poor could want in the wintry season. I was
unused to such wholesale charity; neither do I think it wise;
there can be no spirit either of independance or economy
where the expectation of relief unearned is a habit. Next day
we reached Fountain Dale to dinner. It was a neat, small
house, with tiny grounds, well kept, planted out from a wide
stretch of heath that had once been an oak forest. A chain of
fish ponds, full of well preserved fish, carp, tench and such
like, enlivened the scene, but though all was very tidy, there
was no beauty either there or in the neighbourhood. The
remains of Sherwood forest were not near this bleak and
scantily populated district. There were one or two dull
villages, the ugly little town of Mansfield, very few gentlemen's seats, none with any pretensions, and a general want of
wood. Perhaps if I were to see the country now I should
wonder at these impressions—every body was planting
busily, and thirty years gives a wonderful growth to well
preserved timber.

Berry hill, belonging to Mr Thomas Walker, was the
nearest house to Fountain Dale, just about three miles
off over the heath, a climb the whole way. Mr and Mrs
Walker were hospitable people, very kind, childless, so they

surrounded themselves with relations. Their connexions were all among the mercantile aristocracy of England, a new phase of life to me with my old highland blood, and one at which I opened my eyes with wonder. The profusion of money among all these people amazed *poor* me. Guineas were thrown about, as *we* would not have dreamed to deal with shillings. There was no ostentation, no great show any where, but such plenty, such an affluence of comfort. Servants well dressed, well fed; eating, indeed, went on all day upstairs and downstairs, six meals a day the rule. Well appointed stables, delightful gardens, lights every where, fires every where, nothing wanting, every thing wished for was got; yet, though good humoured and very kindly, they were not really happier one bit than those who had to count their pennies and could only rarely gratify their tastes. Generally speaking, the generation which had made the money in the mills was more agreeable than the generation which had left the mills and was spending the well earned money. The younger people were well educated—so-called—the men were School and College bred, gentle-manly, up to the times; but there was a something wanting, and there was too much vivacity! too much noise, no repose. The young women were inferiour to the young men; they were very accomplished, in the boarding school acceptation of the word, but mind there was not, and manners were defective—no ease. They were good, charitable, and highly pleased with their surroundings and with one another, and extremely proud of their brothers. They had all well filled purses. I do not remember hearing the amount of their regular allowances, but I do remember well the new year's gift at one Walker house. There were four young people of the family, and on lifting the breakfast plate each found a fifty pound note underneath it. William left with me Five pounds for my winter's pocket money. This cut a sorry figure by comparison.

General and Mrs Need were not rich; they lived quietly, had a small establishment, and, to the credit of the rich rela-tions, lived amongst them, apparently on equal terms. Annie, indeed, was the great lady every where, and extremely beloved. Four, I think, of the County gentlemen visited at Berry hill and Fountain Dale: Mr Coke, a book-worm, with an odd wife; Major Bilby and Captain Cope, cadets of good families, in the militia; and Mr Hallowes, a regular country squire, fit for a novel—short, chubby, good-looking, shooting, fishing, hunting, hospitable, kindly, a magistrate, and not an ounce of brains. The beautiful old manor house he lived in stood almost alone. In all our drives I never recollect passing a gentleman's seat; it was a very isolated part of Nottinghamshire, up in the moors. To say the truth, it was rather sleepy work this life in the Forest, and yet the time passed happily. Annie was so bright, so kind, her four boys fine little fellows, and once a fortnight there was an Oyster ploy; the particular friends were invited to meet a barrel of natives and Mr Need, the General's elder brother; by the bye, his wife was a nice, clever woman, unfor-tunately very deaf. At Berry hill I once met Mr and Mrs Lemprière—he was a fat little lively man, the son of the 'Classical Dictionary.'[1]

One visit I did enjoy; it was to the Strutts of Belper and Derby. General Need's father, his friend Mr Strutt, and old Arkwright—a barber, I believe—originated the cotton manufacture of England. Arkwright was the Head, Strutt the Hands, and Need the Sinews, for *he* had had the purse.[2] He was a Nottingham Stocking weaver. Of his two sons, one became a country gentleman, land to the value of £4000 a year having been purchased for him about Mansfield. This was John Need. The other, Sam Need, went into the Army with his younger son's portion, £20,000, into the Cavalry, to India, rose to high command, bore a good name, and married Annie Grant. The four daughters had £100,000 between them. Three of them married in their own Station, and very happily three brothers Walker, all in trade; the fourth, a beauty, won the heart of Mr Abney, a man of family and fortune, which alliance rather separated her from her kindred.

1. John Lemprière (1765?–1824) published his *Bibliotheca Classica* in 1788.
2. This historic partnership, 1771 to 1782, developed the water frame that powered the early Industrial Revolution.

The Strutts were silk weavers. The principal establishment was at Belper, near Derby; such a pretty place, wooded banks and a river, and a model village, the abode of the workmen. Jediah Strutt, who had married a Walker, niece of the General's, was the manager and part Owner of the Belper mills. He had an extremely pretty house in the village, with gardens behind it down to the river, and such a range of glass houses. There were Schools, an hospital, an infirmary, a Library, a chapel, and a Chaplain of their own persuasion (they were unitarians), all so liberally provided, Mrs Strutt and her young daughters all so busy in all these departments, assisted by the dear old Chaplain, who was really the soul of his flock. Then there was the Mill. It was the first of the sort I had ever seen, and it made a great impression on me. I forget now whether the moving power was steam or the pure water of the little river, but the movements produced by either are not easily forgotten. It all seemed to me like magick. Immense rooms full of countless rows of teetotums[1] twirling away by themselves, or sets of cards in hundreds of hands tearing away at cotton wool of their own accord; smoothing irons in long rows running out of the walls and sliding over quantities of stockings; hands without any bodies rubbing as if for the bare life over wash tubs, and when people wanted to reach another storey, instead of stairs they stept upon a tray, pulled a string, and up they went, or down, as suited them.

One huge iron foundry was really frightful; the Strutts manufactured their own machinery, and in this Cyclops den huge hammers were always descending on huge blocks of iron red hot, some of them, and the heat, and the din, and the wretched looking smiths at work there made a very disagreeable impression. It was a pleasant change to enter the packing house. At this time large bales were being prepared for the Russian market; the goods were built up neatly in large piles, high above our head—a string was pulled, a weight came down, and the big bale shrunk into a comfortable seat!

One of the Strutt family, an old uncle, a bachelour and an oddity, was so enamoured of his machinery that he had as much *magick* as possible introduced into his own house;

1. Light tops, spun with the fingers, originally a toy.

roasting, boiling, baking, ironing, all that it was practicable so to manage was done by turning pegs; and being rather a heavy sleeper, a hand came out of the wall in the morning at a certain hour and pulled the bed clothes off him. The whole place was amusing; Jediah and Mrs Strutt very nice, and John Strutt, a younger brother, very nice. We went to a Ball in Derby from Belper, and who should I meet there but our old Edinburgh friend Mary Balfour, now Mrs Meynell. What an ugly man she had married, but he was of high degree; and how very plain she had grown, but she had had a long purse. She was delighted to see me, and, I believe, supposed I had moved into Derbyshire for good, she was so very congratulatory; a second look showed me on the arm of the head of the Strutt family, old Mr Strutt of Derby, so she faded quietly away. This old Mr Strutt was charming, very simple, very clever, very artistick in all his tastes; he had lived a great deal abroad, and at the close of those dreadful Napoleon wars had picked up gems of price of all kinds. His house was a museum; paintings, sculpture, china, inlaid woods, not too many, and all suitably arranged.

We went from this house next day on our way home to lunch in Dovedale at Mr Arkwright's,[1] a beautiful little place in a beautiful valley. Such a luncheon of hothouse fruits. The old gentleman came out of his Mill in his miller's dress and did the honours gracefully. The upper Ten thousand had better look to themselves or they will be shoved from the high places. We paid another visit a little before this time to my old friend Tom Walker of the Scots Greys. He had married a very pretty Irish wife, Constantia Beresford, left the Army, and lived in rather a pretty place not far from Derby. At his house I met two rather agreeable young men, an Irish Mr Bowan, a dragoon, and Count Lapâture, an oddity, but a clever one, though a little fine. I was glad to meet them again at the Derby Ball, where I did not know many people. Another very pleasant acquaintance was Colonel Pennington, an old Indian friend of the General's. He spent a couple of months at

1. Sir Richard Arkwright had died in 1792; this was his son (1755–1843), who was reported to be the richest commoner in England.

Fountain Dale, and left it to return to Bengal to make out the two years required to complete the 32 years of service. He was an artillery officer, had commanded the Force for some years, after indeed creating it, he was thought a great deal of by military men, and was a clever, agreeable companion, but very plain, old, little, shabby. We made him some marmalade, Annie and I, to remind him of his Scotch lady friends, and he wrote for us some amusing verses in return. He was a furious hunter, and regretted nothing in England so much as his stud.

It is strange that during my long stay in Sherwood I never went but once into Nottingham, though only 15 miles from it. My cousin, the rich Miss Launder, lived there, and Doctor Charles Pennington. It is a fine old city with its Castle upon the hill, from which the town slopes to the green plains all round. I rode once or twice to Newstead with Colonel Pennington. Colonel Wildman was not then settled there; it was undergoing repairs, having only just been bought from Lord Byron,[1] and was a fine place certainly, well wooded, with a lake, gardens and shrubberies, but flat, too flat. The house was very fine. One long gallery was divided by skreens into three large rooms, and when filled by the pleasant guests the Wildmans brought there, Annie Need found herself in her right place. When my sister Mary paid her visit to Fountain Dale she and Annie spent half their time at Newstead. Colonel Wildman was West Indian and very rich. He had made one of those queer marriages some queer men make—educated a child for his wife. She turned out neither pretty nor clever, but she satisfied him, and was liked. Haddon Hall was more interesting than Newstead, less attractive, a large high, ugly house. All the reception rooms on the 3rd storey; they were small, low, and scantily furnished; nobody ever lived there, and the Duke of Devonshire's visits were far apart. One thing touched me. The Duke was childless, unmarried; beside the bed on which

1. Byron sold his family home to Colonel Thomas
   Wildman, a Harrow contemporary, for £94,500
   in December 1817. E.G.'s sister Mary was much
   impressed by her visit shortly afterwards.

he lay when at Haddon was a small cot in which slept the little Cavendish boy who was to be his heir. I can't recollect any other incidents of my life in Nottinghamshire.

In May I went up to London with the General. We travelled all night, and about 6 o'clock in the morning I was met on Hampstead heath by my dear little Aunt Frere in her demi-fortune.

Uncle Frere had given up his London house, and lived now in a villa on Hampstead heath, a comfortable house, but ugly, standing in a small square of pleasure ground enclosed by high Walls, shutting out all view of very pretty scenery; London in the distance with its towers and its steeples, and its wide spreading streets, and the four or five miles between the great City and Hampstead Hill a perfect confusion of so called country residences. Life in the forest had been sleepy though enlivened by changes and by the hunter's horn and the bark of dogs, as the horses dashed into the yard on a hunting afternoon, the riders clamouring for bread and cheese and ale, when Annie and I would look out of the back window at what was really a pretty sight. Life at Hampstead was very sleepy, enlivened by nothing, but it was pleasant in a sleepy way, every body was so kind. It was a hot house full of children who did little and servants who did less.

We got up early, as my Uncle had to go to chambers after breakfast. We drove into London nearly every day. We had Freres without end to dinner, such miserable dinners, worse than the breakfasts, for at them we had Twyford sweet brown bread and good butter. We went to bed late, for we were often out at dinner or at plays and Concerts, and twice at the Opera, that was a treat, only no one near me felt the worth of the musick and then we had to drive the four or five miles back, which was very tiring. We always seemed to be busy, yet we did little, there was always a fuss, a quiet fuss, and I was very weary, for we heard nothing, the world was very dead to us, though we were so near the heart of it. And there was no repose, no one was ever left alone. My Uncle and Aunt were all kindness, the children were little things, good and clever, but they were only half alive. I have never since wondered at the wretched health of all that family, the wonder is that any of them lived to grow up after such an exhausting process as was their rearing, no nourishment for either soul or body. No young body could thrive on the unpalatable provisions presented to not very hungry appetites—and no mind could expand where there was so little interest felt in all the improvements of this improving age. They were mostly unnoticed and there was a sort of a religious *bar* which closed the door against all that was bright and beautiful. Yet these religious feelings were not morose, there was no Calvinism in their creed. As far as their lights allowed, they enjoyed the blessings of their lot. I don't know that any of my Uncle's brothers were clever men. Some had got up high but all fell down again. Uncle John made a mill of his Spanish Ambassadorship, Uncle Bartle, who was charming, was outwitted by a woman when acting as Uncle John's Secretary. Between them they caused the retreat to Corunna and the death of Sir John Moore.[1] Excepting these two, they had all the wit to marry rich wives and really only Hatley Frere was below par. My Uncle was a good man of business and a man of good sense, he never seemed to be quite awake enough even to speak distinctly; he drawled his words and through his closed teeth, leaning back in his chair with half closed up eyes, as if quite wearied, as perhaps he was after a hot day's work in chambers. He was a kind, straight forward man, with a great reputation as a man of business, always intent upon giving pleasure to every one around him. My dear, little Aunt was one of the 'blessed who are pure in heart,' and if any of us are ever to 'see God' she will be of them, for her whole life on earth was a continued preparation for heaven. Not a praying, stern, faquir like life of self imposed miseries, hardening the heart and closing it against all the gentle and beautiful influences created to be enjoyed by us; her Christian creed was 'to do good and sin

1. Rt. Hon. J. H. Frere P.C. (1769–1846) (the recently appointed Madrid Ambassador) used every method in his power to persuade Moore to advance from his 1808 winter quarters to attack the French; Sir Charles Oman's *A History of the Peninsular War* argues that Frere was correct in his judgement but his 'uncontrolled expressions showed he was entirely unfit for a diplomatic post'.

not'; self she never thought of except as a means of rejoicing others. She was in truth the minister of comfort to her circle, the sun of her sphere. She yielded to the habits she found, but had she been thrown among a higher order of minds, her naturally great abilities would have developed themselves still more worthily, cramped as they were. She and all belonging to her were happy. What can we wish for more. She had eight children at this time; John and George at School, fine boys, and two little men at School too, a day School, the lessons for which they prepared with me while I was with them. The two elder girls were nearly grown up, pretty, both of them, the two younger ones were nice little bodies very fond of play. Anne was clever, so was poor Willie who did not live.

Uncle William Frere, we called them all Uncles, had married the most accomplished amateur singer in England. At this time she was taking lessons from Velluti; she missed no opportunity of improving herself. He was delighted with her voice and her style, said there were few professional singers superiour to her. She often rode out to Hampstead with her husband, sang to us the whole evening, and rode back again. I often rode in the mornings to her on my cousin Lizzie's quiet pony, and she would sing to me alone as readily as to an admiring crowd. I remembered well what she taught me. I frequently rode into town, frightened a little at first by the noise and bustle of the streets, but I got used to it. Sometimes we cantered over the heath and on to Harrow, which was a great deal pleasanter.

I must try and recollect the names of the few remarkable people I met with. I was twice at the Opera and heard Curioni, Pasta, De Begnis, Camporesi, Madame Vestris and Velluti.[1] The Messiah was admirably given at the Hanover Square Rooms, and Cramer, who was giving lessons to Miss

1. These were amongst the most celebrated contemporary singers of Italian opera, especially Rossini; Giuditta Pasta (1797–1865) was 'the greatest soprano in Europe for more than a decade,' while Giovanni Velluti (1781–1861) was 'the last of the great castrati singers' (*Groves*).

Richards, called, at her request, to hear the little highland girl sing 'Hanouer,' took his violin out of the case, caught up the air, and then played lovely musick of his own as a return for the gaelick Crochallan, and Castle Airley. Sir Robert Ainslie came often to hear the old Scotch ballads, and George Rose to get a listener to his translation of Ariosto, which proceeded but slowly, and never, I believe, was published. Mr William Rose occasionally came to dinner, and that poor, mad poet, Coleridge, who never held his tongue—stood pouring out a deluge of words meaning nothing, with eyes on fire, and his silver hair streaming down to his waist.[1] His family had placed him with a young doctor at Highgate, where he was well taken care of. A nephew of his, a fine young man, a great favourite with my Uncle, often came to us on a holiday; he was a great lawyer afterwards. Miss Joanna Baillie[2] was a frequent visitor; a nice old lady. Then we had Mr Irving of the unknown tongues, the most wonderful orator, eloquent beyond reason, but leading captive wiser heads. Men went to hear him and wondered. Women adored him, for he was handsome in the pulpit, tall and dark, with long black hair hanging down, a pale face set off with teeth superb, and such a pair of flashing eyes. The little chapel he served was crammed with all the titles in London. It was like a birthday procession of carriages, and such a crush on entering as to cause screaming and fainting, torn dresses, etc. Hatley Frere firmly believed this man's rhapsodies, kept him and his wife and their child in his house for ever so long, and brought them up to us for a day. We thought them very dirty; tried the translations I believe, and was busy at this very time calculating the year for the world to end. Happily the period fixed on passed away, to the

1. Samuel Taylor Coleridge (1772–1834) had been a confirmed opium addict by this time for twenty years; in any case his method of conducting a conversation led Mme. de Staël to comment he was great in monologue but bad in dialogue.
2. Joanna Baillie (1762–1851), a prolific Scottish authoress, made her home in Hampstead from 1806 the centre of her literary circle.

exceeding relief of many worthy persons.[1] At a Concert of ancient musick to which my Uncle and Aunt kindly took me I saw another celebrity—the Duke of Wellington. He was standing talking with Rogers the poet, who seized on my Uncle as he was passing to appeal to him on some subject they were discussing, and for five minutes I stood next the great Duke.

My father had pleasant lodgings in Duke Street, where I went when he wished me to see some of his own friends. He took me to the Mackintosh's, where I dined. Sir James was not at home; Lady Mackintosh was kind and agreeable, her daughter Fanny was a nice girl, and Mrs Rich, Sir James's daughter by his first wife, both pleasant and clever. One subject we avoided all allusion to, unfortunate Lady Wiseman, whom we had known so well. Fanny Mackintosh spent most of her time at Holland House with Mary Fox, who was her particular friend; an intimacy my mother would have disapproved of.[2] My father took me also to the Vines; he was a rich merchant, very underbred I thought; she, a quiet little woman, very kind to me. She took me to the grand Review at Hounslow, where we went in Sir Willoughby Gordon's carriage. He was Quarter Master General, and very intimate with Mr and Mrs Vine; they were his neighbours in the Isle of Wight. Of course we were well placed, in the reserve space for the great next to the Duchess of Kent, a plain, colourless woman, ill dressed, whose little shabby daughter, wrapped in a shawl, gave no promise of turning out our pretty queen. Lady Gordon was not with us. She was keeping herself and her young daughters quiet, as they were engaged to a

1. Edward Irving (1792–1834), was a hugely successful popular preacher. His handsome features may have been marred by 'a slight obliquity of vigor' . . . but 'frivolous society in London was provided with a new sensation'. (D.N.B.) E.G.'s mention of his attempted translations of the unknown tongues refers to his belief that the obscure mouthings of a girl, Mary Campbell from Gairlochhead in his native Scotland, revealed the second advent.

2. The Hon. Mary Fox (1806–91) was daughter of Lord Holland, whose nephew, Charles James Fox, kept the Whig interest alive in years of Tory domination.

children's ball in the evening at Carleton house, for these were the days of the regency. She was so obliging as to offer me a ticket for Almack's,[1] which Mrs Vine accepted for me, as she said her sister, Lady Bury, would have great pleasure in being my chaperon; but I had no mind to go. I did not like putting my father to the expense of the dress, and I should have known no body, so the matter was not thought more of, and my little cousins played with the ticket.

My time for leaving these kind relations was drawing near. I had not learned much in that sleepy house, although one way or another I had seen a good deal, and my Uncle had been so good as to take me into his Latin Class with the little boys, whose lessons I was thus able to help. I liked this much, and afterwards found my Latin very useful. George and Willy did not think so.

The Eton holidays were at hand. John Frere and my brother John were to spend them at the Doune. They were to travel with my father and me. How happy they were. We started by coach again, I was getting quite used to this vulgarity, passed through Oxford and thought of my Aunt Mary. On to Liverpool to a good hotel, in the yard of which the boys, to their great delight, discovered a tank full of live turtle; a disgusting sight I thought it, such hideous, apathetick creatures. We walked a good deal about the town; the new streets are handsome, the villas in the neighbourhood very pretty, well kept grounds to most of them. There was no Birkenhead then, but the higher part of the town was sufficient at that time for the retreat of the busy inhabitants. The quays and the squalid lanes in the lower part of the town were as dirty as Glasgow, Bristol or Dublin.

Next day we went on board the steamer for Glasgow.

1. Almack's Assembly Rooms was a fashionable meeting place in St James London; it was celebrated because of an occasion when the Duke of Wellington was refused entry for failing to wear the obligatory knee breeches and white cravat.

# CHAPTER TWENTY-FIVE

## 1823–1827

My Mother and my sisters left the highlands soon after Christmas, and had been ever since staying with poor Aunt Leitch, who was dying. My mother never left her, but she let my sisters visit about among the many friends and relations, Charlotte Ironside with them, and a very pleasant time they spent. Mary Ironside had gone to India with her sister Eliza, a step on her part Mrs Leitch never forgave. Uncle Ralph was at that time living at Tennochside; he used to come in once a week at least to cheer my mother. My father staid only two days in Glasgow. My sister Mary and I and the two boys accompanied him home, leaving Jane as a help to my mother and Charlotte. We went by a fast Coach that beautiful road past Stirling, Crieff, and Blair Drummond to Perth, where we got into the Caledonian Coach, and so on by the old familiar road to our own gate, where a cart was waiting for our luggage. We walked the mile down the heathery brae to the boat at the Doune, and crossed our own clear, rapid Spey at our own ferry.

I was very glad to get home; I was ill, quite exhausted by the life at Hampstead. I had left the forest perfectly well. Week by week, I lost strength while with the Freres; so little sleep, so much worry without much pleasure. My mother was shocked at my appearance. Dr Smith and the highland air and the quiet life soon restored me. Of course during my Mother's absence for such a cause we saw no company beyond the Bellevilles or a stray traveller; but while the boys were with us we were very happy, fishing, shooting, boating, riding, out of doors all day, and I had my flowers to set in order. Mary regretted Glasgow. It was a life of variety much more to her mind than that we led at home. She regretted her young friends too. Still she managed to amuse herself. I forget exactly when my Mother and Jane returned to us, not before winter, I think. There were many things for her and uncle Ralph to settle after poor Mrs Lèitch's death. Charlotte was the heiress. She went to Houghton immediately, leaving Mr Shortridge to sell the house and furniture. Some legacies were left very wisely to the younger Houghton nieces, at least the interest of a certain sum, which on their marriage or death was to revert to their brother William, and so ended the year 1824.

The year 1825 was spent very happily at the Doune in the usual way, William busy, John a season at College in Edinburgh boarded with the Espinasses, and then off to Hartford or Haileybury, I forget which, the Indian College for Civil appointments, where he made a great name. Robert Grant got him the appointment, and there was no demur about it this time. We three girls were a great deal in Morayshire paying long visits, two of us at a time, to our many friends there. We were at Altyre, Relugas, Burgie, Forres House, etc. Altyre was very pleasant, so very easy. It was impossible not to like Lady Cumming, equally impossible not to disapprove of her conduct. She spent her days gardening and fishing—no man could play or land a salmon more dexterously. She was always surrounded by a suite of young men, devoted admirers, some of whose hearts she nearly broke, Sir William looking apparently satisfied. He gave us a Ball, which was extremely well managed, for they had very amusing people staying with them, and they invited all the neighbourhood besides. Poor Rawdon Clavering was there, so much in love with Jenny Dunbar. They married afterwards on nothing, went to the West Indies, lost their health, and she died. And we had those strange brothers whose real name I can't remember, but they one day announced that they were Steuarts, lineally descended from Prince Charles, out of respect to whose wife, who never had a child, the elder brother assumed the name of John Sobieski,[1] the younger brother was Charles. Nobody was more astonished

1. Charles Edward Stuart's mother was Maria Clementina Sobieska. John (c1795–1872) and Charles (c1799–1880) Sobieska claimed to be his legitimate heir.

at this assumption than their own father, a decent man who held some small situation in the Tower of London. The mother was Scotch in some way; her people had been in the service of the unfortunate Steuarts in Italy, and who can tell that she had not some right to call herself connected with them. Her two sons were very handsome men, particularly John Sobieski, who, however, had not a trace of the Steuart in his far finer face. They always wore the Highland dress, kilt and belted plaid, looked melancholy, spoke at times mysteriously. The effect their pantomime produced was astonishing; they were *fêted* to their heart's content; half the Clans in the Highlands believed in them; for several years they actually *reigned* in the north country. At last they made a mistake which finished the farce. Lovat, Fraser of Lovat, had taken them up enthusiastically, built them a villa on an island in the Beauly firth, in the pretty garden of which was a small waterfall. Here Mrs Charles Steuart sat and played the harp like Flora MacIvor, and crowds went to visit them. They turned Roman Catholicks to please their benefactor I suppose, and so lost caste with the publick. Poor Mrs Charles was a meek little woman, a widow with a small jointure whom the Prince, her husband, had met in Ireland. I don't know what took him there, for nobody ever knew what his employment had originally been. Prince Sobieski had been a coach painter, not the panel painter, the Heraldick painter, and most beautifully he finished the coat of arms.

Jane paid a very long visit to Relugas, lovely little place on a wooded bank between the Divie and the Findhorn, and then Sir Thomas and Lady Lauder, who were going to Edinburgh to a grand musical Festival, took her with them, afterwards they went a tour along the Borders, a new country to Jane. One visit they paid was to Abbotsford. Jane was in an extasy the whole time. Sir Walter Scott took to her, as who would not; they rode together all day on two rough ponies with the Ettrick Shepherd and all the dogs. Sir Walter gave her all the border legends, and she corrected his mistakes about the highlands.[1] At parting he hoped she would come

1. For this visit see *Scott's Letters*, Vol. VIII, edited by Sir Herbert Grierson, p. 278.

again, and he gave her a small ring he had picked up among the ruins of Iona, with a device on it no one ever could make out. Mrs Hemans was at Abbotsford, a nice, quiet, little woman, her two sons with her, fine little boys, quite surprised to find there was another lion in the world beside their mother.[1]

The Lauders brought Jane home in great glee and staid a week or more, during which time they held mysterious conferences and went rambles alone, and went on very queerly. I was sure that some secret business was in train, but could not make it out, as I was evidently not to be let into it. At last the discovery came—Sir Thomas was writing his first novel.[2] The hero was McIntosh of Borlam, and the scenes of his exploits were most of them laid in the woods of Rothiemurchus and the plains of Badenoch. 'Lochandhu' really was not bad; there were pretty bits of writing in it, but it was just an imitation of Walter Scott. I believe the book sold, and it certainly made the Authour and his wife completely happy during its composition. Lord Jeffrey, his wife, and Charlotte all came to see us, and Lord Moncrieff, who won my heart, charming little old man. Lord Gillies and Mrs Gillies always came for a few days, and Jane and Emilia Cumming, and the Lady Logie and May Anne and many more, for those two summers were gay. We all went to the Northern Meeting, all five of us; but without my father and mother. Glenmoriston took charge of us and his sister Harriet Fraser, and we went in a very *fast* style, escorted by Duncan Davidson, who unexpectedly arrived for the purpose. Mary was the beauty of the Meeting. She had grown up very handsome, and never lost her looks; she had become lively, and, to the amazement of the family, outshone us all. She was in fact a genius and a fine creature—poor Mary.

In the autumn of 1826, besides our usual visitors, we had Alexander Cumming to bid us good bye before returning to India, a fine, very handsome man, who on account of the

1. Mrs Felicia Hemans, the poetess (1793-1835), visited Abbotsford July 1829.
2. This novel, about one of the leaders of the Jacobite rising of 1715, was published in 1825.

Entail it was intended to marry to Mary, but they did not take to one another, and the Espinasses came, she very absurd, he a clever Frenchman; and Lord Macdonald, 6 feet 4; and then Annie Need. What a happy summer we spent with her, and all the people so delighted to see the Colonel's daughter. Later came her husband the General, and his friend Colonel Pennington, who had been to India and back since he and I parted in Sherwood Forest. He was a very clever man, and a very good man and very agreeable, but old and ugly. How could a young, brilliant creature like my sister Jane, so formed to be a first rate young man's pride, fall to be this old man's darling. But so it was; she did it of her own free will, and I don't believe she ever regretted the step she was determined to take. It was an utterly unsuitable marriage, distasteful to all of us, yet it turned out well; she was content.

The Needs left us in October 1825 taking Mary with them, who was to spend the winter at Fountain Dale. They originally intended to steam from Inverness to Glasgow and Liverpool; luckily this plan was given up. The Steamer was wrecked and nearly all on board were drowned. I don't remember any cabin passenger saved except John Peter Grant of Laggan, the only remaining child of nineteen born to the minister and his celebrated wife, and young Glengarry. Among the lost was one of the pretty Miss Duffs of Muirtown, just married to her handsome soldier husband, and on their way to join his regiment; their bodies were found clasped together, poor things, beside many others unknown. Colonel Pennington had outstaid his friends; he and Jane wandered all over Rothiemurchus, apparently delighted with each other. At last he went, leaving us to prepare for his return at Christmas.

I am not quite sure that my recollections of these two years are quite correct, writing at this distance of time without any notes to guide me; I don't think I have forgotten any thing of consequence, but the dates of these family events are confused. It must have been in September 1825 that the Needs and Colonel Pennington left us. Johnny had gone back to Haileybury, and our diminished party felt dull enough; a weight was over all our minds. We were sitting at dinner on a chill Autumn evening, enlivened by a bright wood fire, and some of the cheerful sallies of poor William, who ever did his best to keep the ball up. The post came in; I gave the key; Robert Allan opened the bag and proceeded to distribute its contents, dropping first one thick double letter into a silver flagon on the sideboard, as William's quick eye noted, though he said nothing. When we all seemed occupied with our own peculiar despatches he carried this hidden treasure to Jane. It was the proposal from her Colonel. She expected it, turned very pale, but kept her secret for two days, even from me, who shared her room. She then mentioned her *engagement* to my father first, my mother next, and left it to them to inform William and me. There never was such astonishment. I could not believe it; William laughed; my father made no objection. My mother would not listen to the subject. More letters arrived, to Jane daily, to William and me full of kind expressions, to my father and mother, hoping for their consent. My father replied for all; my mother would not write; William and I put it off. Annie Need wrote to dissuade Jane, Lord Jeffrey and Miss Clerk to approve, the lover to announce his preparations. My father and William proceeded to Edinburgh to draw up the Settlements. It was found that the fortune was very much smaller than had been expected, and from another source we heard my father would have been glad to have offended the bridegroom, but he was not to be offended; his firm intention was to secure his wife, and he would have thought the world well lost to gain her. Her interests were well cared for. Why not. If old men will marry young women, young widows should be left quite independant as some return for the sacrifice, the full extent of which they are not aware of till too late. Well! the Settlements were made by Sir James Gibson Craig, who well knew how to second my father in arranging them. After all, the young Couple were not badly off—the retiring pay of a full Colonel with the off reckonings, £25,000 in the Indian funds, and a prospect! of Deccan prize-money—some few hundred pounds which he did not get till the year before he died. My Mother wrote many letters to Edinburgh; she certainly did not wish to forward matters, but this spirited pair wanted no help. The Bride asked whether she could be provided with some additions to a rather scanty wardrobe, the best things belonging to Mother and daughter having been settled up for May for her English visit, or whether she should apply to her intended. The Bridegroom set out for the Highlands and had the banns published in *Edinburgh* on his way; a mistake of his man of business which was very annoying to all and caused a good deal of irritation—however, all got right. Jane was determined. She had argued the point in her own strong mind, decided it, and it was to be. Perhaps she was not wrong; the circumstances of the family were deplorable, there did not appear to be any hope of better days, for the girls at any rate, and we were no longer very young. So a very handsome trousseau was ordered, our great Uncle the Captain, kind old man, having left each of us £100 for the purpose, spent long before, I suppose, but Jane said she was entitled to it and so she got more than the worth of it, it added but a small sum to the vast amount of debt.

Colonel Pennington announced that he was engaged to dine with his brother in London on Christmas Day, so the wedding was fixed for the 20th of December 1825.

It was a cold, dull morning. I had been up all night preparing the breakfast, for our upper servants were gone, had been gone since the spring. Miss Elphick, poor soul, had come to be present at the first marriage amongst us. She left us when we left Edinburgh, she had been with the Kirkman Finlays in Glasgow. She assisted my labours by torrents of tears. The Bellevilles were the only guests, Mrs Macpherson so sad. The ceremony was performed in the Library by Mr Fyvie, the young episcopal clergyman from Inverness. My Mother's whole face was swelled from weeping; I was a ghost; William very grave; my poor father, the unhappy cause of our sorrow, did look heart broken when he gave that bright child of his away. The Bridegroom wore his Artillery uniform, which became his slight figure well; he did not look near his age, and he was so happy though so ugly. The Bride stood beside him in her beauty, tall, fresh, calm, composed. It was to be done, and she was doing it without one visible regret. 'I will' was so firmly said, I started. What happened after I never felt. Mrs Macpherson just whispered to me, 'Help them, Eliza,' and I believe I did. I tried I know; dear, kind Mrs Macpherson, what a friend she was, never tiring, always ready, so wise too. The breakfast went off well. The Colonel was so gay, he made his little speeches so prettily, his wife looked quite proud of him. He took leave of the humbler friends in the hall so kindly, and of us so affectionately, that we all relented to him before we parted. We all went down to the boat; the gentlemen crossed the water. On the gravelly shingle beyond was the London built chariot and four horses, the man and the maid, and the two postillions with large favours, a mob of our people round the carriage raising such a shout as their pride—ay, and their blessing—was driven away. She never forgot the home of her fathers, never lost sight of her Duchus; her protecting hand has been the one faithfully held over 'the great plain of the fir trees' from that hour to the day of her death. She has been the nursing mother to all our people, in weal or woe their prop. Beloved every where, she was worshipped there. Doing her duty every where, she has taken the duties of others on herself there. She departed on that wintry day the only unmoved person in the throng; home, to me at least, never seemed like home since.

Colonel Pennington had a hunting box in Leicestershire near the village of Normanton, where they lived till the spring. He then took a pretty, old fashioned place called Trunkwell, near Reading, which they were very sorry to be obliged to leave in a year after, when they fixed themselves at Malshanger for the rest of *his* life, near Basingstoke, in the higher part of Hampshire. It was an ugly house, but very roomy, very comfortable. The garden was good, the grounds pretty, plenty of fine trees, the scenery of the neighbourhood interesting and the place interesting. They improved it much during their time in it; both of them had good taste and delighted in a country life. She liked her garden, her horses, her new acquaintance, and was really very happy, though her husband was not a good tempered man, and certainly often forgot that he had married a girl who might almost have been his granddaughter, so that at first they rather hobbled on at times; but with so really good and clever a man, and so admirable a character as hers, these little points soon wore smooth. They were not at first appreciated; the disparity between them made people suppose all could not be right, that she was either mercenary, or the victim of mercenary relations, but as they were better known they were better understood. Few have left a fairer fame in any neighbourhood, respected, loved, regretted, this is how they are spoken of to this day. Annie Need said a bit of bitter fun about Jane's choice, which she much disapproved. 'It was his mind,' said some of us apologetically; 'she married him for his mind.' 'She could not well have had less body then,' she said tartly enough. Slight as he was, and far from young, he led the Pytchley hunt for many years, he had a fine stud. I think that was the Hunt he belonged to; at any rate Newton Fellowes was the Master.

When the marriage was over. Bride and bridegroom gone, cake cut, guests departed, and my father, my Mother and I were left to spend the remainder of the stern highland winter together, for William went to Edinburgh on business and could not return. Alas! he was imprisoned for debt in the gaol on the Caltonhill. The debt was of his own contracting, for in his College days he had been extravagant; he believed himself to be the heir of wealth, the son of a rich man, and he had the name of a handsome allowance which was never paid him. At the time of the execution of the Trust Deed, he had taken all my father's debts upon himself, bound himself to pay them, and they were upwards of £60,000. Had he been arrested for one of them, I think it would have killed my father; I never saw him so much affected by any thing that ever happened to him; and my poor Mother, who had so gloried in the noble sacrifice of self her son had made, she sank under this; they were very miserable. The debt could not be paid, even by degrees; the sum allowed for the maintenance of the family and the expenses of the forest work was very small, and there were other creditors who would have come forward with their claims had we been able to satisfy this one. Now I saw the wisdom of Jane's marriage, her kind husband sent William money. She wrote pleasant letters; the post was our sunlight; it came but three times a week, but such a full bag; the franks permitted a frequent correspondence.[1] Jane at Normanton, Mary at Fountain

1. This was still her father's privilege as M.P. for Tavistock.

Dale, frequently meeting at the various houses they visited, Aunt Mary from Oxford where she was now established in a small house she had furnished. Other letters and the newspapers, all helped to brighten the long evenings. Mr Caw always came in on the post nights with his little bits of gossip for my mother. He lived at Polchar in his capacity of book keeper, which office he filled remarkably well.

My Mother never went out; my father and I were never kept in, for though cold, it was sunny; hard frost gave us power to walk miles without fatigue. Yes—twice there were heavy falls of snow, which blocked up the hill road; the mail coach could not run, it and the unfortunate passengers were dug out of deep wreaths, and we had no post. So my father took to reading aloud while my mother and I worked. We had given up crossing the hall to the dining room; dinner was laid on a narrow table in the lobby, and wheeled into the Library, my Mother being unfit for the change of apartments. She was well cloked and shawled when she went to bed.

Our establishment consisted of poor Robert Allan, who was butler and footman and gamekeeper, and never could be persuaded to leave a falling house. He had a fault, a serious one, he tippled; but the man was so good, so worthy, it had to be overlooked and he was borne with to the end. Whiskey and all, he never left the family. The cook was Nelly, invaluable Nelly; she had been kitchen maid under Mrs Watling, and now, by the help of my *Cuisinière bourgeoisie*, the best french cookery book ever written, she and I together turned out little dinners that really gave an appetite to my poor father and mother, both of them rather dainty. I always dressed in the evening; it pleased them. We had a bright fire, and we *made* conversation, and sometimes William Cameron spent the evening with us, or rather with my father in the Study; there was always a bed ready for him. William, my brother, wrote cheerfully; his young friends all came to see him, and the Gibson Craigs provided him with any amount of luxuries from Riccarton. Before long he was released; nothing could be made of his confinement, so he was let to return home a little before my father departed for London about Easter. It was a great relief to get William back. I had done my best to carry out his orders, but the distances, the wintry weather, and the difficulty of procuring either money or food, made the position painful.

In the summer of 1826 my father brought Mary back; the fine weather revived our spirits, her cheerful gossip amused our poor mother, and the farm was selling eggs, and wool, and fruit, to the shooting lodges. We had no visitors this season, not even the Grants, but kind Aunt Mary had set us up. She had married a second time, Doctor Bourne, a rich man of great repute as a physician in Oxford.[1] She sent my Mother £60. We had, when my father went to London, three wedders for our supply of meat; we bought a score now, so with the poultry yard, the garden, and the river, we did well till the winter—such a winter, our last in the dear Duchus.

We were quite alone, my mother, my sister Mary, and myself, William off and on as business required; it was a severe winter. My mother kept her room until late in the day; Mary was her maid, and such a tender one. I had my tartan cloke, with a hood and a pair of jail boots, and trotted across the yard to the cellar, and down to the farm to act housekeeper there, then back to the kitchen to manage the dinner. Fine education this, and we were happy, though our troubles were great. We had mutton enough, thanks to dear Aunt Mary, and we sold enough of other things to buy our groceries from Robby Cumming. Inverness had refused to honour my orders; heavy bills were there unpaid. Then there were the servants' wages; William paid the outsiders, but there was nothing for the insiders; how good they were, waiting so patiently, asking for their own as if they were begging for a favour. There had been good stores in the house, but they were vanishing. It was hard to bear up amid such perplexities. In a happy hour I opened my heavy heart to the very kindest friend any one ever had, the Lady Belleville. No good could come of a sinking spirit, the back must bear its burden. Cold and harsh as the world thought Mrs Macpherson, she had a warm heart, with a cool judgment, and untiring zeal in the service of those she loved.

She proposed my writing for the press. I had tried this the

1. Richard Bourne (1761–1829) was Professor of Physic and then of Clinical Medicine at Oxford.

winter before, that heavy winter, wrote what I thought a lively little paper, 'An old story,' from hints furnished by the vanity of our poor cousin Edmund Ironside after a visit of his to the hair dresser in Inverness, copied it fair, and sent it to Blackwood in a fictitious name, desiring an answer to be sent to Mr Sidey the postmaster at Perth, where our bag was made up, there being no post office for years after at Lynwuilg. Day after day did I watch the boy who went to meet the Coach, having the key of the bag, I had no fear of discovery. No answer ever came, the Editor probably never looked at the paper and so lost a story that would have told well in his magazine, for ushered into the library world afterwards by Belleville, it was favourably received by his friend a Mr Fraser, some way connected with the press and brought me £3. It did not go alone, Mary and I between us wrote a bundle of rubbish for the 'Inspector,' and received £40 in return.[1]

We wrote at night in the Barrack room, for we had been obliged to leave our more comfortable apartments on account of the state of the roof over that end of the old house. Whenever it either rained or thawed we had five or six cascades pouring into tubs set round the walls to catch the water. The Barrack room was inconvenient too; the little crooked staircase which led up to it was lighted by a large pane of glass in the roof, a sky light not very tightly fixed. Several times during the snow storms we had to wade through a wreath of snow on the steps underneath it, pretty deep occasionally, so that we were wetted above the ankles; but we did not mind, we took off our shoes and stockings, and dried our feet by a good fire which we had provided for ourselves. Fuel being scarce, we gathered in the plantation as many fallen sticks as, assisted by a few peats taken from the large stacks at the farm, gave us a nice bright fire for our mid night labours. Bits of candle stuck in succession on a save-all, manufactured by our selves out of a nail and a piece of tin, performed the part of lamp, and thus enlightened, we wrote away.

Before Mary came home, it was rather lonely up there

1. *Blackwood's Magazine; Fraser's Magazine for Town and Country; The Inspector, a Weekly Dramatic Paper.*

away from every body, but not dull—where there is an object, the means of attaining that object become a pleasure and in an old patched dressing gown with an old shawl over it, my feet on the warm hearth stone, and two or three potatoes roasting in the ashes, I passed many a happy hour. We worked late, for the Highland winters have very dark mornings, so we rose late. Mary's papers were very clever, very original, they required condensing and a few grammatical corrections, but in themselves they were well deserving of the praise they received.

Dear old Barrack room, the scene of some sorrow, and many pleasures. In our younger days, in John's holidays, we used to give private entertainments there far away from molestation. We contrived a fire, made coffee, boiled eggs, had bread and cheese and butter and porridge. John was the Caterer, and no body ever refused him any thing. How merry we were, hot days or cold ones. Years after, when he was Governour of Jamaica, in one of the few letters he wrote me he recalled the gay doings of the Barrack room, the more enjoyable from their mystery.

When Mrs Macpherson sent us our £40, she sent us also by her Macpherson boy, on his shaggy pony called Rob Roy, a Times newspaper in which was a most favourable criticism of our contributions to the Inspector, especially of Mary's 'Country campaign of a man of fashion.' We were wild; first we skipped, then we laughed, then we sat down and cried. In this state our only thought was, 'We must tell mamma.'

She was alone at work in the Library. We laid our Bank notes before her, presented the praising newspaper and Mrs Macpherson's note. We had dreaded her anger, for she was very proud. Poor woman! that was over; she had suffered too much. 'Dear good children,' was all she said, and then she cried as we did, but happiness prevailed. We had all the fun in the world arranging how to spend our treasure. We were so very badly off for necessaries, we had difficulty in settling what was most wanted. We had no walking shoes. It was amusing to see us in our house shoes—old satin slippers of all colours patched at the sides, looking a little more respectable after we learned to dye them with ink; shabby dress gowns, because we had no plainer for common; the two servant maids as shabby as our selves, saying nothing, good creatures, and very grateful for the share of wages we were now enabled to give them. We three, my Mother, Mary and I, faithfully keeping our secret, for had William known it he would have borrowed some of it, he was so hard up himself, to keep the work going. We thought it best to save a little, have a nest egg, for the hour of need might come again; but it never came, thank God, and the kind friends raised up for us—but I am running on too fast, and my mother thought a few pounds should be spent on me, to enable me to accept a very kind invitation to Huntly Lodge in the spring. Several pretty dresses had been sent to me as presents and never made up, and white muslin was plenty in Robby Cumming's shop, so I set out with the kind Bellevilles for Huntly.

I had always liked Lord Huntly; he had known us young people from our birth and liked us and my father and mother were as intimate with him as they had been with his Mother, the beautiful Duchess, our pleasant neighbour for so many summers. He had married late in life, the unfortunate habit of too many young men of fashion. Lady Huntly was an excellent woman. She brought him a very large fortune, a clear business head, good temper, and high principles. She soon set straight all that she had found crooked. She was not handsome, though she had a good figure, a good skin, and beautiful hands—the Brodie face is very short and very flat and very meaningless; but she suited him, every one liked her, and she always liked me, so the fortnight I passed with her was very agreeable. There were several guests in the house, a large dinner party every day, all of the Gordon name, and staying with their Uncle and Aunt were two of the Montagues, the Ladies Caroline and Emily, and Lord Charles Russell. It was an ugly country, the grounds uninteresting, nothing particular to do except the sorting of what became afterwards a very fine collection of shells and minerals, which she afterwards left, with all that remained of her money, to little Brodie of Brodie, her first cousin. She had no children.

Mary had well filled my place at home. She had a genius for management, and she amused my mother with all her forest tales. Newstead was a never failing subject, for there she got among the great people both of them liked. Colonel Wildman was of the household of the Duke of Sussex, belonged to a crack Cavalry Regiment, was very nice, had married his sister to Sir Robert Gardiner, all brothers all up in high places so that the guests at Newstead were mostly of note. Mary had delighted in the sociable life she had led there. Of course she found the poor old Doune dull after it; had we not had our writings to occupy us her spirits might have got very low, for her fine mind was not sufficient for itself; with a spur and a prop she ran lightly through any life, wanting either she failed; but now at home she had both, and well she did her part. She helped me in all my works and helped our mother, and then skipped merrily up at night to the 'regions of fancy' in our barrack room.

My poor Mother just at this time received a great shock in the death of her eldest brother, my Uncle William Ironside of Houghton le Spring. He was thrown from his horse and killed on the spot. She was much attached to all her family, and she felt this much; but there is a silver lining to most clouds. My father came back in the summer, John followed, and for a few weeks we passed our time as normal. Then came the end.

The Borough of Tavistock, for which my father had sat in the last two Parliaments, was now wanted by the Duke of Bedford for his wonderful son, little vain Lord John Russell.[1] This enforced retirement closed the home world to my poor father; without this shield his person was not safe. He left us; he never returned to his Duchus. When he drove away to catch the Coach that lovely summer morning, he looked for the last time on those beautiful scenes I do believe he dearly loved, most certainly was proud and vain of, though he never valued his inheritance rightly. He went first to London and then abroad, taking John with him. Then came the news of his appointment to a judgeship in India—Bombay; Charles Grant, now Lord Glenelg, had done it,[2] and we were desired to proceed to London

1. Lord John Russell had represented Tavistock 1813–20 but it was his stepbrother Lord William who supplanted E.G.'s father in 1826.
2. The eldest son (1778–1866) of the East India Company Director.

immediately to prepare for the voyage. It was a blessing, and a shock—to me at least; every one else was rejoicing. Letters of congratulation came by every post. My poor mother smiled once more, and set about her preparations for removal with an alacrity that surprised us.

There was a good deal to be done, for the house was to be left in a proper state to be let furnished with the shootings, a new and very profitable scheme for making money out of bare moors in the highlands. We were to take nothing with us but our wardrobes, all else was to be left for sale, and lists of the property left had to be made to prepare the way for the Auction. The stock and crop at the farm, the wine, the plate, the linen, the books, there was the rub, all and everything that was not furniture was to go, even what belonged to my sister and me, except a few pet treasures packed in a small box and left to the care of Mrs Macpherson. She sent them to me, afterwards, and I have a few still, but what belonged to the Doune I gave back to John, and my own small collection of coins I sold during our Irish famine when we were sorely pressed for money; I believe I was cheated for they only brought £50 but it was very welcome at that sad time, a time that set me writing again, and with success.

My mother upset herself by reading old letters before destroying them; she was seriously ill. She warned me not to go through such a trial, and begged of me to burn all letters. I have done so, and regret it. Memory remains, fresh ever, its recollections are often quite as painful as the words of a letter.

William would not let the creditors have the little pony carriage; I don't know that it was exactly right, but nothing was ever said about it. It was given with its two pretty ponies, Sir Peter and Lady Teazle,[1] to Lady Gibson Craig, by whom it was most fully valued. It was the last remnant of our better days. When every other luxury was parted with, that was kept for my Mother's use. She took no other exercise. When my father was at home he always drove her out in it daily. I see them now—he in his gray *woodman's* coat with leather belt holding a short axe and a saw, breeches and long leather

1. Named after the elderly husband and young, frivolous wife in Sheridan's *School for Scandal* (1777).

gaiters, and a hat lined with green and turned up behind, the shortness of his neck bringing the stiff collar of the coat too near the brim of it. She in a drab great coat with a cape, made purposely for all weathers, and a queer misshaped black straw bonnet. Away they went all alone, out for hours, the commonest object of their drive being the pretty hill of the Callert, at the end of the Cambus Mor, which had been lately planted by my mother herself with money left to her by her aunt Jane Nesham. Before Jane married, when my father was away *she* was the driver. She wore a large flap straw hat, such as they all wear now, lined with green, her spectacles on, a plaid thrown round her; standing up at difficult corners, nodding and calling out to every passerby, on she whipped, my Mother, the greatest coward in the world, quite at ease under her guidance. Dear old days, happy through all the troubles. 'Is na the heart tough that it winna break,' said the unhappy Widow Macpherson, who lost her three fine sons in the Spanish war.

The difficulty now was to provide funds for our journey. My Mother had put by £10 of Aunt Mary's money; we had £5 left of the 'Inspector.' Belleville, kind Belleville, brought us £40, part of the produce of another packet of papers already printed, part advanced by him on some more which had been accepted, and would be paid for shortly. The old landau was cleaned, the horses ordered, the heavy trunks packed and sent off to Inverness to go by sea to London, and we were to start in the evening to dine and sleep at Belleville.

It was in August, early in the month; the weather was beautiful, the country looked lovely, the Spey sparkled under the sunshine, the wooded hills on either side stood as they stand now, and we watched the sun setting behind Tor Alvie on that last day, without a tear. Mary and I had determined to be brave. We had called on every one of all degrees; we had taken leave of none, purposely avoiding any allusion to our approaching departure. We denied ourselves the sad pleasure of bidding farewell to favourite scenes. Once unnerved we feared giving way, so keeping actively busy, we went on day by day, looking forward with hope and drawing the veil of resignation over the past.

My father had been knighted, and was safe in France, with

John. William had been in London and Edinburgh and I
know not where else, and had returned to take charge of us.
Poor William, how broken down he looked, how wise and
thoughtful he was; he said a great mercy had been vouch-
safed to us, an honourable recovery was before my father,
happiness and comfort secured to my mother. We should
nourish but one feeling, gratitude; he said this, yet looked so
serious.

On this last day, all packing being done by the help of my
Mother's old maid, whom we had brought over from her inn
at Aviemore to be with her during the night, the only person
in or out of the house who knew how near was our departure,
William and my Mother were in the Study sorting papers in
the large old black cabinet; Mary and I went out for a walk
to the garden for fruit—the pretty garden, all banks and
braes and little dells, with hanging birch all round. It was
just a step into the wood at the upper end and then on to the
Milltown burn, chafing and sparkling in its rocky bed as we
followed it along the path under the Ord. We crossed the
wooden bridge; I had always loved that shady lane with the
old woman in her chair, with her fan, perched up high above,
and the blue Cairngorm at the end. We went on; we caught
the lake, its dark fir skreens, the cottages near this end, the
flour mill, the ruined castle on its island, our own pretty
cottage with its porch and little flower garden and small green
lawn sloping down to the lake, our boat tyed to the old
stump, our cow grazing; we did not enter, we could not have
sat down in the parlour our own hands had fitted up. We
passed on into the path along the shore of the lake, Loch an
Eilein, we did not go on to Loch Gaun, but turned off up the
hill to the sheep cote and so round that shoulder of the Ord by
our own walk, to the seat round the birch tree on the knoll
above the river where we had rehearsed our plays, and where
Jane took the sketch of the Doune which Robson tinted,[1]
then we went down through the wood to the walk by the
Spey, coming out at the gate by the church, and in again to
the planting by the backwater and so to the green gate under

1. G. F. Robson (1788–1833) was well known for his
Scottish mountain scenes.

the beech tree, with few words, but not a tear till we heard that green gate clasp behind us; then we gave way, dropt down on the two mushroom seats and cried so bitterly. Alas! for resolution, had we not determined to avoid this grief. Even now I hear the clasp of that gate; I have heard it all my life, since I shall hear it till I die, it seemed to end the poetry of our existence. We had not meant to take that round; we had gone on gradually, enticed by the beauty of the day, the loveliness of the scenery, the recollections of the life from which we were parting. Long after we returned to the memory of this walk, recalling views, words, thoughts, never to be forgotten, and that we spoke of at sea, in India, at Pau, and at Avranches with a tender melancholy which bound my poor sister Mary and me more firmly together. We had gone through so much, with none to help us. Every body has a life, an inner life; every body has a private history; every body, at least almost every body, has found their own lot at some particular period hard to bear. The trials of our house were severe enough, when our young cheerful spirits felt their bitterness. What must my poor Mother have felt that last sad day. She so reserved, so easily fretted, so weary of suffering, so ill, and so lonely; hers had been a thickly shadowed life, none of it that I can remember really happy.

She had slept well, Mrs McKenzie said; all through the day she was composed, particularly kept busy by William. About 5 o'clock he shewed us the carriage on the shingle on the other side of the river, and putting my Mother's arm within his own, he led her out. No one till that moment knew that we were to go that evening, there was therefore no crowd; the few servants from the farm, joined by the two maids from the house, watched us crossing in the little boat, to which Mary and I walked down alone behind the others. Crossing the hall, William had caught up an old plaid of my father's, which he used to wear when sauntering about the grounds and now was carried off to be put upon the seat of the boat; he called old John McIntosh to row us over—Robert Allan was with the carriage. When leaving the boat, my Mother threw this plaid over the bewildered old man's shoulders. He knew it was the Laird's, and I heard he was buried in it. We entered the carriage, never once looked back, never shed a tear, though the eyes sometimes filled, very gravely we made out those eight miles among those hills and woods, and heaths and lakes, and the dear Spey, all of which we had loved from childhood and which never again could be the same to any of us.

Belleville and Mrs Macpherson received us so kindly, so warmly, cheerfully as of old. The dinner was even pleasant, so skilfully did these best of friends manage the conversation. No one was with them. Mrs Macpherson sat a long while with Mary and me at night, strengthening all right feelings with all her powers of wisdom. She had had two pretty lockets made to enclose her hair, and she cut a long Trichinopoly[1] chain in two to hang them on; these were her parting gifts. Belleville gave to each of us writing cases fully furnished. My Mother, who was a beautiful needle woman, had been embroidering trimmings broad and narrow to be left as remembrances with her friend of thirty years. We avoided a parting, having arranged with William to set off early, before our hosts were up; the only deceit we ever practised on them. We travelled on thro' the bleak hill road, and posting all the way reached Perth to dinner.

Here an unexpected difficulty met us. A coachmaker, not paid for some repairs done to the carriage at various times, seized it for a debt of £40. He was inexorable; we must pay our bill or lose our carriage. William came to me; I never saw him more annoyed; all our imperials and other luggage with their contents seized, like wise. We were in despair, feeling how very little would upset our poor mother—it was the last straw. I recollected kind Belleville's £40 for my unfinished 'Painter's Progress,' very grieved to give it to such a hard man to pay him all when others, more deserving, would only get their due by degrees; but we had no choice, so after a good night's rest we entered our redeemed carriage and drove on to Edinburgh. There the carriage was seized again and allowed to go; we wanted it no longer. We were much annoyed my brother and I by hosts of unpaid tradesmen, whom it was agreed that I should see, as they were likely to be more considerate with me—I, who could do nothing. William kept

1. Famous for its silver.

out of the way and we would not allow my Mother to be worried. The only cross creditor among the crowd was old Sanderson the Lapidary; there really was not much owing to him; a few pounds for setting some of uncle Edward's agates; these few pounds he insisted on getting, and as there was no money to be had he kept a pretty set of garnets he had got to clean, which had been left to me by Miss Neale, the sister of our great Uncle Alexander's Wife; they were set in gold, and though not in fashion then, have been all the rage since. I was thankful to get rid of even one of those unfortunate men, whom I was ashamed of seeing daily at our hotel, Douglas's in Saint Andrew's Square, where we were very comfortably lodged, and where we had to stay for the sailing of the Steamer, which then went but twice a week from Leith to London, and for a remittance to provide for our expenses.

At that season very few of our friends were in town, which was a relief to all, but Lord Jeffrey and Lord Moncrieff came in from their country houses to take leave of us. They were much attached both to my sisters and to me; it was a truly Uncle's kiss and an Uncle's blessing they left with us. I never saw Lord Moncreiff again; Lord Jeffrey lived to greet me with the old warmth years afterwards. What a Society we had lived with, those clever contemporaries of my father took very kindly to his children. We had sufficient intellect to understand their superiority and to shew that our minds were capable of enlargement in such company.

One day and night we spent at Riccarton; neither house nor grounds were then finished. We thought the scale grand, quite suited to the old place and the fine fortune. They were all kind, the whole family, father, mother, sons and daughters. We had been intimate for so long, so much together. Mary was married, the rest were all at home and very sad at the parting. Even William, though he tried to affect high spirits with that strange vulgarity of feeling which he retained till very late in life till long after his marriage with that pretty, lady like Bessie Vivian, who introduced him to society, which improved his ways—he became a polished gentleman and though his father could not turn him into a politician, he made a very useful and agreeable country gentleman,—he gained great credit by the reforms he made in the Edinburgh Record office. He had a good clear head and good business habits, I was sorry to bid him goodbye; his brother, afterwards my brother in law, was I think less attractive.

We were two beautiful days and two calm nights at sea; I recollect the voyage as agreeable, and there were incidents in it of no moment in themselves, and yet that turned to account. Mr and Mrs L'Espinasse and two of their children were on board going to France. She kept out of the way; he was always beside us chattering away in French in his lively style; two foreigners were attracted and edged their way up to the merry party, a Prussian and a Swiss, travelling on business more than for pleasure, but of what sort they did not say. They had scraped acquaintance with another passenger, a very agreeable American, Dr Birkbeck, whose lately published book Mary and I had just been reading, it was lent to us by Belleville.[1] We got on so well with our learned companion that he gave me a copy of his book and a passion flower wreath made in feathers by the nuns of a convent in Canada, very pretty it was and very useful. The only lady we ventured on was a nice looking woman in an Indian shawl, a straw cottage bonnet and a green veil, who was lame and very delicate. On hearing we were bound for Bombay she told us we should find her husband there, a Doctor Eckford, and that he would be glad to hear of her from those who had so lately seen her. She wrote her name on a leaf of her pocket book, and the date, tore it out and gave it to me to show to him. It was so calm we steamed on in sight of the coast a great part of the way; the sea was alive with shipping, mostly small craft, and then we sighted the North Foreland, where the L'Espinasses left us, in a boat which conveyed them to the Boulogne Steamer. We entered the river, when I was actually startled by the sight of two large Indiamen outward bound, floating down with the tide so grandly, moving on their way, their long, long way, with such a silent dignity. There seemed to be no one on board but the crew. As we passed the huge hulls and gazed upon the open cabin windows, our own

1. Morris Birkbeck: his *Notes on a Journey through France* and *Letters from Illinois* were both published in 1818.

destiny, so little liked, seemed to come more certainly upon us, and I know I turned away and wept.

We reached London, or rather Blackwall, in the afternoon, engaged two hackney coaches for ourselves and our luggage—my poor Mother, there was a fall; she did so feel it, and on we went to Dover Street, Piccadilly, where lodgings had been taken for us in the name of General Need. He and dear Annie were there to welcome us, and so began a busy time. It is so long ago, so much was done, so very much was suffered, that I can hardly now, at the end of twenty years, recall the events of those trying days; the order of them has quite escaped me. The few friends in or near London in the month of September gathered round. Dear Aunt Lissy and all her Freres, and good old Sophy Williams, Jane and Colonel Pennington, Lord Glenelg and Robert Grant. Lastly my father and John, he had to come to see Sir Charles Forbes,[1] but it encreased our difficulties for he was watched and tracked, though we had kept very quiet. A violent ringing disturbed us one day, and a violent knocking too, by several parties all insisting on being let in, on seeing some one, on finding Sir John Grant; he was in these lodgings, they were sure he was, he had lodged here before, he certainly had during a sharp fit of illness, and it was a mistake that they had been taken for us, but he knew the old maiden land lady who had been so kind to him would be attentive to his family, and she was; he had won her heart, as he won every one's, and she stood to us well. She said she had let her rooms to General Need, whose wife's trunks with her address upon them were luckily in the hall, and so she got rid of this alarm. For fear of another, it was determined to divide our party. John went to the Freres, Mary was carried off by Jane and her Colonel to Malshanger. My father and mother went to a lodging in a distant street, the General returned to his Cat and Fiddle, leaving dear Annie with me for a little time. Margaret Couper too came now and then to help me, and Mary having left her measure with the required trades people, I got through my work well, Lord Glenelg lending his carriage, for he would

1. Sir Charles Forbes (1774–1849), was a wealthy Bombay merchant and politician.

not allow Mrs Need and me to go to the City or the Dock in a hackney coach without a footman. Our imprudent father could not keep quiet; he was so well known he was followed once or twice, and being so short sighted he might have been seized but for the cleverness of the shop people. So it was resolved therefore to send him away, and on *Sunday* he and John steamed from the Tower stairs to Boulogne. William saw them safe off and then took my Mother to Malshanger. At rest at last, I got on quickly with the necessary preparations. Most of those I had to deal with were so kind, and when Mrs Need had to go home good Mrs Gillio came daily to me; her daughter Isabella was going to Bombay under my mother's care, so that our business was the same. She went with me to the docks to see the ships and arrange the cabins. It was a new and a most wonderful sight to me—a world of shipping up and down, on every side masts and huge hulls filling all space. How any particular vessel was made out our *land* eyes could never discover. We should have been perplexed indeed to make out our *Mountstewart Elphinstone*[1] had we not had a guide. The cabins were furnished, and all the linen of our wardrobes, gentlemen and ladies, supplied by an Outfitter in the Strand, and even our ordinary dresses the few that we required. I had only to get besides, shoes, stockings, gloves, books, stationery, all the little necessaries our toilettes and our occupations needed. My Mother had herself given orders to Miss Steuart for the ornamental dresses, and a tailor had measured us for habits. I saw an Ayah too, a clever little Arab accustomed to wait on ladies. She had come home with a mistress who recommended her strongly, so I hired her to attend on Mary and me. My Mother had engaged in the highlands a pretty half cast girl, the child of a returned soldier, who was anxious to go back to the country she well remembered.

Every one was obliging except old Mr Churton, who had been the family's hosier for years. My father sent me to him with the ready money order, a good large one, as some amends, the only one in his power at present, for old unpaid debts. He refused to have any dealings with it, caught up his

1. Named after the Governor of Bombay, 1819–27.

long bills and a long story, and a grievance, with reflexions on my father's conduct to him which it was not comfortable for his daughter to hear. I told the old cross crab what my father had told me, adding that this was sure money, and that we were going where he would soon save sufficient to pay all his creditors in full. He did not care, he wanted none of this money, nor any orders from the family, nor any speeches either; he wanted nothing but his rights. I had never met with such incivility, was quite unused to be so addressed. I got very faint and queer I fancy, for he seemed frightened and called his sister, who appeared distressed, told the 'dear young lady' not to mind and brought me a glass of wine. But I had recovered, and got grand, and would not touch it, swallowed my tears, and turning to the shopboy, desired him to call up Lord Glenelg's carriage. I walked out à la Princesse, leaving the ill conditioned old man making humble apologies to the air. It was very cruel in him to taunt a young girl with her parents' delinquencies.

As soon as all was in train, all our assistants at work, little Christy and I went down by the coach to Basingstoke. There Jane met us driving her basket phaeton, old Goody herself, and on we went four miles to that most comfortable, thoroughly English place, Malshanger, pretty, in an uninteresting country, being well wooded, the ground undulating, and the neighbourhood thickly studded with gentlemen's seats. It was a very good house, rather large indeed, well sized rooms, cheerful bedrooms, good garden, orchard, paddock, lawn, shrubbery. They made an extremely pretty flower garden afterwards, opening from a Conservatory they added to the Drawing room, and to the charming bow windowed study there was a Verandah covered with creepers. When the flower garden bloomed in front of it, the suite was indeed enjoyable. Jane was very well cared for and very happy. There was a stable full of horses, and servants in plenty. Our kitchen maid Nelly was the Cook, then and ever. The little sister Christy was lady's maid; Robert Allan, Butler—all the old friends established there. We spent three most pleasant weeks at Malshanger. The Colonel seemed so glad to have us, and he was so good natured to us. He rode with me every second day all over those fine Hampshire downs, miles and miles away in every direction, he on his hunters in their turn, I on the 'gentle Mortimer,' which always carried his master to covert all through the hunting season. The intervening days Jane took me off in her basket.

I had got quite out of health; I had been obliged to consult Doctor Wauchope in London, my father being a little uneasy about my altered looks. Little could be done till I got to the country—here I soon recovered and by strictly obeying a few simple rules I was 'all right' before I left these good quarters.

The Colonel and Jane dined out frequently, taking Mary with them. Jane was always handsomely dressed, though she never all her life could put her clothes on neatly. Mary wore plain white muslin and natural flowers in her hair and really she looked beautiful. She was immensely admired, and had she remained longer in this well to do neighbourhood she need never have gone to India. My Mother had gone to Oxford to stay with Aunt Mary in her new home, a very wealthy one. Doctor Bourne, a clever and an amiable man, took good care of my mother, put her into better health, and kept her till William went to bring her up to London a few days before we started for Portsmouth, for the parting had to be borne—poor Jane. Before we left her, William gave us a Deed which Mary and I were to sign. A Deed most improperly asked for, for the true nature of which was not explained to us and which, had it not been for our dear Aunt Bourne, would have left us nigh penniless. It bound us as Securitors for a debt due to Lord Lauderdale, in case of there being no funds at my father's death to acquit it, the interest in the mean while was provided for from the estate. I do not think either my father or Lord Lauderdale knew much about this transaction, it was arranged by the Trustees and the lawyers and William was charged to see the Deed executed—he trusted to Indian funds, and was thankful to get rid by any means of what might have put a stop to India. Debt, that fearful master, tyrant that one by one destroys all good principles, all good feelings, bending at the same time the victim in fetters the most galling—and all the misery caused, all the meanness engendered, all the sad retrospect, all the clouded future, it is the break up of happiness. How the £2,000 given by Government for the outfit (was spent)

I cannot tell, about £400 passed through my hands and paid the Outfitters, the lodgings, the journeys and current expenses. The passage money was of course high, three of the best cabins, and the French expenses and William's—it was little enough I believe. What little personal comforts Mary and I got were provided by good Mrs Sophy Williams. She presented us each with a few yards of lace neatly folded up, and on opening the little parcel, a £5 note was found pinned on the lace. The Freres gave us useful keepsakes and came to see us.

We were filling our carpet bags ready for our early start next morning, when a noisy visitor ran quickly up the stairs, and in bounded William Clarke, just arrived from China. He had in his hand a small case containing a beautiful ivory fishwoman, on her tiny arm a basket full of fish: the old promised wife for our ivory fruiterer. He was in a great hurry to return to clear his ship, and that puts me in mind that among our Edinburgh baggage was a case of whiskey bitters made for the long sea voyage, and a few bottles of fine old Glenlivet; it was seized at the Custom house, and though General Need took a great deal of trouble to represent the peculiar circumstances, we never saw more of our precious contrabands. One of the Clerks told the General confidentially that his Chief considered them quite a prize. I would not carry back my pretty fishwoman to her native tropicks; I sent it and a Bombay work box Uncle Edward had sent me to Fountain Dale to dear Annie. William Clarke, who expected soon to be at Dalnavert, was loaded with messages to the Bellevilles and warmly thanked for his own kind remembrance of us. So he went away.

We had finished all our business with fewer mistakes than could have been expected, considering all that had to be done and how little used to management were the doers, and at 5 o'clock next morning we were picked up by the Southampton Stage, with Lewis Grant in it as our escort. William had gone to France. Sir Charles Forbes, whose essential kindness was almost unexampled, for, without his head and without his purse, my father could never have escaped from some exasperated creditors, had sent one of his head clerks to attend my Mother on her journey. Lewis Grant of Kincorth and his twin brother had been wards of my father; there was an old connexion between us.

Was it Southampton we sailed from, or Portsmouth. I think it must have been Portsmouth, at any rate, it was the same place at which I landed three years later, when my General brought me home.[1] A small inn looking on the harbour—Mrs Gillio was already there with her daughter and her brother, Colonel Grant. He warned us that the Silver Arrow was out after my poor hunted father, scouring the sea and visiting the land. We saw some of the gentlemen bearing it, whom Lewis Grant told that Sir John Grant was not to join his family till the morrow, when they knew the Havre Steamer was expected and that the *Mountstewart Elphinstone* could not sail till the following day, the Captain said, as he was still loading. What should we have done without this friend, who to his sorrow had a part to play and well he played it, for to deception he was forced to stoop, mean deception, my Mother and Mary and I being deceived like the others. The Havre steamer came in, my father and brother not in her. My Mother's anxiety was therefore genuine, we were all three amazed, not knowing what to make of it. Colonel Alexander Grant went about the town making cautious enquiries, Lewis Grant said openly he feared my father had gone up to London and been detained. In the evening he brought us word our ship had moved out to the roads, Spithead, and tho' she would not sail till the following day, the passengers were ordered on board at once. Half bewildered we obeyed at once.

It was late in the September day—the 28th I remember it was, in the year 1827—nearly dark. We got into a good sailing boat and proceeded out to sea, Mrs Gillio, her brother, and Lewis Grant with us. In an hour we reached our huge 'ocean home'; down came the chair, we were soon upon the deck, amid such confusion, all noise, all hubbub, all a dream, but not to last long, for the rumour grew in a moment that the wind had changed. The captain ordered the anchors

1. Her husband was a Lieutenant Colonel down to his
   retiral in 1832; this promotion came in 1854, the year
   E.G. completed her *Memoirs*.

up; our kind friends must go. Mrs Gillio parted with the last of her daughters, her youngest child, and with us whom she loved almost as well. Lewis Grant came up from the cabin, where he had been comforting my Mother. He took leave of my sister and me, a quiet leave. Had he not his romance at the bottom of his honest, warm highland heart. It had laid there, I believe, ever since that Inverness meeting and a little of it lurked there for many a day, at least. I thought so when he and I met again and talked of her 'who had no parallel.' He had mentioned to my mother all his clever arrangement with Captain Henning. She was therefore watching for my father. We stood out to sea and beat about till nearly 10 o'clock, when a Jersey boat sighted our peculiar light, came along-side, and my father and both my brothers came on deck; a few moments were allowed for a few words. My father shut himself up with my Mother; John remained beside Mary and me. William, in an agony of grief I never saw equalled in any man, burst out of our Cabin. We watched the sound of the oars of the Jersey boat as it bore him from us, and then said Mary, pale as a corpse, but without a tear, 'We are done with home.' We got under weigh directly, and favoured by the wind, long before we waked from heavy slumbers, were out of reach of any silver oars.

# CHAPTER TWENTY-SIX

# 1827–1828

I HAD £30 left of the money entrusted to me, this I handed over to poor William, who was to pay the Bill at the hotel out of it and keep the rest. It was not until long after that I heard Colonel Grant had paid the bill and would not accept repayment 'till better days,' which, alas! never in that good man's lifetime came to poor William.

William's story from that period for the next four years would be a good foundation for a novel. His struggles were very hard—he had not learned wisdom. He bore his trials well, and was helped by many friends, proving that there were kind hearts in a world some of us have felt it is a mistake to call so hard as it is reputed. I may touch on his romance again; at present I proceed with my own.

A long four months' voyage in a narrow space amid a crowd of strangers. I could not avoid believing that some of them must have become acquainted with the humiliating circumstances attending our departure; they never showed this, and the Captain, who had been an actor in the miserable scene, was the most delicate of all, apparently ignorant of all; yet in odd ways Mary and I fancied he was more interested in us than in any of the rest of his passengers. We had taken a dislike to the good little man; we had met him at a tea party given by Mrs Gillio for the purpose of introducing him to us. A Captain Gordon was there and his sister in law, Mrs Gordon, a Widow afterwards Lady Stannus, and the manners of these three Indians were so unsatisfactory that our hearts sank at the prospect of Bombay society, they were not first class, certainly. On board his ship no man could be quieter or more agreeable than Captain Henning. My father and mother were the principal people; we had the best accommodation, and we formed a large party ourselves. My father and mother had one cabin, a poop cabin, Mary and I had the other, Isabella's smaller one opened out of ours; opposite to hers was Mr Gardiner; the two deck cabins were occupied by my brother John and the captain. It was quite a home circle apart from every body else; they were all below on the main decks.

Lieutenant Colonel and Mrs Morse were returning to India; a little girl with two brothers who had been at school in England, were going back to their parents in Ceylon; a young Cavalry Officer, a Doctor, and I don't know how many cadets; altogether, with the three mates, between thirty and forty at the Cuddy table,[1] not omitting Mr Caw, that clever, good hearted oddity, who was going with us to India in the hope of being provided for, as his long, unwearied services deserved.

The first feeling that struck me was the absence of all fear; alone on those wide waters, with but a plank between our heads and death, the danger of our situation never occurred to me. There was such a sober certainty of life apparent in the regular routine observed: the early holy stoning [deck scrubbing], the early cleaning, manoeuvring, arranging, the regular bells, the busy crew, the busy cuddy servants, the regular meals, the walks upon the deck, the quiet preparation of all in the Cuddy, of all in our cabins, as if we were to go on thus for ever, as if we had gone on thus for years past; all looked so usual that the terrours which assail the spirits of those on shore who watch the sea never once entered the heads of the most cowardly amongst us. Storms, rocks, fogs without, fires, leaks, want of care within, all so readily arranged before the timid ashore, never once started up in a single mind at sea.

On we sailed, those bright summer days, with hardly breeze enough to fill our sails, skimming leisurely over undulating rather than swelling waves, hardly aware that we were crossing the Bay of Biscay. With Fatima's help our cabin was soon set in order. It was well filled; a sofa bed, a dressing table that closed over a washing apparatus, a writing

1. A cabin near the stern, reserved for officers and cabin
   passengers to use as a dining room.

table, a pianoforte, a bookcase, and a large trunk with trays in it, each tray containing a week's supply of linen. In the locker was a good supply of extra stores, water well bottled, in particular. A swing tray and a swing lamp hung from the roof, and two small chairs filled corners; there was a pretty mat upon the floor, and no little room could look more comfortable. The whole locker end was one large window, closed till we left the colder latitudes, open ever after, and shaded by venetians during the heat of the day. A small closet called a galley, in which Ayah kept her peculiar treasures, had a shower bath in it, readily filled by the sailors, and a most delightful and strengthening refreshment to us. Isabella, in her smaller way, was equally well lodged.

We soon learned to employ our days regularly, taught by the regularity round us. The life we led was monotonous, but far from being disagreeable, indeed after the first week it was pleasant; the quiet, the repose, the freedom from care, the delicious air, and a large party all in spirits, aided the bright sun in diffusing universal cheerfulness. Few were ill after the first weeks, the soreness of parting was over, a prosperous career was before the young, a return to friends, to business, and to pay awaited the elder; and *we* had left misery behind us and were entering on a new life free from trials that had been hard to bear.

It was some little time before I was quite restored to strength—the nervous system had been overstrained as well as the body overfatigued. There was nothing now to disturb either. I occupied myself pretty much as at home, reading, writing, working, shading my charts, and making extracts from the books I read, a habit I had indulged for some years and found to be extremely useful, the memory was so strengthened by this means and the intellect expanded as thought always accompanied this exercise. We were all well supplied with books and lent them freely to one another. Captain Henning had a very good library, and with him and one or two others we could converse pleasantly. Mr Gardiner was very agreeable and soon became a favourite with my father and with Mary. He was a Civilian, not young; he had been ten years in India, and was returning there now after a two years' leave at home. He was about thirty, had held a good appointment, and expected a better. The family was Irish; the father, Colonel Gardiner, had inherited money and made more, and on dying left £100,000 to his five children. A son died, a daughter married a very gallant soldier—Sir Edward Blakeney[1]—two sisters remained unmarried and lived with an Aunt at Twickenham, a Miss Porter, also Irish, their mother's sister. No difficulties could occur to render this intimacy undesirable, so while Isabella and I at the Cuddy door were warbling pretty Canzonettes to our light guitars, and listening in our turn to Mrs Morse, who often brought her harp upon deck in the evenings, Mr Gardiner and his lady love amused us all by the care they took never to be far asunder.

The first Sunday at sea was very impressive. The Bells were rung for prayers, the passengers were seated all round the binnacle, the crew, so trimly dressed, were further back, even the Lascars looked on. The captain read the service, shortened; when he came to 'bless the ship in which we sail,' I know my eyes filled. Our little ship, alone on the wide waters, our little world, as it were, busy with its own little plans and schemes, such a speck in a grand universe; it was very touching. I always liked the Sunday service and always felt more truly religious, more humble, more patient, than I had ever felt in a church on shore; and a funeral at sea—this I did not witness till we were coming home; it is most affecting; that splash into the water after the coffin has been slided through the porthole, shook me from tip to toe; I did not recover it for hours. Such was my father's funeral years afterwards.

So on we sped in our 'gallant ship,' the *Mountstewart Elphinstone*, 600 tons, built by Captain Henning his own self up at Surat, and a very slow sailer! he made her. As we proceeded under brightening skies we ourselves seemed to grow sunnier. We learned to vary our amusements too, I got on famously. The little Ceylon children were very nice,

---

1. Sir Edward Blakeney (1778–1868), later Field Marshall (and C. in C. of troops in Ireland 1836–55 when the married E.G. met him often) married Maria Gardiner.

particularly the little girl; it was a pity to see them lose what they had been learning, so I made them come to me to school for 3 hours daily, Mary, when she was well enough, helping to teach them; however, she soon gave herself something better to do. Then I liked to watch the Captain taking his observation every day at noon, and one of the Officers proposed to me to make a chart of the voyage with the ship's course traced regularly and dated; it was very interesting getting on day by day, sometimes great long runs that carried my dots on ever so many degrees, and then a little shabby move hardly observable. Once, in a calm, we went round in a circle for 3 or 4 days, quite annoyingly.

After crossing the equator we found a charming occupation—a map of the Southern sky. The constellations were so beautiful. We have no idea in these cloudy climates of the exquisite brilliancy of the cloudless ones, the size of the stars too. We marked each as it rose, often staying on the poop till actually ordered away. The Cross, Sirius, Aldebaran, never were such diamonds in a sky. Captain Henning, his old mate, the young Cavalry officer and I, were the *we* who were so busy. Captain Henning was naturally clever, very obliging, but vain and uncultivated, a superiour person when one got over the little under beau manner. The young officer was somebody we should all have heard of had he lived. The Captain was extremely cross at times, but there was too much in his little knot of a head for any of us to resent this.

Besides these more private intellectual pursuits we had publick diversions. Mrs Morse played the harp well, Mr Lloyd sang; every Saturday night the captain gave us a supper; in return each guest spoke or sang, the worse the better fun, but *we* did our best. John, Mary, and I got up many pretty duetts, and glees, and one solo never palled, 'the *wet* sheet and the flowing sea,' though the captain always made me sing it '*taut*,' the '*taut* sheet and the flowing sea,' more correct a great deal but the sound unmusickal.[1]

Another day was for the sailors; they danced and they sang, and did athletick exercises, ending with a supper.

1. The best-remembered poem of the Dumfriesshire
   poet, Allan Cunningham (1784–1842).

Mrs Morse gave a Concert once a week down below in her range of cabins, and my Mother, opening our 4 *en suite*, gave another. Then we played cards in the Cuddy. Every body inclining to be agreeable, amusement was easily managed.

The Cadets killed a shark, and the Doctor dissected the head, giving quite a pretty lecture on the Eye. A nautilus, too, came under his knife, and a dolphin, and flying fish and sucking fish. One day I had been doing my map in the Cuddy, and wanting some pencil or something, went into our cabin; the locker venetians were all open, and there before me, resting on the waters beyond, was an albatross surrounded by her young. Such a beautiful sight. That 'Ancient Mariner' committed a dreadful crime. Another day a storm at a distance revealed to us as it ended a waterspout, which, had it broken on us, would have been our end. It was in hour glass form, spouting up very high. Then we had a near view of Madeira, merely villas among trees on a hill, a town on the shore. A boat or two came off with fruits and took back our letters, but we hardly slackened sail, just passed stately on, all of us absorbed in the vision of the distant peak of Teneriffe, which seemed to tower *through* the skies.

On the line we were becalmed, very hot and very tiresome. We amused several evenings by lowering the boats and taking a rowing circuit of some miles, till to me the feeling of insecurity became oppressive, the ship a speck, and we, some half dozen of us, abandoned as it were without resources on the deep. We had stormy weather near the Cape, bitterly cold; all the thick wraps we were provided with were insufficient to keep us comfortable. One really wild day I had myself lashed to the companion that I might take a steadier survey of the sea 'mountains high.' The waves rose to the mast head, apparently; we were up on top of them one minute, down in such a hollow the next, the spray falling heavy on the deck. The dinner that day little mattered, so few partook. We stouter ones were contented with one dish, a meat dumpling, our portion served to each in a bowl, and the attendant requisites either kept together by padded subdivisions strapped across the table or propt upon the swing trays overhead.

In these latitudes began the sudden showers, so heavy, so incessant, with drops so large, their rattling deafened us. In 3 or 4 minutes a wash hand basin was quite filled; the servants had a grand display of pottery, running about so eagerly to catch an additional supply of that commonest of all Nature's gifts ashore, the scarcest, the most prized at sea, pure water.

We passed very few vessels, two only near enough for hailing, one only able to receive our letters home; yet we went on journalising as if we had next door the penny post box. At length we scented, really and truly scented Ceylon; the mild elastick air which blew from it upon us literally was perfumed by the spice groves it had passed over. I never felt any thing so delicious.

Our vessel was soon surrounded by the singular shaped boats of the Cingalese, a monkey looking race, scarcely a rag upon them, chattering like as many apes, and scrambling about with the wares they had brought for us, and tried to force us all to buy. Their jewellery was false enough, but pretty, their cottons mediocre enough, as were their fruits and vegetables, but we thought these last quite excellent spite of their strangeness to our palates. We had been so long without either, except a few preserved. A whole day we enjoyed ourselves with our savage visitors, amusing ourselves with their gestures, their wares, their extraordinary appearance; the sea alive with boats, the harbour full of shipping, the shore very pretty. We had touched at Point de Galle. At first the charm of green trees, white walls, etc., was sufficient for our admiring eyes. Soon we were calm enough to discriminate, and then it only seemed the more interesting to discover no feature we were used to amid the scenery; roofless houses, closed venetians within verandah shades, no windows visible and for trees, such long, high poles with cabbage heads or wide extending wiry arms, leafless to our ideas. It was like a vision, not like the long desired land.

Poor little Mary and her brothers felt much on leaving us. She had been so happy in our cabin with her studies. Her father, a merchant, a heavy looking man, came for her about noon in a neat boat with an awning over the cushions, under which the poor child threw herself, crying bitterly. Her brothers were calmer, the father very grateful, and so that scene moved away. I never saw Mary again. I wrote to her and sent her presents, and she replied but when I left India I lost all trace of a young intelligent companion, who had beguiled many an hour 'at sea.'

In the afternoon we went on shore ourselves; the captain took us with him to the Master Attendant's house, where he had sent to say we would spend the evening. None but those who have had their limbs cramped up during a long voyage can understand the delight with which the simple movement of one foot fall after another upon firm ground is attended. The sky so bright and sea so clear would have been hot and dazzling otherwise; nothing unpleasant assailed our sensibilities just now; the breeze was cooling, we repeated for ever, and on we went till darkness tumbled down upon us, just as we entered a gate which opened on the bank at top of which was placed Mr Tyndale's bungalow, all fairy land to us, at least. An Indian dwelling consists of one long room, from which sometimes smaller open on either hand; a shaded verandah surrounds it, parts of which are frequently made into chambers as required, by merely dividing them off by a skreen. The simple way of lighting this simple dwelling is by glass cups hanging from the ceiling or stuck against the walls, filled with cocoa nut oil in which floats a cotton wick. The ceilings are mostly breadths of calico sewed together and stretched across the rafters; the floors a composition of lime covered by matting; the furniture scanty, but handsome though bare, no draperies, no covers, nor curtains nor colouring. All must look cool, clean, dark. In such a home we found a set of hospitable people, quite pleased to hear our news from England. They gave us tea, *good bread and butter* and fruit, no fuss, hardly a sound, the shoeless servants quite startling us by offering us refreshments in gentle tones at our elbows when we had never heard them enter the room. There were several men to wait on us, all dressed in close fitting white cotton dresses and red turbans, little black creatures, very ugly, but doing their parts well. The family themselves were no way remarkable, kind obliging persons, it was the surroundings which gave so agreeable an impression—the quiet, the ease, the climate, the beauty of the whole scene which so completely satisfied the feelings. We had left our shawls in a small room near the entrance. On going back to put them on we were astonished at the radiance of the walls; they shone from ceiling to floor in spots all over in a manner incomprehensible to us, till a smiling servant, bringing a tumbler and sweeping some spots into it, revealed a knot of fire flies by the light from which we easily read a book Mrs Tyndale opened. We walked away under stars as bright, and rowed back to our ship over a sea so smooth over which such a fresh, delicious, night breeze played. It was the white day of our voyage.

At day break we were off again. Coasting up within sight of land for the most part, all along the shores of Malabar, not without danger. One night Mr Gardiner, being on deck, became aware of the cause of a great commotion among the watch; a sunken rock had nearly finished our worldly affairs; the captain was called, and by energetick measures we merely saved our distance and our lives. It was cool except for the few hours of midday, very pleasant from the balmy air, the frequent sight of land, and the cheerfulness diffused among our company by the near termination of our long voyage.

We landed on the 8th of February 1828 in Bombay. We entered that most magnificent harbour at sunset, a circular basin of enormous size, filled with islands, high, rocky, wooded, surrounded by a range of mountains beautifully irregular; and to the north on the low shore spread the City, protected by the Fort, skreened by half the shipping of the world. We were standing on the deck. 'If this be exile,' said my father musingly, 'it is splendid exile.' 'Who are those bowing men?' said my mother, touching his arm and pointing to a group of natives with Coloured high crowned caps on some heads, and small red turbans on others, all in white dresses, and all with shoeless feet, who had approached us with extraordinary deference. One of the high caps held out a letter. It was from Uncle Edward, my Mother's younger brother, who had turned the corner round Sir Giffin Wilson's wall so many years ago with his hat pulled down over such tearful eyes, and these were his servants come to conduct us to his country house. All was confusion around us, friends arriving, departing, luggage shifting, each passenger being allowed to carry a bag on shore with necessaries. And it grew dark in a moment, encreasing our perplexity.

At last we were arranged, descended the side of our poor old ship, entered the bunder boat, moved, swung round to the steps of the ghaut,[1] mounted them, found carriages waiting, and away we drove some three miles or so through part of the town and then through a wooded plain, till we stopt at a shabby gate which opened on a narrow road and led us to the wide steps of a portico, reached by a good long flight, edged with two lines of turbaned servants glittering with gold adornments, reflected by the torch each third man bore. A blaze of light flashed from the long building beyond, in front of the entrance to which stood a tall figure all in white, of a most dignified presence, queenlike as a stage heroine, who gave a sign, and from her sides moved on and down the steps four persons in scarlet robes trimmed with gold and bearing in their hands gold sticks the stature of themselves. They opened our carriage doors and out we stept; and thus we were received by my Uncle's wife.

They had come down from Surat, partly to meet us, and partly for my Uncle's health, which repeated attacks of gout had much weakened. He was at this moment on his couch, incapable of leaving it, and still in pain, yet had he made every possible arrangement for our Comfort. The large house of Camballa, which he had hired to receive us in, was of the usual Indian Construction, the large, long centre hall with broad verandahs round it; but such a hall, 80 feet long, 80 feet wide, Verandahs 20 feet wide. It stood on a platform in the middle of the descent of a rocky hill, round which swept the sea, with a plain of rice fields, and a tank, a handsome tank, between the foot of it and the Breach Candi road along the beach. From the hill end of the hall rose a wide staircase in stages; each stage led off on either hand to a terrace, each terrace on the one hand was a flower garden, on the other a covered gallery leading to offices. Top of all, and very high it was, the Terraces were covered in as bedrooms, catching all the air that blew and commanding from their latticed balconies such a view as was alone worth *almost* the voyage from Europe.

1. Bunder is a harbour, hence a boat for short journeys;
   ghat is Anglo-Indian for hindi landing stage.

Dinner was served in one of the Verandahs to the great hall with such a display of plate, so brilliant a light, and such an array of attendants as were startling after our Cuddy reminiscences. I thought of the Arabian nights. The scenes there depicted were realised with a charm belonging to them quite beyond any description to paint and which now at this distance of time rouses the fancy again, and gives them back to memory with a freshness never to be impaired. There was light, vastness, beauty, regal pomp, and *true affection*. All was not gold, however; a better acquaintance with our palace disturbed much of our admiration. Our bedrooms were really merely barns, no ceilings, the bare rafters, bare walls, no fastenings to the doors, the bathrooms very like sculleries, the flowery terraces suspected of concealing snakes, and most certainly harbouring myriads of insects most supremely troublesome, and the tank a nuisance. Very beautiful as it seemed, with its graduated sides descending to the water, interesting from the groups of native women resorting there at all hours with those pyramids of Etruscan shaped pots upon their heads, and their draperied clothing, and winging on with such a graceful step, the tank at night became a nuisance from the multitude of frogs—the large bull frog with such a dreadful croak as deafened us. Still these were minor evils. It was all a stage play life, and we were enchanted with it.

It was some days before our goods were cleared from the Custom House. We had landed in plain white dresses, my Mother and Mary and I, and had merely brought a second of the same sort in our bags; no toilette this to receive the visits of the Presidency. Great expectations had been formed of the new great man, the great Lady his wife, and the celebrated beauties his daughters. It was a bitter disappointment to find people of no mark at all, ladies with no new fashions, the Judge busy, the lady mother ditto, the daughters in white plain dresses, and the handsomer of the two engaged to be married, for Mr Gardiner had not lost the opportunity of securing to himself about the most attractive creature that ever brightened this changing world.

As we were great people, *burra sahibs*, every attention was paid to us. The cannon fired from the Fort when my father went to take the oaths, and every body called on my Lady. It is the custom in this part of India for the older inhabitants to visit the new comers; we, therefore, had to receive a perfect crowd. Many came at the breakfast hour, nine o'clock, the sun had less power thus early, the fashionable part of the society came later, some in carriages of various descriptions, some in palanquins,[1] all the ladies appeared very much dressed, the style of toilette most agreeable in a hot climate being very much more elegant than the every day costume of colder latitudes; the gentlemen in their cool white jackets and trowsers and shirt breasts unconcealed by any waistcoat, looked all so young and so clean that these Civilians quite rivalled the military in uniform.

All these mornings of the first week we were quite busy receiving company; we could hardly find time to unpack our Wardrobes. After luncheon indeed we were free, as no one called afterwards, but then we were tired or we had notes or letters to write, or wished to lie still upon a sofa waiting for the fresh sea breeze. I have lain half dead with exhaustion watching the drops of one of the large chandeliers, as the first intimation of the advancing current was the slow movement of this glittering drop. As soon as we really felt the air, we prepared for our evening airing, and on returning dressed for a party either at home or abroad, for in spite of the heat these gay doings were incessant.

I wish I had preserved a more minute recollection of my first Bombay impressions; they were very vivid at the time, and I remember being struck with surprise that all accounts of India that had ever fallen in my way were so meagre, when materials new and strange were in such abundance. I must brush up memory a bit, try to carry myself back to all the incidents of that interesting time.

The youth of the women, and the beauty of the greater part of them, is one very distinguishing feature of the society; the cheerful spirits of all, gentlemen and ladies, is quite remarkable, to be accounted for, probably, by the easy circumstances of almost all, and the Occupation of their time. There

1. A litter, usually for one, consisting of a large box with wooden shutters, carried on poles by 4 or 6 men.

are no idlers in India. Every man has his employment; he may do it well or ill, but he has it there to do, a business hour recurring with every day, releasing him every afternoon, and well and regularly paid the first of every month. The women must attend to their households and their nurseries with watchful care, or they will rue it, and tho' some may neglect their duties more or less, none can avoid them. Then it is the most sociable country in the world, truly hospitable. Every body is acquainted, every door is open, literally as well as figuratively, there is an ease, a welcome, a sort of family feel among these Colonists in a strange land that knits them altogether very pleasantly. There are gradations in the scale of course, and very rigidly observed too, the ladies in particular preserving carefully their proper position. The Governour does for King, his suite for Court, the Commander in Chief and his suite almost as grand; then the 3 members of Council and their 3 wives! very grand indeed. An Admiral, or rather Head of the Navy. All the Civilians according to seniority, all the military according to their rank; the Judges of the Supreme Court, Officials pertaining thereto; barristers, Merchants—rather below par, with one or two exceptions; attorneys thought little of; Indian Navy ditto; Royal Navy in great repute when a stray vessel came in. A few French and Americans admitted. And several of the natives quite in fashion; rich Parsees, and one or two Hindus. All these elements shook up together very cordially, and there was an undergrouping of lower caste, native and foreign, all in their peculiar costumes, which, with the singular vehicles, the strange scenery, the ocean, and the cloudless sky, made a succession of pictures that would have enchanted an artist eye.

As soon as all the Dignitaries and all the undignified had paid their visits, and what a crowd collected in our Aunt Caroline's fine hall, daily, for a fortnight, my Mother and I had to return this attention. Mary was excused on account of her approaching marriage, which ceremony indeed interrupted our civilities; but we got thro' as many calls as we could, as soon as we had unpacked our finery. My father very wisely built a carriage expressly for this sunny clime, with open sides shaded by venetians and a double roof, with a space between the outer leather and the inner *cork*. It was a delightful contrivance; we never felt baked in it, tho' to say truth it was always disagreeable to me to drive out in the glare of the mid day.

People lived about in so scattered a manner it took us a long time to get thro' our *roster* of several hundreds. Very few inhabited the Fort; a few had cool dwellings on Rampart Row, but only a few. Bungalows on the Esplanade were much more in favour, oddly enough, for they were far from being cool or pretty; they were set down in a long row surrounded by dingy palisades, giving to each house of sticks and mats a bare compound—as the space we should use for garden is called. As these rickety residences cannot be lived in during the rains, they get rather rough usage twice a year, on being first set up, and then pulled down, and few people beautify them with a shrubbery for this space of time. The few tents sprinkled about look prettier, tho' they could not be so comfortable.

The pleasantest houses are those dotted all over the plain and on every rising ground and along the Breach Candi road by the sea, with gardens round them like Camballa, and some little attempt at permanence of construction. The whole scene is very beautiful, the whole style very attractive, and the life, but for the exhausting midday heat, would be very agreeable.

My sister's marriage was a grand affair. I don't remember how many people my Aunt thought it necessary to invite to the breakfast; there were above 20 present at the Ceremony in the Cathedral. We had such a Cousinhood at the Presidency, and Mr Gardiner and Uncle Edward had so many friends, and there were my father's brother judges, etc. Good Mr Carr, now the Bishop, married them.

For so very pretty a girl as Mary then was, so beautiful a woman as she became, there never was a less interesting, I was going to say a plainer, Bride. Her dress was heavy and unbecoming, and a very large veil, the gift of Mr Norris, hid all of her face except the large nose, the feature that had been best concealed. She was perfectly silent before the ceremony and equally silent after it, self possessed all through. She bowed without smiling when her health was drank and she went off with her husband in her new carriage to Salsette as if she had been going out just to take a drive with me.

I never pretended to understand Mary; what she felt, or whether she felt, nobody ever knew when she did not choose to tell them. Like Jane, and I believe like myself, what she determined on doing she did, and well, without fuss, after conviction of its propriety. One thing is certain, she married a most estimable man; and she made a most happy marriage, and whatever she felt towards him the day she became his Wife, she was afterwards truly attached to him and she valued him to the end of her days as he deserved.

We had had plenty to do, she and I, preparing for this event, for Mary, not content with her outfit, ordered considerable additions to her wardrobe, such things as she and our Aunt Caroline considered indispensible in her new position—near £100 my father had to pay. Then there were toilette requisites, a carriage, liveries, horses, servants, linen etc., on Mr Gardiner's part, all to be chosen by her. A friend, Mr Elliot, lent them or rented to them his furnished house at Bycullah, which saved them both trouble and expense, he Mr Elliot being ill and ordered to the Neilgherries; still there were many little matters to settle, and we had no help from my father and mother. They were completely absorbed in the same sort of affairs of their own. Really it was amusing to see persons of their age, who had kept house for so many years, and had full experience of such business, so completely occupied with every the minutest detail of their Bombay establishment. Their house, its situation, furniture, number of servants, etc., one could understand would require attention; but the shape of the turbans, the colour of the cumberbands, *their width*, the length of the robes of the Chobdars, all these minutiae received the greatest consideration. I declare I don't believe the Secretaries to the Government gave half so much thought to their minutes of council. Mr Gardiner and Mary made much shorter work of it, but then certainly they had not so much to do. I had no sinecure listening to both parties, and Aunt Caroline's comments besides.

A short honeymoon satisfied our lovers; they returned after a retirement of 10 days, and then began a round of entertainments to the newly married pair. Every incident was seized on by the community to give excuse for party giving. There was so little to interest any one going forward at any time, the mails being infrequent then, that we all gladly turned attention to the trifles which filled up our lives for want of better things. An Indian life is very eventless; very dull it was to me after Mary married and John left us. Uncle Edward continued so unwell after losing the gout that he was recommended to try a year at the Neilgherries; John went there with them, proceeding afterwards from there by Bangalore to Madras and so to Calcutta, his nomination being to Bengal.

My father and Mother and I removed on their departure to the Retreat, a very fine house belonging to one of the Cowajees, badly situated at the foot of a wooded hill, which intercepted the sea breeze, and on the edge of a tank that overwhelmed us with mosquitoes. We had a large and pretty garden divided into three; one part, round two sides of the house, filled with shrubs and flowers, a piece of higher ground beyond, ending in a long terrace where I liked to walk on moonlight nights, tho' I never sat in a Belvidere two storeys high over looking the road at the end of it, and a rose field of the small single Atta rose, the perfume from which was delightful. The house itself was a palace; a broad gravel terrace surrounded it, with several flights of broad steps at intervals leading down to the road or the gardens. Upon this terrace the verandah of course opened, and into the Verandah opened all the rooms of the ground floor; the centre hall was 60 or 70 feet long, and of sufficient width to allow of three square rooms being partitioned off each end of it; the three at one side we called Drawing rooms. We ate in the hall; at the other side, one room was a spare bedroom, the other my father's study with a bath room thro' it, and the middle room held a very handsome staircase leading up to my Mother's apartment and mine, both were alike composed of three pieces, bedroom, dressing room, wardrobe room which was dark, and contained the large tin cases in which we kept our dresses safe from insects. There were bath rooms and a connecting Verandah in which our Ayahs slept and our tailors worked. Over the hall and Drawing rooms there was no second storey.

Altho' the Drawing rooms were only separated by skreens from the hall, we lived in the hall mostly, on account of the current of air thro' it from its open sides. The kitchens were in a court behind; the stables near them; such of the servants as remained all night slept any where they chose to lay their mats down; they had no bedclothes, neither did they undress. Few of them ate together, the different religions and the different castes of each religion never mixing at meals. They had no settled hours for eating. I used to smell their vegetable curries at all sorts of times, and see piles of white rice, or scones of what looked like barley meal, carried here and there as wanted. The hungry sat in a circle on the ground out of reach of a contaminating presence, dipping their scones or their fingers into the one pot and making a nice mess of it. I have heard of a low caste, or a European, passing between the wind and them making it sinful to finish the polluted repast, which was of course thrown out.

Our Establishment consisted of a Head Servant, a Parsee, who managed all, hired the rest, marketted, ordered, took charge of every thing, doing it all admirably, and yet a rogue. An under steward or Butler, a Mohammedan, who waited on me; 4 Chobdars, officers of the Supreme Court who attended my father there, waited at meals on him and my mother, and always went behind the carriage; they were dressed in long scarlet gowns edged with gold lace, white turbans, gold belts, and they bore long gilt staves in their hands. The Parsee Head wore a short cotton tunick with a shawl round the waist, silk trowsers, very wide, and the high brown silk cap peculiar to the Parsees. My Mohammedan had a white turban, white tunick, red shawl, and red trowsers, tight to the leg. My father's valet was a Portuguese Xian in a white jacket and trowsers, European style. Besides these there were 4 Sepoys for going messages, who wore green and red and gold fancifully about their turbans and tunicks—the family livery; two *hammauls* to clean the house, two *bheasties* to fetch the water, two men to light the lamps, one water-cooler and butter maker (this last piece of business being done in a bottle on his knee), a gardener, a Cook with an assistant, two dhobees or washermen, and a slop-emptier, all these being

Hindus of various castes and going nearly naked, except the cook, who was a Portuguese.

The Stable establishment was on a similar scale: 2 pair of carriage horses, my father's riding horse and mine, a coachman, groom to each horse who always ran beside him whether we drove or rode, and a grass cutter for every pair. Wages had need be small in a country where such a retinue was requisite for three people; no one doing more than one particular kind of service renders this mob of idlers a necessity. My Mother had her maid and I had mine, whose daughter also lived with us and was very useful. We hired a tailour when we wanted one, either a mender, or a mantua maker[1] or a milliner as required.

Our life was monotonous. My father and I rose before the sun, an hour or more, by lamplight, groped our way downstairs, mounted our horses, and rode till heat and light, coming together, warned us to return. I then bathed and breakfasted and lay upon the sofa reading till Fatima came to dress me. I always appeared at the family breakfast, tho' but for form. My father, who had been hard at work, fasting, made a good meal, and my Mother, only just up, did the same. We had frequently visitors at this hour; after they went my Mother walked about with the *hammauls* behind her, dusting her china, of which she very soon collected a good stock—calling out to them *subhr* when she wanted them to go on, and *aste* when they had omitted a cup or vase, for she never could manage their easy language. I wrote or worked or played and sang while the weather remained tolerably cool. In the hot months I never heard of any one able to do any thing. My father went to Court. When it was not term time, my Mother and I sometimes went in the carriage to pay visits. We very often were amused by receiving presents from the natives, and by the arrival of bhorers to tempt us with the newest fashions just received by 'a ship come in last night,' shewn first to us as such great ladies! My father received no presents himself, and permitted us to receive none but fruit and flowers; very valuable ones were at first offered to us but being invariably touched and returned, they soon ceased.

1. An eighteenth-century term for a dress maker.

The flowers generally came tied up with silver twist in the hands of the gardener, but the fruits, fresh or dried, were always in silver bowls, covered with silver gauze and brought in on the head of the messenger. Lady Hood and, they say, Mrs Blair, used to keep the bowls, but we, better instructed, returned the dull looking precious part of the offering with its dirty bit of covering, quite contented with our simpler share.

The Bhorer entered more ostentatiously with a long string of naked porters, each bearing on his head a box. All were set down and opened, and the goods displayed upon the floor, very pretty and very good, and only about double as dear as at home, a rupee for a shilling, about. The native manufacturers are cheap enough, except the shawls; and, by the bye, Mr Gardiner gave me a shawl instead of himself—it cost £100. It is a very good thing to marry the last of a sisterhood, when one meets with such generous brothers in law. At two or rather sooner we had our tiffin, after which one is never disturbed. Particular friends drop in to tiffin sometimes, but they seldom stay long, every body retiring during those hot hours, undressing and sleeping.

At first we took no luncheon beyond a little fruit and bit of bread, my father having a theory that Brahmin fare was what was suited best to India. Neither would he let me take more than a glass of wine at dinner, none at luncheon, only fruit. Also I had to wait for the family breakfast. I was near dying. Luckily this experiment took place before Uncle Edward's departure for the Neilgherries and my Aunt interfered. She could not manage all she wished, so she got Dr Eckford at Barra to give a lecture upon the climate of India and European constitutions—and being rather peremptory in their advice, I got for the future rusks and coffee immediately after coming in from my ride in the morning, meat and better beer at luncheon and a glass of sherry on sitting down to dinner. I got so well, quite fat. As I could never sleep in the day without waking with a headache, I always occupied myself one way or another in my room in the afternoons, in my large and airy room with its shaded verandah—undressing, though, which was a great refreshment, wearing only one of my *unwashed* gingham wrappers, till towards sunset when I took a bath and dressed for the carriage airing, which was never omitted, except in the heaviest days of the rains. It was very pleasant, the drives were beautiful whichever way we went, on the beach, on the Breach Candy road, or the esplanade, and twice a week across the rice fields to Matoonga to listen to the Artillery band, all the Presidency collecting there or on the esplanade. We drove up and down, stopt along side another carriage, sometimes on a cool evening got out and walked to speak to our friends. We were all very sociable, and the Band was delightful, in such good order. The equipages were extraordinary, all the horses fine, but the carriages! very shabby. The smartest soon fades in such a climate; between the heat of one season, the wet of another, the red dust, the insects, the constant use and not much care, the London built carriage makes but a poor figure the second year, and as the renewal of them is not always convenient, and a daily airing is essential, they are used in bad enough condition sometimes, nobody seems to mind so it don't signify.

On the sun going down, which he does at once like a shot, there is no twilight, the crowd separates, the ladies glad enough of a warm shawl on their dark return home, for it was often very cold driving back over the flats. Then, if we were to pass a quiet evening, a very few minutes prepared us for dinner as we wore very pretty toilettes for our airings; but if, as was generally the case, we were to be in company either at home or abroad till midnight, there was great commotion among the Ayahs to have their preparations completed in time. What Servants these Indians are. My Arab, Fatima, was always ready. The very dress I should have chosen laid out, every suitable addition to it at hand—sark, flowers, gloves, pin, scent, handkerchief, all these, and the *curls*, which if worn in that hot land must be false, so brightly brushed beside them. She was so quick in her waiting, so gentle, so quiet, so noiseless. There are many drawbacks to an Indian life, but the servants in Bombay are a luxury.

The society at the time we were there was extremely agreeable. Many of those in high places we had known at home in their less prosperous days. Scotch abounded. My cousins, too, had married well, all the six who had gone out. Poor Kate was dead, the fine girl who had been with us in

Edinburgh. I got on well with them and with their husbands, and often spent a morning with them. We used to congregate at Mrs Bax's with our work in the cool season. Mary Grant and Gregor (one of the Redcastle Grants) lived with us at the Retreat for many months. They had not been good managers and were glad to give up housekeeping for a season. She was very lovely. Mrs Bax uncommonly handsome. Mrs Ward pleased me most, both as to looks and manners; she had married a clever man, and was quite able to profit by the companionship. Little Miss Barra, a good obliging little girl, was quite one of the family party. She came out with us in the *Mountstewart Elphinstone*, and being motherless, was very grateful to us for taking care of her. So indeed was her father, a queer kind of man, and a good Doctor I may say, for he certainly set me up.

When we first came out the dinners were rather appalling; too early in the afternoons, generally between five and six o'clock. Thirty guests, one attendant at least behind every chair. Two to the *Burra Sahibs*, the great people. Stray assistants at the sideboards besides, a military band, a glare of light, the repast handsomely served on silver or plated ware, but of a rather heavy kind as far as the meats went, rounds of beef, saddles of mutton, boiled and roast turkey, pickled pork, one or two hams, fishes and soups, of course, and a second course of sweet things and small birds, but from the first the table was filled up with a number of little plates containing dried fruits, confectionery, sugar plums, and such like. A good deal of wine, good wine, was drunk and some brandy pawnee, but the bitter beer, well frothed up and cold as saltpetre could make it, was the favourite beverage, especially with the ladies. It was well that in the great houses where these great banquets were given the dining halls were of such large dimensions, so open to the air, and the servants so well trained they were never heard. Their bare feet made no sound on the matting, they never spoke, they were machines divining wants, and supplying them magically.

I hear that this cumbrous style of entertainment has been modified of late years among those who were not obliged to give official dinners. My father never adopted much this fashion. His dinners were to sixteen or eighteen people, a small assemblage in that large hall—four small joints only, nicely dressed *entrées* took the places of the beef and the salt pork—the little plates of comfits were dispensed with, so was the military band. The wines excellent, the coolness without a punkah quite pleasant. After dinner small round tables were scattered about with tea and coffee, and additional guests arrived to enliven the evening. Our parties were thought very agreeable, and the style was, I believe, copied—all but the entrées. Our Portuguese cook and my old French book created them and we did not parade our knowledge. Lord Clare [Governor of Bombay, 1830–34] afterwards thoroughly reformed the dinner table and, of course, was imitated—even by the few who had laughed at my father.

The balls were the prettiest assemblies possible, the women so young, most of them so pretty, their dresses so light, their air so happy. The men to suite, many of them in such brilliant uniforms, the numerous rooms large and well lighted, open to the cool Verandahs; excellent music, and grades enough to satisfy vanity. To a stranger there could be nothing more striking than a large ball at Government house, not the house in the Fort, but at Parell, a sort of small palace in fine grounds about four or five miles from the town. There is a very large tank in these grounds, round which on one particular day in the year, occasionally at other times, fireworks are exhibited, such fireworks as we have no idea of in this quarter of the Globe, truly magnificent and truly startling, they cannot be described, only wondered at.

The Governour in my time was the well known Sir John Malcolm, a fine soldierly looking man, coarse in mind and manners, but kind and very hospitable. His wife, with whom he did not live happily, had not come out with him. His married daughter, Lady Campbell, did the honours for a while, but, poor thing, went mad and had to be sent home. She died within a year or two, never recovering her senses. Her husband was very silly. Major Burrowes was an A. de C. and private Secretary, very popular and very agreeable. We afterwards knew him at Cheltenham, a widower with three children, as agreeable as ever, not in despair at having lost a very aerified wife, plain and cross too.

The Commander in Chief was Sir Thomas Bradford,[1] celebrated for his admirable management of the Commissariat during the latter part of the Peninsular war; a very gentlemanly person, liked by those he took a fancy to, disliked by all under his command, and quite a despot in his family, but ruled in his turn by his very odd wife, a confirmed invalid and a very fanciful one. She had been married before to a Colonel Ainslie, and had a son and a daughter of that name with her, aspects of pity to every one. The son, Captain Ainslie, was one of the A. de Camps, and did not fare much worse than the rest of the Staff. The daughter was very hardly dealt with: shabbily dressed, seldom allowed to accept any invitation, nor to speak to any one while driving in the low phaeton with her mother. She was like the Princess in the faery tale, tormented from morning till night. When dressed for a party, a rare pleasure, would be sent to bed; when some grand occasion required a fresh toilette, none was forthcoming, some old faded dress was selected. She was allowed to make no acquaintance, therefore passed the long day alone. If she did get to a dance, she did not have to converse with her partners, who all moved in the melancholy quadrille as if they too were enduring punishment. Major Jameson made us feel quite sorry for her; he was the private Secretary and a favourite, but he could only pity. The single recreation the poor girl had was the evening drive. The little carriage with the four inside was always to be seen among the crowd wherever we congregated, two of the suite as outsiders. The General bowing stiffly but abundantly, the ladies motionless for they knew so few.

Lady Bradford knew nobody for she never visited, and never appeared at the dinners at home. She had been a beautiful woman, now broken down long before her time by asthma and the madeira she took to relieve it. She never dressed but in a close cap and wrapper. When she took her

1. Sir Thomas Bradfield (1777–1853) had served with the
   Portuguese forces in the Peninsular War, not the
   Commissariat.

evening drive she put over the close cap a coarse straw cottage bonnet, and over the wrapper a cloke and she held in her hand a little parasol the size of a plate, which she crooked down by a bend or a joint in the stick, not at the time fashionable. She kept this always up between her and the sun, however low he had sunk, and then between her and the moon or the stars. Poor woman, she had left her Bradford children at home, and was always longing for her letters from those in charge of them. The severe training of her Ainslie children did not turn out well. They both married some years after into the same family, Lord Gray's of Kinfauns in Perthshire. Captain Ainslie married the youngest daughter, Jane, was an unkind husband and turned out dissipated. His sister married the Master of Gray and very nearly ruined him, between expensive dress and gambling. Lady Bradford died at St Helena on her passage home; she did not live to see those little children so beloved. Her devoted husband preserved her body in spirits, and, not properly watching the cask, it was tapped by the sailors, many of whom died from the effects of the poison. I ought to have liked her; she was very fond of me. She delighted in the old Scotch ballads, particularly the Jacobite airs, which I sang to her without musick as she lay half reclining on a sofa in the verandah. She used to 'borrow me of my mother'; that is what she called these short visits and Major Jameson said she really did enjoy this simple musick.

Sir Charles Malcolm, the Governor's brother, was in command of the Navy, a merry, pleasant, rather handsome sailor. No others of the men in high places were any way remarkable, all pleasant enough to meet. To say the truth, I did not take much to the Civilians; the elderly ones were pompous, the younger ones 'upsetting,' looking so absurdly down upon the military, who really were many of them infinitely superiour to them. Mr Bax was an intelligent man, Mr Anderson a clever man; both were kind and cousinly. James Dewar, the brother of our old companion David Dewar, though no great lawyer, was very much to be liked, as was the Advocate Depute [in fact Advocate General], Mr Bridgeman, whose unfortunate Christian name, 'Orlando,' was an unfailing source of fun to Aunt Caroline.

Frequently we were enlivened by chance arrivals; passengers to and from other seaports used to touch at Bombay. In this way we had a peep of Charles Marjoribanks, who was going home for his baronetcy—too late—for he died and George Gordon Glentomie, John Peter Cumming, Archie Arbuthnot, and others, the scene was ever varying.

# CHAPTER TWENTY-SEVEN

# 1828–1829

WE had landed in February and were fairly established in the Retreat by the middle of March. Early in April the hot weather began, encreasing day by day in intensity till the first week in June, exhausting me so completely that, but for the bitter beer, I never could have dragged my failing powers through it. Mr Norris fairly knocked up and had to depart suddenly for the Neilgherries, a bit of good fortune for us, as Mr Gardiner, who had been acting in the Commissariat, was promoted to act for Mr Norris as one of the secretaries to Government; he got also the loan of Mr Norris's very pretty and very cool house on the top of one of the hills near us, Prospect Lodge. This was very pleasant for Mary and me, through having no palanquins, either of us, and walking being impossible, we could not very often meet. Halfway down this hill, at the Hermitage, lived Sir Charles Chambers, a brother Judge of the Supreme Court, a heavy man, related to the Charles Grants, married to a common place wife from Glen Urquhart. At the foot of this hill was Colonel Goodfellow, who commanded the Engineers, with a daughter who played admirably on the pianoforte, and just across our tank lived a Major Griffith, who had charge of the Artillery stores, from which he made most useful presents to Miss Goodfellow and to me. I got a sweeping brush, emery powder, paper of all sorts, ink etc. And besides this he gave us most delightful musick. He was most musick mad; he had organised an excellent Band of stringed instruments, most of them Portuguese, under the direction of the Artillery Bandmaster, and whether they played in his own Compound, or in our fine hall, or better still, from boats on the tank, it was really charming to listen to the well selected and well 'interpreted,' that's the term! good classick musick.

There was one great draw back to our Retreat. The hill which rose at the end of our garden between us and the sea had on its summit the Parsee burying place, a sloping building with a grating over a deep hollow, on which grating were laid the dead bodies of the Parsees; there they lay till devoured by vultures; the bones then dropt through. The condition of the deceased in the new state, or purgatory, into which death has introduced him, is determined by the part of the corpse first attacked by the vultures. An eye ensures happiness, any part of the head is comforting; an arm I suppose is useless as one was dropt in our shrubbery. The vulture is a disgusting bird with its long neck bare of feathers; the first time I saw one seated on my window sill I was really horrified.

The heat encreased, no air by day or by night. We lay on mats with no covering, not even a sheet, as little clothing as possible in the day and all loose, no bands or belts or collars, exertion of any kind exhausting, occupation too fatiguing, even thinking nearly impossible; and the thermometer was not high—94 or 96; it was the moisture of the climate that overcame us; it was completely enervating, and its effect on the skin most thoroughly disgreeable. It was the approach of the Monsoon. Most people left Bombay at this time in search of a drier atmosphere at Poonah or elsewhere. Luckily, this extreme heat did not last long.

The opening of the monsoon is one of the grandest phenomena in nature. About a week or two before the outbreak clouds began to gather over a sky that had been hitherto without relief. Day by day the gloom thickened; at last the storm broke. We were going to sit down to luncheon when a feeling of suffocation, a distant rumbling, a sudden darkness, made us all sensible of some unusual change approaching. The servants rushed to the venetians and closed one side of the hall, with the utmost expedition, the side next the storm; yet they could not save us altogether—from the wind they did, a wind, suddenly rising, burst from the plain with a violence which overwhelmed every opposing object, and while the gust lasted we could hear nothing else, not a step, nor a voice, nor a sound of any kind. It did no harm to our well secured apartment, but it

brought with it a shower, a tempest rather, of sand, so fine, so
impalpable, that it entered like the air through every crevice,
covered the floor, the seats, the tables with a red dust which
well nigh choked us. This was succeeded by a lull almost
awful in its intensity, and then the first thunder growled; at a
vast distance it seemed to rumble, then, strengthening, it
broke suddenly right over the house with a power that was
overwhelming; flash after flash of lightning glared, it was
more, far more, than a gleam; then rain, such as is only
known in the tropicks, poured down in flakes with the din of
a cataract. On came the thunder; again and again it shook the
house, rolling round in its fearful might as if the annihilation
of the world were its dreadful aim.

My Mother and I were as pale as two spectres. In my life,
neither before nor since, I never felt so thoroughly appalled.
It lasted about two hours, after which a heavy rain set in,
falling dully and equally hour upon hour until about tiffin
time the following day, when we had a second thunder storm,
less terrifick, however, than the first, or less to us from
having had that sample. After this the heavy rain continued
unceasingly for 48 hours, making such a noise it deafened us,
completely, we could hear no other sound, and creating
darkness and a chill damp feel equally oppressive. The roads
were soon like streams, the plain a lake, the tanks overflowing. No Europeans stirred out. A party collected at the
Shiltons for tiffin only, remained at this bungalow during
those three first violent days—only such natives stirred
beyond the shelter of a house as could not avoid going out on
business, and they were dressed for the deluge in oilskin
coverings that enveloped the whole person, face and all, out
of which they saw thro' two glass eyes inserted at the proper
place, the most hideous masquerade, but absolutely necessary. The first desperate week over, the rain fell less
constantly and less heavily. We even got a drive sometimes,
as it was occasionally fair for an hour or more but all thro' the
rains, which lasted near 4 months, the weather was extremely
disagreeable in Bombay, hot, chilly, airless, relaxing, every
thing wet we touched. Pans of fire had to be placed in the
rooms frequently. All our clothes had to be dried on cane
skreens made like boxes, or large cases, within which were

the same pans of fire, and still the damp clung to us; yet it was never an unhealthy season.

Up the country the rain was much lighter, more like showery weather at home up at Poonah and beyond. People enjoyed the freshness extremely, while we at the sea side were steaming like the pipes of a factory. The last week rivalled the first very nearly, the Monsoon departing, as it came, in a storm of thunder.

I was glad to see cloudless skies again. October was, however, a melancholy month; pools of stagnant water, decaying vegetation, unpleasant smells, and sickness, such sickness. Now was the time that small white tents filled every space upon the esplanade; the little crazy bungalows that had been hurriedly removed at the first threatening of the rains were now being leisurely replaced, and amongst them and around them was an encampment of the sick from the upcountry stations come down for advice, or for a change, or their furlough to England. The Doctors had busy times moving about in gigs or palanquins doing their best to save the invalids. One of the busiest of these was our Scotch friend, Doctor Eckford. We saw a great deal of him, for we had got very intimate. I had been very ill, an attack of liver, and he was very kindly attentive to me, and had taken quite a fancy to me, on account, I believe, of the leaf I brought him out of his Wife's pocket book. But really, old as I was, I was quite in fashion—a second season of celebrity, a coming out again! Like my father, I have all my life looked 10 years younger than my age; nobody guessed me at 30, and being handsome, lively, obliging and a great man's daughter, I reigned in good earnest over many a better queen! than myself. Of course every eligible was to be married to me, not only that but every body was busy marrying me. 'Now, don't mind them, Eliza, my dear,' said uncle Edward very early in my Indian career; 'don't fix yet, wait for Smith, my friend Smith; he'll be sure to be down here next season, and he's just the very man I have fixed on for you.' Then my Aunt, 'I don't mind your not liking old so and so and that tiresome this, and that ill humoured that, I had rather you married Colonel Smith than any body.' Then my cousins, 'Oh you will so like Colonel Smith, Eliza, every one likes Colonel

Smith, he will make such a kind husband, he is so kind to his horses.' 'My goodness, Miss Grant,' said Mrs Norris, 'is it possible you have refused —— the best match in the Presidency—will certainly be in Council. Who do you mean to marry, pray.' (Every body must marry, they can't help it here.) 'I am waiting,' said I, 'for Colonel Smith.' Great laughing this caused, of course, none laughing more than the intending Bride, to whom this Colonel Smith was no more than a bit of fun, just as likely to be her husband as her most particular admirer, a great fat Parsee.

One morning I was sitting at work; the cooler weather had restored us our needles and I was employing mine for Mary's expected baby, early in November, my Mother lying on the sofa reading, when the Chobdar in waiting announced Colonel Smith. It is customary for all new arrivals to call on the Burra Sahibs. He entered, and in spite of all the nonsense we had amused outselves with, we liked him. 'Well,' said Mary, on hearing who had called, 'will he do?' 'Better than any of your upsetting Civilians,' answered I, 'a million of times, I never liked the Military at home and here I don't like the Civilians. Colonel Smith is the most gentlemanly man I have seen in India.' Mary and Mr Gardiner laughed and neither they nor I thought more about him.

He had come down from Satara, where he commanded, for change of air, not being well. He lived with his friend Doctor Eckford, and we frequently met them in the evenings driving out together and sometimes we met them in society, but our paths did not seem to cross. He paid no particular attention to me neither do I recollect being at all occupied about him, nor did he dine once in my father's house till many months after we had become acquainted. My father and he had got on a sort of pleasant intimacy ages before he seemed to think of me. We used to meet generally in the mornings. We rode always, my father and I, on the Breach Candi road, which was close to us and agreeable from its skirting the sea, and probably the breeze and the sun rise pleased our new companion, as he came a considerable distance to enjoy them. He also seemed to like political disquisitions, for he and my father rode on before deep in Catholick claims which were then being finally discussed in Parliament,[1] while I had plenty to do, by myself, in managing that dreadful Donegal and watching the Parsees' morning adoration of the sun. I had also a certain green book to reflect on; two thick volumes, handsomely bound, lent me, as well as the horse, by Mr Bax; his travels in MS., a small illegible hand and very prosy composition in which the Czar, a grand Duchess, two Archdukes, and Princes, Sultans, and Counts palatine figured in profusion.

These rides in this guise continued all the cold weather, our party latterly reinforced by my cousin John Cumming, who was staying with us, and who sometimes got twisted out of his usual place by me to the side of my father, Colonel Smith exchanging with him for a turn or two, to my father's regret, who on these occasions observed that the Captain had inopportunely interrupted a very interesting argument on the influence of the Irish priesthood over the flocks; that poor Smith was a sad Orangeman, quite benighted, but honest and worth enlightening. It was Mr Gardiner and his radicalism over again.

So began my happy future to gleam on me, particularly after a few, half laughing, half earnest, hints from Dr Eckford, whom my Mother about this time began to talk of as Love's messenger, and then styled roundly Cupid. Such a Cupid. Children, you have seen him, I need say no more. Cupid knew his business well. He threw shafts and bow away as unsuitable to a staid Brigadier and a maiden past her prime. His object was to touch the lady's reason, which he did, no matter how, and the parents too, a matter effected principally by the Irish acres, warranted not to be bog. Who would have thought a marriage thus systematically arranged could have turned out so well. It took a long time for India, tho', and while it was progressing, to the mystification of all lookers on who could not understand why it did not go on in Caesar fashion and be settled on the 3rd day, my Mother's 1st grandchild, dear little Janie Gardiner, was born. It was my

1. Daniel O'Connell's attempt to persuade Wellington's government to pass the Catholic Relief Act dominated the politics of this year.

brother John's birthday, the 23rd of November, and all the cousinhood were assembled at the Retreat to do him honour; Gregor and Mary Grant were indeed staying with us. Mr Gardiner and Mary were expected, but just before dinner they sent their excuse; she did not feel quite well. On leaving the hall a note from Mr Gardiner summoned my Mother, and after the Company departed, I set off myself, up to Prospect Lodge, mounting the long, long, dimly lighted flight of steps that led up the side of the hill without a thought of the snakes at other times I used to be nervous about.

The clock had struck 12; it was the 24th.; 5 minutes after my arrival my little niece was laid upon my knees, and I believe for weeks after I thought of no other existing creature. These Memoirs are but the fair outside, after all, a deal is hid, both as regards myself and others, that it would be painful to record and worse than useless to remember. We 3 sisters had gone thro' much. This blessed baby opened another view of life to all; all loved and welcomed it and leaned on it but our strange mother, who paid it very little attention, never sent for it, never asked for it, never gave it one single gift or even nursed poor Mary. Perhaps she did not like the shove back a grade; there was another generation born and she, the once beautiful wife, was a Grandmother. Somehow she never took to Mary married. She liked none of our marriages. Jane's one could understand her regretting for tho' Colonel Pennington was rich and respected, he was old and ugly. Mr Gardiner, well connected, high in the Civil Service and with £20,000 private property, good looking, gentlemanly, clever, good and six and thirty, he was really a bit of good luck for a tocherless lass, however lang her pedigree. But she never cared for him, for her or their child while they were near her. Afterwards they were highly praised, when they were gone and she felt what they had been to her.

To me I know my baby niece was a perfect delight. All the pleasant cold weather, I walked about with it in my arms whenever it was brought to the Retreat or I could contrive a visit to Prospect Lodge. Mr Gardiner and Mary went very little into company. Before the birth of the baby Mary had been for months very suffering, first the heat and then the rains incommoded her greatly. She never took to her Indian life, never could bear the climate nor suit herself to the ways nor endure the habits nor the society—*that* indeed she undervalued very absurdly and in consequence of her air, she was in turn undervalued herself, so that the spirit of discontent which pervaded the atmosphere around her, quite prevented her life from being a happy one. She never took any exercise, never rose to meet the fresh air in the mornings; the evening drive was often shirked and when the pair in their hideous landaulet did set forth in sulky looking state, they shunned the general meeting place and moved along some byepath all alone. I was a thousand times happier. Our Retreat was a little pompous in some of its arrangements and the fine coach with the Chobdars was a dignified vehicle, rather. I should have preferred Mrs Dewar's gig, for my life was dull, very lonely except just at those hours when meals, the drive or company brought my father, my Mother and myself together. So passed the months until the beginning of March brought a degree of heat again, which poor Mary felt too oppressive. I do believe the poor thing was never well, had never been well from a child and that the merest trifles affected her ill organised frame. At any rate, she was ill, and advised to try the cooler air of the higher land. So an expedition was arranged to Khandalla, a beautiful plain at the head of the pass up the Ghauts on the road to Poonah. These finely shaped, very picturesque mountains enclosed the Bay at its inner extremity, seeming to run near and round it, and to shut it in its 100 wooded islands out from the rest of the world. In reality there was a wide plain to traverse before reaching their base, and the bay to cross before reaching the plain.

As Mary would be dull alone, I was to go with her and her husband, a plan I liked. A change was pleasant, a journey in India new, life in tents! delightful.

The ugly landaulet conveyed the Gardiner *Sahibs*, their baba, and her ama or wetnurse, and a peon to the Bunder. I, escorted by my father, proceeded thither in a queer sort of old pony carriage left especially for my use by Uncle Edward; and strange to say, for an Indian lady, I carried no attendant of any sort with me.

The luggage had gone before with the other servants and the tents. We had a sail of some hours, the scenery so beautiful, varying every moment as we scudded among the islands, then on landing, we rested, while the queer pony carriage which had come over with us was prepared to take us on; it shook us famously and tired Mary, so she took a sleep at the next bungalow, where we left it, and at dusk entered our palanquins, travelling on by torch light, a goodly train, up a steep hill, as I felt from the tilt of the palanquin, tho' I could see nothing. At last it was level ground again, and then a short half hour brought us to our encampment.

I saw, on alighting, only a pretty, oblong room, floor matted, walls and ceiling white as usual, but ceiling domed which was not usual; lamps depending from it, and a well served table laid for dinner with every appendage we were used to elsewhere. We had a pleasant meal in spite of fatigue. Tea, as usual; and then, preceded by a torch bearer, and accompanied by the Head Servant, Mary, her Ayah, who was to wait on me, and Mr Gardiner, highly amused at our state of excitement, I retired to my own tent, which I was lucky enough to get into without entangling my feet in the tent cords. There all was in order like my own bed chamber, my own furniture, most of it, having been transported as if by magick for my use, even to the bath, some books, and the writing table.

After undressing her mistress the Ayah returned, and laid herself down near the door of my tent, inside; a peon stretched himself outside, between the tent and the curtain, and the guard, two or three strong, patrolling around, we all went to sleep as securely as tho' our walls had been of stone instead of canvas.

Next morning, very early, I stept out to feel the cool air and look down on a gully of exquisite verdure opening out into a vast plain of beauty, spreading far away without a limit; the scene around was flat just where we were pitched, but in the distance were rising grounds, woods, and a few shrubs dotted here and there in patches; the road stretched along at a little distance. Very fine the scene was, but it was the air that was so charming. We were just on the brow of the ravine, so that we caught the breeze at once.

Any one looking up at us must have thought the little encampment a very pretty sight, the four larger tents in a semicircle in front, the rowlies for the servants behind, the horses picketted out under the only tope of trees at hand, and beside them the fire, where breakfast was preparing under the cover of the 'cloudless sky.'

How the little baby enjoyed the morning air, sprawling almost naked on its mat after a refreshing bath. We would not let them dress it all the day, there being nobody to remark upon the simplicity of its toilette. We passed our day as usual, books and work—no healthy play, however, the middle hours being very hot, just as sultry as in Bombay, but there was not that relaxing moisture. In the evenings we drove along the road till dark. Once or twice we went as far as the wood of Lanowlie, a beautiful bit of scenery, the wood enclosing both a hill and a tank. The shade appeared to us so irresistible, the glare at our ravine being almost painful, that Mr Gardiner determined on shifting our position. So we had the diversion of moving our camp, striking our tents, packing our goods, travelling our miles, and setting all up again.

The change was delightful, the tents among the trees looked prettier than ever; the horses, in full view, so completely sheltered, were a picture; the air from the water so cool; the flowers in the wood so lovely! I went walking there as far as the creepers would let me, but their trunks and tendrils were so thick, so interlaced among the branches of the forest trees, and there were so many thorns, that in spite of the shade, and a pleasant pathway and the exquisite flowers and the verdure I could get but a little way, and I had to give up the romantick intention of a moonlight ramble therein. I therefore, spent the evening in hanging round my tent large clusters of the blue persian grape, a basket full of which I had bought from a travelling fruitseller. These grapes are extremely delicious, high flavoured, sweet, juicy, yet more of the consistency, size, and shape of a plum than we are used to in grapes. They ripen to perfection at Poonah, and if properly dried make fine raisins. Mary was busy in the same way; our work done, we went to tea, and then to bed after a visit to Janie. I thought, as I turned in to my tent, that a prettier scene had never been fancied. The bright moonlight on the water, the horses beneath the trees, the flickering fire, the white tents with the sleeping figures near them, and the watchful guard moving like dark shadows back and fore. It was gypsey life in its Sunday suit; there was something delightfully free, natural about it, and I thought to myself it would not be at all disagreeable to move thus about with a regiment, especially if one belonged to any one in high enough rank to command as many servants as my civilian brother in law.

And so, I lay me down in peace and took my rest. What waked me? A noise, which once heard can never be forgotten, a noise unlike any other sound in nature, a growl, so deep, so low, so full, so strong, that it almost paralysed sensation. It was just at my ear; there was only a bit of canvas between me and a tiger.

Mine was a single tent, the door of it was open; the moonlight streamed in and shewed me the peon standing upright, shivering with fear, and no Ayah. 'Hush, sahib,' whispered the peon, 'tis the great tiger.'

The wood of Lanowlie was known to the natives as a favourite haunt of this dreadful creature, which is worshipped by some of native tribes of the neighbourhood, and, therefore, is held too sacred to be exterminated. Not very long before our encroachment on his haunts, the post between Bombay and Poonah, a native runner had disappeared, leaving no trace beyond a fragment of turban among some bushes near the road. This came into my mind at the moment—a long one as it seemed; then came the growl again, but not so near; then the scream of the horses, I never heard a horse scream before, nor since; it is a fearful sound, and then came Mr Gardiner's voice. Such a blessed relief. He told me not to fear, that the Tiger had only come to drink at the tank, that the array of human beings would frighten it, that we were all safe, while there were horses, goats and buffaloes to be had, and that the cords and pegs of the tents would ensure the safety of the inmates.

The Ayah, poor soul, had fled at the first alarm to her mistress to call attention to the baby. Mary was with her child in a moment. Next came firing, great firing, the muskets of the guard, Mr Gardiner's pistols; then all the pots and pans began. Every servant seized on one and rattled and shook and beat and thumped; then they screeched and hallooed and screamed; really the tiger must have been more than beast had he remained among such a din. He wisely turned and leaped away, nor did he shew again. Of course our watch and noise continued to make all sure; but he had had enough of us, and we had had enough of Lanowlie. Nothing would induce Mary to risk her precious baby near such a neighbour another day. So a messenger was despatched on the moment to have a boat ready, and at daybreak we broke up our camp in earnest and set out on our return to Bombay.

We drove to the top of the pass, got into palanquins there, and found breakfast ready for us in the bungalow at the foot of the Ghauts. These bungalows are wretched places. A single room unfurnished, bare walls, mud floor, plenty of insects, reptiles even, for scorpions are common in them; no comforts but such as the travellers themselves provided. We were glad enough, however, to find rest and shelter after the excitement of the descent, which in broad daylight gave me here and there a shudder. At one point, a sharp turn brought the side of the palanquin on the edge of a precipice that fell straight down 5 or 600 feet, with not even a bush to break the line till close to the bottom. We crossed the harbour in the afternoon, and just about dark we reached the Retreat, where, instead of sympathy, we were met with shouts of laughter for having quailed before the tiger.

My letters from Khandalla and my more vivid descriptions in conversation had quite bitten my father with a wish to change the relaxing air of the seaside for the freshness of the mountains; but he meditated a much more daring exploit than a visit to the Poonah Ghauts. Colonel Smith, who had been his constant riding companion in my absence, had inspired him with a wish to see more of the country, to try a few weeks of the Mahableishwa hills during the present hot season, when really Bombay was too oppressive. These charming hills were in our new friend's district; he commanded the Brigade at Satara, and Mahableishwa, tho' distant 30 miles, was included. He had been, it seems, most extremely eloquent in his descriptions of the scenery, the lights and shadows, mists, and other phenomena, and had kindly offered every assistance as to preparations, routes, encampment there, etc.

My Mother, who began to have her suspicions as to the cause of all this politeness, exhibited no wish to move. She did not feel it the least too hot where she was, nor did she like the idea of packing, moving, going in boats, in palanquins, over the sea and up precipices, to live in tents without any comforts.

My father, however, was quite taken up with the plan; Colonel Smith dined two or three days running to concoct all the plans properly, tho' they were quickly enough arranged seemingly, for he was listening to my ballads all the evenings, and then one morning he called to take leave. He was to start early next day for Mahableishwa, where he meant to remain till the rains began, would lose no time in doing—I forget what—choosing a spot for our tents, I believe, and would write full particulars of all we were to expect on our journey.

Preparations were accordingly begun. My father and his head Servant Nasserwanjee were closetted for hours for several days, and at last all was announced as ready. My Mother and I did nothing, the ayahs packed our clothes, taking more a great deal than we wished, but Fatima, who had travelled hundreds of miles, hundreds of times, with her former mistresses, Mesdames Hunter Blair and Baker, was not to be thwarted, and she was right; she understood ruralising in India a deal better than we did.

With the exception of our large tin cases, we seemed to have left every thing we generally used behind, for we missed nothing up to the very moment of our departure; yet we must have brought all with us, for I, at least, never asked for a single article afterwards that was not forthcoming. They are wonderful managers, these Indian Servants.

We drove to the Fort, on to the Harbour, descended the broad steps of the ghaut, and entered a very good boat with a neat cabin in it sheltered by an awning. The sail down the coast of Malabar was very pretty indeed, the blue sea under so brightly blue a sky, wooded shores, and a background of mountains. We had room enough to move about, for only the Upper servants were with us, the rest, with the horses, the tents and other luggage, followed in our wake. Near sunset we reached Bancoote; it was quite a pleasure to climb up on our own feet, so seldom used in that country, a rather steep path to a half ruined tower on a point of rock, which was to be our resting place for the night. The view from it was very fine, over land and sea and up a river which flowed rather swiftly round the rock.

We were still admiring it when called to dinner, and there, in the bare walled turret room, was as neatly laid a table and as nice a small repast as any people need ever wish to sit down to. It had all been prepared on board the servants' bunderboat. We had no roasts, but fish, and stews, and curry, rice, fruit, and vegetables, all as well prepared as in the good kitchen at the Retreat. A saunter afterwards, and early to bed, my room as comfortable as in a warm climate was necessary, my own furniture in it, a shawl hung up against the unshuttered window to keep the land wind out and Fatima's little cot close to the door.

Colonel Smith had begged us to get over the bar at the mouth of the river with the morning tide, which served very early, and would help us on in our course up it; we were then to make no delay on leaving the boats but to push on up the mountain to a certain place—Mowlie, I think—where we were to pitch our tents for the night; but my father preferred his own plans. The boats got over the bar, or we had others which were within the bar. I don't know which—we went down to them I know in palanquins, and it was not a short trot; we had had our breakfast first very comfortably in the ruined tower, dressing leisurely, admiring the view, and gathering branches of oleander, almond, and other beautiful flowering shrubs unknown to me.

It was all so pleasant in the cool of the morning, but the river was very far from pleasant in the heat of the noon day; part of the way it was confined by high banks, which reflected the sun's rays, and kept all air from us. We had not brought an awning, and the roof of the cabin soon heated thro'. It was really three or four hours of suffering. On landing, my Mother was so done up that the plan was again departed from, and instead of pushing on up the pass, we resolved on resting—to dine at the spot we had been warned against at the foot of the mountain, a pretty little plain facing the *west*, a rock rising behind it and enclosing it, a hot wind blowing. It was a foretaste of what awaits the doomed, rest there was none. Every stitch of clothes but a gingham wrapper I threw off me, tucked up the sleeves, opened the collar, pulled off my rings, took out my combs, which actually scorched my head, and, creeping below the table in my tent, lay there more dead than alive till the signal for moving was given; dinner was countermanded, and a little fruit welcomed instead. When we were to march my palanquin was so burning I could not breathe in it; they threw *chatties* of water over it, and up rose a steam worse than the scorching. We had to wait half an hour before I could bear its atmosphere.

At last we were off, and as the sun declined and the air cooled, and the ascending path brought the mountain breezes to us, I was able to look up and out, and enjoy the singular scene presented by our party.

A *burra Sahib* needs a large retinue when travelling in the East, or did need it years ago; all may be altered now that we hear of dawks,[1] roads and railroads. First went Nasserwanjee on a *tattoo* ( a little pony ) leading us all, sword in hand, for the scabbard only hung gallantly by his side, the naked blade flourished at every turn above his head; next were some Sepoys or peons, then my Mother's palanquin and her spare bearers, then mine and more peons, then my father's, then the two Ayahs'; then the upper servants on ponies, but without swords; then under servants on foot or on bullocks; the luggage, tents, canteens, trunks, all on bullocks, peons and coolies running beside them to the number altogether of 50 or 60, with the beasts besides and our horses led. It was a long train winding round among the hills, always ascending and turning corners, and when night came on, and the torches were lighted and one was placed in about every fourth man's hand—the effect was wonderfully beautiful, the flames waving as the arms moved, leaves, branches, rocks, gleaming in turn among the dusky train that wound along up the steep pathway. Daylight might not have been so picturesque, but it

1. Anglo-Indian: relays of men or horses used for trans-
   porting mail or passengers.

would have been far more suitable to the kind of journey, and the distance being considerable, many a weary step was taken before we reached our resting place.

It was near midnight when we came to three tents sent by General Robertson for our accommodation. All we wanted was soon ready, for a fire was there, burning in a furnace made of some stones, the usual travelling fire place. Our curry was reheated, I had near a bottle of beer, and my bed being ready by the time this supper was over, I was soon fast asleep in a region as wild as Glen Ennich.

My Mother was quite reconciled to our journey next morning, for a messenger arrived very early with two notes for my father, one from General Robertson, Colonel Robertson then, and one from Colonel Smith; they were notes of welcome, with directions, which warned by the sufferings of yesterday, we obeyed; very kind they were. Every body is kind in India—but it was not that that pleased my mother, it was the messenger. He was one of the irregular horse, a native, light made, handsomely dressed, in coloured trowsers, flowing robe, and yellow cap, I think, and he rode well and caracoled his little spirited horse before us for just as long as we pleased to look at him. She took it into her head that he was one of Colonel Smith's regiment, which regiment was Heaven knows where—in Gujerat, I believe, so she asked Nasserwanjee for a rupee to give to him, and did the civil with the air of a Princess. She certainly, good, dear Mother, liked the rôle of the great lady.

After breakfast we started again on our somewhat perilous road. At least I sometimes trembled a little lest the palanquin bearers should make a false step but on they went through all, and by all, and over all safely, up the steep, very steep rises, down the sharp descents, round those dreadful corners revealing depths that made one shudder. On they went, with their short quick trot that seldom slackened, giving the regular grunt which apparently relieves the chest. They generally have a jar of water slung behind the palanquin a draught of which is the only refreshment I ever saw them take. Parts of this pass were finely wooded, parts bare and rocky, and fine though without water, no roaring cataract nor gliding stream. This is a great want in the landscape throughout India. A long ascent, just as dark, and then a stretch of level road, brought us to the end of our journey. A large double poled tent of Colonel Smith's, which was to be lent to us during our stay on the hills and in which we found his servants and the table laid for dinner. He was himself dining at Colonel Robertson's, so my Mother was able to scrutinise the premises. I was really ashamed of her behaviour. She walked here and there, observed the chairs, the lights, the table linen, and much admired the plate—'Upon my word, Miss Grant, your Colonel is very handsomely supplied, there's really nothing wanting.' The words gave a sort of shock to me. It was the first time I had heard either her or my father connect the Colonel's name with mine. I knew how all these attentions would end from that moment. We had a very good dinner very well served, and retired to our sleeping tents in great good humour. The night was so piercing cold we called for blanket after blanket, the chill of the water next morning was really painful; and as Fatima chose to take the dust of the journey out of my long, long hair outside the tent before I had all my warmer clothing on, I was really shivering. A canter however warmed me and gave me also a good view of the curious place we were settled on. A wide plain on the top of a long ridge of mountains, not much wood near us, but plenty all round, no rising either close at hand, with one exception, a hillock on which stood the Governour's small bungalow, his and the Resident's a little way off, were the only houses at the Station. Everybody else including the sick soldiers sent up there lived in tents, scattered about anywhere in groups of from three to five and six according to the size of each establishment. Riding, we came on the head of beautiful gullies far below us, stretching far out under the morning mist. We looked *down* on mountain tops, stood *above* wooded ravines, which made the scenery so curious.

The air was enchanting, the sun hot in the middle of the day, yet quite bearable, the mornings and evenings delightful, the nights rather cold. The society was on the pleasantest picknicky footing; the way of life most agreeable as soon as we got into it. The first few days we kept our Bombay hours, late dinners, and so on, therefore an exchange of calls with our neighbours was the extent of our intercourse. But as soon as we shewed ourselves well bred enough to conform to the habits of the place we got on merrily: dined at the Robertsons' often, lunched here and there, gave little dinners and little luncheons, and went with parties to the only two lions that there were, the sources of some river and a hill fort. We had Mrs James Farquharson, poor Pauline, and her sister Mrs Simson. A fat man who amused us all, and a thin padre whom we must have amused, for he was always smiling; Sir Lionel Smith, and others.

One very disagreeable circumstance met us there, indeed accompanied us every where, my father's unfortunate dispute with the Government. It had begun some weeks before, and arose thus. Some native case, about Ramchander something else, I may well remember the name, for goodness knows how many times I had to write it over, I often, in any hurry or on confidential affairs, clerked for my father, which had been before the Sudder for some length of time, was removed into the Supreme Court, where the opinion of the 3 Judges on its merits was in direct opposition to that of the Company's.[1] Before my father's appointment, there had been serious misunderstandings between those two powers, each having been in some degree to blame. My father had been well 'advised' by the Board of Controul that it would be very agreeable to have these differences healed and that he could do nothing that would be better approved at home both by the Board of Controul and the Court of Directors than to put an end to these unseemly jarrings. The Bombay Government, anxious to support their own authorities, were delighted at the new Judge's connexion with one of their own servants. Uncle Edward seized on my father at once, seconded by Mr Norris, telling their own version of Sir Edward West's mistakes; but that little wasp with his King's servants and his pomposity and his flattery of similar

1. The case was Moroo Ragonath against his uncle Pandoorung Ramchunder; a writ was issued in February 1829. It turned on whether the court's jurisdiction extended outwith the island and factories of Bombay. Sir Charles Chambers was one of the other judges.

weakness, aided by the heavy weight of Sir Charles Chambers, got the upper hand of the Civil Service, and enlisted my father in right earnest on their own side. The Sudder Adawlut ordered one thing, the Supreme Court ordered another, the Governour in Council interfered, and the King's Judges ignored the Government.

Mr Norris very unluckily had gone to the Neilgherries; the only Indian my father considered to have brains, a mistake rather, but he would take advice from no other. Mr Gardiner came to me one day in real alarm, he was acting Secretary then, to say that a most intemperate paper had been sent in by the 3 judges, and that as they were most decidedly in the wrong, on some points, serious disputes having grave results would be the consequence. I could not speak; he did without effect; I tried my Mother, but she as usual was on the fighting side; these pugnacious women have much to answer for. So the quarrel spread till it became personal. All parties lost temper, all parties listened to tittle tattle, Mr Caw did mischief, poor man, as usual, chiefly by filling my Mother's head with little low whisperings of slights, and slighting words, most of them inventions, and so it went on till both parties appealed to home.

At this point Sir Edward West suddenly died, his Widow followed him in a week or so, leaving one Orphan child, a little delicate girl, to the care of Sir Charles and Lady Chambers. In a month Sir Charles died too. Lady Chambers, poor woman, waited for her confinement, my Mother and I standing Godmothers to the poor posthumous child, Anne Catherine, and then sailing with all the Orphans for England.

The overwork of the Courts quite pleased my father, who went on capitally all his own way, as busy as half a dozen; but the Bombay Government interfering again about that Ramchander business, he, in a pet, closed the Court, a step every body, including my mother, condemned; but he was thoroughly out of temper, and no one to hold him in.

I forget whether he closed the Courts before or after our visit to Mahableishwa, but the dispute was in full vigour at that time, so we were out of the range of all the Governour's civilities, never asked to meet him either—that is, collectively.

I individually was quite his friend, riding with him frequently in the mornings, particularly on the hills, at least till he fancied he might be thought in the way. He used to read me the letters he received from his wife and children, sent me their pictures, newspapers, new books, fruit, flowers, etc. And when it was known that I was soon to remove to Satara, he not only wished me joy with all his heart, and told me I was marrying one of the best fellows in the service, but he confided to me that in the contemplated changes there would no longer be a Brigadier at Satara, the Resident would command what troops were necessary, and that Colonel Smith would be moved. Where would I like to go to. Akmednugger, he called it Nugger, was a good climate and a pleasant place, quite in the way of travellers, he'd send him there if the Station suited me. Only once we got upon the quarrel; he said if I had been my father's Wife instead of his daughter it would never have gone such lengths; so he had listened to gossip too.

I took very much to Colonel and Mrs Robertson; he was delightful, he was quite a Scotchman, mostly a self educated one, and not refined but his innate goodness and long habits of command had given him the manner of a man in authority. He looked great at the head of his own *long* table, beaming his benevolent smiles all round, reading Burns aloud at some of our pleasant gatherings with the accent and the feeling of a country man. Here, too, we made the better acquaintance of Major Jameson, son of old Bailie Jameson at Inverness, connected with the Alves's, Inglis's, and other good northern bodies. Good natured man, he used to devote hours to my mother gossiping with her over all the north *countrie*. She liked him better than any person in Bombay, and was certainly a very great deal happier after he came among us. He was not in my Colonel's regiment, but in one of the other Cavalry ones, and wore the handsome french gray uniform with silver. My Colonel used to meet me most mornings just where the path from our tents joined the road; we then went on together, generally towards Satara. One day either I was earlier than usual, or he was later, at any rate I arrived at the trysting place and he was not there. I did not know that I looked disappointed, but I looked up and down the road, I suppose. 'The Colonel Sahib has gone on,' said the syce,[1] pointing to the fresh marks of a horse's feet. I am sure I blushed, like the 'rosy morn', a little at the man's sharpness, a little at my cool Colonel's easy way of taking matters. Didn't he pay for it. I should think so—he sometimes breakfasted with us, but very rarely, for sooth to say our breakfasts were not tempting to those Indian palates; toast and tea and butter, nothing more, no fish, no rice, no curry.

I had my coffee as usual after my ride, and then I often took a stroll round the tents, and then sat with a book near the curtain, which acted door, looking out on the scene around. Here I passed an hour or so before my father and mother joined me. She never rose early; he had very much given up his morning ride, not liking, perhaps, to meet the Governour. After breakfast we had our usual occupations, visitors or visiting, and then a neat toilette for an early dinner at home or elsewhere. In the evening often a saunter, and I, often a drive in Colonel Smith's gig, none of us having brought up other carriages.

One day I had a ride on an elephant, an extremely disagreeable mode of moving, like a boat heaving up the wrong way. The great beast kneeled down when desired, and I got up his side by the help of a little ladder of 6 or 8 rungs slung to his back, and entered a curricle seat with a head to it. The roll of the creature as it rose was horrid, its awkward walk ditto, I was very glad to get safe on the ground again. Our strolls in the gray of the evening were checked by the appearance of a small green serpent, whose bite was venomous; a peon of the Robertsons' died in consequence, and as we did not know where they might be, their colour concealing them too, we gave up our wanderings.

I was one morning writing at a table near the door of the tent, my toes touching a pile of books on the ground beneath it. Nasserwanjee came behind, and laying one hand on my shoulder to keep me in the chair and the other on the back of the chair, he pulled both back together, asking pardon for the liberty all the while. When I was at a safe distance, two peons moved forward and dashed a billet of wood on one of these

1. Attendant, following a horseman on foot.

little serpents, which had been lying close to the books and my toes—there's a pleasant little interlude in one's occupations. I saw only one other strange animal in these mountains—a large monkey, or an ape rather, which I took for a little old Indian hindu, gray with age, for it was walking upright with a branch in its hand.

And now our time was up, and we were to go back to Bombay, and it was necessary to acquaint Sir John and Miladi that I thought it wiser to go off instead to Satara. It was but 30 miles, every comfort was already there in my Colonel's bungalow, most of my wardrobe was with me, and some furniture. A clergyman was at hand—the smiling one—the Judge could grant the license, and the Resident do all the rest.

My father was delighted, particularly when he heard all the particulars of the Irish estate, the bachelour brother etc. He was charmed, too, at the idea of the mountain wedding, so queer, so primitive. I think he wanted to get rid of me with as little expense, too, as possible. Not so my Mother. She had no wish for any marriage, it would only throw so much more trouble on her. She did not see that either of my sisters had done much for herself by her determination to marry. Jane married to an old man who might be her grandfather, hideously ugly, and far from rich. Mary shut up with her airs and her baby, never seeing a creature, nor of any use to any one. She did not understand this craze for marrying; pray, who was to write all the notes. Colonel Smith was no great catch, just a soldier. An Irish lad who went out as a Cadet, like George McIntosh of the Dell and 50 more such, and a marriage huddled up in that sort of way, in a desert, on a mountain, without a church, or a cake, or any preparations, it would be no marriage at all, neither decent nor respectable; she, for one, should never consider people married who had been buckled together in that *couple beggar* fashion. If there were to be a marriage at all it should be a proper one, in the Cathedral at Bombay by the clergyman who there officiated, friends at the wedding, and every thing as it ought to be.

So there was no help, she was resolute. We had to travel down the ghaut, and along the plains, a 100 miles, I think, for she would have no more sea, and travel back again after the ceremony, at the loss of a month's extra pay, for the Colonel did not receive his allowances when on leave. Well, there was another dilemma. While I had been riding with Colonel Smith, Rose, my mother's pretty half caste maid, had been walking with Serjeant Herring, the officer in charge of the invalids, and when she found that I was to be married, she confided to me that she meant to marry too, that live in that large Retreat without me she would not, could not, that Serjeant Herring had a situation in the hospital department, which gave him enough to support a Wife on very well, that he was a pious young man and very good looking, and would get leave to come down to Bombay for her as soon as he had taken back his invalids. I really was quite frightened; I did not know how to tell my poor mother this bad news. Not so Rose. Strengthened by the love of Serjeant Herring, she could brave greater danger; she should tell my Lady at once and let her get used to it. People were not to live single, people of course must marry, and my Lady etc. So Rose told, and a fine storm we had. I had to bear the worst of it, for it was all thrown on me. I had known of this ridiculous affair, concealed it, encouraged it, planned both Rose's marriage and my own in an artful underhand way—and we should see what would come of it. My poor Mother. She felt deserted, desolate and her natural pride would not let her say so tenderly; there were many such tempers in the olden times.

A third mischance. On our intended line of road there were no traveller's bungalows, none but private ones of the Governour's, into not one of which would she set her foot, and our tents were to go by sea. On this subject she was peremptory, even violent. We were all at a stand still when Major Jameson undertook to manage her. He highly applauded her spirit, approved of her resoloution, and, tho' under all circumstances he thought the Governour's offer of his bungalows extremely obliging, he agreed it was impossible that she could accept it. He knew of proper resting places, having lately travelled that road with Sir Thomas Bradford, to whom he was A.D.C., and so, a goodly company, we set out, Major Jameson and the Colonel riding, my father in a palanquin like the ladies. We travelled long and wearily before reaching the first halting place, a comfortable bungalow where all was ready for a late dinner. The two gentlemen had ridden on, to have every thing ready, my mother and I were not long behind them, but we waited near an hour for my father, who, obliging his bearers to follow some directions of his own, had gone a long round. Good claret, well cooled, and some champagne, greatly enlivened the entertainment, my dear Mother hobnobbing with Major Jameson and asking no questions about the bungalow, taking the Governour's servants and furniture for that belonging to the traveller's restingplace.

So on we went along the line arriving in Bombay in high good humour. All but poor Colonel Smith, whose horse shying or stumbling at the crossing of the stony bed of a river, got so severe a fall, that he nearly fainted and was laid up for some weeks from a strain, in his friend Doctor Eckford's house. When he was able, he removed to the Hermitage, Prospect Lodge I mean, to be close to us, the Norrises having returned from the Neilgherries and resumed possession of their pretty home.

# CHAPTER TWENTY-EIGHT

## 1829

MR GARDINER and Mary had removed to a house in the fort in Rampart row, where they were engaged in packing up their effects, having determined on going home to England. We were all very much distressed at this strange resolution, unwarranted by any real cause; he was in good health, she, never well, no worse in India than at home, and the child was thriving, so that to throw up the service when he was so near the top and return to idle life away on an income very insufficient for her expensive tastes was a piece of folly in the judgement of most others. There were reasons that made Bombay very distasteful to my poor sister, independant of her dislike to the climate, the habits and the society. Mr Gardiner, too, suffered from this mysterious annoyance and I really believe they feared for the safety of the baby—its life had been threatened and with only native servants to watch it, they could never bear it out of their own sight. They fancied, also, that owing to my father's quarrel with the Governour, they had been overlooked in some late appointments, while this was entirely owing to their having refused Tannah when, as is customary, they were passed over next time. However it all was they had determined on going—or rather, she had, for he had never much voice in any matter. They took their passage in a small Liverpool merchantman, 300 tons, and only waited to see me married. The last week of their stay, having sold all they did not mean to carry home, they removed to the Retreat, which I was very glad of for all their sakes. Our dinner party every evening was very pleasant; some of my cousins, or the Norris's, my Colonel, Major Jameson. A fine long marriage Settlement was prepared, for days before our marriage, news arrived of my Colonel's brother's death which made him possessor of the

Irish estate, then valued at about £1200 a year. As we had only been 16 months in India, my father told me he would offer me no additions to a wardrobe he presumed must still be amply provided, he would only buy from Mary her habit, which she had never worn as she never rode and give me that, as my own was growing shabby. My dresses in that climate had grown shabby too—but luckily a box arrived from the London dressmaker on chance, containing 3 very pretty new gowns for me, and a pelisse and hat and feathers for my Mother which she not fancying made over to me. My Colonel too sent me a pretty purse with 30 gold mohurs[1] in it and he ordered mourning for me as he wished me on reaching Satara to put it on for his brother.

My father gave me 20 gold mohurs on my Wedding morning, as I had not spent all Uncle Edward had given me on landing, I felt quite rich for the first time in my life; and I never felt poor again, for though circumstances reduced our future income infinitely below our expectations, we so managed our small income that we never yet have owed what we could not pay, nor ever known what it was to be pressed for money.

My Colonel was married in his Staff uniform, which we thought became him better than his Cavalry light gray. There was a large party of relations, a few friends, and the good Bishop, then only Mr Carr, married us. My Mother, who had become reconciled to my choice, outraged all propriety by going with me to the Cathedral; both she and I wished it, as I was to proceed across the bay immediately after the cere- mony. So it all took place, how, I know not, for between the awfulness of the step I was taking, the separation from my father and mother, whose stay I had been so long, and the parting for an indefinite time from poor Mary, I was very much bewildered all that morning, and hardly knew what was doing till I found myself in the boat, sailing among the islands, far away from every one but him who was to be in lieu of every one to me for ever more. The first movement that occurred to me was to remember Fatima's advice—retire to the inner cabin, take off all my finery.

1. The chief gold coin of British India.

I had been married in white muslin, white satin, lace, pearls, and flowers and put on a cambrick wrapper she had sent on board and had laid ready. The next, to obey my new master's voice and return to him in the outer cabin, where, on the little table, was laid an excellent luncheon supplied privately by my mother, to which, as I had certainly eaten no breakfast, I, bride as I was, did ample justice. Indeed we both got very sociable over our luxurious repast and quite enjoyed the nice cold claret that accompanied it.

We were going to Satara, neither by sea to Bancoote and so up that end of the Ghauts, nor along the plain we had last travelled, but round by Poonah, ascending the Khandala Pass. On landing, therefore, we jogged on in palanquins to the bungalow at the foot of the first ascent, where I had rested with the Gardiners. There I put on my habit, we mounted our horses, and prepared to scale a wall! I could not believe, looking up, that any one would be mad enough to attempt such a climb on horseback; but not liking to make a fuss on such an occasion I stilled my nerves as best I might, and, shutting my eyes, committed myself to the sure feet of the troop horse that had been brought for me, and the care of his attendant who never left his head. After the first pull the ascent was easier, and, more accustomed to the seat, I ventured to look round on the beautiful scenery. Such wooding! such leaves! such creepers! hanging in festoons from tree to tree, sharp rocks around, deep gullies below, and the steep road mounting ever turning sharp corners as usual to rise to fresh grandeur. Not far from the top the tents were pitched on a cool knoll, servants waiting, dinner ready, all prepared as if in an abiding home, so used are Indians to such movings. Next day we past Lanowlie and went on to a bungalow not half so agreeable as the tents, and next day we arrived at Poonah, the most fashionable Station on our side of India.

We took up our abode in a ruinous kind of place just outside the Station, a sort of old temple or garden house or something, where, however, we had two cool rooms, a bath, and a rather untidy but spacious compound. Here I was very glad to rest a whole, quiet day, for the journey had been fatiguing, but my Colonel set off to visit quantities of friends, and, to my dismay, returned towards dusk with Henry Robertson, who was the first who ever called me by my new name, Mrs Smith. He wanted me to dine with him and Jemima, but I begged off, so while we were still at our dessert he and Jemima arrived to join us at tea, and my Cousin Fanny and Mr Ward came soon after, so the next morning I felt confidence enough to face the world, only I was not called on to do it, as we were to continue our homeward journey.

There being a considerable plain to traverse, we applied for an escort, and had a troop of irregular horse sent to us, which materially improved the picturesque of the journey. They were Lancers, and dressed in eastern style, turbans, trowsers, flowing robes, and the smart flag flying. They rode well, and contrasted with the loaded camels, the bullocks, the various attendants, the palanquins, etc. ; I thought, when riding by my husband's side in the cool of the morning, that there had never been off the stage a prettier procession. Our first halt was to breakfast in another temple kind of half ruined building, sheltered by a tope of fine trees, and on the bank of a clear stream. We were to rest here all the hot day, so the camels kneeled down to be lightened of their loads, the bullocks were freed from theirs, the escort dismounted and began to feed and groom their horses beneath the trees, the servants prepared the fires for their meal, and we entered our temple to undress and bathe and put on wrappers, take our breakfast and lie on sofas with our books till time for starting in the afternoon.

The first two hours we used our palanquins, passing at one time through a perfectly deserted town—streets upon streets of really good houses tenantless, not a living creature to be seen in a place of such extent that it took the bearers quite an hour to jog trot thro' it. On the sun going down we took to our horses, and, after a pleasant ride in the dark, reached the cheerful tent, where lights were gleaming, table laid, dinner ready, and all our furniture and toilettes arranged. On the evening of the next day we rode up to Satara, passed the Resident's house, the Lines, and, mounting a gentle rise, stopt at the door of our own home—such a pretty one. Often and often the first impression of it recurs to me.

It was the usual Indian bungalow, one long building

divided into two rooms, with Verandahs all round subdivided into various apartments. The peculiar feature of this very pretty cottage was that the centre building to the front projected in a bow, giving such a charming air of cheerfulness to our only sitting room, besides very much encreasing its size; the Verandah to one side held the sideboard and other necessaries for the table, the other Verandah acted as entrance hall and anteroom. There were no walls on either side between the house and the Verandah, only pillars to support the roof. The back part of the long building was the bedroom, one side Verandah the Colonel's dressing room, the other mine, and the one at the end was furnished in boudoir fashion for me. The bathrooms were in a small court adjoining, the servants' offices at a little distance, and any strangers who came to see us slept in tents. Was there ever any establishment more suited to the country.

We looked over the long Lines of the encampment to a wooded country beyond. To the right were two or three small bungalows at a little distance, the Brigade Major's, the Doctor's, and still further off the Residency. To the left a good way on stretched the native town of Satara, with a hill fort towering above it; altogether a very interesting scene, and the climate when I went there in June really quite delightful.

We rode every morning, drove every evening, and when the rains fell it was in gentle showers like summer rains in England. Sentries guarded our door, and there was a guard besides ready to run all messages. We were waked by the reveillée, but I can't say that we went to sleep at the rappel; our hours in the evening were rather late for an up country station, none of us dining till 5 o'clock. The society consisted of the Resident, Colonel Robertson, with wife and children; his assistant, some young man I don't remember; the Doctor, Bird, who was absent at that time; the Brigade Major Wilson, who had with him on a visit his sister and her husband, Captain and Mrs Law. All these lived like ourselves in bungalows. The Officers belonging to the Brigade lived in tents in the Lines—Major Capon, Captain and Mrs Soppitt, and two or three married lieutenants, whose wives I did pity, poor young things, when I went to return their calls; girls brought up comfortably in England, one, with an ivory handled pen ornamented with turquoises, and a work box having her initials on the lid in brilliants, using her trunk as a seat, the two chairs being presented to us, and the one camp table holding the fine work box. Some seemed dull enough, others radiantly happy, and they were the wise ones. What use was there in repining. People must creep before they fly, as the Irish say, and if the poor lieutenants lived they would rise to rank and all its comforts.

The Resident had company at dinner daily; he was a hospitable man and never seemed better pleased than at the head of his well filled table. We generally dined with him thrice a week at least; once a week they regularly dined with us, the day after our Official dinner. Every Wednesday so many of the Officers, married and unmarried, dined with us, invited by Major Wilson, who kept a roster, and called the names regularly thro'. I used to have a little battle with him when sometimes I wished to have a favourite over again, or out of turn. The next day the Robertsons and other private friends came to eat up the scraps, an entertainment always very pleasant, and called on our side of India a brass knocker, I am sure I don't know why. The Soppitts were good kind people. She pretty and always tastefully dressed, none of the rest interesting, only a Mrs Goodenough played on the pianoforte splendidly. The Surgeon, Doctor Young, was a goose, his Wife a most odious woman, Mr Wilson very nice indeed. Except a stray visitor arrived, we had no relief from the small circle. It would have been stupid for a continuance but for the Robertsons, who suited us perfectly.

Once in three weeks our cousin, Mr Ward, drove over in a gig from Poonah to read prayers to us in the Robertsons' Dining room. Our life was regular enough. We generally rode early, taking the road from the Lines to the river Mowlie, a couple of miles or so thro' a grove of fine trees leading to the broad stream that flowed quietly on beneath hanging banks of wood. In the afternoon we drove through the town and round the fort of Satara, down the long, dingy street guarded about the middle by a lion and a tiger, one at each side, chained of course, but in the open air, plunging about, sometimes with a fierce tug at the chain and a low roar

that made me tremble till well past them; then by a field
where the Rajah's elephants were picketed out, the tame ones
tied by only one leg, a savage one by three. This savage hated
women, and when maddened by the sight of one made most
violent efforts to release himself, so violent that I could not
but fear he might succeed before we got beyond his fury.
These pieces of oriental splendour were far from agreeable to
me. The hill fort rose high above the town; a half ruined
building covered the summit, which the Rajah had lent to the
Robertsons, and thither we often repaired with them to drink
tea and sleep in the cooler air up at that height, the servants of
each family carrying there all requisites necessary for our
separate accommodation.

It was seldom so hot as to prevent me employing myself the
whole day, and I had plenty to do in my new character of
housewife, mending my husband's large and very ragged
wardrobe, that is, making the tailor do it instead of leaning
over his work, needle and thread in hands indeed, but half
asleep. And in overlooking the doings of the head servant,
whom I had soon to make understand that Madame was
supreme, that the way to please Madame was 'to be honest
and just in all his dealings' and that if he did not please
Madame, he would go. When he found that this was in
earnest, that the Sahib was aware of his crooked ways, and
though too indolent to reform them himself, was quite
willing to have them reformed, this rogue gave in, so far, as
not to exhibit his delinquencies too flagrantly. One of his
dodges had been about the poultry. There was a nice poultry
yard full of fine fowl, and a regular sum expended weekly in
feeding them, and yet we never had any fit for the table, all
that we consumed were bought in the bazaar, and were
certainly excellent; ours all died of cramps or cramming, and
the eggs were addled or were stolen by vermin; they did not
thrive in any way. I said they must—we must have so many
eggs and so many fowl per week, and I never would buy one
from that hour; nor did I, nor did we ever want a fair supply
of the very same description, too, that we had bought in the
bazaar. In truth these had been our own, without a doubt,
that we had bought for our Parsee's behoof twice over. The
sheep too; one frequently died, and I announced that the

next we lost he should pay for, and such a casualty never occurred again. So, all through, first with one thing, then with another; the quantities said to be given to the kitchen and the stable were more of every sort than it was possible could be consumed. I boldly diminished them by one half, leaving him quite margin enough after all, as I knew from my father's accounts, which we had regulated by the aid of Mrs Ironside. My Colonel lived for less per month after he married than he had done before, with a larger establishment of course. Batchelours are made to be fleeced very properly. It is the duty of man to have Wife and bairns and if he neglect this law of his kind, let him pay for it, certainly.

Besides these various arrangements Major Wilson helped me in a more elegant employment, the making the entrance Verandah into a perfect greenhouse, in a very short time too; plants grow so quickly in that climate.

When we first reached the Station we were very gay. Mrs Robertson gave us a grand state dinner and a Ball. Major Wilson gave us a dinner, and the Regiments gave us a Ball, which I opened with Captain Soppitt to 'St Patrick's day in the morning.' We danced in the Mess tent, which was very prettily decorated. For this very grand occasion I destined my hat and feathers; being in mourning I could only dress in white muslin, so I thought this handsome hat, which had been considered, when tried on, most particularly becoming, would elevate the plainer part of the attire, and add quite an air of dignity to the Commandant's Wife. It was a *chapeau de paille* shape, of *crêpe lisse*, and really in good taste, but the Colonel was terrified. Such a headgear had never been seen in those regions; plain Mrs Robertson and pretty Mrs Soppitt had never either of them attempted such an outrageous adornment and for *his* Wife to originate such a singularity, he could never stand it; he never had seen ladies wear hats except riding. It was no use talking to him of fashion, beauty, pictures, artists, and so forth; he really was in an agony. So there was nothing for it but to replace my mother's present in its tin case, braid up my long hair in its own peculiar fashion with a pearl comb at the back and a bunch of white roses at one ear, and look girlish instead of matronly. Frequently afterwards his extraordinary dislike to any change in dress he

had not been used to obliged me to appear very unlike the
times, and look dowdy enough for many a year. Latterly, his
eye became more accustomed to all the vagaries of fashion
and so he bore his whims with greater patience—to my great
comfort for it did annoy me more than it ought perhaps, to
wear thin arms when other women cased their in balloons, a
low head beside their towers, and other such peculiarities.
The fate of the hat made me so nervous about a cap in the
shape of a butterfly with spread wings, which had accompanied the last dresses from London, that I never produced it
before any eyes but Mrs Young's, who was poor and fond of
finery, and accepted it with gratitude. It suited her so well,
she looked almost handsome in it, as Colonel Smith remarked in chorus among other voices, wondering where she
could have got so pretty a headdress! These were light
troubles, after all. The only visitors we had were Major
Jameson and a King's Officer, I think named Bonamy,
Captain Bonamy. They came together, staid a week, causing
a round of dinners much enlivened by them. I liked the
Robertson children, poor Tilly and Elphie, ugly little things
but very intelligent. Elphinstone is now a fine young man out
somewhere in India, Matilda in her Satara grave, her mother,
unable to part with her only daughter, kept her on year after
year in that dangerous climate to infancy, and she died of
liver at 9 years old. After we left, mercifully; they had, then,
besides four boys at home.

In the month of October, asthma, to which for many years
my Colonel had been subject, attacked him very seriously.
Night after night he spent in an easy chair smoking
stramonium and appearing to suffer painfully. It is probably
a disease worse to witness than to bear, the breathlessness
seeming to be so distressing. As the fit became worse instead
of better, Doctor Bird, who had returned to his duties,
advised change of air, not to Poonah but to Bombay, to leave
the high ground at once and descend to the Coast for a while,
but not remain there. He told me privately the stomach and
liver were quite deranged from long residence in a tropical
climate and that our best plan would be to return home. This
neither of us wished, and we suggested the Neilgherries;
he said they were only a make shift, present ease, but no

remedy. He advised a consultation on reaching Bombay, after watching the effect of the journey.

As, at any rate, we were not to return to Satara, the new arrangements being to take place after Xmas, we made such preparations as were fitting for the break up there. Discharged the Parsee and all the servants but our personal attendants, packed what furniture we meant to keep in such a way as would render it easy of moving, and all perishable and unnecessary articles were left to be sold. My Grand pianoforte went back to my mother, and with all the quantity of an Indian travelling equipage surrounding us, with the addition of many extras, boxes, cases, horses, gig, servants, etc., we left my first married home, where indeed I had been very happy. Spite of some trials thro' which I think I may say I came well, for I had made a promise to myself to be patient, forbearing, accommodating wherever principle was not concerned, and even then to oppose with gentleness.

I regretted the Robertsons very much, and I regretted a promised visit from the Rajah.[1] The little fat man was coming in state on his elephant with his body guard and a whole long train of attendants to pay a visit of ceremony to the Commandant's wife, and he was bringing shawls, muslins, tissues and pearls to lay at her feet, all which would have been very acceptable; altho' in general the presents thus made are of a very inferiour description. The military are allowed on particular occasions to receive such gifts, the Civilians never; so the Rajah gained by our departure whatever I lost, for he kept his presents. This poor little man was either a most consummate hypocrite, or he was most shamefully illused by those who succeeded General Robertson. On account of political intrigues said to be brought to light, implicating his veracity, indeed his honour, on all points, he was deprived of his dominions, banished to Bengal on a small annuity and overwhelmed with indignities. In our time he was considered perfectly harmless; he had taught

---

1. Pratad Singh: descended from the great
   Sivaji, enthroned 1818; his rule over this small,
   semi-independent principality was little more than
   nominal.

himself English, read the newspapers, after a fashion, and the Encyclopaedia Britannica, which he had bought from the Colonel in 40 volumes, assisted by some interpreter probably little better versed in our language than himself. His principal aim seemed to be to imitate the brilliant style of representation habitual to the French. He had his *Champ de mars*, literally called so, and there he manoeuvred his troops to his own delight, and mine, for they were dressed in every variety of uniform he had been able to pick up at sales of old clothing, horse, foot, artillery of all ages, for he had some Hanoverian Jack boots and feather fringed cocked hats much admired by his Officers, who looked in them, their slight frames swallowed up inside these monstrous habiliments, like so many Tom Thumbs in pewter pots. He was too fat for horseback, he therefore directed operations from his elephant, which was very grandly painted, and hung about with brocade and tassels and gold and silver. He was improving his town too, and had his garden of roses around his palace, neatly kept.

I cannot but think he was honest, for a native, then. We must not judge of them by our standard; truth is not in them; it would be called folly. Their wisdom is cunning, underhand measures are their skill, deceiving is their sagacity; they deal with us as they deal with each other; so the poor Rajah, deprived of his true friend Colonel Robertson, with his shield of integrity, may have fallen into the tricks of his race, or may have been the victim of the intrigues of his brother and successor who bore a very bad character. I have always been sorry for our Rajah.

We required no escort on our return to Poonah, being so large a party. We made out our two days' journey well, and established ourselves in a pavilion in Henry Robertson's compound, where we only slept for we took all our meals with them. He had married, a year before, Jemima Dunlop, a remarkably pretty young woman, Scotch, niece to Mrs Glasgow, well known to my people, as was all her family. She had been a little spoiled and on coming out to India had announced the most high sounding matrimonial intentions; the handsomest, the cleverest, the best born, the best bred man alone was worthy of her name and beauty. So a year passed over, another, and a third. So, dropping a requisite each season, she contented herself with abilities, sinking the other three or outweighing them with worth, which she got into the bargain and had forgotten in her catalogue. She was a very curious woman, exceedingly disagreeable to me, so self opinionated, stingy, dirty and silly, I thought. There was one little baby, a frightful thing kept rolled up in flannel, was four months old and had never been dressed or washed, it looked like, for she did not shine in the washing way. I remember years after when they came to visit us at Baltiboys with the only two children they had left of seven, *he* bathed both boy and girl in a Tub every morning, and the youngest of the two was ten years old.

They were very kind to us at Poonah, gave a dinner party in our honour. We dined out too, at the Wards, and somewhere else, I forget the name. The Wards were living in Wogan Browne's house, a very pretty one, and Fanny had it so beautifully furnished, herself and children so beautifully dressed, and Mr Ward, who managed the Bazaar affairs, kept so good a table, it was quite a pleasure to visit them.

Poonah is a nice place, no beauty of scenery, a wide plain, a wandering town and straggling encampment, always full of people, always full of gaiety, and a delightful dry climate, the very air for me, but not fit for my asthmatick husband; so we determined to move on after a sort of military display was over which was to take place on the following evening, before all the beauty and fashion of Poonah. There was to be a preparatory series of exercises in the morning, to which the Colonel wished to go, and to take me with him, and as my horse was an old trooper bought from Captain Graham of the 4th Dragoons—Sir James' brother—I felt not a bit afraid of either trumpets or firing. It was a very pretty sight; the lines were just forming in the gray half light of the Indian very short dawn. We rode along them in the midst of a party of friends all in high spirits, to take up a good station off the field. When lo! the first bugle call. Hotspur pricked up his ears, seemed every inch of him to grow alive. The second call. Off he set, and scouring the whole plain, planted himself and me in the ranks of his old regiment. I never was so bewildered

in my life, fairly *dazed*, and so unequal to resume the reins
I had let fall to grasp the crutch that Major Willoughby
dismounted, stept forward, took me off my excited steed and
led me to somebody's carriage, where I felt much more
comfortable than at the head of that troop of cavalry, altho'
my abominable Colonel came up in fits of laughing to condole
with me, echoed by his merry companions, none of whom
were *Civilians* to a certainty. I don't suppose riding on
horseback was my forte, for I was always meeting with
disasters, from the day Paddle gave me a bath in the Druie,
to Donegal's capers in the Paddy fields, and this pleasant
Exhibition at Poonah.

As I was not quite sure what sort of figure I had cut in my
habit and hat, and Major Willoughby's arms, I resolved to
efface any disadvantageous impression made in the morning
by an extraordinary display of feminine loveliness at the
Review in the evening, and for this purpose I repaired rather
early after luncheon to our summer house, and ordering a tin
case to be opened, dived down for the box which held the fine
hat and feathers. The box was there—but within it! a riddle
of what had been crape and catgut that fell to dust on being
raised, and some remains of feathers amid a swarm of heaven
knows what kind of creepers; the Ayah must have left the
case open at some time and so let these destructive insects in.
I was wise enough to hold my tongue, the Poonah world
never knew how much elegance it had lost the sight of;
neither did my Colonel till long after. May be the insects
saved us a scene for he might have forbidden the contemplated display—he had very backward notions about dress in
those days. The only smart head tire I had with me was a
cottage bonnet of white net, with a bunch of roses. It very
likely suited me and the Review better than did the hat and
feathers.

We went on in the evening to Dapourie, with Sir Charles
and Lady Malcolm, who were staying there in the Governour's absence, to a late dinner. I rather think they were
honeymooning it, at any rate they had been but a short time
married. She was a very pretty, little, dark, Jewess looking
woman, a Miss Shawe, and he a good sort of rough seaman. He
had not done as much for himself as the other clever brothers

had done for themselves.[1] He had the courage, the daring of the borderer tribe without much abilities. We staid a couple of days in this pleasant spot, a large cool house in pretty grounds, and then we proceeded on our journey to Bombay, where we took up our residence with my father and mother.

Colonel Smith felt better for a day or two, and then he got ill again. Doctor Eckford said he must really do as Doctor Bird had advised, go for 6 months to the Neilgherries; he however recommended a consultation, so Dr McAdam and Dr Penny were called in, and they decided for a voyage home. Whether they were right or wrong, who can say, but they were so uneasy about him that they asked for a private audience of me, and told me he was in serious ill health, had been too long in that climate, that another season could not but go very hard with him, that the Neilgherries was only a palliative, not a cure, and that, in short, were he not to sail for England they could not answer for the consequences.

My father was very unwilling to lose us from India, and gave his voice for the Neilgherry plan; to satisfy me he went again to Doctor McAdam, and on returning told me there was nothing for it but the voyage home. I must own I was very sorry. We had made up our minds to remain 3 years longer, and this sudden retirement from place and pay was a disappointment.

The close of the rains being a very unhealthy time on the Coast we all moved up to Khandalla for ten days, we pitching our tents directly over the deep ravine, my father and mother occupying the bungalow. Here the bracing mountain air, and the fine breeze, tempered by the near neighbourhood of the sea, made the heat of the day quite bearable and the cool nights very enjoyable. We breakfasted at home, spent the mornings as we liked, always dined with my father, and played whist in the evenings. Several travellers paid us visits in passing, all doors being open to all comers in India, which

1. There were ten brothers in this Dumfriesshire family, all of whom had to make their own way in the world. Sir Charles, the youngest, became Vice Admiral in Bombay, where his brother Sir John was Governor: another brother Sir Pulteney became an Admiral.

chance meetings made a pleasant variety, and when the stray guest could play whist I was not sorry to resign my hand to him, for these were in my early gambling days, and I fancy I was not the best of partners, for my husband and myself managed between us to lose as much to our more fortunate parents as paid their boat hire on our return; a piece of luck my father particularly enjoyed the mention of and made a boast of for many a day. He translated two odes of Horace during this visit to the Ghauts, my Mother darning table linen beside him as he wrote. We were by no means so refined in our employments in our tents as were the *burra sahibs* in the bungalow. Doctor Eckford joined us, and we played backgammon etc. And talked and laughed by the hour.

One night we had all gone early to bed; it was calm and dark, no moon, no sound, the sentries being either asleep, or as quiet as if they had been. Suddenly a roar like the roar at Lanowlie broke the stillness, roused us all—it was frightful, such a vicious tone, so near. It came again, and then thro' the ravine came the shriek of a buffalo. The guard stept up to the curtain of the tent and called the Colonel; he valiantly seized a pistol and, wrapping his gown round him, ventured out, to meet Doctor Eckford in similar guise. How I shook within. They soon satisfied themselves that we were in no danger. Our acquaintance the tiger was engaged in deadly conflict with a buffalo, too busy a great deal in the bottom of the dell to have any thoughts of ascending to our height. The poor buffalo had no chance; his moans were soon hushed, and we hoped the horrid scene was over, but another actor had arrived, some other ferocious beast, who set upon the tiger, and really the fearful yells they uttered were terrifying. For a full half hour the battle raged; then all was still. How the combatants had settled matters, which was worsted, or what each suffered, we never knew. In the morning part of the carcase of the buffalo remained on the field, but no other trace of the affray.

My mother at a greater distance had heard none of the outcries. She did not, however, admire such neighbours, and as we had a good many arrangements to make for our voyage, and the cold weather was beginning, we seconded her proposal to return to the Retreat, where I at least had a busy time.

Our preparations for the voyage home were interrupted by the arrival of the two last of the Ironside cousins, Annie and Julia, who had been living since their mother's death with their guardian, Uncle Ralph, at Rothesay, whither he had betaken himself after the sale of Tennochside. This step had been necessitated by the complete derangement of his affairs, into which he had never looked for years. His agent, *Crooky* Shortridge, so called from his hump back, received his rents and answered his calls for money, never intimating that the accounts, which were never looked at, had been very greatly overdrawn. Edmund had larger debts; it had cost much to get him into Mr Kinderley's office, where his foolish and extravagant conduct prevented his remaining. It cost more again to equip him for India, my father having got him a Cavalry Cadetship for Bengal. And lastly, my Uncle had gone security with three others for what had been required to finish the education and provide the equipment of his brother Edward. The necessary funds were furnished by the advice of my father, who was one of the Securities and was never repaid. The other two were James Grant, Corrimo, James Grant, Duke Street, having died bankrupt, and my father's part being in the hands of his Trustees, those from whom the £2,000 had been borrowed came down upon poor Uncle Ralph. The sale paid all debts and left a surplus. It had always been said that there was coal on the estate; this my uncle disbelieved, and took no trouble about it. The Glasgow merchant who bought Tennochside had capital and energy; found the coal, worked the mines, and realised a very handsome income out of them.

My Uncle bore his misfortunes well; he was easy under great trials, like many others; but his temper, never good, became very irritable. He and his wife had never agreed and he and his niece Anne were at open war. She was a saucy, ill bred girl and resented the greater favour shewn to Julia, who was quiet in manner and modest and very handsome. The one most to be pitied of this ill assorted party was my Aunt Judith. All had been hers, and most certainly she had spent none of it; frugality could not have been carried further than by her in every department. What she felt no one ever knew. She went on exactly as usual, silent, grave, stolid, unimpressible, apparently never provoked, and most surely never pleased; the poor Houghton girls were very miserable in a home so unlike their own. We liked them very much but thought Anne the better looking, she had an intelligent countenance and a fine figure, while Julia was dull and fat.

A great many parties were given in honour of the ship's cargo of young pretty girls, and as I am writing of gaieties, I may mention what I had forgotten in its proper place—Mr Bouchier's masquerade. He gave it before I married. He was the head of the post office, a fat, portly man, very good natured, very well off, and a bachelour.

It was great fun choosing our characters, the suitable dresses etc. Our host was the best himself; large, and fat, and fashionably attired, he represented a School mistress with a long sticked fan; his scholars were the tallest young Officers he could get—all in short frocks and red sashes—whom he watched most rigorously, interfering with their partners, gathering them round him and lecturing them on their behaviour by the help of the long sticked fan. The figure that made the most sensation was my Lady Bradford, she had insisted on going, the only time she was ever known to attend any assembly. She had no need for any fancy dress. Her usual attire was quite sufficiently out of the ordinary attire of her sex to pass for a fancy dress—a faded silk, very plain and very scanty gown, and the close cap, made her quite unlike any body else. No one knew her at first; she passed for Jane Shawe. There was the usual number of characters of all times, some very well supported: an Albanian whose beautiful costume was so becoming to handsome Mr Le Geyt that all fell in love with him. Mary was dressed after a print of Celia in 'As you like it.' I was a Hungarian lady of distinction with a wealth of jewels on me that would have frightened me had Mr Forbes told me their value when he sent them. He was the head of Sir Charles Forbes's house at Bombay, a particularly nice person, and able to borrow any amount of jewellery from his native acquaintance. Large, well lighted rooms, the best musick and an excellent supper sent the whole queer looking crowd away happy.

Mr and Mrs Bax at this time made a party to Elephanta, a pretty wooded island about the middle of the Bay, remarkable among all the rest for a cave cut out of the solid rock—the general hindu custom. The supports were huge elephants, by no means coarsely carved. Four of them with arches between, formed the portico, all part of the rock, cut from it like the Temple within. A very large elephant was inside. I forget now if there was any thing else remarkable except the situation and the variety of beautiful flowers, mostly creepers which hung about the stones and the trees. It took us a couple of hours to reach this famous place, where luncheon was soon prepared—the same time to return. Our boat had a good awning, and yet we were all burned nearly black by the fierce sun.

And here I may mention what I had forgotten in its proper place, that on our way to Bombay from Poonah we had stopt to visit another more celebrated excavation, the Temple of Ellora. A wooded hill rises from the plain; at one end a little search reveals a door, not any way remarkable, except that one can't but wonder what it does there. The priest in charge opens it, and reveals such a lovely little display of exquisite carving as is only equalled by Melrose or Roslin; but they were built, they and their pillars, and then ornamented by fine carving. Ellora was cut out of the solid rock, as we cut the props of our coal mines, and the carving was done at the same time with the forming. What a curious people—such patience, such industry and taste too, according to their rights. At Ellora the proportions were elegant, the dome was lofty, the pillars light, unlike Elephanta where all was cumbrous, heavy, suited to the huge animal it was supposed to shelter.

Our newly arrived cousins brought us many kind gifts from the dear ones at home. Jane never forgot us and my good little Aunt Frere well remembered me. She sent me a quantity of useful things, dear in India and sometimes not to be had. Jane had very pleasant news for us. She had become acquainted with the Duchess of Wellington soon after settling at Malshanger, which was not far from Stratfield Saye. I forget what brought them together, I think Colonel Pennington had served under the Duke for a term in India, and Lord Douro hunted with Mr Folyambe's hunt. At any rate, they had grown very intimate, and Jane interested the

Duchess so much about our fine young cousin William
Ironside that he was invited to Stratfieldsaye and when Her
Grace went to see some exhibition or other at Sandhurst, it
was on his arm she walked about, fancy the pride of the
Cadet. She got him his commission and put him into the
Duke's regiment. Jane was so delighted, much more so and
more interested too in that fine young man than were his
sisters, who took it all very coolly, as matters of course, when
I went in great joy to tell them, and never thanked Jane then,
nor for her after care of this their only brother, whom they
lost so early.

I had one regret on leaving Bombay; my father's unfortunate difference with the Governour. Whatever it had been in
the beginning, the shutting up of the Courts had put him in
the wrong at the end. In my opinion, there is a bee in the
bonnet of all the Grants. As a race they are very clever, very
clear headed and very hard working. Under rule and
guidance, they do well, none better. Witness the numbers of
the Clan who have made the name celebrated all over the
world. When they make their own work, they make a mill of
it—they can't sit idle and they never appear to consider the
consequences of their impulsive acts. My husband and I
could have done nothing had we staid. It might have been
arranged perhaps had my poor Mother been in better
humour. This mischief with her was that she never let herself
be natural; none of us could ever find out what she really felt
or what she really wished. She brooded over every occurrence all by herself, and saw every thing through prejudices
not to be got rid of, because they were never named. She had
taken a dislike to the Governour and Sir John Malcolm was
very intimate with my Colonel; he was most anxious to end
this unhappy difference, he spoke both to him and to me, and
empowered him to conciliate my father. He even wrote a note
to be shewn to my father, which would have let him down
easy and by the aid of 'misapprehension,' 'hastiness of
temper on both sides,' 'intermeddling,' he tried to soften
matters. It had a good effect this kind note and Colonel Smith
assuring my father of what I am quite sure was true, that the
*great* Sir John had a high value for the *little* one and believed
him to have been influenced by his brother judges. All was in

good train when my poor Mother interfered. She never knew but the one side of any thing. She burst in with 'proper pride,' 'self respect,' 'high station of a King's Judge' on the one part and ever so many unpardonable 'impertinences' on the other, sparing neither my husband nor me for our uncalled for interference. So it became war to the knife instead of a reconciliation, a great pity.

She was irritated at our departure, which she considered unnecessary. She was good and affectionate, though she would not shew it, and she keenly felt the loss of the last of her children, the one who had stuck by her so long.

Mr Caw was much of the same style; he could not bear to lose any of us; his rudeness to Colonel Pennington was only equalled by his impertinence to Mr Gardiner, and surpassed by his spite to Colonel Smith, yet he would have laid down his life for my sisters and me, in fact, he was jealous of our husbands, he wanted no such fences between the old happy life in the old Country and himself. Never were such queer people as those people of the past age.

After several inquiries, visits to many vessels in harbour, and careful enquiries as to their commanders, we decided to sail in the *Childe Harold*, a new, swift ship, beautifully fitted up, commanded by Captain West, an old experienced lieutenant in the Royal Navy. He was to make a coasting voyage home, which was particularly recommended for Colonel Smith.

This settled, we furnished one of the poop cabins without much cost, as my father made over to us a good deal of our former cabin furniture. The small cabin next us was taken for little Willy Anderson and his maid, who was to act as mine. The Colonel also engaged a native male attendant, as when the violent fit of asthma was on him he was totally helpless and my mother did not think I should continue throughout the voyage able to wait on him alone. The small cabin opposite was taken by Doctor Eckford, who, not feeling well, had resolved to pay a short visit to the Cape. Thus we had prepared for as much comfort as a homeward voyage admits of; it is never so pleasant as a voyage out, for health and spirits are wanting, in general, to those who are leaving their occupation behind them.

We had regrets too, but we left more anxiety than it was easy to bear. The last mail from home brought out the patent for investing Mr Dewar with a knighthood and the Chief Justiceship, he a young man might have been my father's son, not clever, nor in any way qualified for such advancement save as a mark of displeasure with my poor father's folly, Mr Dewar having been acting Advocate General at the beginning of the dispute and so engaged on the side of the local government. My father was lucky not to be required to resign his puisne judgeship; he owed this to Lord Brougham.

I liked David Dewar so well, that James Dewar came in for liking too, and he deserved it from all of us; nothing could be more delicate, more respectful, more considerate than his demeanour to my father during the time they remained so strangely situated on the Bench together. I always heard my father equally commended for bearing this heavy blow so philosophically, and he was wounded on many sides, for they caricatured him as a wild elephant between two tame ones, which was a mistake and they ridiculed him in some places, animadverted on him severely in others: all to a man so sensitive as he really was under that outward stoicism, very, very annoying. It therefore did not surprise us on reaching home to find he had resigned his Bombay judgeship, and had removed to Calcutta with the intention of practising there at the Bar.[1]

My last sight of him in the cabin of the *Childe Harold*, where he and my mother left me late on the evening of the 4th of November; he lingered behind her one moment to fold me to his heart again, neither of us speaking, and then he vanished from my sight for ever. Long I sat listening to the stroke of the oars which carried them back in the darkness to their desolate home. It was a dreary parting.

Mr Anderson had put his little boy to bed in the next cabin, the child being half suffocated with weeping. Oh these

1. He resigned in September 1830 and practised at the
Calcutta Bar for three years before being again
appointed to a Puisne judgeship; he held this post until
his resignation in 1848; he died at sea on his way home
on 19 May 1848.

Indian scenes, a yearly death of the heart for every family. Poor little Willy was a great diversion to my sadness; he was going home under our care, and tho' not an engaging child, he was tractable and a source of employment for I took real charge of him, and I think improved him. He was carefully educated afterwards and has turned out extremely well; the last we heard of him was his having got his troop and married his cousin Helen Grant.

# CHAPTER TWENTY-NINE

## 1829–1830

WE had a pleasant voyage to Colombo, down the coast the whole way, fine, cool weather, the next poop cabin empty, so Willy played there, and I often sat there late and early, our own cabin being disagreeable during the night arrangements. My Colonel slept in a hammock, a large one, which filled up nearly all our space. It was swung low, so after it was up and before it was down it was not easy to move about—it prevented the air circulating to my sofa, too, so that the empty cabin near us was a great comfort.

Doctor Eckford, always pleasant, was a nice, cheerful, clever companion; Captain West remarkably complaisant. The few other gentlemen passengers very inoffensive. There were no ladies; Captain, now Colonel Stalker and an invalid brother, Captain Bradbury, or some such name, a Widower with a little boy, a nice playfellow for Willie. Poor Archdeacon Hawtayne and his Willy, and a very foolish young man, a Mr Mills, whom we smuggled on board after leaving the harbour, or his numerous creditors would have detained him.

Captain West was going to Ceylon for cargo; coffee, spices, etc. He was also to take home invalids from thence, so expected to remain a week at Colombo. We really remained near three. The first day or two we staid in our Cabins, with most of the rest of the ship to ourselves, I sitting under the awning on the poop admiring the pretty Indian view, inhaling the really and truly fragrant air, and thinking over the 21 months that had passed in these strange lands since I had first sighted Ceylon. We then removed to the house of a merchant in the town, a friend of the Captain's, whose immense warehouses, with all the business carried on in his large Court yard, furnished me with hourly amusement.

Here we were discovered by an old Edinburgh friend of mine, Campbell Riddell, and carried off by him to his cool Bungalow on the Coast, where we remained during our stay. It was a charming place, his house hold very well appointed, and he with his Scotch welcome made us feel so quite at home. We spent our mornings in driving out, the sun never preventing exercise in Ceylon, our afternoons upon the beach where the air was delicious, our evenings in company, either at home or abroad. Sir Edward Barnes was the Governour, an old General, extremely fond of his bottle, who had married a young, *very* young and very handsome wife, and who idolised her and the two spoiled children she had brought him. It would be hard to say how the affairs of the island were carried on, the late supper parties affecting most heads next morning. The officials did sometimes appear in their offices before the clerks left them, and the troops were occasionally inspected, but it was perfectly evident that the aim and the end and the business of all the merry party at and about Government House was pleasure, and of a queer kind. A sort of child's play—all excepting the wine part, which indeed required all the strength of manly brains to bear up under, the Governour, who had made his head during a long course of campaigns, not comprehending how difficult some people found it to keep up to his high mark.

We were with their excellencies every evening except the two, when Campbell Riddell entertained them and others, himself. He was a great man, by the bye, sent out by the Home Government as Commissioner to inquire into local abuses, settle some disputed points, put much right that had gone wrong and no wonder, either! Whether he had talents for so grave a charge I should have doubted from early recollection of the rather wild young man who could never settle to business in his own country; but a conciliatory manner, with a most gentlemanly deportment and thorough honesty of purpose, he certainly did possess, and probably he carried out his instructions well, for he was afterwards sent on as Secretary to the Governour at Sydney. He and I were very happy to meet again I know, and soon becoming as intimate as in former days, he confided me his love for a very handsome girl, one of the Rodneys, whom but for her want of education, he would have married at once. The father, Mr Rodney, a man extremely well connected, had come out to Ceylon years before with a wife, who died, leaving him several children. He married again and the same events were repeated. He took a third wife who still lived, a Dutch woman that could scarcely read or write, and thought it needless to give more knowledge to her step children than she possessed herself. I think between her own and former broods, there were altogether 21 young Rodneys, at least they said so, and not a penny of any of them. Two girls, of batch the first, who had had some advantage, were happily disposed of. One had gone to Paris on a visit to her Grandmother, Lady Aldborough, where she captivated a Scotch nobleman, who had a little misgiving in marrying her, and standing somewhat in awe of a naval brother, sent out to the Station where the brother lay a sort of apologetick letter for so rash an act. The brother's Station was Ceylon and he had just despatched to his elder brother such another missive as he had received to excuse his own engagement to the sister of the Paris bride. They were beautiful young women and amiable and both marriages as I have heard turned out well. It did not fare so well with batch the 2nd. Caroline Rodney, very ignorant, her temper very much chafed by her Dutch stepmother's behaviour, brought a deal of ill humour as an accompaniment to her extreme loveliness to poor Campbell Riddell, his lessons in spelling and grammar and sums, in addition, she threw in his face, disobeying also in many ways so that for some years, at least, he had 'to rue the day he sought her.' Whether she got wiser after her children came I know not, but when I saw her it was in the wooing time, all sunshine on both parts.

I found another old friend in Ceylon, Mr Anderson Blair. What situation he filled I don't remember; he lived handsomely and appeared to be happy, and to be liked, especially by the Governour, who found him only too ready to join in the call for another bottle—I remember this used to be said of him, tho' my Mother would never believe it.

The doings of Government House were certainly extraordinary. One night there was a Ball, a supper, rather riotous, throwing about fruit at one another, making speeches, long, rambling and *thick* enough, more dancing, or pulling and pushing rather, from which we were glad to get away. Next night was a Play in the pretty private theatre, 'The Honeymoon,' Lady Barnes acting the heroine. Supper of course in the same style as before, the Governour looking on, A. de C.s applauding. We had then a fancy Ball very well done, Lady Barnes as Queen Elizabeth, beautifully got up and looking wonderfully handsome, her Governour rather old for Leicester. Many characters were well dressed, several well sustained, a few groups very grand. Colonel Churchill was a perfect Henri IV., his Wife such a pretty, impudent Rosalind, with a stupid Celia, but such a Touchstone! some clever young officer. So on of all the rest—rooms large, numerous, well lighted. A grand supper, speeches etc., great noise towards the end. These were all grand affairs; the intermediate evenings, the ladies and gentlemen romped about, playing *petits jeux* with strange forfeits, hide and seek, hunt the whistle, etc. It was all very unseemly, a perfect whirl of riotous folly, very unlike the propriety of a Government House, where there might be mirth and pleasure without such a compromise of respectability.

Campbell Riddell's two quiet dinner parties were really like a return to rational society after a turmoil of disreputables. At the first of these entertainments I was taken to dinner by a grave, particularly gentlemanly man in a General's uniform, whose conversation was as agreeable as his manner. He had been over half the world, knew all celebrities, and contrived, without display, to say a great deal one was most willing to hear. About the middle of dinner Sir Edward Barnes called out 'Sir Hudson Lowe, a glass of wine with you'[1]—people did such barbarisms then—to which my companion bowed assent. Years before, with our Whig principles and *prejudices*, we had cultivated in our highland retirement a perfect horrour of the great, or the little! Napoleon's gaoler. The cry of party, the feeling for the prisoner, the book of Surgeon O'Meara, the voice from St

1. Sir Hudson Lowe (1769–1844) was Governor of
St Helena (1815–21) until Napoleon's death; from
1821–31 he was second in command in Ceylon.

Helena,[1] had all worked the woman's heart to such a pitch of indignation, that this maligned name was an offence to all of us. We were to hold the owner of it in abhorrence, speak to him! never! Look at him, sit in the same room with him, never! Colcraft the Executioner would have been preferred as a companion. None were louder than I, more vehement; and here I was most comfortably beside my bugbear, and perfectly satisfied with the position too. It was a good lesson. They had sent the poor man to Ceylon because he was so miserable at home, the world judging him as we had done, tabooed him remorselessly. He was so truly sent to Coventry that he once thanked Colonel Pennington in a Coffee House for the common civility of handing over a newspaper, saying that any civility was now so new to him he must be excused for gratefully acknowledging it. The opinion of less partial times had judged more fairly of Sir Hudson, his captive, and the Surgeon. Timidity and anxiety made Sir Hudson unnecessarily vexatious, Buonaparte was not in a mood or of a mood to be placable, and Mr O'Meara wanted money and notoriety, which he gained at no expense, not having had much character to begin with, another Colonel Wardle Business.[2]

Our drives about Colombo were merely agreeable; there was no fine scenery, the sea, some wooding and fields, amongst which the frail cabins of the Cingalese were scattered. A country house of the Governour's on a rock starting out of the sea, was cool and pretty. I wondered they did not live there rather than in the dusty town; it would not have been so gay for my lady. It was odd to see the huge elephants working like smaller beasts of burden; they were employed to draw waggons, Artillery guns, etc., and seemed

1. Barry Edward O'Meara (1786–1836) was a surgeon on the *Bellerephon* taking Napoleon into exile; he was persuaded to stay by Napoleon as his physician and quarrelled bitterly with Sir Hudson, the Governor, who forced his departure in 1818. O'Meara's revenge was *Napoleon in Exile; or a voice from St Helena*, published in 1822, a copy of which was in E.G.'s father's library.

2. See 1, pp. 115–6.

to be quite tractable. The climate was very enjoyable, air so balmy; altogether I know I left Ceylon with regret. And our *Childe Harold* was irksome for a day or two. Neither was it improved by the additions to its cargo; bales of cotton, coffee, spices, crowded the deck, making our walk there very confined. The invalid soldiers hung about in idle groups, and the wives and children encreased the confusion. The officers returning in charge of them were very disagreeable, Captain Floyd fine, Mr Bell fault finding; the surgeon, a boy, mischief making; and I lost my spare cabin. It was taken by Mrs Churchill and her little daughter Louisa, on whose account the mother was going home—not that the child's health required Europe, but her education could not be carried on in Ceylon with such parents, in such society, I should think not. It was impossible not to like Mrs Churchill. She was very good natured, quite unaffected, without guile, and so very handsome; but she was all wrong, poor woman, under educated, no principles, idle, frivolous, and had from her birth to the present moment been exposed to the evil influence of bad example. Her father, an Irish judge by name Finucane, had to divorce her mother on account of his own nephew. The mother always denied her guilt, but she lost her cause and her husband would never acknowledge Mrs Churchill, who was born after the separation and brought up under this cloud. When very young, and very beautiful, and very giddy, she was so much distinguished by Colonel Churchill that her character would certainly have suffered had he not married her; this extreme step he showed no intention of taking, but marched off with his regiment from whatever watering place the flirtation had been carried on at. The mother was shrewd enough; she wrote to her five Irish sons stating all circumstances. The brothers *en masse* appeared one morning pistol cases in hand, at Colonel Churchill's new quarters, and introducing themselves, begged to ask him whether he had forgot nothing at his former station.

'Gad,' said he, 'I believe I have forgotten your sister,' upon which there was a grand shaking of hands.

The marriage, thus settled, was soon concluded and then came the question how were the young and very handsome couple to live. Colonel Churchill was of the Marlborough family, his mother a Walpole, little money and less worth on either side. He lived luxuriously on such credit as he could get, helped now and then out of scrapes by various relations. Nobody, however, came forward at this time save Mrs Finucane, who gave sufficient for a fair start, and so the Bride and bridegroom began with rather a flourish at Knightsbridge. They gave the prettiest little dinners ever ordered from the French cook's shop at the corner, good wine, pleasant company, and he was the luckiest dog in the world to have found such a Wife, with such a fortune, as he gave out accompanied her. They were asked out a great deal among the 'first circles,' his connections being all in the red book.[1] She had the good sense to dress simply and to resist a hired carriage, tho' she told me in her natural way that it required all the admiration she received to the full to bear with the straw in the hackney coach, on which she set her dainty feet while bowing Adieux to the noble partners who handed her into such a vehicle. Of course this could not last, and he was fortunately ordered off to Courtray with a draft of men to encrease the Army of occupation,[2] and there he raised the wind in a way he had tried to practise on a smaller scale at Knightsbridge. The little dinners were changed to suppers, play introduced, the Wife's part being to set her bright eyes on the younger men, whom she fascinated readily, without poor thing, I do believe knowing one bit what she was doing. And so, at last some money falling to him, and some arrangement being made about it so as to assure the clearance of his debts in time, family interest got him the appointment of Secretary to the military part of the Government of Ceylon. He had grown a careless husband and she a very indifferent wife by the time we made their acquaintance. Yet they cared for one another in a way. Colonel Churchill made her over to my Colonel's care, who promised, on her landing,

1. A popular name for the *Royal Kalender, or Complete . . . Annual Register*.
2. Courtrai was the headquarters of the Allies' army of occupation in France after the war but this had been withdrawn in 1818.

to deliver her safe to old Mrs Churchill in London, while I undertook friendly offices on board. Little did either of us know the charge she was to be.

The first annoyance was to Doctor Eckford. His cabin was next to hers; part of the partition was movable, a mirrour that slipt down on a spring being touched, and so opened a communication between. Little Miss Louisa soon made this discovery, used, and abused it, bursting forth on the little Doctor at inconvenient moments, so that he never felt secure of privacy; the mother, too, soon began to follow the child, tapping first before shewing herself, but not giving much time between the tap and the apparition. I am quite sure this was all idleness, our medical friend being never attractive and at this moment livid in complexion from liver. He, however, chose to flatter himself with the idea that he was pursued, had captivated! and his serious complaints both to the Colonel and me were sufficient to overset all gravity.

She next tried my Colonel, merely a bestowal of her tedium on any one, but it was disagreeable. Dr Eckford took me every day 3 walks; so many turns upon the deck each time, for the good of my health, hereafter. The first walk was after breakfast always, while the Colonel was shaving, which he had not time for earlier in the morning. A tap at the door one day announced Mrs Churchill, who came to amuse him during the operations. She must have thought she succeeded, for next day she came again, and again, and again. 'Upon my soul,' said the Colonel, 'this is getting too bad, the woman, pretty as she is, is quite a nuisance, a man can't shave for her; Mrs Smith, you must give up your walk and stay and guard your husband.' Not a grateful office to act both guard and spy, but there was no help for it.

So after a few more days she gave up this diversion and took to one less harmless—a regular serious flirtation with Captain Floyd, whom she very nearly distracted spite of his long experience! Dr Eckford informed us he rejoiced in this for his own case but was sorry for the poor *wum*man so exposing herself. Morning, noon, and evening the pair sat close together on the poop, in the Cuddy, or at the Cuddy door, little Louisa always with them, but busy with her doll and books. What they could find to say we used to wonder for neither shone in conversation with others. She spoke little ever and he was a real goose, only good looking. Now and then she would come and sit with me, complain of the long day, the dull voyage, the stupid life, and so on; while we three, the Colonel, the Doctor and I, were quite content, busy and happy, eyes and ears open, and inclined to be pleased, with the weather beautiful.

At length on Xmas morning we came in sight of the Isle of France,[1] and before dinner time we were at anchor in the harbour of port Louis. It was a pretty scene, plenty of shipping on the sea, plenty of wood on the shore, hills in the distance, and a long straggling town lying along the water's edge.

The sailors were all agog to bathe till the captain checked their ardour by the short word 'sharks,' which abounded all about the island; indeed, a poor fellow from a vessel alongside of us had been cut in two that very morning by one of these monsters, which actually bolted the lower part of his body while they were drawing the head and shoulders up on the deck. We saw them playing about in shoals.

The Captain having a good deal of business here we were all to go on shore for a fortnight, which, as before at Ceylon, stretched to a month. These delays must have been very inconvenient to young men with empty purses. Some of them, therefore, had to remain to live on board, merely taking a day's pleasure on land now and then, and the Captain had to provide for them as usual, which he did but scurvily they said, which affair so discontented both parties that there never was any cordial feeling between them again, and this made the remainder of our voyage extremely unpleasant. The idle soldiers got into mischief; the wives took to quarrelling; the two officers could not leave their men, even had they been invited ashore, which they were not, and the surgeon, Mr Mills, and one or two more nursed up such a crop of illhumour that it lasted them all the rest of the way home.

Mrs Churchill had a special invitation to the Governour,

1. Mauritius.

Sir Charles Colville, who sent a carriage for her next day in which she and Louisa and the penniless Mr Mills set off to his country house up among the woods, about 6 miles from the town. Captain West, who was intimately acquainted with the Secretary to the Government—now also at his country house—got the loan of his empty town house for himself and us and Dr Eckford, and this was our principal residence while we remained on the island, altho' we paid two visits, each of some days' duration, one to the Governour, and one to the Secretary, our Landlord, Mr Telfer.

We enjoyed this month extremely. It was hot sometimes at night in the town, but the breeze which came up with the tide always, refreshed the air again and the house was large and roomy, standing back from the street in a courtyard of good size, and with corridors running thro' it, which kept it as cool as could be managed without Verandahs, which luxury and ornament cannot be indulged in here on account of the hurricanes. No year passes without two or three of these destructive storms. The winds are so big, so eccentrick is their course, so overpowering that they sweep off a great deal of property, in spite of every precaution. All buildings are low, there are no projections, nothing that can be caught at, and yet no place quite escapes damage at one time or another.

The scenery is more pretty and quiet and interesting than fine. A plain of fertility beyond the town, bordered by the sea and rising to the mountains, which are some of them picturesquely peaked. 'Peter Botte' very conspicuous. The nutmeg wood belonging to Government, and beautifully kept, is one of the most interesting spots to drive thro' from the beauty of the trees; large, tall, forest trees, they are full of branches and dark leaves, so very fragrant, and the spice in all its stages bursting all around. The nutmeg, quite red when growing, peeps out from its covering of green mace, quite like a flower. The Cinnamon bushes were the underwood, their buds—the cassia buds of commerce—scenting the air. Parrot looking birds were among the branches, and monkeys skipping from tree to tree.

We often drove there, passing on our way by a good house in a large garden, called Madame La Tour's, as unlike as possible to the humble cabins of St Pierre, where stands a monument to *Paul et Virginie*[1] on the spot where her body was washed ashore! underneath which I think they said the lovers were buried! To doubt their existence in the Isle of France would be something too scandalous.

In the evenings we drove in the Champs de Mars, a rather larger space than the Rajah's, but quite as amusingly filled. All here is French, or, more properly speaking, the remains of French.

The Colonists able to remain here with their families—the climate permitting their absolute location—seldom visited the mother country, unless the men found it necessary in the way of business, or an ambitious Mama sent her children for a few years to Paris to acquire higher accomplishments. The inhabitants are therefore essentially French in race, name, language, and habits. We had had the island too short a time to make much change in it. Our few merchants and officials are just a small set of persons unlike the rest, yet all agree comfortably, all being freemen except the servants, who are slaves. Here, again, old prejudices proved deceptive. So happy a set of creatures as these same slaves never did I see in any rank in any country. From morning to night they lightened labour with their songs. I got all the airs in the *Dame Blanche*[2] by heart, hearing them one after the other during all the working hours chorussed out by the dark porters who were busy in a neighbouring store heaving up and down hogsheads of sugar. Every enquiry we made convinced us that unkind masters were rare. Out in the sugar plantations, or in the spice groves, or the Coffee grounds, in the warerooms, in the yards, house or field labour, the powers of the merry slaves were never overtaxed. They were well lodged, well fed, well cared for in sickness and old age, and had plenty to buy dress with, of which they are extravagantly fond, and make a wonderful display of on their numerous holidays. We constantly met or overtook waggon

1.  Bernardin de St Pierre (1737–1814), disciple of Rousseau and novelist, visited the island (1768–70) and wrote this famous novel in 1787.
2.  Opera (1825) by Adrien Boieldieu (1775–1834) based on Sir Walter Scott's two novels, *Guy Mannering* and *The Monastery*.

loads of dark beaux and belles dressed up like actors radiant with mirth, going off a pleasuring to some *Guinguette*,[1] where dancing would conclude the festivities, and every evening crowds of them paraded in the Champs de Mars, the men sometimes in sailor guise with long curls under the jauntily set straw hat, or in more *exquisite* costume, chains and eye glasses much in fashion, attending their ladies in full ball dress, flowers, feathers, flounces, pink crape, blue crape, fans, etc., all in the day light, and all so happy, only—there is a *but* every where—trowsers and petticoats were invariably long enough to touch the ground, for though the slaves may do with his, or her, head what best pleases, neither shoe nor stocking can case the feet; they must be bare, it is the mark of caste, and they feel it, happy as their condition is made; childish and ignorant as they are, they strive to hide the naked feet. Yet they could not exist in freedom—not the old slaves, used to have all provided for them.

Sir Charles Colville told us of a slave he had freed, and made, as he thought, comfortable, with house, and field, and work as a gardener, begging to be made a slave again; he had not the energy to manage his own living. So, as in other cases, we must begin with the young, let the old generations just die away as they are.

The black fashionables were not the only amusing frequenters of the evening promenade. The French, not very particular at home as to their equipages, had certainly not improved their taste in carriage in their colony. Such gigs and phaetons, and post waggons, and extraordinary vehicles of every description, with cracked leather unoiled for years, panels over which the paintbrush could almost never have gone, harness! horses! all so very tatterdemalion! and within, such pretty looking women in such tasteful half dress, so simple, so fresh; hair in such order! it really was a contrast. The men were not so nice: the old ones little and punchy; the younger little and dandified. We visited in one or two merchant families; a call in the evening, a cup of coffee, or fruit, and musick, queer singing, but good playing. In the gay season plays, operas, concerts and balls, publick and

1. Cafés noted for dining and dancing.

private, enliven the cold weather—just now every one that could was getting thro' the heat in the country.

We lived very comfortably in Mr Telfer's house, my black maid and the Colonel's black man to wait on us; both of whom looked down with pity on the two good humoured slaves left in charge of the premises, an old Véronique very fond of a bit of finery, and a Gaspar who slept half his time away. Our breakfasts were very easily managed. Our dinners, wines and all, came from a *traiteur*'s in true French style— little nice dishes admirably cooked, dressed vegetables, *plats sucrés*, and crisp biscuits. It was all so good that I wrote to my father, who was miserable with the Portuguese messes, to advise him to send to the Isle of France for a cook. Mrs Telfer was so good as to consent to assist in the business, and the *Traiteur* promised to choose a *garçon accompli* [ragamuffin, down-at-heel], who would expatriate himself for a bribe.

The scheme was approved and carried into effect, the cook becoming so at home in Calcutta, and I believe so truly attached to my father, and the profits of his kitchen, that he lived with him till his death, when his place was supplied by a *confrère*.

We frequently invited our castaway shipmates to partake of our shore repasts. Mrs Charles Telfer was also a frequent guest, my Colonel being perfectly well and able to enjoy our sociable ways. Our stay was varied by two country visits, one to the Governour, the other to the Secretary. The Retreat was a fine place; the gardens well laid out; the rooms large. There was a numerous suite, too, and nice children, but it was a disagreeable visit. Sir Charles was a dull man, reserved and silent, stiff to every one, but very stiff to us, for he and my Colonel had not got on altogether harmoniously during the time that he had been Commander in Chief at Bombay. His private Secretary was that gigantick Colonel Fraser, who had been such an abominable husband to poor Emmeline McLeod, and to whom therefore I could hardly contain myself to listen, particularly when he had the hardihood to speak.

Lady Colville, one of the Muirs of Caldwell, was deranged, poor thing. She had been quite frantick and had been sent home in durance, placed in a private asylum. She was restored to her husband as cured, but was unsettled in her manners, very easily excited. One evening she was seated near me on a sofa with Mrs Churchill, who was giving a brilliant description of Ceylon merry makings. Lady Colville highly disapproved of such levities and was beginning to express herself very energetically on the subject, fidgetting on her seat too, and twisting herself, and so on, when the head servant, an Englishman, whom I remember remarking afterwards never left the room, came steadily up to her with a tray in his hand, and fixing his eye on her, he said in an odd commanding tone—'Your Ladyship will take coffee?' She was quiet in a moment, took the cup in silence, and we both of us felt that the less we spoke to her the better. In the mornings she was calmer always. I went to her dressing room after my breakfast, which I took in my own room, and she seemed to have great pleasure in making the discovery that patterns of her baby clothes would be useful to me. She collected a little bundle with extreme good nature, adding some fine calicoes etc. to cut up and she sent for a merchant, from whom I bought what else was wanting to give my neat fingers needle work enough to last thro' the rest of the voyage.

We felt it a relief to remove to Mr Telfer's, where we had a kind welcome and no company but the brother, our Captain, and Dr Eckford. We slept in a pavilion in the garden, which left me at liberty for charming wanderings about the wooded hill their cottage was built on. Little Willy had been with these good people from the first, as their only child, a boy of his own age, had been delighted to have a companion.

Here an affair was arranged of which I hardly like to speak, knowing but one side of the story. Judge of it we cannot, tho' the facts acknowledged look ill. This was to be Captain West's last voyage, he now told us; he was to give up his ship on going home, make as much as he could of his part of her and her cargo, and then return with his wife and son and daughter to settle in the Mauritius as part owner of a sugar plantation now in the market. The two Telfers were to have shares; Charles Telfer was to be the manager, and if they could but pick up a few thousand pounds to start with, repair the buildings, purchase more slaves, etc., etc., in a year or two it would be a most remunerating concern.

We all went to see it, an excellent plantation, canes in high order, business going on which much interested us; from the cutting of the canes in the fields, their transport on long waggons, recutting, steeping, boiling in great cauldrons, stirring, skimming, straining, drying, to the packing in the barrels, we saw the whole process, with its rum and molasses, spirit and dregs, hot and sticky, but very amusing.

Dr Eckford was enchanted, his speculating turn quite roused, his vanity flattered by the deference paid him and the idea of proprietorship, and so, cautious and canny as he was, after grave inspection of the books, consultations, calculations and so forth, he offered to buy a share or two himself, and advance the required sum, to start with at 8 per cent—the common rate of interest in the island. I wonder that did not startle him; people must be very much in want of cash when they pay such interest for the loan of it. However he saw no risk, but to make sure of all going right he resolved to remain on the spot for the next few months instead of going on to the Cape; so we sailed without him. To end the tale now, the sugar plantation was a drain on the Doctor's purse for some years. Captain West and the Telfers were equally unsatisfactory as partners, matters grew more than perplexing. The Doctor threatened a visit and legal advice, Charles Telfer cut his throat, the Secretary brother died, Captain West was ruined and the plantation bankrupt. On the Doctor leaving India for good, he called at Port Louis, found Captain West rich, sole owner of the plantation, which he had bought cheap on borrowed money and with £2,000 to indemnify the Doctor for the £5,000 the adventure had cost him.

We soon resumed our sea routine, but not altogether so pleasantly. The steward had been neglectful, and made a poor provision of fresh supplies; the table had therefore fallen off. We had privately supplied ourselves, as we did every where without making a fuss, that would have been useless, and so, faring well in the cabin, were independant of the Cuddy. We could afford a help to Mrs Churchill too; but the friendless and the dogged who fought for the value of their passage money were ill off and cross enough. Major

Floyd consoled himself by complaining to Mrs Churchill for that flirtation recommenced vigorously; I tried to frustrate much of this, and by giving up my pleasant privacy contrived to amuse the Lady sufficiently enough to keep her a good deal from the Cuddy door. She and the Colonel played Piquet and Backgammon while I worked at my tiny wardrobe. She got confidential and told me a deal of her history, poor soul. She might have been a better woman had she been better guided. Idleness was her bane. To get thro' the time she really compromised her character.

On we went, into colder weather; warm wraps were wanted as we neared the Cape—the ugly Cape I must always think it, with that flat topped Table Mountain, woodless shore, and low, objectless town. Yet we were glad to reach it, for our company was ill humoured, fare bad, Captain scowling, except to me. My Colonel, since the colder weather, had been suffering from asthma; he therefore, not being able to dress mostly kept his cabin. The voyage was beginning to be dreary. I suffered a good deal myself, only, having so much to do, I had luckily very little time to think of self.

We did not land the first day, but I bought fresh butter, bread and fruit from the boatmen. Next day the Colonel was so well he went ashore and brought many little delicacies back. He had also heard of an old brother officer being at Wyneberg, about 8 miles beyond Cape Town—Captain Wogan Browne—and had sent off a messenger to offer a day's visit; the answer was an insistence that we should come to him and Mrs Browne for the whole time we were to stay. We gladly consented and passed five very pleasant days in the small house they occupied. Poor Captain Browne was there for health, which utterly failed on his return to his regiment at Poonah, for there he died. She was nursing her only son, a fine boy, tho' with a red head. In the evenings they had a fire, such a charming sight—the fire side is surely more than equal to the moonlight stroll, and certainly superiour to a sofa under a punkah.

The deep sand prevented pleasant walking; it is loose and red, very penetrating. The scenery was disappointing, flat in general, no heath or other flowers in bloom; the cool air was the pleasure and even that was only during the night, and the dawn, and the sunset; the middle of the day was very scorching, as we found when we drove to the grape garden, and walked all thro' among the little bushes on which the over ripe fruit was hanging; a very rich and sweet grape, no mistaking it for the Constantia. When nearly baked we were conducted to a cave as cool as a well, where biscuits and several sorts of Constantia, deliciously cooled wine were presented to us. The Colonel ordered three *awms*[1] some of which we still have, altho' he has always been the reverse of niggardly in his use of it. The oddest thing I saw at the Cape was the sheep going about with little carts behind them to carry their tails in. The appendages are so large, such lumps of fat, that the animals would destroy them and impede its own progress without this assistance. The enormous waggons goods were carried in were drawn by a regular regiment of bullocks, and great noise made with the whip and the tongue of the Conductor.

My colonel bought me a dozen large ostrich feathers here and several bunches of small ones dressed as foxtails etc. for a couple of £; he also replenished our Cabin stores, as did some others unluckily. There had been little doubt from the beginning of the voyage that Archdeacon Hawtayne was not altogether in his senses. Very strange tales of the wildest outbreaks of temper had been current about him in Bombay. His timid young wife was evidently in painful awe of him, for she hardly spoke in his presence. Among the servants it was openly said that at times he used her barbarously, even to shaking and beating her, and nobody doubted that the death in childbed of our friend Kitty was owing to some shock she had received from his violence. Two facts were known, that he had been bound over by the magistrate to keep the peace towards his own head servant and that once, on the company he had invited all assembling at his house to dinner, Mrs Hawtayne was discovered, the image of a ghost, trembling on a sofa, no lights nor attendants, nor any preparations, and the Archdeacon met them with the intelligence that all his household having run away, no dinner could be forthcoming.

1.  Dutch measure of 41 English wine gallons.

It was on account of health that he was returning to Europe. At first he merely appeared excited, restless, wandering in his conversation, gazing up at the stars at night, in one of which he stated that his wife was dwelling and looking down on him with pity. He was also strangely particular about the little boy, whose times of eating he regulated oddly and also had his food prepared in various singular ways—difficult enough to manage on board ship. He was sometimes foolishly indulgent of the child, sometimes harsh and unjust to him. The boy feared him more than he loved him and yet he was the unceasing object of the father's care. He had brought a native servant from Bombay whom he dismissed for some fault at Ceylon, hiring then one of the invalid soldiers.

He had gone ashore at the Cape, and among other things had laid in a great store of water in bottles—the supply from the Mauritius not having kept. A hamper at a time he got up from the hold, any Thursday he required. The Mate once or twice remarked that the Archdeacon had got on to drink a great deal of water. We all remarked that his manner was becoming much more extraordinary, there were frequent quarrels with his servant, loud disputes with the man, and scolding and punishment of the poor child. One day the little creature, who was fond of slinking up to our Cabin and playing quietly with Willy Anderson, rushed up in an agony of terrour, sobbing and screaming out 'hide me, hide me'—and after him the Archdeacon in his shirt and drawers with a whip, rushing about to strike at him. The gentlemen were all on deck. I took the boy in and closed the Cabin door, then opening the looking glass panel, which, as in Mrs Churchill's Cabin, communicated with the small one next to us, which was Willy's, I bid Mary call the Captain. The result of all this was the discovery that the bottles contained rather strong waters, under the influence of which this poor half madman became wholly mad. The Captain from hence forward prohibited any such wares entering that cabin, he possessed of all remaining bottles and after a conference with the Ship Surgeon, a Soldier, Serjeant of superiour character, was appointed to attend upon the poor man with a regular charge upon him, which indeed had become necessary if only to protect the little boy. That night he slept on cushions in Willy's cabin, there was no persuading the poor little thing to go below. I had certainly good nerves then.

The next scene was enacted by the younger Stalker, who now began to have epileptick fits, during which he foamed at the mouth and very much distorted himself. One of them he took while I was seated in the Cuddy near him. I remember gratefully the extreme consideration of all the rest of the party closing round him till they had got me to move away. The unfortunate young man's intemperate habits heightened his disease; how much his good brother suffered under this affliction.

These events carried us on to St Helena, where we were promised fresh provisions and a cow; the one brought from India was said to milk ill, it had therefore been parted with at the Cape. Another had been procured there, the Captain said, but by the most extreme mischance we had sailed without her—the fault of the Steward as before—so were the salt, bad butter, the old biscuit, and the many other deficiencies; a little hard to believe, thought most of us, and very hard to bear. Coarse tea, without milk, brown sugar full of insects, rancid butter, and maggoty biscuits were not Indiaman's fare. At dinner the meat was fresh certainly, but there were no vegetables, with the exception of pumpkin pie. Neither the Colonel nor I could attempt the breakfast. We made Malek prepare us rice and curry or *kabobs* and we flavoured water with apples or lemon, or claret afterwards. I felt this much, being generally ill enough in the mornings at this time.

There were two goats on board expected to kid shortly, which was the hope held out to the discontented—a poor one, as we proved. No wonder so much ill humour prevailed and that the officers and others declined, from the day that we left the Cape, to drink wine with the Captain.

Mrs Churchill got her soldier's wife to make her soup and apple dumplings, and such dishes as her own locker supplied materials for; but really it was very uncomfortable, not unlike starvation. She, and we, had bought tea, coffee, sugar, butter, apples, potatoes, portable soups etc. all in small quantities at the Cape from a sort of forewarning, and well it was that we did so. No body should ever go to sea with a Captain on his last voyage.

We came very suddenly on St Helena. A huge lump, rising out of the sea. A flat top and steep sides, inaccessible they seemed as we coasted round, no way of landing, apparently, till all at once a gully appeared. A zigzag slit thro' the mass of land, running down from high up inland to the sea. A small plain at the bottom just held a little close packed town, and up the steep rock on one side was a set of steps like a ladder leading to a fort upon the top, very pretty, very strange, a want of breadth about it. Several ships were in the roads, boats of all sizes and a few people wandering along the shore. The whole scene struck me as familiar; then I recollected the show box at Moy, at old Colonel Grant's, where I got the porridge breakfast, which the old Lady let me amuse myself with; prints were slid in behind, and, viewed thro' the magnifying peephole, had quite the effect of real scenes. One of these represented St Helena, and very true to nature it must have been to have fixed itself so tenaciously in a childish memory.

We landed in boats on a very loose shingle, thro' which I really could not get; unused to walking for so long, and with more to carry than was convenient, lifting the feet up out of those yielding pebbles was really too much, and at last, nearly fainting, down I lay. The poor Colonel! half a mile more of the same dreadful shingle before us under a hot sun, and no help anywhere; the rest of our party had got on far ahead. There was nothing for it but patience, the very quality in which we were, some of us, deficient. I was so distressed and tried to rouse up, but failed, so began crying. Fortunately—there generally is a fortunately if one waits for it—a second boat landed Mary the maid, to whom I was consigned and by whose stout help after many stoppages in about two hours I reached the boarding house, where the Colonel had engaged a room; there I fainted right off and passed the remainder of the day on a mattress on the floor till sufficiently revived by dinner.

It was a good house in the only street, which consisted of large and small dwellings and some shops on either side of the road that led up thro' the gully; the rock rose up pretty straight behind the row opposite. Our row had a rushing river between it and the side of the mountain, with a steep bank down to the water, which made the look out from the back windows rather pretty. Our host was also a merchant, and a gentleman, it being the custom in this little place for all the inhabitants to keep a sort of inn. Colonel Francis Grant did not, therefore, marry a mere lodging house keeper's daughter. Mr Dunn was a trader and made money by receiving boarders, like others.

Our hostess was a little woman, rather crooked, and not young. She had been a beauty and possessed a voice extraordinary for power and compass; her songs were therefore of a manly cast. All Braham's 'Angel of Life' and such like; the sweetness of tone was gone, but the spirit was there still. I did not like so much noise myself, and thought her style would have been better suited to the top of a mosque, from whence she could have been heard far and near to call the folk to prayers. Each evening we were there, she had an Assembly of the inhabitants in addition to the home party, which consisted of half a dozen from the *Childe Harold* and a whole dozen from another Indiaman, after whose comforts we indeed sighed, for they had cows, new laid eggs, fresh bread, a good cook, and plenty of every thing.

To buy a cow at St Helena was impossible or a goat even; milk was very scarce, and all the butter used in the island came in crocks from the Cape. Every thing was monstrously dear here; 2s. 6d. a pound for sago, 9s. for tea; a bit of ribbon for my bonnet the price of the bonnet itself elsewhere. Our bill at the boarding house was something astonishing, £3 a day, I think, for the maid, the child, the Colonel and me and no separate sitting room, wine extra and beer, and £5 for a carriage we clubbed to take for the morning to visit the Lions of the place—the Briars, the cabin where Napoleon died (the beautiful house near it he never occupied), and his tomb.

The road wound up by the side of the stream, rising at times very suddenly, turning sharp corners as suddenly, frequently high above the water, so that the occasional steepness and the precipice together made timid nerves quake. It was pretty, tho' there was not much wooding and the trees were low, like bushes. The Briars was a cluster of small buildings on a knoll below the road near the river that should have passed as some small farmer's cottage had it not been pointed out to us. Upon the table land we saw the plantations round Government House, where we had been civilly invited to dine by I forget who was the Governour— for we did not go—and then, having ascended the last rise, we looked round on an immense plain bounded by the Ocean. The plain is varied by little heights, little hollows, and some wooding; drives thro' it are agreeable from more variety than one would suppose; the air is delightful. There is no access but by the one precipitous zig zag we had come, along the banks of the only river in the island, and that is a mere brook, or rather torrent; there may be rivulets but we did not see them, there are a few springs. It might be monotonous as a residence; it was certainly grand as a view. The hut Napoleon would not leave was in part fallen from decay; his own room remained, a closet 10 foot square or so, with one small window, dingy green walls. Very wretched.

A very little way off was the prettiest villa ever designed, plenty of space round it, a fine view from all sides, and such a quantity of accommodation inside. A suite of publick rooms, particularly cheerful, good apartments for the attendants, and the Emperour's own wing delightfully arranged, 7 or 8 rooms including a bath and a private staircase. His ill humoured preference of the miserable Cottage punished him severely. Certainly this most charming house, all made in England and merely put together after reaching its destination, was a residence fit for any Prince. I never heard what they did with it. It was too large for any private family, and the Governour was provided for, pulled it to pieces probably and sold the materials.

The tomb was very saddening; 'after life's fitful fever' [*Macbeth* III ii 23] to see this stranger grave. In a hollow, a square iron railing on a low wall enclosed the stone trap entrance to a vault, forget me nots were scattered on the sod around, and *the* weeping willow drooped over the flag. The ocean filled the distance. It would have been better to have left him there, with the whole island for his monument.

On we went again from St Helena to Ascension, miserably enough, the fare more wretched than ever, the ill humour encreasing on that account and added to on another, for we had taken on board at St Helena some new passengers, an old Mr and Mrs Blanch and a young sailor, Mr Agassiz, who had lost his health slave hunting on the Coast of Africa and was going home invalided. Mrs Churchill had varied her attentions to Mr Floyd by latterly paying a deal more to the 3rd mate than was at all fitting, a mere boy, very good looking, better employed about the ship than in gaining expertise in coquetry. The Captain put a stop to his walking arm in arm with her along the deck, but he could not check glances, asides, occasional tender encounters. Indeed she behaved shockingly, for which these two distracted about her, no sooner did fresh prey appear than she cast them off remorselessly—Captain Floyd entirely, the poor mate very nearly. Mr Agassiz she seized on and he paid her off for he became necessary to her. He bewitched her and so imprudent were they both that the Captain had to speak to him. Captain Floyd got savagely sulky, made himself odious. The mate went almost beside himself—the poor boy! heart had given itself away so confidingly and to be cast off as a worn out toy was so cruel a shock; he really pined away, acted quite foolishly. Never was such an unpleasant state of affairs.

For two days these disagreeable scenes went on; the 3rd produced graver matters to think of. About this time last year a vessel homeward bound had in this latitude been attacked by pirates, attacked and overpowered—the surviving men were made to walk the plank, the women after the worst usage left alive in the vessel which was stript and scuttled. It so happened that a cruiser came up with this doomed ship and rescued these unfortunates, several soldiers' wives and one lady, her maid and some children. The lady was the wife of an Officer who remained with his regiment at St Helena, while she returned home on business, taking her little boy and girl with her. She was nearly out of her mind, extremely ill, and on landing sent the maid, with the children, the papers and other effects belonging to them and her husband to his parents, with an injunction to the maid to tell the dreadful tale. She was herself never more heard of. Whether she died or what became of her nobody could ever find out. She said she loathed herself and would never obtrude herself on her beloved husband's sight. The maid described the Pirate as young and handsome, magnificently dressed in a fantastick style and with perfect command over a most horrible looking crew. Whether he it were who reconnoitred us, we could not say, but a most suspicious looking 'craft' bore down upon us, strangely rigged and piratically painted, coming from no regular direction. Several small merchantmen had sailed with us for company's sake, these latitudes being at this time dangerous, and they all began to cluster in our wake at this unpleasant apparition.[1] Mr Agassiz, whose employment it had been to look out for all sorts of contraband keels, said this was not a slaver. As she neared us, he ascended to the mast head and reported that she was all trim and smart and filled with a crowd of active men.

Upon this Captain West began his preparations; all the soldiers were called out in their red coats and dispersed about the deck. The two officers, suitably rigged out, marched here and there. Arms glancing in the sun's rays. The whole crew was called up in full view. Every body on board had a proper place assigned. We ladies with the children were to go down to Mrs Blanch's cabin on the lower deck when directed and our door guarded by Colonel Smith and Mrs Blanch. The soldiers' wives and children to keep below. The Surgeons went to prepare for extremities, and the Archdeacon retired to pray. Perhaps all this was unnecessary, yet it was certainly prudent, and as certainly made us very grave. Mrs Blanch, quite an old woman, was in agonies at the possibility of the treatment she might be subjected to, cried and wrung her aged hands, making her not only ridiculous but troublesome. Mrs Churchill quite shone; roused by the excitement she seemed all alive. 'Pray be quiet, Mrs Blanch,' said she. 'If the worst came to the worst *I* may be in danger enough, but I think both you and Mrs Smith will be respected!' and then she laughed one of those ringing laughs that must have reminded her of her girlhood. She had actually brought down with her some old linen she had for the voyage, scissors, and

1. There was another case of piracy in these waters at this time involving the schooner *St Helena*, which was boarded on 9 April 1830, shortly after this incident.

a housewife, etc., that she might help the surgeons, should it be requisite. Mr Agassiz and Captain West put on their uniforms, and as the English part of the Crew were always as neat as men of war's men, we must have looked rather imposing to our new acquaintance, who soon came boldly within hail. It was before the new system of conversation signals; what we had to say to each other had to be bawled thro' the speaking trumpet. We were informed by 'John Thompson of New York' that he was 'bound for the Cape and else where,' with what, we could not make out, neither did he explain how he had got so much out of his track as to be coming up from the south west on a nor' easterly course. In return we acquainted him that we were 'Captain West, R.N., in the *Childe Harold*, with troops,' which he seemed to think sufficient, for he rolled off and tho' hovering on the outskirts of our horizon for many hours, we saw no more of him nearer and next morning, he had disappeared. Our companions also left us, by degrees, and we in the poop cabin soon resumed that 'evenness and tranquillity of spirit' which not even the jars in the Cuddy could disturb, altho' the poor Colonel had a weary time of it.

From the day we left St Helena asthma had prevented his ever lying down; the hammock was never unrolled. A wrapper, a coverlet, and the easy chair were his doom. At first he could dress and take a walk on deck, latterly he was unable to catch breath enough for the slightest exertion. We had no proper food for him, sago and lemon juice only, and no medicine relieved him, his sufferings were unceasing, his weakness encreased alarmingly for want of proper nourishment; he could not manage meat in any shape. I was really in despair. The soldier's wife made him gruel but he could not bear it; there were no eggs, no milk, chicken broth only. But there came comfort. We had reached Ascension, such a dreadful place, a bare rock, and we were to lay to for a few hours to catch turtle, very abundant there. Two King's ships happened to be doing the same, on board of one of which Mr Agassiz betook himself, and mentioning to the commanding officer how shamefully our Captain was using us in the providing way, that gentleman sent to us, to Mrs Churchill and Mrs Smith, a goat in full milk—was there ever any thing kinder, a perfect stranger he was to all of us. We gave our goat in charge to Malek, who milked her himself and brought his jug of treasure to our cabins, where we divided it honestly. After supplying my Colonel, myself, and the two Willies, there was not much of my share left, but what there was I sent to Mrs Blanch. Mrs Churchill took care of Mr Agassiz, to whom we really owed this unspeakable comfort, and he used to offer his remains to the two disagreeable officers—they, far from being grateful, were indignant at getting so little, demanded their full share of what they insisted was meant for every body, in short were so turbulant that we two owners were afraid of bad consequences. After a consultation it was determined that I should explain, Mrs Churchill not quite liking to encounter Captain Floyd under existing circumstances. A good opportunity presenting itself, I set the matter at rest and amicably. I was sitting inside the Cuddy door with Mrs Blanch one evening, the two malcontents grumbling away outside. Malek was coming from the forecastle with his jug of milk. 'I say, old fellow,' said Captain Floyd, 'hand us over that fine jug of yours. Share alike and fair play, we are not going to let the old gentleman in the sulks there keep all the good things to himself etc.,' nice gentlemanly style! So I just addressed the pair very quietly, told them they were under a mistake about the goat, which was private property, presented especially to Mrs Churchill and me by a private friend, that my sick husband lived almost entirely upon her milk and that until he was supplied, I regretted being unable to offer him and Mr Bell any share of my share, which hitherto I had always given to Mrs Blanch and the little boys. Apologies, bows, smiles and a few epithets, well deserved, applied to the Captain, closed this business, of which we never heard another word, but indeed I got very anxious to reach England. The Colonel's encreasing debility under the obstinacy of his asthma, the uncomfortable atmosphere of our little cabin, always filled with the smoke of stramonium,[1] the cold, the illhumour, the bad fare, the improprieties of Mrs Churchill,

1. Narcotic drug prepared from the Thorn Apple (Datura Stramonium).

the devotion of Mr Agassiz, the despair of the 3rd mate, the sarcasms of Captain Floyd, all combined to render the run from St Helena most disagreeable, tho' we had a good wind. At last, off the Azores we got into what was as good as a trade wind, which sped us on I know not how many knots an hour. We were soon in the chops of the Channel, within a *foot* of never being heard of again too, for the greatest danger almost that can be run at sea we so narrowly missed here. A huge Merchantman tacking her way out, with no lights visible, nor any watch we supposed, bore down full upon us in the darkness of night. Our Captain, who was on deck, *felt* her approach or heard it, seized his trumpet first, and then the helm, and just turned us sufficiently out of the course to avoid the collision. I was lying on the sofa in the gloom of the just vanished twilight; I heard the rush of parting waters, distinguished the encreased blackness as the mass heaved past the windows, and shuddered, at I knew not what, the Captain had given us up. So very near had we been to danger. Hundreds of vessels, they say, are lost in this very way from utter carelessness on both parts. Captain West was prepared on deck, the little swivel loader to be fired if needed—only for this we had been gone. One more escape we had, from fire. The first mate next evening perceived some burning on the lower deck and entered every cabin instantly. The Archdeacon, surrounded by papers in flames on the floor, was vainly endeavouring to check the conflagration he had so unthinkingly raised—he had intended only to burn a few letters.

The coast appeared, first rocky, wild, rough, then came fields and trees, and villages and church spires; then we passed the Needles, and then, sailing on in smooth water with beauty on every side, we anchored in the roads off Portsmouth very early in the morning of some day towards the end of April 1830, St George's day, I think it was, the 23rd. Most of the gentlemen called boats and went ashore. Captain West returned with such delicious things for breakfast, fresh butter, fresh eggs, cream, fine bread. Oh how we enjoyed the feast. It gave us strength for our preparations.

Our two servants bestirred themselves busily. Malek was to remain in the ship in charge of all our heavy luggage; Mary, and the trunks selected, was to land with us. The Colonel was the difficulty; for a week past he had not been able to move hand or foot without bringing on a spasm. They said at Bombay he would never live to reach home. They said at sea he would die on the Voyage, and I believe had we not got that goat, he could not have struggled on under such sufferings. It seemed this last day as if we should never get him safe ashore.

The chair was prepared, he was carried out to it, laid in, lowered to the boat, lifted up and settled among cushions, and the rest of our party seated as could best be managed. We were half an hour or so rowing in, and we landed by the same steps on the same quay, and we had secured rooms at the same hotel looking on the harbour, from which we had started two years and a half before for India. The Captain took the rooms in the morning as the nearest to the water and so the most convenient for the poor Colonel. What was our amazement to see him when the boat struck, rise unassisted, walk up the steps, and along the small portion of the quay in his large cloke which covered his wrapper and seat himself in the little parlour without a gasp. We ordered what was to us the most luxurious repast in the world, tea, bread and butter, eggs and muffins, and did we not enjoy it, our Captain, Mrs Churchill, Mr Agassiz, the Colonel, the 2 children and I. We even played whist, and when we went to bed, the Colonel lay down and slept till morning, the first time he had ventured on such an indulgence for six weeks. We really did feel too happy, I was too happy to sleep, I was tired, too.

We had had the Custom House officers on board early, but they had not been the least impolite—quite the contrary. In the first place, they found nothing contraband, my shawls being on myself and Mrs Churchill, and my trinkets in the Captain's pockets. In the next place they looked for nothing, an old servant of Mr Gardiner's family being Chief of the party. Mr Gardiner had written to him to expedite us on our way, and the civil creature not only let all our packages pass that we wished to take to the hotel, but the trunks (which went to the Custom House) of which I gave him the keys, I am persuaded were hardly looked at—for all their contents were untumbled when they came back to me. A long paper box in which were the Cape feathers and an embroidered muslin gown my Mother had thought of just at the last for Aunt Fanny were all that paid duty—£1 on the feathers, half their cost, on the gown 25/- although we had run it up into a petticoat. They probably thought it decorous to tax something. The good old man had also ordered a set of rooms at the George, higher up the town in case they should be wanted. In short he quite welcomed us home.

Next day I actually walked *with my Colonel* about the town and found it piercing cold up on the Ramparts. I bought a straw bonnet, the Colonel a pair of gloves and a warm scarf for Willie. Before going out I had written two notes, one to Jane to say we should be with her the next day and to ask her to put up Mrs Churchill for two nights, as we really would not lose sight of her, and one to Lady, then Mrs, Burgoyne, whose husband had some command at Portsmouth. She called on us in the afternoon, and tho' very affected and a little airified was cousinly enough. We agreed to stop at her house next morning on our way to Malshanger to see her children. She lived in a pretty villa out of the town, and had all her plain children kept from school and nicely dressed to shew to us; there was good taste about her furniture and her garden, about all but herself. She herself was the same cockney looking, cockney mannered, self important little body that tormented us all as Charlotte Rose.

We were travelling most uncomfortably in two post chaises, Mrs Churchill, Louisa, and I in one, the Colonel, Willy and black Mary the maid in the other. There were three stages; we all met at the first, all met at the second, but we lost sight of the Colonel in the third. Where he had wandered his stupid postboy could not tell; very much out of the road, that was certain, for he did not reach Malshanger for an hour after we had been comfortably seated in Jane's pretty drawing room. Poor Jane, she was watching at the gate. I forget all else almost that day.

The party assembled at Malshanger consisted of Mary, her husband, and *two* children, Tom having been born the previous January, William, Aunt Bourne, and her stepdaughter, Henrietta. We were too large an addition, but it was not for long, as Colonel Smith had determined to go up to town at once to see if any Doctor could get him a bit to rights.

This resolution was hastened by an attack of asthma, the air up on those dry heights of Hampshire not at all suiting him. Asthma attacked him immediately. As his Indian servant would meet him in London, the general voice forbade my accompanying him, indeed I was in no trim for travelling. Besides I stood in need of rest after the discomforts of the voyage and the nights of broken sleep so long continued. He therefore departed on the 3rd morning, with his suite, in Jane's *basket* to Basingstoke, from thence by coach. Poor little Willy, who cried bitterly on leaving his *Aunty* was to be delivered to Miss Elphick at Kensington; she had given up the governess line, having her mother to provide for, and was trying to establish a sort of infant boarding School, which, poor soul, in spite of large help from all of us, she never succeeded in rendering a profitable speculation. Black Mary with whom I was glad to be done, for she was at times when excited rather unmanagable, was to go to the Agent's to resume her sea service, and Mrs Churchill and Louisa were to be deposited at old Mrs Churchill's. We were really glad to part with her. She was an incorrigible coquette, if not worse. After the distracting scene we had unhappily witnessed on her parting from the 3rd mate, and the very tender proceedings with Mr Agassiz, who was to see her again in London, she commenced a flirtation with my brother William, an engaged man at this time, and ought to have been thinking of good Sally, but man like, could not help philandering after a pretty woman. Mrs Churchill was really very inconsiderate, there was no actual harm in her; she was merely amusing herself, was what is called 'fast' in these days, in plain English, indecorous. She went soon after to visit her own Mother at Boulogne, Mr Agassiz her escort. More of her I never heard till some years after, when her husband got some good appointment in Bengal. She and Louisa went to India with them, and there they married their daughter to Colonel, afterwards General and then Sir John Michel,[1] well known in Canada and Dublin.

1. Sir John Michel (1804–86) married Louise Anne, only daughter of Major General H. Churchill C.B., Quarter Master General of the troops in India (D.N.B.).

William went to town but not with Mrs Churchill, he went to play host to Colonel Smith, whom he had invited to his lodgings and who carried a note from me to Mr Robert Pennington, the medical man he meant to consult. We seemed quieter at Malshanger after all these good friends were gone; but not for long. Mrs Guthrie and Mrs Basil Hall came to welcome me home, Mrs Guthrie the same kindly and pleasant person as ever; Mrs Hall kindly too, I believe, but airified by the *passing* fame[1] of her husband. They had come purposely to see me. It is nonsense to expect that early friendship will last under the shade of a total separation. We all declared we were all so happy to meet again, but I really fancied that they, like me, were very nearly indifferent upon the subject. I had never much taken to Margaret. After her marriage she became insufferable to every body but her sister—there was only Jane Guthrie, therefore, to try to care for her. She is to this day a most excellent person, but she is not in my line so that our intercourse is a very ghostlike semblance of the intimacy of our girlish days. Our Christian names in each other's mouths always sounded very hollow to my ears, altho' she and I have retained a warm interest in each other's doings. She was living among people I had never heard of and my Indian past and Irish future were then equally removed from her sympathies. Both sisters were extremely concerned about their dress, a strange affair to my unpractised eyes. Miss Elphick, too, worn a little, not exactly prospering, just able to rub on; and Mrs Gillio, with her warm highland heart. Aunt Bourne, too, had been at Malshanger all along; her rich and happy marriage had ended in a second widowhood, and she was left the charge of a step daughter, who was to her all that her own daughter could have been. Henrietta without being a beauty was very attractive in looks and manners. She was particularly suited to my Aunt, perfectly capable of appreciating her superiourity, and modest and tractable herself. She took to us all, particularly to John Frere, who was also with us for a while, and delighted on moonlight walks in the shrubberies with an

1. For an explanation of Basil Hall's *passing fame*,
   see II, pp. 49–50.

agreeable companion. I have always thought it a great pity these walks were not encouraged. My cousin Freres had not grown up handsome, besides there was a great want of grace in their manner. They were quaint, too, Frerish—that nameless oddity that runs thro' the race. But they were thoroughly amiable, unaffected, well brought up and altogether very pleasing, my dear little Aunt queerer and dearer than ever.

The Gardiners had taken a cottage at a pretty village three miles off down the hill, surrounded the parish church we attended; they took it for six months, and Jane and I hoped it might suit them for a longer time. It was so very comfortable, an old, good sized farm cottage, with a porch, and a draw well, and latticed windows, and a new front, with large rooms, and large windows looking on a flower garden, a well cropped kitchen garden behind. The house was furnished and the rent was low, though not a cheap country, no expensive establishment could have been kept there. They should have been tired of their wandering adventures. Their voyage in that little boat had been very boisterous. They escaped shipwreck by a mere chance; instead of landing at Liverpool they were stranded on the coast of Galloway, landed in boats, started with half their luggage for London, in post chaises, and after a London lodging and other discomforts, took a house at Ham, too near Mr Gardiner's aunt Miss Porter at Twickenham, whose interference with their domestick arrangements made their moving again almost a necessity. They tried Cheltenham, Leamington, Matlock and then eagerly responding to Jane's proposal of this cottage, which accidentally offered itself, they arrived at Malshanger, bag and baggage, to look at it. A few days sufficed to settle them most comfortably, having a talent for this sort of business. They looked very happy there, always cheerful, every thing nice about them, the children, neat and merry, dear little things. Jane and I often drove there in the basket cart with 'Goody,' and while she wandered through the village visiting all the poor people who shared her bounties, I sat quietly by Mary's work table in the window opening on the garden, where Mr Gardiner delighted in being busy, little Janey in her short white frock and broad blue sash trotting up and down the room, and baby Tommy on my knee.

All parties were anxious that my Colonel and I should settle in that neighbourhood; there was a very desirable place, Tangier, close to Malshanger, to be let, but we could not take it. The sharp air of these Hampshire heights quite disagreed with him. Besides that, duty and early attachments recalled him to his own green isle. In London, where he remained three weeks, he was comparatively well. Asthma attacked him directly he returned to us. Mr Pennington told him the disease was a consequence not a cause, but it was now chronick and would not cure, though it would be relieved, and his health, which was much deranged, should strengthen. He advised him to seek for an air that suited him, and *stay* in it and trust to time. An Indian *stay* anywhere; foolish Mr Pennington. It was plain he could not stay at Malshanger, so he left us for Dublin.

My sisters and I had a subject of anxiety in William's engagement to Sally Siddons; about this time she came on a visit to Mary, her sister Elizabeth followed to Malshanger; William, of course, was with his affianced. The news of their engagement had not reached Bombay when we sailed. I met it in England, I must say, with dismay. I feared it would really overset my father and that my Mother would give way to a violence of disapproval that would make all concerned very uncomfortable. For myself, I had yet to find out that worth would, and should, outweigh quarterings, that good sense and high principles in a woman are worth to her family more than all the more brilliant qualities, which are more attractive, and that no rank in life honourably supported ought to place a bar between a gentleman and a gentle-woman. So, liking her father and admiring her mother, our near connexion was a bitter pill. Very anxiously we all awaited our Indian letters, Jane, Mary, and I were grave, William in a fever, Sally calm. Mrs Siddons had written to my father detailing the whole progress of the attachment, which, when mentioned to her, she would not sanction without this consent. She touched on William's faults of character, but believed them to have been redeemed by the way in which he had supported adversity, which belief alone could have induced her conditionally to consent to give him such a daughter, knowing too, that she must lose her for their destination was to be Calcutta. William was keeping his terms at the Temple, Lord Glenelg having obtained permission for him to proceed as a barrister to Bengal. The last paragraph of Mrs Siddons' letter probably did no harm; it stated that Sally's fortune would at the least be £10,000.

My father received this letter alone and alone he determined to consider it before venturing to inform my Mother. This naive admission sufficiently explained his own feelings. He passed a sleepless night, and when at dawn he made up his mind to rouse his sleeping partner with the news, he found he might have saved himself all his perturbation. My Mother had heard nothing for a long while that had given her so much pleasure. A most cordial invitation to William and his Wife accompanied the consent to the marriage; Jane gave a grand dinner, the daily ones were small enough, Colonel Pennington produced champaign, and an evening of happy family cheerfulness followed. My Mother was very wise. She made the best of it, not her usual way.

It was a fine summer. I thought I should have enjoyed the power of wandering out in the open air at every hour after the imprisonment of India—and so perhaps I might, but I had not the power, for I was ill, very uneasy and not able to exert myself. I had had to hire a little maid to wait upon myself in order to secure some attendance in my room, Jane in that immense large house having but two women servants and an old Molly, who came in after weeding the shrubbery to wash up dishes. There was always company in the house, additions frequently at dinner, besides one or two regular parties of the neighbours, and two of the little Penningtons, Charles and Annie, were living there. Georgina came afterwards, and the father and mother, neither of whom I liked. I therefore fared but badly as to attendance. So I proposed to Jane to hire a maid, to wait entirely on me, do out my room etc., and to pay her board so that she would cost her nothing. Jane was charmed. She knew a young woman that would exactly suit. She would arrange it all, the plan was excellent. I hoped so, for as it was I was rather miserable. Poor little Sarah, on the 29th. May, Royal oak day, we went all to lunch with Mary and to see the villagers dance upon the green, the queen, footing it merrily in her white dress with her garland of oak leaves round her straw hat, was pointed out to me as my future maid, which not a little startled me, and Mary advised me to cry off. But as the engagement was made, and only conditional, I did not like to disappoint either Jane or her protégée, as she could easily be left when we moved if she did not suit me. But she was the nicest creature possible, a good housemaid, quick and neat at her needle, clearstarched well, was always busy and always merry and I felt sure that when I had her to myself, we should get on admirably.

As it was, I had her not, or very little. Jane expected her to be obliging, the housemaid begged for help, the Cook Nelly! insisted upon help, the little Penningtons were given over to her. So what with dressing them, and waiting on them, cleaning other rooms than mine, going messages, shelling pease, basting meat etc., I was nearly as forelorn as before. I might ring but was I answered? Sarah had just stept out to the farm for eggs, to the garden for parsley or had gone with Master Charles to lead his donkey. I daresay it was very good for me to try to wait upon myself, however, as Mr Workman of Basingstoke, who was to attend me, was not easy about me, as he told Jane, a proper monthly nurse was sent for to town, and down came Mrs Stephens, the usual assistant of Mrs Guthrie. Under her government, Sarah had to mind her own mistress, as the mistress herself, much to her own benefit, had to mind the nurse. She was a skilful person, and I do believe by her care of me she prepared me so properly for what I had to go thro', that she was the principal means of saving my life and Janey's. It was a case similar to the Princess Charlotte's, whatever that was, for I am sure I don't know.[1] I took ill on the last day of June, Saturday, the day King George the 4th. died. On Tuesday the 3rd. of July that little blessing to her parents saw the light about 9 o'clock in the morning. Poor Jane, who never left me, had given me over. The clever little strange Doctor, however, brought us both thro'—there never was a better recovery either, altho' the nurse had to leave us in 10 days being engaged elsewhere.

1. She had given birth to a still-born boy and died shortly afterwards.

Before I left my room, I had a peep of my husband on his way from Dublin to London, and he returned only to take me away, being ordered by his doctor to Cheltenham for a long course of the waters. He came back in a very pretty *britchska*[1] he and William had chosen for me; *Annie Need* and these two travelling together in it. After a few days we packed up and packed off, and then indeed I felt I was gone out from among my own kindred, and had set up independently—a husband—a baby—an end indeed of Eliza Grant.

And here I think I'll leave my Memoirs for the present. You know, dear children, what my Irish life had been, the friends we found, the friends we made, the good your dear father did. Ten months in Dublin sufficed to shew us a town life was not then suited to us. We resolved to settle among our own people, your father finding in his own old neighbourhood all those companions of his youth whom he had left there more than thirty years before. A very happy life we led there. First in the pretty cottage at Burgage which we improved without, and within, and made so comfortable, and then in our own fine house built by ourselves, such a source of happy occupation to the Colonel for years and the means of raising his tenantry from debt and apathy and wretchedness to the thriving condition in which we now have them. It would take a volume to describe our slow but regular march of improvement, never wearying in well doing, bearing patiently with ignorance and all its errours, and carefully bringing up our own dear children to follow us in doing likewise. One only trouble assailed our happy home, the want of health—that miserable asthma breaking him and breaking me and stepping in between us and many enjoyments. The purse, though never heavy, was never empty, our habits being simple. On looking back I find little essential to regret and much, Oh so much, to be truly thankful for.

Dublin, February 1854                                        E.S.

1. An open carriage with removable folding top and space for reclining when used for a journey.

# POST SCRIPT TO THE
## MEMOIRS OF A HIGHLAND LADY

P.S. On looking over these recollections I find I have made no mention of Castle Grant, the old residence of our Chief from whom our family are lineally and not very recently descended—who the Grants were, where they came from and when, is very debatable ground among antiquaries. They were a formidable clan when they were first heard of in the history of their country. Some of them in very early days had certainly settled in Glen Urquart. Some had rather gone eastward or settled independantly about Lochindarb, a bare and bleak plain stretching on toward the Spey, near the banks of which the Chief finally established himself. A high tower on a bleak moor—the tower was added to and the village of Grantown was built and the tower of Muchrath, a sort of outpost was erected. This tower and a sufficiency of land was left to the second son of the Laird of the day, known as Patrick Grant of Muchrath. Somewhere about the year 1400, his mother was a daughter of the Earl of Athol, a Stuart not a Murray, her grandmother was a daughter of the Earl of Argylle, for the Grants were a potent Clan and their Chiefs had married well. This Patrick of Muchrath was my immediate ancestor, the founder of our house, for when the Shawes were attained and forfeited the lands of Rothiemurchus, the king bestowed them on the Laird of Grant 'gin he could tak' them', and the Laird of Grant made them over to the most energetick of his sons, Patrick who gave up the wild heath of Muchrath and brought with him to his new & beautiful conquest the stone which had been placed over the doorway in the old tower recording the date of his possession. This stone was built in to the front wall of the small house at the Dell where he had lived for many years.

My father and mother were much at Castle Grant during the early years of their married life. Sir James Grant the last baronet and his amiable wife were thoroughly hospitable, their large straggling house was always filled with relations and with friends and the dinner table in the great hall easily held the 40 or 50 guests, all chance comers of respectable degree were welcome. There was not exactly a 'below the salt' but practically the guests at the Tower end of the table never intruded into the drawing room. Good Sir James always hoped to die a Laird of Grant and he did, his eldest son succeeded to an Earldom and a fine estate near Elgin, where poor man he lived under the care of his sister the Lady Anne, for with the title of a Seafield and the estate of Cullen came a fearful inheritance, disease of the brain. His second son Colonel Francis Grant and my father fell out about politicks and the quarrel never healed.

I was only once at Castle Grant, shortly before we went to India. My Mother and Mary and I formed part of a large assemblage of relations brought together by Lady Anne in the hope of rousing her brother. We were all very merry, very happy but poor Lord Seafield remained quiet, harmless as ever—still he had sense—he took Mary by the hand one day and led her into the picture gallery and stopt before a picture of the Brigadier, who married Queen Anne's maid of honor. Mary was his image, a true Grant with the blue eyes and the fair skin and the fair hair—poor old Seaforth![1]

I have no memory for more.

1. The Good Sir James (1738–1811) was the eighth baronet.
   His eldest son, Sir Lewis Alexander (1767–1840), the fifth
   Earl of Seafield from 1811, was one of fourteen children,
   all of whom apart from two died young or did not marry.

# Index

*"Reawaken[s] my awe at the strangeness of our world."*
Will Self

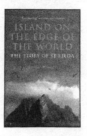

# Island on the Edge of the World:
# The Story of St Kilda

## Charles Maclean

When missionaries and tourists first discovered St Kilda in the late nineteenth century, they found a Utopian society unchanged for 2000 years. In exchange, they brought money, disease and discord. By 1930 this forgotten society had disintegrated, and the last remaining islanders were evacuated.

This account of human endeavour in the unending struggle between man and nature movingly shows how the destruction of St Kildan culture is a microcosm of a process which is still taking place all over the world.

"A story like a marvellous pebble, wet from the sea, strange and comic like all things out of step with time, sad as the old songs the women sang, splendidly told . . ."    *Sunday Times*

"A fascinating book . . . Charles Maclean is an excellent writer . . . he describes the story of St Kilda with powerful compassion."
Magnus Magnusson

1 84195 755 0 (10-digit ISBN)
978 1 84195 755 5 (13-digit ISBN)

£6.99

Buy direct from Canongate
**www.canongate.net**
"A cool club stocked with well-read friends rather than a lazy corporate exercise." GUARDIAN